DESERT SHIELD
TO
DESERT STORM

**Redondo Beach
Public Library**

DESERT
SHIELD
—— *to* ——
DESERT
STORM

THE SECOND
GULF WAR

Dilip Hiro

Routledge
New York

Published in 1992 by
Routledge, an imprint of
Routledge, Chapman and Hall, Inc.
Copyright © 1992 by Dilip Hiro

Printed in the United States of America
on acid free paper

First published in London in 1992
by HarperCollins Publisher

Library of Congress Cataloging-in-Publication
data is available

ISBN 0-415-90656-3
ISBN 0-415-90657-1 (pb)

CONTENTS

APPENDICES

ILLUSTRATIONS

The Iraqi Prime Minister, Abdul Karim Qasim
Popperfoto
The UN Security Council on 18 August 1990 *Sipa/Rex
Features*
President Bush and Emir Jaber al Sabah of Kuwait
Popperfoto
Palestinians carry an injured woman away from the holy
Dome of the Rock *Associated Press*
A Palestinian during a pro-Saddam Hussein
demonstration *Frank Spooner Pictures*
General Norman Schwarzkopf, Dick Cheney and
General Colin Powell *Frank Spooner Pictures*
The US Secretary of State James Baker with King Fahd
ibn Abdul Aziz *Popperfoto*
President Bush with President Hafiz Assad of Syria
Popperfoto
James Baker and the Iraqi foreign minister Tariq Aziz
Frank Spooner Pictures
Victims of an Iraqi Scud attack on Tel Aviv being
removed, 20 January 1991 *The Independent*
Dead Iraqi soldiers and their equipment scattered in the
desert *Rex Features*
Iraqi prisoners of war in Kuwait *Popperfoto*
The aftermath of the US-led coalition's attack at the
Mitla ridge *Rex Features*
President Bush with Douglas Hurd *Popperfoto*
A Kuwaiti welcomes the victorious troops of the
US-led coalition forces *Frank Spooner Pictures*
General Schwarzkopf and Prince Khalid ibn Sultan of
Saudi Arabia *Associated Press*
Jalal Talabani with Ayatollah Muhammad Taqi
Moderasi, and Aziz Muhammad *Popperfoto*
Jalal Talabani with President Saddam Hussein
Popperfoto
A Kuwaiti soldier at a border post, with a burning oil
well in the background *The Independent*

ABBREVIATIONS

ABC American Broadcasting Company

ACC Arab Co-operation Council

AH *Anno* Hijra (Migration of the Prophet Muhammad)

ALARM Air Launched Anti-Radiation Missile

APD Arab Projects and Development

Aramco Arabian American Oil Company

Awacs Airborne Warning and Control Systems

BBC British Broadcasting Corporation

b/d barrels/day

BNL Banca Nazionale del Lavoro

CBS Columbia Broadcasting Service

CIA Central Intelligence Agency

CNN Cable News Network

CSCE Conference on Security and Co-operation in Europe

DIA Defence Intelligence Agency

EC European Community

EST Eastern Standard Time

FAE Fuel Air Explosive

FBI Federal Bureau of Investigation

GCC Gulf Co-operation Council

GMT Greenwich Mean Time

IAEA International Atomic Energy Agency

ICO Islamic Conference Organization

ID Iraqi Dinar

IKF Iraqi Kurdistan Front

KD Kuwaiti Dinar

KDF Kuwait Democratic Front

KDP Kurdish Democratic Party

KIA Kuwait Investment Authority

KIO Kuwait Investment Organization

KOTC Kuwait Oil Tanker Company

KTO Kuwait Theatre of Operations

mb/d million barrels/day

MODA	Ministry of Defence and Aviation	PNC	Palestine National Council
MP	Member of Parliament	PUK	Patriotic Union of Kurdistan
NAM	Non-Aligned Movement	RAF	Royal Air Force
Nato	North Atlantic Treaty Organization	RCC	Revolutionary Command Council
NBC	National Broadcasting Corporation	RDF	Rapid Deployment Force
		RFFG	Reserve Fund for Future Generations
NORAD	North American Aerospace Defence Command	SAIRI	Supreme Assembly of the Islamic Revolution in Iraq
NPPF	National Progressive and Patriotic Front	SGR	State General Reserves
		SSD	State Security Department
NSC	National Security Council	TPC	Turkish Petroleum Company
OAPEC	Organization of Arab Petroleum Exporting Countries	UAE	United Arab Emirates
		UN/UNO	United Nations Organization
OPEC	Organization of Oil Exporting Countries	UNHCR	United Nations High Commissioner for Refugees
PFGK	Provisional Free Government of Kuwait	UNHUC	United Nations Humanitarian Centre
PFLP-GC	Popular Front for the Liberation of Palestine–General Command	UNIIMOG	United Nations Iran–Iraq Military Observer Group
PLF	Palestine Liberation Front	Unikom	United Nations Iraq–Kuwait Observation Mission
PLO	Palestine Liberation Organization		

US/USA	United States of America
USS	United States Ship
USSR	Union of Soviet Socialist Republics
WASP	White Anglo-Saxon Protestant
WML	World Muslim League

MAPS

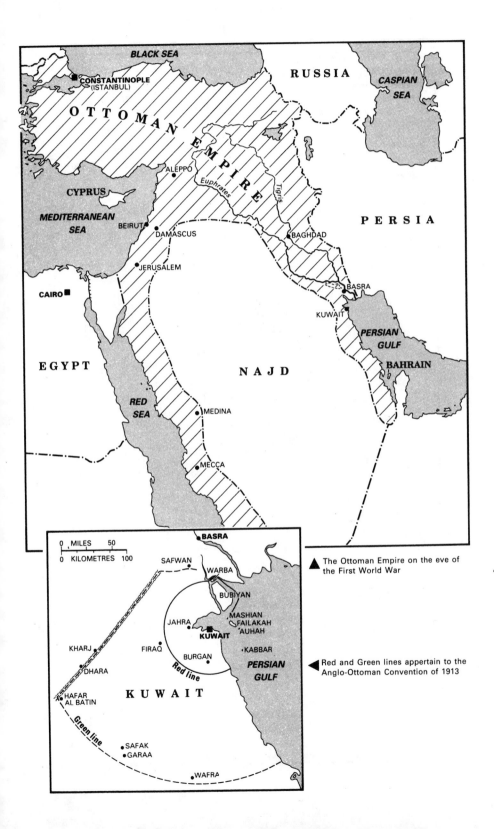

BLACK SEA

RUSSIA

CASPIAN SEA

CONSTANTINOPLE (ISTANBUL)

OTTOMAN EMPIRE

ALEPPO

Euphrates

Tigris

PERSIA

CYPRUS

MEDITERRANEAN SEA

BEIRUT

DAMASCUS

BAGHDAD

JERUSALEM

CAIRO

BASRA

KUWAIT

PERSIAN GULF

EGYPT

NAJD

BAHRAIN

RED SEA

MEDINA

MECCA

0 MILES 50
0 KILOMETRES 100

BASRA

SAFWAN

WARBA

BUBIYAN

MASHIAN
FAILAKAH
'AUHAH

JAHRA

KHARJ

FIRAQ

KUWAIT

KABBAR

BURGAN

PERSIAN GULF

Red line

DHARA

HAFAR AL BATIN

KUWAIT

Green line

SAFAK
GARAA

WAFRA

▲ The Ottoman Empire on the eve of the First World War

◀ Red and Green lines appertain to the Anglo-Ottoman Convention of 1913

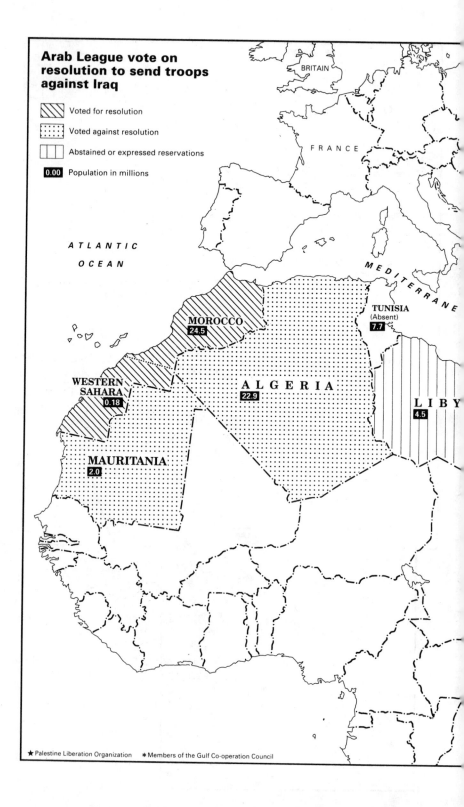

Arab League vote on resolution to send troops against Iraq

Voted for resolution

Voted against resolution

Abstained or expressed reservations

0.00 Population in millions

BRITAIN

FRANCE

ATLANTIC

OCEAN

MEDITERRANEAN

MOROCCO
24.5

TUNISIA
(Absent)
7.7

WESTERN
SAHARA
0.18

A L G E R I A
22.9

L I B Y A
4.5

MAURITANIA
2.0

★ Palestine Liberation Organization   ✳ Members of the Gulf Co-operation Council

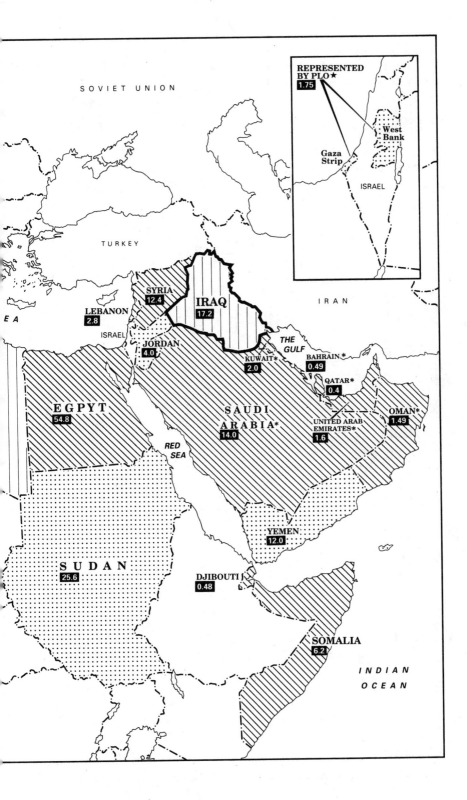

SOVIET UNION

REPRESENTED
BY PLO ★
1.75

West
Bank

Gaza
Strip

ISRAEL

TURKEY

IRAN

SYRIA
12.4

IRAQ
17.2

LEBANON
2.8

E A

ISRAEL

JORDAN
4.0

THE
GULF

KUWAIT*
2.0

BAHRAIN*
0.49

QATAR*
0.4

EGPYT
54.8

SAUDI
ARABIA*
14.0

UNITED ARAB
EMIRATES*
1.6

OMAN*
1.49

RED
SEA

YEMEN
12.0

SUDAN
25.6

DJIBOUTI
0.48

SOMALIA
6.2

INDIAN
OCEAN

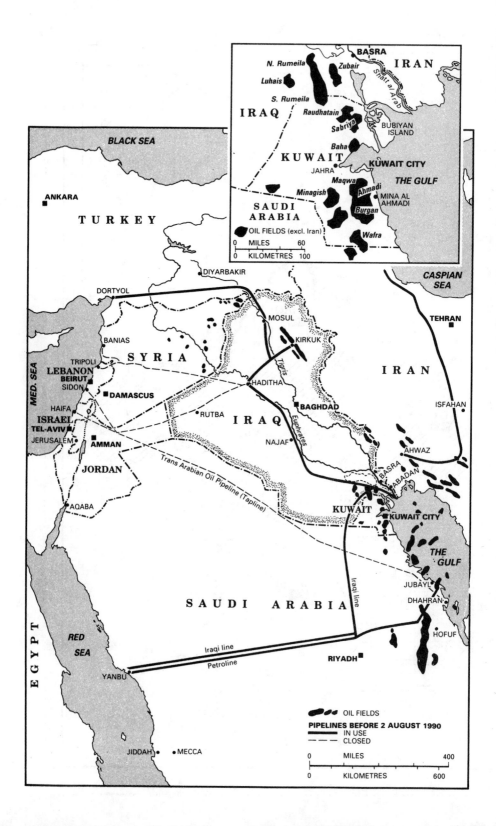

BASRA
N. Rumeila
Zubair
IRAN
Luhais
Shatt al Arab
S. Rumeila
IRAQ
Raudhatain
Sabriya
BUBIYAN
ISLAND
Baha
KUWAIT
JAHRA
KUWAIT CITY
Maqwa
THE GULF
Minagish
Ahmadi
MINA AL
AHMADI
SAUDI
Burgan
ARABIA
Wafra
OIL FIELDS (excl. Iran)
0   MILES   60
0   KILOMETRES   100

BLACK SEA
CASPIAN
SEA
ANKARA
DIYARBAKIR
DORTYOL
TEHRAN
TURKEY
MOSUL
BANIAS
KIRKUK
SYRIA
Tigris
TRIPOLI
LEBANON
HADITHA
IRAN
BEIRUT
SIDON
DAMASCUS
ISFAHAN
MED. SEA
HAIFA
RUTBA
BAGHDAD
ISRAEL
IRAQ
TEL-AVIV
Euphrates
JERUSALEM
NAJAF
AHWAZ
AMMAN
BASRA
ABADAN
JORDAN
Trans Arabian Oil Pipeline (Tapline)
KUWAIT
AQABA
KUWAIT CITY

SAUDI   ARABIA
THE
GULF
JUBAYL
DHAHRAN
Iraqi line
RED
HOFUF
EGYPT
SEA
Iraqi line
Petroline
RIYADH
YANBU

OIL FIELDS

PIPELINES BEFORE 2 AUGUST 1990
IN USE
CLOSED

0   MILES   400
0   KILOMETRES   600

JIDDAH
MECCA

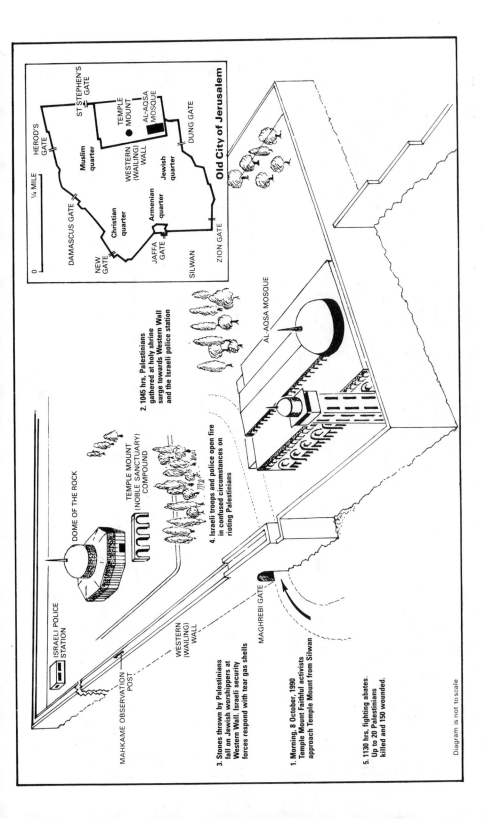

Old City of Jerusalem

0   ¼ MILE

ST STEPHEN'S GATE

HEROD'S GATE

DAMASCUS GATE

NEW GATE

Christian quarter

JAFFA GATE

Armenian quarter

Muslim quarter

TEMPLE MOUNT

AL-AQSA MOSQUE

WESTERN (WAILING) WALL

Jewish quarter

DUNG GATE

ZION GATE

SILWAN

ISRAELI POLICE STATION

DOME OF THE ROCK

TEMPLE MOUNT (NOBLE SANCTUARY) COMPOUND

MAHKAME OBSERVATION POST

WESTERN (WAILING) WALL

MAGHREBI GATE

AL-AQSA MOSQUE

2. 1005 hrs, Palestinians gathered at holy shrine surge towards Western Wall and the Israeli police station

3. Stones thrown by Palestinians fall on Jewish worshippers at Western Wall. Israeli security forces respond with tear gas shells

4. Israeli troops and police open fire in confused circumstances on rioting Palestinians

1. Morning, 8 October, 1990 Temple Mount Faithful activists approach Temple Mount from Silwan

5. 1130 hrs, fighting abates. Up to 20 Palestinians killed and 150 wounded.

Diagram is not to scale

Allied command structure

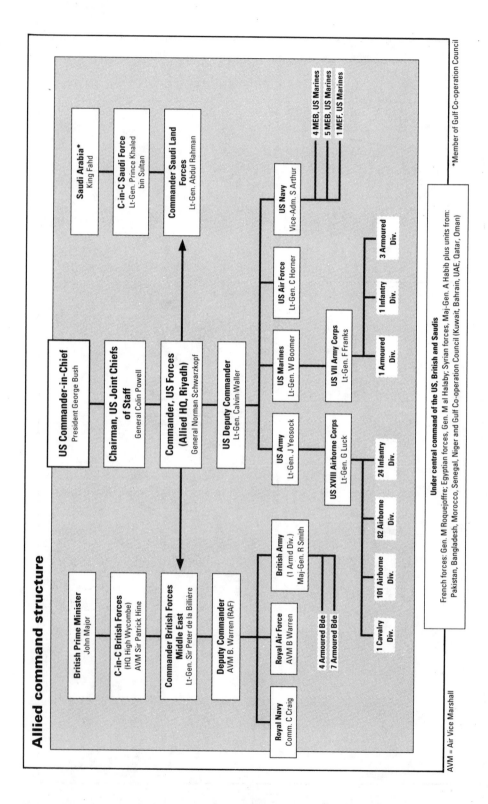

US Commander-in-Chief
President George Bush

Chairman, US Joint Chiefs of Staff
General Colin Powell

Commander, US Forces (Allied HQ, Riyadh)
General Norman Schwarzkopf

US Deputy Commander
Lt-Gen. Calvin Waller

Saudi Arabia*
King Fahd

C-in-C Saudi Force
Lt-Gen. Prince Khaled bin Sultan

Commander Saudi Land Forces
Lt-Gen. Abdul Rahman

US Army
Lt-Gen. J Yeosock

US Marines
Lt-Gen. W Boomer

US Air Force
Lt-Gen. C Horner

US Navy
Vice-Adm. S Arthur

US XVIII Airborne Corps
Lt-Gen. G Luck

US VII Army Corps
Lt-Gen. F Franks

1 Cavalry Div.

101 Airborne Div.

82 Airborne Div.

24 Infantry Div.

1 Armoured Div.

1 Infantry Div.

3 Armoured Div.

4 MEB, US Marines
5 MEB, US Marines
1 MEF, US Marines

British Prime Minister
John Major

C-in-C British Forces
(HQ High Wycombe)
AVM Sir Patrick Hine

Commander British Forces Middle East
Lt-Gen. Sir Peter de la Billière

Deputy Commander
AVM B. Warren (RAF)

Royal Navy
Comm. C Craig

Royal Air Force
AVM B Warren

British Army
(1 Armd Div.)
Maj-Gen. R Smith

4 Armoured Bde
7 Armoured Bde

Under central command of the US, British and Saudis

French forces: Gen. M Roquejoffre; Egyptian forces, Gen. M al Halaby; Syrian forces, Maj-Gen. A Habib plus units from: Pakistan, Bangladesh, Morocco, Senegal, Niger and Gulf Co-operation Council (Kuwait, Bahrain, UAE, Qatar, Oman)

*Member of Gulf Co-operation Council

AVM = Air Vice Marshall

Principal targets in Iraq

- AIR BASE
- AIR DEFENCE COMMAND CONTROL CENTRE
- NAVAL BASE
- BALLISTIC MISSILE PLANT
- CHEMICAL/BIOLOGICAL WEAPONS PLANT
- NUCLEAR WEAPONS RELATED PLANT

```
0        MILES       120
0      KILOMETRES    200
```

TURKEY

SYRIA

TALL AFAR   MOSUL   ARBIL

KIRKUK

Tigris

BAIJA

Euphrates

SAMARRA

BALAD

H1   I   R   A   Q

FALLUJA   BAGHDAD

RASHID

SALMAN PAK

H2   HABBANIYA   TUWAITHA

RUTBA   MAHMUDIYA

H3   KARBALA   ISKANDARIYA

HILLEH

IRAN

MUDAYSIS

AMARA

WADI KHIRR

QURNA

GHALAYSAN   NASIRIYEH

BASRA

JALIBA

SALMAN   SHUAIBA

UMM QASR

JORDAN

SAUDI ARABIA

KUWAIT

KUWAIT CITY

THE GULF

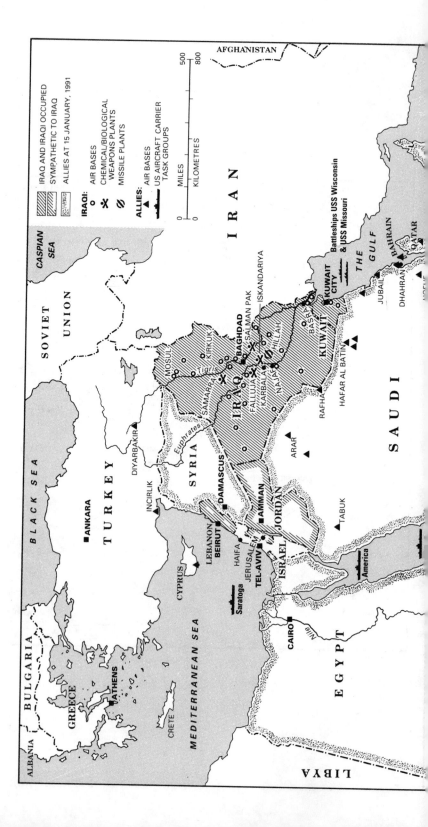

AFGHANISTAN

IRAQI:
○ AIR BASES
✗ CHEMICAL/BIOLOGICAL WEAPONS PLANTS
∅ MISSILE PLANTS

ALLIES:
▲ AIR BASES
⚓ US AIRCRAFT CARRIER TASK GROUPS

IRAQ AND IRAQI OCCUPIED
SYMPATHETIC TO IRAQ
ALLIES AT 15 JANUARY, 1991

MILES   500
KILOMETRES   800
0   0

CASPIAN SEA

SOVIET UNION

IRAN

BLACK SEA

TURKEY

ANKARA

DIYARBAKIR

INCIRLIK

SYRIA

DAMASCUS

MOSUL

KIRKUK

Tigris

SAMARRA

IRAQ

FALLUJA

BAGHDAD

SALMAN PAK

ISKANDARIYA

HILLAH

KARBALA

NAJAF

Euphrates

ARAR

BASRA

KUWAIT

KUWAIT CITY

Battleships USS Wisconsin & USS Missouri

BAHRAIN

QATAR

THE GULF

JUBAIL

DHAHRAN

HAFAR AL BATIN

RAFHA

SAUDI

TABUK

AMMAN

JORDAN

ISRAEL

JERUSALEM

TEL-AVIV

HAIFA

LEBANON

BEIRUT

CYPRUS

Saratoga

MEDITERRANEAN SEA

CRETE

GREECE

ATHENS

BULGARIA

ALBANIA

America

CAIRO

Nile

EGYPT

LIBYA

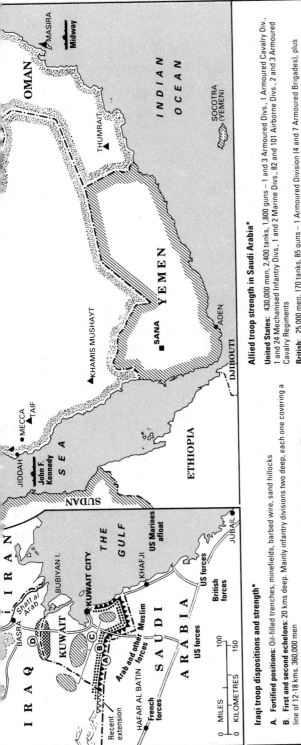

Allied troop strength in Saudi Arabia*

United States: 430,000 men, 2,400 tanks, 1,800 guns – 1 and 3 Armoured Divs., 1 Armoured Cavalry Div., 1 and 24 Mechanised Infantry Divs., 1 and 2 Marine Divs., 82 and 101 Airborne Divs., 2 and 3 Armoured Cavalry Regiments

British: 25,000 men, 170 tanks, 85 guns – 1 Armoured Division (4 and 7 Armoured Brigades), plus support units

Saudi Arabia: 40,000 men, 200 tanks

Egypt: 35,000 men, 450 tanks – two armoured divisions, supporting units and 145 Commando Regiment plus a further 5,000 in the UAE

Syria: 20,000 men, 200 tanks

French: 9,000 men in 6 Light Armoured (Daguet) Div.

Other contingents from Gulf Co-operation Council (Bahrain, Kuwait, Oman, Qatar & UAE), Bangladesh, Morocco, Niger, Pakistan and Senegal. Total: 26,000 men

Iraqi troop dispositions and strength*

A. Fortified positions: Oil-filled trenches, minefields, barbed wire, sand hillocks

B. First and second echelons: 20 kms deep. Mainly infantry divisions two deep, each one covering a line of 12-18 kms. 360,000 men

C. Mobile armoured reserve: 100,000 men, tanks, armoured personnel carriers, artillery

D. GHQ reserve: 120,000 men in eight Republican Guard Divisions

There were also 100,000 men on border with Syria and Turkey, and 200,000 men on border with Iran

0 MILES 100
0 KILOMETRES 150

*All figures are estimates at 13 January, 1991

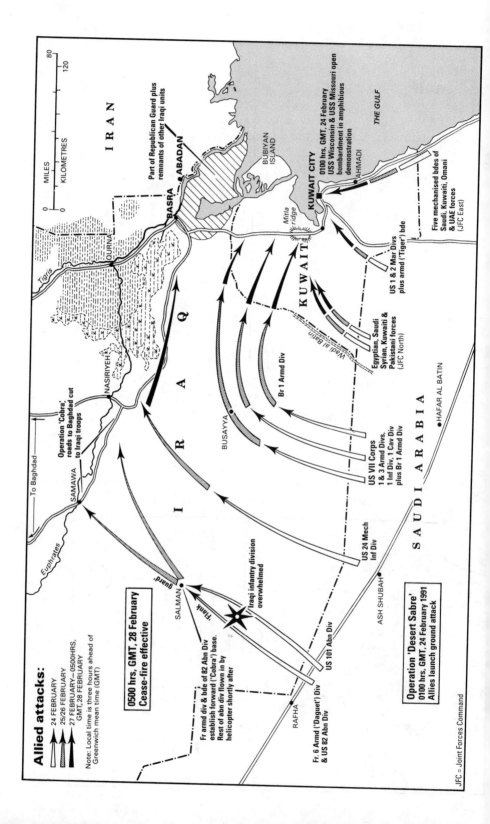

Allied attacks:

24 FEBRUARY

25/26 FEBRUARY

27 FEBRUARY—0500HRS,
GMT, 28 FEBRUARY

Note: Local time is three hours ahead of
Greenwich mean time (GMT)

0 — MILES — 80
0 — KILOMETRES — 120

I R A N

Part of Republican Guard plus
remnants of other Iraqi units

ABADAN

BASRA

QURNA

Tigris

Euphrates

NASIRIYEH

Operation 'Cobra',
roads to Baghdad cut
to Iraqi troops

To Baghdad

SAMAWA

I R A Q

BUSAYYA

BUBIYAN
ISLAND

Mitla
ridge

KUWAIT CITY

0100 hrs, GMT, 24 February
USS Wisconsin & USS Missouri open
bombardment in amphibious
demonstration

THE GULF

AHMADI

K U W A I T

Wadi al Batin

Br 1 Armd Div

US 1 & 2 Mar Divs
plus armd ('Tiger') bde

Five mechanised bdes of
Saudi, Kuwaiti, Omani
& UAE forces
(JFC East)

Egyptian, Saudi
Syrian, Kuwaiti &
Pakistani forces
(JFC North)

US VII Corps
1 & 3 Armd Divs,
1 Inf Div, 1 Cav Div
plus Br 1 Armd Div

US 24 Mech
Inf Div

S A U D I   A R A B I A

HAFAR AL BATIN

0500 hrs, GMT, 28 February
Cease-fire effective

SALMAN

guard

'flank'

Iraqi infantry division
overwhelmed

ASH SHUBAH

Fr armd div & bde of 82 Abn Div
establish forward ('Cobra') base.
Rest of abn div flown in by
helicopter shortly after

US 101 Abn Div

RAFHA

Fr 6 Armd ('Daguet') Div
& US 82 Abn Div

Operation 'Desert Sabre'
0100 hrs, GMT, 24 February 1991
Allies launch ground attack

JFC = Joint Forces Command

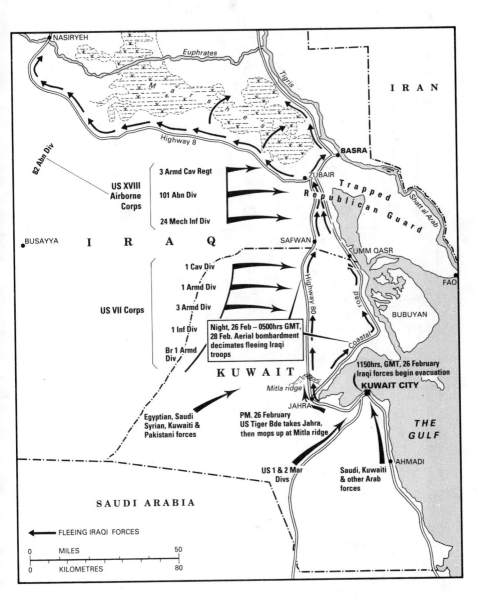

NASIRYEH

Euphrates

Tigris

IRAN

Highway 8

BASRA

ZUBAIR

Trapped Republican Guard

Shatt al Arab

82 Abn Div

3 Armd Cav Regt

US XVIII
Airborne
Corps

101 Abn Div

24 Mech Inf Div

BUSAYYA

I R A Q

SAFWAN

UMM QASR

FAO

1 Cav Div

1 Armd Div

US VII Corps

3 Armd Div

1 Inf Div

Br 1 Armd
Div

Highway 80

Coastal road

BUBUYAN

Night, 26 Feb – 0500hrs GMT,
28 Feb. Aerial bombardment
decimates fleeing Iraqi
troops

K U W A I T

Mitla ridge

1150hrs, GMT, 26 February
Iraqi forces begin evacuation

KUWAIT CITY

JAHRA

Egyptian, Saudi
Syrian, Kuwaiti &
Pakistani forces

PM. 26 February
US Tiger Bde takes Jahra,
then mops up at Mitla ridge

THE
GULF

AHMADI

US 1 & 2 Mar
Divs

Saudi, Kuwaiti
& other Arab
forces

SAUDI ARABIA

FLEEING IRAQI FORCES

0	MILES	50
0	KILOMETRES	80

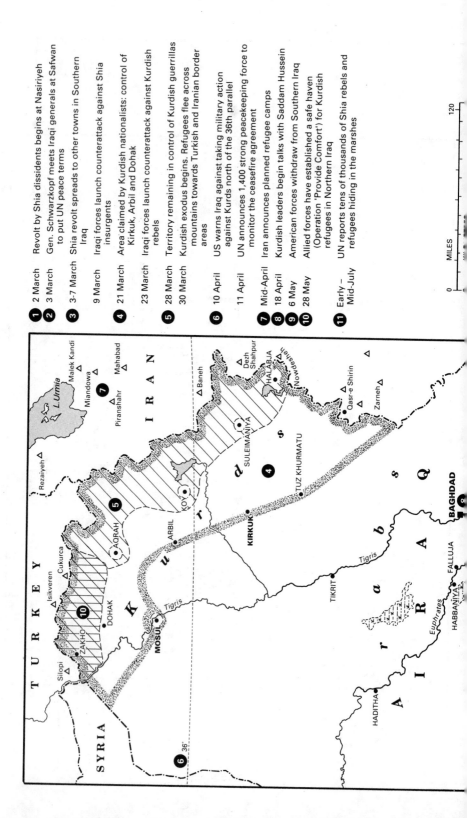

1	2 March	Revolt by Shia dissidents begins at Nasiriyeh
2	3 March	Gen. Schwarzkopf meets Iraqi generals at Safwan to put UN peace terms
3	3-7 March	Shia revolt spreads to other towns in Southern Iraq
	9 March	Iraqi forces launch counterattack against Shia insurgents
4	21 March	Area claimed by Kurdish nationalists: control of Kirkuk, Arbil and Dohak
	23 March	Iraqi forces launch counterattack against Kurdish rebels
5	28 March	Territory remaining in control of Kurdish guerrillas
	30 March	Kurdish exodus begins. Refugees flee across mountains towards Turkish and Iranian border areas
6	10 April	US warns Iraq against taking military action against Kurds north of the 36th parallel
	11 April	UN announces 1,400 strong peacekeeping force to monitor the ceasefire agreement
7	Mid-April	Iran announces planned refugee camps
8	18 April	Kurdish leaders begin talks with Saddam Hussein
9	6 May	American forces withdraw from Southern Iraq
10	28 May	Allied forces have established a safe haven (Operation 'Provide Comfort') for Kurdish refugees in Northern Iraq
11	Early – Mid-July	UN reports tens of thousands of Shia rebels and refugees hiding in the marshes

0   MILES   120

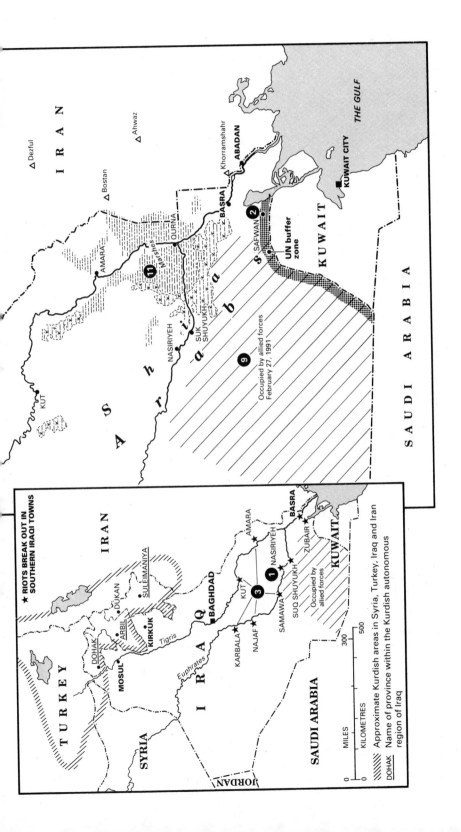

Map (main): IRAN, Dezful, Ahwaz, Bostan, Khorramshahr, ABADAN, BASRA, AMARA, Marshes, QURNA, KUT, KUWAIT CITY, THE GULF, SAFWAN, UN buffer zone, KUWAIT, NASIRIYEH, SUK SHUYUKH, SAUDI ARABIA, Occupied by allied forces February 27, 1991

A l - A h w a r (Ash-Shatt al-Arab)

Inset map: RIOTS BREAK OUT IN SOUTHERN IRAQI TOWNS, TURKEY, SYRIA, IRAN, JORDAN, IRAQ, SAUDI ARABIA, KUWAIT, BASRA, AMARA, NASIRIYEH, ZUBAIR, KUT, SUQ SHUYUKH, SAMAWA, NAJAF, KARBALA, BAGHDAD, KIRKUK, ARBIL, DOHAK, MOSUL, DÜKAN, SULEIMANIYA, Tigris, Euphrates

MILES / KILOMETRES 0 300 500

Occupied by allied forces

/// Approximate Kurdish areas in Syria, Turkey, Iraq and Iran
DOHAK Name of province within the Kurdish autonomous region of Iraq

PREFACE

Since the military conflict between Iraq and the US-led coalition took place in the Gulf, it seems logical to call it the Gulf War. But this term had been in vogue in the 1980s, and was applied to the warfare between Iran and Iraq which lasted from September 1980 to August 1988: a fact of which I, as the author of a book on the subject, am particularly aware.

To minimize the confusion, therefore, I often describe the Iran–Iraq armed confrontation as the First Gulf War, and that between Iraq and the US-led coalition as the Second Gulf War.

Indeed, the latter is a direct descendant of the former. It was in the course of the Iran–Iraq War that Baghdad increased the size of its military from 242,250 troops to nearly 1,200,000, and raised huge foreign loans, including about $14 billion from Kuwait. Both these factors came to play key roles in the two-year interregnum between the end of the First Gulf War and the Iraqi invasion of Kuwait.

However, the border dispute between Iraq and Kuwait has a long history, dating back to the era of Ottoman Turkish rule in the region. That is why I begin this book with a chapter tracing the roots of the dispute to earlier times. This chapter also outlines the nature of the state and society in Iraq and Kuwait, and the history of the First Gulf War, which in later years impinged directly on Kuwait.

The second chapter describes the situation in Iraq following the ceasefire in the Iran–Iraq War: its attempts to assume the leadership of the Arab world, and its growing alienation from America. It also sketches in the background of the worsening relations between Israel and the Palestinians, whose cause Iraq took up with renewed enthusiasm. It felt encouraged by the internal discontent in Kuwait to press its demands for concessions on border demarcation, and angry at Kuwait's attempts to undermine Iraq's economy by flooding the international oil market with over-supplies, thus depressing the price.

The next section of the book, entitled 'The Crisis', deals with the situation created by Iraq's invasion and occupation of Kuwait, starting with the responses of America and the United Nations.

Chapter 3 covers the first three weeks of the Gulf crisis. And Chapter 4 outlines the events from 23 August to 17 September 1990, the day the American secretary of defence dismissed General Michael Dugan, the US air force chief of staff, for revealing Washington's offensive strategy of bombing Iraq. The following chapter describes, primarily, the domestic problems facing President George Bush (1989–). Chapter 6, starting with the 8 October 1990 killings of the Palestinians in Jerusalem, dwells on the responses of various parties to the event, and their impact on the ongoing Gulf crisis. President Bush's announcement of doubling the US forces in the Gulf region marks the beginning of the next chapter, which ends with the United Nations Security Council's adoption of a resolution, on 29 November 1990, authorizing 'all necessary means' to reverse the Iraqi aggression. Chapter 8 describes the events until 16 January 1991, when the Second Gulf War erupted.

The final part of the book, entitled 'The Military Solution', is divided into three chapters: the air campaign until 23 February; the ground war until 28 February; and the aftermath, which continues.

In the concluding chapter I give an analytical summary of the causes of the outbreak of the war as well as the impact it has had on the region and the outside powers, including the United Nations.

To produce contemporary history, one has to rely largely on the media. There, a resident of London is especially privileged. He has access to five quality British newspapers as well as the *International Herald Tribune*, which carries important news stories and comments published simultaneously in the *New York Times*, the *Washington Post* and the *Los Angeles Times*. English translations of significant radio and television broadcasts in the Middle East are published daily by the US government as the *Foreign Broadcast Information Service* and by the British Broadcasting Corporation as the *BBC Summary of World Broadcasts*.

Since there is no standard way of transliterating Arabic names and words, spelling Arabic words can be a nightmare. There are 52 different ways of spelling Hussein, for example. There is no uniformity even for such common words as Moslem/Muslim. When it comes to looking up an index, a particular difficulty arises where the same place or person is spelled with a different first letter – as in Arbil/Erbil/Irbil; or Gadhafi/Qadhafi. In each case I have chosen one of the most widely used spellings in the English-language print media, and stuck to it – except when the spelling of a book author is different from mine. There I have simply reproduced the published spelling in quoted matter.

There is also no standard definition of the Middle East. Some authors apply the term to the geographical area extending from

Morocco to Pakistan, and Turkey to Sudan, including the island republic of Cyprus; others restrict it to the Arabic-speaking section of the region and Israel, leaving out Turkey, Cyprus, Iran, Afghanistan and Pakistan. Still others narrow it further by excluding Arab North Africa – Morocco, Mauritania, Algeria, Tunisia and Libya – as well as Djibouti and Sudan. I use the term in the narrowest sense.

The right name for the gulf that divides Iran from the Arabian Peninsula is also debatable. The internationally recognized term is the 'Persian Gulf', but Arabs like to call it the 'Arab Gulf', and the international media 'the Gulf'. I have used the last name, but have listed the two others in the index.

Confusion can also arise regarding dates due to large differences in local times in the Gulf and on the eastern coast of America. To dispel it, I have always used Greenwich Mean Time (GMT). Eastern Standard Time (EST), applicable to New York and Washington, DC, is five hours behind GMT, except during spring and summer months, when it is four hours behind. Gulf time is three hours ahead of GMT throughout the year. In other words, the clocks in Baghdad are seven to eight hours ahead of those in New York or Washington, depending on the season.

The dinar is the Iraqi unit of currency, and is noted as ID. In 1990 the official exchange rate was 0.3109 to one US dollar. The dinar is also the Kuwaiti unit of currency, and is noted as KD. Its official exchange rate in 1990, before the Iraqi invasion, was 0.292 to one US dollar.

The following Arabic words signify religious or secular titles of a leader: ayatollah, emir, hojatalislam, imam, sayyid, shaikh and sultan.

To help the reader place a political leader in time, I state in brackets, following the first mention of the leader's name, the years when he/she was, or has been, in power.

Last, but not least, my thanks to Heather. But for her diligent assistance in researching this book, it would have taken longer to materialize.

London   Dilip Hiro
21 August 1991

INTRODUCTION

Several features of the Second Gulf War make it unique among the armed conflicts of this century: the numbers of troops and amount of military hardware assembled in the region; the complex, fragile coalition that America managed to put together and hold; the frenetic diplomatic activity before and during the hostilities; the role of the United Nations; the unprecedented co-operation between Washington and Moscow in resolving the crisis by reversing the Iraqi invasion of Kuwait; the round-the-clock media coverage in the West of the 42-day war; and the role of television, particularly the Atlanta-based Cable News Network, as an instant diplomatic tool.

During the initial two weeks of their air campaign, the allies dropped more conventional explosives on Iraq and Kuwait than in the whole of the Second World War, which lasted 310 weeks. In the first 12 hours of the hostilities, the US-led coalition dropped more bombs on enemy territory than the United States had done in its 17-day air campaign, codenamed 'Linebacker-2', in Vietnam in 1972. The 600,000 gallons of fuel consumed by one US armoured division of 350 MI Abrahams tanks was nearly twice the total used by the US 3rd Army during its drive into Germany from France in 1944–5. To sustain its 430,000 troops at the start of the Second Gulf War, the Pentagon moved 6 million pounds of materiel daily.[1]

The Gulf crisis emerged on the heels of the end of the Cold War, which resulted in a 'cold' victory for the West, captured dramatically in the dismantling of the Berlin Wall in November 1989. It was a by-product of the break-up of the Moscow-led bloc. The collapse of this bloc, accompanied by an apparent weakening of the Soviet Union, led to a dramatic rise in the exodus of Soviet Jews, most of whom went to Israel. This increased fears in the Arab world for the future of the Palestinians in the Occupied Territories. These were shared by Iraq's president, Saddam Hussein (1979–), who was disappointed at the diminution of the power of Moscow, a long-term ally of Baghdad, and its predominant arms supplier.

He saw the hand of Washington in the newly adopted policy of Kuwait and the United Arab Emirates of exceeding the limits on their oil output specified by the Organization of Petroleum Exporting

Countries (OPEC), thus lowering the oil price, in order to harm Iraq's economy and lessen its diplomatic and military power. Since he was in no position to challenge Washington, Saddam Hussein turned on his weak neighbour, Kuwait, activating a border dispute which had deep roots.

To his surprise and disappointment, Iraq's invasion and occupation of Kuwait acquired an international dimension to an extent that the Iraqi president had not predicted. Further diplomatic and military setbacks ensued for him as the Soviet Union co-operated actively with America at the United Nations Security Council, thus providing the UN with the pre-eminence it had not enjoyed since its founding in 1945.[2]

Once America became militarily involved in the Gulf crisis, with its troops stationed in Saudi Arabia, its defence department (popularly known as the Pentagon, because of the shape of its headquarters) mounted psychological warfare against Iraq. Since journalists were the unwitting carriers of the disinformation peddled by the Pentagon, the media became contaminated.

As the crisis matured, and war preparations intensified, the allies' disinformation campaign gathered momentum. On the eve of hostilities the Pentagon introduced a 'pool' system, whereby a small proportion of the 1,600 accredited journalists was allowed to proceed to the forward lines, and their stories were shared with the rest of the press corps. 'US commanders will maintain extremely tight security throughout the operational areas and will exclude from the area of operation all unauthorized individuals,' stated the Pentagon press guidelines. This meant arresting journalists who turned up unescorted in the battlefield, and cancelling their accreditation. During the first four weeks of the war, the US field commanders detained at least 24 reporters on this count, including Chris Hedges of the *New York Times*, who was interviewing Saudi traders along a road some 50 miles from the Kuwaiti frontier. Certain correspondents were barred from press conferences because of their persistently 'impolite' line of questioning. It was thus that General Norman Schwarzkopf, the commander of the US Central Command, was able to joke publicly at his press conference on 27 February 1991 that the media had 'aided and abetted' allied deception tactics by saying that an amphibious attack on the Iraqi forces was imminent.[3]

As for the Iraqi side, the government had total control over the media, with President Saddam Hussein himself directing the day-to-day management. When it came to dealing with foreign correspondents,

Iraq's information ministry drew on the experience it had accumulated during the eight-year war with Iran: a conflict in which the Western media were more anti-Iranian than anti-Iraqi. It exposed reporters to the situations and information which it wanted to see highlighted.

The behaviour of the Iraqi information ministry was in line with the overall set-up in the country: a one-party state dominated by the Sole Leader, Saddam Hussein. Though Kuwait, a monarchy, was not in the same category as Iraq, it was a country ruled by a venal oligarchy, intent on curtailing the limited rights accorded to its citizens by the 1962 constitution.

While particular elements contributed to the creation of the Gulf crisis and the subsequent warfare, the general contributory factors were the absence of power sharing and public accountability (inherent in a parliamentary democracy), and inequitable distribution of wealth in the Arab world (due to unequal oil reserves and population density), against the background of the unresolved Palestinian problem dating back to 1948.

During the subsequent 30 years – while the membership of the Arab League nearly trebled,[4] the Arabs fought two major wars with Israel, and the oil-producing states prospered as never before – the independent Arab countries evolved as highly centralized states, with their presidents or kings acting as autocrats. Their rule rests, primarily, on strict control of the upper echelons of the military and intelligence services, and the media; nothing more.

In this context, which excludes free debate and the weighing of the pros and cons of an issue over an extended period of time, sudden switches of policy have become a rule, rather than an exception. Treachery and double-dealing are as much a way of political life in the Middle East as 'conspiracy'. Hence, what may seem baffling behaviour to the Western observer or reader is routine for most Arab leaders as well as non-Arab specialists on the Middle East.

In other words, the short-term interests of an Arab ruler, or his motivation, can and do change so swiftly that he undertakes a sudden U-turn without any regard to his past position, and without worrying about the impact of his action on his fellow-citizens, or the fortunes of the clandestine opposition at home or abroad. This applies as much to his domestic policies as it does to inter-state relations, whether the foreign country be Arab or non-Arab.

It would be useful to bear the above points in mind while reading this book.

PART I

HISTORICAL BACKGROUND

1 IRAQ AND KUWAIT:
NEIGHBOURS OR ONE FAMILY?

'Iraq has decided to ... demand the land [of Kuwait] arbitrarily held by imperialism, which belongs to the province of Basra.'

> Abdul Karim Qasim, the Iraqi prime minister,
> 25 June 1963[1]

'Nations are not only measured by the size of their population or the extent of their territory, but [also] by their people's capacity for achievement.'

> Shaikh Jaber III al Ahmad al Sabah,
> the Kuwaiti emir, 2 February 1987[2]

The Kuwait crisis of August 1990 was the third in a century, the first one occurring in July 1897 and the second in June 1961, not to mention the semi-crisis of March 1939. Each of these centred on the identity of Kuwait vis-à-vis Iraq. As such, it impinged directly on the future status of Kuwait's ruling dynasty, the al Sabahs, part of the Amarat clan of the Anaiza tribe.

Originally based in the Arabian hinterland, the Anaiza tribe had migrated to the northern shores of the Gulf following a severe drought in 1710, and settled along the sea at Kuwait (lit., Little Fort). It developed trading facilities there, and accepted the suzerainty of the Ottoman Turks who held sway in the region. Over the decades pearling and sea-trading brought prosperity to the tribe.

Communal affairs were conducted by three leading families: the al Jalahimas, al Khalifas and al Sabahs. The al Khalifas managed local commerce, the al Jalahimas seafaring trades, and the al Sabahs public administration and defence. Out of this arose, from 1752 onwards, the dynastic rule of the al Sabahs, the first ruler being Shaikh Sabah I al Sabah, and the second, Shaikh Abdullah I al Sabah (1756–1814).

The Ottoman Turkish sultans honoured the al Sabahs as their officials and considered Kuwait part of Ottoman Iraq. However, the incursion of the British into Kuwait in 1776 – marked by the opening of a base by the (British) East India Company – began to undermine Ottoman authority there.

In the late nineteenth century – when Kuwait had become a centre of rivalry between Ottoman Turkey, Britain, Russia and Germany – the British were alarmed by German plans to extend the proposed Berlin–Baghdad railway to Kuwait, which was to be used as a terminus and coaling station. They were particularly upset by the policy of Shaikh Abdullah II al Sabah (1866–92) of strengthening Kuwait's ties with Istanbul. Matters came to a head during the rule of Shaikh Muhammad I al Sabah (1892–6). He found himself sandwiched between pro-Ottoman elements, advocating formal integration of Kuwait with Iraq, and pro-British elements, insisting on strengthening the administrative independence that Kuwait enjoyed under the Ottomans. The latter were led by Mubarak, a half-brother of Shaikh Muhammad I.

Encouraged by Britain, Mubarak assassinated Muhammad I in May 1896, and seized power. But it was not until early 1897 that the Ottoman sultan recognized the official status of Shaikh Mubarak I by appointing him *qaimmaqam* (i.e. provincial sub-governor) of Kuwait. This seemed a stop-gap affair, with Istanbul preparing to impose direct administrative control over Kuwait so as to abort any breakaway designs that Mubarak might have. In July 1897, fearing a military move by the Ottomans, Mubarak I appealed to the British to guard the Kuwaiti shoreline. They responded quickly and deployed their gunboats, thus creating the First Kuwaiti Crisis. Relations between Ottoman Turkey and imperial Britain reached a low point, with the Ottomans protesting vehemently against British interference in the internal affairs of their empire. In the end, to avoid a military clash with Britain, a superpower, Istanbul let the status quo prevail.

This in turn encouraged Shaikh Mubarak I (1896–1915) to sign a secret treaty with the British in January 1899. In exchange for an annual subsidy of 15,000 Indian rupees (£1,500), the Kuwaiti emir accorded Britain the right of exclusive presence in Kuwait and control of his foreign policy.[3]

During his visit to Kuwait in 1903, Lord Curzon, the governor-general of India, reiterated London's commitment to Shaikh Mubarak I. Encouraged by such declarations, the shaikh expanded his realm by seizing adjacent areas. However, he suffered a severe political setback when the British, pursuing their higher interests, signed an Anglo-Ottoman Convention in July 1913 which recognized Kuwait as 'an autonomous caza [i.e. administrative unit] of the (Ottoman)

Empire' under Shaikh Mubarak as Ottoman *qaimmaqam*. His complete autonomy was recognized within an inner (red) circle of 40-mile radius, centred on Kuwait port, which included not only the islands of Warba and Bubiyan but also Mashian, Failakah, Auhah and Kabbar. Beyond that, in a segment of land with a radius of 140 miles, centred on Kuwait port, marking the outer (green) boundary defined by the Convention, Shaikh Mubarak was authorized to collect tributes from the tribes.[4]

However, the outbreak of the First World War in June 1914, when the Ottomans sided with the Germans, invalidated the Convention, and allowed London to announce that Kuwait was an 'independent shaikhdom under British protectorate'.

The disintegration of the Ottoman empire at the end of the First World War in November 1918 left Britain as the sole imperial power in the region. At the same time it sharpened the rivalry which had grown between the Kuwaiti emir, Shaikh Salim I al Sabah (1917–21), and the ruler of Najd, an adjoining territory, Abdul Aziz ibn Abdul Rahman ibn Saud (1902–53).

Shaikh Salim I insisted on Kuwaiti frontiers being drawn according to the outer (green) boundary defined by the Anglo-Ottoman Convention of 1913, the high point of Shaikh Mubarak I's expansionist activity. Abdul Aziz ibn Saud opposed this, arguing that Kuwait was no longer in control of the disputed lands, and that the Convention had not been ratified. To make the point, in May 1920 ibn Saud's forces attacked a Kuwaiti detachment recently stationed in the southern area contained in the 1913 Convention's outer boundary, and forced it to retreat. Britain intervened diplomatically, but failed to reconcile the warring parties. In early September ibn Saud declared that he did not recognize Shaikh Salim's domain beyond the surrounding walls of Kuwait port. The next month his forces raided Jahra, 25 miles west of Kuwait port, well within the inner (red) boundary defined by the Convention. Shaikh Salim I appealed to London for assistance and, as before, the British obliged. Determined to frustrate ibn Saud's ambition to absorb Kuwait into his domain, the British deployed gunboats, armoured cars and aircraft to such an extent that his forces retreated without a fight.

Border disputes occurred not only between Kuwaitis and Najdis but also between Kuwaitis and Iraqis. Indeed, relations between Kuwait and Iraq were to bedevil the region for the rest of the century, with Iraq – whether under a pro-Western monarchy or a leftist republican regime – periodically attempting to reclaim Kuwait as a lost member of its family with a view to re-creating the situation which had, in its view, existed in the Ottoman era.

Of the three political entities involved, two – Iraq and Kuwait – were under Britain's tutelage, with Iraq being its temporary charge and the tiny Kuwait being a permanent one. Britain was concerned about the raids that the bedouin followers of ibn Saud, unused to recognizing artificial land borders, conducted inside the territories of both Kuwait and Iraq. To stabilize the situation, Sir Percy Cox, the British high commissioner in Baghdad, called ibn Saud to a conference in late November 1922 at the seaport of Uqair (near Bahrain). It was also attended by Major John More, British political agent in Kuwait, representing Shaikh Ahmad al Sabah (1921–50). The end result was the Uqair Protocol of 2 December 1922, imposed by Cox. It defined the boundaries between Iraq and Najd, and Kuwait and Najd. In both cases, to overcome the stalemate, Cox carved out neutral zones where tribes from the adjoining countries were given equal rights to water and pasture. (In 1975 Iraq and Saudi Arabia agreed to divide the neutral zone equally.) The Uqair Protocol confirmed the inner (red) line of the 1913 Anglo-Ottoman Convention so far as Kuwait's southern border with Najd was concerned. But it did not define Kuwait's northern frontier with Iraq. 'I still do not know what the frontier between Iraq and Kuwait is, and I shall be glad if you will kindly give me this information so that I may know it,' wrote Shaikh Ahmad al Sabah to the British political agent, Major More, on 1 April 1923. Major More advised Shaikh Ahmad to state his claims. On 4 April he did so by reiterating the outer (green) line of the 1913 Anglo-Ottoman Convention as it applied to the area north of Kuwait port. The same day Major More informed Sir Percy Cox in Baghdad of Shaikh Ahmad's claim. On 19 April Cox replied that Shaikh Ahmad 'could be informed that his claim to the frontier and islands indicated is recognized in so far as His Majesty's Government are concerned'.[5] In other words, two British officials defined the Kuwaiti–Iraqi border, awarding the crucial area between the inner (red) and outer (green) lines of the Anglo-Ottoman Convention to Kuwait, limiting Iraq's access to the Gulf to a mere 36 miles of coastline infested with swamps and marshland, thus denying it the possibility of a deepwater harbour and constraining its ability to become an important naval power in the region. King Faisal I of Iraq (1921–33) was disappointed. But, with his country under British mandate, he had no choice but to ratify Iraq's boundaries with its neighbours as decided by British officials. He ratified the frontier with Kuwait through an exchange

of letters with the Kuwaiti shaikh in August 1923. Forty years later
these boundaries were to be recognized afresh; but this did not alter
the fact that the Kuwaiti–Iraqi frontiers were fixed originally by an
imperial European power, which controlled both territorial entities.

The British mandate over Iraq was the result of the Allies' victory in
the First World War over the Central Powers – including the Ottomans
who had been ruling Iraq since 1638 – and a decision by the League
of Nations Supreme Council in April 1920. This awarded Britain the
mandate for the Ottoman provinces of Basra, Baghdad and Mosul (to
be constituted later as Iraq), and France the mandate for Greater
Syria (Syria, Palestine and Lebanon) minus Palestine, which went to
Britain.

Both mandate powers had to contend with a strong wave of Arab
nationalism demanding total independence. The Syrian National
Congress, meeting in Damascus in February–March 1920, proclaimed
the independence of Greater Syria and the formation of a national
government under Faisal I ibn Hussein as a constitutional monarch.
A similar gathering in Baghdad, guided by al Ahd (The Covenant), a
group dominated by nationalist Iraqi military officers who had opposed
Ottoman suzerainty in the past, declared Iraq to be independent under
the constitutional reign of Abdullah ibn Hussein, a younger brother
of Faisal I. (They were sons of Hussein ibn Ali, the Hashemite king
of Hijaz, which contained the holy shrines of Islam at Mecca and
Medina.) These declarations of independence were rejected by Britain
and France.

In July 1920 the French defeated the forces of King Faisal I, and
imposed their mandate. Faisal I then accepted the throne of Iraq
offered to him by Abdullah, who was to be pacified by the British
with the offer of ruling the land east of the river Jordan, to be called
Transjordan (later Jordan).

Britain spent the best part of the summer and autumn of 1920
crushing the popular movement against its military rule in Iraq.
Later, in March 1921, London opted for indirect rule of Iraq through
a local government with an Arab leader. Finding Faisal I suitable for
the position, the British installed him as king in August.

To formalize its relations with Iraq, Britain incorporated the terms
of its League of Nations mandate into a treaty. The Iraqi government
deliberated for more than a year before endorsing it. The Anglo-Iraqi
Treaty of October 1922, which vested economic and military control
of Iraq in British hands, was then placed before a constituent assembly elected in March 1924. The reluctant members ratified it only

after the British high commissioner had threatened to suspend the constitution.

One of the major points of friction between Iraq and Britain was the future status of the Mosul province (with a predominantly Kurdish population), believed to be rich in oil, which had fallen into British hands three days after the Armistice of Mudros signed on 30 October 1918 to end the First World War. In March 1925 the Iraqi government granted an oil concession to the Turkish Petroleum Company (in which the British government had a 75% stake), giving it highly favourable terms. Four months later the Arbitration Commission of the League of Nations decided against Turkey, and awarded Mosul to Iraq, provided Iraq remained under British mandate until its acceptance as a member of the League of Nations. This set a positive seal on Iraqi–British relations. Aware of the fact that the Sunni Kurdish inhabitants of Mosul helped balance the predominantly Shia populations of Basra and Baghdad provinces, the Sunni-dominated government of Iraq played down its differences with Britain. The TPC's 1927 discovery of oil in commercial quantities in Mosul province further improved Anglo-Iraqi relations.

By holding parliamentary elections, Faisal I legitimized his regime. This suited Britain, whose interest in Iraq was heightened by the discovery of oil in Mosul. Aware of the economic benefits of petroleum, the Iraqi government improved its relations with London. It was against this background that in September 1929 Britain agreed in principle to sponsor Iraq's membership of the League of Nations.

In November 1930 a 25-year-long Anglo-Iraqi Treaty was drafted, to be implemented after Iraq had entered the League of Nations as an independent state. The new treaty required the Iraqi monarch to formulate a common foreign policy with Britain and allow the stationing of British forces in his country, in exchange for a British guarantee to protect Iraq against foreign attack. This was the price London extracted from Baghdad before ending its mandate on 3 October 1932.

On the eve of its application for League of Nations membership, Iraq was asked for a copy of the border agreements it had made with its neighbours. In his letter of 21 July 1932 to the British high commissioner in Baghdad, the Iraqi prime minister confirmed Iraq's border with Saudi Arabia and Kuwait as defined by the Uqair Protocol and the subsequent letters exchanged between Sir Percy Cox and Major John More.[6] However, this did not stop popular and official attempts in Iraq to draw Kuwait back into the Iraqi fold.

A few years later the Basra-based Association of the Arab Gulf urged a union between Iraq and Kuwait: a call taken up by the Iraqi monarch, Ghazi ibn Faisal (1933–9), who resorted to making nightly broadcasts on his private radio station calling on Kuwaitis to join the 'Iraqi family'.[7] The young ruler shared the aspirations of his people and military officers for complete independence from London. In October 1936, at his behest, the armed forces commander-in-chief, General Bakr Sidqi, overthrew the pro-British government of Yasin Hashemi.

Following the signing of the Iran–Iraq Frontier Treaty on 4 July 1937 – whereby Iraq conceded the *thalweg* (the median line of the deepest channel) principle for the Shatt al Arab waterway, marking the common border, for four miles opposite Abadan – the Iraqi foreign minister, Tawfiq al Suwaidi, explained to the British foreign secretary, Lord Halifax, that Iraq would like to lease a piece of territory from Kuwait to construct a deepwater harbour and link it to the Basra–Baghdad railway line. 'In the light of Iranian threats to the Shatt al Arab, we wish to start a project to guarantee an outlet to the sea via Kuwait,' wrote Iraq's deputy foreign minister to the British government on 7 September 1938. London replied that since Iran was an ally of Britain, Baghdad need not fear it, and that Kuwait was unlikely to allow the digging of a canal through its territory. 'If Kuwait was to give the island of Warba to Iraq, then the whole of the Abdullah [Khor] Waterway would come under Iraq's rule and guarantee a safe port for us [at Umm Qasr],' wrote Suwaidi in his note to London in late September.[8] But nothing came of this proposal either.

Disappointed and angered by the failure of his government's initiatives, and aware of the agitation for a written constitution and parliament that had erupted in Kuwait in 1938, King Ghazi encouraged the Kuwaiti opposition to overthrow Shaikh Ahmad al Sabah, making liberal use of his private radio station. Iraqi newspapers followed suit, promising the Kuwaitis better living standards if they joined the more advanced Iraqis.

Tension rose in the spring of 1939 as King Ghazi moved his troops to the Iraqi–Kuwaiti border. London warned that it would intervene militarily if his forces attacked Kuwait. In the event, nothing violent happened. On the night of 4 April 1939, the monarch was killed in a sports car accident. And with him died the escalating Iraqi–Kuwaiti crisis.

While Faisal II, the four-year-old son of Ghazi, became the titular head of state, power passed to his pro-British uncle, Abdul Ilah, who acted as regent. With the outbreak of the Second World War in

September 1939, tensions between the pro- and anti-British factions within the Iraqi ruling hierarchy became acute. Having failed to persuade his cabinet colleagues to declare war against Germany, the pro-British Prime Minister Nuri al Said resigned in March 1940. He was succeeded by Rashid Ali Gailani, a pan-Arabist nationalist. In April 1941 Gailani led a successful coup against the British, which led to the fleeing of the regent and his royal charge as well as Nuri al Said.

But Gailani was unable to withstand a British counter-offensive in May. The regent, the young king, and Nuri al Said returned to Baghdad in June 1941. The triumphant British reinstalled Nuri al Said as prime minister. But it was not until 1943 that he felt secure enough to proclaim war against Germany.

Following peace in August 1945, Nuri al Said allowed political parties, except the Communists, to function freely. He played an active role in the formation of the Arab League, and sent troops to fight in the Palestine War of 1948–9. But they performed poorly. The disappointed Iraqis blamed the incompetence and corruption of the ruling oligarchy – headed by Regent Abdul Ilah – for national humiliation on the battlefield.

Nuri al Said's increasingly dictatorial ways, his manipulation of the electoral system and elections, and the banning of political parties in early 1949 widened the chasm between the rulers and the ruled which had been created by the Palestine War fiasco.

The coming of age of Faisal II (at 18) in 1953 made no difference to the sharing of power by Regent Abdul Ilah and Nuri al Said. By deciding to enrol Iraq into the British-sponsored Middle East Treaty Organization (popularly known as the Baghdad Pact) in 1954, Nuri al Said showed disregard for the nationalist leanings of the military officer corps. His refusal to condemn the October 1956 Anglo-French–Israeli aggression against Egypt, ruled by the charismatic Gamal Abdul Nasser (1954–70), damaged the regime's popular standing beyond repair.

In Kuwait, Britain's position became virtually untenable when its part in the tripartite invasion of Egypt, the leader of Arab nationalism, was revealed. There were popular demonstrations against the aggressors in the capital.

This disturbed not only London but also Washington. For by 1955, during the rule of Shaikh Abdullah III al Sabah (1950–65), Kuwait had become the leading oil exporter in the Gulf; and it maintained this position for the next decade, in the process accumulating large

sums in US dollars (the currency used for oil transactions) at Britain's
central bank, the Bank of England, and providing a crucial support for
the British pound sterling. For a tiny country of 6,880 square miles
(17,818 square kms), no larger than Wales, this was a considerable
achievement.

Extraction of petroleum by the Kuwait Oil Company (owned jointly
by British and American interests), which had begun in 1938 after
four years of exploration, was interrupted by the Second World War.
It was only after 1946 that oil output and exports reached commercial
proportions. The closing down of the oil industry in neighbouring
Iran in 1951–3 (due to the dispute between the British-owned Anglo-
Iranian Oil Company and the nationalist prime minister Muhammad
Mussadiq) led to a rapid increase in Kuwait's oil production.

Not surprisingly, when on 14 July 1958 the clandestine Free Officers'
Group,[9] led by Brigadiers Abdul Karim Qasim and Abdul Salam Arif,
overthrew the pro-Western regime in Baghdad, assassinating the royal
family and prime minister Nuri al Said, both London and Washington
were shocked and alarmed.

The main concern in leading Western capitals was to safeguard
Kuwait and its oil reserves. As it happened, on the day of the revolution
in Iraq, the British foreign secretary, Selwyn Lloyd, was in Washington.
After his meeting with John Foster Dulles, US secretary of state, Lloyd
sent a secret cable to the prime minister, Harold Macmillan (1957–63).
'One of the most reassuring features of my talks here has been the
complete United States solidarity with us over the Gulf,' stated Lloyd's
cable. 'They are assuming that we will take a firm action in Kuwait.
They themselves are disposed to act with similar resolution in relation
to the Aramco [Arabian American Oil Company] oilfields in the area of
Dhahran, although the logistics are not worked out. They assume that
we will also hold Bahrain and Qatar, come what may. They agree that
at all costs these oilfields [in Kuwait, Saudi Arabia, Bahrain and Qatar]
must be kept in Western hands. The immediate problem is whether
it is good tactics to occupy Kuwait against the wishes of the ruling
family . . . To produce tolerable conditions for a long term operation,
we should have to take control of the whole of Kuwait and run it as
a Crown colony. For a short term operation we could hold the oil area
alone, but that would no doubt mean a Nasserite regime in the rest
of Kuwait . . . The advantage of this action would be that we could
get our hands firmly on the Kuwaiti oil.' In the end, however, Lloyd
opted for keeping out of Kuwait. 'On balance, I feel it is very much to
our advantage to have a kind of Kuwaiti Switzerland where the British

do not exercise physical control . . . If this alternative is accepted, we must also accept the need, if things go wrong, ruthlessly to intervene, whoever it is [who] has caused the trouble.'[10]

America went beyond holding consultations with Britain. President Dwight D. Eisenhower (1953–60) combined despatching 10,000 American marines to Lebanon,[11] then in the midst of civil strife, to protect its pro-Western government against a defeat by the local Arab nationalist forces, with 'apparent authorization' of the use of nuclear weapons 'to prevent any unfriendly forces from moving into Kuwait'.[12]

The financial and economic dependence of Britain on Kuwait had been underlined some months earlier, in January 1958, by Selwyn Lloyd. His major concerns included Britain's free access to Gulf oil production 'on favourable terms and for [pound] sterling', and 'suitable arrangements for the investment of the surplus revenues of Kuwait' in Britain. Reflecting this perception, recently declassified US policy papers reaffirmed that 'the UK asserts that its financial stability would be seriously threatened if the petroleum from Kuwait and the Persian Gulf area were not available to the UK on reasonable terms, if the UK were deprived of the large investments made by that area in the UK and if [pound] sterling were deprived of the support provided by Persian Gulf oil.' These British needs, and the fact that 'an assured source of oil is essential to the continued economic viability of Western Europe', provided some reason for the US 'to support, or if necessary assist, the British in using force to retain control of Kuwait and the Persian Gulf'. Indeed, in November 1958, the US National Security Council recommended that America 'be prepared to use force but only as a last resort, either alone or in support of the United Kingdom', if these interests were threatened.[13]

The July 1958 revolution in Iraq accentuated differences between the independently minded Arab nationalist Baghdad and the British-protected Kuwait. Following Iraq's withdrawal from the pro-Western Middle East Treaty Organization, and its formal adoption of a non-aligned foreign policy, popular pressure grew on the Kuwaiti emir, Shaikh Abdullah III, to abrogate the 1899 Anglo-Kuwaiti Treaty.

He found himself under an external threat as well. Once the republican regime in Iraq had consolidated its hold, its leader, Prime Minister Abdul Karim Qasim, began reviving the old claim that Kuwait was an integral part of Iraq. This worried Shaikh Abdullah, especially as he was negotiating an end to British protection. In order to widen his popular base, he promised his subjects a constitution in 1960.

As the British government pondered ending its protection of Kuwait, it called on the Chiefs of Staff Planning Committee to report on 'the practicability of an operation to dislodge Iraqi forces from Kuwait', bearing in mind in particular that 'the West is anxious to preserve continued access to oil'. In its report to the Chiefs of Staff, the Planning Committee stated that the Foreign Office felt that 'an operation to recapture Kuwait from the Iraqis might well be less objectionable politically – even if delayed – than an attempt to forestall Iraqi intervention'. The documents prepared for the British defence officials' meeting with their American counterparts in April 1960 argued that 'a successful military solution requires that Western forces should be poised to intervene quickly before hostile public opinion has time to build up.' However, the record of the subsequent Anglo-American defence meeting was withheld for fifty years instead of being released thirty years after the event for the benefit of researchers and historians. Significantly, the papers of Prime Minister Harold Macmillan showed that he considered the creation and maintenance of an independent Kuwait as the cornerstone of Britain's Middle East policy at a time when the Trucial States (later renamed the United Arab Emirates), Bahrain and Aden were British colonies, and Oman and Jordan were tied closely to Britain. 'All these commitments are really in support of our interest in the security of Kuwait,' Macmillan wrote in October 1960.[14]

The Anglo-Kuwaiti talks led to an agreement. On 19 June 1961, Edward Heath, as Lord Privy Seal, informed the House of Commons that the 'obsolete and inappropriate' Anglo-Kuwaiti Treaty of 1899 had been formally replaced by a concord of 'close friendship' which acknowledged Kuwait's full independence and sovereignty. The new relationship centred on a renegotiated Anglo-Kuwaiti defence agreement, entitling Kuwait to call on London to assist it in defending itself against foreign invasion. Since Britain had moved its troops and tanks from Kuwait to neighbouring Bahrain, it was in a position to meet its military obligations quickly.

On 25 June the Iraqi leader, Qasim, publicly demanded that Kuwait be returned to Basra province, and described the Kuwaitis who had signed the new agreement with Britain as 'irresponsible people under the sway of imperialism'. This was the beginning of the Second Kuwaiti Crisis.

As rumours circulated that Qasim had despatched two brigades from Basra, thirty miles north of the Kuwaiti border, to attack Kuwait, Shaikh Abdullah III, commanding no more than 1,500 Kuwaiti troops, appealed on 30 June for military assistance to Britain and Saudi Arabia. The next day British troops began arriving by air and sea from Bahrain, Aden and Cyprus. Within a week 6,000 British soldiers and their armour were in place. A smaller force arrived from Saudi Arabia.

Kuwait lodged a complaint with the United Nations. At its Security Council meetings the Iraqi ambassador to the United Nations denounced the military build-up as a 'sordid operation', a 'military adventure reminiscent of the Suez [aggression of October 1956]', and an 'aggressive act accompanied by a singularly unconvincing attempt to hide behind the mantle of the Shaikh of Kuwait'. The Soviet Union vetoed a resolution approving United Nations membership for Kuwait on the ground that the renegotiated Anglo-Kuwaiti defence agreement had left Kuwait still under 'foreign domination'.[15]

In contrast, Prime Minister Harold Macmillan made out that the British government's action was guided above all by compassionate concern for a weak country threatened by a powerful neighbour. 'We could not afford to leave Kuwait hopelessly undefended against forces poised to attack,' he told the House of Commons. But the real motives had been spelled out long before by Dick Beaumont, head of the Foreign Office's Arabia Department, and declassified thirty years later. 'The United Kingdom's irreducible interest in the Gulf was the protection of Kuwait's oil,' he wrote in 1960. 'Kuwaiti independence will not be preserved unless any government which might wish to subvert or overthrow it is convinced of Her Majesty's government's willingness and ability to defend Kuwait by force of arms if necessary.'[16]

As for the Kuwaiti government, it combined its complaint to the United Nations with an appeal to the Arab League, which had accepted its application for membership on 22 June. Employing the means it came to adopt repeatedly in later years, especially during the 1990 crisis, its finance minister toured Arab capitals pledging large sums of money to win support. At the Arab League meeting the decision to aid Kuwait was unanimous, with only Iraq opposing. Nasser, then president of the United Arab Republic, consisting of Egypt and Syria, came out strongly in favour of assisting Kuwait – motivated partly by his animus towards Qasim, who had refused to amalgamate Iraq with the United Arab Republic. The result was the despatch of a 2,000-strong Joint Emergency Force of the Arab League – consisting of units from Jordan, Saudi Arabia, Sudan and the United Arab Republic – to replace the British troops. This, in effect, defused the Second Kuwaiti Crisis – publicly. But there was a clandestine aspect to it: Kuwait's agreement to pay $85 million in grants to Iraq, a very substantial sum in those days.[17] This arrangement set a pattern which was to repeat itself in the coming decades: when threatened by Iraq with annexation, the al Sabahs bribed their powerful neighbour to back off.

The British troops finally left on 19 October 1961. The Arab world could claim, rightly, that it had found and implemented an Arab solution to the crisis. As the situation stabilized, the Arab League's Joint Emergency Force began withdrawing from Kuwait in stages, the last units leaving the emirate in early 1963.

However, the basic threat to Kuwait's territorial integrity, inherent in its smallness and geographical position and heightened by its stupendous oil riches, had not been totally banished. This was highlighted by Qasim on 29 December 1962. 'We could occupy Kuwait militarily in half an hour,' he told visiting Syrian journalists. 'No power on earth can prevent us from doing so.'

The following February Qasim was overthrown, and assassinated, by military officers belonging to the Arab Baath Socialist Party, which had been formed clandestinely in Iraq about a decade earlier. This, and the departure of the last foreign troops from Kuwait, prepared the ground for the approval of Kuwait's application for UN membership by the Security Council on 7 May 1963.

On 4 October 1963 the representatives of Iraq and Kuwait signed in Baghdad 'Agreed Minutes Regarding the Restoration of Friendly Relations, Recognition and Related Matters', thereby formally recognizing the boundary between Iraq and Kuwait, and the allocation of offshore islands, as specified and agreed in the exchange of letters between the Iraqi prime minister and the Kuwaiti emir on 21 July 1932 and 10 August 1932.[18] But the exchange of envoys did not take place until Kuwait had signed a lucrative contract with Iraq to buy 120 million gallons of water daily from the Shatt al Arab.

The post-Qasim regime was run by members of the Arab Baath Socialist Party. This had originated as the Arab Baath Party in Damascus in April 1947, following a pan-Arab congress. Its founders were three teachers: Michel Aflaq, a Greek Orthodox Christian; Zaki Arsuzi, an Alawi Muslim (i.e. like the Shias, a follower of Imam Ali); and Salah al Din Bitar, a Sunni Muslim. The party's basic principles were described as: the unity and freedom of the Arab Nation within its homeland; and a belief in the 'special mission of the Arab Nation', the mission being to end colonialism and promote humanitarianism. To accomplish it the party had to be 'nationalist, populist, socialist and revolutionary'. While the party rejected the concept of class conflict it favoured land reform; public ownership of natural resources, transport and large-scale industry and financial institutions; trade unions of workers and peasants; co-option of workers into management; and acceptance of 'non-exploitative private ownership and inheritance'.[19] It stood for a representative and constitutional form of government, and for freedom of speech and association within the bounds of Arab nationalism. Its programme was summed up by the slogan: 'The eternal mission of the Arab Nation: Unity, Freedom, Socialism'.

According to the Baath Party, Arabs form one nation which is currently divided into various regions (countries). Therefore the party has at the top the National Command which encompasses the whole Arab world and which serves as the central executive authority. Under it are certain Regional Commands pertaining to those Arab states where the party is strong enough to justify establishing one. Below a Regional Command are branches, composed of sections, made up of divisions, each one consisting of a few three-member cells.

The party became active in Iraq in 1952, and two years later it claimed membership of 208 there. It held its first (clandestine) regional congress in late 1955 when it decided to co-operate with other nationalist groups. But it played only a marginal role in the military coup which destroyed the monarchy in 1958.

Some Baathist activists, including Saddam Hussein, attempted unsuccessfully to assassinate Qasim in October 1959 because he refused to further Arab unity by agreeing to amalgamate Iraq with the United Arab Republic. Despite being suppressed by Qasim, the party increased its size. By the time the Baathists, joined by non-Baathist sympathizers, overthrew Qasim in February 1963, the party had 850 active members and 15,000 sympathizers, and its own militia, called the National Guard. But once in power, the Baathists fell out among themselves on the questions of union with Nasser's Egypt and the degree of socialism to be achieved, thus allowing the prestigious but non-Baathist Abdul Salam Arif to usurp power as president in November 1963.

In 1965 his government revived the 1937 plan to construct a deepwater harbour at Umm Qasr and connect it with the Basra–Baghdad railway. This brought to the fore the idea of leasing Kuwaiti soil on the mainland and/or its offshore islands. Knowing that Kuwait was keen to demarcate the Kuwait–Iraq land frontier, Baghdad linked the issue with its proposal for leasing Kuwaiti territory. Kuwait seemed willing to lease the small Warba Island to Iraq for 99 years. However, the negotiations came to a sudden halt when the Iraqi president died in a helicopter crash in April 1966.

His brother, Abdul Rahman Arif, succeeded him. Politically vulnerable, he spent too much of his time protecting his position, and
balancing various groups among military officers, to pay much attention to foreign affairs. In December a dispute between Syria and the
(Western-owned) Iraq Petroleum Company over oil transit fees led to
the stoppage of oil exports through the Mediterranean terminals. This
played havoc with the economy, making Baghdad more aware of the
economic weakness entailed by lack of proper access to the Gulf. The
dispute dragged on until March 1967.

Three months later, in June 1967, came the Third Arab–Israeli War.
The Arif regime was exceedingly slow to react. Only after the people
had taken to the streets, demanding participation in the fight, did the
government send a token force to Syria. By the time it arrived there,
the war was practically over.

The fiasco was widely blamed on the incompetence of President
Abdul Rahman Arif. This undermined his authority, and created an
environment in which an alliance of Baathist leaders and non-Baathist
military officers overthrew him on 17 July 1968. Within a fortnight
the Baathists got rid of their non-Baathist allies, and assumed total
power.

But the party in 1968 was quite distinct from what it had been five
years earlier. It was more down-to-earth than before, having learnt
to concentrate on such practical issues of policy as land reform. It
was better organized and bigger, with 5,000 active members; and
yet more conspiratorial and more paranoid about co-operating with
non-Baathist elements.

The ruling five-member Baathist Revolutionary Command Council,
headed by President Ahmad Hassan Bakr, a former major-general,
set out to institutionalize the interweaving of the party with the
state machinery and with secular society at large. It decided to
transform the military into an organ of the Baath by placing party
members with freshly acquired military training in crucial positions
and directing them not to execute any significant order without
clearance from Baath headquarters. The same strategy was used for
domestic intelligence services. Concurrently, the military hierarchy
ordered that the ranks and officers be imbued with Baathist ideology.
In addition, the party set up its own bureaus in parallel with such
major institutions as the military, police and intelligence. The interim
constitution of July 1970 formalized party supremacy by stating that
the Revolutionary Command Council (RCC), the highest state body,
had the right to select new members of the Council from 'among

the regional [i.e., national] leadership of the Arab Baath Socialist Party'.

Earlier, in November 1969, RCC membership was expanded to fifteen, with all but one of the ten fresh members, including Saddam Hussein (a close adviser to, and a relative of, President Bakr), being civilians. Thereafter the Bakr–Hussein duo came to dominate the party and the state as a result mainly of their cunning elimination of their RCC colleagues, with six of them removed from the RCC within two years.[20] While Bakr focused on widening his power base in the officer corps, Saddam Hussein tightened his grip over the RCC's National Security Bureau, which specialized in gathering information on domestic opposition; the Public Security Directorate, engaged in routine intelligence gathering at home; and the party's militia, the National Guard. Together, Bakr and Hussein gained a degree of power neither could have acquired alone.

The party leadership set up cells in government departments, professional syndicates, educational institutions, publicly and privately owned businesses, trade unions, agricultural co-operatives and women's associations. These cells were all the more effective because the Baathist cadres were required to keep their party affiliation secret. The party units met regularly to evaluate the performance of the government departments in the light of Baathist principles and guidelines, and report to their headquarters. A similar procedure was followed in the armed services. By the time the Baathists held their Eighth Regional Congress in January 1974, *inter alia* to clarify the party–state relationship, their ranks had swelled to 20,000.

In external affairs the Baathist regime hardened the anti-American stance it had inherited from Abdul Rahman Arif who, following the June 1967 Arab–Israeli War, had severed diplomatic links with Washington. Relations with Moscow became increasingly cordial.

Early in July 1971 a delegation led by the Soviet vice-prime minister, Vladimir Novikov, signed an Iraqi–Soviet protocol of co-operation in Baghdad. During a return visit to Moscow in February 1972, Saddam Hussein, then deputy head of the RCC and assistant general-secretary of the Baath Party, declared that 'the firm strategic alliance between our peoples, parties, and governments is the foundation on which [our] economic, technical, cultural and other relations are being built and will continue to be built.'[21] He stressed ideological concurrence – opposition to Western imperialism, Zionism and the American designs for peace in the Middle East – as the common ground for mutual friendship.[22] This led to the conclusion of the Iraqi–Soviet Treaty of Friendship and Co-operation on 9 April 1972.

Soviet success in developing the Rumeila oilfields in southern Iraq showed the Iraqis that they need not be totally dependent on Western capital or expertise for the progress of their vital oil industry. This encouraged it to nationalize the Iraq Petroleum Company, which it did in June 1972.

The IPC retaliated by taking action against the purchasers of its oil. This led to a severe drop in Iraq's oil revenues and created financial uncertainty, with the government unsure of its ability to pay the military and civil service. Baghdad was compelled to seek a large loan from Kuwait. After dragging its feet for several months Kuwait finally rejected the Iraqi request in early 1973. Iraq moved its troops to the Kuwaiti border, and demanded the right to build oil facilities including a deepwater oil terminal off Bubiyan Island. Kuwait refused. On 20 March, Iraqi armour attacked two Kuwaiti border posts and took up positions inside Kuwait. The Kuwaiti emir raised the alarm, and appealed to the Arab League for assistance. Saudi Arabia despatched its forces to show solidarity while working behind the scenes to defuse the crisis. The pro-American Shah of Iran (1941–79) was quick to warn pro-Soviet Iraq of serious consequences if it attacked Kuwait. In the end, Baghdad withdrew its forces after it had received an undisclosed amount of money from Kuwait, following Saudi mediation. In August, in his talks with the Kuwaiti crown prince in Baghdad, Saddam Hussein, then deputy head of the Iraqi Revolutionary Command Council, suggested dividing Bubiyan Island in two, with Iraq keeping the eastern half and Kuwait the western. But nothing came of the proposal.[23]

While Iraq welcomed Moscow's material and moral aid to the Arabs in the October 1973 Arab–Israeli War, and sent its troops to Syria to fight the Israelis, it did not join the Arab oil boycott of Israel's supporters which was decided unanimously at the meeting of the Organization of Arab Petroleum Exporting Countries (OAPEC) in Kuwait. This was an illustration of Baghdad's determination not to let its membership of a supra-national Arab organization, or its close ties with Moscow, inhibit it from pursuing an independent foreign policy: a fact which remained unchanged for the next seventeen years and which impinged, dramatically, on the conscience of the world community in the summer of 1990.

On its part, the Soviet Union had no compunction in offering recognition to Kuwait after the departure of the British troops in October 1961. The Kuwaiti emir accepted this in principle, if only to bolster the international status of his emirate, then under threat from Iraq. The exchange of envoys occurred in March 1962. Reviewing Kuwait's foreign policy, soon after the accession of Shaikh Sabah III al Sabah in late 1965, an editorial in the Moscow-based *New Times* lauded Kuwait for following a neutralist line in external affairs.[24]

OAPEC's oil boycott led to a steep rise in petroleum prices. Among the beneficiaries was Kuwait. In 1975, when Kuwaiti oil production was running at only two-thirds of the 1973 level of 3 million barrels per day (mb/d), the government's annual oil revenue soared to $7,200 million. Since the state budget could only absorb $2,900 million, the rest was available as investment and aid abroad.[25] Kuwait became a force in the international monetary system.

As for Iraq, its income shot up from $75 million in 1972 to $8,000 million in 1975.[26] The Baathist regime enlarged its popular base by awarding hefty wages and salary increments, expanding educational, health and public welfare services, and implementing ambitious economic projects. Simultaneously, the Baath Party tightened its grip over the military, police and intelligence. A well-planned internal security system held Baathist members responsible for the safeguarding of their street or neighbourhood.

By the mid-1970s, though still deputy head of the RCC, Saddam Hussein had outstripped President Bakr in leadership, cunning, ruthlessness, determination, organizational ability and charisma. As a youthful, energetic figure, he appealed to those Baathists who believed in strong ideology and commitment to progressive socio-economic policies.

Saddam Hussein took an active interest in foreign affairs and the politics of oil. Soon after the nationalization of the IPC on 1 June 1972, he visited Paris to sign a contract to sell France about a quarter of Iraq's oil output. It was while he was attending a summit meeting of the Organization of Oil Producing Countries (OPEC) in Algiers in March 1975, that he concluded an accord with the Shah of Iran to settle the border issue.

His agreement to share the fluvial border of the Shatt al Arab with the pro-American Iran did not mean that Saddam Hussein had altered his radical views on America, oil and the Gulf monarchies. His address on 12 June 1975 to the Iraqi ambassadors to Western Europe and Japan aptly summed these up; and, despite the convulsions that Iraq and the Gulf region were to undergo during the next fifteen years, they remained virtually unchanged. In his opinion, the US had gone beyond considering oil as a strategic material in which it ought to acquire self-sufficiency. 'Oil has become a decisive element in American global policies with particular effect on its relations with Western Europe and Japan,' he stated. 'Hence the United States will not be content with the present status quo . . . America and some European states will have the lion's share of the joint oil [resources] of Saudi Arabia, Kuwait and other countries . . . The question of what the future will bring is the one in which the will of the people plays a crucial part. It may be that the future will favour the United States for some time, but in the longer term, the future will favour the peoples . . . It has become evident that America's involvement in an area of conflict as a party hostile to the will of the peoples . . . will turn this [popular] will towards an anti-American stand, regardless of the strong grip of America's local allies, the reactionary regimes [of the Gulf].'[27]

Among the region's reactionary regimes that Saddam Hussein had in mind was the one in Kuwait, then preparing to celebrate the fourteenth anniversary of its independence, which had brought in its train a constitution (promulgated in December 1962) and a parliament.

Kuwait's constitution guaranteed 'personal liberty' and 'the freedom of the press'. However, while allowing the citizen 'freedom to join trade unions or contract out of them', it barred the formation of political parties. It assigned the task of safeguarding these freedoms to an independent judiciary.[28] It specified an elected National Assembly of 50 members. Though it preserved the ruler's prerogative to appoint the council of ministers (who automatically became members of the National Assembly), thus denying the elected body any executive authority, it gave the Assembly such powers as approving or disapproving the ruler's ministerial appointments, all official legislation, and the government's policies in foreign affairs, oil, defence, finance and other matters. Also the National Assembly was given the prerogative of choosing the crown prince (and thus the future emir) out of a short list of three.

Having conceded a popularly elected parliament, Shaikh Abdullah III al Sabah (1950–65) and his successors tried to determine its composition by manipulating the electoral system, and by co-opting the tribal and mercantile leaders into their scheme. The franchise was limited to about 10 per cent of the male citizens – that is, those Kuwaiti men, aged 21 or above, who could prove that their ancestors lived inside the walls of the capital in 1920 or before.[29] The ten five-member constituencies were so demarcated that each had a large bedouin area; and an elector was allowed to vote anywhere he wished. This allowed the pro-emir candidates to ferry the bedouin voters *en bloc* to those constituencies where the support for them was known to be low.

Aided by such tactics, and by the willing co-operation of the leaders of the dominant Ajman and Awazim tribes, Shaikh Abdullah III al Sabah had little difficulty in getting a parliament in January 1963 which was a virtual rubber-stamp.

Trouble arose after his death in 1965, when his successor Shaikh Sabah III al Sabah (1965–77) appointed a new council of ministers. Several parliamentary deputies found these appointments so unacceptable that they resigned in protest. To forestall any future repetition of such an embarrassing event, the emir decided to see a totally pliant parliament elected at the next poll. The result was open vote-rigging in January 1967. The opposition protested, demanding a re-run, but in vain.

By comparison the election of 1971 was free, but hardly fair. As in the past, a large majority of seats went to the nominees of the monarch and his cabal of thirty to forty tribal leaders. The remainder were taken mainly by the nominees of the fifteen super-rich merchants, who stood at the apex of a 5,000-strong merchant community, with the rest – about half a dozen seats – going to the most politically conscious of the Kuwaitis: the nationalist-leftist professionals and intellectuals led by Dr Ahmad Khatib.

The Arab–Israeli War of October 1973, and particularly the use of oil as an effective diplomatic weapon by the Arab states, moved the opinion of the press and the public towards the positions taken by the nationalist-leftist deputies.

Overall, therefore, despite the above-mentioned limitations, the National Assembly established itself as a fairly independent forum, voicing popular views on many internal and external matters. Of course it represented only a minority of the Kuwaiti nationals, who in 1975 were about 44 per cent of the population estimated at one million. Among the non-Kuwaitis, the 250,000 Palestinians were the largest single group. Due to their disproportionately high presence in educational institutions, the civil service and the media, the Palestinians had considerable influence on Kuwaiti public opinion, and thus on parliament.

Though the Fourth National Assembly elected in January 1975 continued to be dominated by the conservative tribal-merchant bloc, the tone of parliamentary debates became increasingly strident. The radical minority succeeded in making the conservative majority back its demand that oil production be pegged to a maximum of 2 mb/d, that the Western-owned Kuwait Oil Company be nationalized, and that the press laws be liberalized.

The nationalist-leftist bloc in Kuwait's parliament was actively sympathetic towards the Palestinians, the largest expatriate Arab community in the emirate. The intervention of the Syrian forces in the Lebanese civil war (1975–90) against the leftist Lebanese–Palestinian alliance angered most Palestinians, and created tension in Kuwait. Disruption of the press in Beirut, regarded as the freest in the Middle East, encouraged the Kuwaiti papers (largely staffed by the Palestinians) to provide uncensored news. This alarmed and angered not only the Kuwaiti emir but also the royal family of neighbouring Saudi Arabia. The latter was particularly stung by anti-Saudi statements made by some Kuwaiti parliamentary deputies which were reported in the local press.

Accusing the National Assembly of wasting time on debating legislation and indulging in 'malicious behaviour', the emir suspended it in August 1976. He also restricted press freedom and suspended four important articles of the constitution.[30] He acted in close collaboration with the Saudi royal family. In September 1977 he dissolved the Assembly, thus repeating the Kuwaiti history of two generations before.

Nearly forty years earlier, a demand by the notables for power-sharing had arisen in the wake of petroleum fees and advance royalties paid by the Kuwait Oil Company to the emir from 1934 onwards. They argued that these payments should be treated as government income and used for public services. The emir's refusal to concede this point enlarged the ranks of those demanding political reform. In 1938 they became divided into moderate and radical factions, the former favouring calling on London to intervene directly and impose reform, and the latter advocating union with Iraq. It was against this background that Shaikh Ahmad yielded by asking the Merchant Society to select a 14-member council, and then directing it to produce a constitution. The council's five-point draft constitution specified a popularly elected 20-member legislative assembly with powers to approve or disapprove '[all] internal concessions and lease monopolies as well as external agreements and treaties'. Since this would have interfered with Britain's colonial administration of Kuwait and, more importantly, the British companies' objective of extracting the best possible terms for oil concessions, London refused to countenance the constitution. The emir therefore rejected the document, and dissolved the council.[31]

However, in September 1977 the dissolution of parliament elicited different reactions from the two important sections of society: the educated urban dwellers, and mercantile and tribal leaders. The former denounced the emir's decision while the latter endorsed it.

If the urban educated class had any hopes that the demise of Shaikh Sabah III al Sabah on 31 December 1977, followed by the accession of Shaikh Jaber III al Ahmad al Sabah to the throne, would lead to the restoration of the National Assembly, these were soon disappointed.

Aware that the absence of parliament provided the emir with greater latitude in conducting foreign affairs, Izzat Ibrahim (Duri), a close aide to Saddam Hussein, proposed to the Kuwaiti government, during his visit to Kuwait in early 1978, that it should partition Bubiyan Island and allocate one part to Iraq to secure 'the Arab nation's interests in the Arabian Gulf'. As before, the Kuwaitis gave the Iraqi official a polite hearing, and nothing more.

Shaikh Jaber III continued the domestic policies of his predecessor, showing no sign of reviving parliament, confident of the backing he had from influential business leaders on the issue. After all, by barring non-Kuwaitis from owning land or real estate, or a majority share in any business, the al Sabahs had laid a firm foundation for the future prosperity of Kuwaiti businessmen and real-estate owners. The oil price boom of late 1973, which in turn led to zooming imports and accelerated economic activity, brought untold riches to this social class. For instance, by the mid-1970s private investments abroad of the top fifteen merchants' families alone were estimated to be in the region of $6,000 million.[32]

However, within a couple of years, the merchants' endorsement of the strangling of the National Assembly soured into grumblings against the emir. The reason was that, with the scrutinizing gaze of the National Assembly removed, the ruling family had taken to lining its private pockets at the expense of the state and the long-established merchants.

'Before [the dissolution of the National Assembly] the shaikhs were not really in business, but now they are everywhere,' said Ahmad, the American-educated forty-year-old son of an important merchant. 'Shaikh Mishaal al Sabah, a brother of the ruler, who heads security, owns a factory for building material. It seems a South Korean [construction] company won a contract on one condition: they would buy material from him. The shaikhs get a cut from every contract, whether military or civil.' That such complaints were widespread and well-founded became apparent when Abdullah Nafissi – a political

scientist whose book entitled *The Other Face of Kuwait* illustrated
how the ruling family was making money at the expense of the state
– was arrested and expelled.[33]

A glimpse of the super-affluent lifestyle of the al Sabahs in the
mid-1970s was provided by an American air stewardess. Many years
later, she recalled meeting the eldest son of Shaikh Sabah III al Sabah
on a flight from Las Vegas to New York. The young shaikh, who had
been gambling in Las Vegas, was wearing *five* of the medallions that
the leading casino, Caesar's Palace, handed out to heavy gamblers. The
stewardess ended up dating his cousin. 'They would go to London to
party, and return to New York to go to the dentist.' In New York they
would rent a palatial suite at the Waldorf Hotel, and buy luxury cars.
Then would follow sessions with salesmen to equip the vehicles with
custom-made fittings and accessories.[34]

While disaffection against the al Sabahs was growing in Kuwait, Iran
underwent a republican Islamic revolution in February 1979, resulting
in the overthrow of the corrupt, autocratic monarch, Shah Muhammad
Reza Pahlavi. The revolutionary movement was led by Ayatollah
Ruhollah Khomeini (1979–89), a towering Islamic personality of Shia
persuasion.

As early as 1974 Khomeini had declared himself against monarchy,
and based his argument on the Hadiths, the sayings and doings of
Prophet Muhammad. 'Tradition relates that the Prophet said that the
title of King of Kings, which is [today] borne by the monarchs of Iran,
is the most hated of all titles in the sight of God,' Khomeini stated.
'Islam is fundamentally opposed to the whole notion of monarchy
. . . Monarchy is one of the most shameful and disgraceful reactionary
manifestations.'[35]

Once in power, Khomeini lost no time in attacking the Gulf rulers
as 'mini-Shahs'. He regarded them as corrupt men who fostered what
he called 'American Islam' or 'golden Islam'. He was scathing about
their policy of depleting the valuable oil resources of their countries
to satisfy the ever-growing demands of America, which he described
as the Great Satan, the number one source of corruption on earth. He
denounced them for denying their subjects any role in the decision-
making processes of the state. The creation of a representative system
in Islamic Iran, with a popularly elected president and parliament,
made his argument for republicanism attractive to many in the Gulf
monarchies.

Khomeini's onslaught, and the fear that the downfall of the Shah
would embolden republican forces in their own countries, made

the Gulf monarchs nervous. They were ill-equipped to tackle the threat stemming from Khomeini's salvos, since they had all along sought legitimacy of their rule within Islamic precepts. Khomeini's view, based on an interpretation of the Sharia – Islamic law (consisting of the Quran and the Hadiths) – that hereditary power is unIslamic, was the most serious ideological threat they had faced so far.

They were aware that Khomeini's attack on dynastic rule and his condemnation of the policies and personal lifestyles of the Gulf monarchs had been particularly well received by the Shia ulama (i.e. religious-legal experts) in the region. This made Bahrain, with 60 per cent Shia population, the most vulnerable to revolutionary upheaval. The next in line was Kuwait, a quarter of its nationals being Shia. In July 1979 a delegation of local Shia leaders flew to Tehran to congratulate Khomeini, and 30 former parliamentary deputies petitioned the emir to revive the National Assembly and desist from amending the 1962 constitution.

The Iranian revolution was viewed favourably not only by the Shia minority – composed of bedouins, poor urban dwellers and merchants – but also by the Palestinians. The growing popularity of the protest movement, centred on the Shia mosques in Kuwait City, added to the ruling family's worries, apprehensive that the movement might encounter receptive minds among the substantial Shia segment within the armed forces.

Shaikh Jaber III al Sabah tried to tackle the rising protest by following a stick-and-carrot policy. He put further restrictions on press freedom and banned public meetings of more than twenty people without prior permission by the authorities.[36] He initiated a policy of wholesale expulsion of 'undesirable' aliens: mainly Shia Iranians. In February 1980 the emir decided to placate the populace by appointing a constitutional commission of thirty-five members (including eight Shias) to recommend amendments to the constitution with a view to reviving the institution of an elected assembly of some kind. By the end of February 1981 the constitution had been amended, and elections to the National Assembly held under it.

Having conceded parliamentary elections, the emir tried to make sure the opposition candidates were defeated. He succeeded to a large extent. None of the nationalist-leftists, including the veteran Ahmad Khatib, was elected. Of the many Islamic fundamentalist candidates only six managed to win. Shaikh Jaber III had good reason to feel satisfied: he had defused a threat to the ruling dynasty and fostered a parliament willing to do his bidding most of the time.

More importantly, however, Iran's Islamic revolution created major problems for the secular regime of Iraq. It accentuated the Shia problem which had its roots in the Ottoman era. The Sunni Ottomans had excluded Shias from public office, and denied to Shia ulama certain privileges given to Sunni ulama. On the other hand the Ottoman sultans had let Najaf and Karbala – the holy cities containing respectively the shrines of Imam Ali and his son Imam Hussein, the most revered figures of Shias apart from Prophet Muhammad – function as semi-independent enclaves. When the secular Baathists seized power in mid-1968 their government imposed strict censorship of religious publications, shut down various Islamic institutions, began harassing Shia ulama and, for the first time in Iraqi history, allowed the sale of alcohol in the Shia holy places. These steps goaded Shia clergy to rally their followers to protest, a development which in turn brought government repression.

It was against this backdrop that in 1969 al Daawa al Islamiya (The Islamic Call) was formed clandestinely in Najaf. In December 1974 Shia religious processions turned into indignant political demonstrations against the Baathist regime. Shias felt, rightly, that they were grossly under-represented in the upper echelons of the police, military, intelligence, civil service and the ruling party's hierarchy. The tension between the Shia masses and the regime erupted violently at the height of a Shia ceremony in early February 1977 when the government sealed off Karbala. The police intercepted a procession of pilgrims on its way from Najaf to Karbala. This triggered off riots. The police opened fire, killing several dozen people.

Some Baathist leaders, headed by President Bakr, wanted to conciliate Shia dissidents and accommodate party ideology to the rising wave of Islamic revival, while others, led by Saddam Hussein, the second most powerful leader, advocated repressing Shia protest and adhering strictly to the party policy of separation between religion and politics. Saddam Hussein won.

He grasped the gravity of the situation if only because Shias formed 70 per cent of the Arab population, which was about 80 per cent of the total, the rest being Kurds. Unlike the Kurdish insurgents, who were confined to the mountainous region in the north, Shia activists were part of the mainstream both socially and geographically. So Saddam

Hussein combined relentless persecution of Shia militants with a policy of promoting loyal, moderate Shias to middle-level ranks in the state and party hierarchies. The strategy seemed well tailored to contain Shia discontent.

But Saddam Hussein's plan was upset by the victory that the predominantly Shia revolutionary forces in Iran, led by Khomeini, won over an apparently invincible Shah in early 1979: it raised the expectations and aspirations of Iraqi Shias to an unprecedented degree.

For Tehran, three factors made Iraq the primary target for instigating the next Islamic revolution: the secular nature of the Baathist regime; the oppression of the Shia majority; and the existence of six Shia holy shrines within its boundaries, in Najaf, Karbala, Kadhimain and Samarra.

Thus both republican, socialist Iraq and monarchical Kuwait found themselves threatened by the emergence of a revolutionary Islamic regime in Iran, though for different reasons. But the tension between Iraq and Iran was the more severe, and escalated into a shooting war on 22 September 1980.

Saddam Hussein, exercising supreme power as the president of the republic as well as of the Revolutionary Command Council since July 1979, had territorial and political aims in invading Iran: to recover the eastern half of the Shatt al Arab boundary he had conceded to Iran in March 1975; to crush Iranian agitation among his country's Shia malcontents; and, as an ambitious corollary, to overthrow Khomeini's Islamic regime.

Before launching his attack Saddam Hussein consulted the rulers of Saudi Arabia and Kuwait on visits to the capitals of these countries on 5 and 12 August respectively. During the eight-year war that ensued they consistently provided him with money, diplomatic support, logistical back-up and intelligence. The 1980–88 Iran–Iraq conflict, later to be known as the First Gulf War, brought Iraq and its monarchical neighbours – Kuwait, Saudi Arabia and Jordan – closer than ever before.

The First Gulf War: 1980–88

Having a substantial Shia minority of its own, and lacking military muscle to protect its vulnerable oil facilities or to stand up to either of the belligerents in the First Gulf War, Kuwait found itself particularly vulnerable to threats from Iran. At the beginning of the hostilities, Tehran warned that it would take 'appropriate action' against any regional state that transformed its discreet backing for Baghdad into active co-operation. To show that it meant business, Iran staged air raids on Kuwaiti border posts on 12 and 16 November 1980 in retaliation for alleged Kuwaiti involvement in the Iraqi military effort. Under the circumstances the Kuwaiti regime continued its policy of permitting the media to take up a pro-Iraqi stance while banning its officials from endorsing this stand.

After initial successes the tide began to turn against Iraq on the battlefield, and Kuwait increased its financial and logistical aid to its northern neighbour, with 500 to 1,000 heavy trucks a day carting goods to Iraq. To its interest-free loan of $2 billion to Baghdad in the autumn of 1980, it added two further sums of $2 billion each in April and December 1981.[37] Iran disapproved of Kuwait's actions. On 1 October 1981 the Kuwaiti oil installations at Umm Aayash were hit in an air raid. Though Tehran denied responsibility the Saudi-based Awacs (Airborne Warning and Control Systems) reportedly tracked the attacking planes from their Iranian base. The moral was clear: Kuwait must pay a price, periodically, if it persisted in its policy of allowing Iraq to use its ports, airfields and highways.

In 1983 Iran mounted a series of major offensives against Iraq, which the latter was able to repulse, but at a great cost in men and materials. This had a mixed impact on the Gulf monarchies. Freshly impressed by Tehran's power, the Lower Gulf states of Oman, the United Arab Emirates and Qatar became genuinely neutral. In contrast, Saudi Arabia and Kuwait drew nearer to Iraq. Here again there was a difference. Kuwait's backing for Iraq stemmed from two factors: its growing anxiety about the internal subversion likely to be undertaken by Kuwaiti Shias, and genuine fear of Iraq, which now proposed leasing Bubiyan Island to improve its defences against Iran. Rioting by Kuwaiti Shias during their Ashura ceremony (to mourn the death of their much revered Imam Hussein) in October 1982, which the authorities blamed on Tehran, highlighted the ruling dynasty's anxiety about Iran. To counter the Iraqi pressure, the Kuwaiti government consolidated its hold over Bubiyan by building a bridge between the mainland and the offshore island in early 1983.

In the absence of any such competing territorial claims straining relations between Saudi Arabia and Iraq, Riyadh's links with Baghdad grew tighter. At the September 1982 Arab summit in Fez, Iraq backed the peace plan offered by the Saudi monarch, Fahd ibn Abdul Aziz

(1982–). When the Iranians staged their offensive at Mandali on 1 October 1982 with a view to capturing Baghdad, the Saudi king telephoned Saddam Hussein to reassure him of his backing. Riyadh Radio warned that Iran would face war with 'the whole Arab world' if it refused mediation and broke through the Iraqi defence lines.[38] Such a statement implied that Saddam Hussein was struggling on behalf of the Arabs as a whole, and concurred with his interpretation of the continuing hostilities between Iraq and Iran: in the name of Islam, Khomeini was attempting to expand his Persian empire, and in fighting to preserve its territorial integrity Iraq was resisting his designs on behalf of the whole of the 'Arab homeland'. Not surprisingly, the failure of the Iranian offensive was welcomed as much in Baghdad as in Riyadh. In March 1983 Crown Prince Abdullah ibn Abdul Aziz declared: 'Iran cannot enter Baghdad because that would mean an all-out war with Iran [by us].'[39]

The events of 1983 established clearly that alone among the Gulf states Saudi Arabia had emerged as the most important regional supporter of Iraq. During that year there were a dozen exchange visits involving top officials of the two countries, including Saddam Hussein's arrival in Riyadh on 15 January. In his talks with King Fahd he reportedly secured the monarch's permission for an oil pipeline through Saudi territory. Equally importantly, Saudi Arabia persuaded France, a major arms supplier to the kingdom, to deliver five highly advanced warplanes, called Super-Etendard, to Iraq. The deal was facilitated by Saudi Arabia's agreement to pay for the jet fighters in oil – out of the 200,000 b/d that it had contracted to ship to Iraq's customers. This arrangement came into being due to Riyadh's reluctance to provide cash to Baghdad because of falling oil prices and its much reduced OPEC quota – down from 9.5 mb/d in 1979 to 4.5 mb/d in early 1983. During that year Saudi Arabia ran a deficit of $15.5 billion in its current trade account, in contrast to its surplus of $7.6 billion in 1982. Riyadh helped Baghdad in another way. It provided 10 per cent down payment to the foreign companies signing contracts with Iraq, and guaranteed the balance.[40] Deprived of the generous oil income of the immediate past, Kuwait too opted for supplying petroleum to Baghdad's customers: 130,000 b/d.[41]

Following bomb explosions in December 1983 at the US and French embassies in Kuwait, the international airport and the compound of an American residential complex accommodating US Hawk-missile experts, relations between Kuwait and Tehran deteriorated sharply.

Though none of those arrested for these acts was Iranian, the government deported hundreds of Iranian residents. In contrast, Saddam Hussein's retaliatory ground-to-ground missile strikes against five Iranian towns won the grateful appreciation of the Kuwaiti emir, and further strengthened mutual Kuwait–Baghdad ties. The same happened during the Iranian offensives of February–March 1984. In the wake of Iraq's loss of the Majnoon Islands to Iran, Kuwait announced a 'public mobilization plan'.

The Tanker War, from February 1984 onward, had a direct impact on the Gulf states, particularly when Iranian retaliation took the (unacknowledged) form of attacks on ships trading with Kuwait or Saudi Arabia. The constituents of the six-member Gulf Co-operation Council (Bahrain, Kuwait, Oman, Qatar, Saudi Arabia and the United Arab Emirates)[42] succeeded in convincing the Arab League foreign ministers' conference in Tunis on 20 May 1984 that Tehran's attacks on Saudi or Kuwaiti vessels outside the Iraqi-declared war exclusion zone constituted acts of Iranian aggression.

A denouement between Tehran and Riyadh was reached on 5 June 1984 when the Saudis shot down an Iranian F-4 fighter which they claimed had intruded into Saudi airspace and ignored two warnings. According to an account given by a top Saudi official to a group of Western journalists in Jiddah three years later, Tehran began sending up its warplanes after losing its F-4. 'The Iranians sent up eight, we sent up 15; then they had 20,' he said. 'By the end we had 25 F-15s and 18 F-5s in the air ... Then we heard one command from the Iranians to their pilots – RTB – Return to Base.'[43] If true, this incident showed that neither party was willing to go over the brink and declare war against the other.

Iran did not wish to be diverted from its primary conflict with Iraq. As for Saudi Arabia and Kuwait, they had good reasons to refrain from joining the fray. They seemed to have heeded both friendly advice from Damascus (which sided with Iran) and dire warnings from Tehran. 'The lifestyle of the littoral states of the Persian Gulf ... depends on ports, installations and their oil pipelines,' said Ali Akbar Hashemi Rafsanjani, speaker of Iran's parliament. 'All of them could be destroyed by shelling, let alone air attacks.'[44] In any case these countries needed time, equipment and practice to make their defences effective. America came to their aid. Besides airlifting fresh weapons to Saudi Arabia, Washington upgraded its military links with Kuwait, sending military personnel to Kuwait to upgrade its US-made Hawk anti-aircraft missiles. The Pentagon also extended the Saudi-based Awacs cover to Kuwaiti refineries and desalination plants.

This caused much resentment among Arab nationalist officers in the Kuwaiti military. More than two dozen of them plotted to overthrow the al Sabah regime. But their plan was discovered in early February 1985, leading to the arrest of their leader, Colonel Abdul Rahman Fakhru. He was sentenced to ten years' imprisonment.[45]

However, elections to Kuwait's Sixth National Assembly were held as scheduled on 20 February 1985. The electorate was limited to 56,000. While formal political labels remained banned, the nationalist-leftists contested under the unofficial banners of the Democratic Group (headed by Ahmad Khatib) and the National Bloc, and the Islamic camp under the labels of the Reform Society (of the Muslim Brotherhood), the Salafi, and the pro-Iranian Cultural Association. In a house of 50, the nationalist-leftists secured five seats, and the Islamic groups eleven.

The emir expected that the re-emergence of the nationalist-leftists in the National Assembly after an absence of four years would be a desirable counter-weight to the growing influence of the Islamic fundamentalists. The fundamentalists, sympathetic to Iran, wanted Kuwait to stay out of the First Gulf War, and were critical of Iraq for demanding not only money from their country but also 'land', meaning specifically the offshore islands of Bubiyan and Warba. In practice, to the chagrin of the ruler, the nationalist-leftist and Islamic groups began co-operating with one another in parliament.

On 25 May 1985 a suicide bomber driving a car packed with explosives made an unsuccessful attempt to assassinate Shaikh Jaber III al Sabah. Claiming that the action had been directed by Iran,[46] and intent on showing Iraq's solidarity with Kuwait, Saddam Hussein resumed air raids on Tehran (which he had suspended in June 1984 after intercession by the United Nations), and intensified attacks on Iranian ships in the Gulf. On 30 May and again on 4 June 1985 Iran's vital Kharg Island oil terminal was subjected to particularly severe air strikes by Iraq. In return Iran deployed its F-4 fighters based on Lavan Island to strike ships trading with Kuwait or Saudi Arabia near the Qatari coast.

To the surprise of many, the Iranians were successful in their February 1986 offensives in capturing 320 square miles of Iraq's Fao Peninsula, and retaining most of the territory in the face of repeated Iraqi counter-offensives.

Since its offshore island of Bubiyan was only fifteen miles from the Fao front, Kuwait felt seriously threatened by Tehran's military success. It condemned Iran's moves, and put its forces on alert. Reversing its policy of excluding Gulf War footage from its television screens, the Kuwaiti government began transmitting material supplied by Iraqi television. The Kuwaiti press adopted a blatantly pro-Baghdad stance, highlighting for example news of private donations for Iraq's war effort. By late March these were to reach a total of $525 million.[47] The government renewed its countersale petroleum contract with Baghdad. 'Financially, politically, in the mass media, everything had become territory for Iraqi propaganda,' said Abdul Reda Assiri, a political scientist at Kuwait University. 'Kuwaitis not only loved Saddam Hussein, but [also] worshipped Saddam.'[48] Riyadh was equally concerned about Iraq. On 12 February 1986 King Fahd reportedly phoned Saddam Hussein to enquire about the Iranian offensive; and over the next fortnight there were four high-level contacts between Riyadh and Baghdad.

Tehran repeated its public disapproval of the aid that Saddam Hussein's Arab neighbours were providing him. 'These countries should remember that we are now on their borders,' Rafsanjani said on 28 February 1986. 'Iran will no longer accept that your ports should receive arms shipments for Iraq, that your roads should be used to strengthen the Iraqi army, and that Iraqi oil should pass across your territory.'[49]

But such tactics proved counterproductive. At their meeting in Riyadh from 1 to 3 March 1986, Gulf Co-operation Council foreign ministers combined their condemnation of Iran's occupation of Fao and its threats against their countries with praise for Iraq for its readiness to end the conflict peacefully. Following this, GCC chiefs of staff decided to despatch the GCC Rapid Deployment Force, consisting of two brigades made up chiefly of Saudi and Kuwaiti troops, from Hafar al Batin, Saudi Arabia, to the Saudi–Kuwaiti border.[50]

In early March Iran hit four ships leaving or approaching the western side of the Gulf in as many days in retaliation for Iraq's attacks on four Iranian tankers plying between Kharg and Sirri Islands during the previous week. Thus Iran proved its potential for enforcing its threats against Iraq's allies.

Kuwait was the more vulnerable. Unlike Saudi Arabia (and like Iran), it was totally dependent on tankers for exporting its petroleum. So, to avenge itself for Iraqi attacks on its tankers, Iran began attacking Kuwaiti tankers. This worried the al Sabah regime.

At home, too, the Kuwaiti government felt harassed. In early 1986 the Islamic camp in the National Assembly took exception to the liberal reform of universities proposed by the education minister, Hassan Ali Ibrahim. He yielded to the opposition's fierce criticism, and offered his resignation in May. The emir refused to accept it. Stung by this, the opposition turned its attention to the alleged misdeeds of the minister of oil, Shaikh Ali Khalifa al Sabah, and the minister of finance, Jasim Khurafi. The fact that the oil minister was an eminent member of the al Sabah family worried the emir. The ruler seemed to have reckoned that parliamentary investigation into Shaikh Ali Khalifa al Sabah's running of the oil ministry as well as the past record of the finance ministry would lead to a parliamentary examination of the ruling family's role in the disastrous collapse of Kuwait's unofficial stock exchange, Suq al Manakh, in September 1982, leaving $97 billion in paper debts.[51]

As if this were not enough, the Kuwaiti petroleum complex at Mina Ahmadi was set on fire on 17 June. The fire raged for two days. The saboteurs claimed to belong to the Revolutionary Organization: Force of Prophet Muhammad. They were almost certainly Shias, either native-born or Lebanese (resident in Kuwait). This event shook the administration and angered the National Assembly. Afraid that the legislators would insist on investigating the incompetence of several ministries, including oil, the whole cabinet decided to resign in late June.

Faced with the collapse of his government, Shaikh Jaber III did what his predecessor had done in similar circumstances: he dissolved the National Assembly and imposed censorship. Significantly, his action (taken on 3 July 1986) received approval not only from the Saudi king but also from the Iraqi president.[52]

On 6 July the emir met General George Crist, commander-in-chief of the US Central Command, in charge of American military activity in the region, reportedly to discuss US aid in training a Kuwaiti guard to protect oil installations. Three months earlier, during his visit to Kuwait, Richard Murphy, US assistant secretary for the Near East, had stated that Washington would provide security for Kuwait in the event of a foreign invasion provided the emirate requested it.[53] What Kuwait faced from Tehran was something less than outright invasion of its territory; but attacks on its tankers were threatening a vital source of its income. One way to safeguard its vessels, the Kuwaiti government reckoned, was by securing American as well as Soviet protection for them.

It decided to act in September, but was diverted in early November when the hitherto clandestine Irangate affair surfaced in America to reveal that the second administration of President Ronald Reagan (1985–8) had been supplying weapons and spares to Iran in return for assistance in the release of the American hostages held in Lebanon by pro-Iranian groups. This was seen in Kuwait (and other Gulf states) as part of a 'conspiracy' to prolong the First Gulf War, and keep Iraq busy on its eastern front in order to divert Arab resources and energy away from tackling the Palestinian–Israeli problem.

However, on 10 December the state-owned Kuwait Oil Tanker Company (KOTC) sought information from the American Coast Guard concerning procedures for the reflagging of foreign vessels to US-flag ships. A fortnight later the KOTC informed the American embassy in Kuwait of its interest in reflagging its tankers.[54]

Because of the disarray in which the Reagan administration found itself in early 1987, due to the discovery of the Irangate affair, it was unable to respond positively to the Kuwaiti request for providing a naval escort to its reflagged oil tankers. But the situation changed when Washington learned on 2 March that Moscow had agreed to lease three of its own tankers to Kuwait. This was widely publicized in the American media – although not the interconnected fact that a few weeks earlier Kuwait had allowed the Soviet Foreign Trade Bank to raise a $150 million loan through a Kuwaiti investment company.[55] Indeed, this was to set a pattern to be repeated in late 1990 during the Third Kuwait Crisis: Kuwaiti financial aid in exchange for Soviet diplomatic backing. For now, the Kuwait–Moscow deal provided the US administration with a rationale for meeting the Kuwaiti request, as well as securing Congressional and popular support for it by raising the Soviet bogey. Two months later, in order to comply with American law, Kuwait agreed to transfer the ownership of half of its twenty-two tankers to the US-based Chesapeake Shipping Incorporated so as to secure American naval escort. This greatly strengthened military-economic ties between Washington and Kuwait.

Ironically, the matter acquired urgency by virtue of an Iraqi action. On 17 May 1987 two Exocet missiles fired by an Iraqi warplane hit an American frigate, USS *Stark*, about 85 miles (140 kms) north-east of Bahrain, killing 37 crewmen. Saddam Hussein apologized for the attack which, he claimed, was accidental. But an Iranian official described it as 'a serious and dangerous trap' laid by Baghdad to entangle both superpowers in the war.[56] Washington put its naval force on high alert and authorized it to fire on any craft believed to be of 'hostile intent'. The incident raised tensions in the Gulf, with the US reaffirming its decision to go ahead with the reflagging of the Kuwaiti tankers, and Richard Armitage, assistant defence secretary, publicly stating on 29 May: 'We can't stand to see Iraq defeated.'[57]

On 16 May and again on 19 June two tankers carrying Kuwaiti oil – one of them Soviet-registered – were hit by sea mines off the coast of Kuwait. By mid-June mines, believed to have been laid by Iran, had been detected at the approaches to the channel leading to Mina Ahmadi oil terminal in Kuwait. It took the US and Saudi navies about a month to make the channel and the approaches mine-free. On 7 July Iraq attacked Kharg as Tehran fortified its strategically placed islands of Abu Musa and Greater and Lesser Tunb near the Hormuz Straits.

Rafsanjani, known as a pragmatic figure in Tehran, instigated the despatch of a high-powered Iranian mission to Kuwait to persuade its government in secret talks to suspend the US reflagging of its tanker fleet in exchange for an Iranian guarantee to end attacks on Kuwaiti shipping.[58] Kuwait turned down the offer, and reflagged the remaining nine tankers. This action confirmed Iran's earlier assessment of Kuwait as summarized by its foreign minister, Ali Akbar Velayati. In a letter to the United Nations secretary-general, he had said that Kuwait had 'virtually turned [itself] into an Iraqi province' having placed its resources 'at the disposal of France, America and the Soviet Union', and added: 'As long as Iran's oil exports are threatened by Iraq, Iran cannot allow Iraq to receive guaranteed oil [income] in order to beef up its war machine through Kuwaiti tankers flying whatever flag.'[59] By attacking a Kuwaiti freighter outside the Hormuz Straits on 31 August, Tehran gave vent to its anger at Kuwait's stance.

At the end of seven years of warfare with Iran, in September 1987, Iraq possessed nearly 400 combat aircraft – six times the strength of Iran's airworthy warplanes. But at 193, Iraq's attack helicopters were less numerous than Iran's 341. On the ground Baghdad owned 4,500 tanks and 3,200 armoured combat vehicles versus Tehran's respective totals of 1,570 and 1,800. Iraq had 2,800 major artillery pieces whereas Iran had 1,750.

Baghdad had managed to replace its substantial losses in warplanes and other military hardware by continuing to borrow large sums. Its total foreign credits – excluding $45 to $55 billion in economic and military loans and grants from Gulf Co-operation Council members

– amounted to $50.5 billion, or three times its Gross Domestic Product.[60]

By continually extending its conscription rules Iraq had increased its professional military troops to 955,000, far above the 655,000 troops in Iran, which was three times more populous. Iraq's Popular Army (with some female units), estimated to be 650,000 strong, was slightly larger than Iran's Revolutionary Guards Corps at 620,000. Thus the Baathist regime had put under arms nearly 1.6 million men in a country with a total of 2.7 million males aged 18 to 45. Its achievement looked all the more impressive in contrast to the Iranian total of approximately 1.28 million men under arms out of a total of some 9 million males aged 18 to 45.[61] Achieving the target of putting 60 per cent of the Iraqi males aged 18 to 45 years into military uniform meant worsening the labour shortage that already existed, something that Baghdad overcame by engaging more than a million foreign workers.

In the diplomatic arena, by accepting the United Nations Security Council's comprehensive ceasefire Resolution 598 of 20 July 1987, Iraq had improved its position considerably. Iran, on the other hand, continued to be equivocal about this resolution. Goaded by GCC members, the meeting of the Arab League foreign ministers on 25 August condemned Iran's occupation of Iraq's territory, denounced mine-laying in the Gulf, and approved Kuwait's actions to protect its security as well as economic interests.

In mid-January 1988, the confidence of GCC states, particularly Kuwait, was enhanced by the visits to the region by the US defence secretary, Frank Carlucci, and the Egyptian president, Hosni Mubarak (1981–). Carlucci announced that there were no plans to reduce the US naval presence in the Gulf. The news was well received by Kuwait, which had by now allowed the US to anchor two supply barges within its territorial waters to act as floating bases, and re-registered 17 of its original 22 tankers under the American and British flags.[62] Both Kuwait and Saudi Arabia had by then renewed for one more year their oil countersale agreement with Iraq.

In mid-April 1988 Iraq's recapture of its territory in the Fao Peninsula, achieved with a liberal use of chemical weapons, and followed by America's mauling of the Iranian navy, boosted the confidence of Kuwait and Saudi Arabia. They noted that the US administration reacted sharply to the damage caused by a mine to one of its warships by knocking out two Iranian oil rigs, and that it responded to the subsequent moves by Tehran with unexpected speed and vigour, in the process sinking or damaging five Iranian vessels. Most importantly, the Reagan administration's actions received enthusiastic backing from both US Congress and public opinion. Kuwait, Saudi Arabia and Iraq felt reassured of the American resolve to checkmate Iran militarily in the Gulf.

Iraq's offensive in the Shalamche area in the southern sector on 25 May 1988, which involved an extensive use of chemical agents, succeeded in expelling the Iranians from Iraqi territory. And so too did its assault in the Majnoon Islands a month later, once again executed with a liberal use of poison gases. Iran left the Halabja area in Iraqi Kurdistan on 12 July, and Iraq pulled out of the Iranian enclave in the Naft-e Shah region in the central sector.

These events prepared the ground for Iran's unconditional acceptance of Security Council Resolution 598 on 18 July 1988. Now Baghdad demanded that 'all issues' must first be settled through direct negotiations before a ceasefire could come into effect, with UN observers being allowed to enter Iraq. These demands were a façade and a delaying tactic behind which Saddam Hussein wanted to press home the military superiority his country had acquired over Iran. Soon the Iraqis mounted lightning offensives against Iran in the southern and central sectors. These enabled Saddam Hussein to impress on his people and others that Iraq was militarily superior to Iran, and concurrently to enhance Baghdad's strategic position before the ceasefire. In a sense he wished to transform what was, by most accounts, a military draw into an outright victory.

At the Security Council Iran rejected Iraq's demand for direct talks since that amounted to a unilateral amendment of Resolution 598. Tehran's stand was backed by almost all Security Council members; and Saddam Hussein withdrew his demand on 6 August. Two days later the Security Council unanimously approved the implementation details of Resolution 598. On 20 August the ceasefire came into force, thus ending nearly eight years of war. If Saddam Hussein had had his way, hostilities would have ceased in June 1982 when Israel invaded Lebanon, so that Iran and Iraq could have joined hands to fight Israel. But this was not to be.

Iraq's defensive struggle against an Iran on the offensive from mid-1982 onwards helped Saddam Hussein to forge national unity to a degree not thought possible before. Most Iraqi Shias remained loyal to the state. Their failure to respond to repeated calls by Khomeini to revolt against the Baathist regime stemmed from three major causes. Divided by clan and tribe, they had failed to evolve a corporate sectarian identity; with an enemy at the frontier, nationalist feeling took precedence over sectarianism; and most Shias shared with their Sunni fellow citizens a fear of violent disruption of their lives in the wake of an Iranian victory. Whatever the reasons, the Shias' behaviour reassured the Iraqi leader who, reversing the earlier neglect of the religious question by the Baath Party, enthusiastically and publicly adopted Islamic symbols and rituals, and inducted the clergy, Sunni and Shia, into the war propaganda machine.

Kurdish nationalists remained unreconciled. But the fact that they were confined to a certain region proved to be both their strength and their weakness. While their geographical specificity allowed the regime to isolate them, they proved difficult to suppress, settled as they were in a mountainous terrain.

The long conflict with Iran engendered a powerful military-industrial complex, and militarized Iraqi society. Under the pressures of warfare Saddam Hussein, a politician initially determined to keep the armed forces under strict civilian control, let military service and soldierly values dominate society and the ruling party. The Iraqi media widely publicized Saddam Hussein's conferences with senior defence officers, which far outnumbered his meetings with high political or administrative officials. It was significant that most of the deputies elected to the Second National Assembly in October 1984 had been active in the war effort. With the size of the regular military approaching one million (four times the figure at the start of the war in 1980), and the Popular Army well past the half-million mark, Saddam Hussein realized that the armed forces were a far more effective tool to integrate society and state than the Baath Party. Not surprisingly, he instructed party cadres to imbibe military values and uphold discipline, patriotism and martyrdom.

In the course of the war the Iraqi leader upgraded the professional expertise of the military while downgrading the importance of Baathist ideology among the officers. This lessened the interest of the armed forces hierarchy in domestic politics, and increased their commitment to defending the country.

The war brought about a marked change in the Baath Party itself. In the name of increasing production, the importance of Baathist socialism was minimized and the private sector encouraged to grow at the expense of the public sector. The concept of Arabism was made subservient to the idea of Iraqi nationalism, which was used as the paramount force to motivate citizens to join the war effort. Also, the Baath Party's commitment to radical republicanism was quietly dropped in order to secure and maintain the active backing of the Gulf monarchies, particularly Saudi Arabia and Kuwait.

While Saddam Hussein was the main player in mounting the invasion of Iran in September 1980, he seemingly acted in collusion with his close neighbours in the Gulf: Saudi Arabia and Kuwait. As the war dragged on, he became more dependent on his Arab and non-Arab allies. Only by borrowing enormous sums could he continue the hostilities and concurrently provide consumer and other goods to his countrymen.

And only by internationalizing the conflict – specifically, getting the American navy involved in the Gulf shipping – did the Iraqi president finally achieve an end to the war, something he had been pursuing for the better part of eight years. In this he was helped actively by Kuwait, with the latter approaching the superpowers to provide naval escort for its oil tankers. Kuwait was merely an extreme example of the wariness and alienation that the Gulf monarchs felt towards the Islamic Republic of Iran. Of these the rulers of Saudi Arabia and Kuwait mattered most to Iraq. During the eight years of warfare, despite a barrage of blandishments and threats emanating from Tehran, they did not loosen their close alliance with Baghdad.

Riyadh played a crucial role in bringing about a rapprochement between Baghdad and Washington, strengthening Iraq's hand very considerably. But for the timely economic intervention by the United States in 1983, and again in 1986, to help it financially, by providing subsidized American foodgrains bought with US credits, Iraq would have been in dire economic straits. Washington's decision to provide credit of $460 million to Baghdad for the purchase of 147,000 tons of American rice in early 1983 had wide and favourable international repercussions for Iraq, then in the midst of a severe economic crisis. It reassured many governments and banks in Europe, Japan and the Middle East of the future viability of the Saddam Hussein regime, and revived its badly bruised credit-worthiness. In June 1983, ignoring the fact that Iraq was on the US state department's list of 'nations that support international terrorism', Washington authorized the sale of 60 helicopters to Baghdad for 'agricultural use', well aware that the helicopters could easily be adapted for military purposes. This further bolstered Iraq's standing in the region and outside.[63]

There was also an ongoing arrangement between Riyadh and Baghdad (blessed by Washington) for the transmission of intelligence on Iran, gathered by American-piloted Awacs operating in the Gulf since the outbreak of the war. This proved invaluable to the Iraqi high command in forging advance plans to blunt the many offensives Tehran mounted.[64]

Last but not least came the agreement between the US Central Intelligence Agency and Iraqi intelligence for exchange of information. In the course of public hearings concerning the Irangate scandal, it emerged that this agreement was implemented soon after the US embassy in Baghdad reopened on 22 November 1984, enabling the CIA to deal with its Iraqi counterpart through the American mission. However, it now transpires that this clandestine agreement went into operation two years earlier (when Iraq was still on Washington's list of 'terrorist nations') – through the US embassy in Amman, with King Hussein of Jordan personally overseeing the transfers of information from both sides.[65]

The United States had no particular affinity, political or economic, for Iraq. If anything, as Moscow's long-time ally and Israel's militant enemy, which harboured such Palestinian extremists as Abu Nidal, Baghdad aroused much antipathy in Washington. However, America was intensely hostile towards the Islamic revolution in Iran, apprehensive that an Iranian victory over Iraq would change the balance of power irrevocably, and damagingly, in favour of Tehran and against the West. This is what drove it to court Baghdad.

In any event, the outbreak of the First Gulf War in September 1980 was clearly linked with events in Iran (the failed monarchist coup in July 1980) and America (the presidential election in early November 1980).[66] Like many other countries the US was surprised by the spirited resistance that Iran offered to the invading Iraqis and the success it had in expelling them. So long as stalemate prevailed on the front lines Washington was content to maintain a semblance of neutrality in the war. But as the scales began to tilt increasingly in Iran's favour in late 1983, the US altered its policy, stating publicly that Iraq's defeat would be against its interests. With every Iranian military success – from the Majnoon Islands in 1984 to Fao in 1986 and Shalamche a year later – the US increased its backing for Baghdad, culminating in an unprecedented naval build-up in the Gulf and, for all practical purposes, the opening of a second front against Iran in the summer of 1987.

The containment of Iran's Islamic revolutionary movement achieved by Iraq, coupled with Baghdad's loss of interest in pursuing its radical, republican cause, made the Gulf monarchies secure. Their corporate organization, the Gulf Co-operation Council, became well-established.

Such was the situation in the Gulf in the late summer of 1988.

2 PRELUDE TO THE CRISIS

'There is no place among the ranks of good Arabs for the faint-hearted who would argue that as a superpower, America will be the decisive factor and others have no choice but to submit.'

President Saddam Hussein addressing the Arab
Co-operation Council summit, 24 February 1990[1]

'I cannot conceive of any government in Israel agreeing at any time to prohibit Jews from living in any part of Eretz Israel.'

Prime Minister Yitzhak Shamir addressing the
Israeli parliament, 22 February 1990[2]

'The Iraq of 1990 and beyond is not the Iraq of 1981, when the Israelis hit the Tammuz scientific reactor . . . when we were preoccupied with a fierce war with Iran.'

President Saddam Hussein, in a speech on
17 July 1990[3]

'The Kuwaitis boast of their aid to Iraq, but it was Iraq that defended their thrones and wealth with blood. We sacrificed our brothers, fathers and sons to let them enjoy life.'

Ahmad Khalis, an Iraqi university student in
Baghdad[4]

Since Iraq ended its hostilities against Iran with military superiority, its president convinced the Iraqis that their country had won the longest conventional war of the century. And they believed him. They danced in the streets at the start of a long holiday as the government greeted the ceasefire in the early hours of 20 August 1988 with a 101-gun salute.

But there was one section of Iraqi society which did not join these celebrations: the Kurdish nationalists who had backed the Kurdish

Democratic Party and the Patriotic Union of Kurdistan, which had actively co-operated with Iran in its war with the Saddam Hussein regime.

By amalgamating the Kurdish province of Mosul with the Baghdad and Basra provinces of Mesopotamia to create modern Iraq after the dissolution of the Ottoman empire, the British created the Kurdish problem for the central government of Iraq. As descendants of the Indo-European tribes who settled in south-eastern Turkey, north-eastern Iraq and north-western Persia, Kurds traced their distinct history as a mountain people to the 7th century BC, appearing as Medes in the Bible. Racially, they are different from Turks and Semite Arabs, and their language, a member of the Indo-European family, is akin to Farsi (Persian). After the dissolution of the Ottoman empire the Kurds in Mosul province mounted periodic rebellions, first against Britain, the mandate power, and then against the central Arab authority in Baghdad. In 1927 the importance of the Kurdish area rose sharply when a British-dominated company struck oil near Kirkuk, the largest find in the world until then. A Kurdish insurgency for independence led by Shaikh Ahmad Barzani in 1931–2 was crushed in 1935 by a joint Iraqi–Turkish campaign, a strategy to be re-employed half a century later in the midst of the Iran–Iraq conflict. During the Second World War Mustafa Barzani, a brother of Ahmad, led another rebellion which failed. He escaped to Iran where, under the banner of the Kurdistan Democratic Party, he founded the Kurdish republic of Mahabad in 1946. When the republic was crushed by the Shah of Iran, Barzani fled to the Soviet Union.

Following the 1958 coup Barzani returned to Iraq, and backed the new regime under Qasim. In exchange Qasim legalized the KDP, and promulgated a constitution which stated: 'Arabs and Kurds are associated in this nation.' This was a formal recognition of the Kurds – who formed 16–25 per cent of the national population – as a distinct ethnic minority. However, when Barzani advanced a plan for autonomy Qasim rejected it; and in September 1961 he mounted an all-out campaign against Kurdish insurgents. It was not until June 1966 that a 12-point agreement was signed between Barzani's KDP and the Baghdad government. It included the official recognition of the Kurdish language and proportional representation of Kurds in the civil administration. But in the absence of mutual trust the agreement failed to resolve the problem.

The Baathist seizure of power in July 1968 made little difference to the Kurdish problem. The KDP resorted to an armed struggle in March

1969. This reached a stalemate – and paved the way for a settlement between the warring parties in early 1970, facilitated by the mediation of Yevgeny Primakov, then deputy director of the Institute of World Economy and International Relations, Moscow. The result was a 15-point agreement between the KDP and the central government, to be implemented over the next four years. The interim constitution of July 1970 recognized the Kurds as one of the two nationalities of Iraq, and the Kurdish language as one of the two official languages in the Kurdish region. But once again, due to mutual distrust, the accord failed to hold.

By March 1974 the Baghdad government had enforced the Kurdish autonomy law, stemming from the 1970 accord, as planned, including the appointment of a Kurd, Taha Muhyi al Din Maruf, as vice-president of the republic. This set the scene for the convening of a (nominated) legislative council in Arbil, the capital of the Kurdistan Autonomous Region, comprising the provinces of Dohak, Arbil and Suleimaniya. Protesting against the exclusion of such oil-rich areas as Kirkuk, Sinjar and Khanaqin from the Kurdish region, the KDP demanded that the enforcement of the autonomy law be postponed until a fresh census revealed the exact distribution of Kurds in north-eastern Iraq. Baghdad ignored the demand, and the KDP resumed its armed struggle against the central authority. At its peak the fighting involved 45,000 Kurdish guerrillas who pinned down four-fifths of Iraq's 100,000-plus troops and nearly half of its 1,390 tanks. According to a United Nations assessment, the conflict led to 60,000 civilian and military casualties, and the destruction of 40,000 homes in 700 villages, leading to the displacement of 300,000 people.[5] Barzani claimed to have liberated 25,000 square miles with a population of 1.5 million Kurds adjacent to the Iranian border. This was achieved with the direct assistance of the Shah of Iran, who was intent on destabilizing Iraq for having signed a friendship and co-operation treaty with Moscow in 1972. Besides supplying US and Israeli arms to the Kurds on a large scale, the Shah used his forces to cover the Kurdish insurgents with artillery fire and anti-aircraft missiles. The resulting tension between Baghdad and Tehran reached such a pitch by early 1975 that there was a serious possibility of a full-scale war between them. Aware of the dangers of such an eventuality, the two neighbours encouraged mediation first by Turkey and then by Algeria. This was successful, and led to the conclusion of an accord signed in Algiers on 6 March 1975 by the Shah of Iran and Saddam Hussein.

The Algiers Accord signified victory for Iran, and incorporated the

Iranian demand, first made over sixty years earlier, that the *thalweg* principle be applied to the frontier along the Shatt al Arab. It was a bitter pill for Iraqi leaders to swallow, and they did so only because the Iranian-backed Kurdish insurgency had left their armed forces and their ammunition exhausted.

During the course of the 1980–88 hostilities with Iran, too, the activities of the Kurdish insurgents compelled Iraq to deploy many divisions in the north to the detriment of its war effort elsewhere. Taking advantage of the pressure of the war on Baghdad, the KDP, now led by Masud Barzani, a son of Mustafa Barzani, and the Patriotic Union of Kurdistan, headed by Jalal Talabani, set up liberated zones respectively along the borders with Iran and Turkey.

Once Baghdad and Tehran had decided on a ceasefire on 8 August 1988, Saddam Hussein acquired greater flexibility in deploying his forces. To settle scores with the Kurdish insurgents for their unpatriotic stance during the war and achieve a lasting solution to the endemic Kurdish problem, on 6 August he pressed his troops into action against the forces of the KDP and PUK, using air raids and chemical weapons. Reports of Iraqi use of poison gases against Kurdish villages began filtering out of the area from 17 August onwards, with Masud Barzani claiming in late August that so far 500 Kurds had been killed and 3,000 injured in the campaign mounted by some 60,000 Iraqi troops using artillery, tanks, aircraft and chemical weapons.[6] By then the Iraqi armed forces had become adept at using chemical agents for both offensive and defensive purposes. From a modest start in 1983, when the Iraqis deployed poison gases as a defensive weapon *in extremis*, causing injuries to 574 Iranian soldiers, they increased their use to the extent that during the first quarter of 1988 alone they had wounded 13,673 Iranian combatants.[7] Later, during the second and third quarters of 1988, the Iraqis had made ample use of their chemical arsenal in their offensives against the enemy: a fact recognized among others by a CIA report which concluded that use of chemical agents by the Iraqis was the 'decisive factor' in the war.[8] Now, as a result of the Iraqi military campaign, Kurdish refugees began pouring into Turkey, some of them being subjected to poison gas attacks as they fled.

It was against this background that on 29 August the UN Security Council, acting on an earlier report of its fact-finding mission, unanimously condemned Iraq's use of chemical weapons in the First Gulf War and added that it would immediately consider measures against Iraq if it deployed them again. Therefore the need to establish that Baghdad had employed such arms in its Kurdish areas became crucial.

Unsurprisingly, Baghdad denied deploying poison gases against 'Kurdish terrorists', with its ambassador in London, Muhammed al Mashat, dismissing such a claim as 'an outrageous lie'. By waging an intense military campaign for about a month the Baghdad government wrested control of some 4,000 square miles of northern Iraq from the Kurdish nationalists. In the course of it, 65 villages were subjected to chemical attacks and a majority of the 3,800 Kurdish villages were depopulated, with nearly 100,000 Kurds driven into Turkey and Iran, and many more either ferried to easily controllable settlements away from the international border or to concentration camps in southern Iraq.[9] Having achieved his political objective, Saddam Hussein extended a general amnesty to the Kurds on 6 September for a month, and appealed to the refugees to return home.

The Saddam Hussein government's deployment of poison gases against its own citizens in peacetime exceeded even its earlier shocking behaviour. On 16 March 1988, during the course of its fight with the Iranian forces in the area, the Iraqi air force had dropped chemical bombs on the Kurdish town of Halabja, killing at least 4,000 people and injuring 10,000.[10] Baghdad's routine use of chemical agents in Kurdistan aroused revulsion in the West, including America. Reflecting this, the US Senate voted on 9 September 1988 to impose economic sanctions against Iraq for its 'gross violation of international law'. The endorsement of this bill by the House of Representatives, followed by the president's signature, would have deprived Iraq of loans and loan guarantees worth $800 million, and imports of 'sensitive' high-technology products. The Iraqi administration responded by organizing a 150,000–250,000-strong anti-American demonstration in Baghdad.[11]

Unable to decide conclusively whether or not the Iraqis had used poison gases, America and Britain decided to take the matter to the United Nations. However, that did not stop the US secretary of state, George Shultz, from stating that, based on 'the examination of Kurdish refugees by US embassy personnel in Turkey' and 'other sources', the Iraqis had deployed chemical weapons against the Kurds. The 'other sources' turned out to be US intelligence agencies which had intercepted Iraqi military communications.[12]

In mid-September, when the United Nations Security Council decided to send an investigation team to Iraq, the government in Baghdad refused to receive it. 'The Kurds are Iraqi and it is an internal issue,' said Adnan Khairallah, Iraqi defence minister. 'So what is the role of the UN in this issue? I want to deal with a certain segment of my population in the way I want.'[13] Responding to the Iraqi refusal, Britain's foreign secretary, Sir Geoffrey Howe, stated that if conclusive evidence were obtained, 'punitive measures' against Iraq had not been ruled out. But these were empty threats since neither Britain nor America had yet come up with an incontestable way of ascertaining the facts.

Meanwhile the US Senate pursued its anti-Iraq bill, much watered down from its original version, by attaching it to an administration tax bill, in order to circumvent a possible presidential veto. The final compromise bill specified two phases. The first phase provided immediate prohibition of the sale of American military equipment and sensitive technology to Iraq, as well as loans, financial or technical aid from international financial institutions. This ban could be set aside only if Iraqi guarantees not to deploy chemical weapons proved reliable. The second phase would involve the president choosing one of the following options: denying Iraq access to the American export-import bank; imposing restraints on Iraqi imports and exports; and downgrading diplomatic relations.[14] In short, because of the equivocal attitude of the White House, nothing came of the moves by the US Congress.

Two conclusions could be drawn from this episode. By virtue of its long and friendly association with the American establishment in the course of the Iran–Iraq War, Saddam Hussein's regime had established a strong pro-Iraqi lobby in the US; and by refusing to yield to pressure from Washington and London, Saddam Hussein reasserted his independence of action, and showed that he was his own master.

His government adopted an equally tough stance when conducting peace talks with the Iranians in late August 1988 under the chairmanship of the United Nations secretary-general in Geneva. It demanded the immediate clearance of the Shatt al Arab under the UN aegis. Tehran argued that, according to the 1975 Algiers Treaty, clearing the waterway was the joint responsibility of Iran and Iraq. Baghdad stated that the 1975 Treaty no longer existed; Tehran stressed that, being a border agreement, it was valid for ever, and that such a document could not be abrogated unilaterally. So the intermittent negotiations dragged on during the following two months, with neither side prepared to budge.

Having thus established his strength in both domestic and foreign fields, the Iraqi president could afford to relax his grip over government and society, if he so wished. And he did, nominally. He offered amnesty to Iraqi political offenders inside the country and outside. In late

November 1988 he announced what seemed an Iraqi perestroika. He promised a new constitution and electoral law introducing a multi-party system. His information minister, Latif Jasim, declared that, following the end of hostilities with Iran, a free press had become of 'paramount interest'.

Saddam Hussein combined his promises of political liberalization at home with an attempt to secure a higher profile for Iraq in the Arab world. He made an unscheduled trip to Cairo to discuss with President Hosni Mubarak the formation of a council of those non-Gulf Arab states – Egypt, Jordan and North Yemen – which had aided Iraq during the war. The idea had originally come from King Hussein ibn Talal of Jordan (1952–) after the Arab League summit in November 1987 had allowed the member states to re-establish, on an individual basis, diplomatic links with Egypt, which had been suspended from the League following its signing of a peace treaty with Israel in March 1979. The Jordanian monarch wished to see Egypt fully integrated with other Arab states. Later that year he discussed the idea of establishing a council of those Arab countries outside the GCC which had actively assisted Iraq in the First Gulf War. He visualized the grouping to be modelled upon the European Community. Mubarak showed interest because, among other things, he felt that joining such a grouping would ease the formal re-entry of Egypt into the Arab League. But he balked at King Hussein's suggestion that the proposed co-operation council should have a military dimension. The Egyptian president consulted the Saudi monarch, and both agreed that the council should exclude military and intelligence matters.

With the First Gulf War ending in August 1988, the matter acquired urgency: this was well illustrated by Saddam Hussein's trip to Cairo in late November.

According to an Egyptian version of the events leading up to the formation of the Arab Co-operation Council in Baghdad on 16 February 1989, the other members pressed Egypt hard to turn the proposed council into a defence and security organization with its own integrated military and intelligence structure. But its president refused.[15] Thus the ACC emerged as a group committed to co-operation only in economic and other non-military fields.

King Hussein, historically dependent on foreign aid to sustain his country, saw in the ACC a mechanism by which oil-rich Arab states could aid the less fortunate Arab countries on a multilateral basis. This was also the hope of North Yemen, one of the poorest Arab states but one with excess manpower at home. It saw a welcome opportunity in directing its workers away from Saudi Arabia to Iraq, thus lessening its economic dependence on the Saudi kingdom.

The interlinking of Iraq with pro-Western Egypt and Jordan in a European Community-style organization was well received in Western capitals, particularly Washington. It was seen as a way of taming Saddam Hussein's militancy: an objective the US had been pursuing by strengthening economic ties with Iraq with a view to making it progressively dependent on Washington.

Among Iraq's Gulf neighbours, Saudi Arabia seemed to have no objection to the new council so long as it did not dabble in military matters. At the same time it disliked the idea of being surrounded, geographically, by the members of a grouping to which it did not belong. Hence it was thought prudent to safeguard Saudi borders with Iraq by signing a non-aggression pact with Baghdad. This happened on 27 March 1989 during King Fahd's visit to Baghdad. The accord spelled out the principles of 'non-interference in the internal affairs of the two sisterly countries' and 'non-use of force and armies between the two states'.[16]

Earlier, Saddam Hussein had offered a similar accord to Kuwait during his meeting in Baghdad in early February 1989 with the Kuwaiti crown prince and prime minister, Shaikh Saad al Sabah. But the latter had left without responding to this proposal by Saddam, as well as the one about Iraq leasing the offshore island of Bubiyan. The prime reason for Saddam's Bubiyan proposition was to strengthen Iraq's access to Umm Qasr by constructing maritime facilities on the offshore island. Besides the age-old apprehension about Iraq's aggressive intent, the Kuwaiti leaders now had to take into account the reaction of Iran with which they had only recently re-established diplomatic links. Tehran was likely to disapprove of any territorial change that enhanced the military-strategic position of its rival, Iraq. At a more practical level, however, Shaikh Saad al Sabah had no problem in concluding a contract for the purchase of 350 million gallons of drinking water and 500 million gallons of irrigation water daily from Iraq.[17]

By entering into a formal supra-state Arab organization, Saddam Hussein consolidated the prestige he had acquired in the Arab world during the Iran–Iraq War as the untiring Arab hero battling the Persian adversary at the eastern frontier of the Arab world, and finally forcing him to stop fighting. Unsure of how the peace talks with Iran would go, he had refrained from reducing the strength of his armed forces, which stood at 1.2 million on the ceasefire day, two-and-a-half times the size of the Egyptian military, the next largest force in the Arab world.

With a fivefold increase in the Iraqi military, and a corresponding expansion in the size of the officer corps, Saddam Hussein faced the daunting task of ensuring that the military officers remained unanimously and unquestioningly loyal to him during peacetime. That this objective was not always achieved manifested itself in the periodic attempts at a coup by dissident officers. The first such report came from Iranian sources in early November 1988 which claimed that the Iraqi government had executed four high-ranking military officers for 'attempted subversion'. Another plot, to shoot down Saddam Hussein's plane on his flight back from Egypt after a surprise visit there, was also aborted. The next one was planned for 6 January 1989, the army say, and involved an attack on the review stand during the traditional army parade. The plan was discovered by Iraqi intelligence.[18] One way for Saddam Hussein to make himself indispensable to the Iraqi state and society was to ensure that there was no other leader, civilian or military, who was even remotely capable of replacing him. Given that the armed forces had emerged as the single most important national institution, held in higher esteem than the Baath Party, the Iraqi president needed to be certain that no other military officer became popular enough to be considered as an alternative leader. Little wonder that by the autumn of 1988 the two generals – Mahir Abdul Rashid and Thabit Sultan – who had risen in stature and popularity due to their outstanding performance during the First Gulf War had been either put under house arrest (Rashid) or involved in a fatal helicopter accident (Sultan).[19] Such events, however, did not interfere with routine state business like parliamentary elections, which were held on schedule on 1 April 1989. Interestingly, only half of the successful candidates were Baathist, the rest being carefully selected independents or members of the minor leftist or nationalist groups allowed to function as part of the Baathist-dominated National Progressive and Patriotic Front.

Given that power was highly concentrated among Saddam Hussein and his senior advisers, most of whom were his close relatives, he could not always separate family matters from state affairs. His estrangement from his wife, Sajida, and his deep involvement with his mistress, seriously damaged his relationship with his brother-in-law, Adnan Khairallah, who had been defence minister since 1978. On 5 May 1989 Baghdad Radio announced that he had been killed in a helicopter crash and buried within hours of the accident. He was returning from the Kurdistan region when, according to the state radio, his helicopter hit a fierce sandstorm. The truth was probably nearer to the disclosure made by 'Captain Karim' – later identified as Mizhir Affat – a 'close and intimate' bodyguard of Saddam Hussein for five years, after his defection in the winter of 1990. According to him, four detonator charges were placed on Khairallah's helicopter by Hussein Kamil Hassan Majid, a son-in-law of the Iraqi president, on the direct orders of Saddam Hussein. Majid did so while Khairallah was having lunch with Saddam Hussein at a military garrison near Mosul.[20]

Adnan Khairallah's death meant tighter control of the defence ministry by Saddam Hussein, who had all along fashioned Iraqi foreign policy. Among other things this meant a continued hard line towards Iran on peace talks, with repeated stress on an immediate exchange of prisoners of war, twice as numerous in Iraq's case as in Iran's, coupled with ignoring Tehran's pleas to vacate 920 square miles of Iranian territory.

The one country which had been decidedly unhappy at the end of the First Gulf War was Israel. It was deeply concerned about the enormous increase in Iraq's military power, its successful deployment of ground-to-ground missiles (modified Scuds called 'Al Hussein') with a range of 350 miles, and its development and use of chemical weapons, which were widely interpreted as balancing the Israeli arsenal of nuclear weapons, reportedly consisting of 200 nuclear warheads and 47 atomic bombs in 1990.[21] The destruction of the Iraqi nuclear reactor near Baghdad on 7 June 1981 by Israeli aircraft had not deterred Saddam Hussein from acquiring nuclear arms. Such indeed was the conclusion implied in what Israeli sources told the *Washington Post* in late March 1989. Baghdad was developing nuclear warheads for delivery by ground-to-ground missiles, which too were under development, the Israelis said, and Saudi Arabia was partly funding the project, with Pakistan providing technical assistance. King Fahd stated that his country would give aid to Iraq to rebuild its nuclear power plant destroyed eight years earlier by Israel, although not for developing or producing nuclear arms.[22]

Saudi Arabia had earlier agreed to provide free building materials for the rebuilding of Basra, devastated during the First Gulf War. The complete project was expected to cost $4.9 bn, and was part of the overall Iraqi strategy of preserving and enhancing its access to the Gulf for economic and diplomatic reasons. It combined its reconstruction of the war-damaged Basra with the expansion of facilities at Umm Qasr and Zubair ports. The reopening of the Basra oil refinery, with half its pre-war capacity, in February 1989 was followed by the shipment of oil products from Zubair to Dubai. Overall, though, Baghdad's reconstruction plans were hamstrung by the urgent demands of debt servicing and high defence expenditure. Its income was limited by the OPEC quota of 2.64 mb/d of oil. Little wonder that the government decided to extend the austerity programme it had introduced in 1983. To curtail public expenditure, it began a demobilization programme in late 1988, starting with the troops who had served the longest, and reduced the army by 200,000 in a year.[23]

Its economic salvation lay in reaching an accord with Iran. The death on 3 June 1989 of Ayatollah Khomeini, the Iranian leader implacably opposed to Saddam Hussein, raised hopes in Baghdad that the successor regime in Tehran would be more amenable to compromise. To encourage such a development, the Iraqi president halted all activities, including radio broadcasts, of the Mujahedin-e Khalq, the best organized anti-Khomeini Iranian group based in Baghdad.[24] But the post-Khomeini regime of Ayatollah Ali Khamanei followed the earlier official line, insisting that Iraq must relinquish forthwith the occupied Iranian territory; and Iraq continued to demand an immediate exchange of about 100,000 prisoners of war held by the two sides.

At the second Arab Co-operation Council summit in Alexandria on 17 June 1989, Saddam Hussein secured the council's backing for his claim to all of the Shatt al Arab, disputed by Iran. The ACC also supported Iraq's call to the UN to clear the Shatt al Arab of the debris of the Iran–Iraq War.

While stalling peace talks with Iran, the Iraqi government continued its long-term aim of achieving self-sufficiency in arms and ammunition, as well as military parity with Israel. This decision had been taken in 1974, after the dramatic rise in the oil price which made such an objective achievable – and the implementation was put into the hands of a three-member committee, including Saddam Hussein and Adnan Khairallah. It consulted a Beirut-based company named Arab Projects and Development which, in 1975, advised repatriation of Arab scientists and engineers from abroad to Iraq. By appealing to their Arab nationalism and offering them handsome salaries, APD brought some 4,000 Arab scientists and engineers to Iraq from the West and Egypt. In 1978 APD recommended that Iraq should focus on chemical and biological weapons because their technology was simpler to obtain and master than that of nuclear arms. Saddam Hussein agreed, but insisted that the nuclear option should be pursued concurrently. This programme was in train under the nuclear co-operation treaty that Iraq had signed in 1974 with France, the one advanced Western nation which had forged close ties with Baghdad. The French aim was primarily to have favoured access to Iraqi oil, and secondarily to become an alternative source of supplies of heavy weaponry to Iraq, thus reducing its total reliance on Moscow for the purpose. In 1975 France contracted to supply Iraq with two nuclear reactors – one of 40 megawatt capacity and the other of 500 kilowatt – to be operated on enriched uranium.

Israel set out to sabotage the Iraqi nuclear programme. In 1979 Israeli agents destroyed two reactor cores in a French warehouse shortly before they were to be shipped to Iraq. On 13 June 1980, Yahya Mashad, the Egyptian physicist who headed Iraq's atomic energy programme, was murdered in a hotel room in Paris, where he had arrived to discuss the French reactor. On 7 June 1981, Israeli aircraft destroyed the nuclear reactor at Tuwaitha near Baghdad, eliminating Iraq's ability to produce plutonium, the ingredient for nuclear arms. As France was unwilling to rebuild the plant, Iraq activated the co-operation agreement it had made with Brazil on nuclear research for peaceful purposes, although this was a poor substitute for the French option. Meanwhile, the chemical weapons programme continued, with APD being able to buy a blueprint for a plant from an American company, and then deciding to assemble the factory by itself by procuring parts piecemeal for 'a pesticide plant' from mainly West German sources through Turkish intermediaries. By early 1979 the first chemical arms factory, worth $60 million, was ready near Akashat in north-west Iraq. The Iran–Iraq War provided an incentive to accelerate the programme; and Iraqi forces used chemical agents extensively in 1988, first against their Iranian enemies and then against the Kurds of Iraq. Also scientists and engineers busied themselves developing plants capable of manufacturing cholera, typhoid and anthrax strains at Salman Pak (near the capital) and in north Iraq. By 1988 Iraq had completed its chemical weapons self-sufficiency programme.[25]

In the conventional arms field, however, Iraq planned to become an exporter. It began organizing annual international military exhibitions. The scale of such fairs could be gauged by the fact that the April 1989 exhibition attracted 168 British companies, including the giant arms manufacturer British Aerospace. At this fair Iraq exhibited not only the Assad Babil (Babylonian Lion) tank, an Iraqi version of the Soviet T-72 tank, with its electronics and 125mm guns manufactured in Iraq, but also a Soviet MiG-23 modified for in-flight fuelling. In early July Baghdad claimed to have successfully tested an Adnan-1 Airborne

Warning and Control System, believed to be a modified Soviet Ilyushin Il-76 plane.[26]

Inevitably, such a massive arms development and production programme, involving missiles, chemical weapons, nuclear devices and satellite launching equipment, was bound to result in occasional mishaps. On 18 August 1989 there was a massive explosion at a military plant near Iskandariya, where *inter alia* experiments on different explosives for the non-nuclear part of an atomic bomb and fuel for Condor-2, a two-stage solid fuel missile with 1,000 km range, were being conducted. Unconfirmed reports claimed that 700 deaths had occurred. After a London newspaper had published a report of the accident on 6 September the Iraqi authorities stated that nineteen people had been killed by a fuel depot blast.

Aware that in September 1988 Israel had launched its first satellite, Ofeq (i.e. Horizon), with its own rocket, Shavit (i.e. Comet), and aware too that the Israeli satellite, which stayed in orbit for three months, had military purposes,[27] Iraq pursued its own satellite launching programme vigorously.

Hussein Kamil Hassan Majid, Iraq's minister of industry and military industrialization, claimed that on 5 December 1989 Iraq launched its first space rocket, Tammuz-1, from Al Anbar space centre 30 miles from Baghdad. He also claimed that Iraq had developed two further missiles with a range of 1,850 kms (1,110 miles) one of them called Al Abid. Its range was twice that of Al Abbas, or thrice that of Al Hussein at 570 kms (360 miles). The range of Al Hussein was twice that of the Soviet-made Scud-B. Al Abid was believed to be a three-stage rocket, 24.4 metres long, and weighing 48 tonnes; and it was meant to be used for placing satellites in orbit. On 8 December the US Defence Intelligence Agency confirmed the launch of 'an Iraqi rocket capable of putting a satellite in orbit', followed by sources at NORAD (North American Aerospace Defence Command) stating that following the Iraqi launch 'three objects had been tracked which had orbited the earth four or five times'. Later reports said, however, that the Iraqi rocket flew for only 130 seconds and reached an altitude of about 20 kilometres before dropping back to the ground, and that it was a single stage, liquid fuel device.[28]

In contrast to these mishaps, the *Mideast Markets*, a British newsletter, published a fairly detailed report in December 1989 which claimed that Iraq was co-operating with China to manufacture nuclear weapons and had established a network of companies in Europe to procure equipment and expertise. Until the 1981 Israeli raid on the

Iraqi nuclear reactor, the West had believed that Iraq planned to make a bomb from plutonium obtained from spent nuclear fuel rods. Now, it seemed, the intention was to use uranium enriched by centrifuges. The research on this process was being conducted at a facility at the Saad-16 complex near Mosul, designed by an Austrian company, Consultco, and built by West Germany's Gildemeister, with equipment supplied by a subsidiary of a German company called MBB. As for the components for the centrifuge, China had reportedly agreed to help.[29]

Such projects continued against the backdrop of severe economic constraints on Baghdad. 'Iraq has a tremendous number of problems on its plate at present – its debt servicing, continued high defence expenditure, and a huge programme of economic reconstruction and reform,' said Donald Twyford of the United Kingdom's Export Credit Guarantee Department in late 1989 at a seminar on Iraq in London. 'Iraq is economically and politically committed to paying back its [non-Gulf] debts,' stated Sadoun Hamadi, Iraq's deputy prime minister. 'But our country's resources are limited mainly because our oil production share in OPEC is limited.' Therefore, the Iraqi official added, the Baghdad government was expanding its austerity programme started during the war, which also underpinned its economic reform aimed at revitalizing the economy. Privatization plans, launched earlier, had thus far seen $2.2 billion-worth of public sector companies sold to private citizens.[30]

To curtail public expenditure the defence ministry had demobilized 200,000 soldiers, bringing the total military strength down to about one million. This in turn created problems between the demobbed troops and the Arab expatriates, mainly Egyptian, who had kept the civilian economy, including agriculture, running during the war. In the autumn of 1989 there were violent clashes between returning Iraqi soldiers and Egyptian workers, which resulted in the death and injury of several hundred Egyptians. The fear of attack, and a new law limiting the size of remittances (to help Iraq save its foreign exchange), caused an outflow of thousands of Egyptians back to their country. Among other things such a development ran counter to the raison d'être of the Arab Co-operation Council. While Saddam Hussein addressed Egyptian workers to reassure them, one of his deputy prime ministers, Taha Yassin Ramadan, flew to Cairo and signed an agreement covering payments overdue to Egyptian workers and companies, and promising an inquiry into the death of Egyptians in Iraq.[31]

While the Iraqi and Egyptian governments were engaged in solving this pressing problem, the attention of the Western world was focused on the rapid changes occurring in Eastern Europe, with the breaching of the Berlin Wall on 9 November being the most dramatic. The sudden decline in Soviet power in Europe, vis-à-vis the Western camp led by America, had a knock-on effect on the non-European countries allied with Moscow, which felt weakened. Among them was Iraq, an ally of the Soviet Union for three decades.

In contrast Israel, the Middle Eastern country intimately linked with America, felt strengthened. Pressured by Washington, Moscow liberalized its emigration law, creating the prospect of more than a million Soviet Jews migrating from the USSR over the next five years or so. By severely limiting the number of Soviet Jews it was prepared to accept, America directed most of them to Israel. It was estimated that about 100,000 Soviet Jews would settle there in 1990, an eight-fold increase over the previous year.[32] Both the right-wing Likud Bloc (with 41 parliamentary deputies out of 120) and the left-wing Labour Alignment (with 38 parliamentary seats), partners in the National Unity government of Israel since November 1984, were jubilant at the prospect, while being at odds on the fundamental issue of how to further the Arab–Israeli peace process. On 22 February 1990 the Labour Party Central Committee gave Likud two weeks to accept a Labour compromise plan for talks with Palestinians or face the collapse of the National Unity administration. The Labour formula urged Israel and the Palestinians to withdraw all preconditions, and authorized Cairo to name the Palestinian delegates, adding that these names could include Palestinian residents of East Jerusalem (a territory that Israel had annexed soon after the 1967 Arab–Israeli War) with additional homes in the Occupied Territories as well as one or two deported Palestinians.[33]

Labour's position partially took into account the Palestinian insistence that East Jerusalem was part of the Occupied Territories of the West Bank and Gaza, forming 23 per cent of the Palestine which existed under British mandate, that Israel had seized from Jordan and Egypt (respectively) in the June 1967 Arab–Israeli War.[34] This was an issue of extreme importance to Palestinians and other Arabs. They feared that the Israeli authorities would settle the Soviet Jews in the Occupied Territories, and that American aid running at a record level of $2.98 billion – $1.19 billion for military purposes and $1.79 billion for civilian – might be used towards this end. Arab League foreign ministers, meeting in Tunis in early February 1990, resolved to launch a diplomatic campaign to warn the international community that the immigration of Soviet Jews to Israel would curtail the chances of peace in the Middle East.[35]

Just then Iraq urged the UN High Commissioner for Refugees (UNHCR) to condemn the emigration of Soviet Jews to Israel as 'a blatant violation of the 1949 Geneva Convention', which forbids an occupying power to interfere with the demography of the territory under its occupation. Iraq called on the High Commissioner to 'take effective measures to deter the Zionist entity from its continued violations of human rights, instead of adopting abstract resolutions calling on the occupying authority to adhere to international charters on human rights and international treaties'.[36] When voting was held in mid-February 1990 on a resolution calling on the UNHCR to act against Israel's settlement of Soviet Jews in the Occupied Territories, the US abstained.

The American gesture did not lead to any softening of the Israeli stance. Yitzhak Shamir, the Israeli prime minister, followed up his statement on 8 February that there was need for a 'big Israel' to accommodate the new influx with one a fortnight later: 'The Israeli government has no policy of directing where the new immigrants should live.'[37]

It was against this background that Saddam Hussein held discussions with Arab Co-operation Council officials in Baghdad on 16 February 1990, the second anniversary of the ACC. Assessing the international situation, he remarked that both superpowers would lose strength in the absence of active rivalry to dominate the globe, and implicitly provide an opportunity to the Arab world. 'Arabs possess an extraordinary ability to accelerate the creation of an international balance . . . because of the region's geography and because of the possession of a source of energy unparalleled in the world,' he stated. 'All the major influential powers are affected by this source: be it the US, Japan, Europe or even the Soviet Union.' Given this, he was displeased about the continued American military presence in the Gulf when the reasons which initially brought it about had ceased to exist. There was no longer war between Iran and Iraq – with the concomitant threat to the Arab Gulf states from Iran – and no danger to US interests in the region from the Soviet Union, increasingly embroiled as it was with its deepening domestic crises. It was about time Washington declared its intention to withdraw from the Gulf, with an understandable proviso that it would return if the situation changed.[38]

On 21 February the US state department published its annual report on human rights, with a dozen pages devoted to Iraq. 'For years, execution has been an established Iraqi method of dealing with perceived military and political opponents,' it said. 'Both physical and psychological torture are used . . . Given the rigid chain of command within the government, torture could not be practiced without the authorization of senior officials.' This encouraged the Foreign Affairs Committee of the House of Representatives to propose a resolution condemning Iraq for its 'gross violations of human rights': a move that offended Baghdad.[39]

At the fourth ACC summit in Amman on 23–24 February the Iraqi leader offered his thesis on America in sharper terms. 'It has become clear to everyone that the US has emerged in a superior position in international politics,' he began. 'We believe that America will continue to be able to depart from the restrictions that govern the rest of the world during the next five years until new balancing forces are formed. Moreover, the indisciplined and irresponsible [US] behaviour will engender others' hostility if the US embarks on rejected stupidities. Given the relative erosion of the role of the Soviet Union as the key champion of the Arabs in the context of the Arab–Zionist conflict and globally, and given that the influence of the Zionist lobby on US politics is as powerful as ever, the Arabs must take into account that there is a real possibility that Israel might embark on new stupidities within the five-year span I have mentioned. This might take place as a result of direct or tacit US encouragement.' He then alluded to 'American support for an unprecedented exodus of Soviet Jews to Palestinian territory. This would not have happened under the cover of human rights if the Americans had not pressured the Soviets, exploiting the Soviet Union's special circumstances [of political and economic weakness] in order to incorporate the issue into their bilateral agreements with Moscow.' Additionally, there was rising American support for Israel's 'strategic arms stockpiles' (to be enhanced from the Nato arsenals being whittled down), and it was to be allowed complete latitude to deploy them as and when necessary. Saddam Hussein concluded therefore that Washington was 'not interested in peace as it claims'.[40] Little wonder that the ACC summit decided to 'work to end' Jewish emigration from the USSR and Eastern Europe to 'the occupied Palestinian and Arab territories'. This statement reflected ACC leaders' thinking that the retreat of the USSR from the Middle East and the influx of Soviet Jewish settlers would whet Israel's appetite for expansion and entrench its intransigence towards the Palestinians.

A rebuttal from the Bush administration would have drawn Saddam Hussein's attention to the fact that the peace process was progressing, thanks to American efforts. The US had helped bring about a meeting of Shimon Peres, the Labour leader in charge of Israel's foreign ministry, with President Mubarak in Cairo on 24 January, where Peres had publicly agreed to accept a Palestinian delegation to the peace negotiations which included East Jerusalem residents and deportees. The intention was to arrange an Israeli–Palestinian meeting in Cairo, with the Egyptians playing host. On the Soviet Jewish settlement issue, the Israeli government had stated in late January that it did not have 'an official policy' of settling Soviet immigrants in the Occupied Territories.[41]

With Likud refusing to accept the Labour ultimatum of 22 February regarding the terms of advancing the peace process, the scene was set for a confrontation between the two parties. On 12 March the Labour Party Central Committee authorized Labour parliamentarians to terminate their coalition with Likud if they felt that this would advance the peace process.

Following the passing of a no-confidence motion by 60 votes to 55 on 15 March 1990, the National Unity government fell. Then followed an extended period of uncertainty, with the leaders of Likud and Labour trying to cobble together a workable coalition while the Shamir government functioned as caretaker. The instability in Israel worried Saddam Hussein: it was a virtual repeat of the situation that prevailed in February 1981 when Menachem Begin, the Likud leader, headed a caretaker administration until the general election scheduled for early July. During that similar state of Israeli politics the caretaker prime minister had ordered the bombing of the Iraqi nuclear reactor on 7 June 1981; and the action had helped his party, Likud, to improve its chances dramatically at the polls. The Israeli success in knocking out the Iraqi nuclear facility had left a deep scar on the psyche of the Iraqi leader and government. They were determined never to let such a thing happen again; and they had since then directed much of their military strategic thinking towards that end.

·Unlike in 1981, the prime Iraqi military project that interested Israel concerned ballistic missiles, especially Condor-2, a missile to be powered by solid fuel. Codenamed Project 395, it had three sections: DO1, concerned with research and production of solid fuel, was conducted at a military plant near Iskandariya; DO2, dealing with the engineering aspect, was based at a complex near Falluja; and DO3, focused on testing, was based near Karbala. The DO1 military plant had experienced a massive explosion in mid-August 1989, and the Iraqi authorities probably attributed the explosion to sabotage organized by Israel. The attempt by a London-based Iranian journalist, working for a British paper, to penetrate this secret military installation further strengthened Iraqi paranoia.

The journalist was Farzad Rabati Bazoft, a 32-year-old Iranian Kurd and a British resident since the age of seventeen, who had been working for the London-based *Observer* on a freelance basis since late 1986. After he had obtained British travel papers (not a passport) in early 1988 with the assistance of the newspaper, he began visiting Iraq mainly to cover the First Gulf War. On 6 September he undertook an Iraqi government-sponsored trip to cover the elections to the Legislative Council of the Kurdistan Autonomous Region. That day a British paper published a report on the Iskandariya explosion. While in Baghdad, many Western reporters, including Bazoft, tried to pursue the story through official channels, but were rebuffed. They gave up, except Bazoft.

On 12 September, accompanied by Daphne Parish – a nursing administrator at Baghdad's Ibn al Bitar hospital (run by an Irish charity) – with whom he had become friendly during his earlier visits, he set out for Iskandariya in a four-wheel-drive car, the couple wearing white coats and posing as an Indian doctor and his nurse. Advised by Parish not to act like a 'James Bond', he seems to have behaved in a restrained fashion. They drove around the perimeter fence. Next day Bazoft returned to the site alone, still disguised as an Indian doctor, discovered a crater 80 feet wide, made sketches, took pictures and collected soil samples, a loose shoe and some clothing. He approached the British embassy to arrange to transport the soil samples by diplomatic bag. The official statement that this request was refused by the embassy was later contested by Simon Henderson, author of *Instant Empire: Saddam Hussein's Ambition for Iraq*, who claimed, from information supplied to him by a former British intelligence official, that Bazoft who had been on 'the books of British intelligence', had been provided with special containers to collect soil samples by a contact at the British embassy in Baghdad, who later sent the samples to London by diplomatic bag for chemical analysis.[42]

On 15 September Bazoft was arrested. Six weeks later, on 31 October 1989, he made a 25-minute confession on Iraqi television. He said that in 1983 he met 'some Israeli intelligence officers living in Britain', and became friendly with them; and in 1987 he was recruited to spy on Iraq. 'The Israeli intelligence agents exploited me and my work to serve their interests.' In 1987, continued Bazoft, he was desperate to stay in

Britain, but had no way of doing so. The Israelis, who had befriended him, came to his rescue: they found him a job with the *Observer*. He was 'thrilled by the status that working for the *Observer*' conferred on him 'after years of doing odd jobs, often in fast-food restaurants'. It was 'like a gold mine'. The Israelis then trained him to gather information and write intelligence reports. He said that the British authorities knew he was working for Israel. 'I went to one of the important military establishments [of Iraq] with the nurse Daphne Ann Parish who acted as a guide and gave me assistance while I was taking pictures and [soil] samples.'[43]

It was not until 8 March 1990 that Bazoft was produced before a revolutionary court in Baghdad. There he withdrew his confession, but that seems to have made no difference to his case. On 10 March he was convicted of espionage and given a (mandatory) sentence of capital punishment. Daphne Parish, as a co-defendant, was sentenced to 15 years in jail.

The British prime minister, Margaret Thatcher (1979–90), said that she was 'horrified and taken aback' by these sentences, with William Waldegrave, minister of state at the Foreign Office, warning the Iraqi ambassador in London of 'grave consequences for Anglo-Iraqi relations' if Bazoft were executed. On 11 March, following his lunch with Thatcher in London, King Hussein of Jordan agreed to plead with Saddam Hussein to spare Bazoft's life. The next day the European Community headquarters in Brussels appealed to Iraq for clemency. When the British foreign secretary Douglas Hurd requested a meeting with Saddam Hussein, the response from Baghdad was that the Iraqi president was 'not prepared to reduce the sentences of Mr Bazoft and Mrs Parish while under political and media pressure'. Arguing that Iraq's action was 'in harmony with the Iraqi law which provides for the death sentence on any spy', its information minister, Latif Jasim, said: 'The fabricated clamour against us constitutes blatant interference in our internal affairs'.[44] The first indication that the British diplomatic offensive had misfired came in the afternoon of 14 March when, addressing a gathering of peasant leaders, Saddam Hussein declared, 'The Iraqis are masters of themselves.' Some members of the audience had been assembled to give accounts of the suffering experienced by their fathers under British rule. Once they had gone through this exercise, Saddam Hussein sought, and won, the approval of his audience for the execution of a 'British spy who worked for Israel'.[45] On the morning of 15 March Bazoft was hanged.

The British government recalled its ambassador from Baghdad, and cancelled visits to Britain by Iraqi officials.[46] It persuaded the European Community to issue a strong condemnation of the Iraqi action.

In Baghdad, the ruling National Progressive and Patriotic Front, headed by the Baath Party, strongly denounced 'the suspect and hostile British campaign against Iraq', and repudiated 'the illegal British interference in Iraq's internal affairs' regarding 'the just sentence passed on spy Farzad Rabati Bazoft, a British subject of Iranian origin'.[47] Tens of thousands of Iraqis marched in the capital protesting against Western and Israeli denunciations of Bazoft's execution.

The Iraqi campaign was aided by the unsavoury details of Bazoft's life which were leaked within hours of his execution. In June 1981 he had been arrested for armed robbery near Oxford and sentenced to 18 months in jail. He was to have been deported to Iran following his release in early 1983, but his appeal against the deportation was upheld because of danger to his life in Iran. He moved to London, where he did odd jobs in fast-food restaurants. In 1984, partly inspired by an older friend, Michael Mifud, a Gibraltarian businessman who had once been a journalist, he began writing for an Iranian monarchist paper in London. Between 1987, when he was attached to the *Observer* as a freelance, and 1989 – said the British foreign secretary to the House of Commons – Bazoft had offered Scotland Yard information four times on subjects which were 'unconnected with Iraq'; and the Yard did not consider his offerings worth following up. According to the *Sunday Times*, these had to do with 'Middle East terrorism', most probably pro-Khomeini individuals or groups threatening anti-Khomeini Iranians.[48]

An examination of his background led many experts on intelligence services in Britain and elsewhere to conclude that Bazoft was a suitable quarry for recruitment by secret services. 'The fact that he was appealing against his deportation order meant that his existence would have become known to MI5 in one form or another,' said a Special Branch source in London. Rupert Allason, who, as Nigel West, has written several books on espionage, said: 'It is highly likely Bazoft will have tried to capitalize on his knowledge and background by offering information to the Israelis. Mossad [the Israeli secret service] almost certainly snapped him up, and might well have been unaware of his criminal background.'[49] On the other hand, on his return from the site of the military factory on 13 September 1989, Bazoft openly talked about his trip. Also, after the First Gulf War ceasefire in August 1988, his freelance earnings had declined to such an extent that he had had to give up an apartment he had bought on a mortgage. The truth was probably well captured by a remark made by one of his Iranian friends. 'Bazoft was caught in the cross-fire of intelligence services,' he said. 'Low-level officials were giving him information although the Iraqis were aware that he came from the Kurdish area of Iran. He was letting himself be used.'[50]

Such nuances were lost on the Iraqi media and government. 'As far as the Iraqi regime was concerned, the man was in fact or potentially in possession of secret information which could fall into anybody's hands,' remarked a senior Arab political figure. 'It scarcely mattered whether it was for Israel or the *Observer*.'[51] Also the Baghdad regime was genuinely surprised and puzzled by all the fuss made in Britain about Bazoft, who possessed nothing more weighty than a British *laisser-passer*, and was in its eyes just another 'interfering Iranian'.

Unsurprisingly, the Iraqi papers daily published supportive statements from all over the Arab world, from the ACC secretariat to the Arab Dentists' Union. Along with this went angry editorials and condemnation of Britain, ranging from its human rights abuses in Northern Ireland to the arrogant behaviour of the British royal family. Some commentators wanted to know when, if at all, the British government had modified court verdicts in response to foreign requests. Others wondered why such Asian states as Malaysia and Singapore which execute Westerners for drugs offences were not subjected to the same kind of vilification. Finally, most commentators stressed that while spying might have been downgraded to a frivolous topic in the Western media, it was a deadly serious subject in the Middle East.

The last point was underlined by the fact that Saddam Hussein visited Riyadh, where he obtained King Fahd's endorsement for Iraq's right to implement its laws against those who threatened its security.[52] Bahrain followed the Saudi lead, as did Kuwait. On 26 March came the Arab League's 'denunciation' of 'interference in Iraq's internal affairs by Britain and other members of the European Community'.[53]

Summarizing the general Arab reaction to the Bazoft episode, Leslie Plommer, a Cyprus-based British journalist, wrote: 'Bazoft's activities have aroused much suspicion and little sympathy throughout an area where real and imagined conspiracies are a way of life, and death.'[54]

As it was, the renowned Egyptian journalist Muhammad Heikal – whose career included being the right-hand man of President Gamal Abdul Nasser – had been warning in his recent columns, syndicated throughout the Arab world, that Iraq's combined military and economic power was reaching a magnitude that 'outside powers' found 'impermissible' for any Arab state.[55]

Saddam Hussein was aware of this. What seemed to have alarmed him all the more was the enormous publicity given to the Bazoft affair in the Israeli media, and the 'solutions' that were openly discussed. While expressing solidarity with a fellow-journalist, the commentators in Israel turned to what Bazoft was trying to investigate: the burgeoning Iraqi arsenal of ground-to-ground missiles and chemical weaponry. In the course of the debate that followed in the Israeli print and broadcast media, many of the participants openly advocated destroying Iraq's chemical arms manufacturing facilities through surgical strikes – the type that had been used in June 1981 to bomb the Iraqi nuclear reactor near Baghdad. Iraqi fears were heightened when on 22 March Gerald Bull, a Canadian scientist who had helped Iraq to develop long-range artillery, was assassinated near his flat in Brussels. Bull believed that huge guns could be used to replace first-stage rockets in firing satellites, or missiles, into orbit. After he had established his company, Space Research Corporation, in Brussels in the early 1980s, Iraq became his principal customer, and a Bristol engineer, Christopher Cowley, his right-hand man. Cowley went on to place orders for Iraq's 'Project Babylon' to procure superguns from abroad.[56] Bull's murder, carried out professionally, was believed by many observers to be the handiwork of the Israeli secret service, Mossad, and was reminiscent of what had happened to Yahya Mashad, the Egyptian physicist in charge of Iraq's nuclear programme, in June 1980. These developments were instrumental in the statement by the Arab League on 26 March 1990 endorsing Iraq's action in the Bazoft affair.

The furore over Bazoft had hardly subsided when on 28 March British officials, working in conjunction with their American counterparts, arrested five people – one Iraqi, one Lebanese and three Britons (of foreign origin) – at London's Heathrow airport for trying to smuggle into Iraq (from the US) forty high-speed electronic capacitors, known as krytrons, which can be used as triggers for nuclear explosions. These arrests were advertised by the authorities as the culmination of an Anglo-American operation which had begun eighteen months earlier. What angered and puzzled Iraq was that ten months before the US authorities had blocked the delivery of 185 high-speed capacitors by an American company, but had not publicized the fact.[57]

It is worth noting that Israel had developed its nuclear arms manufacturing capacity, and built up its nuclear arsenal, through clandestine means. It acquired its first main 24-megawatt nuclear reactor from France in 1958 without the knowledge of its chief patron,

America, and commissioned it as a 'textile factory' near Dimona in the Negev desert. During the decade 1957–67 Israel obtained at least 200 lbs, perhaps as much as 572 lbs, of weapons-grade uranium, surreptitiously, through a front company in the US. In 1968 Israeli agents hijacked a ship carrying 200 tons of uranium oxide from Antwerp, Belgium, to Genoa, Italy, thus providing the Dimona reactor with enough fuel for eight years. In 1985 an American businessman was arrested for selling 810 krytrons to Israel in 1980–82.[58]

Washington's change of stance made Baghdad suspicious of American intentions. Its suspicions were aroused further when, on 30 March, US intelligence sources leaked information to the *New York Times* saying that Iraq had built six launchers for its modified Scud missiles (called Al Hussein) in western Iraq, and that this brought Tel Aviv within the range of its ground-to-ground missiles.[59] These news stories soon became the nucleus around which the media in Britain and America seemed to have built a virtual campaign which presented Saddam Hussein as a power-hungry megalomaniac about to hold the world to ransom with his nuclear armoury, who needed to be brought to heel. Baghdad viewed this as a continuation of the anti-Iraqi campaign in progress since the Bazoft episode to create a political environment for an Israeli attack on Iraq.

There were additional factors which made the Iraqi leader conclude that a surgical strike by Israel was imminent. One was the continuing political deadlock in Israel since 15 March. Secondly, Israel had taken to describing Iraqi military co-operation with Jordan as menacing, thus preparing the ground for attacking Iraq. Thirdly, the concerted attempts to paint Saddam Hussein in devilish colours – a treatment that had previously been accorded to Colonel Muammar Qadhafi of Libya – seemed to point towards an assault on the demonic leader's country.

It was against this backcloth that Saddam Hussein made a television broadcast to the military on 2 April. Alluding to the murder of Gerald Bull, the Canadian inventor of long-range artillery, he compared the Western media's silence over this incident to the outcry raised by it over Bazoft's execution. Bazoft, he asserted, was attempting to collect information meant to facilitate a surgical strike on an Iraqi target by the 'Zionist entity'. He revealed that several Western firms, acting on behalf of Western intelligence agencies, had repeatedly tried to implicate Iraq by offering to sell it fissionable material, but Iraq had rejected such overtures. The incident at London airport concerning the krytrons was along such lines. He described the hullabaloo in the West about the krytrons as 'part of the Western–Zionist plot' to deprive Iraq of the technology it needed to protect itself and to create a pretext for Israel to attack Iraq. There was no reason for his government to produce nuclear weapons, he asserted. 'Why should we need an atomic bomb? Don't they know that we have the binary chemical weapons to cause fire to devour half of the Zionist entity if the Zionist entity, which has atomic bombs, dared attack Iraq?'[60]

Saddam Hussein's dramatic warning proved to be a double-edged sword. While it probably succeeded in dissuading Israel from mounting a raid against Iraq, it exacted a heavy political price from him by severely damaging his standing in Washington. The state department described it as 'inflammatory, outrageous and irresponsible'. John Kelly, assistant secretary for Near Eastern Affairs, and Dennis Ross, head of the state department's policy planning bureau, recommended limited sanctions against Iraq to secretary of state James Baker. He agreed, and passed the matter on to his department's under-secretary for political affairs, Robert Kimmit. It took several weeks for the state department's modified policy to manifest itself as the refusal of Washington to renew credits to Baghdad to purchase American foodgrains.

Meanwhile, on the advice of President Mubarak of Egypt, a delegation of five US senators, headed by Senator Bob Dole, the Senate minority leader, on a tour of the Middle East, met President Saddam Hussein in Mosul on 12 April. They presented him with a letter expressing 'very deep concerns' about his chemical and biological weapons. In reply, Saddam Hussein repeated the resolution that had been adopted by the ACC a week earlier urging 'comprehensive removal of all weapons of mass destruction' in the region.[61] Significantly, this was a repeat of the offer Baghdad had made two years earlier, during the Iran–Iraq War, when world attention was being focused on its use of chemical agents.

But so long as there was no agreed programme of disarmament in the non-conventional field in the Middle East, Iraq felt that it had the right to arm itself in such a way as to counterbalance Israel's nuclear arsenal. Its officials argued that if the West considered the nuclear 'balance of terror' to be the operative element in containing the East–West confrontation, and finally dissipating it, then the Arabs should be free to pursue the same strategy in their confrontation with Israel. In their view, what had made the Jewish state uncompromising on Palestinian rights since its founding in 1948 was the fact that it enjoyed military superiority over its adversaries, and only a strategic military balance would produce genuine peace in the region.

However persuasive this argument might have seemed to objective observers, neither the US administration nor Congress was convinced. Indeed, when Congress reconvened on 19 April, after the Easter recess, a motion was tabled in the Senate calling for economic sanctions against Iraq.

This happened in an atmosphere of rising apprehension in the West about Iraq's military intentions. On 11 April British customs officers, acting on a tip-off, confiscated a consignment of eight 6-metre-long steel tubes, about to be loaded on to an Iraq-bound ship. It was alleged that these were part of 52 barrel sections intended for different sized superguns: one of 1,000mm bore and 175 metres long, and the other of 350mm bore. Two engineering firms, Forgemasters of Sheffield and Walter Somers of Halesowen, Birmingham, were involved. By the time the British authorities acted, 44 similar sections of steel tubing had already been shipped to Iraq. Both Baghdad and the British companies insisted that the consignment was part of a petrochemical pipeline order that had been cleared earlier by the department of trade and industry in London. On 18 April the British government stated that it was 'fully satisfied' that the steel segments were to be assembled to make an artillery piece. Two days later it announced that two earlier shipments of similar steel tubing, which were on their way to Iraq overland, had been confiscated by Greek and Turkish customs at its request. It seemed that the British authorities acted after they had discovered a connection between the Iraqi order for the steel tubing and Space Research Company, the Brussels-based company owned by Gerald Bull, who had been assassinated a few weeks earlier. Bull was a proponent of high-powered artillery pieces, and had a long record in developing them. Under HARP, the High Altitude Research Project funded by the American and Canadian governments in the late 1960s, he had developed a supergun which could fire a 600-pound rocket-boosted shell over 1,150 miles.[62] He met Saddam Hussein in Baghdad at the time of Iran's Basra offensive in early 1987. As the Iraqi leader was deeply interested in developing a weapons delivery system that was immune to an anti-missile missile shield, he encouraged Bull to design superguns for his forces. Out of this arose Baghdad's 'Project Babylon'.[63]

Those who disagreed with London's interpretation argued that a gun of such gargantuan dimensions was technically unfeasible. In any case, given its missiles and aircraft, Iraq had no need for such a weapon. As for Baghdad, it repeated the argument offered earlier about the high-velocity capacitors that a legitimate technology purchase was being portrayed as part of an underhand weapons development and procurement plot.

Baghdad viewed the new controversy in the same light as the seizure of its consignment of krytrons and the Bazoft episode: a well-orchestrated attempt to vilify Iraq. The fact (revealed later) that the inspectors of Britain's department of trade and industry had ignored eleven similar tip-offs[64] validated the Iraqi assessment. The Western official and media campaign centred on these episodes was, according to Baghdad, designed to present Iraq as a menace to regional peace in order to provide Israel with a pretext to attack it. In Saddam Hussein's view, what had brought about this state of affairs was Arab technological progress in general and Iraq's strategic parity with Israel in particular. To ward off any strike by Israel, Baghdad resorted to repeating with rising vehemence its resolve to return an Israeli blow with an equally strong blow. Indeed on 18 April Saddam Hussein declared that Iraq would retaliate against 'any country that attacked an Arab state'.[65]

In America the changed policy towards Iraq manifested itself in the state department's statement on 21 May that it was suspending action on Baghdad's request for a $500 million loan guarantee from the US Commodity Credit Corporation. This was a political decision, but to soften the blow for the Saddam Hussein regime, Washington attributed it to 'possible irregularities' reported by its department of agriculture, including the possibility of kickbacks in Iraq's purchases of sugar, rice and corn.[66]

In the background was a scandal involving Iraq and an American branch of the Banca Nazionale del Lavoro, the biggest bank of Italy, which is 74.5% state-owned. In early September 1989 the US Federal Bureau of Investigation stated that it was investigating possible irregular transactions by the Atlanta, Georgia, branch of the BNL. It had been found to have extended $1.72 billion in credits to Iraq, with $720 million guaranteed by the US department of agriculture's Commodity Credit Corporation, and another $1 billion by the Central Bank of Iraq. A large proportion of the $1 billion loan had been used to finance trade and investment in defence equipment and missile-related technology. Most of the credits had been secured in the first half of 1989, and the manager of the Atlanta branch, Christopher Drogoul, a naturalized American of French–Algerian origin, was the key operator. Most of the loans were used to procure high technology defence equipment, including missile parts, which were airlifted as 'agricultural machinery and

machine parts' from various parts of North America and Western
Europe to Rome's Fiumicino airport from where they were forwarded
to Baghdad by Iraqi Airways. Further investigation revealed that the
middle-rank executives at BNL's head office in Rome had been aware
of the unauthorized payments. The scandal led to the resignation of
the bank's president and director-general.[67] However, by the latter
half of May 1990, when the US state department decided to suspend
extending credits to Iraq for the purchase of American foodgrains, the
FBI had not obtained sufficiently strong evidence to charge anybody.

Baghdad construed Washington's action as a further example of its
increasingly anti-Iraq position, and prepared to neutralize this by
rallying the Arab world behind itself at the forthcoming extraordinary
summit of the Arab League in Baghdad on 28 May. The idea for such
a gathering had been canvassed by Jordan and the PLO, whose leaders
were particularly alarmed by the massive influx of Soviet Jews into
Israel – a consequence of the end of the Cold War – which they
saw as impelling the Israeli government to make its occupation of
the West Bank and Gaza irreversible, and transforming Jordan into
an alternative homeland for Palestinians by inducing a forced mass
exodus from the Occupied Territories. Since neither Jordan nor the
PLO was strong enough to abort such an Israeli plan they needed to
ally themselves with a regional power. In Iraq they found one.

The PLO was undergoing a crisis of identity. Nearly a year after the
spontaneous uprising of the Palestinians, the intifada, in the Occupied
Territories on 9 December 1987, the Palestine National Council (parliament in exile) accepted by 253 votes to 46 the UN Security Council
Resolutions 242 (of 1967) and 338 (of 1973), long regarded by the West
as the cornerstones of efforts to resolve the Arab–Israeli conflict. So
far the PLO had rejected Resolution 242 because, while insisting
on recognition of the independence of every state in the region, it
referred to the Palestinians as refugees rather than as a social entity
entitled to self-determination. It had also rejected Resolution 338
because, while guaranteeing Palestinians 'their legitimate national
rights' without specifying what these were, it recognized Israel's
right to exist within secure borders. By recognizing Resolutions
242 and 338, the PLO implicitly recognized Israel. At the same
session, in Algiers in mid-November 1988, the PNC declared the
independence of its own state of Palestine, claiming that its right to
do so derived from the UN Security Council Resolution 181 of 1947
which called for the partition of Palestine between the Arabs and the
Jews. The PNC also voted to pursue the path of negotiations for a

peace settlement through an international conference which would include the PLO as an individually recognized representative of the Palestinians, alongside Israel and the permanent members of the UN Security Council. This meant a formal renunciation of the use of armed struggle by the PLO to achieve an independent Palestinian state, a commitment confirmed by Yasser Arafat some days later at a press conference in Geneva. With this the stage was set for formal talks between the PLO and the US. Following mediation by Egypt, a dialogue ensued between PLO officials and American diplomats in Tunis, the headquarters of the PLO. However, over the next eighteen months, these low-level talks yielded nothing of substance. The PLO, which had strengthened its ties with Egypt during this period, began to drift away from Cairo – and towards Baghdad. In an interview with the *Washington Post*, Abdullah Hourani, a PLO executive committee member, attributed this change to Iraq's 'growing economic, political and military power in the region', with Iraq creating 'the material base for a balanced settlement in the region'.[68]

Out of this arose a close alliance between Iraq, the PLO and Jordan, intent on rallying the Arab world against the Israeli–American axis. Its hands were strengthened by the events in Israel of 20–22 May 1990.

On 20 May, Ami Popper, a young Israeli, shot and killed seven Palestinian workers while they waited in Rishon LeZion to be hired as casual labourers. The confrontations that followed between the Palestinians and the Israeli troops in the Occupied Territories were so severe that they claimed seven more Palestinian lives. In the two days of rioting that spread to the Israeli towns of Nazareth, Lod, Haifa and Beersheba as well as the Golan Heights, eight more Palestinians were killed, and another 722 injured. The matter was placed immediately before the UN Security Council. On 26 May fourteen of the fifteen Council members supported a resolution to despatch a UN team to the Occupied Territories, but it was vetoed by the United States. Israel announced that it was prepared to receive a team sent by the UN secretary-general, but the Arab countries said that a team despatched by the Security Council would be 'a more appropriate' international response.[69]

It was against this backcloth that Arab League leaders met in Baghdad on 28 May. 'It behoves us to declare clearly that if the Zionist entity attacks and strikes [us], we will strike back powerfully,' Saddam Hussein said in his public address to the summit. 'If it uses weapons of mass destruction against our nation, we will use against it the weapons of mass destruction in our possession.' He went on to link Israel with the US. 'It would not have been possible for the Zionist entity to engage in aggression and expansion at the Arabs' expense if it did not possess the force and political cover provided by America – the main source of the Zionist entity's aggressive military force, and the main source of its financial resources,' he explained. Aware of the American dependence on Arab oil, he warned, 'Nobody . . . has the right to enjoy our [oil] resources and wealth at the same time he is fighting us and opposing our scientific and technological progress.'[70]

At the summit there was a consensus that the Arab countries needed to forge a strategy to counter American support for Israel. Being the entity most threatened by Israeli actions, the PLO was given the privilege of moving the main resolution. It offered a strongly anti-American motion which the Gulf monarchies were unwilling, and Egypt was reluctant, to endorse. It fell on Iraq to reconcile these disparate responses by agreeing to a moderating of the PLO draft, taking into account President Mubarak's argument that, since Washington provided Cairo with $2.2 billion in annual aid, it would be untrue to state that America posed a threat to Egypt.[71] Indeed, because of its overdependence on American handouts, and its peace treaty with Israel, Egypt had been able to apply only limited pressure on America and Israel on behalf of the PLO, which had eschewed terrorism and other violent means to achieve its goals. To strengthen its case against Washington, Baghdad leaked a US state department document which purportedly urged the Arabs to recognize Israel and accept the right of Soviet Jews to immigrate into Israel, and urged heads of state in the region to avoid 'excessively ardent language' if they wished to be taken seriously. In the end the summit adopted a resolution which was judged by most observers as highly critical of the US.

The summit resolution described the emigration of Soviet and other Jews to Palestine and other Occupied Arab territories as 'a new aggression against the rights of the Palestinian people and a serious danger to the Arab nation as well as a gross violation of human rights, the principles of international law and the Fourth Geneva Convention of 1949'. This 'massive and premeditated process' was a 'dangerous threat to pan-Arab security' and deserved to be tackled on a collective basis. Calling on the UN Security Council to guarantee that Jewish immigrants were not settled in the Occupied Palestine and Arab territories, including Jerusalem, it demanded a UN agency to monitor implementation of such a resolution. Referring to 'the hostile tendentious political and media campaigns, and the scientific and technological ban against Iraq', the Arab leaders affirmed Iraq's 'right to take all appropriate measures to safeguard and protect its national security and provide the requirements for development, including the possession of advanced science and technology and to use them for internationally legal purposes'. They also reiterated 'the right of Iraq and all Arab states to reply to aggression by all means they deem fit to guarantee their security and sovereignty'.[72] The threats to Arab security and sovereignty were perceived not only in terms of the frustration of the Palestinian uprising, the dramatic rise in Jewish immigration, and the stalemate in the peace process, but also the officially inspired campaigns by America and Britain against Iraq and Libya, and the growing threat to the existence of a vulnerable Jordan.

By stating that Jewish immigration was a threat to the 'Arab national interest', the summit resolution strengthened the hands of Jordan and the PLO. And by holding America responsible for the Israeli policies of 'aggression, terrorism and expansion', it undermined Washington's credibility as a mediator in the peace process. Finally, by assigning Iraq a pivotal role, the summit rectified the balance of power within the Arab League which, since the suspension of Egypt from the Arab League in 1979, had moved towards Saudi Arabia. To strengthen its ties with the Palestinians and the PLO, Baghdad announced emergency aid of $25 million for the intifada.[73]

Any satisfaction that Saddam Hussein may have derived from the summit's decisions was to prove transitory. The regional focus was soon to shift away from the Palestinian issue – and towards Iraq's worsening relations with its small neighbour to the south: Kuwait.

On 30 May, a pro-Iraqi Palestinian group, the Palestine Liberation Front (PLF), headed by Abu al Abbas, tried to land on Tel Aviv's Nitsanim and Gaash beaches in six speedboats. The attempt failed. Four Palestinians were killed, and 12 captured. The PLF announced that its action was in response to the murders of seven Palestinians at Rishon LeZion, on 20 May.

The next day, declaring that the PLO was not responsible for the attempted attack on Israel, Yasser Arafat stated that only the Palestine National Council could decide what to do about the PLF leader, Abu al Abbas. Washington said that it was 'not satisfied' with the PLO response. Senior PLO officials argued that their agreement with the US exempted attacks on military targets inside Israel, and that in *Al Siyasa*, a Kuwaiti newspaper, Abu al Abbas had declared that the aim of his guerrillas was to storm an Israeli military officers' camp.[74]

That Arafat was in tune with his constituency inside the Occupied Territories became apparent when, protesting against Washington's use of the veto at the UN Security Council on 26 May, the Palestinian leaders from the West Bank and Gaza severed contacts with US officials in Tel Aviv and Jerusalem, and urged Arab leaders to initiate sanctions against America including 'the use of the oil weapon'.[75]

The hardening of Palestinian attitudes coincided with the formation of the most right-wing government in Israeli history. On 11 June the hardline administration of Yitzhak Shamir received the backing of 62 out of 120 parliamentary deputies. It included David Levy as foreign minister, Moshe Arens as defence minister, and the ultra-hawkish Ariel Sharon as housing minister in charge of settling Jewish immigrants. Within days this cabinet issued policy guidelines which stated, *inter alia*, that 'the government will place immigration and absorption [of immigrants] foremost among its national objectives', and that 'the eternal right of the Jewish people to Eretz Yisrael is not subject to question and is intertwined with its right to security and peace.' The latter policy was translated by prime minister Shamir thus: 'The Israeli government would not encourage Soviet Jews to settle in Judea, Samaria and Gaza [i.e. the Occupied Territories] but it would not prevent them from doing so either.'[76]

With this, the downward spiral in the relations between the major parties accelerated. On 13 June US secretary of state Baker coupled his plea to Shamir to make the necessary compromise to get the Israeli–Palestinian talks started with a warning to the PLO that if it wanted its dialogue with the US to continue it must condemn the Palestine Liberation Front's landing on the Israeli beaches and discipline those responsible. Five days later Saddam Hussein reaffirmed his threat to attack Israel if it were to attack Iraq or others in the Arab world. The 'others' included Libya, since a Libyan ship was believed to have dropped the PLF guerrillas in speedboats near the Israeli shore. On 20 June President Bush announced the suspension of US dialogue with the PLO due to its failure to condemn the aborted attack on Israel or discipline those responsible, adding that if the PLO acted against them, bilateral talks would resume.[77] Saudi Arabia urged the immediate resumption of dialogue, as did Jordan and Egypt. But nothing came of these appeals to Washington.

King Hussein of Jordan compared the rising tension in the region to the hair-trigger period before the June 1967 Arab–Israeli War. His officials predicted an Israeli attack on either Jordan or Libya. Jordan was a potential Israeli target because it had entered into military co-operation with Iraq and because its monarch had not ruled out inviting Iraqi troops into his country.[78]

With the tension between Iraq and Israel rising sharply, Saddam Hussein moved to seek rapprochement with Iran. In a letter to Iran's supreme leader, Ayatollah Ali Khamanei, and its president, Rafsanjani, on 21 April (during the holy month of Ramadan), he proposed direct talks between Rafsanjani and Khamanei on the Iranian side and Izzat Ibrahim and himself on the Iraqi side in Mecca. In their reply on 1 May, the Iranian leaders suggested that preliminary meetings should be held in their respective capitals as a prelude to the summit, and that these should be conducted within the context of UN Security Council Resolution 598, and only after Iraq had withdrawn from the occupied Iranian territory. They stated that the 1975 Algiers Treaty should be excluded from the talks, implying thereby that it remained valid and was not negotiable. Responding on 19 May, Saddam Hussein did not address the Iranian leaders' preconditions, and instead emphasized once again 'the unity among Muslims to confront the aggressions of Israel and the imperialists'. On 26 May Iran's National Security Council met to consider the Iraqi president's second letter. It seems to have decided to respond to it positively.[79] As a result the foreign ministers of Iran and Iraq held direct talks on 3 July 1990 in Geneva in the presence of the UN secretary-general, something they had not done since the opening round after the August 1988 ceasefire. Later both sides declared that the negotiations would be conducted within the context of Resolution 598.

The other area where Saddam Hussein had continued his policy of relaxation was in the domestic economy and politics. That he was acutely aware of the events in Eastern Europe was obvious from a speech he delivered to Baath Party officials in February 1990. He explained to his audience that those developments had resulted from 'uncorrected mistakes'. The governments there had interfered in everything – from 'the thread to the needle, their marketing and their availability' – and set his regime apart from such a system. 'If we had done that, we would be at loggerheads with the people,' he said. Actually, the decentralization and privatization of Iraq's highly centralized economic system with a dominant public sector had begun in the course of the Iran–Iraq War in order to raise output. In practice it amounted to reducing the size of the bureaucracy, privatizing state assets and stimulating the private sector. Also greater autonomy was given to the managements of public sector undertakings. As a result, after the 1988 truce, many agricultural projects, hotels and tourist services, as well as 47 light industrial units, were sold to the private sector. Direct government control was to be limited to such strategic economic activity as the petroleum, defence and heavy industries. However, the lifting of marketing and price controls soon after the ceasefire led to high price rises. It took some time for the government to bring the inflation rate down to 12–15 per cent. That is why Saddam Hussein in a speech in February 1990 could afford to urge Iraqis to air their grievances 'freely so that the authorities could respond positively to complaints'. Also, according to the official media, his earlier proposals for political liberalization were being studied by a high-powered committee.[80]

The other regional country where the authorities found themselves having to liberalize the political system was Kuwait. Once the Iran–Iraq War ended in August 1988, the emir of Kuwait lost his chief reason for continuing press censorship and ruling without a parliament. Those who wanted the National Assembly restored were encouraged and excited by the movement for democratization in East Europe that gathered momentum in the autumn of 1989. They took to organizing a series of *diwaniyas* (informal gatherings) in the homes of eminent citizens, including 32 of the 50 members of the dissolved National Assembly. A petition initiated by the Group of Thirty-two calling for the restoration of parliament was signed by 25,000 voters, constituting 40 per cent of the total electorate. But this had little impact on the ruling family. While conceding the principle of 'public political participation', Crown Prince Shaikh Saad al Sabah said, 'The problems of the old National Assembly required some new form of democracy.'[81] In response, the Group of Thirty-two organized rallies at the homes of former parliamentary deputies. On 22 January 1990 police violently broke up one such gathering, injuring many participants. To calm tempers, the crown prince announced a round of consultations with tribal, religious, business and community leaders to work out a new formula for the functioning of a restored parliament. These talks went on for a couple of months. Apprehensive of the palace's plan to alter the 1962 constitution, the Group of Thirty-two warned on 20 April against amending the constitution, something only the National Assembly was empowered to do. The warning was ignored. Three days later the emir announced a 75-member National Council (with 25 members nominated by the ruler) as a 'transitional body' for four years, which would propose, *inter alia*, non-binding recommendations for 'new controls' over parliamentary life. It was to have none of the legislative powers of the National Assembly or its independent authority.

The Group of Thirty-two, also called the Constitutionalists, rejected the emir's decree. On 25 April, the Eid al Fitr (lit., Festival of Breaking the Fast), supporters of the Group of Thirty-two marched to the house of Ahmad al Sadoun, former parliamentary speaker. Finding it surrounded by barbed wire and special forces personnel, they proceeded to the residence of Saleh al Fadal, former deputy speaker, only to be teargassed by the special forces.[82] Some days later, the Trade Union Federation's traditional May Day rally was banned so that it could not be used by the opposition.

Government repression only steeled the resolve of the Group of Thirty-two to stick to its decision to boycott the impending elections to the National Council, a step endorsed by many professional bodies. Of the Group of Thirty-two (former parliamentary deputies) only one decided to contest elections.

In the run-up to the poll on 10 June the Constitutionalists kept up their agitation, which resulted in the arrest of 17 of their leaders, including the veteran Ahmad Khatib. There were 348 candidates for the 50 elected seats. Despite the wide choice, the overall turn-out was down by a quarter from the 85 per cent recorded at the last parliamentary election, with some suburbs of Kuwait City registering an all-time low turn-out of below 40 per cent.[83] The result was a chamber in which the elected segment was dominated by pro-government deputies slavishly loyal to the emir through ties of clan and tribe – further strengthened by the 25 nominees of the ruler. This meant smooth sailing for the government led by prime minister Shaikh Saad al Sabah, who was also the crown prince.

While the emir of Kuwait had good grounds to feel that he had virtually solved his pressing domestic problem, he had reason to fret over his relations with the powerful neighbour to the north: Iraq. The nub of the problem, in Baghdad's eyes, was the open flouting of the OPEC output quota by Kuwait (as well as the United Arab Emirates). Overproduction by these states in the spring of 1990 depressed the oil price well below OPEC's reference price of $18 a barrel, fixed in November 1989. During a closed session of the extraordinary Arab summit in Baghdad on 30 May the Iraqi president addressed the gathering on the subject. He alluded to 'the failure by some of our Arab brothers to abide by the OPEC decisions when they flooded the world market with more oil than it needed, thereby enabling clients to buy below the fixed [OPEC] price.' He added that 'for every US dollar drop in the price of a barrel of oil, the Iraqi loss amounted to $1 billion annually'. The total loss to the oil-producing Arab countries was manyfold. After urging that the matter be viewed from 'a pan-Arab angle', he said, 'War is fought with soldiers and harm is done by explosions, killing and coup attempts, but it is also done by economic means sometimes.' He added, 'I say to those who do not mean to wage war on Iraq, that this is in fact a kind of war against Iraq. Were it possible, we would have endured . . . But I say that we have reached a point where we can no longer withstand pressure.'[84] The Iraqi leader knew well the efficacy of the economic tool. During the First Gulf War, Kuwait and Saudi Arabia had succeeded in damaging Iran's economy by causing an oil price collapse from over $30 a barrel in late November 1985 to under $10 in early April 1986 by flooding the market. Tehran never recovered sufficiently from this near-fatal blow to its economy to wage its war with Baghdad vigorously. Iraq's economy suffered, too, but unlike Iran, it received substantial financial and other aid from Saudi Arabia and Kuwait – not to mention the US and other Western nations – to withstand the oil price crash.[85]

Now, Saddam Hussein's plea seemed to have fallen on deaf ears. Overproduction continued, and depressed the price to $11 a barrel in June, a level at which Iraq's oil income was barely enough to meet current expenses, leaving nothing to meet the repayments on foreign loans or pay for the minimum reconstruction that was needed. In late June a desperate Saddam Hussein sent a personal message to the Kuwaiti emir, warning him to curb Kuwait's excess output (of 600,000 b/d over OPEC's quota of 1.5 mb/d) as it was having a 'negative impact on Iraq and OPEC's vital interests'. He addressed a similar missive to the ruler of the UAE.[86] Iraq's deputy prime minister, Sadoun Hamadi, told Kuwaiti officials that the oil price needed to be raised to $25 a barrel.

To resolve the worsening problem, Saddam Hussein proposed a summit meeting of the Arab Gulf members of OPEC: Iraq, Kuwait, Qatar, Saudi Arabia and the UAE. Having agreed to the idea of such a gathering in principle, King Fahd tried to rally fellow-monarchs against Iraq's move to raise the petroleum price to $25 a barrel, aware that a high oil price was detrimental to the economy of the West, particularly America, whose interests were dear to the Saudi royal family for political and personal reasons. Most of the private investments of some 4,500 male Saudi royals, running into tens of billions of dollars, were in American financial institutions and real estate. (So too were the investments of some 1,200 al Sabahs of Kuwait.)

Two days before the meeting of the oil ministers of the Arab Gulf members of OPEC on 11 July 1990, Iraqi intelligence secured the intercepts of a telephone conversation between the Saudi king and the emir of Qatar, Shaikh Khalifa ibn Hamad al Thani (1972–). To Saddam Hussein, these tapes established conclusively that the two rulers were plotting against Iraq's interests.

King Fahd started the conversation.

Fahd: We have had enough: Israel threatens Iraq and now Iraq threatens Israel. Now we're back to the same old story of [President] Nasser before 1967 [Arab–Israeli War]. We want to think the matter over.

Khalifa: I shall always be with you.

Fahd: I wanted to tell you that I told Hisham [Nazer, Saudi oil minister] to tell his brothers not to pay attention to what the Iraqi minister said. Iraq is in trouble. There's a sensitive situation between Iraq and Israel . . . The important thing is that we put everything in order during these two months [until September], especially when things become quiet and we follow a defensive stand. Two months are left to us. As Gulf states, we shall meet and organize matters. The same applies to Iraq. The Iraqis have lost their temper . . . And you know when someone loses his temper his speech is unreasonable.

Khalifa: True, their speech is unreasonable.

Fahd: We don't want that.

Khalifa: I am sure it is unreasonable.

Fahd: We don't want problems with Israel. We don't want problems with Iran.

Khalifa: True.

Fahd: But we are envied as Gulf states. Yet where were those who now envy us when we were poor? They did not say our brothers have nothing.

Khalifa: No, they did not . . .

Fahd: All I want to do is stop the bad temper. When things become quiet it will be easy to talk to Iraq. Saddam thinks highly of you. All we must do is to stop this bad temper. I told my minister to meet their minister in Iraq tomorrow. Before you meet with Iraq, all of us must agree [on policy] as Gulf ministers. Keep quiet even if the Iraqi minister says something bad. These people, the Iraqis, have got themselves into a problem with Israel, but they have nothing to do with Israel. 700 kilometres separate them from Israel. The matters must be settled wisely . . .

Fahd: They [Iraqis] have given themselves the same problems as Nasser, and he could not solve them. How can we fight the whole world? Between [the two of] us, I think the Palestinians have pushed matters too far. They are losing nothing.

Khalifa: True.

Fahd: I hope Abu Ammar [i.e. Yasser Arafat] will be reasonable. I told our brothers, the Palestinians, that we will do our best so that they might not lose the West Bank and Gaza. I don't want to see the West Bank and Gaza lost by sheer words.

Khalifa: That'd be disastrous.

King Fahd then pointed out that the Iraqis were proposing the summit conference for a time when Shaikh Khalifa would be away.

Fahd (continuing): As a principle, when they mentioned that idea, I said it can't be. Let oil ministers meet first, and discuss with one another. It will be better if ministers of oil, foreign affairs and finance meet in every country to discuss the matters from all political, financial, social and oil aspects.

Khalifa: True.

Fahd: At that time you might think of a summit meeting. But don't think of holding a summit if there's a chance of failure.

Khalifa: And Kuwait?

Fahd: Probably our brothers, the Iraqis, will agree to dismiss the idea of a summit meeting.

Khalifa: God be praised.

Fahd: It's easy to start a conflict but it is very difficult to stop it. Israel is our number one nightmare. It has 200 nuclear warheads and 47 atom bombs. Its people are crazy. All our Palestinian brothers have to do is to do their best, and we will help them. They have got to put their hand on the West Bank and Gaza. They don't have to go to the extreme. In that case Israel would make them real colonies.

Khalifa: We have to gain one position after another.[87]

Several conclusions can be drawn from this conversation. Saudi Arabia behaved as leader of the Gulf states, with other states quite content to play second fiddle. Yet it was mortally afraid of Israel. Its monarch grew nervous watching the tension between Israel and Iraq rise. The inclination on his part to be cautious bordered on impotence. His persistent tendency to advise the PLO and its leader to tone down their rhetoric after they had renounced the armed struggle seems odd, especially when evidence on the ground showed that the Israeli government was for all practical purposes colonizing the West Bank and Gaza. More specifically, this conversation provided Saddam Hussein with concrete proof of an 'economic conspiracy' by the Gulf monarchs against his country, which had protected them from the expansionist designs of Iran.

Unknown to the Iraqi president, then, was another document which, if genuine, showed co-ordination between Kuwait's State Security Department (SSD) and the US Central Intelligence Agency. It was a memorandum, dated 20 November 1989, by the director-general of the SSD, Brigadier Fahd Ahmad al Fahd, to the interior minister, Shaikh Salem al Salem al Sabah, summarizing the agreements reached by him with William Webster, director of the CIA, during their meeting at the CIA headquarters in Langley, Virginia, on 14 November 1989. 'We agreed with the United States side that visits would be exchanged at all levels between the State Security Department and the Central Intelligence Agency, and that information would be exchanged about the armaments and social and political structures of Iran and Iraq,' read paragraph 2 of the memorandum. 'We agreed with the American side that it was important to take advantage of the deteriorating economic situation in Iraq in order to put pressure on that country's government to delineate our common border,' stated paragraph 5. 'The Central Intelligence Agency gave us its view of appropriate means of pressure, saying that broad co-operation should be initiated between us, on condition that such activities are co-ordinated at a high level.' Significantly, the last paragraph referred to 'a special telephone [in Mr Webster's office] at our disposal to promote rapid exchange of views and information that do not require written communication'.[88]

For the present, however, the meeting of the petroleum ministers of Iraq, Kuwait, Qatar, Saudi Arabia and the UAE held in Jiddah on 11 July went some way towards the Iraqi objective of $25 a barrel. It unanimously urged OPEC to freeze the ceiling on the overall output of 22.1 mb/d to help raise the price per barrel from $14 to the $18 target which had been set in November 1989.[89]

However, on 13 July, this stand was repudiated by the Kuwaiti oil minister, thus rekindling Saddam Hussein's apprehension, built up over many months, that the Gulf monarchs were lining up against Iraq's economic interests. On 9 July, the day the Saudi and Qatari rulers agreed to undermine Saddam Hussein's proposal for a summit, the Kuwaiti government welcomed the foreign minister of Iran for the first time since the 1979 revolution. Its decision to resume the ferry service with Iran while continuing to stall Baghdad's suggested resumption of air travel between Iraq and Kuwait also upset the Iraqi government.[90] Equally disturbing to Baghdad was the visit to Cairo on 14 July by President Hafiz Assad of Syria (1970–) – an arch-rival of Saddam Hussein who had sided with Iran during the First Gulf War – after an interval of thirteen years. It went down badly with the Iraqi president, and cooled his relationship with President Mubarak.

While the threat of Israel appeared to be rising, support for Iraq from fellow Arab countries seemed to be declining – a process in which, according to Saddam Hussein, America and Britain played important roles. In an interview with the *Wall Street Journal*, published on 28 June, he said: 'British and US diplomats are combing the Gulf warning rulers to fear Iraq.'

Little wonder that on 15 July Iraq's foreign minister, Tariq Aziz, sent a letter to Chadli Klibi, the Arab League secretary-general, in which he complained about the oil policies of Kuwait and the UAE, and laid specific territorial and financial claims against Kuwait.

'Precisely since Iraq began to raise its voice calling for regaining the Arabs' rights in Palestine and drawing attention to the dangers of the American presence in the Gulf, the Kuwaiti government began to adopt an unjust policy aimed at harming . . . Iraq,' wrote Tariq Aziz. 'The government of the United Arab Emirates participated with the Kuwaiti government in this regard.' The oil glut created by these states, he continued, had caused the price to fall below OPEC's 'minimum price' of $18 a barrel – to between $11 and $13 a barrel. Since 'a drop of $1 in the price of a barrel of oil leads to a drop of $1 billion in Iraqi revenues annually', he argued, Baghdad had lost many billions of dollars due to the policies of Kuwait and the UAE. Despite the Iraqi president's appeal to these states at the Baghdad summit (in late May) they had continued the policy of overproduction of oil. 'We have no choice but to deduce that he who deliberately, directly and openly adopts this policy, or he who supports or instigates it, is implementing part of the imperialist-Zionist plan against Iraq and the Arab nation,' he stated.

Secondly, Tariq Aziz added, since 1980 Kuwait had been extracting oil from the 'Iraqi Rumeila oilfield' (which extended three miles into

Kuwait) and, based on the prices between 1980 and 1990, 'the oil stolen by the Kuwaiti government from the Rumeila oilfield . . . amounts to $2.4 billion [at the rate of 25,000 b/d]'. Finally, he summarized Iraq's assessment of the Iran–Iraq War and the financial aid it had received from the Gulf states to conduct it. 'The war which Iraq was obliged to wage was not only intended to defend Iraq's sovereignty, but also to defend the eastern flank of the Arab homeland, especially the Arabian Gulf region,' Tariq Aziz wrote. 'This was confirmed by the Gulf leaders themselves in the strongest words.' In a war that lasted eight years, 'the value of the military hardware for which Iraq paid hard currency . . . amounted to $102 billion.' Because the conflict severely disrupted Iraq's petroleum production (of 3.6 mb/d before the war) and exports, Baghdad lost $106 billion in oil revenue. Among the countries that benefited from the decrease in Iraqi oil exports were Kuwait and the UAE. 'How can these amounts [i.e. the interest-free loans from Kuwait and the UAE to Iraq up to 1982] be regarded as Iraqi debts to its Arab brothers when Iraq made sacrifices that are many times more than these debts in terms of Iraqi resources during the grinding war and offered rivers of blood of its youth in defence of the [Arab] nation's soil, dignity, honour and wealth?'[91] While no figures were mentioned, it was widely believed that Kuwait's interest-free loans (in cash and oil countersales) to Iraq amounted to $10 to $14 billion.[92]

Two days later, in a television speech on the 22nd anniversary of the Baathist coup, Saddam Hussein issued a public warning to the Arab countries conspiring with the US to hurt Iraq. He distinguished between the 'old method' of military means and the 'new method' of economic warfare. 'This new method, which has appeared within the ranks of the Arabs, seeks to cut off livelihood while the old method, which has already been contained [by Iraq], sought to cut off necks,' the Iraqi leader said. At the behest of the US, certain Arab states had deliberately overproduced oil in defiance of the will of the OPEC majority. As a result of the fall in oil prices from $27–$28 a barrel which prevailed 'not very long ago', Iraq had been losing $14 bn a year. 'Raising our voices against the evil [of over production] is not the final resort if the evil continues,' he warned. 'There should be some effective act to restore things to their correct position . . . Iraqis will not forget the saying "Cutting necks is better than cutting the means of living".' He then went on to explain why the US was intent on lowering the oil price steeply. Its need to import oil was increasing 'at high rates corresponding to its increasing demand', and 'now that it has the opportunity, the United States is determined to become the only superpower without competition', it is 'working to guarantee the flow of oil to it at the cheapest price'. Moreover, the US wanted 'an increasing strategic reserve of oil' in order to withstand any disruptions caused by strife and wars in the Middle East likely to result from America's superpower ambitions and Israel's expansionist policies. 'If bought at a price lower than its true value, the oil reserve [of America] will not be as heavy a burden to the US Treasury as it would have been if bought at its true value.' Given this, Saddam Hussein argued, 'the policies of certain Arab rulers are American-inspired and detrimental to the interests of the Arab nation'.93

On an OPEC quota of 1.5 mb/d, with 700,000 b/d meant for export, Kuwait was overproducing by 500,000 b/d, thus increasing its input into the international oil market by about 71%. Additionally, the UAE was injecting its overproduction of 450,000 b/d into the market. Given the extreme sensitivity of the petroleum market to demand and supply, a total excess of 950,000 b/d was enough to depress prices considerably.

The low oil price of course reduced the revenues of Kuwait and the UAE as well as those of other oil producers. But given the enormous oil reserves of these two tiny emirates – at about 100 billion barrels each – and their healthy bank deposits and foreign investments, their economies were immune to any fall in petroleum prices. In 1989 Kuwait earned $7.7 billion from oil exports and $8.8 billion from its over $100 billion-worth of foreign investments. With more than half of its foreign income coming from investments, Kuwait was inclined to favour lower petroleum prices: cheap oil kept the Western and Japanese economies healthy and stock markets buoyant. According to the Bank of International Settlements, Kuwait had $16.3 billion in assets, twice its liabilities. In contrast, Iraqi deposits amounted to $5.36 billion against liabilities of $7.5 billion.94

While the Iraqi National Assembly backed Saddam Hussein's attack on the oil policies of Kuwait and the UAE, the Kuwaiti National Council, meeting in a closed session on 18 July, denounced Iraq's memorandum to the Arab League for 'its violation of the rights of neighbourliness and its shunning of the Arab and Islamic frater-nity'.95

In his reply to Iraq's letter on 19 July, Kuwait's foreign minister, Shaikh Sabah al Sabah, described Iraq's charges of Kuwaiti installa-tions on Iraqi territory as 'a falsification of reality'. He referred to 'repeated Iraqi attempts to dig oil wells within Kuwaiti territories, which inflict severe damage on the reserves of the part of the [Rumeila]

field within Kuwaiti territories'. He proposed an Arab League committee to settle the border dispute. Regarding the 'deterioration of the [oil]
price', he described it as 'an international problem in which numerous
sides – producers, consumers and OPEC members and non-members –
were involved.'96

On 19 July the US state department expressed 'strong commitment'
to 'supporting the individual and collective self-defence of our friends
in the Gulf, with whom we have deep and long standing ties'.
The 'friends' in this case were apparently Kuwait and the UAE.
Baghdad took unkindly to this, with an editorial in the Baathist
Party newspaper, *Al Thawra* (The Revolution), on 21 July expressing
astonishment at the American position.

To lower tension, King Fahd despatched his foreign minister to
mediate between Baghdad and Kuwait City. And, responding to an
invitation by President Mubarak, Tariq Aziz arrived in Cairo on
22 July.

The next day, as Mubarak flew to Baghdad to cool tempers against
the background of the despatch of 30,000 Iraqi troops to the Kuwaiti
border, Washington confirmed that its six warships in the Gulf,
including four frigates, had been put on alert, and that they had
joined an exercise with the UAE navy as a signal of support for the
UAE and Kuwait.97

On that day, the Iraqi government paper, *Al Jumhuriya* (The
Republic), singled out the Kuwaiti foreign minister, Shaikh Sabah
al Sabah, a brother of the emir, accusing him of turning himself into
'a tool to implement the American policy in Kuwait, including the
undermining of Iraqi–Kuwaiti relations', and 'the focal point of the
conspiracy [being] implemented by the Kuwaiti government against
Iraq and the Arab nation'.

It was against this charged atmosphere that Saddam Hussein had
a two-hour meeting with the US ambassador to Iraq, April Glaspie,
in his office on 25 July. He handed her a long message to President
Bush in which he surveyed Baghdad–Washington relations since their
resumption in November 1984. 'When planned and deliberate policy
forces the price of oil down without good commercial reasons, then
that means another war against Iraq,' he wrote. 'Military war kills
people by bleeding them, and economic war kills their humanity by
depriving them of their chance to have a good standard of living . . .
We do not accept that anyone could injure Iraqi pride or the Iraqi
right to have high standards of living. Kuwait and the UAE were
at the forefront of this policy aimed at lowering Iraq's position and

depriving its people of higher living standards.' He then referred
to the US statements pertaining to 'its friends' in the region. 'You
know you are not the ones who protected your friends during the
war with Iran,' Saddam Hussein continued. 'I assure you, had the
Iranians overrun the region, the American troops would not have
stopped them, except by the use of nuclear weapons . . . So what
can it mean when America says it will now protect its friends? It
can only mean prejudice against Iraq. This stance plus manoeuvres
and statements which have been made [by America] has encouraged
the UAE and Kuwait to disregard Iraqi rights.' He well understood
Washington's statements about wanting 'an easy flow' of petroleum.
'But we cannot understand the attempt to encourage some parties to
harm Iraq's interests . . . If you use pressure, we will deploy pressure
and force . . . Everyone can cause harm according to their ability and
their size. We cannot come all the way to you in the United States,
but individual Arabs may reach you . . . We don't want war because
we know what war means. But do not push us to consider war as the
only solution to live proudly and to provide our people with a good
living.' He concluded his message by saying to Glaspie: 'I hope the
[US] president will read this himself and will not leave it in the hands
of a gang in the state department. I exclude the secretary of state – and
[John] Kelly [assistant secretary for the Near East], because I know him
and I exchanged views with him.'

Saddam Hussein and April Glaspie then conversed in the presence
of the Iraqi foreign minister, Tariq Aziz.

> *Glaspie*: As you know, he [President Bush] directed the United
> States administration to reject the suggestion of implement-
> ing trade sanctions [against Iraq] . . . I have a direct instruction
> from the president to seek better relations with Iraq.
>
> *Saddam Hussein*: But how? We too have this desire. But matters
> are running counter to this desire.
>
> *Glaspie*: President Bush is an intelligent man. He is not going to
> declare an economic war against Iraq. You are right. It is true
> what you say that we do not want higher prices for oil. But I
> would ask you to examine the possibility of not charging too
> high a price for oil.
>
> *Saddam Hussein*: $25 a barrel is not a high price.
>
> *Glaspie*: We have many Americans who would like to see the
> price go above $25 because they come from oil-producing
> states.

Saddam Hussein: The price at one stage had dropped to $12 a barrel, and a reduction in the modest Iraqi budget of $6 billion to $7 billion is a disaster.

Glaspie: I know you need funds. We understand that, and our opinion is that you should have the opportunity to rebuild your country. But we have no opinion on the Arab–Arab conflicts, like your border disagreement with Kuwait. I was in the American embassy in Kuwait in the late 1960s. The instruction we had during this period was that we should express no opinion on this issue, and that the issue is not associated with America. James Baker has directed our official spokesmen to emphasize this instruction. We hope you can solve this problem via Klibi [Arab League secretary-general] or via President Mubarak ... I now speak of oil ... We can see only that you have deployed massive troops in the south ... When this happens in the context of what you said on your National Day [17 July] ... that the measures taken by the UAE and Kuwait are, in the final analysis, parallel to military aggression against Iraq, then it would be reasonable for me to be concerned. And for this reason, I received an instruction to ask you, in the spirit of friendship, not confrontation, regarding your intentions.

Saddam Hussein: It is natural for you as a superpower to be concerned. But what we ask is not to express your concern in a way that would make an aggressor believe he is getting support for his aggression. We want to find a just solution ... But at the same time, we want the others to know that our patience is running out regarding their action, which is harming even the milk of our children ... We sent them [Kuwait and the UAE] envoys and handwritten letters. We asked King Fahd to hold a four-member summit, but he suggested a meeting between oil ministers [in Jiddah] ... Only two days after that meeting [on 11 July] the Kuwaiti oil minister made a statement that contradicted the agreement ... Also after the Jiddah agreement, we received some intelligence that they were talking of sticking to the agreement for two months only. Then they would change their policy.[98]

Glaspie: Mr President, it would be helpful if you could give us an assessment of the effort made by your Arab brothers and whether they have achieved anything.

Saddam Hussein: On this subject, we agreed with President Mubarak that the prime minister of Kuwait would meet with the deputy chairman of the Revolutionary Command Council [Izzat Ibrahim] in Saudi Arabia, because the Saudis initiated contact with us, aided by President Mubarak's efforts. He just telephoned me a short while ago to say that the Kuwaitis have agreed to that suggestion . . . He told me they were scared. They said [Iraqi] troops were only 20 kilometres north of the Arab League [border] line. I said to him that regardless of what is there, whether they are police, border guards or army, and regardless of how many are there, and what they are doing, assure the Kuwaitis and give them our word that we are not going to do anything until we meet with them. When we meet and when we see that there is hope, then nothing will happen. But if we are unable to find a solution, then it will be natural that Iraq will not accept death, even though wisdom is above everything. There you have good news.

Aziz: This is a journalistic exclusive.

Glaspie: I thought to postpone my trip [abroad] because of the difficulties we are facing. But now I will fly on Monday [30 July].[99]

It transpired later that after receiving Glaspie's account of this meeting and the message from President Hussein, the Bush administration effectively approved the line she had taken. Indeed, responding to the Iraqi leader's message, President Bush sent him a 'presidential message' on 28 July via the US embassy in Baghdad. In it, he reportedly told Saddam Hussein that the US wanted to improve relations with Iraq, but advised him against pursuing 'threats involving military force or conflict' to resolve Iraq's grievances against Kuwait, and added that the US would 'support other friends in the region', meaning the moderate Gulf states.[100]

However, Bush's well-known opposition to economic sanctions against Baghdad was not enough to deter the US Senate from passing a motion on 27 July, by 80 votes to 16, to impose an arms and technology embargo against Iraq and terminate $1.2 billion loan guarantees that Washington provided Baghdad to enable it to buy American farm and commercial products. Expressing the Bush administration's view of sanctions, attached to a farm bill, Senator Richard Lugar, a Republican, said: 'Passage of this legislation would badly undercut any possibility we have of influencing Iraqi behaviour in areas from the [Middle East] peace process to human rights, terrorism to [nuclear] proliferation.'[101] The state department reiterated Lugar's line.

Washington's positive attitude towards Baghdad had developed in the course of the Iran–Iraq War. Saddam Hussein was seen as a strong, secular leader, well-motivated and capable of containing the revolutionary Islamic tide rising from Tehran, intent on drowning the ruling families of the Gulf states possessing nearly half of the world's petroleum reserves. America's neutrality in that conflict did not inhibit it from aiding Iraq materially and providing it with military intelligence on Iran, or from destroying or disabling half of Iran's navy. Over the years the Baathist regime of Saddam Hussein came to be perceived in Washington as secular and tolerable, a stabilizing influence in a region prone to volatility. Its regime came off rather well when compared to those in such Arab countries as Syria (penniless, tied to Moscow), Lebanon (wracked by a long and bloody civil war), Libya (headed by a megalomaniac maverick), or Egypt (highly bureaucratic, debt-ridden). The continued estrangement between Iran and the United States even after the death of Khomeini, a vehemently anti-American leader, encouraged Washington to cultivate Baghdad as a counterweight to its regional rival, Tehran. The Iraq connection had proved quite lucrative to the farming community in the US, with Iraq emerging as the leading buyer of American farm produce. The oil companies and other businesses too found Iraq attractive: it had the second largest petroleum reserves in the Gulf, a population as large as all of the Arabian Peninsula countries combined, and a strong and varied economy. Moreover, Iraq quickly filled the gap left in American oil imports when President Reagan banned the import of Iranian oil in early 1987.

However, whatever may have been the rivalries of Iraq and Iran more than three years earlier, now they joined hands at the OPEC meeting in Geneva on 25 July to push for a reference price of $21 a barrel. Assisted by Saudi Arabia, they achieved their objective. At the same time the overall OPEC output was raised slightly to 22.5 mb/d, with the Iraqi quota fixed at 2.7 mb/d.

With that matter settled, regional attention once again turned to the Iraq–Kuwait crisis. Aware of Baghdad's animus towards his foreign minister, Shaikh Sabah al Sabah, the Kuwaiti emir named Shaikh Saad al Sabah as the head of the Kuwaiti delegation to meet its Iraqi counterpart led by Izzat Ibrahim, deputy president of the RCC.

The two delegations arrived in Jiddah on 31 July with different expectations. The Iraqis came simply to secure their 'rights', territorial as well as financial, which included not only obtaining $2.4 billion for the Iraqi oil that Kuwait had allegedly stolen but also a loan of $10 billion to surmount the current financial crisis. The Kuwaitis arrived to haggle, intent on exploiting Iraq's weakened economic situation to settle once and for all what mattered most to them: frontier delineation.

After meeting for an hour and a half in the evening, they adjourned the session first for prayers, and then for dinner hosted by King Fahd. According to one version, after the king's departure, Izzat Ibrahim and Shaikh Saad resumed the negotiations informally. The Kuwaiti crown prince insisted that they discuss the border demarcation before anything else. This angered the Iraqi leader. Tempers flared. 'Don't threaten us,' Shaikh Saad reportedly said to Izzat Ibrahim. 'Kuwait has very powerful friends. You'll be forced to pay back all the money you owe us.'[102] This seemed in tune with the guideline reportedly specified by the Kuwaiti emir to Shaikh Saad: not to make any concessions to Iraq in the negotiations, and to remember that this position was based on the advice given to him by the US, Britain and Egypt. 'Whatever you hear from the Saudis and the Iraqis about Arab brotherhood and solidarity, don't listen to it,' stated the Kuwaiti emir's memorandum of 29 July 1990 to Shaikh Saad. 'Both have their own interests. The Saudis want to weaken us and exploit our yielding to the Iraqis so that in the future we shall yield to them the [jointly owned] Neutral Zone, and the Iraqis want to compensate for their war from our accounts.'[103]

Of the 'powerful friends' mentioned by Shaikh Saad, America was the most important. 'We remain strongly committed to supporting the individual and collective self-defence of our friends in the Gulf,' stated the US defence department on 31 July. 'We also remain determined to ensure the free flow of oil through the Hormuz Strait and defend the principle of freedom of navigation and commerce.'[104] At the same time it leaked information to the *Washington Post* that satellite pictures showed that six Iraqi divisions, consisting of 95,000 soldiers, were deployed near the Iraq–Kuwait frontier.

These actions of the Pentagon and the behaviour of Shaikh Saad al Sabah in Jiddah seem to have convinced Saddam Hussein that further negotiations with the Kuwaitis were futile: an assessment which paved the ground for the decision by the Iraqi high command on the night of 31 July–1 August to invade Kuwait.[105]

In Jiddah it was announced on 1 August at 14.34 GMT (17.34 local time) that the Iraqi–Kuwaiti talks had failed. By then the Iraqi delegation was back in Baghdad. 'The talks collapsed because Kuwait did not give in to Iraqi demands to write off debts and to relinquish some of its territories,' said a Kuwaiti official in Jiddah. 'The two sides failed to reach an agreement because Iraq did not see any serious sign by the Kuwaiti officials in tackling the major damage inflicted on Iraq due to their recent behaviour and positions taken against Iraq's fundamental interests,' said Sadoun Hamadi, one of the members of the Iraqi delegation.[106] Expecting the worst, the Pentagon put its naval force in the Gulf on high alert.

But the al Sabahs did not show the same degree of alertness or preparedness, as the next twelve hours were to reveal.

PART II

THE CRISIS

3 SADDAM'S BLITZKRIEG, BUSH'S LINE IN THE SAND

'Never in history has so much been lost so quickly by so few.'

Christopher Dickey, an American journalist, on
the loss of Kuwait to Iraq[1]

'A line has been drawn in the sand. The United States has taken a firm position [on the Iraqi invasion of Kuwait].'

President George Bush, 8 August 1990[2]

'The invasion is a black and white situation. We condemn it. But the reasons for the invasion are not so black and white.'

Egyptian diplomat on the eve of the Arab summit
of 10 August 1990[3]

'In Saddam, Arabs see a man of action – the first leader in years to shape events rather than submitting to them.'

Algerian civil servant in Algiers[4]

'The crisis over Kuwait marks a watershed for the Bush administration. Success will boost world morale and the world economy. It will strengthen the president's domestic leadership. Failure will blight all future domestic and international efforts.'

Henry Kissinger, former US secretary of state[5]

Iraq's invasion of Kuwait on 2 August 1990 aroused an immediate outcry in the world community, with the United Nations Security Council passing a resolution demanding an immediate Iraqi withdrawal the same day. Further resolutions from the Security Council, as well as the Arab League and the Gulf Co-operation Council, followed. The non-Arab response reached a climax with Washington ordering military intervention, codenamed Operation 'Desert Shield'. Then, on 10 August, the Arab summit condemned the Iraqi action by a majority vote, and pledged military assistance to Saudi Arabia. Two days later Saddam Hussein tried to place his invasion and annexation of Kuwait in the larger context of other occupations in the Middle East, and offered a three-point plan to resolve the present crisis along with the earlier, continuing ones in various parts of the region. His initiative was rejected by the US as well as Egypt. Undeterred by this, King Hussein of Jordan stepped in to mediate in what had by 14 August evolved as an Iraqi–American confrontation.

The end of Phase One of the Kuwait crisis, and the beginning of Phase Two, were marked by Saddam Hussein's climb-down on 15 August in his peace talks with Iran.

Phase One

The Iraqi military started moving into Kuwait at 2.00 a.m. (local time) on 2 August. It was led by six divisions of the élite Republican Guard. Two of these, including armoured brigades, advanced the 75 miles from the Iraqi–Kuwaiti frontier to the capital. They were assisted by Special Forces which were brought into Kuwait by ship and helicopter some hours after the border crossing. Helicopter-borne troops took over the offshore islands.

During the second stage of the offensive Iraq's fighter aircraft hit key installations in and around Kuwait City while its commandos and airborne units attacked the emir's residence, Dasman Palace, the radio and television station, and the Central Bank. The main thrust of the Iraqis was aimed at the palace, facing the sea, and the military barracks and airport at Jahra, west of the capital, housing an élite brigade. The Dasman Palace was attacked by Iraqi units in armoured personnel carriers which had been brought in by landing craft. More Iraqi troops arrived in helicopters, which landed on the roof and in the garden of the palace. By then, early dawn, most of the inhabitants of the palace had fled in a convoy of Mercedes-Benz limousines.

The emir was reportedly tipped off an hour before the invasion. According to a version released by Washington soon after the Second Gulf War, Crown Prince Saad telephoned the US embassy in Kuwait at 04.00 local time (21.00 EST on 1 August) requesting immediate military assistance to halt the Iraqi invasion, but insisting that the request 'not be made public or treated as official'. By adding diplomatic and legal problems to the already difficult task of mounting swift military operations against Iraq, Crown Prince Saad complicated matters for Washington, thus aborting any chance of instant positive response from the White House. At 05.30 local time Crown Prince Saad telephoned the US embassy again, saying he was willing to make an official request and make it public. By then it was too late for the United States to provide effective military assistance. According to another (unofficial) version, around 04.30 local time the Kuwaiti emir and his immediate entourage rushed to the US embassy to board an American military helicopter (brought in earlier from one of the US warships) bound for Bahrain. The rest of the residents of the Dasman Palace drove south into Saudi Arabia. From Bahrain the emir and his entourage were later to fly to Dammam, Saudi Arabia. In the chaotic hurry that preceded the escape, one senior member of the royal family, Major Ahmad al Sabah, was left behind. Assisted by crack Kuwaiti troops guarding the palace, he resisted the Iraqis for a couple of hours, and died in the process. The palace was then sealed off by some of the 350 Iraqi tanks which arrived in the capital at dawn. The airport and military barracks also fell to the invading force. While the battle was being waged in Kuwait City, motorists in Baghdad sounded their horns and flashed their lights, celebrating the news that their army had successfully invaded Kuwait. Iraqi radio and television stations broadcast patriotic songs and mobilization orders for the armed forces.[6]

By 11 a.m. flag-waving Iraqi troops controlled most of the key buildings in the Kuwaiti capital; and Baghdad Radio was in a position to announce that the regime of Emir Jaber al Ahmad al Sabah had been toppled. Iraq's casualties were put at 500, Kuwait's at more than twice this figure.[7] While the 20,300-strong Kuwaiti military was no match for the 100,000 battle-hardened Iraqi troops, many observers felt that the Kuwaitis could have performed better. 'They could have fought much more in the streets,' remarked an Arab diplomat in Dubai. 'The air force fired a few shots, then fled with its planes to Saudi Arabia and Bahrain. If the army could have held out in Kuwait City for three or four days, there would have been enormous pressure on the Americans to help them.' Later, it emerged that on the eve of the Iraqi invasion the Kuwaiti defence minister, Shaikh Nawaf al Sabah, had reduced the state of alert, which had been at its highest in mid-July, withdrawn the Kuwaiti tanks from the border, and ordered the troops not to fire on Iraqis if they crossed over. He had taken these measures because he 'didn't want to provoke the Iraqis'.[8]

In purely military terms, the Iraqi action was considered well planned and efficiently implemented. Among those who expressed 'grudging admiration' for Saddam Hussein's military leadership were 'anonymous Israeli intelligence officers'. They were impressed with the performance of his forces in a night operation and the skill with which he deceived Western intelligence about the timing of his offensive.

As for the politics of the episode, Baghdad claimed that it had responded to an appeal from 'young revolutionaries [in Kuwait] who wanted its support in a coup to install a new free government'. By the mid-afternoon of 2 August the Provisional Free Government of Kuwait (PFGK) was claiming on state radio that it had deposed the emir. It ordered an indefinite curfew. Almost simultaneously Iraq's ruling Revolutionary Command Council stated: 'We announce to anyone who dares to challenge [us] that we will turn Iraq and the dear Kuwait into a graveyard to anyone who tries to commit aggression or [be] moved by the lust of invasion.' It called the al Sabah family 'traitors and agents of Zionist and foreign schemes'.[9]

President George Bush ordered an immediate US economic embargo against Iraq, which in turn suspended debt repayments to America. Washington, London and Paris froze Iraqi and Kuwaiti assets. Moscow halted its arms sales to Baghdad. While America and Britain called for collective international action, Iran demanded an immediate Iraqi evacuation of Kuwait.

The fifteen-member United Nations Security Council passed Resolution 660 condemning the Iraqi invasion and demanding that 'Iraq withdraw immediately and unconditionally all its forces' to their positions of 1 August. It called on Iraq and Kuwait to begin negotiations immediately to resolve their differences. Fourteen votes were cast in favour of the motion, with the ambassador of Yemen, the only Arab member, failing to exercise his vote owing to lack of instruction from his government.[10]

There were many in the Arab world and outside it who wondered why Saddam Hussein had not opted for capturing only the disputed border area and/or the two Kuwaiti offshore islands of Bubiyan and Warba. One theory was that he calculated that a limited move of this kind would create as much negative response in the Arab world as a total seizure of Kuwait, and so he might as well go in all the way.

Iraqi officials were aware of discontent in Kuwait prevalent not only among the non-national Arab majority but also among the nationals. They knew of the agitation for restoration of the National Assembly that had racked the emirate since the winter of 1989–90, and felt that disaffected Kuwaitis, who were openly critical of the al Sabahs, would welcome the forces of Saddam Hussein, whom they had applauded publicly during and after the Iran–Iraq War.

As for the non-Kuwaiti section of society, the Palestinian, Egyptian and Jordanian inhabitants had contributed enormously to building the infrastructure of the state and creating its immense wealth, but had been denied the political and economic benefits stemming from full citizenship. In a larger context they felt aggrieved that the Kuwaiti ruling family had concentrated far more on forging links with Western, especially American, interests than alleviating the misery that existed in poor Arab countries. 'We see five million Egyptians scattered around the Arab world and Europe like slaves of the old times, children dying in the Sudan ... a bankrupt Jordan, a bankrupt Syria, a bankrupt Lebanon, while these ruling Gulf families put their money into Europe and America,' said Tariq Masarma, a Jordanian commentator. 'They are building hotels, not states.'[11]

More specifically, conscious of the conflict that had existed between the Kuwaiti emir and the alliance of the former parliamentary deputies and the Constitutionalists, the Iraqi government tried to co-opt the latter. But the attempt failed. Therefore the nine-member Provisional Free Kuwait Government, headed by Colonel Ala Hussein Ali and announced on 4 August, consisted of four colonels and five majors. They were all members of the (nomadic) bedouin tribes who by and large had been deprived of the right to own land or vote, and who also formed the bulk of the Kuwaiti military ranks and officer corps.

The PFGK immediately ordered the formation of the Popular Army in Kuwait to replace the old army and take over from the Iraqis as they withdrew according to a schedule agreed a day earlier. 'Based on an understanding with the Provisional Free Government of Kuwait, a plan has been drawn up to begin the withdrawal of these [Iraqi] forces [which came to help the revolutionaries] in accordance with a timetable as of Sunday [5 August], unless something emerges that threatens the security of Kuwait and Iraq,' ran a statement by the ruling Revolutionary Command Council. 'There can be no return to the defunct regime after the sun of dignity and honour has risen in Kuwait, and the relationship between Kuwait and Iraq at present and in the future will be determined by the Iraqi people and the Kuwaiti people.'[12]

To consolidate its position at home the PFGK conferred citizenship rights on non-Kuwaiti Arabs. 'Brother Arabs, the Provisional Free Government of Kuwait greets you and calls on you to understand the uprising of your free brethren,' its communiqué said. 'You are our kith and kin, and what is ours is yours, and our task is yours.'[13]

As it happened the Iraqi aggression occurred on a day when the foreign ministers of the 45-member Islamic Conference Organization were in session in Cairo. The twenty-one Arab League ministers immediately convened a special session. Sadoun Hamadi arrived from Baghdad, and presented an uncompromising stand. On the night of 3 August the Arab League ministers passed a resolution by fourteen to one (Iraq), with five abstentions and one walk-out, which read in part: 'We condemn the bloodshed and the destruction of buildings [in Kuwait], and we call upon Iraq to immediately and unconditionally withdraw its troops.'[14] The countries voting in favour of the resolution were: Algeria, Bahrain, Djibouti, Egypt, Kuwait, Lebanon, Morocco, Oman, Qatar, Somalia, Saudi Arabia, Syria, Tunisia and United Arab Emirates. Those abstaining were: Jordan, Mauritania, the Palestine Liberation Organization, Sudan and Yemen. The Libyan representative walked out. While rejecting foreign intervention in the crisis, the resolution called on Iraq to end its bid to change the government in Kuwait by force and negotiate its dispute with its neighbour.

This move was warmly received by King Fahd as he presided over an emergency meeting of senior Saudi princes at the Salam Palace in Jiddah, the summer capital, where the emir of Kuwait had sought refuge.

In contrast, the Arab League resolution went down badly in Baghdad. The Iraqi president, it transpired, had been reassured by King Hussein that President Mubarak, conscious of his membership of the Arab Co-operation Council, would refrain from condemning the action of a fellow-member, Iraq, and use his influence to prevent the Arab League from putting Iraq in the dock. King Hussein also claimed to have talked (along with President Mubarak in Alexandria, the summer capital of Egypt) to President Bush on the evening of 2 August during the latter's return flight from Aspen, Colorado, to Washington, and got an agreement from him not to intervene with any Arab leaders for 24 hours as he and Mubarak worked to defuse the crisis. But earlier that day, while signing the executive orders on freezing Iraqi and Kuwaiti assets at 5 a.m., Bush had instructed his national security adviser, Brent Scowcroft (in the absence of the secretary of state, James Baker), to pressure Arab countries to condemn Iraq's invasion. This resulted, *inter alia*, in an urgent message from Washington arriving on the desk of the Egyptian foreign minister on 3 August, reminding him of the size of the military hardware the US had sold to Egypt and other

Arab countries, and warning him that if they failed to take a strong stand on the Iraqi invasion they would 'no longer be able to count on America'.15 The subsequent promise of the Bush administration to write off its $6.75 billion military loans to Cairo, and to continue to provide more than $2 billion a year in aid, showed that there was a trade-off between the US and Egypt – with Mubarak reversing the joint decision he had taken with King Hussein to refrain from an immediate condemnation of Iraq, which Saddam Hussein had insisted on.

Furthermore, once the Egyptian foreign ministry had issued a statement condemning Iraq on the afternoon of 3 August, it suited Mubarak to gain the stamp of Arab League approval for it. He also feared that if Saddam Hussein managed to consolidate his position in Kuwait, that would terminate his own role as the head of Arab diplomacy in resolving the Palestinian–Israeli problem. It all meant a setback to the peace efforts of King Hussein, who had embarked upon shuttle diplomacy and succeeded in organizing a mini-summit of the heads of Egypt, Iraq, Jordan, Saudi Arabia and Yemen in Jiddah on Sunday 5 August.

The Iraqi invasion seemed to have caught both President Bush and the British prime minister Margaret Thatcher off guard. The American spy satellite pictures showed that by Monday 30 July, Iraq had moved 100,000 troops up to the Kuwaiti border. But they lacked the elements essential for an offensive: communications, artillery, ammunition and logistical back-up for the invading armoured troops. It was not until Wednesday 1 August that all these components were found to be in place. Any American military response was bound to revolve around the Centcom (Central Command), which could mobilize up to 400,000 troops, and which exercised operational control over all US forces in South Asia, the Middle East and East Africa, encompassing 19 countries. Its mission was to defend US interests in the region: strategic oil reserves, shipping lanes and international waterways. Its commander was General Norman Schwarzkopf, a veteran of 38 years' service in the US armed forces. Centcom had evolved out of the Rapid Deployment Force, established by President James Carter (1977–80) in February 1979 to safeguard Gulf oil supplies and build up the American Fifth Fleet operating from the island of Diego Garcia, near Mauritius, in the Indian Ocean.16 Out of the RDF's contingency plans, which visualized fighting the Soviets or Iran in the Gulf, evolved a secret Operations Plan 90–1002. It required a massive air and sea lift of troops as well as deployment of heavy armour and anti-tank forces on the ground. At a private briefing on 1 August at the US defence department the

Centcom commander, Schwarzkopf, pointed out that Operations Plan 90–1002 had not visualized Iraq as the enemy or the loss of Kuwait.

Later on 1 August, by about 21.00 EST, all the important officials in Washington knew that Iraq had crossed into Kuwait. Soon the National Security Council's Situation Room in the White House and the Crisis Situation Room in the Pentagon became beehives of activity. (Secretary of state Baker was in Irkutsk, a Siberian city, for meetings with the Soviet foreign minister, Eduard Shevardnadze, and the US ambassador to Iraq, April Glaspie, was on holiday in London.) Before midnight the White House had condemned the aggression.

At the National Security Council meeting on the morning of 2 August, the seriousness of the Iraqi action was discussed, with Schwarzkopf outlining two military responses: Tier One, consisting of punitive air strikes against Iraqi targets, using US naval aircraft; and Tier Two, Operations Plan 90–1002, designed to defend Saudi Arabia. Treasury secretary Nicholas Brady pointed out that by taking over Kuwait Iraq had doubled its oil reserves to 20 per cent of the total world reserves. With this, argued President Bush, a former oilman, Iraq would be able to manipulate oil prices and hold the US and its allies 'at its mercy'. Higher prices would fuel inflation, worsening the 'already gloomy condition' of the American economy, he predicted. Richard Cheney, secretary of defence, stated that the 'marriage of Iraq's military of one million men with 20 per cent of the world's oil' presented 'a significant threat'. Between safeguarding Saudi Arabia and ejecting the Iraqis from Kuwait, he favoured the former. However, the meeting ended inconclusively.[17]

In the afternoon Bush left for Aspen, Colorado, to deliver a speech at the Aspen Institute on International Affairs and meet Margaret Thatcher, another major speaker there. Given the historical link between Britain and Kuwait, Thatcher was deeply concerned about Saddam Hussein's invasion. She reportedly warned Bush during their two-hour meeting at the mountain lodge of Henry Catto, the US ambassador to Britain, that if the Iraqi withdrawal was 'not swiftly forthcoming, we have to consider the next step'. Taking his cue, Bush said at a press conference later: 'We're not ruling any options in, but we're not ruling any options out.' By the time he returned to Washington, he was reportedly at one with 'Thatcher's rhetoric'.[18]

The NSC and the state department spent this day and the next focusing on the diplomatic and economic aspects of the crisis, with the armed forces leaders concentrating on working out military options, bearing in mind that the implementation of Tier Two, Operations

Plan 90–1002, rested on the availability of military bases inside Saudi Arabia.

So the attention of the top administration officials turned to convincing the Saudi ambassador to the US, Prince Bandar ibn Sultan, that the US was serious and would do 'what is necessary' to protect Saudi Arabia, and that the Saudis too would have to show they were serious and would 'accept' US troops. Scowcroft said as much to Prince Bandar, a son of Prince Sultan, the Saudi defence minister for 28 years, during their meeting on 3 August. Trained as an air force pilot, and married to Princess Haifa, a daughter of King Faisal ibn Abdul Aziz (1964–75), Bandar was appointed ambassador to the US in 1983, when he was 34. During that period he had established himself as a vocal, outgoing diplomat with high-level contacts in the American administration.

Later that day, to demonstrate that the US was 'serious', Cheney and General Colin Powell (chairman of the Joint Chiefs of Staff) showed Bandar 'top secret' satellite photographs to convince him that one of the three Iraqi armoured divisions was advancing through Kuwait to the Saudi frontier. Powell then outlined the 'top secret' Operations Plan 90–1002, involving 100,000 to 200,000 combat troops and three aircraft carriers. This reportedly impressed Bandar. He told his interlocutors that when King Fahd had talked to Saddam Hussein about the movement of Iraqi troops towards the Saudi border, the latter had told him that this was 'an exercise'. When the first Iraqi incursion had occurred on 3 August, the Saudis used the hotline between Riyadh and Baghdad, and the Iraqi chief of staff said that it was a mistake, and that he would 'cut off the arm of any Iraqi soldier who put his finger over the border'. However, there had been a second incursion six hours later, which had prompted another hotline call to Baghdad. The Iraqi officer at the other end had replied that he knew nothing about any incursion. Then, according to Prince Bandar, six hours later there was a third incursion. This time the Saudis had failed to reach any Iraqi with authority on the hotline. (Interestingly, Prince Bandar did not reveal the size of the Iraqi troops involved, and refused to do so later when asked.) After his meeting with Scowcroft and Powell, Prince Bandar telephoned King Fahd; and the monarch reportedly said that if he had seen the overhead satellite pictures with his 'own eyes' then he should tell 'them to come [to Saudi Arabia] and bring the overheads'.[19]

Bush spent the weekend of 4–5 August at the presidential retreat of Camp David in the mountains of Maryland designing a multifarious strategy: economic, diplomatic and military. On Saturday morning he had a meeting with Dan Quayle, vice-president, John Sununu, White House chief of staff, James Baker, Brent Scowcroft, Richard Hass, the Middle East expert at the NSC, Richard Cheney, General Colin Powell, General Norman Schwarzkopf, Paul Wolfowitz, policy undersecretary at the defence department, William Webster, director of the CIA, and Marlin Fitzwater, White House press secretary.

Schwarzkopf presented Operations Plan 90–1002 in two parts: (a) deterrence piece; and (b) war-fighting piece. With the US navy in place, what was needed immediately for deterrence was more air power combined with a credible size of ground forces in Saudi Arabia – something that could be achieved within a month. To have the full deterrence piece in the region, involving 200,000 to 250,000 troops, would need four months. As for expelling the Iraqis from Kuwait, it would take at least twice as long to assemble the war-fighting piece, which would be twice as large as the deterrence piece. When the discussion turned to using only air power, Powell and Cheney argued that air power by itself was not enough to do the job, and that land power was the key back-up to air power. 'If you want to deter,' said Powell, 'don't create a phoney deterrence.' In short, there was no alternative to having US military bases on Saudi soil. 'My worry about the Saudis is that they're going to be the ones who are going to bug out at the last minute and accept a puppet regime in Kuwait,' said President Bush. 'We should be asking them how committed they are.' This was a chicken-and-egg problem, said Scowcroft, with the Saudis unsure of how much they could count on the US. Powell worried that even if the Iraqis withdrew from Kuwait, it was going to be 'a different emir and a different situation', and that the status quo in Kuwait and elsewhere in the region would have been changed irrevocably. 'That's why our defence of Saudi Arabia has to be our focus,' Bush concluded. At this point the deputies to the principals departed, leaving the conference room to eight senior officials: Bush, Quayle, Sununu, Baker, Scowcroft, Cheney, Powell and Webster. They reportedly discussed intelligence reports which showed that, following the pattern of the past, King Fahd and his senior advisers were seriously considering defusing the crisis by offering financial aid to Saddam Hussein. The meeting apparently decided to work to reverse this process. The matter became urgent as, later in the day, President Bush received a telephone call from President Mubarak telling him that he had received 'an authoritative report' that King Fahd had decided *not* to invite the American troops.[20]

Leaving aside intelligence reports provided by the CIA or its Egyptian counterpart, the fact that the government-controlled or -guided media in Saudi Arabia had yet to inform their audiences or readers of the Iraqi invasion of Kuwait indicated that King Fahd, the sole wielder of state power, had yet to finalize his response to the crisis.

President Bush telephoned King Fahd to tell him that the Iraqi troops were massing along the Saudi border and that he needed to act. Fahd replied, politely, that while they required some American assistance for their air force they did not need the US army. That afternoon Prince Bandar left Washington for Jiddah to join the intense discussion among senior Saudi princes there. On his arrival he was told that, following President Bush's warning, the Saudi defence ministry had sent scouts into Kuwait, who had reported that there was 'no trace of the Iraqi troops heading towards the [Saudi] kingdom'. Bandar replied that he had seen the US satellite pictures showing something to the contrary.[21] Now, the credibility of President Bush depended on these 'top secret' photographs. These were also to be the main tool of Cheney, assigned by Bush to go to Saudi Arabia, to persuade King Fahd to invite the American forces into his kingdom.

The accidental straying of an Iraqi patrol into the poorly demarcated Kuwaiti–Saudi Neutral Zone came in handy to Bush at the White House as well as to the hawks in the Salam Palace in Jiddah as ominous evidence of Baghdad's plan to invade Saudi Arabia. The Saudi kingdom put its troops on red alert. While Saudi Arabia had spent $46.7 billion during 1982–9 on importing arms, mainly from America, Britain and France – nearly half the amount spent by Iraq during its eight-year war with Iran – its 67,800-strong military was no match for Iraq's huge and battle-hardened army.[22] Bush warned that America would 'react strongly' to any attack on the Saudi kingdom. Baghdad denied any such plans.

In a sense Bush was trying to overcompensate for his failure to draw the right conclusions from the 'useful and timely information' provided by the CIA and the Defence Intelligence Agency. Between the two agencies, the CIA had offered a softer interpretation. At first it guessed that Saddam Hussein was sabre-rattling to influence the 25 July OPEC meeting towards raising the oil price. Later, over the weekend of 28–29 July, the movement of Iraqi troops was attributed to a possible or probable plan to take over the disputed border strip and occupy Kuwait's two offshore islands. Accepting these interpretations and Saddam Hussein's assurances to April Glaspie on 25 July, as well as to President Mubarak and King Hussein, the White House and the state department had concluded that the Iraqi troop build-up was aimed at intimidating rather than invading. (Incidentally, this was also the assessment of Soviet military intelligence. A Novosti report, published in the *Rabochaya Tribuna* (Workers' Tribune) of 14 October 1990, said that Soviet military intelligence thought that Iraq had massed troops along the Kuwaiti border in order to occupy the 'disputed northern part of Kuwait'.)[23]

Now, at Camp David, Bush mounted a diplomatic blitzkrieg on the telephone, contacting a dozen foreign leaders, mainly Western but also some Arab, including the exiled emir of Kuwait. He asked them to back an economic embargo against Iraq at the United Nations Security Council and to despatch troops to Saudi Arabia to form a multinational force in order to deprive Baghdad of the argument that the Saudi leaders were acting as agents of American imperialism.

On his return to the White House on the evening of Sunday 5 August, Bush called the Baghdad regime 'international outlaws and renegades', and demanded a total Iraqi pull-out from Kuwait. Expressing disappointment at the reactions to Baghdad's aggression in the Arab world, he urged Arab states to condemn it and help expel the Iraqis from Kuwait. 'I view very seriously our determination to reverse out this aggression,' Bush said. 'This will not stand, this aggression against Kuwait.'[24]

Economic reprisals were already in train. Without waiting for the UN resolution on sanctions, the West and Japan had acted swiftly against Iraq and its newly acquired territory of Kuwait. On 3 August, Japan and major West European countries began freezing Kuwaiti assets. Japan also suspended oil imports from Iraq and Kuwait. Petroleum prices reached $24 a barrel, an increase of 50% over the past month's figure; and the stock markets in New York, Tokyo and London plunged. The next day, 4 August, European Community foreign ministers meeting in Rome agreed to ban all Iraqi and Kuwaiti oil imports, to freeze Iraqi and Kuwaiti assets, and to suspend all arms sales as well as scientific and technical co-operation. Elsewhere, China joined the Soviet Union in halting all arms exports to Iraq.

The rush to freeze Kuwaiti assets abroad had to do with their size. Most conservatively, these amounted to over $100 billion, and stemmed mainly from the Reserve Fund for Future Generations. Established in 1976, it was built up by injecting 10% of oil revenues into it each year, bringing the cumulative total to $85 billion by 1989. Seven-eighths of this sum was invested abroad, and managed mostly by the Kuwait Investment Authority, a department of the finance ministry. The KIA controls the London-based Kuwait Investment Organization which administers the portfolio which had grown to over $100 billion by mid-1990. The overseas investments are in equities, government securities and property in all major economies worldwide – with about 40% invested in North America, 20% in Japan and the Far East, 20% in Britain, and the remainder in Germany, France and Spain. Then there were valuable Kuwaiti assets in oil and gas in the form of refineries and petrol stations whereby Kuwait Petroleum International, controlled by the state-owned Kuwait Petroleum Company, sells 250,000 b/d of refined oil products in Europe. Finally, about $6 billion of the State General Reserve, amounting to $30 billion, was invested abroad.[25]

'Nominally, there is provision for legal separation of royal family and state wealth, but in reality the signatories controlling the dispersal of [state] funds are all members of the royal family or their associates,' noted David Watts of *The Times*. 'The control of the royal family over the country's assets is virtually total.'[26] Given that the personal wealth of the al Sabah family amounted to $60 billion, the Kuwaiti ruling family controlled, directly or indirectly, $160 billion.

Had the Provisional Free Government of Kuwait been recognized by the West and Japan, Baghdad would have inherited more than $100 billion-worth of assets of the previous regime. Additionally, Iraq would have gained by acquiring the Kuwaiti state assets within the country, including its oil production capacity of over 2 mb/d, and having its debts of $10 to $14 billion to Kuwait cancelled. Finally, it would have nearly doubled its oil reserves by adding Kuwait's 94.5 billion barrels to its own 100 billion barrels, thus bringing its total to nearly 20% of global reserves, almost rivalling Saudi Arabia, which possesses 25.5% of world oil reserves.[27] This, and the unrivalled military power of Iraq in the region, would have made Saddam Hussein the most powerful figure in the Gulf, able to dictate the extraction rate of petroleum and thus its price: a position thus far enjoyed by Saudi Arabia, which aligned its oil policy with that of America.

Little wonder that, according to the *Washington Post* of 6 August, the CIA director William Webster had been instructed by President Bush to plan covert operations that would destabilize the Iraqi regime and overthrow Saddam Hussein: he posed a threat to vital US interests that extended well beyond the immediate Kuwaiti crisis. The means to be employed were: (a) strangling Iraq's economy, (b) fomenting discontent and subversion within the Iraqi military, and (c) supporting internal and external resistance to Saddam Hussein.[28]

On Sunday 5 August, according to the government-controlled radio stations in Baghdad and Kuwait, the Iraqi troop withdrawal from Kuwait had begun at 8 a.m. local time as planned, and the recently formed Kuwaiti Popular Army units were taking control as the Iraqis left.[29] The 3 August agreement between the two governments specified full Iraqi pull-out unless 'something emerges that threatens the security of Kuwait and Iraq'. That is where the Iraqi threat to Saudi Arabia, real or contrived, and the American response to it, became crucial elements.

While both Washington and Riyadh kept saying that Iraq was preparing to move into Saudi Arabia, King Hussein of Jordan claimed that Saddam Hussein had told him he would not invade the Saudi kingdom. The Iraqi ambassador to the US denied categorically that his country had any plans to invade Saudi Arabia, a neighbour with which it had 'excellent fraternal relations'. The matter would have been cleared up at the mini-summit of Arab leaders, including Saddam Hussein and King Fahd, in Jiddah on 5 August, had that meeting not been cancelled by King Fahd, the host. After the war he explained his decision publicly. 'I know since 1975 that Saddam is only interested in media publicity, so my position was that if he wants to talk to me, it is only for this purpose,' King Fahd said. 'I said if he wants to talk to me let him put it down in writing that he will leave Kuwait without conditions, then I will talk to him.'[30]

On 6 August Saddam Hussein called Joseph Wilson, the US chargé d'affaires in Baghdad, to the presidential palace to take an urgent message to President Bush. In it he made three points. 'Kuwait was a state without borders, and whatever happened with the entry of the Iraqi forces cannot be measured in the framework of the relationship between states in the Arab world,' Saddam Hussein said. His second point concerned Saudi Arabia with which, he claimed, Iraq had developed 'an excellent relationship' since 1975, and referred to Iraq's non-aggression pact with the Saudi kingdom of March 1989. 'We don't understand the meaning of your [Bush's] declarations that you are afraid of Iraq's intentions with respect to Saudi Arabia and that after Kuwait will come Saudi Arabia,' Saddam Hussein continued. 'Your worries are unfounded, but if you are showing that worry in order to make Saudi Arabia worry, that is something else . . . We are ready to give them [our Saudi brothers] any guarantees they want, to remove that worry.' The final point concerned Saddam Hussein's promise to 'certain Arab officials' that he would not use force against Kuwait 'under any circumstances', and the conveying of this pledge to the

Americans. 'I did not give that promise to any Arab,' Saddam Hussein stated. 'What happened is that some Arab leaders were talking to me about the massing of [Iraqi] troops on the Kuwaiti border, and they were telling me that the Kuwaitis were afraid and worried. I told them that I promised that I would not take any military action before the meeting in Jiddah that we had agreed upon. This is what happened. There was no military action before the [Jiddah] meeting. We were waiting for the return of the vice-president [of the RCC, Izzat Ibrahim] from Jiddah to take a decision.' He then explained the speed with which 'the operation' was undertaken. 'The possibility arose before the Jiddah meeting, and in accordance with the patriotic movement in Kuwait,' he said. 'But it was not the first priority on the list. We were putting more effort into asserting our rights through negotiations.'

The Iraqi president then addressed the general issue of Baghdad–Washington relations. 'Why do you want to be our enemies?' he asked President Bush in his message. 'In our view, you could look after your interests better through a strong nationalistic and realistic regime in the area [like Iraq's] than through the Saudis. You are talking about an aggressive Iraq, but if Iraq was aggressive during the Iran war, why did you maintain relations with it? You are talking about the 2 April communiqué [against Israel]: we never issued such a communiqué before, during or after the war with Iran. Why did I issue that communiqué? It was because some Western and American circles were urging Israel to attack us; and the communiqué's aim was to put an end to all aggression. We believe that it promoted peace. If we had remained silent, Israel would have attacked us, and we would have counter-attacked.'

When the meeting turned into a dialogue between Joseph Wilson and Saddam Hussein, the American envoy mentioned his agenda: the nature of the Iraqi invasion of Kuwait, and Iraq's intentions regarding Saudi Arabia. 'The withdrawal of our forces [from Kuwait] has to be based on an international agreement,' Saddam Hussein said. 'It is not in anyone's interest that the Iraqi army withdraw in a hurry, leaving Kuwait to the warring parties. The Provisional Government took our advice to form separate militias, and we advised them to be self-sufficient and to use the Popular Army.'

Wilson asked for an assurance that Iraq did not intend to undertake 'any military action' against the Saudi kingdom. 'You can offer that assurance to the Saudis and to the world,' the Iraqi president said. 'We will not attack those who do not attack us. We will not harm those who do not harm us ... If things remain as they are, they would remain our brothers, except if you played a disruptive role, and made them move against us, then everyone would have to fight for his legitimate right ... We will only get disturbed if they [the Saudis] provide an opportunity for an action against Iraq.' He then asked Wilson if America wanted to 'push Saudi Arabia to take an action against Iraq [such as closing Iraqi oil pipelines to the Red Sea] which would trigger an Iraqi reaction' leading to US action against Iraq. Wilson replied that Washington had no intention of 'pushing' Saudi Arabia in any direction.[31]

As it was, that day, 6 August, Saudi Arabia was 'pushed' to seek American military intervention. At 11 p.m. local time (4 p.m. EST), Cheney telephoned Bush (then in a meeting with prime minister Thatcher) from Jiddah to say that he had secured the Saudi invitation for US forces, but on three conditions: the US should give it in writing that it would leave Saudi Arabia when the Iraqi threat was over, and that it would obtain Saudi approval before initiating any offensive military action against Iraq, and thirdly, Washington should keep Riyadh's invitation secret until the first American troops had landed on Saudi soil.[32] Apparently, Cheney succeeded in scaring King Fahd with satellite pictorial evidence that Iraqi warplanes were being loaded with chemical bombs and that Iraq had positioned surface-to-surface missiles in Kuwait aimed at Saudi targets. But that was not enough for the Saudi monarch to overlook the prospect of the American troops on Saudi territory acting as an independent force to achieve their anti-Iraqi objectives without giving much thought to the impact of their actions on Saudi interests and sovereignty. That is why he insisted on a written guarantee from President Bush to leave his kingdom once the job on hand was accomplished.

With the Saudi invitation secured, Bush, as commander-in-chief of the US, immediately ordered General Powell to (a) deter further Iraqi aggression, (b) defend Saudi Arabia, and (c) improve the overall defence capabilities of the Saudi peninsula. This was the start of Operation 'Desert Shield'. Significantly, there was no mention here of expelling the Iraqis from Kuwait. Since a minimum force of 300,000 US armed personnel was needed to engage Iraq, and since transporting them was expected to take about four months, Bush concluded that it was no use fighting for Kuwait now, but a line had to be drawn on Saudi Arabia.

In New York the UN Security Council voted by 13 votes to nil for Resolution 661 which, invoking Chapter VII of the UN Charter, specified mandatory economic sanctions against Iraq and occupied Kuwait including a worldwide ban on their oil exports. On the suggestion of Ethiopia, the resolution allowed food into Iraq and Kuwait 'in humanitarian circumstances'. It was only the third time (the earlier examples being Rhodesia and South Africa) that the UN had taken such a step. By affirming 'the inherent right of individual or collective self-defence, in response to the armed attack by Iraq against Kuwait, in accordance with Article 51 of the Charter [of the United Nations]', Resolution 661 set the scene for 'defensive military action' in the future. Also, Security Council resolutions under Chapter VII have the force of international law, although the Council has no means of enforcing them.

Following the UN sanctions resolution, Turkey banned tankers loading Iraqi petroleum at its Yumurtalik offshore terminals. Its officials expected that the oil storage facilities would be full within five or six days – necessitating closure of the second of Iraq's 800-mile oil pipelines with a total capacity of carrying 1.6 mb/d,[33] the first one having been shut off earlier due to falling demand. So the only overland outlet for Iraqi petroleum left was the one running through Saudi Arabia to the Red Sea.

Having taken the unpalatable decision to invite the US military into their kingdom, Saudi leaders worked hard to soften its negative impact on their subjects as well as on other Arabs and Muslims. One way was to present the arrival of American troops as part of a multinational effort to aid Saudi Arabia militarily. Thus the role of the governments in Egypt and Morocco, friendly to Washington as well as Riyadh, became crucial. The US defence secretary understood this, and promised to help. During his subsequent stopovers in Alexandria and Rabat, he pressured his hosts to announce immediately the dispatch of their forces to Saudi Arabia.

As it was, responding to a private call from King Fahd, President Mubarak had begun sending Egyptian troops to Saudi Arabia on 4 August. By 6 August about 2,000 Egyptian soldiers were deployed at Hafar al Batin, near the Kuwaiti border, which was also the headquarters of the one-brigade-strong Rapid Deployment Force of the GCC. But Mubarak suppressed the news so as to give time for the 100,000 Egyptians in Kuwait to leave without harassment by the occupying Iraqi forces, and to show the world that he airlifted the troops only *after* the Arab League had accepted the Saudi request for military assistance. This was also the case with King Hassan of Morocco. Both Arab leaders were embarrassed by the hasty statement on 7 August by the American delegation led by Cheney that Egypt and Morocco had agreed to send troops to Saudi Arabia and participate in a multinational force being assembled by the US. Due to the inconvenient leak by Cheney's spokesman, the Moroccan government let its 1,200 troops linger in Cairo while Mubarak hotly denied the American statement.[34] He did so partly because he had just denied having made such a commitment during his meeting with Izzat Ibrahim, vice-president of the ruling Revolutionary Command Council of Iraq: a fellow-member with Egypt of the Arab Co-operation Council, and with which it had developed intimate military links during and after the Iran–Iraq War. On the other hand Mubarak was only too aware of the dependence of the heavily debt-ridden Egypt on America, a fact which limited his area of manoeuvre.

While the Arab countries were not expected to respond formally to Washington's invitation to join a multinational force under its leadership until after the Arab summit on 10 August, Britain agreed to do so immediately.

Fearing air strikes by America or Israel, Saddam Hussein ordered air raid drills for his citizens, the revival of plans to evacuate the four million residents of Baghdad, and the formation of eleven new army divisions. On 7 August, while the Provisional Free Government of Kuwait declared Kuwait a republic, Saddam Hussein addressed the nation on television on the eve of Victory Day, to celebrate the victory that Iraq claimed to have achieved over Iran in the First Gulf War which, according to Baghdad, lasted from 4 September 1980 to 7 August 1988. 'It is our duty to say that the Day of the Call [by the Kuwaiti people], the 2nd of this month . . . is the legitimate new-born child of 8th of August 1988.'[35]

However, issuing such uncompromising statements did not inhibit Saddam Hussein from attempting to make a deal with President Bush: a pattern he repeated a few times during the 24-week crisis.

Around this time, according to Kuwaiti sources, the Iraqi president addressed a letter to his American counterpart. In it he offered to withdraw from Kuwait *and* co-operate on oil pricing provided America recognized the services Iraq had rendered to its interests and the Arab Gulf states' security and welfare by defeating Iran in the 1980–88 war at an immense cost to its economy and manpower. As a *quid pro quo* for these services, (a) Iraq should be allowed to retain Bubiyan and Warba islands, and an area of northern Kuwait bordering Iraq; (b) the US should promise to see that Iraq's wartime debts to both Western and Arab nations were written off; and (c) suitable funds should be provided to rehabilitate Iraq's war-shattered economy. Bush promptly rejected the offer.[36]

Senior American officials had no qualms about making deals with such loyal Arab allies as the Egyptian president. On 7 August, in the course of his meeting with Mubarak, Cheney did exactly that. Mubarak gave permission for American military aircraft to enter Egyptian airspace. He also agreed to lobby the Arab summit (scheduled for 10 August in Cairo) to pass a resolution against Iraq, and to send his troops, publicly, to Saudi Arabia as 'part of a totally Arab force' to be (formally) devised at the summit. In return Cheney promised to see Cairo's military debts of $6.75 billion to the US written off.

While Cheney's plane flew west, 48 advanced F-15s of the US air force and a brigade of 2,300 men from the 82nd Airborne Division were in mid-air, flying east and planning to arrive in the Eastern Province of Saudi Arabia on the morning of 8 August. Cheney arrived in Washington about the same time as the American warplanes and troops landed in Dhahran.

Thus bolstered, King Fahd decreed the closure of the Iraqi oil pipeline to Yanbu, pushing the total reduction of Iraq's exports to 90%. The official reason given was that due to a steep fall in demand the storage tanks at Yanbu had become full, necessitating the shut-off. With this the rubicon was crossed.

Future historians debating the chance that Arab diplomacy had to secure a peaceful solution to the crisis between 2 and 7 August will encounter conflicting accounts of the events.

They will find at least three versions dealing with the Saudi call to the US for military assistance. (1) A Washington Version: the US defence secretary arrived in Jiddah on 6 August with sufficient intelligence data to convince King Fahd that Iraq was about to invade his country. Consequently, Fahd reluctantly asked for US troops which were despatched from America the next day, 7 August. (2) A Non-Saudi Arab Version: the evidence provided by the Pentagon was not enough for King Fahd, who wanted a strong Arab dimension to his call for armed assistance by foreign powers. Only after President Mubarak had agreed to send a sizable number of Egyptian troops to his kingdom as part of an Arab multinational force did the Saudi monarch agree to allow US forces into his kingdom.[37] (3) A Saudi Insider Version: according to the sources close to Prince Sultan ibn Abdul Aziz, the idea of letting US troops into the kingdom was accepted by King Fahd within 24 hours of Iraq's invasion of Kuwait. Initially he was reluctant. But he gave in to the pleas of his brother and defence minister, Prince Sultan, who, 'in a state of agitation', warned that without Washington's aid they would be unable to withstand an Iraqi invasion. Acting on the instructions of King Fahd, the Saudi ambassador to Washington, Prince Bandar ibn Sultan, met the US national security adviser, Brent Scowcroft, on 3 August, and made a formal request for the American military presence on Saudi soil. The subsequent visit of the US defence secretary on 6 August was merely to discuss arrangements for the deployment of US forces.[38] All those statements about Fahd's refusal to call in the American troops until and unless he had first secured a pledge from sister Arab states to despatch their forces to Saudi Arabia were, according to this version, so much window-dressing.

The Washington Version has been described at length by Bob Woodward of the *Washington Post* in his book *The Commanders*. There are two major deficiencies in it. Woodward did not interview President Bush. And he used only one source to describe the Saudi side of the story: Prince Bandar, a 41-year-old diplomat-operator 'whose fingerprints', in his own words, 'were all over the Iran-Contra affair', and whom Cheney considered 'a little bit off the wall and not necessarily a 100 per cent clear channel to King Fahd'.[39] Since the only Saudi version has been offered by sources close to Princes Sultan and Bandar, it is one-sided. It ignores altogether the contrary and powerful pressures applied to King Fahd by Crown Prince Abdullah ibn Abdul Aziz and Prince Salman ibn Abdul Aziz, the influential governor of Riyadh. Given the poor state of King Fahd's health and his legendary reluctance to take decisions, it is hard to believe that he accepted the principle of calling in US troops within 24 hours of the Iraqi invasion. As for the remaining version, apparently originating in Cairo, it is more a complement to the central story rather than the main story itself. In any case, the two non-American versions need to be fleshed out – with the assistance of reliable Arab sources – before a sound judgement can be passed.

However, the fundamental flaw with all three versions lies in the basic premise on which they are built: a serious threat to Saudi Arabia from Iraq. Even if Saddam Hussein was prepared to discard the March 1989 non-aggression pact he had signed with King Fahd, he could not afford to overlook the Carter Doctrine of 1979, publicly adopted by the next US president Ronald Reagan, which included a tenet summarized by him in October 1982 thus: 'An attack on Saudi Arabia would be considered an attack on the United States.' If the Iraqi leader had wanted to capture the Saudi kingdom he would have done so immediately after seizing Kuwait. 'A Saudi military expert said that Saddam Hussein missed his chance to invade Saudi Arabia immediately after his army took over Kuwait, when it could have pushed on along the coastal road to the Eastern Province [of Saudi Arabia],' reported Youssef Ibrahim in the *New York Times*.[40] Secondly, if the Iraqi president had been serious about attacking the Saudi kingdom he would have secured Iraq's eastern front by making peace with Iran, something he was to do thirteen days *after* invading Kuwait.

Hard evidence of Saddam Hussein's aggressive intentions towards Saudi Arabia was reportedly provided by the pictures taken by US spy satellites. In the past such photographs have been doctored to serve a political purpose. The best-known example was provided by the evidence collected by the US President's Special Review Board, chaired by John Tower, a former US senator, published in February 1987. 'We all recognized that the [satellite] information need not be accurate and that it was highly perishable given the dynamic nature of the conflict [between Iran and Iraq],' wrote Lieutenant-Colonel Oliver North, deputy director for political-military affairs at the National Security Council, to Vice-Admiral John Poindexter, the National Security Adviser, on 10 February 1986 in his memorandum *Next Steps for Iran*. 'In short, we believe that a mix of factual and bogus information can be provided at this meeting [with the Iranians] which will satisfy them about "good faith".'[41] At this meeting in Tehran, doctored satellite pictures exaggerated the size of the Soviet force along the Iranian border to 36 divisions! Equally, the satellite intelligence information pictures supplied to Iraq during the First Gulf War were often altered to make them misleading or incomplete. It would seem that this practice continued in the run-up to the Second Gulf War. Satellite pictures taken on 11 and 13 September by Soyuz-Karta, a Soviet commercial satellite agency, and bought by the *St Petersburg Times* of St Petersburg, Florida, showed that the Iraqi force in Kuwait was about one-fifth of the 250,000 troops and 1,500 tanks claimed by the US administration.[42]

Leaving aside the doctoring of satellite pictures, it is difficult for a layperson to read and interpret them. 'The place where it starts to get tricky is that you've got these pictures of tanks at the border,' said John Pike, director of space technology at the Federation of American Scientists in September 1990. 'But do they show that these tanks are about to invade or [merely] digging in?' As most people are unaccustomed to 'reading' these pictures, naïve policy-makers accept the interpreter's word for it. Before the Iraqi invasion, when the satellite pictures showed Iraqi troops gathered at the Iraq–Kuwait border, the 'governing wisdom' was that Saddam Hussein could invade, but 'we don't think he will'. After the invasion, when Iraqi troops were at the Saudi–Kuwaiti border, the 'governing wisdom' was that Saddam Hussein could invade, and 'we think he will'. 'Satellite pictures can tell you a lot about capabilities but not about intentions,' concluded Pike.[43] The scouts of the Saudi military discovered no sign of the Iraqis heading towards the Saudi border. Between an eye-witness account and a satellite picture, which one is more reliable?

Future chroniclers will be intrigued, too, by the overall description of the events from 2 to 10 August by King Hussein, one of the few insiders with unhindered access to Saddam Hussein before and during the crisis, and a friend of the West since his accession to the Jordanian throne in 1952.

King Hussein's version, articulated by his palace spokesman to Martin Woollacott and published in the *Guardian* on 20 August, ran as follows. Before the Kuwait–Iraq meeting in Jiddah on 31 July, Mubarak announced that he had Saddam Hussein's word that 'there would be no use of force against Kuwait'. This negated the purpose of Iraq's massing of troops along the Kuwaiti border, depriving Saddam Hussein of leverage and encouraging Kuwaiti leaders to dig in their heels. The outcome was the collapse of the talks and the Iraqi invasion. After that King Hussein (together with President Mubarak) secured a promise from President Bush that he would not intervene with any Arab leader for the next 24 hours while they, King Hussein and Mubarak, tried to get Saddam Hussein out of Kuwait. According to King Hussein, the Iraqi president agreed to withdraw from Kuwait if the Arab League would desist from condemning Iraq. But Mubarak reneged on his promise when the Egyptian foreign ministry (responding to pressure from the US state department) condemned Iraq on the afternoon of 3 August. Following this, the Arab League foreign ministers did the same by a majority vote later that day. This destroyed the opportunity of a successful resolution of the crisis at the Arab mini-summit in Saudi Arabia scheduled for 5 August. 'At that time, the [Jordanian] sources say, Iraq was still genuinely ready to withdraw,' wrote Martin Woollacott. 'But its reaction to the Arab League condemnation was to name the Provisional Government [in Kuwait] whose personnel had earlier been deliberately left unclear.' The third missed chance was just before King Fahd accepted American troops on Saudi soil on 7 August. 'Again, according to the [Jordanian] sources, the Iraqis were still ready for a phased withdrawal, although now the Provisional Government [of Kuwait] would have had to be represented at the talks.'[44] Saddam Hussein's reaction to the Saudi decision to invite US forces was to merge Iraq and Kuwait. The graduated nature of Iraqi responses demonstrated that it wanted to bargain but was denied the opportunity, the Jordanian sources concluded.

The bitter despair expressed by King Hussein over the way the Gulf crisis had developed reflected the mood of his nation. Thus he came to act more like a constitutional monarch rather than the royal autocrat he had often seemed until November 1988 when he ordered free and fair elections in Jordan. Of the 80 elected deputies 32 were Islamic fundamentalists. Given this, and the fact that three-fifths of the country's 4 million nationals were of Palestinian origin, who regarded Saddam Hussein as a modern-day Saladin (Salah al Din Ayubi) destined to liberate Jerusalem from the infidel, King Hussein had little choice but to tilt in the direction of the Iraqi leader. The pressure of the Gulf crisis seemed to have dissolved all traditional antagonisms. 'It's king and country, Muslim and Christian, secular and religious, Palestinian and Jordanian, all together,' said a Jordanian intellectual.[45]

Since Saddam Hussein presented himself as the most convincing champion of the Palestinian cause, he won overwhelming support among the Palestinians. Their bitter disappointments since the 1948–9 Arab–Israeli War had made them so acutely aware of the failings of the Arab political order that they could not help rejoicing at the thundering blow he had struck at it. They had nothing but contempt for the West which had acquiesced in what they saw as repeated Israeli aggressions, major and minor.

As for Israel, its reaction to the Iraqi invasion was mixed. It felt confident that an inter-Arab crisis of such a magnitude would diminish pressure on it to resolve the Palestinian issue. At the same time it felt threatened by Iraq's strength, ruthlessness and military expertise. It reckoned that, deterred from attacking Saudi Arabia, Saddam Hussein would turn to striking Israel in order to unite the Arab world behind him. Lacking a common border with Israel, the Iraqi leader was likely to use Jordan as the staging area for his forces. Israel therefore warned Amman that it would regard the entry of Iraqi troops into Jordan as a threatening move, and would respond 'appropriately'.

A communiqué issued by Iraq's Armed Forces General Command on 8 August claimed that Israel 'has painted its planes with US markings and some of its pilots, who will carry out the aggressive missions, have been provided with American identity cards and names in order to escape Iraq's direct military retaliation against Israel'. It warned of appropriate Iraqi response to this 'hostile action' by Israel.[46] Following this, the Israeli press reported on 10 August that Washington 'had explicitly promised Israel it will strike with maximum force at Iraq should the Iraqi president move against the Jewish state'.[47]

On 8 August the Provisional Free Government of Kuwait decided to appeal to 'the kinfolk in Iraq' to agree that 'Kuwait should return to great Iraq, the motherland', and for 'the hero Saddam Hussein to be our leader and protector of our march'. Iraq's Revolutionary Command Council accepted the Kuwaiti appeal. 'What has befallen other states in the Arab lands befell Iraq when colonialism divested it of a dear part of it, namely Kuwait, and kept Iraq away from the waters to prevent it from acquiring part of its tactical and strategic capabilities, and thus kept part of its people and part of its wealth away from the origin and the well-spring,' its communiqué said. 'Based on all this . . . the RCC has decided to return the part and branch, Kuwait, to the whole and root, Iraq, in a comprehensive, eternal and inseparable merger unity.'[48] Kuwait's Colonel Ala Hussein Ali was appointed an Iraqi deputy prime minister, and the rest of his cabinet colleagues were named as advisers at the presidential office.

That morning, President Bush addressed the American nation on television from the Oval Office. 'As today's president, I ask for your support in a decision I've made to stand up for what's right and condemn what's wrong, all in the cause of peace,' he said. 'At my direction, elements of the 82nd Airborne Division as well as key units of the United States Air Force are arriving today to take up defensive positions in Saudi Arabia.' He referred to the Iraqi invasion of Kuwait which, he said, came 'just hours' after Saddam Hussein had 'specifically assured numerous countries in the area that there would be no invasion'. Bush listed four goals: Iraq's immediate, unconditional and complete withdrawal from Kuwait; the restoration of Kuwait's legitimate government; achieving the security and stability of the Persian Gulf; and the safeguarding of American lives. 'Our country now imports nearly half the oil it consumes and could face a major threat to its economic independence,' he said. 'Iraq has amassed an enormous war machine on the Saudi border, capable of initiating hostilities with little or no additional preparations . . . The sovereign independence of Saudi Arabia is of vital interest to the United States.' Alluding to 'the long standing friendship and security relationship between the United States and Saudi Arabia', President Bush stated that 'US forces will work together with those of Saudi Arabia and other nations to preserve the integrity of Saudi Arabia' and to deter further aggression by Iraq. 'The mission of our troops is wholly defensive,' he concluded. 'Hopefully, they will not be needed long. They will not initiate hostilities, but they will defend themselves, the Kingdom of Saudi Arabia, and other friends in the Persian Gulf.'[49]

With the arrival at Dhahran airport of the first units of an expected 40,000 US troops, Saudi Arabia moved more of its forces to the Kuwaiti–Saudi frontier. In Cairo, President Mubarak called an emergency Arab summit on 10 August.

By now more than 50 warships from several nations, including three US aircraft carriers, were either in the Gulf or approaching it, tightening the blockade of Iraq. Among the foreign vessels steaming to the Gulf were two Soviet warships.

Moscow had supported the two Security Council resolutions on Iraq, and stated that it would apply economic and military sanctions against Baghdad. 'Despite the Soviet Union's friendship and co-operation with Iraq, the USSR must base its assessment of events on principles and then determine further Soviet actions,' said Alexander Byelonogov, deputy foreign minister. 'The expectations of those who counted on the aggravation of Soviet–American relations – on a new East–West confrontation – have been dashed, and [instead] the Iraqi invasion has cemented Soviet–American co-operation, with the two capitals maintaining close and permanent contacts.'[50] This was bad news for Saddam Hussein who, according to the *Sovyetskaya Rossiya* (Soviet Russia) of 8 August, was enraged by the suspension of Soviet weapons deliveries, and the lack of support or understanding from the Kremlin. This was apparent in his 4 August reply to the letter from President Mikhail Gorbachev (1985–), necessitating an immediate missive in return from the Soviet leader.

Having condemned Iraq for its aggression, and taken a common position at the United Nations, Moscow lost no time in speaking out against using force against Baghdad. Valentin Lozinskiy, the Soviet ambassador to the United Nations, cautioned America and Britain against taking unilateral military action against Iraq without seeking the approval of the Security Council.[51]

On 9 August the Soviet Union voted for Security Council Resolution 662, which declared that 'annexation of Kuwait by Iraq under any form or whatever pretext has no legal validity, and is considered null and void'. The vote was unanimous, with Cuba and Yemen too backing it.

Among the three Western permanent members of the Security Council, France followed the example of America and Britain in despatching its warplanes and battleships to the Gulf to act as a 'vigilant' attack force if other Arab states were threatened, or French citizens were detained in Iraq.

Fearing American aerial and/or sea attack, Iraq began deploying a growing number of anti-aircraft guns, artillery and rocket-launchers in Kuwait City and along the coast. It ordered the closure of all foreign embassies in Kuwait City within two weeks since the state of Kuwait had ceased to exist. It also closed the international borders of Kuwait, thus trapping thousands of Westerners, including nearly 5,000 Britons.

With hundreds of US troops arriving in Saudi Arabia by the hour, the monarch could no longer keep his subjects in the dark regarding the momentous events of the past week, something the state-controlled or -guided media had so far done. He addressed the nation on 9 August. 'Painful and regrettable events have been taking place since the dawn of last Thursday, 11th Muharram 1141 AH [2 August 1990 AD] in a way that took the whole world by surprise – when the Iraqi forces stormed the sisterly state of Kuwait in the most vile aggression known to the Arab nation in its modern history,' he said. 'The Kingdom of Saudi Arabia declares its categorical rejection of all the measures and declarations which followed that aggression ... Oh brethren, that regrettable event was followed by Iraq's massing of huge forces on the borders of the Kingdom of Saudi Arabia. Faced with these bitter realities, and out of the Kingdom's eagerness for the safety of its territory and the protection of its vital and economic constituents ... the Kingdom of Saudi Arabia expressed its wish for the participation of fraternal Arab forces and other friendly forces. Thus the governments of America and Britain took the initiative ... to send air and land forces in order to back the Saudi armed forces in performing their duty to defend the homeland and citizens against aggression.' He concluded with an assurance to his subjects that 'The [foreign] forces which will participate in the joint training between them and the Saudi military will be present temporarily in the Kingdom's territory, and will leave immediately when the Kingdom of Saudi Arabia so wishes.'[52]

Having delivered the speech, King Fahd flew to Cairo to attend the emergency Arab summit. The conference opened the next morning, 10 August, with an address by the host, President Mubarak, and was in session when Baghdad Radio broadcast a statement by Saddam Hussein entitled: 'Save Mecca and the Tomb of the Prophet from Occupation'.

'The situation of the Arabs has changed ... after the foreigner entered our land,' Saddam Hussein stated. 'Through its partitioning of the [Arab] lands, Western imperialism founded weak mini-states and installed the families who rendered it services that facilitated its [exploitative] mission . . . Imperialism attended to its interests in oil . . . when it established these dwarf oil states. Thus it prevented the majority of the sons of the people and the [Arab] nation from benefiting from their own wealth. As a result of the new wealth passing into the hands of the minority of the [Arab] nation to be exploited for the benefit of the foreigner and the few new rulers, financial and social corruption spread in these mini-states . . . [and from there to] many quarters of the majority of the Arab countries.' It was against this background that Iraq responded to 'the call' to save Kuwait from 'the scourge of weakness and corruption and isolation which kept it away from its kinsfolk in dear Iraq'. This response humiliated 'corrupt and traitorous people' as well as 'the imperialist and Zionist circles'. Because Iraq represented the Arab nation's 'capability' to uphold its honour and rights, 'the imperialists, the deviationists and the lackeys of the foreigners have joined ranks against Iraq', and 'the American forces came, and the doors of Saudi Arabia were opened to them under a false claim that the army of Iraq would continue the militant struggle against it. Neither denial nor explanation has worked. This means there are deliberate arrangements to commit aggression against Iraq . . . The rulers there [in Saudi Arabia] not only disregarded their people and the Arab nation . . . but [also] challenged God when they placed Mecca and the tomb of the Prophet Muhammad under foreign protection.' He called on 'Arabs, Muslims, believers in God', to 'stand up for Mecca, which is the captive of the spears of the Americans and the Zionists. Revolt against injustice, corruption, treason and treachery! Revolt against the spears of the foreigners that defiled your holy places!' He urged the Egyptians to 'prevent the foreigners and their fleets from passing through the Suez Canal and crossing Egyptian airspace lest your airspace and water be polluted', and called on the 'Sons of the Strait of Hormuz' to prevent the foreigners' fleets from passing. He concluded with an exhortation to his listeners to 'Resist the invader, denounce them, and expose the collaborators, the conniving ones and the defeatist and impotent ones, and support Iraq!'[53]

In response, the Muslim World League, based in Mecca, explained that the conflict along the Saudi–Kuwaiti borders was 1,500 kilometres (900 miles) away from the two holy Islamic sanctuaries, which were not 'under American or any other occupation'. The

Saudi ambassador to the US, Prince Bandar ibn Sultan, said, 'The [Islamic] holy places are in safe hands, and it is very regrettable that the Iraqi president is now repeating the empty rhetoric made before him by Khomeini.'[54]

While the Saudi-funded Muslim World League came to the rescue of King Fahd with one voice, the same could not be said of the religious establishment in the Saudi kingdom. The seventeen-member Supreme Religious Council was seemingly split on the issue of non-Muslim troops' presence on Saudi soil. On 9 August, the day the government publicly acknowledged the arrival of American troops in Saudi Arabia, it published prominently the opinion of several lesser known members of the Supreme Religious Council supporting the official decision, with the state-run television carrying their endorsement on several news bulletins for two days. However, the names of the two most respected Council members – Shaikh Abdul Aziz ibn Abdullah ibn Baz and Shaikh Muhammad ibn Saleh ibn Uthaimin – were not mentioned. This meant that they disagreed with the published opinions, and were opposed to the deployment of American troops, despite the fact that King Fahd had consulted leading theologians before his meeting with Cheney on 6 August.[55] Ibn Baz, the most distinguished member of the Council and rector of the Islamic University of Medina, is more widely known inside Saudi Arabia than anybody except the monarch and the crown prince. And Ibn Uthaimin's scholarship has made him known outside Saudi borders. Given the significance of their silence it was unlikely that the Saudi government would let the matter rest. It was bound to exert maximum pressure on the two religious leaders to toe the official line.

In order 'not to give ephemeral legitimacy to foreign intervention which is in the interests of neither the Arabs nor world peace and security', Tunisia stayed away from the summit in Cairo. A seven-point resolution placed before the conference endorsed UN Security Council Resolutions 660, 661 and 662; coupled a denunciation of Iraq's aggression against 'the fraternal state of Kuwait' with a demand for the immediate withdrawal of Iraq from Kuwait; and accepted the request of 'Saudi Arabia and other Arab Gulf states to dispatch Arab forces to support their armed forces in the defence of their territories and territorial integrity against any foreign aggression'. It was backed by twelve members (Djibouti, Egypt, six GCC states, Lebanon, Morocco, Somalia and Syria), and opposed by three (Iraq, Libya and the PLO). Algeria and Yemen abstained. Jordan, Mauritania and Sudan expressed reservations about the resolution.[56] A majority resolution of the Arab League is binding only on those who have voted for it.

The rift in the Arab League was symptomatic of Arab opinion in newspaper editorials as well as in the streets and bazaars. Those who opposed Saddam Hussein's action did so on the principle that resort to violence within the Arab family must be rejected; seizing land by force constituted a grave threat to the Arab world and international security, and severely undermined the Arab case against Israel for occupying Palestinian and other Arab territories. Iraq's invasion and annexation of Kuwait, a fully-fledged member of the United Nations, were unprecedented in the post-Second World War period, and could not be allowed to stand.

Significantly, one of the two members which sided with Iraq in opposing the Arab League resolution was the PLO. It was only too conscious of the 23 years of Israeli occupation that the Palestinians in the West Bank and Gaza had suffered and the impotence of the UN and the Arab League in the matter. What appealed to the PLO and its constituents was the vigour with which the Iraqi leader had championed the Palestinian cause, both diplomatically and materially. This was one of the two major reasons which made Saddam Hussein popular not only in the Occupied Territories but also in Jordan, Yemen, Sudan and most of North Africa; the other was Washington's military intervention on behalf of Riyadh and against Baghdad, which generated Arab nationalist fervour. Taking their cue from what was happening in Jordan, thousands of young men in Libya, Tunisia and Algeria converged on the Iraqi embassies to volunteer to defend Iraq. 'They support Saddam Hussein because he is strong,' explained a Jordanian journalist. 'They are sick of their leaders like President Mubarak bowing to American pressure.' Washington's assertion that it was defending small nations against brutal aggression was dismissed as hypocritical. 'What did the Americans do to stop the [June 1982] Israeli invasion of Lebanon? What have they done about the bloody occupation of the West Bank and Gaza [since June 1967]?' These questions were often flung at Western journalists in the streets of most Arab cities. What made the situation worse this time around for the proponents of such nationalist views was the control over the bulk of Arab petroleum that they saw the US acquiring. 'Arabs had always hoped that oil was part of their strategic weapon to be used for their own interests to implement the goals of the Arab nation,' said Mazzan Bakr, a Palestinian journalist. 'Americans have often accused Arabs of using oil as a weapon, but by going to [Saudi] Arabia, they are now using it as a strategic weapon themselves.'[57]

America's confidence was well reflected in the departure of President Bush on Friday 10 August for a vacation in Kennebunkport, a seaside resort in Maine. He had obviously achieved the prime objective of deterring further aggression by Iraq, if it had any such plans. Baghdad's repeated denials of any aggressive designs, topped with a formal letter to the UN secretary-general on 13 August – in which its foreign minister described the claims of an impending Iraqi invasion of Saudi Arabia as 'groundless and baseless', and offered to 'provide the necessary guarantees on a bilateral level and through the Arab League' to reassure Saudi Arabia[58] – were ignored by US officials and media. They had kept up a steady stream of news flashes claiming that the number of Iraqi forces had increased from 100,000 to 120,000 and then to 170,000, and that they were in 'an offensive posture'. This had helped Bush gradually to raise the threshold of 'necessary' US force in the Gulf from the original 40,000 to 100,000 – so long as war did not erupt.[59]

Bush had reason to feel satisfied with the result of the Arab summit, particularly with the stance of Syria, a radical state and long-time ally of Moscow, which had parted with such traditional allies as Algeria and Libya and adopted a hard line against Iraq, starting with a public condemnation of Baghdad's action on 4 August. 'The world would resemble a jungle if every country were to impose its illegitimate viewpoints through aggression and the use of force,' the Syrian president, Hafiz Assad, declared three days later.[60] Bush showed his appreciation by sending the US assistant secretary for the Near East, John Kelly, to Damascus to meet Assad on 9 August, and followed this up with a phone call to the Syrian leader from Kennebunkport reportedly to congratulate him on despatching two army divisions to the Iraqi border, an action originally suggested by his own emissary.[61]

Syria applauded the Cairo summit as 'a success' which had 'limited the current crisis and averted the dangers of foreign intervention in the region'. The official comment published and broadcast in the state-controlled media failed to mention the arrival of American forces in Saudi Arabia. Soon the government announced that it would send troops to Saudi Arabia as part of the 'Arab force' which was there to 'prevent American military intervention in the Iraqi–Kuwaiti crisis', and that these troops would be deployed at the Saudi–Kuwaiti border to serve as 'a deterrent to Iraqi expansion southward and to any American move toward Kuwait'.[62]

Finding himself on the defensive, politically, Saddam Hussein tried to gain some area for manoeuvre. On 12 August, Sunday, he offered a three-point peace initiative. 'I propose that all issues of occupation . . . be resolved according to one set of basic principles and premises to be laid down by the UN Security Council,' he said. 'First, the preparation of withdrawal arrangements . . . for the immediate and unconditional withdrawal of Israel from the occupied Arab territories in Palestine, Syria and Lebanon; Syria's withdrawal from Lebanon; a withdrawal between Iraq and Iran; and the formulation of arrangements for the situation in Kuwait . . . The implementation of the programme should begin with the enforcement of all the applicable UN Security Council and UN [General Assembly] resolutions . . . until we get to the most recent occupation . . . Second, we propose the immediate withdrawal from Saudi Arabia of US forces and other forces . . . [to] be replaced by Arab forces whose size, nationality, duty and deployment will be defined by the UN Security Council . . . Third, all boycott and siege decisions against Iraq should be frozen immediately.'[63]

While the Iraqi leader's proposals were rejected promptly by the White House, they were received positively by Yemen, where the ruling coalition – consisting of the General People's Congress and the Yemeni Socialist Party – called for an emergency Arab summit to support Iraq's proposals for settling the Gulf crisis.

Saddam Hussein's initiative was welcomed enthusiastically by Palestinian and Jordanian press and people, with the Palestinians in Nablus, the largest city in the West Bank, mounting a pro-Saddam demonstration. 'There is an absolute consensus among Palestinians that Saddam Hussein has made the right connection,' said Daoud Kuttab, a Palestinian commentator. 'His proposals expose the double standard of the West.' The extent of his popularity could be judged by the fact that in Jordan some 40,000 people signed up at the Iraqi embassy to fight for Iraq.[64] Such partisans readily accepted the Iraqi leader's analysis that there could be no satisfaction of Arab aspirations and no justice for the Palestinians until the corrupt allies of the West in the Arab world had been destroyed, starting with the emir of Kuwait.

Having lost his throne, but not the recognition of his government by the international community, the Kuwaiti ruler maintained close contacts with Washington and London. He requested these capitals to impose a naval blockade of Iraq under Article 51 of the UN Charter, which gives UN members the right to protect themselves when attacked or to ask fellow-members to come to their aid. But UN lawyers argued that this article prohibited unilateral action by any single country once the Security Council had taken measures, such as economic sanctions, to maintain international peace and security. When America and Britain justified giving orders to their naval ships to interdict vessels trading with Iraq or to turn them away, by claiming a formal request from Kuwait, several Security Council members, including France, Canada and the USSR, disputed this reasoning. So did the UN secretary-general, Javier Pérez de Cuellar.[65]

In any case, with Iraqi exports down to 10 per cent of the pre-invasion level, and imports curtailed to the same extent, Baghdad had to take drastic measures to withstand the economic siege. It revived the death penalty for hoarding food which had been imposed during the Iran–Iraq War, with Saddam Hussein appealing to Iraqi women 'to feed their families half their usual fare'.[66] Given that Iraq imported 70 per cent of its food annually, at a cost of $3 billion, such advice seemed appropriate. It was only a matter of weeks before the authorities reintroduced rationing of basic necessities as they had done during the war with Iran. Since a typical Iraqi family spent half its budget on food, the official steps taken to ensure adequate supplies at reasonable prices were likely to keep any popular discontent, emanating from the UN embargo, to a manageable level. Such measures, however, were unlikely to stem the outflow of non-Iraqi workers who, at 1.4 million, were nearly a third of the national workforce of 4.25 million.[67]

The UN economic boycott intensified Baghdad's policy of transferring Kuwaiti assets to Iraq, the reason given being that the Kuwaiti state under the emir had allegedly stolen Iraqi petroleum worth $2.4 billion. The transfers of Kuwait's gold, local and foreign currencies, civilian aircraft, cars, oil tankers, and military hardware, including US-made Hawk anti-aircraft missiles, during the first week after the invasion were estimated to be worth $3 billion.[68] Such gains, however, were small compared to the losses inflicted on the Iraqi economy by the international blockade.

While Iraq was compelled to tighten its belt, Kuwait and Saudi Arabia were generous in aiding such countries as Turkey to overcome the losses due to the observance of an embargo against Iraq. While Riyadh promised to supply oil to Ankara at a discount, the Kuwaiti crown prince, Shaikh Saad al Sabah, promised substantial aid to Turkey during his meeting with the Turkish president, Turgut Ozal, on 14 August.[69]

Saddam Hussein pressed on with his programme of absorbing Kuwait into Iraq as an additional, nineteenth, province, and presented a hard line on the issue in public. In private, though, he kept up his efforts to reach a compromise with the US, and encouraged King Hussein of Jordan to act as a mediator. After meeting Saddam Hussein in Baghdad on 13 August, the Jordanian monarch flew to the United States with a message for President Bush from the Iraqi leader.

King Fahd was equally busy on the diplomatic front, focusing on assembling a large body of troops from Muslim countries in his realm. He despatched an emissary to South and South-east Asia for this purpose: he succeeded in Pakistan and Bangladesh, but failed in Malaysia and Indonesia. The Pakistan government agreed to let its 5,000 officers, technicians, pilots and naval officers, seconded earlier to Saudi Arabia, fight Iraq if necessary, and agreed 'in principle' to join the 'Islamic contingents' going to the kingdom. Bangladesh too made a similar promise.[70]

However, the Saudi king overlooked an important Muslim neighbour: the Islamic Republic of Iran. Actually, he could not have acted otherwise, since his government had broken off diplomatic ties with it in 1988.[71]

As it was, Iran, which had been a victim of Saddam Hussein's aggression a decade earlier, lost no time in condemning Iraq for its invasion of Kuwait. Arguing that once again Iraq's aggressive actions had opened the Gulf to foreign powers, Iran's foreign minister, Ali Akbar Velayati, called on Baghdad on 7 August to 'abandon its ambitions over the offshore islands of Kuwait'. He added, 'We cannot accept any change in Kuwaiti borders, neither in land nor in water.' Two days later, during his tour of the Gulf states, he said: 'Iran will not tolerate any alteration in the political geography of the region.'[72]

On 15 August, to the great surprise of Tehran and many other capitals in the region and outside, Iraq offered wide-ranging concessions to Iran in its peace talks.

Phase Two

In his letter of 8 August, President Rafsanjani had proposed that 'peace talks should be based on the 1975 [Algiers] Accord'. He had also stated that holding negotiations 'at a level higher than what is currently under way in Geneva is acceptable only when we could achieve specific results out of the current Geneva talks', and that the withdrawal of the Iraqi forces from the occupied Iranian territories 'can [be] accomplished in a matter of one or two days'.[73]

'In harmony with the spirit of our initiative which we announced on 12 August 1990, through which we meant to achieve a lasting and comprehensive peace in the region . . . so as not to get any of Iraq's potential diverted from the field of the great battle . . . to avoid the mixing of trenches . . . and as a fruit of our direct dialogue, which has continued since our letter to you on 21 April 1990 and until your last letter to us on 8 August 1990', Saddam Hussein offered Rafsanjani on 14 August: 'First, [we] approve your proposal as contained in your reply letter dated 8 August 1990 . . . considering the 1975 [Algiers] Accord closely connected with the principles cited in our letter dated 30 July 1990 . . . Second, we are ready to send a delegation to you in Tehran, and to receive your delegation in Baghdad, to prepare the agreements and sign them . . . Third, our withdrawal will begin as of Friday 17 August 1990 . . . Fourth, all prisoners of war held in Iraq and Iran should be exchanged immediately and comprehensively.' He told the Iranian president that 'everything you wanted, and on which you have been concentrating, has been achieved', and once documents are exchanged, 'we can start a new life under the canopy of Islam's principles . . . and keep away those who are fishing in murky waters off our coasts. We may also co-operate to keep the Gulf . . . free of foreign fleets and foreign forces that are lying in wait for us.'[74]

Saddam Hussein's unconditional acceptance of Rafsanjani's proposals was received by Iran with surprise and elation, with its foreign minister calling the Iraqi leader's offer 'the greatest victory for the Islamic revolution in its history'.

The possibility of such a move was implicit in the fact that on 21 April 1990 Saddam Hussein had taken the initiative in addressing a personal letter to Rafsanjani suggesting a meeting between them in Mecca within the next week or so. Between this overture and the meeting of the Iraqi and Iranian foreign ministers in Geneva in mid-July, it later transpired, Saddam Hussein had sent a 'secret message' to Rafsanjani, advising him not to make a 'negative' interpretation of 'certain events' likely to occur in the Gulf region, and that once the situation had settled down after those 'events', Iran and Iraq would emerge as the dominant powers in the region, and they could regulate Gulf affairs 'in a partnership'.[75] After the foreign ministers' Geneva meeting, the pace of correspondence between their presidents had quickened, with Saddam Hussein following up his telegram to Rafsanjani on 30 July with a letter on 3 August.

Once Iraq had annexed Kuwait, its access to the Gulf widened to such an extent that it could afford to share the Shatt al Arab with Iran according to the 1975 Algiers Accord. And once the Iraqi president agreed to concede this point to Tehran, thus taking a major step towards signing a peace treaty, he could safely plan withdrawing the bulk of his 300,000 troops facing Iran along the 730-mile international frontier, and redeploying them elsewhere.

In retrospect it could be seen why Saddam Hussein had so far refused to concede Iran's reasonable demands. In the wake of the August 1988 ceasefire, it was necessary for him to claim victory and maintain a certain tension with Iran. By so doing he managed to delay massive demobilization, which was likely to create social problems by making redundant hundreds of thousands of mainly Arab expatriate workers, and to keep his military and officer corps occupied along the border – away from the capital and any chance of a possible coup against him. Now, however, having antagonized his affluent Arab neighbours to the south, he found himself in need of mending his fences with his eastern neighbour. And he did so with alacrity. Knowing the anti-Western, anti-Zionist politics of Iranian leaders, he tried to woo them by using that sort of rhetoric. But, knowing his track record and his propensity for sudden U-turns, Tehran remained sceptical.

The Iraqi president's decision was greeted with surprise by all world leaders, including Thatcher and Bush. They also perceived in it much military cunning, and inferred that he planned to consolidate his hold over Kuwait.

As for Saudi Arabia, there seemed no evidence that Saddam Hussein was planning to attack it. This created a dilemma for Bush and his policy-makers. How were they going to sell the idea of war with the Iraqi leader to Americans who, according to the Times-Mirror Centre for the People and the Press, showed uncommonly high interest in the Gulf crisis, with 66% following the story 'very closely' – compared to 60% for the US invasion of Panama in December 1989 and 58% for the American air strikes against Libya in April 1986.[76] The first step, they concluded, was to launch a propaganda blitz against the person and policies of Saddam Hussein.

Bush took up the job with enthusiasm. Giving a pep talk to the Pentagon staff on 15 August, he depicted the Iraqi leader as a liar and a mass murderer. Implicitly comparing him to Adolf Hitler (1932–45), Bush said, 'A half-century ago our nation and the world paid dearly for appeasing an aggressor who should, and could, have been stopped. We are not about to make the same mistake again.' He stressed that there was 'no substitute for American leadership', which could not be effective 'in the absence of American strength'. He repeated the

American objectives in the Gulf as outlined a week earlier in his television address. 'The free flow of oil', he argued, was necessary to protect 'our jobs, our way of life, our own freedom, and the freedom of friendly countries around the world', which would 'all suffer if control of the world's oil reserves fell into the hands of Saddam Hussein'. Bush ridiculed the Iraqi president's interpretation of his 'unprovoked invasion of a friendly Arab nation' as 'a struggle between Arabs and Americans', and added: 'It is Saddam who lied to his neighbours . . . Saddam has claimed that this is a holy war of Arab against infidel. This from a man who has used poison gas against the men and women and children of his country, who invaded Iran in a war that cost the lives of more than half a million Muslims, and who now plunders Kuwait. Atrocities have been committed by Saddam's soldiers and henchmen. The reports from Kuwait tell a sordid tale of brutality.'[77]

Saddam Hussein was stung by Bush's charge of lying. Assuming that this charge was based on his having broken his promise to President Mubarak that he had no intention of attacking Kuwait, he repeated publicly what he had told Bush in a private message on 6 August through the American chargé d'affaires in Baghdad. 'You, US President, lied to your people when you told them that you were massing troops to protect American interests in Saudi Arabia,' he stated. 'Now you are telling them that they are there to force Iraq to withdraw from Kuwait.' Saddam Hussein then turned to the comparison with Hitler. 'Whoever does not want history to link him with the base characteristics of Hitler must search thoroughly for peaceful means and not rush into preparations for war,' he said.[78]

By now the Gulf crisis had turned into a dramatic struggle between two antagonists: George Bush and Saddam Hussein. Even allowing for the vastly differing socio-cultural features of the Arab Muslim world and the White Anglo-Saxon Protestant (WASP) segment of American society, the two leaders were poles apart: Bush, a patrician from the sophisticated eastern seaboard of America; and Saddam, son of a poor peasant from a village in central Iraq.

Saddam (lit., Clasher/Fighter) Hussein was born to Subha and Hussein Majid on 28 April 1937 in a landless family of the Albu Nasir tribe's Began clan (of Sunni persuasion) in Auja, a village near Tikrit, a town on the Tigris River, about 100 miles north of Baghdad. Saddam's father died before his birth, and his mother, Subha, remarried Ibrahim Hassan, an illiterate peasant. He treated Saddam harshly and instead of sending him to school made him work as a farmhand or shepherd. At ten Saddam ran away from home to live with his maternal uncle Khairallah Talfa, a teacher, who had lost his military post in 1941 for backing the nationalist Rashid Ali Gailani against the British in the Second World War, and was fervently against British imperialism. Khairallah sent his son Adnan and Saddam to the same school in Tikrit, where many of the teachers were admirers of Gamal Abdul Nasser.

In 1955, when he was eighteen, Saddam went to Baghdad for further schooling and became involved in oppositional activities. (He had already shown a flair for handling small arms.) At 20 he joined the Baath Party as an associate member. After the 1958 republican coup he engaged in fights between the Baathists and the followers of Prime Minister Abdul Karim Qasim. He was part of the six-man Baathist team that tried, unsuccessfully, to assassinate Qasim in October 1959, and received injuries to his leg in the shoot-out. He escaped to Syria, and then to Egypt.

Once in Cairo, he received a government stipend – arranged through the Egyptian intelligence agency, the Mukhabrat – to pursue his studies. He joined a private college and finished his high school education at 24. Then, it is said, he joined Cairo University to study law.

Soon after the Baathists seized power in Baghdad in early 1963, Saddam Hussein returned to Iraq and married Sajida Talfa, a schoolteacher and a daughter of his uncle Khairallah Talfa. (Some biographers claim that Sajida had been brought over to Cairo to join Saddam if only to help moderate his violent streak, which often led him to pick fights with those Iraqi and non-Iraqi students who disagreed with him.) During the brief Baathist rule he was made a full member of the party (with a total national membership of less than 1,000), and appointed an interrogator at a prison.

In opposition, the Baath Party persecuted by President Abdul Salam Arif once again turned into a conspiratorial organization. Saddam Hussein moved up the ranks and joined the party's regional command, where 50-year-old General Ahmad Hassan Bakr, a cousin of Khairallah Talfa and a founder member of the Baath in Iraq, played a leading role. Because of his involvement in a failed Baathist coup attempt in October 1964, Saddam Hussein found himself behind bars. He escaped in July 1966. Later that year he was elected assistant general secretary of the Baath, now led formally by Bakr. For the next two years Saddam worked hard to reorganize the party and supervised its rejuvenated militia, called the National Guard.

He was only 31 when the Baath captured power in July 1968. Though not a member of the governing Revolutionary Command Council, he was quite influential thanks to his close relationship with Bakr. In November 1969 he secured a place on the RCC. Thereafter the Bakr–Hussein duo came to dominate the party, mainly as a result of their cunning decimation of their RCC colleagues.

The Mafia-style manner in which General Bakr and his Baathist military colleagues removed from power the two leading non-Baathist military conspirators, Abdul Razzak Nayif and Ibrahim al Daoud, a fortnight after the 17 July 1968 coup, was a foretaste of the brutal means that the top Iraqi leaders came to employ to deal with rivals and dissidents. While Saddam Hussein was not the initiator of this style, he adopted it with ease, and transformed it into a brutally effective means of achieving his escalating ambition. He had many opportunities in the party and state to use his considerable conspiratorial abilities, developed during his formative years as an underground Baathist activist often on the run. While busying himself with restructuring and strengthening the party, he tightened his grip over the intelligence and security apparatus of the government. As a youthful, energetic figure, who became a member of the ruling Revolutionary Command Council in November 1969, he appealed to those Baathists who believed in a strong ideology and commitment to socio-economic progress.

Those senior figures in the party or government who crossed him paid dearly. Hardan Tikriti, a prominent Baathist, defence minister and a member of the RCC, was one such. After his abrupt dismissal from his posts in October 1970, he went into exile in Kuwait. In March 1971 he was assassinated by Iraqi agents.

By 1972, the 35-year-old Saddam Hussein had become vice-president of the RCC, the second most powerful position in Iraq. He represented Iraq in signing important foreign agreements during his trips abroad, first to France and then to the Soviet Union. At home, among other things he applied himself to solving the endemic Kurdish problem.

By the mid-1970s he had outstripped Bakr in leadership, cunning, ruthlessness, organizational ability and charisma. It was he who signed the Algiers Accord with Iran in 1975. However, he still needed Bakr, a former military officer with an avuncular personality, whose comparative moderation and piety went down well with the older, conservative segments of society. But the Shia problems, which escalated into a series of crises in 1977–8, strained the long-sustained alliance, since Bakr advocated compromise and Saddam Hussein confrontation.

In mid-July 1979, on the eve of the eleventh anniversary of the Baathist coup, Saddam Hussein secured the resignation of Bakr on 'health grounds'. Having reached the peak he wasted no time in consolidating his position and removing any possible challenge to his supremacy. Two weeks later he discovered a major 'anti-state conspiracy' involving 68 top Baathist civilian and military leaders. Following a summary trial by a specially appointed tribunal of half a dozen of his closest allies on the RCC, 21 of the accused were executed. They included five of the twenty members of the RCC, including Adnan Hamadani, a long-standing, close personal friend of Saddam Hussein, and Muhyi Abdul Hassan Mashhadi, secretary of the RCC, who had been bold enough to suggest that the successor to President Bakr ought to be elected through a free vote of the RCC. The executions were carried out by Saddam Hussein and the remaining members of the RCC, thus sealing a bond of blood among them. The confessions and trials were filmed. Saddam Hussein arranged a showing of the film to several hundred party leaders, and later ordered the circulation of a video version among the party cadres. Having decimated all doubters at the highest level, the Iraqi president carried out a widespread purge of dissident elements in trade unions, the Popular Army, student unions, and local and provincial governments, resulting in the executions of up to 500 party leaders.[79]

The purges carried an unmistakable message to politicians, trade unionists and military officers: the young president would brook no dissent, and would mete out the harshest punishment to anybody who dared to oppose him. He combined these moves with such popular actions as raising the salaries of the military, police, intelligence, civil service and judiciary. Thanks to the doubling of oil prices that occurred in the late 1970s, his regime could well afford to do this. This strategy of ruthless suppression of opposition at higher or more fundamental levels, sweetened with open-handed generosity towards large constituencies, was a replica of the one Saddam Hussein had been following concerning the Shia problem – a problem which ultimately led to his invasion of Iran in September 1980.

In the course of the eight-year conflict, Saddam Hussein further monopolized power, militarized Iraqi society, and fostered a personality cult to the extent that every shop, office, public building and most homes displayed his portrait – with clocks, watches and calendars being adorned with his face; paintings, murals and cardboard cut-outs, some of them several storeys high, depicting him as a field marshal, a comforter of bereaved children, a bedouin or a Kurd in traditional dress, a cigar-smoking politician, an air force pilot, a devout Muslim at prayer and a businessman.

At the same time he enlarged and sharpened the repressive instruments of the state. His adversaries therefore had no option but to try to get rid of him through assassination. There was at least one major attempt every year to eliminate him. Sometimes this came close to success. For instance, on 11 July 1982 a group of Iraqi soldiers belonging to al Daawa al Islamiya, an Islamic fundamentalist group, ambushed Saddam Hussein's motorcade with machine-guns and rocket-propelled grenades as it made its way to Dujayal, a town 40 miles north of Baghdad, where the Iraqi president maintained a weekend retreat. The attack killed ten of his bodyguards. His car was hit, but he was unhurt. The government reprisal was brutal: it resulted in 150 casualties and the destruction of parts of Dujayal.[80] During the First Gulf War he came under severe pressure by several members of his inner circle to step down to meet the Iranian demand for a ceasefire three times – in June and October 1982, and again in mid-1985. Each time he used his armoury of cunning, conspiratorial skills, daring, ruthlessness, tenacity, a loyal and efficient intelligence apparatus, and a flair for populist gestures and action to the full – and survived. The end result was that by the time the conflict ended in August 1988 Saddam Hussein had emerged as a larger-than-life leader, indestructible, and destined to play a leading role on the Arab and world stages.

Part of his success in the war with Iran was due to the assistance he received from the two Reagan administrations, of which George Bush was an integral part. The very installation of Reagan in the White House was intertwined with the eruption of the First Gulf War in September 1980 and the possibility of the release of the 52 American hostages held by Iran on the eve of the US presidential elections in early November 1979. The fate of the American captives in Tehran played a major role in the design of the election campaigns by the incumbent chief executive, Jimmy Carter, and his challenger Ronald Reagan, running on the Republican ticket along with George Bush standing for vice-president.

George Herbert Walker Bush was born on 12 June 1924 in Milton, Massachusetts, in an aristocratic family with a history of political office. His father Prescott, before taking his seat in the US Senate, was a merchant banker with Brown Brothers Harriman, the finance house of Averill Harriman, one of the pillars of the American and British establishments. The Bushes traced their forebears to the Pilgrim Fathers, who arrived in New England in 1620, with their family home at Kennebunkport, Maine, emerging as the seat of an eminent

American dynasty. On his maternal side George Bush was related to a family that had owned plantation estates in South Carolina.

As a boy George went to a prestigious boarding school, Phillips Andover College, where he was captain of the soccer and baseball teams, an experience in leadership which schooled him to play as a team, not a solo, member. On his eighteenth birthday, in 1942, he volunteered for the war, and saw action as a navy pilot in the Pacific. He won a Distinguished Flying Cross for flying on to attack a Japanese radio and communication centre after his bomber had been hit. He ditched in the sea, and was luckily rescued by a US submarine.

In early 1945 he married Barbara McCall, a daughter of a publishing mogul. Later that year he enrolled at Yale, the university of his father and grandfather, to major in economics. Here again he captained the baseball team.

After his graduation in 1948 he was offered a job in the family's banking firm, but turned it down. Instead, as one version would have it, he and his wife put their worldly possessions into an old car, and drove to the oil wells of Texas. The place they rented in a shantytown slum of Odessa, Texas, offered a bathroom which had to be shared with a local whore. After working as a clerk in an oilfield supply store of the International Derrick Company for a couple of years, Bush established an oil development company dealing in royalty rights for petroleum and gas properties. In 1953 in partnership with two friends, he set up the Zapata Petroleum Corporation followed by the Zapata Offshore Company. This was the beginning of George Bush's life as a wildcat Texan oilman, which after 14 years and 129 oil wells transformed him into a self-made man of considerable wealth. Another version has it that, far from being adventurous, George Bush had decided to work for the International Derrick Company owned by Dresser Industries of which his father, Prescott Bush, was a director. It was only after the family bank had offered a guarantee of $100,000, later raised to $500,000, that George took to wildcat drilling. None the less, he proved to be an energetic, gregarious, and popular citizen of Midland, Texas, and a devout Episcopalian, the American equivalent of the Anglican Church.

His first attempt at a national elective office – a seat in the US Senate – on a Republican ticket in 1964 failed. But two years later he aimed lower by contesting a seat in the House of Representatives from an affluent district in Houston, the capital of Texas, where he was now based. He won. In 1968 he repeated the performance. But his second attempt to enter the US Senate in 1970 failed.

He spent the next seven years serving the Republican administrations of Richard Nixon (1969–74) and Gerald Ford (1974–6), or the Republican Party, in various positions. During 1971–3 he was the US ambassador to the UN, followed by a year as chairperson of the Republican Party National Committee. Then came a stint as the Chief of the US Liaison Office in Peking in 1974–5. From there he went on to become the director of the CIA in 1976–7.

With a Democrat, Carter, in the White House, Bush found himself without an official position. He decided to seek the Republican nomination for president, won a number of primaries, and became Ronald Reagan's strongest rival. In May 1980 he withdrew from the contest, and asked his delegates to switch their backing to Reagan. Two months later, at the party convention, Reagan adopted him as his running mate. They won handsomely. Bush became vice-president in 1980, and retained the job in 1984 after the second victory for the Reagan–Bush ticket at the polls.

During his eight years as the Number Two man in the Reagan administrations Bush acquired a reputation as a ditherer, a man of 'permanent indecision' and little conviction, ready to trim his sails for expediency. After he had won the Republican Party ticket for presidency in mid-1988 he had to work hard to live down his popular image as a wimp. In the process he conducted a dirty campaign against his rival, Michael Dukakis, the governor of Massachusetts, which was based on two simplistic, highly charged points – 'No new taxes' and the granting of furlough to a convicted black murderer, Willie Horton, in Massachusetts – and wrapping them in the American stars and stripes. It worked. He overcame his wide lag behind his adversary in the opinion polls, and went on to win by a huge margin.

Once in power he enjoyed its privileges and trappings with the ease of a patrician. As an aristocratic Easterner he had an abiding interest in external affairs. Given Ronald Reagan's lack of interest in international relations, as vice-president Bush had had much opportunity to concentrate on these. He continued to do so after winning the presidential contest, leaving the management of domestic issues almost totally in the hands of John Sununu, his chief of staff.

Bush's installation at the White House in January 1989 coincided with the virtual collapse of the Soviet Union as a superpower rival to the US. This period handed him a series of easy victories. By the early summer of 1990, however, the situation was swinging against him. The trouble surfaced on the home front, his weaker suit. Faced with a severe crisis in the budgetary deficit, he had to renege on his election promise of 'No new taxes', to the delight of his Democratic adversaries, who controlled both houses of Congress. On top of this came the deepening crisis of the savings and loans banks. Besides damaging an economy in recession, it threatened to embroil the president personally since his son Neil, a director of a savings and loans bank, was being accused of having received a bribe from a client seeking a huge overdraft.

Against this background the Kuwait crisis came as a godsend to Bush. It provided him with the moral crusade he had always yearned for, and to which he could relate as a veteran of the Second World War. His Episcopalian upbringing, puritanical background and experience of fighting Nazi Germany and militaristic Japan confirmed his belief that evil existed on this planet and that it ought to be confronted and destroyed. The evil was now personified by Saddam Hussein – the president of Iraq, which until the UN embargo sold a third of its oil exports to the US – an Arab leader whom Bush had been cultivating before 1 August as a pillar of stability and moderation in the Middle East. Once the Gulf crisis erupted, Bush took personal control of tackling it. He resorted to applying intense pressure on allies and adversaries, often in telephone conversations.

Bush seemed well suited to handle the crisis, as his consistently high ratings in the opinion polls on the subject confirmed. He knew more about petroleum than any other president. As a former member of the House of Representatives, he had a better understanding of Congress than his two predecessors, Reagan and Carter. (In sending a letter to Congressional leaders, explaining his despatch of American forces to the Gulf, he acted wisely.) A spell as director of the CIA had equipped him to evaluate intelligence reports. Finally, as a former US ambassador to the United Nations, Bush was well versed in the conduct of international diplomacy.

In the diplomatic field Bush was ably assisted by his secretary of state, James Addison Baker, aged 60. A Houston lawyer and long-standing personal friend of Bush, Baker had served the Reagan administrations as White House chief of staff and secretary of the treasury. Though born in Texas into a family of lawyers, Baker had been educated at the exclusive Hill School, Philadelphia, and Princeton University. While at Yale, Bush had been initiated into the Skull and Bones secret society (of the White Anglo-Saxon Protestant ilk); Baker belonged to Ivy, the exclusive dining club at Princeton.

Bush trusted Baker's instincts and judgement and assigned him the task of rallying international backing for Washington in resolving the

Gulf crisis. His immediate objective was to secure the world community's support to obtain Baghdad's permission for 'the nationals of third countries' to leave Kuwait and Iraq. The matter came to the fore with the Iraqi forces' order of 15 August to some 4,000 Britons and 2,500 Americans in Kuwait to assemble the next day at specified hotels in the capital. Very few of them turned up, and there were no Iraqis at the hotels to receive those who did. But the word went round that they were to be transported (eventually) to Baghdad. This was confirmed by Saadi Mehdi Saleh, the speaker of the Iraqi National Assembly, which decided to detain the nationals of those governments that were participating in the economic embargo against Iraq and preparing to attack it. Most of the 8,000 Western and Japanese nationals in Kuwait and 3,400 in Iraq were involved. The British foreign secretary Douglas Hurd called the Iraqi decision 'the tactics of the outlaw down the ages'.[81]

On 18 August, the Security Council adopted Resolution 664 demanding that Iraq 'permit and facilitate the immediate departure from Kuwait and Iraq of the nationals of third countries', and 'rescind its orders for the closure of diplomatic and consular missions in Kuwait'. The vote was unanimous.

That day, as 41 Britons were moved from their hotels in Baghdad to unknown destinations – 35 Americans had been sent to undisclosed locations the day before – Saadi Mehdi Saleh announced the National Assembly's decision that groups of Western 'guests' were to be housed at the country's military and strategic installations. 'The use of innocent civilians as pawns to promote what Iraq sees to be its self-interest is contrary to international law and indeed to all acceptable norms of international conduct,' said Marlin Fitzwater, the White House press secretary.[82]

Baghdad explained its action. 'The world is aware that these [Western] governments . . . are gearing up to commit aggression against Iraq and the Arab nation,' the communiqué stated. 'Foremost of [our] sacred missions should be the protection of peoples from aggression and injustice and the assurance of peace, and any conduct that in the end promotes this noble and humane objective gains deep legitimacy, which is the substance of divine, secular and international laws.' It was therefore decided, continued the statement, 'to play host to the citizens of these aggressive nations as long as Iraq remains threatened with an aggressive war'.[83]

With nearly 59,000 US military personnel, 500 planes and 59 warships already in the Gulf, with a further 45,000 marines en route, and three US battleships firing warning shots at two Iraqi tankers in the Persian Gulf and the Gulf of Oman, following their refusal to halt to be searched by the American navy,[84] the fear in Baghdad of an attack by the United States was real. Washington tried deliberately to foster such feelings, with a clear indication that something had to give before the 24 August deadline fixed by Iraq for the closure of all foreign embassies in Kuwait City. Mixed with this were emotional interviews conducted with the Westerners held hostage in Iraq and their anxious families at home. The Pentagon gave briefings to the print and broadcast journalists, embellishing them with maps and scenarios of war plans, and their editors invariably turned them into lead stories.

In America, and to a large extent in Britain, major television networks succumbed to jingoism, with television commentators, almost always defence correspondents, peppering their reports with 'Growing feeling that war can't now be avoided' and 'Imminent sense in the Bush administration that war is approaching'. As Marvin Kalb, a former Columbia Broadcasting Service (CBS) reporter now running a think-tank on the press, put it: 'When boys go to war, the [television] networks [go] too. Despite all their efforts to be realistic and neutral, if you put a whisper of the possibility of war in the hollow chamber of network TV, it will come out of the other end as a shout.'[85]

Typical of the war fever encouraged in the media by American and British officials was the front-page headline in the London *Sunday Times* of 19 August: 'US ON BRINK OF WAR WITH IRAQ: SADDAM TO STARVE HOSTAGE BABIES' (the latter part of the headline being based on the statement by an Iraqi official that 'the foreigners held in Iraq would suffer the same food shortages [due to the economic blockade] as Iraqis'). The text underneath repeated the Pentagon claim that it would destroy Iraq's 500 combat planes within 24 hours and defeat all of its ground forces within ten days. The CIA put out a story that Baghdad was only two years from making a nuclear weapon. This was a deliberate ploy to wrong-foot the Iraqis. But Iraq could not afford to take chances. Its motto seemed to be: better accept the enemy's disinformation and stay on guard rather than be caught off-guard.

That day, 19 August, Saddam Hussein addressed an 'open letter' to the families of 'foreigners in Iraq', expressing his 'pain' at the decision of the National Assembly to detain their family members in Iraq, and proposing a five-point plan 'to secure freedom for all'. (1) The UN Security Council, with US approval, should pledge that America would withdraw from the region in no longer a period than it took to build up its military presence in the region. The Council should give an undertaking to Saudi Arabia that it would stand militarily against Iraq – collectively, along with those countries that abided by its resolution – if Iraq tried to attack it. At the same time Iraq and Saudi Arabia should promise not to attack each other. (2) The Security Council should promise peace and security in the 'whole region' according to Iraq's 12 August peace initiative, and foreign forces should withdraw from the holy lands of Hijaz and Najd [i.e. Saudi Arabia]. (3) If either (1) or (2) were accomplished, then foreigners would be allowed immediately to travel as they chose. (4) If the above were not possible, then it would be enough for the American president to make a 'public commitment in writing to withdraw his troops and those of his allies from the land of the Arabs and the holy places of Muslims according to a timetable no longer than it took for their [military] build-up', to pledge 'not to use force against Iraq', [and] 'to lift the blockade on Iraq by all sides immediately'. Then, the Iraqi government would allow 'the foreigners concerned to travel outside Iraq'. (5) The question of Kuwait should be left to Arabs to resolve 'as an Arab issue'. This is what had happened earlier to such issues as the Western Sahara, involving Morocco and other concerned parties, and the Syrian 'occupation of Lebanon'.[86]

The US president (as well as the British prime minister) rejected Saddam Hussein's deal promptly. He had responded similarly to an earlier offer – made by the Iraqi foreign minister Tariq Aziz in an interview with American Broadcasting Company (ABC) television in Baghdad on 15 August – to hold open-ended discussions with America on the Gulf situation. Bush replied that such talks could take place only after Iraq had withdrawn from Kuwait.

Behind these public policies certain clandestine moves were afoot, at least on the Iraqi side. Equally significant was the fact that Baghdad made no mention of its precondition about the US troops' withdrawal from Saudi Arabia in a deal that it offered Washington secretly through a former high-ranking US official. This was part of the Iraqi regime's 'deniable diplomacy', whereby it made compromising moves towards America through a third party with the proviso that if the story leaked it would deny it unequivocally (so as to preserve its credibility among its own nationals regarding its official stand that Kuwait was an eternal part of Iraq).

The proposal from Iraq's foreign ministry and 'higher-ups' was carried by an Iraqi-born American citizen (with extensive business ties in Iraq), and another American 'close to the White House chief of staff John Sununu'. They were in Baghdad when Iraq invaded Kuwait. When they sought to leave they were advised by a high official close to Saddam Hussein to stay while the Iraqi authorities prepared a 'message' for the Bush administration.

Iraq's proposal was finally delivered to Brent Scowcroft, the national security adviser, on 23 August, and published in the New York-based *Newsday* a week later. It consisted of a deal, and an offer of a mutually advantageous agreement with America. In exchange for Iraq conceding withdrawal from Kuwait and allowing foreigners to leave the country, it should be given the following concessions: the lifting of UN economic sanctions, a 'guaranteed access' to the Persian Gulf through the Kuwaiti islands of Bubiyan and Warba, and full control of the Rumeila oilfield that extends slightly into Kuwaiti territory from Iraq. In addition, Iraq's proposal included efforts to negotiate an oil agreement with the US 'satisfactory to both countries' national security interests', develop a joint plan to 'alleviate Iraq's economic and financial problems' and 'jointly work on the stability of the Gulf'.[87]

The White House confirmed that Scowcroft had recently met 'a former official of a previous [US] administration' who had 'relayed ideas concerning the Persian Gulf situation'. However, it added, 'there was nothing in this particular proposal that merited its pursuit.'[88] On its part, and as expected, Baghdad declared that the *Newsday* report was 'wishful thinking by the enemies of the Arab nation'.

These developments unfolded in an atmosphere electrified by an unguarded comment by Cheney on 17 August that US troops might still be in the Gulf in 1992, an election year in America. In the first fortnight Bush's principled, bold response and instinctive American patriotism had triumphed. But doubts crept in later, created by the rapid US military build-up in the Gulf, which in turn engendered the unappetizing options of a shooting war or an expensive, debilitating stalemate.

American analysts and opinion-formers divided into doves, hawks and middle-roaders. The hawkish position was articulated by Henry Kissinger, former US secretary of state, in an article in the *Los Angeles Times* of 19 August. By deploying so many troops, and stating categorically that it would accept nothing less than Iraq's complete and unconditional withdrawal from Kuwait, the US had passed 'the point of no return', he argued. So now it was essential either to topple Saddam Hussein or to obliterate his military power. 'If it should be concluded that sanctions are too uncertain and diplomacy unavailing, the US will need to consider a surgical and progressive destruction of Iraq's military assets – especially as an outcome that leaves Saddam Hussein in place and his military machine unimpaired might turn out to be an interlude between aggressions,' he wrote.

Kissinger's stance happened to coincide with that of the Israeli government which – while following Bush's advice to keep a low profile and deny Baghdad ammunition to denounce Washington's build-up as part of a 'Zionist plot' – maintained an active lobby behind the scenes in the US. It aimed to pressure Washington to take 'decisive military action' against Baghdad even at the cost of endangering the lives of Western hostages. 'In a carefully aimed briefing for American journalists last week, Israeli military officials advocated a massive American air strike against Iraqi military targets,' reported Anton La Guardia in the *Daily Telegraph* of 23 August. The Israelis felt that 'any delay in taking action could allow pro-Iraqi unrest [in the Arab world] to undermine moderate Arab countries which support America's stance.' However, public support in the US for such a policy was slim, as the latest opinion poll indicated. It showed 78% opposing a first strike against Iraq, with roughly the same percentage approving Bush's handling of the crisis by sending American forces to the Gulf.[89]

The doves' stance stemmed from a humanitarian instinct against war-making, or healthy scepticism about the doings of politicians in power, or the isolationist streak in America, traditionally associated with conservatism (except when fighting Communism). Rebutting the government's line that the American way of life was at stake, Dr Michael Sandel, political scientist at Harvard University, stated, 'It is not our highest values that are threatened, nor our democratic principles. It is a way of life dependent on cheap oil and profligate energy use.' Galen Carpenter, foreign policy director of the Cato Institute, a right-wing think tank, said, 'The Bush administration never allowed time for [other] interested parties to deal with Iraqi aggression on their own, nor did it give the Arab League time to formulate a solution. As Washington rushed into the conflict it seemed almost grateful for the opportunity to demonstrate America's continuing global leadership in a post-Cold War setting.'[90]

The middle positions were often taken by members of Congress who were anxious to see that they were not deprived by the chief executive of their constitutional authority to declare war, something Presidents Lyndon Johnson (1963–8) and Richard Nixon had done. 'Quite frankly, I never contemplated talk of 250,000 American troops in Saudi Arabia, nor talk of an American presence there for several years,' said Senator Joseph Biden, chairperson of the Senate Judicial Committee. 'This calls for not only some consultation but quite extensive debate with Congress.'[91]

Among America's leading Western allies, Britain followed Washington's lead unquestioningly. Its government was in tune with popular feelings. A Gallup poll published on 12 August showed that 83% backed Prime Minister Thatcher's decision to send troops to prevent an Iraqi invasion of Saudi Arabia (under Operation 'Granby') while 13% disapproved. Sending further troops if necessary was backed by 69%, and opposed by 24%.[92]

The situation was different in France, a close friend of Iraq for nearly twenty years. The government was divided, with the defence minister, Jean-Pierre Chévènement, a founder-member of the Iraq–French Friendship Society, advocating a non-hostile approach to Saddam Hussein – backed by the foreign minister, Roland Dumas, who stressed the importance of an Arab solution to the crisis, and the interior minister, who was concerned about the damaging consequences of a war with Iraq on relations between the white Christian majority in France and the black-and-brown Muslim minority of three million (of North or West African origin). While going along with the official policy of bolstering the French military presence in the Gulf by despatching reconnaissance squadrons to the UAE and air instructors to Saudi Arabia to maintain the Mirage fighters of the Kuwaiti government-in-exile, and ordering the assembling of a fleet of seven warships and an aircraft carrier, Chévènement leaked a statement to Agence France-Presse in which he expressed his fear that the military build-up in the Gulf 'had heightened the risk of a full-blown war by raising the stakes to such an extent that there was no longer time to explore properly other options: economic sanctions and negotiations.' In this he differed with the French president, François Mitterrand. In a nationwide television speech on 21 August, Mitterrand conceded the failure of his hopes that the Arab world could solve its own problems, and referred to the plight of Western hostages in Iraq. He acknowledged that France was now enmeshed 'in a logic of war', and concluded that the problem now was 'how to extricate ourselves from a potential war while ensuring that the fundamental rights laid down in international law are respected.'[93]

The French ground forces' presence in the UAE was complemented by that of the US air force's 50 F-16 warplanes and 16 transport aircraft. The emirates' government tried to enhance its fighting capability by calling on its 15- to 40-year-old male citizens to volunteer for military training.

While Gulf Co-operation Council defence ministers assembled in Jiddah to mobilize the troops of its Peninsula Shield Rapid Deployment Force to its full strength of two brigades, Syria finally confirmed that it was sending 1,200 troops to Saudi Arabia in accordance with the Arab summit resolution of 10 August, and 'to safeguard Muslim shrines in Saudi Arabia'. Endorsing the view that the Gulf should not be left to 'foreign forces', the official spokesman in Damascus said that 'Arab troops could gradually replace these foreign forces', and that by despatching its forces to Saudi Arabia, Syria was making 'a serious attempt to prevent the partition of the Arab nation'. Behind all such statements was the hard, but unpublicized, fact that the Syrian president had been given immediate financial aid worth $500 million by Riyadh, with a promise of a further $500 million, if he sent his forces to the Saudi kingdom.[94]

As the richest country in the region and the one which felt most threatened by Iraq, Saudi Arabia had been generous in its hand-outs to Arab and non-Arab states to secure their military assistance. It estimated the direct and indirect costs of the Iraqi invasion and its aftermath at $11 billion in three months, the direct expenses being its increased military expenditure and the cost of housing and feeding the Kuwaiti refugees, and the indirect ones being 'lost economic opportunities'. However, the Iraqi invasion and the prelude to it had caused oil prices to rise from $16 a barrel to nearly $30 (on 22 August), thus nearly doubling Riyadh's petroleum revenue. On top of that, following the UN sanctions against Iraq and occupied Kuwait – which had been allocated respective OPEC quotas of 2.8 mb/d and 1.5 mb/d during the pre-invasion period – the Saudi kingdom promised to raise its oil output from 5.4 mb/d (its OPEC quota) to make up for the boycotted Iraqi and Kuwaiti supplies. It did so, by 2 mb/d, on 19 August.[95]

The other major country to benefit from the oil price increase was the Soviet Union which, with 12.2 mb/d output, was the world's largest producer. It was estimated that each $1 increase in the price of petroleum earned Moscow an extra $2 billion a year in exports. But this was not enough. Such was the parlous state of the Soviet economy that President Mikhail Gorbachev was prepared to seek, and accept, financial aid from any country – including the Saudi kingdom, one of the most anti-Communist states in the world, and one of the few which did not have diplomatic links with Moscow. Aware of this, and aware of the denunciation of Iraq voiced repeatedly by the Soviet president as well as his foreign minister, Eduard Shevardnadze, the Saudi ambassador to the US, Prince Bandar ibn Sultan, visited Moscow to meet Shevardnadze with the (unpublicized) purpose of providing economic aid to the Kremlin.[96]

In a sense the wheel had turned full circle. Bandar's father-in-law, Prince (later King) Faisal ibn Abdul Aziz, had arrived in Moscow in 1932 seeking financial assistance from the Soviet Union, which had been the first country to recognize the founder of Saudi Arabia, King Abdul Aziz ibn Abdul Rahman ibn Saud, and his domain in 1926, a year before Britain did. In 1931 the Kremlin gave credits to the Saudi monarch to help him overcome the financial crisis he faced due to a sharp fall in the number of Muslim pilgrims to Mecca and Medina caused by the world recession. Seven years later, in the course of widespread purges in the USSR, the Kremlin recalled its (Tartar Muslim) consul to Saudi Arabia, put him on trial, and did not replace him. Thereafter diplomatic ties between the two countries atrophied, with Moscow denouncing Saudi Arabia as a reactionary monarchy and Saudi Arabia condemning the USSR as a militantly atheist state, and financing numerous anti-Communist projects worldwide.[97] A thaw in Moscow–Riyadh relations in the late 1970s turned into a freeze with the Soviet military intervention in Afghanistan. Following the Soviet withdrawal from Afghanistan in early 1989, and the granting of religious freedom in the USSR, the two sides had taken tentative steps to re-establish links. The Kremlin's consistent condemnation of Iraq's aggression against Kuwait pleased Riyadh. This was the backdrop to Prince Bandar's visit to Moscow when it was agreed 'in principle' to restore diplomatic ties.

Ironically, Iraq, the country whose actions had caused a jump in petroleum prices, was unable to gain anything out of the rise. The UN embargo was being stiffly enforced, with an American destroyer in the Red Sea even turning back a Sudanese-flagged Cypriot ferry, loaded with cars for Jordan, as it tried to enter Aqaba. When on 22 August the *Ain Zalah*, an Iraqi tanker, began unloading crude at the Yemeni port of Aden, the Yemeni government came under such pressure from the US that it terminated the operation after five hours.[98]

Bush, assisted by Thatcher, continued his efforts to obtain Security Council approval for the implementation of the anti-Iraq sanctions by military means, if need be. Their success came on 25 August, when the Security Council passed Resolution 665, calling upon 'those Member States co-operating with the Government of Kuwait which

are deploying maritime forces to the area' to use 'such measures commensurate to the specific circumstances as may be necessary under
the authority of the Security Council to halt all inward and outward
maritime shipping in order . . . to ensure strict implementation of the
provisions related to such shipping as laid down in Resolution 661
(1990).' The voting was 13 to none, with Cuba and Yemen abstaining.
This was the first time that the United Nations had authorized the use
of force (implied in the phrase 'such measures commensurate to the
specific circumstances as may be necessary') by its members without
a UN flag or UN command structure to implement it.

Both America and Britain were adamant about keeping their embassies in Kuwait open, defying Baghdad's deadline of 24 August for the
closure of all foreign missions in Kuwait City. To establish that the
situation was returning to normal in the occupied emirate, and that
the Saddam Hussein regime was not prepared to tolerate any breach of
law and order there, it executed 20 people, many of them Iraqi soldiers,
for looting, and hung their bodies in the streets.[99]

All along, Baghdad continued to consolidate its military position in
Kuwait by digging in and increasing the size of its troop deployment,
a process much facilitated by its evacuation of the occupied Iranian
territories by 21 August. Along with this went the policy of placing
Western and Japanese hostages at key military and strategic sites in
Kuwait as well as Iraq.

Iraq's war machine was mainly of Soviet origin, 11 of the 17 Iraqi
air squadrons consisting of Soviet aircraft, and over 4,200 of Iraq's
5,500 tanks being Soviet-made, including 1,072 T-72s. The role of
some 3,000 Soviet military experts maintaining these weapons, and
training the Iraqis, was therefore important, and vexing to the US.
When Washington raised the issue of Soviet military advisers in Iraq,
it got an evasive reply. 'These military personnel are fulfilling their
contractual duties, and they will leave when their contracts expire,
these being of 10 to 365 days' duration,' Colonel Valentin Ogurstov,
a Soviet defence ministry spokesman, said. 'There are misgivings
in the armed forces about Moscow abandoning its long standing
close relationship with Iraq. It is not easy for us to move from
fully-fledged relations to zero.'[100] Alexander Bovin, a leading Soviet
commentator on the Middle East, conceded as much in his column
in *Izvestia* (News) on 23 August: 'The Soviet line on Iraq represented
a difficult U-turn for Moscow,' he wrote. 'While Moscow is relying on
the UN and collective action, Washington banks on its own strength
and independent action.'

While the Bush administration was keen not to break with the Gorbachev government on any aspect of the Gulf crisis – a development bound to be exploited by Baghdad – it retained the independent initiative it had acquired since 2 August, which allowed it the freedom to alter its stance suddenly and radically. For example, once the 24 August deadline approached, the Bush administration decided to turn off the 'war is imminent' tap, and turn on the diplomacy tap. It seized on the forthcoming meeting between the UN secretary-general Pérez de Cuellar, and the Iraqi foreign minister, Tariq Aziz, as a convenient peg to do so. On 24 August, 'non-attributable' briefings were given by the US administration to the American and British press corps in Washington, playing down the threat of hostilities and playing up the chances of a diplomatic solution.[101]

This manoeuvre could be seen as part of the classical psychological warfare meant to be directed as much at the public at home as the adversary abroad. On the domestic front, well-doctored information – or news, in the common parlance – is deployed to arouse the martial spirit of the nation, mobilize public opinion behind the military conflict, suppress or discredit dissent, and prepare citizens for the human and material sacrifices required for victory. On the battle front, censored information – propaganda, in other words – is used to keep the enemy guessing, sap his resolve to fight, and mislead him about both the tactics and strategy to be employed against him. Interestingly, sudden changes of policy and emphasis were adopted by Washington in late autumn and early winter too – when it had the disadvantage of working towards a universally known deadline of 15 January 1991, which robbed it of surprise, an important element in any war, as Saddam Hussein's action in Kuwait amply showed.

However, irrespective of the real motivation behind the U-turn in the Bush administration's policy, it could not escape the fact that it was now engaged in television warfare with its adversary, signalled by Tariq Aziz's long interview with Ted Koppel of ABC-TV on 15 August offering the US open-ended talks on the Gulf crisis – and with CNN virtually replacing diplomatic cables as the immediate means of communications between the two governments. Iraq's information ministry took to contacting CNN two hours before issuing an important statement so that its schedule could be cleared to carry the Iraqi statement live. Equally, the Pentagon let a CNN reporter film the radar and weapons system of an F-15 warplane to warn Iraqis of the devastating potential of the aircraft.

But, in terms of popular impact, all this was small fare compared to the televised visit that Saddam Hussein paid to a group of fifteen British hostages, including children, somewhere in Baghdad on 23 August. The Iraqi television broadcast was picked up by CNN and transmitted worldwide. In his first public appearance since the Gulf crisis began, the Iraqi president wore a business suit and displayed the amiable disposition of a caring father. 'Your presence here and in other places is meant to prevent the scourge of war, to avoid war,' he explained to the group of British men, women and children. 'What would make us happy would be to see you back in your countries or roaming the streets of Baghdad in the normal way.' A young British man remarked that the last Iraqi initiative was 'quite reasonable', and asked, 'Will there be another?' Saddam Hussein replied, 'There is always something new. Initiatives can be developed.' He added, 'We have threatened none of them [America and Britain] . . . [Yet] in the past few days I have come across articles published in Western papers . . . [urging] President Bush to strike at Iraq and actually use force against Iraq despite the fact of your presence here.'

However, the centrepiece of his meeting was his behaviour towards the children. Fondling them, he asked if they were getting milk and playing football with Iraqis. When a British woman said she was worried about her child's education, he promised to send 'experts from the ministry of education'. Ruffling the hair of Stuart Lockwood, a seven-year-old boy wearing blue shorts, Saddam Hussein said, 'When he and his friends, and all those present here, have played their role in preventing war, then you will all be heroes of peace.'[102]

At one level this was grotesque exploitation of hostage children, which deserved to be denounced as 'shameful theatricals' (as it was by the US state department) or 'a repulsive charade' (as it was by the British foreign office); at another it was a masterpiece of public relations meant to reassure the world that Iraq's 'foreign guests' were safe and well, and that the Iraqi president cared for them personally.

What was not realized by most specialists and the general public abroad was that Saddam Hussein had perfected the art of public relations during the eight-year First Gulf War. For example, he made a point of personally awarding cars, television sets or land to the families of soldiers killed in the conflict, and acting as the caring father figure, offering solace to the bereaved; appearing in the Kurdish region of Iraq in Kurdish dress; praying at the holy shrines of Shias in the Shia-dominated cities; and so on.

Now, Saddam Hussein's televised meeting with British hostages was first league stuff, with the daily propaganda warfare conducted by both sides over the ether acting as background. Baghdad set up radio stations directed at specific audiences: the Voice of Egypt of Arabism for Egyptian listeners; the Holy Mecca Radio for Saudi audiences; and Voice of Peace (Sout al Salam), in English, targeting the American troops in the region. 'Your wife is waiting for you,' was the usual refrain of the broadcaster addressing US forces in English. 'Remember what the gasoline emirs are doing with the American girls.' Holy Mecca Radio played a different tune. 'This is Holy Mecca,' it would begin. 'Have pity on the holy land of Islam which has been defiled by the American infidel.' This touched a sensitive nerve since Muslim opinion varied from wary to hostile towards the Christian military presence in Saudi Arabia, with many religious scholars citing the Prophet Muhammad's decree banning Christian and Jewish tribes from the holy land, and arguing that all of Saudi Arabia constituted the Muslim holy land. The radio station of the Kuwaiti government-in-exile (now based in Taif, Saudi Arabia) would retort with descriptions of the events of the seventh century when Muslim refugees from the oppression of Arab infidels sought the help of the Negus in Ethiopia, a 'just' Christian king. They did so because Prophet Muhammad had told them to.[103]

On the diplomatic front Baghdad was intent on securing the departure of all foreign missions from Kuwait City as an essential step towards consolidating its hold over Kuwait as the nineteenth province of Iraq.

4 DIPLOMACY, HOSTAGES AND MILITARY BUILD-UPS

'To let the world know everything about the whole situation, let us have a debate between me and them [Mr Bush and Mrs Thatcher] on television for the whole world to see.'

Saddam Hussein addressing a group of European and Japanese hostages, on 28 August 1990[1]

'Let Saddam Hussein comply with the UN resolutions, and then we will talk.'

Marlin Fitzwater, White House spokesman[2]

'There are only two groups that are beating the drums of war in the Middle East: the Israeli defence ministry and its amen corner in the US.'

Patrick Buchanan, an American columnist[3]

'Saddam Hussein tells you that this is a struggle between Iraq and America. In fact, it is Iraq against the world.'

President George Bush addressing the Iraqi people in a television speech, on 16 September 1990[4]

'We are ready for dialogue with the US. Iraq will be prepared to guarantee America's strategic interests in the Middle East.'

Taha Yassin Ramadan, vice-president of the Iraqi RCC, 22 September 1990[5]

By the time 24 August, the Iraqi deadline for the closure of foreign missions in Kuwait, arrived, the crisis had shaped up as a confrontation between Iraq and America, with each side acting as a mirror image of the other, alternating threats with gestures of conciliation, going feverishly ahead with the military build-up while not discouraging intermediaries from devising peace plans.

Baghdad knew that the US did not have enough forces on the ground to initiate a land war to retake Kuwait. However, the fear of US air strikes on Iraqi targets in mid-August was real, with Pentagon briefings, uncritically disseminated by the Western media, painting scenarios that varied between a four-hour air war which would cut off the Iraqi military high command from its armed forces and an aerial bombardment of several days' duration to annihilate Iraq's military and economic targets. Along with this went an aggressive verbal style, well illustrated by the statements made at the first press conference given by General Norman Schwarzkopf – 6 foot 3 inches tall, weighing 252 pounds – in Riyadh. 'I think the Iraqis are a lousy bunch of thugs,' he said. 'I hope they're hungry. I hope they're thirsty. I hope they're running out of ammo [ammunition].'[6]

Baghdad was careful not to give any excuse to Washington to resort to military action. But, increasingly aware that more needed to be done to discourage US 'surgical strikes' against Iraq, it resorted to taking Western and Japanese hostages and dispersing them to strategic sites, starting with 35 Americans on the night of 17–18 August.[7]

In the Arab world there were many supporters of Saddam's move, who were ready to rationalize it. 'First, it frustrates [the West's] superior power to dictate what should be the object of rational negotiations,' said a Palestinian intellectual and film-maker. 'Second, it tries to move the common people in the West into thinking, and applying pressure on their politicians . . . Finally, the move gives time to everybody to re-think the whole thing again.' However, in this case 'everybody' meant, primarily, Arabs and Westerners: peoples whose perceptions of the crisis varied widely. 'The West is treating this as a war game, with [its] newspapers printing maps bristling with tanks and aircraft symbols and likely missile targets,' a Jordanian businesswoman in Amman said. 'The most the West was worried about was the price of petrol and the collapse of stock markets. Your children are not going to be bombed so you cannot feel as we feel. The only thing stopping the West from looking at everything as a disposable item on the war board was the presence of so many Westerners in Iraq [and Kuwait].'[8]

On the other hand, even setting aside the immorality and illegality of taking civilians as hostages, this move hurt Iraq's national interest. It provided a strong cement to hold together the anti-Iraq coalition at the United Nations, and steeled its resolve to isolate Iraq diplomatically and economically. Aware of this, the Iraqi leader seemingly decided to use the hostage card to reduce his country's diplomatic isolation and, in the process, to project himself as a discriminating as well as caring politician. He classified the hostages according to the policies followed by their countries. First of all came those governments which had not participated in the military build-up against Iraq. For example, when the president of Austria, Kurt Waldheim (1986–), arrived in Baghdad on 25 August he was welcomed enthusiastically, and his request for the release of 80 Austrians was granted promptly. But the criterion of non-combativeness towards Iraq applied only to four other countries – Finland, Portugal, Sweden and Switzerland – with an aggregate of 490 hostages,[9] a small proportion of the total.

It was only after Saddam Hussein had, on 28 August, extended the exemption to all women and children among the Western and Japanese hostages, totalling over 3,000, that the malign consequences of Iraq's action were considerably reduced. Characteristically, the Iraqi president reached this decision during or shortly after his meeting that morning with the second group of hostages, Western and Japanese, an encounter that was once again televised. One Englishwoman was shown asking Saddam Hussein, 'How can you use children as pawns in something they don't understand?' And Kevin Bazner, a 35-year-old American, remarked, 'It would be a gesture of sincerity to release all women and children.' Saddam Hussein replied, 'No one should cause harm to anyone unless . . . there is no other alternative.' Later that day, after consulting the National Assembly speaker and other members of the Revolutionary Command Council, he ordered that all foreign women and children would be free to 'stay or leave'.[10]

Most observers noticed that the Iraqi president offered this concession to the West and Japan on the eve of the meeting of his foreign minister, Tariq Aziz, with UN secretary-general Pérez de Cuellar in Amman.

As for Washington, the state department's statement welcoming Saddam Hussein's move as 'a significant step in the right direction' was coupled with President Bush's preference for a peaceful solution to a swift military strike against Iraq, stated in an address to 150 Congressmen. This tied in neatly with the briefing Scowcroft gave to the *Washington Post* in which he stated that though President Bush had repeatedly equated the Iraqi leader with Adolf Hitler, America was 'willing to accept a diplomatic solution to the crisis, but only after Saddam withdraws from Kuwait and allows the Kuwaiti government to return to power'. If at that point Saddam needed 'some face-saving device, the United States would be prepared to see that occur'.[11]

However, this conciliatory gesture did not stop the Bush administration from making it clear to Pérez de Cuellar in private that his brief was to reiterate the Security Council resolutions and the need for compliance with them, *not* to enter into negotiations with Tariq Aziz on their implementation. (In the event, nothing came of these talks.)

This schizoid stance by Washington could be seen either as part of a shrewd psychological warfare against the Iraqi leader or a genuine reflection of the divided counsel President Bush was receiving from his four close advisers, or as a combination of both.

Baker was against the US nailing its colours too high on the mast, and advised that the administration should avoid for as long as possible being pushed into the corner of military action. A pragmatic man, he preferred compromise to confrontation. He was backed by Brent Scowcroft, who argued that the Gulf crisis should be seen through a long and wide lens and who, in the process, emerged as a theoretician of the 'new world order'. A retired air force general, Scowcroft, a 64-year-old Mormon, was a strategic thinker and foreign policy professional.

At the other end of the spectrum was Dick Cheney, 48, a former Congressman from Wyoming and chief of staff under President Gerald Ford, who had displayed a cool, intelligent manner during the initial days of the crisis but who had by now virtually concluded that the Iraqis would have to be forcibly expelled from Kuwait and that military means needed to be seriously considered.

In between was Colin Powell, at 53 the youngest chairman of the Joint Chiefs of Staff in American history. He had come a long way from his upbringing in a poor Jamaican immigrant family in the Bronx, New York. During the Reagan years, having served the defence secretary, Caspar Weinberger, as a military assistant, he had moved up to serve as deputy to the national security adviser, Frank Carlucci, and then, following the Irangate scandal in November 1986, had himself become national security adviser. By then he had established himself as the best trouble-shooter in Washington, and as someone well-informed in international and defence affairs. He was a man of strong views, who knew how to promote them. But, unlike Baker, a wheeler-dealer, with whom he shared a propensity for compromise, he was at heart a military man: ready to fall in line with what the commander-in-chief, the US president, wanted. In the current crisis, he believed that time must be given for a political solution, but not too much time. Once he found Bush intent on getting the Iraqis out of Kuwait, he advised that (a) Saddam Hussein must be made to realize that he was risking an all-out war with the US which he was bound to lose, and (b) sufficient force must be despatched to the region, with Plan 90–1002 assuring America of full control of the air and sea, and the ground troops to include heavy armour to make the combined force credible as both deterrent and fighting machine. Aware of the failure of the US strategy of incremental rise in its military capability in Vietnam, he was a strong advocate of putting the maximum force upfront with a view to taking the combat into Iraq, and not fighting a limited war and then seeking negotiations.

Baker and Scowcroft argued that if the Iraqi president evacuated Kuwait and released the hostages, then not going along with the offer he had made through back-channels would seem 'unreasonable'. Cheney advocated a hard line, arguing that allowing Saddam Hussein to stay in power in Iraq would be potentially dangerous to the region as well as to the Bush presidency. A cautious man, General Powell was reluctant to advise war without the support of the US Congress and public, something unlikely to happen if Saddam Hussein withdrew.

A similar split existed in Baghdad. When asked by an Austrian journalist on 25 August 1990 whether he had a message for the American people, Saddam Hussein replied: 'I have sent a letter to Bush and a letter to the Americans ... We are [merely] defending ourselves. He who wants to live and not die should seek peace. What I want to say, and this is not a threat but ... a fact, that whoever attacks Iraq will find in front of him columns of dead bodies which have a beginning but may not have an end ... So US officials should seek political solutions to world problems and should forget that they can get anything they want.'[12]

That day, echoing the stance of his president, Iraq's information minister, Latif Jasim, warned that his country would retaliate with force if any of its ships were sunk or damaged by the naval vessels currently enforcing a tighter blockade against it. 'We will sink one of their ships – maybe two – and if they attack us we will attack them.'[13] Yet two days later US intelligence reports indicated that Baghdad had reversed its policy and ordered its merchant shipping crews not to resist attempts by foreign naval forces to inspect their vessels.

Behind this cat-and-mouse game, both sides continued to build up their military forces, with Iraq concentrating on turning Kuwait into a fortress and the Americans reinforcing their presence in the Saudi kingdom. The Iraqi army strength in Kuwait, according to the Pentagon, stood at 190,000, with its military hardware amounting to 1,000 tanks, 1,200 armoured vehicles and 800 artillery pieces. The troops of the anti-Iraq coalition totalled 130,000, including 40,000 Americans. The Arab segment of it included 9,000 soldiers of the

GCC Rapid Deployment Force, the contingents of 2,000 and 1,200 special forces commandos from Egypt and Syria respectively, and 1,200 Moroccans from a motorized brigade assigned to guard a refinery in Saudi Arabia.[14]

By late August there were foreign forces in all of the Gulf monarchies, the latest one to invite them being Qatar (preparing to welcome troops from America, Britain and Egypt), following the examples of Saudi Arabia and the UAE (already host to armed forces from the US, Egypt and Pakistan). Bahrain had, after its independence in 1971, signed an agreement with Washington to provide it with naval facilities, allowing it to base the US Middle East Force there. Oman, a protectorate of Britain from 1871 to 1971, had been giving air and naval facilities to the US military on its offshore island of Masirah since 1977.[15]

GCC states were being courted by Iran, with its foreign minister visiting their capitals (except Riyadh, with which Tehran had no diplomatic ties) and reminding the rulers that his country had all along warned them of Baghdad's aggressive intentions. 'Iraq must definitely pull out of Kuwait,' said President Rafsanjani in his Friday sermon on 24 August. 'Its move cannot be tolerated under any circumstances.' He acknowledged that the Iraqis had made peace with Iran. 'But that is a separate issue,' he said. 'Iraq must evacuate [Kuwait].' A deplorable result of the Iraqi aggression was that it had drawn foreign forces into the region. 'One possibility is that they [alien forces] would put a stop to aggression, which we do not mind,' he continued. 'We warn that once the calamity is over . . . then these forces . . . [should] return to their own homes.' Following the foreign policy guidelines laid out by Ayatollah Khomeini, the founder of the Islamic republic, Rafsanjani stated that 'We would have preferred regional countries, including the pro-Western ones, to deal with the crisis themselves.'[16]

So far as the human dimension of the Gulf crisis was concerned, the pro-Western regimes in the region were handling it well. They played host to the Kuwaiti nationals who fled from the emirate in their thousands (with the non-Kuwaitis escaping through Jordan). Saudi Arabia became the most favoured refuge for the Kuwaitis, followed by Bahrain and the UAE, where in late August 1,500 Kuwaiti exiles were arriving daily. Not surprisingly, anti-Baghdad feeling was rife in the UAE, particularly in Abu Dhabi and Dubai, which witnessed two anti-Iraq demonstrations, the second attended by 10,000 people.[17]

On the other hand there were frequent, and massive, demonstrations in favour of Iraq and Saddam Hussein not only in the West Bank, Gaza and Jordan but also in Yemen, Sudan, and the countries of the Maghreb – Algeria, Libya, Mauritania, Morocco and Tunisia. One sign of the times was that in the Old City of East Jerusalem cassettes of Iraqi ballads had replaced the strident songs of the intifada as the favourite music of the Palestinians. The official stance of the PLO was more restrained. In a communiqué of 19 August it came out in favour of a solution to the crisis which would guarantee the territorial integrity of Iraq, Kuwait and Saudi Arabia – followed by a statement by a member of the PLO Executive Committee and the chairperson of the Palestine National Fund, Juwaid Ghusain, that Iraq's occupation of Kuwait was 'illegal'.[18]

Once American troops had begun arriving in Saudi Arabia, the Arab countries had divided on the simple question of the presence of non-Arab forces in the Saudi kingdom. After meeting the Iraqi president in Baghdad on 28 August, Yasser Arafat expressed the need to 'fight the American and foreign presence in the region'. Libya's leader, Colonel Muammar Qadhafi, an Arab nationalist, was opposed to this military intrusion of the US into the Arab world. So too was President Zine al Abidine ben Ali of Tunisia, who had until recently been a favourite of Washington. Responding to the Islamic fundamentalist pressures at home, he had decided to change the overall direction of Tunisia's policies away from economic affairs and the US to political matters and Europe and the Arab world. The regime of Colonel Maayouya Ould Sidi Ahmad Taya in Mauritania had been friendly with Baghdad and its ruling Baath Party for several years, and had reportedly allowed the use of its territory for the testing of Iraqi intermediate and long-range missiles. In Algeria the government condemned the Iraqi invasion of Kuwait while deploring the presence of alien forces in Saudi Arabia and the UN sanctions against Iraq. It was aware of the popularity of the Iraqi leader among ordinary citizens, and of the strength of the Islamic fundamentalists in Algeria, who as elsewhere in the Arab and Muslim world were backing Saddam Hussein. The military junta in Sudan, led by General Omar al Bashir, being of Islamic fundamentalist hue, was sympathetic towards Baghdad. In both parts of the recently unified Yemen, north and south, the bias was also in favour of Saddam Hussein. Iraq had provided military officers and training to North Yemen for many years. And the Marxist state of South Yemen had been staunchly anti-American. Unsurprisingly, an official radio broadcast in Yemen stated that 'the main threat to the region is the build-up of US and Nato forces, and the escalation of psychological and propaganda warfare against Iraq and the Arab nation with the objective of pushing our region to the brink of military confrontation.'[19]

However, the situation in the two states which counted most, Egypt and Syria, was mixed. There were persistent reports that Saddam Hussein's daring and continued defiance of America had aroused admiration for him among ordinary Syrians, but living as they were in a police state – and conscious of the implacable hostility of their president, Assad, towards the Iraqi leader – they dared not show their pro-Saddam feelings. When they did, as happened in a few East Syrian towns bordering Iraq on 26 August, and later in and around Damascus, they were shot down in their dozens by the security forces.[20] As someone who ran a similar type of repressive regime himself, Saddam Hussein seemingly gave up hopes of being lauded as an Arab hero in the streets of Damascus or any other Syrian city.

In Egypt, however, the Iraqi leader felt he had a chance. During the 1980s, relations between Baghdad and Cairo had improved from cordial to intimate, with hundreds of Egyptian military advisers and experts and thousands of Egyptians serving in the Iraqi armed forces, and the Iraqi government lavishing expensive gifts, including prestigious Mercedes-Benz cars, on Egyptian ministers and newspaper editors to build up goodwill. Now Saddam Hussein tried to stoke up support through the Voice of Egypt of Arabism. 'The oil of the Arabs is for the Arabs,' he said in a speech directed mainly at the impoverished people of Egypt, a country of 54 million. He contrasted the lack of opportunities for Egyptians with the luxurious life of the Gulf royal families. The al Sabah family had a fortune of $60,000 million, he said, and King Fahd of Saudi Arabia had personal assets of $18,000 million. Even giving a fraction of the oil income of the Gulf monarchies to Egypt could release it from its dependence on American aid of a little over $2,100 million a year. But while Egyptians shared with other poor Arabs a loathing for the al Sabahs and other oil oligarchs, the experiences of over one million of their compatriots working in Iraq during and after the First Gulf War had been far from happy.[21] More importantly, Egyptian media reports of the appalling state of tens of thousands of Egyptians fleeing Kuwait and Iraq through Jordan in the wake of the Iraqi invasion, severely damaged the prospect of a pro-Saddam Hussein upsurge in Cairo or anywhere else in Egypt.

Meanwhile, the Arab leaders close to the Iraqi president, particularly King Hussein and Yasser Arafat, redoubled their efforts to devise a peace formula acceptable to all. On 28 August King Hussein unveiled his peace plan, which had Arafat's backing: (1) a simultaneous withdrawal of Iraqi troops from Kuwait and foreign troops from Saudi Arabia, with Iraqi troops in Kuwait replaced by an Arab peacekeeping force; (2) a referendum/election in Kuwait within six months of Iraq's withdrawal to choose a new government and a new parliament, with the new administration signing an agreement giving Iraq certain rights over Kuwait which would otherwise be autonomous – followed by a regional non-aggression pact.[22] 'The idea was to turn Kuwait into another Monaco, a constitutional monarchy that would sign an agreement with Iraq, giving it control over certain administrative aspects, on the understanding that the emirate, mirroring the relationship between Monte Carlo and France, would have self-rule,' explained the London-based pro-PLO *Al Quds al Arabi* (The Holy Jerusalem). Iraq, which on 19 August had formed a committee to study the possibility of turning Kuwait into a 'free zone', accepted the plan. But the London-based *Al Sharq al Awsat* (The Middle East), owned by the Saudi royal family, attacked it, saying that it was 'no more than a carefully worked-out manoeuvre to buy time for Iraq', and that it would result in a semi-autonomous Kuwait under the tutelage of Baghdad.[23]

None of this interfered with Iraq's efforts to consolidate its hold over Kuwait. On the day King Hussein announced his peace plan, the Iraqi government paper, *Al Jumhuriya*, stated that Iraq's territory would be extended southwards to include a Kuwaiti frontier post, that this strip of territory would be renamed Saddamiyat al Mitla, and that the rest of Kuwait would be known as the nineteenth province of Iraq. The official map released next day incorporated these changes, with Kuwait City renamed Kadhima, its name in the Ottoman era.

By then, confident that the US would not be in a position to mount a sustained attack on Iraq for about three months,[24] Saddam Hussein and his aides concluded that the longer their country stood alone facing the US-led forces gathered in northern Saudi Arabia the greater would be its chance of emerging as the shining symbol, as well as substance, of Arab independence, and the popularly acclaimed leader of the Arab world.

President Saddam Hussein articulated his strategy in an interview with French television. He argued that Western victory in the Gulf would require not only defeating Iraq's military and destroying its economy, but also overthrowing his regime: a monumental task. He would 'win' just by hanging on, he maintained. Time was on his side, and ultimately the Americans would have to withdraw, 'humiliated', he concluded.[25] His unexpressed estimation was that with time the

US-led coalition would fall apart, providing him with the chance to compromise by accepting an 'Arab solution', the sort he had offered to the US through back-channels.

Meanwhile, he and his government tried to use US television networks to get their message across directly to the American people. His hour-long interview with Dan Rather of CBS-TV on 29 August, conducted like a summit between two leaders, was a propitious start for him. 'Every signal he sent out, including his body language, said that he is not feeling cornered, and indeed he thinks George Bush is the one cornered,' Rather said. 'He's not a person I'd want to fight.'[26]

None the less, there was a strong case to be made that the Iraqi leader's strategy was flawed. He had made a series of miscalculations. He had clearly underestimated the reaction of the world community, especially the Western powers, to his invasion of Kuwait. This was pointed out by no less a regional leader than President Rafsanjani, who referred to the time during 'the last stages of the [Iran–Iraq] war' when Iran began harassing Kuwaiti ships. 'No sooner had we turned against Kuwait than the Americans, the English and all other satanic forces arrived in the region and stood against us,' he said in his sermon on 24 August. 'The same number of ships and navies came [as now]; and they even entered into war with us . . . It could have been foreseen [by Saddam Hussein] that any aggression against Kuwait would bring about a similar development.'[27]

Saddam Hussein's second major miscalculation was that he failed to see that with the termination of the Cold War in favour of the US, Moscow would not veto any anti-Iraq resolutions at the UN Security Council. His thinking had not caught up with the contemporary political situation.

Within weeks Saddam Hussein's disappointment with Moscow had reached such a level that on 25 August Baghdad Radio announced that the previous day President Gorbachev had sent him a message at 5.30 p.m. 'calling for the adoption of measures of a radical nature', and asking for a reply the same day by 7.00 p.m., failing which the USSR would be 'compelled' to vote for the US draft resolution presented to the Security Council concerning the embargo against Iraq. (Later it transpired that what was described by Baghdad Radio as Gorbachev's call for 'the adoption of measures of a radical nature' was indeed a warning by him to Saddam Hussein that if Iraq failed to evacuate Kuwait it would face more rigorous enforcement of economic sanctions, and asking him pointedly whether he proposed to withdraw or not.) Baghdad replied that the short time given to respond showed that the letter was just an excuse for Soviet inaction on the Security Council resolution. The exchange of letters between the two presidents had begun soon after the Iraqi invasion, with Saddam Hussein rebuffing Mikhail Gorbachev's calls for the evacuation of Kuwait, rationalizing the Iraqi action in Cold War language by condemning Kuwait's royal rulers as 'greedy capitalists'. Sadoun Hamadi visited Moscow on 20 August, but failed to bring about a change in Soviet policy. Now, Gorbachev was under mounting pressure by President Bush to back the US-drafted resolution, allowing 'minimum force' to enforce sanctions against Iraq, that was to be presented to the Security Council.

On Moscow's insistence the words 'use minimum force' were replaced by 'use such measures commensurate to the specific circumstances as may be necessary' in the American draft at the Security Council. After it was adopted as Resolution 665 on 25 August, the Soviet Union announced that its navy would *not* enforce the UN blockade against Iraq.[28]

In a way this was a reflection of the division between the defence and foreign ministries in the Kremlin, the former advocating a tilt towards Iraq, and the latter total alignment with Washington, with the Soviet foreign minister, Eduard Shevardnadze, summarizing his ministry's policy thus: 'Unless we find a way to respond to it [the Iraqi invasion of Kuwait] and cope with the situation, our civilization will be thrown back half a century.'[29]

Soviet defence officials were apprehensive of America's intentions in the Gulf, and said as much publicly. 'The US has been trying to acquire bases in Saudi Arabia for 40 years without success,' wrote *Krasnaya Zvezda* (Red Star), the Soviet army paper, on 31 August. 'Iraq's aggression has given it these bases almost automatically.' The matter was raised a week earlier by senior Soviet officials with Prince Bandar ibn Sultan during his visit to Moscow to convey a message to Gorbachev from King Fahd. Tass, the Soviet news agency, quoted Prince Bandar as saying that the troops of America and other countries would leave 'either in the event of their mission having been fulfilled, or if we ask them to leave'. But this statement was considered inadequate by the military high command, which persisted in highlighting the scale of the problem. In an interview with Tass, General Vladimir Lobov, the chief of staff of the Warsaw Pact, said that, since the presence of US troops in Saudi Arabia 'extends Nato's borders into the Middle East', it 'drastically changes the strategic balance in the region'. As Iraq is only 200 miles from the borders of Georgia, Armenia and Soviet Azerbaijan, the new development gave America 'a unique opportunity to exert pressure on events in the [Soviet] region'.[30] Later he told a Supreme Soviet committee that the shift in US forces could complicate talks in Vienna with America on reduction in conventional weapons.

Overall, senior defence officials in Moscow were unhappy with Gorbachev's apparent lack of resistance to Washington's designs to dominate the Gulf in the aftermath of inflicting a military defeat on Iraq, a long-time Soviet ally now virtually abandoned by the Kremlin. They were equally upset by America's attempts to create ill-will between Baghdad and Moscow by circulating baseless stories, mainly through the CIA, such as that the Soviet defence ministry was supplying secret information about Iraq's armed forces to the Pentagon.

Besides the military establishment in Moscow many Soviet opinion-formers cautioned against using force to settle the Gulf issue. 'All states involved should display caution, circumspection, and self-control,' said *Pravda* (Truth), the Communist Party daily, in its editorial of 2 September. It pointed out that the UN Security Council had condemned Iraq five times in August. 'But the only acceptable response is collective effort and the use of political means,' it continued. 'A military solution would entail huge human and material losses, and a sharp deterioration in the international situation. Not only would people and oil refineries fall victim but also something ephemeral at first glance but in reality very important – the emerging process of East–West relations, international life as a whole, and the process of détente.'

Many Soviet analysts described the Gulf crisis as 'the first potential North–South military confrontation', in which they did not want their country to take sides. Then there was the fear of a revival of the arms race between the superpowers. 'The war in the Gulf will whet the appetite again of the American military–industrial complex and start an arms race just when we thought it was dying down,' remarked a member of a Soviet think-tank on foreign affairs.[31]

While applauding the end of the Cold War, the Kremlin did not wish to take the new Soviet–American co-operation to the extent of appearing to have become a supporter of US military intervention in the Third World, let alone an ally in such an operation.

President Gorbachev combined his private warnings to President Bush that massive US military action against Iraq would 'dwarf the Iraqi aggression against Kuwait' with a public appeal to Washington 'to prevent escalation [in the Gulf], and be calm and consistent', and urged a political settlement, suggesting that the key to solving the crisis was through 'the Arab factor'.[32]

'The Arab factor' came to the fore in the form of a seven-point peace plan, for implementation under joint UN–Arab League supervision, unveiled by Libya on 1 September after consultations with Iraq, Jordan and Sudan: (1) Iraqi troops should withdraw from Kuwait and be replaced by UN forces; (2) US and other international forces should pull out of Saudi Arabia and be replaced by Arab and Muslim troops; (3) the UN embargo against Iraq should be lifted; (4) the disputed part of the Rumeila oilfield as well as Bubiyan and Warba Islands should be ceded to Iraq; (5) as for restoring the al Sabah dynasty, the views of the Kuwaiti people should be respected, and they should be allowed to decide 'their own system'; (6) the issues of debt and compensation between Iraq and Kuwait should be settled through negotiations; and (7) to ensure that there was no transgression of OPEC quotas in the future, there should be a 'unified Arab oil policy' to be implemented 'forcibly'.[33]

Libya had offered this plan after voting against each of the five anti-Iraq resolutions debated at the meeting of the Arab League foreign ministers in Cairo on 30–31 August: (1) support for the UN secretary-general in the implementation of Security Council Resolutions 660, 661, 662, 664 and 665; (2) as the occupying power Iraq must protect civilians and their properties in accordance with the Islamic law and the Fourth Geneva Convention of 1949; (3) Iraq must refrain from hindering the legitimate right of foreign nationals in Kuwait and Iraq to depart any time they wanted; (4) Iraq's decision to close down the diplomatic missions in Kuwait was null and void; and (5) regarding compensation to Kuwait for the damage resulting from the Iraqi invasion, the Kuwaiti delegation offered a review of the huge material losses caused by Iraq's actions. The twelve members voting for the resolutions were the same as at the 10 August summit (see p. 128). But unlike on that occasion, the pro-Iraqi as well as neutral members (with the exception of Libya) stayed away.[34]

The Libyan plan proved abortive. Saudi Arabia and Kuwait turned it down, with the Kuwaiti Crown Prince Saad al Sabah specifically rejecting the idea of a plebiscite in Kuwait to decide the type of government.[35]

Similarly, the talks between Pérez de Cuellar and Tariq Aziz in Amman on 31 August and 1 September proved 'inconclusive'. Pérez de Cuellar said that Aziz had promised that Iraq would not initiate military action. 'I feel he [Pérez de Cuellar] came to Amman in a straitjacket,' said Tariq Aziz. 'The margin of manoeuvre on his side was very limited. He is a servant of the Security Council where the powerful have the clout.'[36] Moreover, in this case, the initial, seminal resolution, 660, made no specific mention of the secretary-general. This was in striking contrast to Security Council Resolution 598 of 20 July 1987, which dealt with a ceasefire in the Iran–Iraq War. Five of its ten clauses requested the secretary-general to implement the specific provisions of the resolution and 'keep the Security Council informed' on the implementation of the resolution.[37] It is possible that in this case the Security Council's permanent members ignored the secretary-general's role because he was away on a tour of Latin America when the Gulf crisis erupted, and they drafted the resolution in a hurry.

The two Security Council resolutions which needed to be implemented on an ongoing basis concerned the economic embargo against Iraq. While a pro-Iraqi state like Libya offered to load any Iraqi ship docking in Libyan waters with free food and fuel, the American, British and French warships kept up their vigilance against vessels travelling to or from Iraq. On average the US navy questioned through radio contact 50 ships a day in the Red Sea, Arabian Sea and Gulf of Oman, and boarded two for inspection – mainly in the Red Sea. On 30 August American warships searched the Sri Lankan *Kota Wirama* and barred it from entering Aqaba on the grounds that it was carrying chemicals intended for Iraq. Five days later a party from USS *Goldsborough* boarded the Iraqi freighter *Zanubia*, in the Gulf of Oman, found it carrying tea from Sri Lanka to Basra, and prevented it from delivering its cargo by escorting it to Muscat, Oman.[38]

By all accounts the economic blockade of Iraq was almost 100 per cent effective, imposing a loss on Iraq of $80 million daily in lost oil revenue alone and another $54 million to occupied Kuwait.

It was also damaging the economies of Turkey, Jordan and Egypt. But they were being compensated by grants and cancellations of loans not only by the oil-rich states of Saudi Arabia, Kuwait and the UAE but also America, West Germany and Japan. Conscious of the fact that UN trade sanctions against Iraq would cost Egypt $2 billion annually, President Bush decided to ask Congress to cancel the $7.1 billion military debt that Cairo had built up since the US-brokered Camp David Accords of September 1978. Saudi Arabia and the UAE agreed to compensate Turkey for its loss of revenue due to the closure of the Iraqi oil pipeline by supplying it with 3 million tons of oil, with the exiled ruler of Kuwait offering an initial grant of $300 million.[39]

On 30 August 1990 the *Washington Post* reported that the Bush administration had put together an 'Economic Action Plan' to defray the cost of the deployment of US forces in the Gulf and aid the states hurt by trade sanctions. Of the $23 billion (later raised to $25 bn) to be collected from wealthy countries over the next year, half would go to funding Operation 'Desert Shield', now costing $46 million a day, and the remainder to such regional states as Turkey, Egypt and Jordan. Saudi Arabia would pay $4 billion immediately and another $500 million a month to cover food, water, and transportation and other costs for the foreign troops on its soil; Kuwait $3 billion immediately (raised to $5 billion a week later, with half for 'Desert Shield' and the other half to the countries sending troops to Saudi Arabia or suffering from the UN embargo) and $400 million every month; and the UAE coupling an immediate payment of $1 billion with a promise of $100 million a month to follow – giving a total from the three Gulf states of $8 billion immediately and $1 billion each month. Japan and West Germany would offer, respectively, $1.3 billion and $600 million immediately and $60 million and $40 million monthly.[40]

While Kuwait's ruler could meet this commitment out of the income from his $160 billion foreign investment, the governments of Saudi Arabia and the UAE could easily afford their contribution out of the increased revenue from oil created by the rise in both output and price. At $28 a barrel petroleum was now selling at twice the rate prevailing three months earlier. The OPEC meeting of 29 August decided by ten votes to three (Iran, Iraq and Libya) to free its members from following the production quotas. The next day Saudi Arabia announced an increase in its output of 2 mb/d (to 7.5 mb/d), the UAE and Venezuela by 500,000 b/d each, and Indonesia by 250,000 b/d.

The oil-rich Gulf states' funding of the military build-up by the anti-Iraq coalition worried the Iraqi president, and he said as much to his friends, including Abu Iyyad, the second-in-command at the PLO. Following this, in an interview with the Paris-based *Libération* on 4 September, Abu Iyyad outlined Saddam Hussein's position. He would welcome negotiations with the West provided he received guarantees about protection from attack on Iraq or from air strikes against Iraq's chemical weapons plants or nuclear laboratories by the American forces in the Gulf. 'The Iraqi leader is not convinced that, even if he withdraws [from Kuwait], and releases the Western hostages, he will escape a devastating attack by the rapidly increasing American military machine in the region,' Abu Iyyad said. He added that Saddam Hussein would be willing to give up Kuwait in return for its oil-rich border strip and Bubiyan Island, and an assurance that Shaikh Jaber al

Sabah would not be restored to power. 'This is a new Iraqi position,' Abu Iyyad concluded. By all accounts it was an authoritative leak of what the Iraqi president had offered his American counterpart through unofficial channels. But it had no chance of being accepted by the US as it would have left Saddam Hussein with at least some of the spoils of his aggression. (This position was stretched to such an extent that, replying to those Americans who argued that Washington's case against Saddam Hussein would be stronger if the US sought the election of a democratic government in Kuwait, Baker stated that 'dictators like Saddam Hussein' might get the idea that 'they can bring about change in another country by using military force'.)[41] In public, however, the White House repeated what it had said before: 'Saddam Hussein must withdraw from Kuwait unconditionally, and then we will talk to him.' As the weeks and months unrolled this refrain was to repeat itself with little, if any, variation: a press leak of a deal offered by Baghdad to Washington, reiteration by Iraqi officials that Kuwait was an eternal part of Iraq, and a statement by the White House that the pre-condition for any US–Iraq talks was the unconditional evacuation of Kuwait by Iraq's forces.

In the absence of any progress on his wish to conduct direct talks with the US, Saddam Hussein stuck to his strategy of bolstering the Iraqi military in Kuwait and raising political tension against his Arab adversaries, primarily King Fahd and President Mubarak.

This was the basic thrust of his radio and television speech on 5 September addressed to 'the Iraqi people, faithful Arabs and Muslims everywhere'. He began by referring to the 'manifestations of solidarity and demonstrations' in favour of Iraq by 'the steadfast stone-throwing people' of Palestine as well as others – citizens of Jordan, Yemen, Tunisia, Algeria, Libya, Sudan and Mauritania. This 'gathering of the faithful', Saddam Hussein continued, assumed 'intermingling of the Arab and non-Arab' on the basis of the Quranic verse: 'Verily, the most honoured of you in the light of God is [he who is] the most righteous among you.' Referring to the era of Prophet Muhammad, he stated that 'the most vigorous opponents of the values of the [Islamic] message were among the ranks of the Arabs.' In contemporary times King Fahd, President Mubarak and their allies were 'repeating the role of Abu Rughal, who acted as the guide of the Abyssinian Ibrahah on the road to [attack the Kaaba in] pre-Islamic Mecca, who was to be defeated by God with flights of birds and stones of baked clay.' To compound their sin, they had invited 'invading armies that have occupied and desecrated the land housing the sacred shrines of Muslims and Arabs'. It was the duty of the faithful to liberate the Muslim shrines in Mecca and Medina from 'captivity and occupation', Saddam declared. Promising that Iraqis would not rest until the last 'soldier of occupation' had departed from 'the land of Arabism in Najd and Hijaz [i.e. Saudi Arabia]', he appealed to 'the enduring and afflicted people of Hijaz; the oppressed people of Najd and the Eastern Province; the people of Mecca, Medina, Hail, Riyadh and Jiddah; the fraternal people in dear Egypt; and all the sons of our [Arab] nation wherever they disagree with their rulers regarding dignity, sovereignty, justice and faith, to revolt against treason and traitors, and against the infidel foreign occupation of the land of their holy shrines.' He called on the believers to fight, and cited the Quranic verse: 'If there are 20 amongst you, patient and persevering, they will vanquish 200; if 100, they will vanquish 1,000 of the unbelievers; for those are a people without understanding.' However, according to Saddam Hussein, 5 million Iraqis had volunteered for the military and the Popular Army to 'sacrifice their lives for principles and the homeland', not to mention the more than one million combatants in Iraq's military. 'Consequently, the invaders need to assemble a minimum of 12 million combatants,' he argued. 'Oh brothers, you know that the air force cannot settle a ground battle, regardless of the sophisticated weaponry.' He concluded that 'Palestine will be liberated from the Zionist invaders', and that 'the Arab and Islamic nation' will see a sun 'that will never set'.[42]

This speech summed up both Saddam Hussein's politico-military strategy and, equally importantly, the guidelines that his government had provided the Iraqi media. News from abroad, particularly from the Arab countries, was presented in such a way as to show that Saddam Hussein's strategy was working. In the war conditions that prevailed during the eight years of the First Gulf War the Iraqi media became proficient in tailoring the presentation of reality, political as well as military, to fit the perceptions of the Leader President. The current crisis, which had all the hallmarks of developing into a military conflict, provided a chance for the media to give a repeat performance.

'Papers and television constantly strive to give the impression that Iraq has wide support, inside and outside the Arab world; that America's unjustified intrusion is the only problem; that President Bush is beginning to back down; that war is now unlikely; and that the sanctions will be ineffective,' reported Martin Woollacott from Baghdad in the *Guardian* on 6 September. 'Once the country has got through the present trouble, there will be a crock of gold for everybody.' In a recent television interview Sadoun Hamadi, Iraq's deputy prime minister, had painted a rosy picture of the future for Iraq, possessing one-fifth of the world's petroleum reserves (following the annexation of Kuwait), and an annual oil revenue of $46 billion.[43]

But this optimistic talk masked deep worries at every level of society. Many Iraqis were confused and depressed by the volte-face of their president in his peace talks with Iran. 'Iraqis fought for eight years for, they were told, the Shatt-al-Arab,' said one Iraqi, insisting on anonymity. 'Now the president has given it away overnight. People are asking what was the war for. All that sacrifice?'[44]

The economic penalty for the Kuwaiti invasion was mounting daily, fuelling inflation and crippling Iraq's forty-plus major capital projects, including the world's largest petrochemical complex, due to lack of supplies and spares. Its oil wells were functioning at 20 per cent of capacity, producing just enough to meet the domestic demand.

In its battle to overcome the ill effects of the UN economic embargo, Iraq instituted rationing for bread, sugar, tea and cooking oil (all of which were wholly or largely imported) – something it had done during its war with Iran. Having endured rationing for the best part of eight years, most Iraqis adjusted without much difficulty. Monthly rations for heavily subsidized essentials cost about three Iraqi dinars per adult in a family where the major breadwinner earned ID 85 a month. The government had large stocks of wheat, and its policy of confiscating food and other supplies from Kuwait eased the situation. By exempting peasants from military service, providing cheap credits, and ordering farmers to plant 80 per cent of their land with wheat or maize, the government took steps towards achieving self-sufficiency in food.

In a way, Iraq had no choice but to withstand the consequences of the UN embargo on its own – after the failure of its attempt to persuade Iran not to participate in sanctions. During a clandestine visit to Tehran in early September 1990 the Iraqi foreign minister, Tariq Aziz, had offered a set of economic proposals to President Rafsanjani. These included Iraq paying $25 billion as war reparations to Iran, and the establishment of an 'Iran–Iraq Economic Co-operation Council', which would co-ordinate supplies to Iraq while selling Iraqi oil abroad through the pipelines of Iran. While Rafsanjani was reportedly non-committal, his later words and deeds made plain his rejection.[45]

Meanwhile, the pillage of Kuwait continued, with food and other supplies there being confiscated and shipped to Iraq. 'The once proud Kuwait City is a scared, half-empty town,' reported Caryle Murphy in the *Washington Post*. 'The streets are still littered with smashed cars and half-burnt Iraqi military vehicles hit by Kuwaiti resistance fighters. Crack Iraqi troops man road blocks, looking for Westerners and seizing guns from Kuwaitis. The business district is still closed, with many shops looted.'[46] In the hunt for Westerners, food and Kuwaiti resistance fighters, the Iraqi troops had taken to breaking into houses, shops and warehouses, and pillaging them. Looting seemed to have become systematic, with even street lights and traffic signals being despatched to Iraq.

Representatives of the Kuwaiti government-in-exile were active in publicizing the misdeeds of the Iraqi occupiers. Inside Kuwait, opposition to the Iraqi occupation consisted of the Constitutionalists, the pro-Sabah elements and the pro-Islamic nationalists. When the Constitutionalists were approached by the Iraqis to form the post-Sabah government, they refused. But they did not resort to armed resistance to the occupiers. In contrast, the Islamic elements, consisting mainly of Shia Kuwaitis, took to arms and made sporadic and small-scale attacks on Iraqi soldiers at night. Saddam Hussein responded to the situation in Kuwait in the same way he had done to armed opposition at home. He used state terror efficiently, and suppressed the Kuwaiti resistance.

But while the result he achieved was the same in both cases, there were certain basic differences. Because of the international nature of the crisis, Saddam Hussein's actions were being monitored closely outside the region, particularly in Western capitals. This in turn made the Iraqi president look outwards, to try to comprehend the words and deeds of the Western media and politicians to an extent he had never done before. He took to gleaning the foreign press. Yet this was not enough to compensate for his basic lack of understanding of the non-Arab world. He did not speak any foreign language, and his travels outside Arab countries were limited to the Soviet Union – with one brief visit to France in 1972. His understanding of American state and society was woefully inadequate and deeply flawed. In a sense he was a typical small-town Iraqi, introverted, but with a strong will bordering on obstinacy.

Refusing to accept that the Washington–Moscow co-ordination on resolving the Gulf crisis was solidly rooted, Saddam Hussein tried to undermine it. As Gorbachev and Bush prepared to meet on 9 September, he sent his foreign minister, Tariq Aziz, to the Soviet capital. 'The Soviet Union is ready to listen to us, and this is constructive,' Tariq Aziz said after his meeting with Gorbachev. 'It doesn't have a hostile attitude behind its position [on the Gulf crisis]. Without hesitation I can still call the Soviets our friends.' Addressing the same press conference, Gennady Gerasimov, the Soviet foreign ministry spokesman, said that there was 'little chance' of Moscow cancelling the twenty-year Friendship and Co-operation Treaty it had signed with Baghdad in April 1972.[47] However, non-partisan observers took a less sanguine view of the Aziz–Gorbachev meeting. 'Tariq Aziz's long-standing crony in the Kremlin was Andrei Gromyko [Soviet foreign minister until 1985], who hailed Iraq as a staunch anti-imperialist country,' said one Soviet diplomat. 'I don't think there is anyone significant there now who speaks Iraq's language.'[48] On the other hand, President Gorbachev had combined his call for Iraqi withdrawal with convening a Middle East international conference that would tackle the Gulf, Palestinian and Lebanese crises.

On 8 September, in the afternoon, Saddam Hussein addressed a 25-minute message to Bush and Gorbachev through an Iraqi News Agency broadcast on Baghdad Radio. 'While you will be in a position to make decisions that affect humanity you will be flanked by angels on one side and devils on the other, each side arguing its case according to its own instincts,' he began. 'You should remember that the Arab nation is one even if it was fragmented as it is now.' He complained that the UN Security Council had never before adopted such 'hasty and emotional' resolutions as the ones against Iraq, and alluded to the 'rabid campaign that preceded the events of 2 August led by the heads of the American and Zionist organizations' to expose the 'concealed motive' in 'the emotional campaign within the Security Council' by the US, which had proceeded 'unilaterally to adopt more unjust resolutions against Iraq'. As for the USSR, Saddam Hussein continued, its leader 'must remember that for some time now politicians all over the world have been worried about the superpower status of the Soviet Union, especially after America began to act unilaterally in the world, and behave arrogantly in the absence of the party that in the past used to guide it to a more balanced path.' He urged 'the concerned politicians' to 'choose this critical issue and time to restore to the Soviet Union its superpower status by adopting a just and fair position, and rejecting America's shunning of the just solution to the regional problems contained in our initiative of 12 August.'[49]

Since the last superpower summit in June in Washington, the position of both Gorbachev and the Soviet Union had deteriorated

– with the worsening of the economic crisis, as well as ethnic and nationalist unrest in various republics of the USSR, damaging the popularity and authority of Gorbachev and the overall standing of the Soviet Union. The Gulf upheaval had intensified disagreements between Gorbachev's military and civilian foreign policy advisers, and complicated his relations with the Arab world.

It seems doubtful that Bush and Gorbachev discussed the Iraqi leader's publicly issued 'message' to them during their seven hours of talks in Helsinki on 9 September.

'Today, we once again call upon the government of Iraq to withdraw unconditionally from Kuwait, to allow the restoration of Kuwait's legitimate government, and to free all hostages now held in Iraq and Kuwait,' their joint communiqué stated. 'Nothing short of the complete implementation of the United Nations Security Council resolutions is acceptable. Nothing short of a return to the pre-2nd August status of Kuwait can end Iraq's isolation . . . We are determined to see this aggression end and, if the current steps fail to end it, we are prepared to consider additional ones consistent with the UN charter. We must demonstrate beyond any doubt that aggression cannot and will not pay. As soon as the objectives mandated by the UN Security Council resolutions mentioned above have been achieved . . . the presidents direct their foreign ministers to work with countries in the region and outside it to develop security structures and measures to promote peace and stability. It is essential to work actively to resolve all remaining conflicts in the Middle East and Persian Gulf.' Within this overall context Bush and Gorbachev agreed that emergency food supplies could be flown into Iraq and Kuwait in 'humanitarian circumstances' so long as they were strictly monitored, with special priority being given to meeting the needs of children.[50]

At the joint press conference Gorbachev summarized his assessment of the situation. During 'phase one', a strategic approach had been implemented in which the world community had shown unprecedented solidarity, further aggression had been stopped, the oil fields in the region had been protected, and a UN embargo had been instituted. During 'phase two', the focus should be on finding a political solution, particularly when 'Our two states and the United Nations have a huge arsenal of means at our disposal to resolve the situation through political means', and 'Using military means will drag us into a situation with unpredictable result.' He therefore ruled out a Soviet military presence in the region beyond its three warships currently in the Gulf. In contrast, Bush, committed to building up an impressive

US war machine in the region, wanted to keep open the option of an attack on Iraq by the US and its allies. It was the same when it came to the question of linking the Gulf crisis with the Israeli–Palestinian conflict. 'I see the implementation of the UN resolutions [on Iraq] as separate and apart from the need to solve other questions,' said Bush. 'These issues are not linked.' Gorbachev disagreed. 'There is a link because the failure to find a solution in the Middle East at large also has a bearing on the "acuteness" of the [Gulf] crisis,' he said. Finally came the length of American forces' presence in the Gulf, an issue that seemingly bothered Gorbachev. 'US troops will stay in the Gulf until we are satisfied that the security needs of the area have been met and these [UN] resolutions have been complied with,' stated Bush. 'I made it very clear to President Gorbachev that we have no intention of keeping them there a day longer than is required.'[51] At the same time, reversing the policy of the past US administrations, Bush invited the Soviet Union to play an 'expanded role' in the Middle East.

On bilateral relations, Bush promised the Soviet leader that he would do more to persuade the US Congress to give Moscow economic aid. This was a sweetener to keep Gorbachev in line. But however pressing was the need for the Soviet leader to secure foreign financial and technological assistance, he was not prepared to forge a partnership with Washington whereby an East–West condominium settled the fate of the world; nor did he want to see America emerge as the world policeman. Instead, he wanted a regional solution to be devised through political means by the Arabs under the aegis of the United Nations.

With the financial estimates of Operation 'Desert Shield' rising by the week, the US Congress was not in a mood to provide economic aid to Moscow. Many members of Congress felt that Washington's allies were not doing enough to foot the bill for tackling the Gulf crisis. Indeed, on 10 September the US Senate called on President Bush to produce an official check-list of allies' contributions by 30 November.

But, to the White House, the more worrying aspect of Operation 'Desert Shield' was the failure to harmonize the armed forces of the US and its Arab allies both in reality and in their public statements. This was not due to lack of trying. In late August His Royal Highness General Khalid ibn Sultan, the commander of the Arab-Islamic Forces, was presented to a press conference in Riyadh by William Lynch of William Lynch Marketing Consultants of Chicago. A graduate of Britain's Royal Military Academy at Sandhurst, Prince Khalid

also went to Fort Leavenworth Staff College, an air war college in
Alabama, and to the US navy's post-graduate school at Monterey. On
his return home, as the eldest son of Prince Sultan ibn Abdul Aziz,
minister of defence and aviation of Saudi Arabia, Prince Khalid soon
rose to become the commander of the country's air defence forces.
Yet, facing local and foreign journalists, he was nervous. He refused
to tell how many Arab and Muslim troops were deployed in the Saudi
kingdom, or how his forces would respond if Iraq attacked America's
'other Middle East ally, Israel'. But he did say, 'I am sure that if any
action is done from Saudi soil, I know for a fact that it would have
to be discussed between King Fahd and President Bush.'[52]

This upset General Schwarzkopf, who wanted a totally free hand for
the US in military matters. He conveyed his objections to the White
House. President Bush contacted the Saudi ambassador, Prince Bandar
ibn Sultan (a younger brother of Prince Khalid), and conveyed his fears
that a stipulation about prior permission from King Fahd before the
Saudi-based American troops could mount operations against Iraq
could leave US military 'hamstrung in certain situations'. Prince
Bandar reportedly replied that US forces had been invited to Saudi
Arabia on the 'clear understanding' that their role was to be defensive.
Bush then stated that the strategy of giving the trade embargo time to
work precluded a military offensive 'for the time being'. The issue was
thus left unresolved. But to put the record straight, Prince Sultan, the
Saudi defence minister, stated publicly on 1 September that US forces
would not be allowed to launch 'hostage rescue operations' from Saudi
territory, and that 'Our kingdom will not serve as a theatre for action
that is not defensive.' It was then revealed that the previous week
he had refused to allow the US to station B-52 bombers at a base
outside Jiddah because of the offensive capabilities of these warplanes.
The line taken by Prince Sultan was that the US must first secure
authority for military action against Iraq from the Security Council,
and then consult King Fahd before mounting such an operation.[53] In
the end, Washington did what Riyadh insisted on; but that was some
three months later.

The Washington–Riyadh discord on the US military aims and
methods had hardly subsided when James Baker stirred up the problem. Appearing before the House of Representatives Foreign Affairs
Committee, the US secretary of state said that the administration
was planning a long-term military presence in the Gulf even if Iraq
withdrew from Kuwait. He outlined a new 'regional security structure'
to counter the future military potential of Iraq, stating that such an

arrangement would probably include an international arms boycott of Iraq, the further arming of its Arab neighbours, and a US naval or land force in the region. The resulting organization, he said, would be something 'similar to Nato'.[54] The Saudis reminded Baker that a 'regional security structure' already existed, and it was called the Gulf Co-operation Council. The fact that Baker modified his statement the next day – saying that the Bush administration had just 'begun its thinking about a new security arrangement for the long term', and that his earlier remarks should 'not be equated with the idea that somehow we are calling for a Nato of the Middle East' – did not set at rest the worries he had aroused not only in Riyadh but also in Tehran and Moscow, among other capitals.

Having invited the largest American deployments since the Allies' 1944 landings on the Normandy beaches of France, the Saudi officials watched their guests warily, making sure that their country did not get dragged into an armed conflict with Iraq because of the angry impatience of President Bush. At every airbase the air forces of America and Britain were told in no uncertain terms that they were under the overall command of Prince Turki ibn Nasser ibn Abdul Aziz, the commander of the Saudi air force. Under the rules of engagement publicized on 9 September, US fighter and helicopter pilots were forbidden to fire on Iraqi intruders without express Saudi permission, except when the American plane or helicopter was being attacked. As for the ground troops, Prince Khalid placed the troops of the Arab-Islamic Forces between the Kuwaiti border and the US military further south. Two Saudi armoured brigades, one mechanized brigade, and one airborne brigade, posted near Hafar al Batin and at Khafji, formed the first line of defence. Two mechanized brigades of the GCC Rapid Deployment Force, one brigade of Egyptians, 3,000 Syrian commandos, 2,000 Pakistani infantrymen, and 1,200 Bangladeshi soldiers together constituted the second line of defence. Then, from 100 miles south of the Kuwaiti border, below the 27th parallel, in an arc formation, was deployed the third line of defence, consisting of 70,000 Americans, including 40,000 marines (with the overall total scheduled to rise to 100,000 by mid-September). While Schwarzkopf's headquarters described the interposition of the Arab-Islamic Forces as a 'trip wire' tactic for the benefit of the US forces, Prince Khalid's office stressed that it underlined the 'primarily Arab nature' of the dispute. When Baker asked Riyadh for funding for Operation 'Desert Shield', the Saudis were quick to respond positively, aware that money provided them with another means of control over the Americans. With $100 million a day in windfall oil profits, they could easily afford to be generous paymasters.[55]

The other Gulf country which benefited from the upsurge in the oil price was Iran. Ever since the steep fall in petroleum prices in the winter of 1985–6, Tehran had been in financial straits. It had canvassed OPEC members at the fateful July 1990 meeting, successfully, to raise the reference price of oil. And at the August meeting along with Iraq it had opposed, unsuccessfully, an overall production increase for OPEC and the abandonment of the quota system.

Significantly, the Iraqi oil minister, Abdul Rahim Shalabi, was a member of the high-level delegation, led by Tariq Aziz, which arrived in Tehran on 9 September to confer with Iran's foreign minister Velayati. The Iraqi visitors were driven through the streets of Tehran where murals portraying Saddam Hussein as a bloodthirsty Dracula, or as clutching the bombs being dropped on Iranian cities, had been painted over.

The leaders of the two countries agreed to resume diplomatic relations. Aziz offered a non-aggression pact between Iran and Iraq, and also a friendship and co-operation treaty. President Rafsanjani called for a speedy demarcation of the Iran–Iraq border and its reopening to Shia pilgrims from both countries.

At a more mundane level, according to 'Arab oil industry officials', Iran agreed to accept 200,000 b/d of Iraqi petroleum and refined products in return for food and fuel. On 13 September the *Tehran Times*, a paper close to President Rafsanjani's office, denied that Iran had decided to break UN sanctions by entering into a barter deal with Iraq. However, a week earlier the same newspaper had stated that 'Iranian officials are convinced that the Muslim Iraqi people should not pay for the mistakes of their government', and that 'Iran is able to solve the Iraqi people's needs for medicine and food, as these items are not banned by the UN sanctions.' Since the Iraqi oil imports were for internal Iranian consumption, and could be delivered to Iran through the already existing pumping facilities, no overt proof of the deal was expected to become available to outsiders.[56]

Actually, Saddam Hussein was offering Iran far less than he did to other Third World countries on 10 September. Referring to 'the oil monopolies making illegal profits' out of the Gulf upheaval (because of the 50% increase in the oil price during the five weeks of the crisis) and the inability of poorer nations to cope with the price rise, and in appreciation of the Third World's 'just position' on the Palestine issue, Saddam Hussein declared his 'readiness to supply needy Third World countries with Iraqi oil free of charge'. This arrangement, he surmised, would not contravene the economic embargo against Iraq, as it did not involve buying and selling. He invited such states to apply stating the quantity and type of crude oil they needed. In case Iraq was unable to ship the petroleum to them, they must arrange the transportation at their own expense. This offer, he assured them, was not linked to 'the kind of decision you make or to your position on the current [Gulf] crisis'.[57]

This was the Iraqi leader's way of illustrating to the superpowers that their détente did not address the problems of the Third World, and that, despite its own economically dire situation, Iraq was willing and able to aid the needy states. The practical problem that these countries faced was transporting the free Iraqi oil. They were only too aware of the daunting problem of circumventing the naval blockade, and the risk they ran of being penalized by the UN Security Council if they succeeded. In the end no Third World state was able to make practical use of the Iraqi offer.

Soon, however, the Iraqi president was to receive public support for his anti-American stance from an unexpected quarter: Ayatollah Ali Khamanei, the Supreme Leader of Iran.

Addressing a gathering of the 'outstanding children of the [Iranian] martyrs' in Tehran on 12 September, Khamanei said, 'We are strongly opposed to the presence of America in this region, to the greed of America . . . and to America's demanding, bullying and shameless attitude.' He questioned the grounds on which the United States insisted on providing security for the region. 'What has the security of our region to do with you?' he asked Washington. 'It is the business of the nations of this region,' he asserted, reiterating a foreign policy doctrine of Khomeini, the founder of the Islamic Republic of Iran.

Ayatollah Khamanei condemned those 'nations and governments who allow the aggressor America to come here to plan in accordance with its own interests and to set up a security system in the Persian Gulf', and warned that 'Muslims and Muslim nations' will not allow it. 'Anybody who stands up to fight and confront America's aggression, greed, plans and policies aimed at committing aggression in the Persian Gulf region will have participated in the jihad on the path of Allah (jihad fi sabilallah), and anybody who is killed on that path is regarded as a martyr.' He added, 'We shall not permit the Americans to establish a foothold for themselves in the region, where we are present . . . and [we shall not permit the Americans] to turn it into a sphere of their power, and to acquire the power to administer the affairs of Muslims, especially the affairs of the sacred regions of Muslims and their two holy shrines.' He was surprised that the Americans had not learnt a lesson. 'They have seen how in Lebanon a handful of committed Muslim youths evicted them from the country.' He recalled how, when 'the whole of Europe, Nato, the Warsaw Pact and Arab reaction' had 'stood against the Islamic revolution' in Iran, and 'persuaded Iraq, stoked the war against us and surrounded us', Iran had not extended 'a begging hand towards anyone'. In contrast, 'They [the Saudis] have invited the Americans and . . . are now waiting to see when they will make a decision and what sort of decision.' He condemned those governments which intended to defend themselves by 'the hand of aliens', thus humiliating their own nations.[58]

Hojatalislam Sadiq Khalkhali, chairman of the foreign affairs committee of the Iranian parliament, called for the creation of a 'broad military alliance' between Iran and Iraq against Israel and America. 'Such a military alliance is what all Muslim people in the region want and desire,' he said.[59]

These statements came against the background of reports that Iran planned to open its frontiers with Iraq, and that it was receptive to the idea of supplying food and medicines to its neighbour. This was bad news for the Bush administration which, according to Baker, had made 'overtures' through third parties to Tehran regarding the Gulf crisis. Now, responding to Khamanei's fatwa (religious decree), the US state department said, 'The Iranian position appears to be based on a misunderstanding of what we mean by regional security structures and arrangements.'[60]

Khamanei's strictures were directed as much at Riyadh as they were at Washington. 'There is suspicion in Iran that Saudi acceptance of the American military aid has more to do with the al Saud royal family seeking to safeguard its own power and interests than to protect the country's border,' reported Celia Hall, a British journalist, from Tehran.[61]

Conscious of the unease prevalent in the Muslim world about the Saudis' invitation to the US to intervene militarily from their soil, the Saudi-funded World Muslim League (WML) invited 350 Muslim religious scholars from 80 countries to Mecca to discuss the matter. On 12 September, at the end of a three-day conference, the WML adopted a 14-point resolution. 'Regarding seeking help from foreign forces, and following a review of studies by religious scholars, the conference believes that the help sought by the Kingdom of Saudi Arabia from foreign forces to support its [own] forces is self-defence and was necessitated by a legitimate need, and that the Islamic Sharia [law] allows such a measure as long as it is within the limits defined by it,' stated the resolution. 'Once . . . Iraq has withdrawn from Kuwait and when there is no longer a threat against Saudi Arabia and the states of the region, the [foreign] forces should leave the region.' It called on Muslim countries to establish a permanent Islamic force under the supervision of the Islamic Conference Organization (ICO) to which its members could appeal in case of armed conflict among them.[62]

The reference to the 'studies by religious scholars' had to do with the fatwa (religious decree) issued by the seventeen-member Supreme Religious Council of Saudi Arabia on 13 August which stated that it was the 'duty of those in authority' to 'take every means that halts the advance of evil and secures safety for the people', and that the 'current circumstances' dictate that 'the man in charge of the affairs of Muslims' should 'seek the assistance of the one who has the ability to attain the intended aim'.[63]

That Washington's ability far exceeded merely 'halting the advance of evil' was becoming apparent daily. Following their trip to the region in early September, a group of sixteen US Senators put it about that '15 October is the D-Day', the date when America would mount an offensive to expel the Iraqis from Kuwait.

General Powell undertook a tour of the Gulf in mid-September aiming, *inter alia*, to boost the morale of the US forces. In a speech to the crew of USS *Wisconsin*, after alluding to President Saddam Hussein as 'this joker we've got up there in Baghdad', Powell challenged him. 'We can't take this kind of crap any longer,' he said. 'If somebody wants to fight with us, then don't play around: kick butt.'[64] Such talk was partly an element of the psychological warfare that had been unleashed against the Iraqi leader since 3 August, and partly based on the confidence gained by the American military and civilian leaders after they had substantially resolved the question of the operational command and control of the US and other forces. 'There is a separate chain of command for Saudi forces, and a separate chain of command for US forces,' said a Pentagon spokesman. 'The Saudis would be notified if the US launches any attack.' This implied that the Saudis did not have a veto.[65] Regarding the US assault on Iraq, the situation had been made murky by General Schwarzkopf's statement that it would take two more months before he had all the ground troops he needed in place, and that the delay was due to the difficulty of moving heavy military hardware by elderly US naval ships, and the demands on the limited field workshop facilities to cope with the effects of desert sand on tanks and helicopters.[66]

While such mixed signals confused Baghdad, they also complicated matters for the authorities in Riyadh so far as the public opinion in Saudi Arabia and other Muslim countries was concerned. A major motive for convening the World Muslim League conference in Mecca was to convince Muslims abroad that the massive US military presence in Saudi Arabia did not constitute a religious or cultural threat. 'Muslim delegates were able to see with their eyes that not a single American army boot had set foot on Islam's holiest shrines,' reported Robert Fisk of the *Independent* from Jiddah.[67]

Yet doubts about the American enterprise remained. 'There is the question of the concern felt by the public in the streets about the United States because of its strategic alliance with Israel,' said Abdullah Omar Nassif, the secretary-general of the Islamic Conference Organization, the parent body of the World Muslim League. 'You have to know that among Muslims, among the general public, there is a worry. If this force in the Gulf was under a UN banner there wouldn't have been any problem. People would have accepted it because all Muslim countries have signed the charter of the United Nations. But because the force came individually [from Western countries], it made people agitated, and they thought this was another colonial force coming in.'[68]

The argument that the necessity for calling in foreign troops had arisen out of the invasion of Kuwait by Saddam Hussein was offered not only by those who had been assembled in Mecca or Jiddah by the Saudi authorities but also, quite independently, by President Assad of Syria. He and his senior officials deplored the Iraqi aggression against Kuwait as 'an example of the law of the jungle dominating intra-Arab relations' and stressed that such an action strengthened 'Israel's case for retaining Occupied Arab Territories', giving it a free hand to 'gear up for new incursions'. Moreover, they argued, Saddam Hussein's action had diverted attention away from the Arab–Israeli conflict epitomized by the Palestinian intifada.[69]

However, the intifada, being a movement inspired and manned exclusively by the Palestinians in the Occupied Territories, had nothing to do with Assad. Indeed, its independent dynamic had the inadvertent effect of reducing Assad's influence in the region. This had come at a time when Syria's superpower ally, the USSR, beset with mounting economic and ethnic problems at home, had lost its motivation and resources to back its foreign allies. In late 1989 the

Soviet ambassador reportedly told Assad that the Kremlin could no longer underwrite his quest for strategic parity with Israel, that future Soviet military assistance would be sufficient only to deter or repel an attack by Israel, and that Syria would have to pay in hard currencies for its purchase of Soviet arms. This change of policy after nearly four decades of close co-operation came at a time when economic aid to Damascus from the oil-rich Gulf monarchies had tapered off after the expiry of the ten-year agreement they had signed with Syria at the 1978 Arab summit in Baghdad in the wake of Egypt's concord with Israel. Syria's isolation in the Arab world was exposed when it became the only state (other than Lebanon, which followed the Syrian lead in foreign affairs) to boycott the May 1990 Arab summit held in Baghdad.

Leaving aside brief periods of mutual understanding, even sympathy, relations between Damascus and Washington had been correct at best, and belligerent at worst. During the June 1967 Arab–Israeli war Syria severed its diplomatic links with America. But following the October 1973 conflict it co-operated with the US in working out a disengagement agreement with Israel.

Resumption of diplomatic ties in June 1974 led to an improvement in mutual relations – up to a point. 'We want good relations with the US, but not at the expense of our relations with the Soviet Union,' said a senior Syrian official in early September 1975.[70] With Syria's direct involvement in the Lebanese civil war in June 1976, Damascus–Washington relations became entangled in the Lebanese imbroglio. The Israeli invasion of Lebanon in June 1982 – followed by America's military involvement in Lebanon, and its attempts to forge a peace treaty between Lebanon and Israel – and the inclusion of Syria on the US state department's list of nations that support international terrorism, strained Damascus–Washington ties to breaking point. US intelligence sources alleged that the Damascus-based Popular Front for the Liberation of Palestine-General Command (PFLP-GC), led by Ahmad Jibril, was responsible for the blowing up of a Pan-Am airliner near the Scottish town of Lockerbie in December 1988, causing the deaths of 278 people. This was one of the subjects discussed when Baker met his Syrian counterpart, Farouk al Shaara, and President Assad in Damascus on 14 September. The Syrian officials reportedly told Baker that if the US had 'hard evidence' against the PFLP-GC, their government would try the accused. They assured him that they were preparing to send more troops to Saudi Arabia.[71]

Indeed, arrangements were already afoot to transport 8,000 Syrian troops with their Soviet-made T-72 tanks in Soviet ships from Latakia.

Voicing the official line the officer in charge, General Muhammad Deeb Dahar, said: 'Our mission is exclusively defensive . . . to prevent war between Arab brothers.' There were also the pecuniary considerations, the price-tag for the Syrian services to Riyadh being $1 billion.[72]

But above all else, the Syrian president's action stemmed from his personal animosity towards Saddam Hussein, something that had over the years become integral to Syria's foreign policy. The two leaders had much in common. Like Saddam, Hafiz Assad (b. 1931) came from a poor peasant family in the village of Qurdaha in the mountainous coastal region of northern Syria. At sixteen he joined the Arab Baath Socialist Party. Unlike Saddam, however, Hafiz succeeded in enrolling at a military college, and graduated as a pilot. He moved up the party ladder to become a member of its five-member Military Committee in 1960, when he was 29. In March 1963 this Committee became the real architect of the successful Baathist coup. During the June 1967 Arab–Israeli War Assad was defence minister. Syria's poor performance in that conflict weakened the civil leadership of the party and state, opening a way for Assad – then both defence minister and commander of the air force – to assume full power in a bloodless coup in November 1970. As he consolidated his presidential authority, other members of the Military Committee fell by the wayside. In the October 1973 Arab–Israeli conflict he co-ordinated his war plans with President Anwar Sadat (1970–81) of Egypt. But after the ceasefire Sadat went his way – towards Washington – leaving him, an ally of Moscow, on his own. Alarmed by Sadat's decision in September 1978 to make unilateral peace with Israel, the Iraqi leaders invited Assad to Baghdad, where they offered to unite Iraq and Syria to create a powerful eastern front against Israel. Assad accepted the proposal. But the dramatic events in Iran in late 1978 and early 1979 caused a miscarriage of the Iraqi–Syrian unity plans. While Assad, a follower of Alawism (a sub-sect within Shia Islam), openly praised the Iranian revolution and immediately recognized the Khomeini regime, Baghdad maintained a stony silence.

Soon after assuming the presidency of Iraq in July 1979, Saddam Hussein encouraged the major opposition force in Syria, the Muslim Brotherhood, to mount an armed struggle against the Assad regime. The high point of the Brotherhood's violent activities was an assassination attempt on Assad on 25 June 1980 when two hand grenades were lobbed at him. He managed to kick one away, and his bodyguard threw himself on the other. Assad unleashed unprecedented repression against the Brotherhood which reached a peak in February 1982 when, in an effort to crush the insurrection in Hama, between 5,000 and 10,000 people were killed in three weeks of fighting, and large parts of the city were razed to the ground.[73] With this, human rights activists abroad put Assad in the same bracket as Saddam Hussein, 'the butcher of Baghdad'. But unlike the Iraqi leader, who seemed to stand up well to the rigours of his office and the long-lasting war with Iran, Assad suffered a severe heart attack in November 1983. He survived, but emerged as a leader more content to respond to events than to shape them.

Yet Assad lost none of his calculating skills. 'The Syrian leader is acknowledged even by his enemies as the Arab world's master strategist: shrewd, stubborn and calculating, inexhaustibly patient and serpentine in biding his time for the main chance and then pouncing on it,' wrote David Hirst of the *Guardian*.[74] He quickly measured the potential of taking an anti-Saddam position: funds for Syria from the Gulf monarchies, a free hand in shaping the outcome of the Lebanese civil war, and a US promise for a just and comprehensive peace in the Middle East. He soon won the promise of an economic aid package from the European Community to compensate Syria for the loss of transit trade and the remittances sent by Syrian workers from Kuwait. There was of course the risk that should hostilities erupt, Syria, the fountainhead of pan-Arab nationalism, would end up fighting a fellow Arab state, alongside non-Arab troops. But, in Assad's estimation, it was a risk worth taking as it was likely to be outweighed by actual and potential rewards.

As an insurance policy, however – in case Iraq's president emerged unscathed from the Gulf crisis – Assad and the Syrian media refrained from attacking Saddam Hussein personally. In a sense they were reciprocating the Iraqi leader's gesture of sparing Assad the kind of derogatory epithets he was throwing at King Fahd and President Mubarak. 'Pan-Arab nationalism emerged from the heart of Syria, and we still hope the Syrian people will manage to make their voice heard in support of Iraq,' said a senior official in Baghdad in mid-September.[75]

By then this was a forlorn hope, as was the insistence of the Syrians as well as the Egyptians that they were in Saudi Arabia for purely defensive reasons. The contrary evidence appeared in the *Washington Post* of 16 September, and was provided by General Michael Dugan, US air force chief of staff (since June) in his interview with the paper's reporters in Dhahran. He said that other chiefs of staff as well as General Schwarzkopf shared his view that 'Air power is the only answer that's available to our country' to deal with Iraq's 'huge land army and tank force', and 'the only way to avoid a protracted land war that would probably destroy Kuwait'. Until a fortnight ago, Dugan continued, 'US target planners had assembled a somewhat conventional list of Iraqi targets which included, in order of priority: Iraqi air defences; airfields and warplanes; intermediate range missile sites, including Scud ground-to-ground missiles; communications and command centres; chemical, nuclear and munitions plants; and Iraqi armour formations . . . That's a nice list of targets . . . but that's not enough.' Stressing that 'The cutting edge [of any US attack on Iraq] would be in downtown Baghdad', he directed his planners to research 'what is it that psychologically would make an impact on the population and regime in Iraq . . . to find centres of gravity where air power could make a difference early on'. He then cited 'Israeli sources' advising that 'the best way to hurt Saddam' was to target his family, his personal guard and his mistress. Since Saddam was a 'one-man show' in Iraq, Dugan continued, 'if and when we choose violence he ought to be at the focus of our efforts'. Given that Iraq had 'an incompetent army', an air defence relying heavily on Soviet-made SA-6 surface-to-air missiles, and an air force with 'very limited military capability', the US ought to rely heavily on its superior air power. Conceding that 'there are a lot of things that air power cannot accomplish' and that the US air force had 'great difficulty in driving people out of the jungle' in Vietnam, he said: 'There's not much jungle where we're going.' He was prepared to give some role to the armed services other than the air force. Marine and army ground forces could be used for diversions and flanking attacks and to block an Iraqi counter-strike on Saudi Arabia, he added. Also, ground forces might be needed to reoccupy Kuwait, but only after air power had so shattered enemy resistance that soldiers can 'walk in and not to have to fight house-to-house'.[76] What Dugan was describing was a military doctrine stated in Manual FM 100–5, known as AirLand Battle, developed mainly by General John A. Starry of the US Army's Training and Doctrine Unit, and formally adopted by the Pentagon in 1981, which could be simply translated as: 'Strike deep and throughout Iraq'.

By revealing that the US had already mapped out its offensive strategy of bombing Iraq, Dugan embarrassed the White House in more ways than one. The action resulted in his instant dismissal.[77] Explaining it, a defence department spokesman said that the point was not whether what Dugan said was true or not, but that 'he spoke out about items that were not his to discuss on the public record in a very tense situation.' More specifically, said Richard Cheney, defence secretary, 'He had violated a host of standing orders prohibiting discussing [publicly] strategy and tactics, playing down other US armed services, and estimating opposing forces.' Much worse than that was Dugan's failure to comprehend that 'A very fragile, a very important international coalition has been put together to halt Saddam Hussein's aggression . . . [and that] the conduct of US national security policy is an extremely delicate task.'[78]

Dugan's dismissal on 17 September did not mean the scuttling of the offensive strategy he was advocating, as subsequent events were to reveal. But it could be seen, retrospectively, as marking the end of the defensive phase of Operation 'Desert Shield' and the beginning of the offensive phase. (In Kuwait, too, 17 September 1990 signalled the start of the next phase. On that day Iraqi troops went around the streets of Kuwait City announcing that those who wished to leave were free to do so, thus planning to empty the capital of anti-Iraqi elements, and implementing further integration of Kuwait into Iraq.)

In the US, given the public concern among politicians and commentators about the prospect of tens of thousands of American casualties in a war that could drag on for many months, the option of an exclusive, or almost exclusive, air campaign had much appeal. But the feelings and opinions of the governments and peoples in the Arab countries allied to Washington ran in a contrary direction when considering the prospect of extensive death and destruction of fellow Arabs in Iraq and Kuwait. As the head of the anti-Iraq coalition of disparate parts, Bush was likely to find his hands tied to an extent he had not realized in the early days of his enthusiastic canvassing of the Kuwaiti cause. His other problem was that the Arab leaders were likely to graduate their backing for his lead only to the extent that he had been able to muster popular support at home for his handling of the crisis. So far, he had done well.

But, as the debate began revolving more and more around the number of American 'body bags', his Democratic rivals in Congress became increasingly wary of backing the president: a development likely to curtail Bush's area of manoeuvre in tackling the Gulf crisis.

5 BUSH AND THE DOMESTIC FRONT

'Operation "Desert Shield" will provide air cover for the Savings-and-Loan banks scandal and the budget deficit.'

Peter Hart, a Democrat pollster[1]

'Mr Bush likes to govern by consensus . . . To a fault, he likes to be all things to all people.'

Peter Pringle, British journalist[2]

'The strategy of deliberate drift [of Bush] burdens the US with a host of problems that have become worse over the past decade: drugs, homelessness, racial hostility, education, environment.'

Time editorial[3]

While President Bush was engrossed in tackling the Iraqi invasion of Kuwait he let a simmering domestic crisis reach boiling point. It concerned reducing the federal budget deficit and involved dealings with the US Congress, which controls the government's purse strings. The president and Congress were agreed on the goal, but they differed on the means. The Democrat-controlled Congress wished to increase income tax on the rich whereas the chief executive was intent on keeping his election pledge not to raise taxes.

Many Democrat, and some Republican, lawmakers were also unhappy at the way Bush was handling the Gulf crisis. He seemed to be leading the country towards a military confrontation with Baghdad without showing any sign of seeking authorization for war from Congress. This caused grumbling on Capitol Hill, which in some cases erupted into angry questioning. 'Do we have a president? Or a Caesar? A monarch? A potentate?' asked Representative Henry Gonzales in a letter to Tom Foley, speaker of the House of Representatives, on 19 September 1990. 'What happened to . . . the power invested in Congress to declare war?'[4]

Gonzales was among many national legislators who insisted on Congress exercising its constitutional authority to declare war, which had been strengthened by the 1973 War Powers Resolution. This gave Congress the authority to limit the stay of US forces abroad. Within 60 to 90 days of the initial deployment of troops abroad in an area 'where hostilities are imminent', Congress must act to authorize the president to keep them there, failing which they must be brought home. Since its enactment the War Powers Resolution had been used once – by President Reagan – to despatch US marines to Lebanon in September 1982. Congress limited their deployment to 18 months.[5] However, on the whole, Reagan regarded this law as imposing unreasonable limitations on the president as commander-in-chief. Bush agreed with this interpretation, and wanted the law repealed.

It was against this background that on 11 September 1990 President Bush forwarded to the Senate Republican leaders a draft resolution on the Gulf crisis. It backed 'the actions taken by the president in support of the goals [in the UN resolutions], including the involvement of the UN and of the friendly governments. The Congress urges continued action by the president . . . to deal with Iraqi aggression and to protect American lives and vital interests in the region.' The Democrats on Capitol Hill were against the draft resolution as it smacked of the Tonkin Gulf Resolution passed by Congress on 7 August 1964, which President Lyndon Johnson later claimed had endorsed (in advance) the military policies he pursued in Vietnam. That resolution read in part: 'The Congress approves and supports the determination of the President, as the commander-in-chief, to take all necessary measures to repel any armed attack against forces of the United States and to prevent further aggression.' It also authorized the president to 'aid any Southeast Asian state' in pursuance of the above objectives.[6] The manner in which President Johnson, a Democrat, had misused this resolution had left a deep mark on the collective memory of Congress.

At the same time, now, with elections to the House of Representatives and a third of the Senate seats due in November, most Democrats did not wish to be seen to be tying the president's hands to the extent that they could be accused of sending heartening signals to the Iraqi leader. So they concentrated on attacking the Bush administration's record of backing Saddam Hussein until the day of his invasion of Kuwait, reminding the White House, to its great embarrassment, that on 31 July 1990 John Kelly, assistant secretary for the Near East, had told the House Foreign Relations Committee that 'the US has no defence treaty with Kuwait and no obligation to come to its aid if attacked by Iraq', and opposed the enforcement of the US

Senate resolution specifying sanctions against Baghdad. When Kelly was called to testify again on 19 September before this committee, its Democrat chairperson Lee Hamilton reminded him of the stand he had taken seven weeks earlier. Thus pushed, Kelly referred the committee members to a remark made by President Bush at a recent conference. 'The previous US policy in the Gulf did not produce results,' Bush had admitted. 'Was he [the president] wrong?' Hamilton asked. 'It [the policy] did not succeed,' Kelly replied. 'That's for sure,' Hamilton said. This exchange was shown on the major television networks' news programmes.[7]

There were many Democrats who argued that the idea of US troops in Saudi Arabia had been sold to the American people on the false premise that Saddam Hussein was an Adolf Hitler, and that there was as much at stake here as during the Second World War. Firstly, if Saddam was a Hitler, then Bush and his Republican predecessor, Reagan, were partly guilty of making him powerful. Unlike the Germany of the 1930s, Iraq had imported its chemical weapons plants; and all its tanks, warplanes, missiles and radar systems had been purchased abroad, thanks to the governments or arms merchants of the USSR, France, China, America, Brazil and West Germany. Secondly, comparing Saddam Hussein to Hitler and his invasion of Kuwait to the German takeover of the Sudetenland (a province of Czechoslovakia) in 1938 was flawed. Whereas Hitler's Germany was the second most powerful industrial nation in the world, with the largest air force in Europe and possessing most of the tanks in European arsenals and a fresh, eager army moving against an unprepared neighbour, Saddam Hussein's Iraq was entirely dependent on the nations now lined up against it for its warplanes, tanks and artillery; its military was far from vigorous after an eight-year conflict which had ended in a draw, and its current adversaries included the most powerful countries on the planet. At $59 billion, Iraq's gross domestic product was half that of Belgium, a country of less than 10 million people but with a sophisticated arms industry.

In any event, Hitler's Germany did not face a worldwide economic embargo after its 1938 aggression. According to a study by two economists, Gary Hufbauer and Kimberley Ann Elliot, the UN sanctions would reduce the GNP of Iraq and Kuwait by 40%, allowing for seepage through Iran, Jordan and Yemen. While food supplies were not expected to be seriously blockaded, the critical question was the degree to which spare parts could be available for its military and civilian industries, and Iraqi oil sold, for example, across the Iranian border.[8]

The economic embargo, however, was not an end in itself. It was a means to resolving the crisis – without violence. There was no slackening of Arab endeavours to find a political solution. The Arab mediators found Iraq in a mood for compromise. Taha Yassin Ramadan, its first deputy prime minister, said on 17 September that Iraq was willing to withdraw from Kuwait if this led to an international conference to solve the Palestinian problem. 'Any chance for peace should be within the framework of a foreign withdrawal from the Arab Gulf lands and an Arab settlement of the Kuwaiti issue,' Ramadan stated. 'We will discuss all issues: the Gulf, Lebanon and Palestine.' This had the backing of Saddam Hussein. During dinner with a senior Arab diplomat at a military camp forty miles from Baghdad, he told his guest that he was prepared to consider withdrawal from Kuwait provided (a) the compromise did not appear to have been proposed by Iraq, and (b) he could show some tangible gain for Arabs, such as American endorsement of an international peace conference on the Israeli–Palestinian issue.[9]

On 19 September, King Hassan of Morocco, after consulting King Hussein of Jordan and President Chadli ben Jedid of Algeria, offered a five-point plan: Iraqi withdrawal from Kuwait; an Arab summit to be held immediately; withdrawal of non-Arab troops from Saudi Arabia; a 'special relationship' between Iraq and Kuwait; and an international peace conference on the Middle East to consider the Palestinian and Lebanese problems. Both Washington and Riyadh rejected the proposals. Commenting on Baghdad's insistence on linking the Kuwait crisis with the Palestinian issue, the state-controlled Saudi television drew a parallel between the two situations. The Iraqi troops' mistreatment of the Kuwaitis was a mirror image of the Israeli forces' mistreatment of the Palestinians on the West Bank and Gaza, it said. America specifically rejected the last two points, arguing that these would amount to rewarding Saddam Hussein for his aggression.[10]

On 14 September Iraqi troops raided the residence of the French ambassador in Kuwait in the course of a campaign to flush out Westerners, particularly 750 Americans and 500 Britons, known to be hiding from the authorities. They detained four French citizens, one of them a military attaché. The incident enraged President Mitterrand. Next day he gave his fourth televised press conference on the Gulf crisis, after an emergency cabinet meeting, and announced a new, harder French policy towards Baghdad. He had moved adroitly. First he obtained the backing of his Socialist Party by reprimanding his defence minister, Chévènement, for being slow in responding to the crisis and failing to ask for an emergency session of the parliament to debate it. Second, having got the right-of-centre opposition to support him, Mitterrand isolated the right-wing National Front, leaving only the Communists offering equivocal criticism and winning a huge majority in parliament for a tough stance in the Gulf. Now, reacting to the Iraqi troops' violation of diplomatic immunity, the French president announced the despatch of 4,000 ground troops, backed by tanks and warplanes, to Saudi Arabia.[11]

Furthermore, at the Security Council, France initiated a stiff motion against Iraq. Passed unanimously on 16 September, Resolution 667 'strongly' condemned 'aggressive actions perpetrated by Iraq against diplomatic premises and personnel in Kuwait, as well as the abduction of foreign nationals'. Baghdad rejected the resolution as 'unjust and humiliating'.

Flushing out foreign nationals from their hiding places in Kuwait was one of the measures Baghdad was taking to consolidate its hold over Kuwait. So too was Saddam Hussein's decision to appoint Ali Hassan Majid, the erstwhile minister for local government, as the civilian governor of Kuwait. A cousin of the Iraqi president, Majid had been director-general of the Public Security Directorate until the early 1980s and was given a seat on the Baath Party's regional command in July 1986. Nine months later he was appointed general military commander of the Kurdistan region charged with defeating Iran's strategy of making steady gains in Iraqi Kurdistan. After the First Gulf War ceasefire, Majid used poison gases against the Kurds.[12]

Now, as governor of Kuwait, Majid decided in mid-September to allow all those Kuwaiti nationals to leave who wanted to, except males aged 18 to 45 who were liable for Iraqi conscription. Three thousand Kuwaiti nationals passed through the Kuwaiti–Saudi border at Khafji on the first day. According to their reports, there were about a dozen troop concentrations between the border and Kuwait City, with Ahmadi turned into a major military encampment. There were a large number of tanks and anti-aircraft batteries along the ring road that bypassed Kuwait City. Inside the capital there were checkpoints every 200 yards, manned by Iraqi troops, looking for Westerners and confiscating weapons from Kuwaitis. The Iraqi units were apparently preparing to defend themselves against an American offensive.[13]

'Kuwait is a nation of burnt-down buildings, stripped-down cars, roads torn up by tanks, dying plants ignored by the Iraqis, and empty supermarket shelves,' said Khalid, a 38-year-old Kuwaiti businessman. After the first ten days following the invasion, looting by Iraqi soldiers and poor, non-Kuwaiti residents, particularly Palestinian youths, stopped. In its place came formal requisition by the Iraqi authorities. Once a Kuwaiti businessman had submitted the inventory of his stock to the Iraqi authorities, they would requisition all or part of it and issue him a promissory note in Iraqi dinars as payment. The removal of food from shops and warehouses to Iraq was thus orderly and on a large scale. As for public property, Kuwait City's modern science research centre, for instance, was stripped of its computers and other sophisticated equipment. Items from the National Museum were being shipped to Iraq. The city's 25 hospitals were either closed for lack of staff, equipment or medicine, or had been taken over by the Iraqis as military billets. A few banks were open and allowed withdrawals of 225 Iraqi dinars a week.[14]

For about a week following the invasion there were anti-occupation marches, often led by women, but these stopped after 10 August when Iraqi firing on a demonstration led to the death of one woman. For the next fortnight Kuwaiti nationalists, mainly Shia, directed sniper fire at Iraqi outposts and military trucks. (Unlike urban-based Shias, by and large, the members of the disenfranchised bedouin Kuwait tribes remained neutral, and the Sunni merchant families cautious.) With most of the Iraqi troops deployed along the coast and outside Kuwait City to forestall anticipated American attack, the Kuwaiti resistance scored well. On 22 August, however, Iraqi forces moved into the city's residential quarters, carried out house-to-house searches, and summarily executed those possessing weapons. Reprisals for attacks on the Iraqi military were severe. When the bodies of four dead Iraqi soldiers were found near a school in early September, the authorities burnt down 15 houses nearby, and the personnel of the Special Forces, wearing shoulder flashes 'Squad 65' and 'Squad 68', arrested all the young men living near the site. Severe repression, lack of ammunition and permission to leave Kuwait virtually put an end to resistance by mid-September.[15]

In early October the London-based human rights organization Amnesty International produced a report based on evidence collected from scores of interviews with those who had left Kuwait. 'Their testimony builds up a horrifying picture of widespread arrests, torture under interrogation, summary executions and mass extra-judicial killings,' the report concluded. 'Scores of hangings of those suspected of opposing Iraq's annexation of Kuwait have been reported in the grounds of Kuwait University. Those hanged were summarily executed without any form of trial after being accused of criminal offences.' These offences included possession of opposition literature, the Kuwaiti flag or a picture of the emir, and refusal to replace the emir's picture with Saddam Hussein's. Some 200 Kuwaitis who had been killed by the Iraqi military had been taken to hospitals, where documents certifying that they had died in hospital were obtained by force.[16]

While the internally organized resistance against the Iraqi forces inside Kuwait died down by mid-September, the externally organized resistance against them continued. It was directed primarily from the Saudi border town of Khafji, and secondarily from Hafar al Batin. From Khafji, the opposition beamed radio and television signals, and smuggled newspapers and pamphlets, into Kuwait. The headquarters of the national committee which guided the resistance was based in Khobar, Saudi Arabia. By early September it claimed to have killed 200 Iraqi troops.

The national committee, which was also charged with the welfare of the Kuwaiti refugees, set up sub-committees in all Saudi provinces. It was funded by the Kuwaiti government-in-exile functioning from the Sheraton Hotel near Taif, Saudi Arabia. It allocated $55 million a month for the welfare of the Kuwaiti refugees.

The number of Kuwaiti refugees swelled, reducing the number of those still resident in Kuwait to about half the pre-invasion total of 700,000. Among non-Kuwaitis, the same was true of the Palestinians, down by nearly half from their pre-invasion total of 350,000. But the most steep fall was among Asian expatriates – Indians, Pakistanis, Bangladeshis, Sri Lankans and Filipinos – down from 800,000 to 200,000. As they were the backbone of the Kuwait labour force their departure destroyed the Kuwaiti economy, already crippled by the stoppage of oil exports.[17]

Unlike the Kuwaitis and Palestinians, who took refuge respectively in Saudi Arabia and in Jordan and the Occupied Territories, the Asian expatriates were stranded in the refugee camps of Jordan for several days or several weeks. On 6 September Jordanian officials said that an estimated 605,000 people had entered Jordan from Kuwait and Iraq since 2 August, and that 105,000 were currently being held in 17 refugee camps.[18]

Jordan was not in a position to handle this level of human traffic, and appealed for international help. It received some, but not enough to help it recoup all the expenses it had to incur to house and feed such a large number of refugees and transients. Even without this calamity, Jordan expected to suffer an annual loss of $2.1 billion for abiding by the UN sanctions against Iraq made up of the loss of the remittances of 200,000 Jordanians working in Iraq and Kuwait, exports to these countries, customs duties on Iraqi foreign trade passing through Jordan, the rise in the oil price and a steep fall in tourists. In the course of the First Gulf War its economy had become integrated with Iraq's. Before the embargo, Jordan imported 83% of its oil needs of 70,000 b/d from Iraq at the fixed price of $16.40 a barrel in repayment of the $550 million it had lent Baghdad during the Iran–Iraq War. In the changed circumstances, Riyadh offered to supply 33,000 b/d to Jordan at the market price, then fluctuating between $30 and $35 a barrel. When King Hussein pointed out that his country lacked hard currency to pay for the Saudi oil, King Fahd reportedly told King Hussein that he was prepared to write off up to $40 million of Jordanian liabilities towards Saudi oil companies. The Saudi monarch expected a political *quid pro quo*. Yet King Hussein continued to appeal to the West to seek a compromise with Saddam Hussein. He also criticized the Saudi monarch for failing to act as the Custodian of the Holy Shrines (his official title) by inviting non-Arab, non-Muslim troops to his kingdom. In mid-September he allowed the convening in Amman of the Popular Forces Conference for Solidarity with Iraq, which was attended by twenty radical groups from the Arab world. The conference condemned the Saudi alliance with the US, angering King Fahd who cut off oil supplies to Jordan saying that Jordan had failed to pay $48 million it owed Saudi oil companies for the oil delivered so far. His foreign minister asked the Jordanian ambassador to Saudi Arabia to reduce his staff. The envoy refused, and flew home in protest. Riyadh expelled Jordanian diplomats, alleging that they were helping Iraqi diplomats to gain access to areas off-limits to them since the Kuwaiti invasion.[19]

The other neighbour to upset King Fahd was Yemen. Its president, Ali Abdullah Saleh, a pan-Arab nationalist, was ideologically close to Baathism, and his country (North Yemen, before May 1990) had been a traditional recipient of aid from Baghdad. Saleh stated that Yemen was 'opposed' to Iraq's invasion of Kuwait, but was 'strongly opposed' to the build-up of US-led forces in the Gulf, arguing that it endangered '[Arab] sovereignty, oil resources and Arab national security'. He refused to 'sell' the loyalty of Yemen, a thinly disguised reference to the Saudi way of conducting diplomacy – through the cheque-book. Saudi Arabia expelled many Yemeni diplomats claiming, as in the case of their Jordanian counterparts, that they were helping the Iraqi diplomats to gain access to areas off-limits to them since the invasion. Also, Riyadh withdrew exemptions to Yemenis who hitherto had been allowed to enter the Saudi kingdom without visas or sponsors and allowed to engage in commerce. The forced repatriation of tens of thousands of Yemenis inflamed public opinion in the republic against Riyadh, thus reinforcing the policy their government was pursuing.[20]

As for Iraq's neighbours, Jordan continued its friendly attitude towards Baghdad, with its monarch addressing an open letter to the American people calling for a negotiated settlement to the Gulf crisis, and for an early withdrawal of American and other foreign forces from Saudi Arabia; Syria and Turkey continued to pursue an anti-Iraq policy; and Iran continued to balance its call for the Iraqi pull-back from Kuwait with the withdrawal of all foreign troops from the Gulf.

During his four-day visit to Tehran, Assad tried to persuade President Rafsanjani to join the anti-Iraq coalition militarily, but failed. The Iranian leader focused on the Western military build-up in the Gulf region. 'We are certain that the American and Western military presence is not for saving Kuwait,' Rafsanjani said. 'They have come to serve more important objectives, among them the problems Israel faces. We should not allow foreign forces and those hegemonist powers, who are all geared up to tighten their grip on vital oil resources in the Persian Gulf, the Red Sea and other sensitive points of the world to remain in the region.' He added that the presence of foreign troops was hindering the regional Arab countries from finding a solution to the crisis, and that he favoured the solving of all the problems, including the Lebanese and Palestinian ones. Assad's stress lay elsewhere. 'Today we are witnessing the presence of foreign troops in the region as a result of the Iraqi occupation of Kuwait,' Assad said. 'We are sincerely calling for the elimination of the cause so that the effect can be removed.'[21]

Like Iran among the regional states, France in the anti-Iraqi coalition tried to find some balance. Its military contribution to the Saudi defences was second only to America's. It had deployed 14 warships, 30 combat aircraft, and more than 13,000 men, including 4,200 ground troops equipped with 42 anti-tank helicopters and 48 tanks.[22] Unlike the British contingent, scheduled to become 15,000 strong, the French contingent, under the command of General Michel Roquejoffre, was to become an integral part of the strategic group of Saudi, Egyptian, Syrian and Moroccan forces, with no direct link with the Americans or Britons. (Nor was the French force to be under the direct command of Prince Khalid ibn Sultan.) Yet the French president kept his diplomatic options open.

This became apparent when he delivered a speech to the UN General Assembly on 24 September. In an attempt to reverse 'the logic of war' that prevailed, he offered a four-point plan to establish 'the logic of peace'. The first phase required an Iraqi declaration of 'intent' to withdraw from Kuwait. The second phase consisted of (a) UN supervision of the Iraqi evacuation, (b) freeing of all hostages, (c) restoration of Kuwait's sovereignty, and (d) confirmation of the 'democratic will' of the Kuwaiti people (a hint here of a possible UN-supervised plebiscite in Kuwait after the Iraqi withdrawal). The third phase involved tackling the problems of Lebanon, the Palestinians and 'full security' of Israel. In the final phase, he continued, we could begin to 'think of a reduction of arms in the Middle East, from Iran to Morocco'.[23]

Among the Security Council's five permanent members, China declared that it was 'impressed' with the Mitterrand plan. Qian Qichen, the Chinese foreign minister attending the UN General Assembly session, was said to have stated in his talks with his British counterpart, Douglas Hurd, that 'war in the Gulf would be catastrophic, and therefore a peaceful solution was essential'.

The Mitterrand plan also elicited a positive response from Iraq. On 27 September Baghdad Radio broadcast a political commentary by the Iraqi News Agency, which described France as 'the only paragon' among Western 'villains'. 'The French speak in a non-hostile tone,' it said. 'Mitterrand is seeking [political] solutions to the region's problems.'[24]

The INA commentary had appeared four days after a hardline communiqué issued by a joint meeting of the RCC and the leaders of the Baath Party's Regional Command. 'Honest nationalists, be they rulers or leaders of the national liberation movements, should beware of turning into a means of pressure [on Iraq] in their search of so-called compromises,' it said. 'If we feel that the people of Iraq are being strangled, and there are some who are directing a bloody strike against the Iraqis, we will strangle all those who are the cause of such a state of affairs.' The countries hinted at were Israel and Saudi Arabia, and 'strangling' them meant launching attacks on Israel (in general) and Saudi oilfields (in particular). The next day, in his address to the visiting Islamic and Palestinian delegations, Saddam Hussein was more explicit. If the Iraqi people's plans to re-integrate Kuwait into Iraq were frustrated by the Western and Arab forces assembling in the

Gulf, Iraq would destroy all Middle Eastern oilfields and bring Israel into the fray, he warned.[25]

What lay behind the Iraqi president's hardline stance was the strengthening of the Iraqi defences of Kuwait: he had by now moved most of his 300,000 battle-experienced troops from the Iranian border to Kuwait. During his hour-long journey from Basra to Fao (near the Iraqi–Iranian border) in late September, Patrick Cockburn of the *Independent* saw little sign of Iraqi infantry and none of armour or artillery. All the troops and hardware had been despatched to Kuwait or west of Basra in Iraq, he reported. It was thus that Saddam Hussein had, according to the Pentagon, managed to bolster the Iraqi military presence in Kuwait to 430,000.[26]

The strengthening of Saddam Hussein's military muscle in Kuwait occurred at a time when President Bush was entering a rough patch at home. This was because of his failure to secure the co-operation of the US Congress, dominated by Democrats, on major issues. Congress had already used its leverage to make the president retract, to his great embarrassment, his 'No new taxes' election pledge.

On the Gulf crisis the Bush administration faced two major domestic problems. Firstly, it failed to get Congressional endorsement of its policies in the early phase of a tide of patriotic enthusiasm for its stand. Now Democrat members of Congress had taken to attacking the administration for its previous policy of cultivating Iraq – with Baghdad–Washington trade rising six-and-a-half times in six years, from $571 million in 1983 to $3,600 million in 1989 – and providing it with military and economic aid. The credits for American foodgrains to the Saddam Hussein regime had grown from $215 million in 1983 to $1,045 million in 1989, the second largest sum provided by the US for the purpose. By then Washington had granted 486 export licences worth $730 million involving sensitive technology for Iraq, and a further 160 were pending on 2 August 1990. Just a day before, according to the House of Representatives Government Operations Sub-committee on Commerce, Consumer and Monetary Affairs, the Bush administration had approved a sale to Iraq of $695,000-worth of advanced transmission devices, and two weeks before another sale of $4.8 million in advanced technology products. When the US commerce department had tried to tighten export policy after Saddam Hussein's statement against Israel on 2 April 1990, it had been rebuffed by the state department.[27]

Secondly, there was disarray in the Bush administration's senior ranks. The most public, and severely damaging, example of it was the unseemly dismissal of General Dugan. Nobody among Bush's close aides was entirely certain what the president wanted to do. They saw a 'perpetual ditherer' in charge, with the weeks of hard, tense personal diplomacy and other work manifesting themselves in his suddenly aged, tired looks.

He faced a complex set of problems in the Gulf. In order to hold the US–Arab alliance together, it was crucial for him to keep Israel out of the fray. The statement on 29 September by a senior White House official that 'Our message number one, two and three to Israel is to keep out of this at all costs' reflected the desperation of the US administration on the subject. So far Israel had done so, contenting itself with demanding and securing American weapons. But Iraq was intent on getting Israel involved, by mounting missile attacks for instance, so there was no guarantee that Israel would stay out. Secondly, much to the chagrin of Washington, Tehran had emerged as a strategic actor in the Gulf drama, with a great potential to sabotage the UN embargo. It could use its position to extract major concessions from the anti-Iraq coalition.

Finally, the more Washington committed itself to safeguarding or restoring the feudal, autocratic monarchy of Saudi Arabia or Kuwait, the greater was the chance of such a system becoming destabilized because of its exposure to republican, democratic ideas and people from abroad, and the resulting loss of fear and reverence for their rulers among their subjects. An increasing number of members of Congress were asking why troops from a democratic republic should be seeking to restore one autocratic potentate and safeguard another. A group of sixteen US senators on a tour of the region in early September got a taste of the arrogance of the al Sabahs when the emir of Kuwait refused to receive them in Taif, and instead despatched a group of officials to meet them in Jiddah. They were incensed. A few weeks later even a senior state department official had to concede publicly that the al Sabah family was one of 'the less popular regimes in the Arab world'.[28]

General Dugan's disclosure of the American strategy for military action in the region confirmed the suspicions of the Arabs, including those in Saudi Arabia, that Washington was more interested in annihilating Iraq than in restoring Kuwait to the al Sabahs. Dugan's revelation that Israel had transferred to the US its 'Have Nap' missiles with one-ton warheads for use against Iraq by American B-52 bombers provided further evidence of American–Israeli collusion to destroy the Arab world's most powerful nation.

This information rekindled the tension which had all along existed in the Saudi royal family regarding the kingdom's relationship with the US and which reached a high point in the mid-1970s following a dramatic leap in oil prices. It revolved around the speed of economic development and the extent to which it was necessary to compromise with orthodox Islamic values and practices. Those who advocated a slower pace of industrialization and closer adherence to the teachings of the Quran and the Sharia were also the ones who stood for a sharper struggle against Zionism and greater support for the Palestinians. Led by King Khalid ibn Abdul Aziz (1975–82) and Prince Abdullah ibn Abdul Aziz, they came to represent the Arab nationalist trend within the royal family. Those who stood for a fast pace of industrialization, accompanied by greater religio-cultural liberalization at home, advocated still closer ties with America, leading to the formal signing of a long-term security treaty with Washington. Headed by Crown Prince Fahd and his brother Prince Sultan, they came to be identified as the modernist-Americanist trend within the ruling family.[29] The inception of the 1979 Islamic revolution in Iran, followed by the lowering of American prestige in the region, weakened the Fahd–Sultan wing. The establishment of the Gulf Co-operation Council in 1981 provided a semblance of regional security and self-reliance. On the other hand, the succession of Fahd to the throne in 1982 gave an upper hand to the modernist-Americanist section within the royal family. This was counterbalanced to a certain extent by the elevation of Abdullah to crown prince, a traditionalist-nationalist who was popular with the religious establishment. As the commander of the well-armed National Guard, reputedly better trained than the regular military troops, Crown Prince Abdullah was a powerful figure. At the beginning of the Kuwait crisis, he was said to have argued against inviting the US military, while Prince Sultan, the defence minister, pressed for it. Once King Fahd, a full brother of Sultan, decided to call in the Americans, Abdullah had no choice but to fall in line. But this did not mean that basic differences between the crown prince and the king on formulating the kingdom's foreign and defence policies had been resolved.

In Washington differences sharpened on the advisability of using force. The situation reflected national sentiment. While overall backing for Bush on his handling of the crisis was high, in the upper 70s, there was deep division about the use of force against Iraq, with only 48% in favour, and the permanent stationing of US forces in the Gulf, with 52% opposing it.[30] There was much support for an

economic embargo, at least among American politicians. The House
of Representatives Foreign Affairs Committee unanimously praised
Bush for his reliance on international sanctions approved by the UN
Security Council. 'The United States shall continue to use diplomatic
and other non-military means, to the extent possible, in order to
achieve those objectives and policies, while maintaining credible US
and multinational deterrent military force,' its resolution stated. It
refrained from giving Bush open-ended support for military action.[31]

The Security Council tightened the screw further on Baghdad. On
25 September 1990, the foreign ministers of the Permanent Five –
meeting for only the third time in the 45-year history of the UN
– voted to extend the application of the embargo against Iraq to
all means of transport including aircraft, and threatened Iraq with
'potentially severe consequences' if it failed to withdraw from Kuwait.
The motion (Resolution 670) was carried by fourteen votes to one,
with only Cuba voting against, and Yemen, yielding to pressures
from Saudi Arabia and America, siding with the majority. The UN
secretary-general said that the organization faced an unprecedented
test, and it needed to show that 'the way of [economic] enforcement
is qualitatively different from the way of war'. Appealing to Baghdad,
he said, 'What is demanded of Iraq is not surrender, but the righting
of the wrong that has been committed.' Baghdad Radio denounced the
UN resolution as 'unjust', adding that it had been passed at the behest
of President Bush.[32] The Iraqis noted too that the Soviet Union was in
the chair at the Security Council when the motion was debated and
carried.

As if this were not enough, on the same day the Soviet foreign
minister, Eduard Shevardnadze, declared in his speech to the UN
General Assembly that the USSR might support the use of force if
Iraq's occupation of Kuwait continued. Aware that a week earlier
the Saudi foreign minister, Prince Saud al Faisal, had said that his
government would 'welcome' Soviet troops on Saudi soil, Baghdad
viewed Shevardnadze's statement with great concern. 'In a tone that
clearly shows the bribes given by the Americans and its allies, the oil
shaikhs, USSR foreign minister Shevardnadze spoke from the United
Nations forum in a threatening voice,' wrote the political editor of the
Iraqi News Agency. 'We tell Shevardnadze, if you are not concerned
about relations of friendship with the Arabs and want to be dragged
into the alliance of American hostility, then the Arabs will not be
concerned about the likes of you.'[33]

Iraq could take comfort from the fact that the Soviet military did not endorse the foreign ministry's position. In an interview with the *Washington Post*, the chief of the Soviet general staff, General Mikhail Moiseyev, warned against a military conflict in the Gulf. 'In the event of some military action, Iran will join the Iraqi side,' General Moiseyev said. 'This would not be simply some kind of conflict: this would be a world war ... Such a war will not bring any glory either to the American people or to the people of Iraq.' He drew an analogy with the First World War. 'The First World War in 1914 also started because of some minor thing,' he said. 'Today we should do our utmost to avoid that.'[34]

Aware of the CIA- and DIA-inspired stories in the Western press that the USSR had been co-operating actively with America by providing it with valuable military information on Iraq, General Moiseyev tried to put the record straight. He said that he had supplied technical information to the US embassy in Moscow regarding Soviet-made weapons used by Iraq, and added, 'The CIA already has as much information [on these weapons] as I do.'[35]

Not to be outwitted in this game of bluff and counter-bluff, *Al Qadisiya*, the newspaper of the Iraqi armed forces, reported on 28 September that Iraq's military possessed powerful electronic warfare equipment to counter the radar and other reconnaissance installations of the enemy. It claimed that, financed by Kuwait and Saudi Arabia, Egypt and Israel had set up an intelligence station in the Negev desert to pick up data on the movement of Iraqi troops.

All such information was of course classified. What was widely known, however, was the set of arrangements made by the industrialized nations to deal with shortages of petroleum and refined products in case of disruption of supplies. Overall, government stocks in the West and Japan were sufficient to last 98 days compared to the standard requirement of 90 days. The commercial oil company stocks amounted to 70 days' supplies, fifteen days above the standard requirement.[36]

Yet oil markets were nervous, with the price of a barrel fluctuating around $35. On 27 September, Shaikh Ahmad Zaki Yamani, director of the London-based Centre for Global Energy Studies and a former Saudi petroleum minister, confirmed an earlier report by the Kuwaiti foreign minister that Iraq had mined all Kuwait's oil wells, and that it could destroy them at the touch of a button. 'In the event of a war Iraqi oil wells might also be destroyed,' he continued. 'If ever the Iraqis can inflict damage on oil installations in Saudi Arabia this ... might push the price above $100 [a barrel] unless the major consumers – America,

Europe, Japan – opened up their strategic reserves and did something drastic.' This, and the firing of shots across the bows of the Iraqi tanker *Tadmur* by USS *Elmer Montgomery*, caused the oil price to rise above $40 a barrel, a record for over a decade. The next day, President Bush ordered the release of supplies from the strategic reserves stored in salt caverns in Texas and Louisiana, the first time this had been done apart from the test run in 1985.[37]

With the petroleum price at its highest level in twelve years, the oil revenues of the Gulf states shot up. At $35 a barrel, Saudi Arabia and the UAE were earning $4–5 billion a month more than they would have at $20 a barrel. Even allowing for the huge sums that Saudi Arabia was having to spend to finance the presence of American and other troops on its soil, as well as providing economic aid to the states hurt by the embargo against Iraq, it had plenty to spare to buy weapons and plan on doubling its military to 130,000. It submitted an arms shopping list worth $21 billion to the US administration, a record. Responding to pressures from the US Congress as well as the Israeli government, the White House trimmed this down to $6.7 billion, with a promise to Riyadh to consider a fresh application in January 1991. The list included advanced M1 A2 tanks, anti-tank missiles, helicopters and Patriot anti-missile missiles.[38]

Leaving aside the political ramifications of the transaction, its economic aspect could only benefit the US: it would narrow Washington's trade deficit. Then there was the deeper and longer-running problem of covering the federal budget shortfall, an issue that had bedevilled relations between Congress and the presidency throughout the 1980s, with a Republican president intent on not raising taxes while maintaining high defence spending, and a Democrat-led Congress, while not unhappy about reducing taxes, being more interested in continuing adequate funding of social welfare, pensions and medical care. The two sides compromised on the sums, and ended up taking the same old route of borrowing the deficit. This transformed the US from the world's largest creditor nation in 1981, with a surplus of $141 billion, to the world's largest debtor, with debts of $620 billion. At $260 billion, interest on domestic public debt was one of the three largest items of federal expenditure along with defence and social security. On top of that, foreigners with capital had lost interest in investing in the US. In the first six months of 1990 direct foreign investment in America was $10.5 billion, down from about $32 billion in the corresponding period of 1989. The comparative figures for the two periods for the sale of US Treasury Bonds were: $2 billion (versus

$12 billion); and for other securities $6 billion (versus nearly $20 billion).[39]

The White House's more particular and pressing problem, however, was how to forge a compromise with Congress in time for the new fiscal year beginning on 1 October 1990. Bush intervened personally, but was rebuffed. During the Reagan presidency, when Congress proved obstructive, the chief executive would appeal directly to the American people through a television speech, getting his way by whipping up grass-roots pressure on members of Congress. When President Bush tried to do the same, the effect was the reverse. This failure was partly due to an appalling television performance, partly due to the political arrogance stemming from an approval rating of over 70% in the polls, and partly due to the absence in the Bush White House of the raw political skills of Reagan's active supporters.

On 5 October, thanks to an unexpected alliance between right-wing Republicans and liberal Democrats in the House of Representatives, the House rejected a bipartisan agreement – reached after months of secret negotiations between the White House and Capitol Hill – to curtail the $290 billion budget deficit by $41 billion in the coming fiscal year, and by $500 billion over five years. As a result, such non-essential federal services as the management of the Grand Canyon, Yellowstone Park and the Statue of Liberty closed down. To keep the essential federal government running the Congress passed a 'temporary spending bill' to cover the expenses for the next fortnight, until 19 October, while the two sides bargained feverishly to conclude a new deal. The ultimate point that Bush had to face was: would he yield to a Democrat-supported increase in income tax for the rich if Congress agreed to his proposal for a cut in capital gains tax?

Now the wimp in Bush came to the fore. He signalled that he would accept the deal; then, yielding to the Republican legislators' argument that his capitulation would whet the Democrats' appetite, he reversed his stance. During the next 24 hours Bush changed his mind twice, thus completing a quadruple somersault. On 10 October, while he was jogging in St Petersburg, Florida, reporters asked him to explain his behaviour. 'Read my hips,' he replied, and jogged on. Little wonder that within six weeks he lost twenty points in his approval rating, the steepest fall in popularity for a president outside major scandals.

Even in tackling the Gulf crisis, he seemed to be modifying his stance. In his address to the UN General Assembly on 1 October, he reiterated that annexation of Kuwait 'will not be allowed to stand', and that Saddam Hussein could face military action possibly under the

UN flag. However, he added that the US sought 'a peaceful outcome, a diplomatic outcome'. After an Iraqi pull-back from Kuwait, he believed that 'There may be many opportunities: for Iraq and Kuwait to settle their differences permanently, for the states of the Gulf themselves to build new arrangements for stability, and for all the states and peoples of the region to settle the conflict that divides the Arabs from Israel.' Bush combined this public move with a private one. He participated in the drafting of a letter to Saddam Hussein from President Gorbachev. 'Iraq has to withdraw if war is to be avoided,' it said. 'But if the Iraqi president decides to withdraw he can look forward to international conferences on regional disputes.' The letter was to be delivered in person by Gorbachev's special envoy, Yevgeny Primakov, to the Iraqi leader.[40]

Bush's speech at the UN resulted in a considerable easing of tensions in Baghdad. At the diplomatic reception there to celebrate German unity on 3 October, Arab diplomats told the US chargé d'affaires, Joseph Wilson, that they were 'encouraged' by Bush's speech, and asked if it meant a new American policy. When they were told there was no change in Washington's stance, they refused to believe it. In reality Bush's apparent sign of 'Give diplomacy a chance' was a convenient cover-up for the fact that the American build-up was taking longer than expected primarily because nearly half of the US naval transport ships either were out of action or had broken down in operation.[41]

While Bush's words carried more weight than Mitterrand's, the latter's plan was more comprehensive, and accepted the principle of linkage between the Gulf crisis and the Palestinian problem. Little wonder that in his message on Prophet Muhammad's birthday, 30 September, Saddam Hussein described the French president's address to the UN General Assembly as 'different in its language from others . . . We have to encourage any behaviour by foreigners, including those who have become involved in the naval build-up, to pull back while not bargaining over our principles.' He added that 'Iraq is launching contact with the French government with the aim of formulating a precise viewpoint . . . so that action could be launched on clear and solid foundations.' After elaborating on his 12 August initiative, and proposing that foreign troops in Saudi Arabia be replaced by an Arab force under the UN aegis and that Kuwait's historical connection with Iraq be recognized and the opinion of the Kuwaiti people be considered, he concluded: 'We will not dispute where the starting point [for a peace process] should be.'[42]

Mitterrand's plan gained further credence when it received a 'general welcome' from King Fahd during the French president's meeting with him in Saudi Arabia on 4 October, with the proviso that the return of the al Sabah family to Kuwait as the ruling oligarchy had to be a *sine qua non*.

The talks in Baghdad on 5 October between Saddam Hussein and Yevgeny Primakov, a Soviet Presidential Council member who had known the Iraqi leader since 1969, centred on the Mitterrand plan. 'I am not pessimistic any longer towards the prospect of a political solution to the crisis,' Primakov said after the meeting. 'I am greatly satisfied by my talks.'[43]

Saddam Hussein was to receive an unexpected boost from his strongest constituency outside Iraq: the Palestinians under Israeli occupation.

'Anyone with a sense of humanity must sympathize with the Palestinians. Their lands are occupied, they have no political rights, and they are daily victims of a misguided policy which believes that the security of Israel must rest on closed universities, illegitimate settlements and even collective punishments.'

Douglas Hurd, British foreign secretary,
4 October 1990[1]

'I don't want to mix these two questions [the Gulf crisis and the Palestinian issue], but one cannot try to defend human rights here and neglect them there.'

President François Mitterrand, 9 October 1990[2]

'If there is to be a political solution to the Gulf crisis, then linkage is the best and only way. International legality is indivisible.'

Jamil Hilal, PLO spokesman, 11 October 1990[3]

'They fail to understand that Israel is Washington's only reliable ally [in the Middle East]. The Arabs need the US more than Bush needs the Arabs.'

Prime Minister Yitzhak Shamir, in an interview
with the *Ma'ariv* (Twilight), 19 October 1990[4]

In early September, when the 27-month-old Palestinian intifada was going through its quietest phase, it was announced that a foundation stone for the 'Third Temple' of the Jews would be laid by the Temple Mount Faithful at the Temple Mount, in the Old City of Jerusalem, on the Feast of the Tabernacles (8 October).

The Old City and other parts of (Arab) East Jerusalem were captured by Israel from Jordan in June 1967. The Temple Mount is the site of two Jewish temples successively built and destroyed in biblical times, leaving only the Western (Wailing) Wall below the Mount, where Jews go to pray. The ground of the Mount itself is regarded as too sacred for modern Jews to tread on, and the signs in the narrow lanes of the Old City leading to it warn them away. This policy is crucial in maintaining interreligious peace, for the Mount is also sacred to Muslims. Known to them as Haram al Sharif (i.e. the Noble Sanctuary), its vast compound includes the Al Aqsa mosque and the Dome of the Rock. This, the site of Prophet Muhammad's 'night journey' to heaven, is Islam's third holiest shrine, after Mecca, the prophet's birthplace, and Medina, where he was buried.

The Temple Mount Faithful, a group of about 1,000 people led by Gershon Salomon, believe that Jews should reclaim the Mount and build a temple there. Whenever its members tried to enter the compound in large numbers, the authorities compromised by letting a few do so through the Israeli-controlled Maghrebi (i.e. Western) Gate under heavy guard to pray for a while and then depart. This time, however, in mid-September the Israeli high court banned the Temple Mount Faithful from entering the area. But the group let it be known that it would not abandon its march on 8 October.

In his sermon on Friday 5 October the preacher of the Al Aqsa mosque, Shaikh Fadhallah Silwadi, called on his co-religionists to congregate at the Noble Sanctuary on the following Monday morning to frustrate the plans of the Temple Mount Faithful.

On that morning Temple Mount Faithful activists gathered at Silwan, just outside the Old City walls, and began marching towards the Mount as planned. Word reached the 3,000-strong Palestinians gathered at the holy shrine. They became agitated; and around 10.45 a.m. they surged towards the Western Wall and the Israeli police station. They threw stones which landed in the Western Wall square where Jewish worshippers were gathered. The Israeli security forces fired tear gas shells at the Palestinians.

After the first round of stones and tear gas, one or more of the following incidents triggered a massive burst of fire from the Israeli police and troops: (a) a gun dropped by a fleeing Israeli soldier was picked up by the rioting Palestinians, and this alarmed the soldier's colleagues who started firing; (b) Israeli soldiers from the Mahkame observation post built into the Western Wall shot dead a young Palestinian waving a Palestinian flag, which enraged the crowd; (c) a few of the armed Jewish settlers (from the Occupied Territories) present at the scene began firing their personal weapons.

Whatever the primary cause, by 11.30 a.m., following the Israelis' use of tear gas, plastic bullets and live ammunition, 18 to 20 Palestinians lay dead, and another 150 were wounded. Since most of the Jewish worshippers, having said their prayers, had left the Western Wall square by the time the stone-throwing started, only about 20 of them were hurt. The Israeli police post on the Mount was burnt down.

Monday 8 October 1990 became the bloodiest day of the Palestinian intifada, and in fact of the twenty-three years of Israeli occupation of the West Bank (including East Jerusalem) and Gaza.

As expected, reactions were varied, with the Israeli authorities crying 'premeditated conspiracy', the Arabs 'a bestial massacre', and others taking positions in between.

Prime Minister Shamir saw Israel as 'a victim of a satanic plot'. His police minister, Ronnie Milo, had 'no doubt whatsoever' that this was a pre-planned provocation,'arranged by Palestinian militants to incite violence to divert attention away from the Gulf crisis and revive the flagging intifada'.[5]

Palestinian leaders from East Jerusalem appealed to the UN Security Council. 'We do not understand how the Security Council can ignore our plea for protection when it is prepared to send troops to fight a war in the Gulf region,' it said. 'Once again we issue a plea to the civilized world ... Protect us against Israeli soldiers, settlers and armed religious zealots.'[6] The PLO stated that the massacre vindicated its contention that 'the Gulf and Palestinian problems are linked'. Its central committee demanded UN sanctions against Israel and the deployment of an international force to protect Palestinians in the West Bank and Gaza from the occupying forces of Israel.

Elsewhere in the Arab world, the sharpest response came from Baghdad. It ordered three days of national mourning, and demanded that the UN Security Council should behave in 'the same severe way' it had showed 'in response to the events in the Gulf'. Stating that Israel had no choice but to leave the Arab lands, Saddam Hussein warned that Iraq had a 'powerful new weapon', Al Hijaara al Sijjil (The Powerful Stones) – named in honour of the stones thrown by the Palestinians at their Zionist enemies and capable of reaching 'the targets of evil' – which would be used 'when the time of reckoning comes'. The Jordanian government denounced 'the horrible massacre of our Palestinian people', and appealed to its citizens to 'remain vigilant in protecting this dear homeland as a bastion of steadfastness against aggression'.[7]

To America's main Arab allies – Egypt, Saudi Arabia and Kuwait – the shedding of Palestinian blood in Jerusalem brought shame and humiliation, embarrassingly establishing the point that while the US president was intent on setting Kuwait free from Iraq he was not particularly interested in liberating the West Bank and Gaza from Israel. The Saudi and Kuwaiti rulers condemned Israel strongly. President Mubarak warned that the Jerusalem killings could lead to 'grave consequences' in the Gulf crisis, thus establishing, if only implicitly, a connection between the Israel–Palestinian issue and the Iraq–Kuwait problem. Syria, on the other hand, persisted in its refusal to accept any linkage between the two issues. Indeed its foreign minister, Farouk al Shaara, argued that the Iraqi invasion of Kuwait had created 'the circumstances for Israel's action against the Palestinians'.[8]

Outside the Arab world, France took a strong stand. Addressing the National Assembly on 10 October, the French foreign minister, Roland Dumas, called on the world community to 'support the Palestinian aspirations', and added that France would back a demand for a Security Council mission to the Occupied Territories. 'The UN finds itself confronting these problems, which risk becoming interlinked, because the question presents itself in the same terms,' explained Mitterrand two days later. 'We cannot seek to uphold the [international] law here, and neglect it there.'[9]

In contrast, America and Britain were only mildly critical of Israel. President Bush called the event 'saddening' and his secretary of state Baker described it as a 'tragedy in Jerusalem', as if it involved an element of inevitability. 'When Iraqi troops opened fire with live rounds on Kuwaitis demanding the end of Iraqi occupation [on 10 August] – killing one woman – the Americans rightly condemned the Iraqi brutality as "murder",' noted Robert Fisk in the *Independent* of 10 October. 'Yet when the Israelis kill 19 Palestinians, demanding the end of Israeli occupation in East Jerusalem, the Americans call it a "tragedy".'

The news of this 'tragedy' hit the Bush administration when it was in the midst of an internal crisis created by the impasse on the federal budget deficit. It was taken aback by the vehemence with which its Arab allies reacted to the violent deaths of the Palestinians in Jerusalem. While it tried to absorb this shock, it received a warning from the Soviet Union and the European Community that American refusal to join the international condemnation of Israel at the UN Security Council could threaten anti-Iraqi solidarity. Washington's dilemma was that if it got tough with Israel, this would be construed as a success for Baghdad. If it failed to do so it would weaken the position of the Saudi king, who would be perceived as conniving in Israel's desecration of the Noble Sanctuary, Islam's third holiest shrine, while having invited infidel troops to protect his own realm.

As the news of the killings spread in the Occupied Territories, there were spontaneous demonstrations, resulting in the imposition of a curfew on large areas of the West Bank, Gaza and East Jerusalem, the deaths of three more Palestinians, and the arrests of scores of Palestinian leaders, including Faisal Husseini, believed to be closely allied with the PLO. The clandestine Unified National Leadership coupled its call for a week of mourning with a declaration that 'Every [Israeli] soldier setting foot on the land of the state of Palestine is a fair target to be liquidated.'[10]

As the Palestinian protest continued, and as fresh evidence (offered by Zeev Schiff, military correspondent of *Ha'Aratez* (The Land) among others), refuted the Israeli authorities' allegations of a pre-planned attack by the Palestinians, the government appointed an independent committee of inquiry headed by General Zvi Zamir, former head of Mossad, the Israeli secret service, to report on the killings, scrapping the earlier internal police inquiry.[11]

This was in part meant to pacify Bush, who needed to mollify the Arab members of his anti-Iraq coalition. They had gone along with his insistence on not linking the Palestinian issue with the Gulf crisis, aware that such a step would result in entangled procrastination on the Kuwaiti occupation, thus paving the way for some gains by the Iraqi president. Yet, to retain credibility among their own people and the pro-Iraqi members of the Arab League, they needed an assurance from Washington that once it had reversed the Iraqi aggression it would deal sternly with its long-time protégé: Israel. However, such a pledge would in itself have established the very linkage between the two crises that the anti-Iraqi Arab capitals and Washington were keen to avoid. In short, the Temple Mount killings had done for Saddam Hussein what he himself had failed to achieve.

At the same time, despite the continued pro-Iraqi tilt of the PLO in the Gulf crisis, it managed to retain the unanimous backing of the Arab countries at the United Nations, where it had enjoyed a permanent observer status since 1974, and where its representative, Zehdi Labib Terzi, had drafted, or supervised the drafting of, all the resolutions on Palestine for debate by the Security Council or the General Assembly. Along with two Palestinian committees within the UN secretariat there was a powerful Palestinian committee at the General Assembly. They held conferences and seminars, and arranged tours of the West

Bank and Gaza. Through those members of the Security Council which belonged to the 103-member Non-Aligned Movement, the PLO could convene a Security Council meeting whenever it wished.

Now, as the Security Council met on 9 October, at the initiative of Yemen, to debate the Jerusalem killings, almost all the speakers compared the Israeli occupation of the Palestinian territory to the Iraqi occupation of Kuwait. They recalled that twice in the current year the US had vetoed resolutions condemning Israel's actions in the Occupied Territories. It had done so in May regarding a motion stipulating the despatch of a fact-finding mission by the Security Council to report on the condition of Palestinians living under Israeli occupation. Because of the US veto, all that had happened was a short trip to Israel and the Occupied Territories by Jean-Claude Aimé, the UN secretary-general's special assistant for the Middle East. Now, in view of the Council's Resolution 666 reminding Iraq of its responsibilities to the civilians in occupied Kuwait under 'international humanitarian law including, where applicable, the Fourth Geneva Convention', the seven Third World members of the Security Council – Colombia, Cuba, Ethiopia, Ivory Coast, Malaysia, Yemen and Zaire – wanted to make Israel meet its obligations towards Palestinian civilians under its occupation. They wanted to send a Security Council commission to Israel to report on how to safeguard Palestinian civilians. Once they had received the backing of France and Canada, they were certain of getting their resolution adopted, a prospect America dreaded. Washington's options were: abstaining, voting for the resolution and abandoning Israel, or vetoing it and endangering its strategy of maintaining a UN-based international consensus against Iraq. Abstaining on such a vital issue hardly befitted the world's sole superpower. President Bush thus faced an acute dilemma.

He resolved it by ruling out the use of the US veto to protect Israel, and concentrating on getting the draft Security Council resolution softened in two aspects: its condemnation of Israel, and the provision for a Security Council fact-finding mission to be sent to the Occupied Territories. The American decision not to exercise its veto made the sponsors of the draft resolution amenable to Washington's views on the subject. This led to a protracted debate in the Council and behind-the-scenes horse-trading.

At home the White House was in the midst of a continuing battle with Congressional leaders on the federal budget deficit against the background of a fast-approaching deadline: midnight, 19 October.

Bush appeared beleaguered, unable to provide resolute leadership. This caused a deep slump in his popular standing: down from 76% in early September to 55% in mid-October.[12]

Aware of Bush's vulnerability, the pro-Israel lobbies got to work. The American Israel Public Affairs Committee condemned the Bush policy at the UN as 'harsh and hypocritical, caving in to the political needs of our new-found Arab allies, including the practitioners of international terrorism and human rights violations such as Syria.' Orthodox Jewish leaders called for a 'Sabbath of protest' on 20 October against the US efforts at the UN. Even liberal Jews (such as those in 'Americans for Peace Now'), opposed to the Israeli occupation of the Arab territories, complained about Bush's efforts at the Security Council.

The Israeli government too did its best. Prime Minister Shamir telephoned his personal contacts in America, warning that if Washington left Israel deserted and vulnerable at the United Nations, the Jewish state would have no choice but to look after its own security, and if the US shied away from destroying the military threat to Israel from Baghdad, then Israel might act on its own. Among those Shamir contacted was Armand Hammer, an influential businessman of long standing. Hammer reportedly passed on the sombre message to President Bush who, in turn, called President Mitterrand to convey Israel's desperation and persuade him to moderate the draft resolution condemning Israel.[13]

On 13 October the Security Council unanimously adopted Resolution 672, a watered-down version of the draft that the Third World members had offered. After expressing 'alarm' at the violence of 8 October at the Haram al Sharif in Jerusalem, it condemned 'the acts of violence committed by the Israeli security forces', and called upon 'Israel, the occupying power, to abide scrupulously by . . . the Fourth Geneva Convention, which is applicable to all the territories occupied by Israel since 1967'. Welcoming the secretary-general's decision to send a mission to the region, the Council requested him to submit his 'findings and conclusions' before the end of the month.[14]

The next day Israel's cabinet decided unanimously not to receive the UN secretary-general's mission. 'To receive a [UN] delegation in these circumstances would be to accept that Jerusalem is not our legal capital, and to bring into question Israeli sovereignty,' said David Levy, the foreign minister.[15]

On 15 October James Baker sent a letter to Levy. 'If you reject the UN mission I am worried that Israel, and not Iraq, will be the focus of world attention,' he wrote. 'There will be some who will compare you unjustly to Saddam Hussein and to his rejection of the Security Council resolutions.' Appearing on an American television programme, Dan Quayle, US vice-president, elaborated the American stance. 'I hope Israel and the cabinet and the prime minister recognize how far the [American] president went to make sure that the Palestinian question is not related to Saddam Hussein,' he said. 'We will urge co-operation [from Israel], but we are not going to let Israel become the issue in the Middle East. The issue is that Saddam Hussein invaded Kuwait.' Bush underlined the last point on 15 October when, addressing a Republican Party election meeting in Dallas, he referred to two children in Kuwait being arrested and executed by the Iraqi troops in the presence of their parents for distributing opposition leaflets. 'This is Hitler revisited,' Bush said. 'But remember, when Hitler's war ended, there were the Nuremburg trials [in which Nazi soldiers were held individually accountable for their crimes].'[16]

Such a strong anti-Saddam statement by Bush was meant in part to pacify Shamir in Jerusalem. Yet he remained adamant. On 17 October the US joined Britain and the Soviet Union in urging the UN secretary-general to despatch an investigative team to Israel despite its refusal to co-operate.

On 18 October Israel responded by accusing Washington of 'humiliating and endangering Israel' by supporting the Security Council resolution on the Jerusalem killings. The next day in a long interview with the *Ma'ariv*, Shamir was more outspoken. President Bush, he argued, was 'messing with Israel' because he had no clue as to how to deal with Iraq. 'Bush and Baker are boiling mad with us,' Shamir stated. 'They say in Washington that Israel's refusal [to co-operate with the UN mission] may sabotage American efforts in the Gulf. That's just talk. Who is preventing them from dealing with Iraq?' He accused Bush and Baker of abandoning Israel to secure an Arab coalition against Iraq.[17]

President Bush received flak from the Arab side as well. An extraordinary meeting of the Arab League foreign ministers in Tunis on 18 October combined its condemnation of Israel for 'its new aggression against the [Al Aqsa] mosque of Jerusalem and the Dome of the Rock, and for the killings of the Palestinian people' with criticism of Washington's response, demanding that it should 'change its policy to favour the national rights of the Palestinians and Arabs, and stop aid to Israel'. Earlier, though, it had rejected by 11 votes to 10 the PLO's draft resolution which denounced 'the US government's procrastination and evasiveness during the UN Security Council debate, affirming American bias towards Israel's policy of repression and terror'.[18]

The Arab League's statements made little impact at the Security Council, where the UN secretary-general decided, in view of Israel's continued refusal to co-operate, against despatching a UN mission there.[19]

Critical well-wishers of Israel felt that by refusing to co-operate with the UN investigation, it had inadvertently brought the PLO right back to centre stage, and thus played into the hands of Saddam Hussein and other radicals. Others felt that, despite Israel's intransigence on the UN mission issue, its strategic alliance with America remained intact. While the détente between Washington and Moscow had reduced the significance of the United States–Israel military axis, the importance of intelligence co-operation between the US and Israel remained as high as before, with the superpower heavily dependent on its regional ally in the matter. Israel's military strength made it a highly valued friend to America. Also, Israel continued to be popular among the US public and politicians. To a considerable extent, this stemmed from the sharing of such socio-political values as democracy and multi-party politics and, at a popular level, the similarity of appearance, dress and speech of the American and Israeli spokespersons on television. These factors enabled the pro-Israeli lobbies to continue to wield much influence on US politics and media, and fairly quickly relegate a bitter, public squabble currently in progress to a minor quarrel within a family.

This became obvious when Israel announced its plans to construct 15,000 new apartments for Jewish immigrants in East Jerusalem (which the US, according to President Bush, considered part of the Occupied Territories), with its foreign minister, David Levy, adding that Israel would continue to settle Soviet Jewish immigrants in the Occupied Territories. This contravened the statement made in his letter of 2 October 1990 to US secretary of state Baker that 'Israel's policy was not to direct or settle Soviet Jews beyond the Green Line [the Israeli border before the 1967 Arab–Israeli War]'.[20]

Tension in the Occupied Territories was high, with Israeli troops injuring fifty Palestinians in a clash at a Gaza refugee camp on 18 October. That day the Palestinian leaders boycotted a scheduled meeting with British foreign secretary Douglas Hurd, who was touring the region. On the previous day Hurd had said that the PLO had made 'a serious mistake' by supporting Iraq; but a lasting settlement, which must include secure borders for Israel as well as 'legitimate rights for Palestinians', would still require the reconciliation of Israel with Palestinian nationalism through Israel's talks with 'representative Palestinians'. The Palestinian leaders objected to this, arguing that it suggested Britain was supporting the Shamir government's concept of a non-PLO, alternative leadership in the Occupied Territories. Hurd tried to pacify the Palestinians by saying that the British position was that it favoured self-determination for the Palestinian people, and adding that 'Whether or not that leads to a Palestinian state is a matter for them and [their] negotiation [with Israel].'[21] But this did little to lower the temperature in the Occupied Territories where, on 21 October, in revenge killings a young, deranged Palestinian, named Omar Abu Sirhan, murdered three Israelis in the Baka district of Jerusalem. Israel sealed off its (pre-1967) boundaries to the Palestinians in the Occupied Territories, thus turning a third of the total Palestinian labour force of 370,000 out of work.[22]

In America, too, tension of another sort remained high: the unprecedented impasse between the president and Congress remained unresolved as the end of the two-week period covered by the 'temporary spending bill' of 5 October approached. The deadline was then extended to 24 October.

In between the two 'temporary spending bills', unknown to the public President Bush had received another piece of bad news on 11 October. It came from General Schwarzkopf who, instructed by Bush, had devised an American attack plan codenamed Operation 'Night Camel', to be launched on a moonless night: the American warplanes and helicopters had night vision, something the Iraqi aircraft lacked. Presented by Schwarzkopf's chief of staff, Major-General Robert Johnston, to the president, it consisted of four phases. In phase one, aerial attacks would target (a) Iraq's command, control and communications (to cut off the Iraqi high command in Baghdad from its forces in southern Iraq and Kuwait), (b) its air force and air defence systems, and (c) its chemical, biological and nuclear arms facilities. Phase two would attempt to sever Iraqi troops from their supplies by bombing, continuously, Iraq's munition and supply centres as well as its roads and transport facilities. Phase three would concentrate air attacks on the entrenched Iraqi ground forces. Once these air phases had been implemented within a week, a land assault on the Iraqi troops in Kuwait would follow. Phase four involved a three-pronged ground attack: US marines staging an amphibious assault from the east; US army attacking the Iraqi defence lines in the south; and Egyptian units assaulting the enemy further to the west while protecting one of the American flanks. The military planners envisaged lethal artillery duels, resulting in the deaths of 20,000 American troops. Finding this scale of casualties unacceptable, Bush rejected Operation 'Night Camel', or, more specifically, the last phase of it. Military experts criticized this phase because it overlooked two basic rules of war: 'Don't attack the enemy's strength' and 'Go where the enemy is not'.[23] Following this, Schwarzkopf needed more time to produce a revised assault plan.

Bush also had a diplomatic problem. He did not have the agreement of the Arab allies that they would participate in an American-led offensive against the Iraqis. In an interview with the Abu Dhabi-based *Al Khalij* (The Gulf) on 8 October, Major-General Muhammad Ali Bilal, the commander of the Egyptian troops in Saudi Arabia, had stated that 'The Egyptian forces in Saudi Arabia will not participate in any offensive.' So had the commander of the Syrian troops in the Saudi kingdom, Major-General Ali Habibi, in an interview with the same newspaper a day earlier.[24] However, through persuasion and pressure, Washington felt the Arab allies could be brought into line.

But what if Saddam Hussein decided to pull out of Kuwait completely or mostly, keeping only the disputed border strip and the islands of Bubiyan and Warba? That would have deprived Bush of achieving his real strategic objective, through military action against Iraq, of weakening it, without crushing it altogether, to ensure that neither Saddam Hussein nor his successor was able to dominate the region with the planet's largest source of petroleum. Little wonder that the prospect of Saddam's total or partial withdrawal from Kuwait was labelled by the White House as 'the nightmare scenario'. Therefore, the White House decided, means had to be devised to punish the Iraqi leader even if he implemented Security Council Resolution 660. It launched the idea of demanding reparations from Iraq and, working in conjunction with London, formally placed it before the Security Council, in the hope that even if the Iraqi leader sidestepped the political cost of his aggression he would be unable to survive the humiliation stemming from having to reimburse Kuwait for the damage caused.

The Kuwaiti government-in-exile was of course busily taking note of the destruction that the Iraqi troops had caused. It had also started paying generous monthly stipends to its nationals. More importantly, in mid-October it convened a Popular Conference – in response to the rising criticism by American politicians about 'our boys' shedding blood for the 'feudal autocrats' of the Arabian Peninsula, and President Mitterrand's specific mention of the 'democratic will of the Kuwaiti people' in his speech at the UN General Assembly. Most observers noted that after the Iraqi invasion the al Sabahs had resorted to acting even more selfishly and high-handedly than before, for example making arbitrary use of Kuwait's national assets nominally held by the Kuwait Investment Authority. 'They have been behaving more like arrogant shaikhs than ever before, and monopolizing everything as if they were more interested in preserving their own rule than the existence of Kuwait itself,' said one Kuwaiti critic.[25]

Of the thousand-odd Kuwaiti exiles who gathered in Jiddah for the Popular Conference on 13 October, the vast majority were loyalist parliamentarians and civil servants. But also present were Ahmad Khatib and his Constitutional and Democratic Grouping. They had arrived on the understanding that the ruler would promise restoration of the 1962 constitution (based on the twin concepts of the al Sabahs as rulers of 'the hereditary emirate of Kuwait', and the people as 'the source of all power') while they would pledge support for the restoration of the al Sabahs as rulers. Acting for the emir, Crown Prince Saad al Sabah told the assembly that in a liberated Kuwait the al Sabah regime would 'consolidate' freedoms granted by the 1962 constitution.

Nobody could say for certain when Kuwait would be liberated. So long as the anti-Iraqi coalition partners were building up their forces there was no chance of war. At the current rate, it seemed in Baghdad, the coalition would not be ready to fight until well into November. Yet, leaving nothing to chance, the Iraqi president and his senior aides studied thoroughly foreign news stories, the statements of the various commanders in Saudi Arabia, and the intelligence reports from their embassies in the Arab countries, to figure out when an assault on Iraq was imminent and try to avoid it. Avoidance of war had become the cornerstone of Saddam Hussein's Gulf policy. Indeed, in early October he approached the US to re-establish military contacts in order to avoid large-scale hostilities, but the White House did not respond.[26] His non-military intentions were, however, often masked by his statements about military and economic retaliation in case of a first strike by the US-led forces: these statements sounded like threats to mount pre-emptive strikes against Iraq's enemies. While he was prepared to reach a compromise he was particular to see that any concession he made was not interpreted as a sign of weakness. A similar feeling was prevalent in the opposing camp, particularly among the American hawks and the Kuwaitis. Baghdad believed that time was on its side as it would allow pro-Iraqi sentiment in the Arab world to solidify and manifest itself in the streets. And it felt confident that it would be able to withstand the UN embargo well into 1991 by managing the economy efficiently through rationing.[27]

The Baghdad government considered it equally important to keep up the morale of the people. This was done in various ways. Through print and broadcast media the public was constantly told that there was growing support for Iraq in the Arab world and outside; and that there was growing discord in the enemy camp as well as rising opposition to President Bush in America. 'A feeling of normality pervades Baghdad, encouraged by government propaganda that speaks of worldwide support for Iraq's occupation of Kuwait,' reported Marie Colvin of the *Sunday Times*. 'TV news shows film of demonstrators from Washington to Whitehall [in London], with protesters shouting "Hands off Iraq". The footage is shot close-up so that it is not apparent that only a handful of protesters are present.'[28]

Concurrently, Baghdad used the approximately 3,700 Western and Japanese hostages in two ways. It placed 661 of them, including 260 Britons and 103 Americans,[29] at strategic military and economic sites in order to inhibit allied attacks while gaining time to strengthen Iraq's military capability, particularly its air defences. Meanwhile it was reinforcing the Iraqi military presence in Kuwait and southern Iraq to compel the US to increase its troops in Saudi Arabia – a time-consuming process – which in turn bought Baghdad a further period of peace. As for those Western and Japanese hostages who had not been placed at strategic sites, Saddam Hussein decided to use them as an emotional tool to alienate the Western and Japanese peoples from their governments, and show that Iraq was not isolated.

It was in this context that Saddam Hussein began receiving well-known politicians from the West and Japan interested in winning the freedom of their fellow-citizens held hostage. He met visitors from Finland, France and Spain. Then, on 21 October, he held a three-hour meeting in Baghdad with Edward Heath (1970–74), a former British prime minister, and promised him the release of 38 sick and elderly British hostages. Stressing that detaining thousands of foreigners as hostages had created ill-feeling for Iraq in Britain, and prevented a diplomatic solution, Heath urged Saddam Hussein to withdraw the hostages from military and civilian installations. After the meeting Heath told a press conference, 'There is a fear of lightning attack here either by the US or someone else [presumably Israel]. The belief remains that the hostages act as a prevention against a sudden US attack.' From his talks it had emerged, he added, that Saddam Hussein would 'do anything possible' to bring about a peaceful solution to the present crisis. Unknown to Heath, the current prime minister of Britain, Margaret Thatcher, had a day earlier rejected a message from Saddam Hussein through Primakov that he would be prepared to withdraw from Kuwait if a 'face-saving' formula could be found, insisting that he must leave unconditionally.[30]

While the concession to Heath consisted of freeing elderly and sick British hostages, the Iraqi president had something more sweeping in mind for France, which had about 330 citizens in Iraq and Kuwait (including 77 held at strategic sites). 'My proposal reflects the attachment and the friendship felt by Iraq toward France, and the refusal by France to adopt the hostile tactics of Bush or to use arms against Iraq, as expressed in popular demonstrations, messages and meetings,' he said in a letter to the Iraqi National Assembly. Tariq Aziz, who had forged strong Iraqi–French links during the First Gulf War – and who had reportedly had a secret meeting in Tunis with Claude Chausson, the French commissioner of the European Community, and two other French envoys, to discuss Primakov's ideas for a diplomatic solution to the crisis (such as an Iraqi pull-back on condition that Iraq retained the disputed border strip and the two offshore islands) – participated in the parliamentary debate. 'I understand that French forces would not be used in military action against Iraq,' he said. 'French opinion on all Middle East questions, including the Palestinian cause, has undergone a real revolution . . . President Mitterrand's speech to the UN last month was a new phenomenon in the Western position.' He distinguished between different Western governments thus: 'The US is an imperialist state, while the British regime of Mrs Thatcher has kept its old colonial reflexes. However, we cannot attribute the same attitude to the French government.'[31] The National Assembly decided to release all French citizens.

More importantly, for Baghdad, a promising hint came from the Saudi defence minister, Prince Sultan, in his briefing to a group of local newspaper editors and 'Arab media figures' on 21 October in Jiddah. Having reaffirmed the Saudi position that Iraq must withdraw unconditionally from Kuwait and allow the reinstatement of the legitimate government of Emir Jaber al Ahmad al Sabah there, he stated, 'The Iraqi leadership will not be harmed by withdrawing from

a brotherly Arab country and by saving the blood of the Arab nation.'
Turning to the territorial root of the problem, Prince Sultan said, 'If
Iraq has claims, we shall all respond. Any Arab who has a claim
against his Arab brother must make that claim in a magnanimous
way rather than by using force ... There is no harm in an Arab
country giving its sisterly Arab country anything – be it land, money
or a sea inlet.' He then pointed out that 'in drawing borders in all
Arab regions we have given parts of our land and territorial waters
to our Arab brothers magnanimously.'[32] This was no more than what
President Bush had hinted in his UN General Assembly speech three
weeks earlier, but an out-of-context citation of Prince Sultan's words
offered to Western news agencies by a Qatari journalist present at
Prince Sultan's briefing made it appear as if the Saudi defence minister,
repeating his performance of two months earlier, was breaking ranks.
Among those who were upset by this was General Schwarzkopf. On
the other hand, the mellow tone of Sultan's briefing was in line with
that of recent statements made by other leading Saudis, including
King Fahd, who had appealed to Saddam Hussein to see the error
of his ways. The change of tone in Riyadh was partly explained by
a realization that Saudi oil production facilities could suffer severely
in a war with Iraq, which Riyadh increasingly saw as unlikely to result
in a quick victory.[33]

Such a development made Saddam Hussein hopeful that the longer
he could stave off a military confrontation with the US-led alliance,
the better were his chances of causing a rift within it. There were signs
that Baghdad's appeal to pan-Arab and Islamic solidarity was paying
dividends. The Muslim Brotherhood, the most significant Islamic
fundamentalist movement with branches in most Arab countries,
which had so far received funds and inspiration from Saudi Arabia,
had by and large settled for backing Saddam Hussein. Moreover, the
situation in Syria held some promise. There was a gaping contradiction
between the official policy on the Gulf crisis and popular feeling. 'The
majority of ordinary Syrians are sympathetic to Iraq,' said an Iraqi
opposition leader based in Damascus. 'There is no acceptance of Syria
and the US working together [against Iraq].'[34]

This was the case despite the dramatic success President Assad
had notched up in the 15-year-old Lebanese civil war. Since 1976
some 40,000 Syrian troops had been occupying about two-thirds of
Lebanon, yet Assad had been unable to impose his will completely
on his weak neighbour. Indeed, following the failure of the Lebanese
parliament to elect a president of the republic in September 1988,

General Michel Aoun, the military chief, had declared a 'war of liberation' against Syria: an enterprise which was covertly backed by America and Israel. They had drawn a 'red line' around the Christian enclave controlled by Aoun, who occupied the presidential palace at Baabda near Beirut, which he refused to vacate when the Lebanese parliament elected Elias Hrawi as president in late 1989, confident that neither the Lebanese troops loyal to the president nor the Syrian forces would dare to attack him. On the evening of 12 October 1990, while Aoun addressed his supporters from the palace, someone from the crowd fired two pistol shots at him but missed. The next morning Syrian aircraft bombed Aoun's palace. But Aoun had left by then for the safety of the French embassy. From there he called on his forces to surrender. Yet the fighting went on for several hours. By the time it finished there were 800 casualties, military and civilian, and the Syrian-backed President Elias Hrawi was the victor. On 13 October Hrawi's men occupied the presidential palace.[35]

It was significant that Washington set aside its 'red line' in Lebanon and let Syria intervene militarily to defeat Aoun and his forces, who had all along been pro-Western. It did so as a concession to Syria for joining the anti-Iraqi coalition. It even persuaded Israel to follow suit.[36]

The uncontested control of President Hrawi over Lebanon did not help President Assad much to overcome the unpopularity he seemed to have gained as a result of joining an alliance led by America, which had traditionally been portrayed as an enemy of Syria and Arab nationalism, and a strategic ally of Israel which had been occupying the Golan Heights captured from Syria in June 1967. Unable to express their disagreement with the official policy, many Syrians turned to the mosque as an implicit protest against a secular state and to seek solace in a time of trouble.

Assad's government tried to overcome the problem by organizing an unprecedentedly comprehensive series of policy briefings for the party and military leaders. It lost no time in clutching at the news of Washington supplying weapons from the Nato armoury to Israel, and on 24 October publicly accused the US of 'deception', alleging that American military moves in the Gulf were related 'not only to the Iraqi invasion of Kuwait but also to a wider plot aimed at undermining Arab military and economic power.' On 28 October both Damascus Radio and *Al Thawra*, the Syrian government newspaper, hectored Washington for providing additional military aid to Israel, describing it as 'a move that would only reinforce [Israeli] aggression', and urged the Arab states to 'revise their attitude toward the US administration in the light of its attitude toward Israel'. The Syrians were particularly incensed about the US decision to 'lease' Israel two Patriot anti-missile missiles, thus destroying the strategic balance in missiles that Syria and Israel had so far maintained. 'We interpret this as the US exploiting the moment to give more and more military aid to Israel,' said a Syrian spokesman.[37]

However, such statements by Damascus did not mean that Assad was about to leave the anti-Iraq coalition or renege on the promise he had made to Riyadh to despatch more troops to Saudi Arabia. In short, Syria was playing hot and cold in the same way as the US was, though for different reasons.

President Bush followed up his dove-like speech to the UN General Assembly on 1 October by initiating talks with Congressional leaders four days later concerning the possible use of force against Iraq. (These were sufficiently serious to move Representative Les Aspin, chairperson of the House Armed Services Committee, to tell the *New York Times* a few days later that 15 October was 'the day of the offensive'.)

The state of flux, real or contrived, was well captured by the meeting that General Powell, accompanied by Cheney, had with President Bush and Scowcroft on 5 October at the Oval Office. There Powell presented two basic options: containment of Iraq through sanctions, and an offensive against it. 'There is a case here for the containment or strangulation policy,' Powell told Bush. 'If you do not want to make more military investment, here is the alternative . . . It will work some day. It may take a year, it may take two years, but it will work some day.' In military terms, he added, he could 'live with either containment or an offensive option'. Powell fielded a few questions from those present. Then he asked Bush, 'Where do you want to go, Mr President?' Regarding 'containment', Bush replied: 'I don't think there's time politically for that strategy.'[38] This somewhat ambiguous reply by Bush summed up the current policy of his administration. Washington was issuing dovish and hawkish signals simultaneously, partly to satisfy Gorbachev's insistence on a political solution, partly to keep the disparate anti-Iraq coalition together, and partly to confuse Saddam Hussein.

Following an agreement between Bush and Gorbachev in Helsinki that the US would not use force until all the Soviet negotiating resources had been exhausted, Yevgeny Primakov, a member of President Gorbachev's council of ministers, was assigned the task of finding a non-military solution to the crisis. After his meeting with Saddam Hussein on 5 October, it was decided that he should brief the various capitals – Washington, Rome (then holding the six-monthly presidency of the European Community), Paris and London as well as Cairo, Damascus and Riyadh – on it, and then return to Baghdad for a second round of talks.

In his briefings to the Western capitals in mid-October, Primakov summarized his talks in Baghdad thus: having realized the opposition that confronted him, the Iraqi president was considering how best he could extricate himself from Kuwait without loss of face, and was ready to withdraw on certain conditions. But since conditional withdrawal was unacceptable to the leading permanent members of the Security Council he might compromise by accepting an undertaking that Iraq's territorial claims on Kuwait would be open to negotiation after the Iraqi pull-back which would be undertaken after he had received a guarantee against a US military strike against Iraq.[39]

At home, US secretary of state Baker was dovish. In his 16 October testimony to the US Senate Foreign Relations Committee, he said that the sanctions against Iraq were 'tightening with increasing severity' (causing Iraq a daily loss of $80 million in oil revenue), and added that 'blockades, sanctions and containment have a chance of bringing about the desired outcome short of war'. War, he feared, could be highly destabilizing across the entire Middle East, as it would spread to Israel and Jordan immediately. Secondly, if Iraq were crushed, then the Gulf region would be 'open to domination by Iran'. However, Baker was opposed to a deal with Saddam Hussein on the offshore islands or 'anything else', and confirmed that he had offered a compromise and that President Bush had found it unacceptable, saying that there could be talks with him only *after* Iraq had left Kuwait.[40]

The hawkish position in the Bush administration was articulated forcefully by Paul Wolfowitz, policy under-secretary of defence. He wanted swift military action against Baghdad on the ground that if Iraq's military power survived the current crisis, it would dominate the Gulf, with Saddam Hussein being able to press his thumb on the Western world's economic jugular whenever he wished to. Several days later hawkish views were to be expressed by William Webster, the CIA director. According to him, the UN sanctions were having 'no significant impact on Iraqi military capabilities', and he had 'no real confidence that the area will ever be secure again as long as Saddam Hussein is still there . . . unless he is dissociated from his weapons of mass destruction.'[41]

In retrospect, it can be seen that Washington had entered the second phase of its psychological warfare against Saddam Hussein. This consisted of combining the military build-up and tough rhetoric with shuttle diplomacy and a determined effort to refocus the world's concern on the Gulf crisis after a fortnight's attention to the Israeli–Palestinian issue in the wake of the events of 8 October in Jerusalem. The US administration's overall aim was to make its allies unresponsive to any new plan for a negotiated settlement from the Iraqi president that he might offer during the next few weeks while escalating its war objectives far beyond the UN mandate – to overthrowing Saddam Hussein.

On 24 October the White House reached a final compromise with Congressional Democrats on the budget deficit, thus ending a long, bruising battle. (That day, to keep the anti-Iraq coalition intact, the US voted with the rest of the members of the Security Council for Resolution 673, which called on Israel to reconsider its refusal to receive the UN secretary-general's envoy.) Now President Bush could concentrate fully on the Gulf crisis. He and Cheney were waiting for Powell to return from Riyadh after his consultations with Schwarzkopf on the size of the increase in US troops needed to turn them into an offensive force.

They knew that an increase was inevitable. On 25 October, in an interview with CBS television, replying to a (planted) question as to whether the Pentagon was getting ready to send another 100,000 troops to the Gulf, Cheney replied: 'It's conceivable that we'll end up with that big an increase.' This would raise their total to 310,000, or 60 per cent of the highest level of US deployment during the Vietnam War. In another interview he confirmed the figure 100,000, and then added that this would not alter the relief of forces already there after six to eight months. 'There clearly will be a rotation policy.'[42] Responding to the American move, Baghdad said that its army was strong enough to repel an assault by 700,000 enemy troops.

General Powell returned to Washington on 25 October with a request from General Schwarzkopf for a doubling of the US army, navy, air force and marines, the increase in ground troops to be achieved by moving three armoured and mechanized divisions of US VII Corps based in Europe to the Gulf. Schwarzkopf's request stemmed from the increased Iraqi strength in Kuwait, now put at 28 divisions (somewhat exaggeratedly) and thus upsetting CIA predictions that Saddam Hussein could not deploy more than 14 divisions in the Kuwaiti Theatre of Operations. (While waiting for a formal meeting of top policy-makers on 30 October, Powell was instructed by President Bush to transform the contingency plan for the offensive into a 'Second Phase Deployment Plan'.) Reversing its policy of deriding the Iraqi military's morale and capabilities, the Pentagon had taken to exaggerating them, putting out stories about its improved chemical weapons capacity, nerve gas delivery systems, air-burst gasoline bombs (or fuel-air explosives, FAEs), captured US-made Hawk missiles, a new line of defensive earthworks along the Kuwaiti–Saudi border, and the planned total destruction of Kuwaiti oil wells. The intention was to prepare public opinion for increasing US military deployment in the Gulf to meet the growing Iraqi menace.

Already the signs in Saudi Arabia were clear that the US was building a formidable offensive military machine. 'For more than 100 miles along the Kuwait highway in eastern Saudi Arabia, the great multinational army is spread across the desert, the terrain now humped and distorted by thousands of armoured vehicles, command bivouacs, missile sites, encampments, camouflage-draped artillery emplacements, and by fleets of bulldozers cutting revetements and bunkers into the powdery sand,' reported Robert Fisk of the *Independent* on 29 October 1990. 'The dust of a hundred new military roads hangs in the air while beneath it, in the fog, are the soldiers: American, British, Saudi, Egyptian, Moroccan – whose presence or blood is supposed to liberate Kuwait.' No longer was it possible to call it a defensive operation. 'The forward movement of units, the repositioning of the 24th and 101st US Infantry Divisions ... the shift of Harrier close support helicopters nearer to Kuwait, the very strength of the forces ... speak not of military option but military intention.'[43]

These developments occurred at a time when public opinion had turned against war. A *Wall Street Journal*–National Broadcasting Corporation poll published on 26 October showed that, in the wake of a 20-point slide in the president's popularity from 76% to 56% due to the three-week budget deficit crisis, support for the military option had declined from 56% a month earlier to 47%. A poll published in *Newsweek* three days later showed 69% saying that the president should pay more attention to a diplomatic solution. Those opposed to war took to the streets on 20 October in more than a dozen American cities. Some 15,000 protesters marched in New York, shouting such slogans as 'Hell no, we won't go/We won't fight for Texaco'. Their sentiments were shared among others by 81 Democratic members of the House of Representatives who on 26

October declared: 'We are emphatically opposed to any military action.'

None of this had any impact on the Bush administration. Addressing the Los Angeles World Affairs Council on 29 October, Baker dwelt on the fate of the 103 American hostages being used as human shields by the Iraqis, and condemned this as 'simply unconscionable'. He warned, 'We will not rule out a possible use of force if Iraq continues to occupy Kuwait.'[44] Significantly, that day the UN Security Council adopted Resolution 674 by thirteen votes to none, with two abstentions (Cuba and Yemen), reminding Iraq that it was liable for any loss, damage or injury to Kuwait and third states and their nationals and corporations resulting from its occupation of Kuwait.

On 30 October, at a two-hour meeting with the top military and civilian leaders at the White House, the president listened to Powell explaining Schwarzkopf's request for doubling the US forces in three months, given the constraints of the US transportation system. It was obvious that Bush and Cheney had ruled out the sanctions option, which was widely expected to become effective in ten months. The chief reason for not considering the embargo option seriously was the fragility of the anti-Iraqi coalition. Bush and Cheney feared that 'some outside event' could shatter the alliance. Once the option narrowed to an American offensive the question of timing had to be settled. There, Bush took note of the advice given three weeks earlier by Major-General Johnston. He had marked the period 1 January to 15 February as 'a window of opportunity'. Weather conditions would deteriorate in March bringing in both heavy rains and high temperatures. Besides, the holy month of Ramadan – when Muslims are enjoined to fast from sunrise to sunset, and not to engage in warfare – was due to start on 17 March.

The next day, 31 October, Bush secretly approved a timetable for mounting an air campaign against Iraq in mid-January 1991 and a large-scale land offensive in mid-February 1991.[45]

His second major decision was to secure a UN mandate for war; and for this it was vital to hold the anti-Iraq coalition together. This was Baker's primary charge as he set out on a tour of the Middle East and Europe, the secondary one being to solicit ideas from the allies on how to raise pressure on the Iraqi leader during the current phase of confrontation with him. Baker's tour was also meant to pacify an increasingly fretful American public at home as well as the troops in the Gulf, who were anxious to learn the next step in the resolution of the three-month crisis.

Meanwhile, the Primakov mission continued. Having briefed Cairo and Damascus on his way to Baghdad, the Soviet envoy had an hour-long meeting with Saddam Hussein there on 28 October. He passed on a personal letter to him from President Gorbachev. The talk was described as 'broad, deep and useful' by Saddam Hussein in an interview with Cable News Network.

At a press conference in Paris on 29 October, Gorbachev announced that he had received two telegrams from Primakov saying that Iraq had 'modified' its previous intransigent position – by, *inter alia*, not even mentioning that Kuwait was an integral part of Iraq. The Soviet president revealed that the Primakov mission was not 'just one independent branch' but 'part of the process involving many countries, with some of the parts being secret', and added: 'Certain countries might undertake a particular role. I am thinking of Saudi Arabia [where that day Primakov was meeting King Fahd] . . . they might take an initiative.' President Mitterrand agreed that the 'Arab factor' must be brought into play.[46]

Baghdad's response was positive. A senior Iraqi official told visiting Jordanian journalists that Iraq sought 'a serious political process and movement towards a diplomatic solution', but needed guarantees that it would not be used by the US as a cover for a surprise attack on his country. 'Iraq told Primakov it would free all hostages in exchange for a Franco-Soviet commitment to a peaceful solution,' he said.[47] Washington reacted negatively. Senior US officials were quoted as having been 'chagrined' by Gorbachev's suggestion of an inter-Arab conference to resolve the crisis, something that was bound to lead to 'the kind of bargaining' that could result in 'an incomplete compliance with the UN demands'.[48]

At a Republican fund-raising event on 31 October, Bush referred to the United States flag flying over the American embassy in Kuwait where 'our people are being starved by a brutal dictator'. Complaining about the conditions inside the besieged embassy, Bush said, 'I've had enough with that kind of treatment of Americans. Look back into history, into what happened when Hitler invaded Poland, and there is a direct parallel to what has happened in Kuwait. The Death's Head regiments were those SS (Schutz Staffel – i.e. Protection Forces) troops and they came in and systematically wiped out a lot of Polish people, lined up the kids and shot them. And the same things are going on in Kuwait today. It has been brutal.' It is interesting that Bush made the statement about the American mission just two days after Margie Howell, wife of the US ambassador in Kuwait, had been quoted as saying that 'My husband and his staff of 26 are not short of food or water, and are in good shape and morale' – and this had been confirmed by the state department, which said: 'The US embassy has three or four weeks' tinned food left, a thriving vegetable garden, and a [water] well producing enough brackish water for showers and washing the embassy cars.'[49]

The contradictory statements made by the president and his state department stemmed from the basic contradiction in what the US wanted to achieve simultaneously; this had led to alternate hot and cold cycles, each one lasting no more than a few days. On the one hand the Bush administration wanted to maintain psychological pressure and the military threat against Saddam Hussein in the hope that he would 'fall on the floor and come to Jesus', on the other it did not wish its domestic audience to take its bellicosity at face value, get over-excited on the eve of the Congressional poll and expect precipitate action and results.

Saddam Hussein was caught in a similar trap. While increasing the battle-readiness of his troops and bolstering Iraqi air defences, he was careful not to whip up anti-American feeling through an orchestrated media campaign lest it should lead to an unexpected incident (such as the killing of one or more of the 350 American hostages in Iraq) which might provide Washington with the pretext it was looking for to attack Iraq. Nor did he choose to engage in public name-calling with George Bush. When asked by a CNN reporter how he felt when he heard Bush 'equating you with Adolf Hitler', Saddam Hussein replied, 'Do you not think he [Bush] is closing the door to dialogue and peace with that head of state [i.e. himself] by making such descriptions at this phase [of the crisis]?'[50]

Aware of Bush's lack of interest in talks, Saddam Hussein had to look out for the most opportune time for the American president to attack Iraq even though such a step would jeopardize the lives of 741 hostages – 430 of them British and another 103 American – held at strategic sites (the remaining 2,300 were detained at hotels and other civilian premises). He reckoned that Bush might implement his 'Destroy Iraqi military in four days' plan during the run-up to the US Congressional election on 6 November. He therefore took seriously Baker's statement of 29 October about 'not ruling out a possible use of force', and put the Iraqi forces on 'extreme alert'. 'The [Iraqi] president underlined the need [to the military high command] for extreme alert in the face of the treacherous designs of the American enemy and its allies in the coming days,' reported the Iraqi News Agency on 31 October. 'He instructed the high command to review preparations for urban warfare in Kuwait.'[51]

Concurrently Saddam Hussein intensified his hostage diplomacy. With the departure of women and children in September, the number of Western and Japanese hostages fell to about 3,700. About 40 per cent of these were British: 600 in Kuwait (520 in hiding, 80 placed at strategic sites), and 850 in Iraq (350 on sites, 150 held in hotels, and 350 working and living at home). Nearly 30 per cent of the total were American: 700 in Kuwait and 350 in Iraq (with 103 held at strategic sites). The Japanese were the next largest group: 327 (including 141 at strategic sites) in Iraq, and 8 in Kuwait. At 327 (including 67 held at strategic sites), the French were the next in size before their release was ordered by the Iraqi National Assembly on 23 October. Then came the Italians – 315 in Iraq and 2 in Kuwait; followed by West Germans: 245 (with 77 at strategic facilities) in Iraq and 20 in Kuwait. Next was Ireland – 229 in Iraq, 30 in Kuwait; followed by Holland with 155 in Iraq and 5 in Kuwait.[52]

Following the wholesale release of the hostages from France, a country which had despatched troops to Saudi Arabia, popular pressure mounted on the government of Germany (West Germany before 3 October) – a state which was barred from sending armed forces to a region outside Nato – to gain the freedom of its nationals trapped in Iraq and Kuwait. The hands of the German chancellor, Helmut Kohl, a Christian Democrat, were tied because of the decision by the European Community summit on 29 October not to send representatives of their governments to Baghdad to negotiate the release of hostages, and to discourage others from doing so. Aware of the willingness of Willy Brandt (1969–74) – a former chancellor of West Germany, a Nobel peace prize winner, and the current chairman of the Socialist International – to attempt to gain the freedom of West German and other Western captives, Kohl tried to get the UN secretary-general to name Brandt as his envoy for the purpose. This move failed. Undeterred, Bonn declared on 1 November that 'a mission of leading personalities, acting on their own responsibility, is the most suitable way to underscore to the Iraqi leadership the demand for the release.' In this way Bonn meant to place a multinational mantle on the Brandt mission. London criticized Bonn for disregarding the EC's decision.

Such a public display of dissension among the European Community's leading members pleased Baghdad, which had by now perfected its version of 'hostage diplomacy'. Its elements were local as well as Western and Japanese media, senior politicians (often retired or in opposition) from the West and Japan, and Western peace groups. The path blazed by Edward Heath was to be trodden soon by Yasuhiro Nakasone (1982–7), a former Japanese prime minister, and Willy Brandt. The dual purpose was to undermine Washington's claim that Baghdad was diplomatically isolated, and to divert Iraqi and world attention away from the Kuwait crisis.

Indeed, building on the idea broached by Saddam Hussein to Primakov that all hostages would be freed if a guarantee was given by Moscow and Paris that the crisis would be resolved peacefully, the speaker of Iraq's National Assembly, Saadi Mehdi Saleh, said on 3 November that all 'foreign guests' would be free to leave if there was an undertaking of non-aggression against Iraq either from the five permanent members of the UN Security Council, or from two or more of the following countries – the Soviet Union, France, China, Japan and Germany – with at least one being a permanent member of the Security Council.[53] Since Japan was one of the states included in the list by the Iraqi parliamentary speaker, the subject was most probably discussed during the four-hour meeting between Saddam Hussein and Yasuhiro Nakasone on 4 November.

In the end, nothing came of the Iraqi proposal, chiefly because the US was resolutely against bargaining on the hostage issue, arguing that holding foreign nationals by Iraq was illegal to start with. Any softening on this issue would have given wrong signals to its allies, the Bush administration thought. And this was the last thing it wanted to do as Baker commenced his eight-day tour of seven important capitals on 4 November.

His first stop was Riyadh. Trouble was brewing under the surface there, with the differences within the Saudi royal family regarding the duration of the US military presence in the kingdom still unresolved. Crown Prince Abdullah ibn Abdul Aziz, commander of the National Guard, charged with maintaining internal security, was unhappy at the fast escalating strength of the US forces. To distance himself from the way the Gulf crisis was being handled by King Fahd and defence minister Sultan, he returned to Riyadh while the rest of the royal family were still in the summer capital of Jiddah. The crown prince reflected rising public unease at the growing Western military deployment, a subject which formed the core of many Friday sermons delivered from the pulpits of mosques. The more vehement ones were taped and sold as cassettes. The clandestine trade in these recorded sermons reached such proportions that the Saudi secret police moved in to curb it.[54] The militant Saudi priests argued that the Kuwaiti rulers had been punished for deviating from the true path of Islam through debauchery, arrogance and corruption. They were critical of such heretical practices in Saudi Arabia as the performances of singers on television, and warned their audience that the infidel forces in the kingdom could not be trusted, and that what was afoot was a conspiracy to destroy Islam in its birthplace.

Crown Prince Abdullah represented the traditionalist-nationalist school of thought in the ruling family. During the previous two decades this strand among commoners had been strengthened by the rise of a new breed of Islamic fundamentalists (partly in response to the events in Iran). Now Saudi society was broadly divided into two camps: Islamist and modernist. The former included orthodox ulama (religious scholars) as well as militant fundamentalists intent on reducing, and finally eliminating, all Western influence, while the latter encompassed religio-cultural liberals and secularists, ready to back such reforms as abolishing tribal quotas in the armed forces and allowing women to become nurses. The modernists wished that such changes could come from within rather than as an offshoot of the arrival of American forces in the kingdom. They were actually as uneasy about the prospect of seeing the Saudi military subordinated to General Schwarzkopf as the traditionalist-nationalists were. The Saudi rulers were aware of the prevalence of this sentiment.

No wonder that at the top of the agenda of the Baker–Fahd meeting on 5 November was the question of the operational command and control of the multinational forces stationed in the kingdom. It was resolved. 'US and Saudi forces would operate under a joint command in defence of Saudi Arabia,' an official Saudi communiqué stated. 'But beyond the borders of Saudi Arabia, US troops would operate under American commanders once any operation was approved at the highest political level by both governments.' The Pentagon rationalized the joint command on the grounds that it was 'necessary' within the boundaries of Saudi Arabia since it was 'their sovereign territory', and at the same time the US could not release its soldiers to serve under another command because of 'the amount of stuff [military hardware] we've got down here'. The fact that command outside Saudi soil was ceded to the Americans meant that Riyadh's original objections to any counter-offensive operations from its territory had softened.[55]

London had already submitted the operational control of its units to the Americans. This reflected well the attitude of the British government and people who were strongly supportive of the US.

An opinion poll in Britain in late October showed 60% approving military action in the Gulf and 31% disapproving.[56]

The position of the French in the command structures was unclear, a symptom of the somewhat equivocal position that Paris had taken vis-à-vis Washington. The reasons for this were both historical and contemporary. Since the late 1970s France had maintained close military ties with Iraq, supplying it with military hardware worth about $25 billion until mid-1990. France valued highly its links with North Africa, where opinion was running almost universally in favour of Iraq and Saddam Hussein. Pro-Iraqi sentiment was also strong among the nearly three million Muslims of North and West African origin living in France. Finally, public opinion in the country was averse to the use of force against Baghdad. A poll published in *Le Monde* in late October showed that only 22% thought that the presence of the French task force in the Gulf was 'a demonstration of France's willingness to launch a military attack on Iraq'.[57]

Little wonder that during his visit to Cairo on 4 November to meet President Mubarak, Mitterrand said that more time should be given to UN sanctions, and that on his return to Paris the next day he had an hour-long meeting with King Hussein to be briefed on the latter's talks with the Iraqi foreign minister in Amman. In fact, the French president was at the heart of diplomatic moves under way outside America, whose secretary of state was then untiringly flying from one capital to another in the region (his last stop there being in Ankara on 7 November), telling Washington's allies that US air power alone could not win the war, and that they had to be prepared to join a massive ground offensive. If nothing else, these globe-trotting activities of leading Western and Arab officials succeeded in returning world attention to the Gulf crisis – away from the Palestinian deaths in Jerusalem and their aftermath.

General Zvi Zamir's commission's report on the incident, based on the testimony of 124 witnesses (of whom only two were Palestinian) and published on 26 October, had absolved the police and paramilitary border police of using excessive live ammunition. While conceding that 'in some cases uncontrolled live fire was used', particularly after the return of the police and paramilitary border police to the Temple Mount for mopping-up operations, it concluded that, overall, they were justified in firing live ammunition when their lives were in danger at several stages of the riot, and tear gas and rubber bullets had failed to disperse the crowd. The report concentrated on technical failures as well as planning and operational failures of police and paramilitary border police.[58]

'The report was written for the benefit of the White House in Washington and the United Nations in New York,' stated Nahum Barnea, a columnist in the Israeli mass circulation daily *Yediot Aharonot* (Latest News). 'The Israeli government wanted a propaganda document, and that's what it got.' The military correspondent of *Ha'Aretz*, Zeev Schiff, pointed out that 'The commission does not deal with the central question: why were so many killed and wounded?' Apparently, the White House was not convinced. Commenting on the report, the US state department said, 'Both the president and secretary [of state] have said that the use of live fire resulting in the deaths of many people appears to have been excessive use of force.'[59]

At the UN Security Council, the secretary-general submitted his report by 30 October as required by Resolutions 672 and 673. It said that since Israel had refused to receive the UN mission he was unable to collect the required information, and ended with the recommendation that the Security Council should convene a conference of all 164 UN members to discuss the measures that the UN should adopt to make Israel comply with the Fourth Geneva Convention of 1949 which protects civilians in times of war and occupation.[60]

The secretary-general's report was released on 2 November. Next day Palestinian support for it in the Gaza refugee camps led to rioting. It was so serious that the attempts by the Israeli security forces to quell it resulted in 300 injuries in three days, and an indefinite curfew for 180,000 Palestinians.[61] But by then the attention of the world had returned to the Gulf and scant heed was paid to the sufferings of the Palestinians.

All in all, the period 8 October to 7 November had gone well for President Bush. Despite the universal condemnation of the unprecedented Israeli violence against the Palestinians in Jerusalem, he had managed to block any linkage of the Gulf crisis with the Palestinian issue, and to keep the fragile anti-Iraqi coalition together. At the same time, unknown to the world, he had decided to acquire an offensive capability in the Gulf in order to expel the Iraqis from Kuwait militarily.

7 DESERT SHIELD
INTO DESERT SWORD

'We are not on some exercise. This is the real world situation, and we are not walking away until our mission is done, until the invader is out of Kuwait.'

President George Bush, addressing US forces in
Saudi Arabia, 22 November 1990[1]

'We are not intimidated by the size of the armies, or the type of [military] hardware the US has brought.'

Saddam Hussein to Anker Jørgenson, former Danish
prime minister, 12 November 1990[2]

'Today, the worldwide march to freedom is threatened by a man hell-bent on gaining a choke hold on the world's economic lifeline. Energy security is national security.'

President George Bush, addressing US forces in
Saudi Arabia, 22 November 1990[3]

The mid-term elections in America on 6 November produced no surprises. As in previous such polls there was a slight drift away from the party of the incumbent president. In the 440-strong House of Representatives the Republicans lost 9 seats to the Democrats, retaining 168, and in the 100-strong Senate one seat, reducing their total to 44. In other words, Bush had failed to transform his much approved handling of the Gulf crisis into an electoral asset for his party.

Once the election was out of the way, President Bush made public his secret decision of 31 October. On 8 November he ordered the despatch of extra troops to the Gulf to give the US offensive capability. The order involved moving three armoured divisions and one armoured cavalry regiment (from Germany), and two corps headquarters and one infantry division (from the US), three aircraft carriers with task forces, one battleship with escorts, 40,000 marines, and an unspecified number of National Guard units. Though the White House deliberately avoided quantifying the addition, the *Washington Post* estimated that the final overall total of US forces in the Gulf would be 430,000, twice its current strength.[4] By the time the deployment was complete, the US military would have six of its 14 aircraft carrier groups in the Gulf – as many as it would have deployed against the Soviet Union in case of a full-scale war – and two-fifths of its total Marine force of 195,000 stationed in the Gulf.

Following the abolition of the military draft in 1973, the Pentagon adopted the 'total force' policy, which counted all types of reserves (ready, standby and retired) as part of overall US force totals. The active units of the US armed forces added up to 2,118,000, with about one-tenth being women; and the reserves to 1,819,000; giving the grand total of 3,937,000 under full mobilization. America's active, standing army was 761,000 strong, with the 'ready reserves', consisting of the National Guard and army reserves, amounting to 1,043,000. Ready reserves were attached to the standing units of the army. (The same arrangement applied to the other wings of the armed forces.)[5] Their period of active duty, once called up, was increased from 180 days to 360 days by a change in the law made by Congress before it disbanded in early November. Instead of calling up certain units of the 'ready reserves', as Bush did, he could have declared a national state of emergency and mobilized all the reserves for two years. But this was considered politically unwise as it would have fuelled anti-war protest.

On 9 November, reversing the earlier decision, Cheney said that his department was no longer planning to rotate the US troops already in the Gulf or heading for it, and that they would stay 'until the crisis is over'. What he did not say was that there were not enough troops under arms to allow the Pentagon to introduce rotation while maintaining a strength of 430,000 in the Gulf. This meant that the crisis had to be resolved before long as lack of rotation was going to cause severe problems of morale by the end of the winter. The signs were already there. Soldiers' grumbling came to the surface during Baker's visit to US military camps in Saudi Arabia on 4 November. Walking among a group of soldiers, Baker asked for their thoughts on the crisis. One of them described his experience in the Saudi kingdom as 'hell on wheels', and another complained bitterly about the lack of alcohol. Later, soldiers shouted at Baker, 'When can we go home?' Still others said, 'Let's do something or go home.'[6]

Along with the US its Arab allies too were in the process of increasing their commitment. The Egyptians were set to raise their military presence from 14,000 to 25,000, and the Syrians from 3,000 to 15,000. By now, the anti-Iraqi coalition had assembled nearly 1,800 warplanes and helicopters, and 70 naval ships.[7]

The multinational forces were assembled to confront the Iraqis whose military strength and deployment were described by the Pentagon thus. Iraq was still developing its belt of 'obstacle defence' along the southern Kuwaiti border with its four-tier defences: (1) minefields and rows of razor wire, (2) concrete obstacles to stop tanks, (3) ditches seven feet deep (called tank traps), some of them filled with oil and napalm to create a barrier of fire, and (4) bulldozed sandhills, called berms, to act as barriers to armour and to channel the attacking tanks into a chosen killing ground. The berms also made attacks by low-flying helicopters or planes much more hazardous. Behind them were dug-in mortar, machine gun and artillery pieces concentrated on the breaks in the berms. In the rear of the defence belt was the first echelon, mainly an infantry line with a network of trenches and well-dug-in command bunkers. Then came the second echelon, consisting of three to four armoured or mechanized (equipped with artillery) divisions, dug in (and therefore difficult to destroy from the air) for 'counter-penetration', to block any allied incursion. These two echelons totalled 150,000 troops. Another 100,000 were deployed along the Kuwaiti coastline. Then came the third echelon, made up of two to three armoured or mechanized divisions, which was the 'mobile reserve'. Within two weeks it had moved from the mid-west of Kuwait to the west of Kuwait Bay and north of the new southern boundary of the expanded Basra province for 'counter-attack', to recover any lost ground. The move was made because the Iraqis expected a US attack against their central/southern front and a simultaneous amphibious landing from the east. To repel the marines' landing the Iraqis had stationed fully laden oil tankers with a view to blowing them up to create a sea of fire in front of the attacking force. The fourth echelon, consisting of five divisions of Republican Guards with modern T-72 tanks, straddled the (original) northern border of Kuwait, to repel a flanking attack from the west or to reinforce the central front. All this was part of the southern sector (called by the Pentagon the Kuwaiti Theatre of Operations, KTO). There were two more sectors in Iraq: one east of Baghdad, facing eastwards; and the other facing the Kurdish region in the north-east. The borders with Iran, Turkey and Syria were thinly guarded. To counter US air superiority the Iraqis had reportedly acquired a new radar known as monopulse, which was difficult to be tracked and destroyed by the missiles available in the American armoury. Also Iraq seemed to have many more ground radars to guide its air defence missiles than had been realized by the Pentagon a month earlier. Consequently, the US military had to revise upwards its earlier estimates of the time and cost of winning its air campaign against Iraq.[8]

As for the Iraqis' fighting ability, a realistic assessment was provided by a publication of the US Deputy Chief of Staff for Intelligence, Washington DC, entitled *Desert Shield Order of Battle Handbook*. A copy of the handbook was issued to each of the American combat troops in the Gulf. It described the Iraqi army as 'one of the best-equipped and most combat experienced in the world . . . distinguished by its flexibility, unity of command and high level of mobility.' Instead of minimizing Iraqi logistical expertise, as had been done so far by senior American and British military commanders, the handbook stated that 'The Iraqi army can conduct multi-corps operations spread over 100 kms or more and is capable of co-ordinating air and artillery, timing of movements and operations, co-ordinating complicated logistical requirements, and getting supplies, equipment and troops to the right place at the designated time.' It discussed Iraqi military tactics in great detail, and included the Iraqi army's 'entire brigade and divisional structure during offensive and defensive operations' and 'operational planning' for chemical weapons. 'Chemical weapons are utilized when planners assess fire support or force size as insufficient to attain the objective,' stated the handbook. 'Once authorization for chemical weapons use is given, corps commanders are given chemical rounds to be delivered by artillery. Chemical warheads include three types: a lethal mustard agent, an incapacitating agent, and tear gas.'[9]

Overall, the Iraqi strategy of buying time by placing Western and Japanese hostages at strategic sites and raising the stakes for the US-led forces to retake Kuwait by reinforcing its troops in the emirate seemed to be working. According to Pentagon sources, an armoured assault on the Iraqi frontline along the Saudi–Kuwaiti frontier which was expected to last hours, resulting in light casualties, in late September was now expected to take days and result in 'heavy casualties'. It was part of Baker's mandate to convey to the allies the hard fact that the war could not be won by US airpower alone and that 'heavy ground commitments and high casualties from all' would be expected.[10]

Staving off US military action had also benefited Saddam Hussein at home. In the early days of the crisis there were doubts among ordinary Iraqis about the wisdom of marching into Kuwait. But as weeks went by, with Baghdad consolidating its hold over Kuwait and Iraqi propaganda building up a credible case of the 'child returning to his mother', the early doubts disappeared. Also, the initial complaints at the reintroduction of military conscription after a lapse of two years proved transient. The grumbling over rationing and high prices continued, but given the brutal efficiency of the intelligence services and the repressive arms of the state, it was unlikely to escalate into anything serious. Equally, the ever-present threat to the Saddam Hussein regime from among the home-based dissidents, actual or potential, in the upper echelons of the military, had no better chance of success now than before the crisis. The replacement of Lt-General Abdul Karim Nizar Khazraji, 70-year-old army chief of staff since early 1987, by his deputy, Lt-General Hussein Rashid Wendawi, aged 51, was probably a sign of the government promoting younger, hard-core loyalists. (The change was made in August, but made public three months later, on 8 November.) A native of Tikrit, the home town of the Iraqi president, Hussein Rashid Wendawi had been commander of the Presidential Guard (later renamed the Republican Guard) in 1986. His force was despatched to the frontline east of Basra in early 1987 when the Iranians launched massive human wave assaults to capture Basra. Following his success in blunting the Iranian offensives, he was honoured by Saddam Hussein, and promoted in July 1987 to command the First Army Corps in the north.[11] As the Iran–Iraq War had amply shown, external pressures on Saddam Hussein were unlikely to undercut his power.

During the current crisis, however, the Iraqi president had indeed given himself an unusual instrument to wield against his adversaries: the hostages. He used it not only to protect his strategic sites but also to exert pressure on enemy governments by creating discord between them and their opposition politicians backed by substantial popular opinion. He had attracted such leading political figures as Heath, Nakasone and Brandt to Baghdad for talks, and rewarded them, with Brandt leaving with 206 Western hostages, including 140 Germans.[12] Since Saddam Hussein's high-profile public relations exercise depended on the fact that he had Western and Japanese hostages in his power, he was unlikely to release them all at once.

Those who wanted to use the interregnum between peace and war to find a political solution were active, too. The German foreign minister, Hans Dietrich Genscher, proposed that the EC troika of its past, present and future presidents – Ireland, Italy and Luxembourg – should team up with Algeria, Jordan and Tunisia to formulate a peaceful solution to the crisis. The PLO representative in London, Afif Safieh, revealed that the PLO was trying to arrange a meeting between

King Fahd and President Hussein. A meeting of the foreign ministers of Saudi Arabia, Egypt and Syria on 10 November urged a peaceful solution, and agreed to try to lower tensions. In an interview with the Cairo-based *Mayu* weekly, President Mubarak appealed to Saddam Hussein to withdraw, and added, 'We will deploy Arab disengagement forces between you and Kuwait.' When asked about the stand Egypt would adopt in case war plans required land forces to advance towards Iraq 'to bring about stability', he replied: 'We have no objections to marching towards Kuwait as peace forces. As for Iraq, this is not our business.'13

About then King Hassan of Morocco issued a public call for an extraordinary Arab summit, which was backed by the PLO, Jordan and Mauritania, all of them friends of Iraq. But Baghdad was sceptical. On the eve of his departure for Rabat to seek clarification about the proposed conference, Taha Yassin Ramadan, Iraq's first deputy prime minister, stressed that 'Arab summits should not be gatherings to conspire against the [Arab] nation as was the case with the conspiratorial Cairo summit [of 10 August] whose resolutions were produced by agent Hosni [Mubarak] and traitor [King] Fahd', and that 'Arab summits are not meant to translate ready-made resolutions that have been prepared by the Zionist US defence department but to decide on an agenda through prior consultation and careful study so that it covers all Arab causes, the foremost being the Palestine cause.' He insisted on consultations with Iraq on 'the place and the circumstance' in which Saddam Hussein could attend such a meeting. In turn, King Fahd stated that he would attend only if Iraq agreed to withdraw from Kuwait beforehand. The next day Presidents Mubarak and Assad said that Iraq was putting up too many conditions.14 In the event, King Hassan's initiative failed.

Then there was the international forum of the UN Security Council with power concentrated among its five permanent members. Here Iraq's isolation was lessened by the arrival in Baghdad of China's foreign minister, Qian Qichen. Saddam Hussein was aware of the probable US move to obtain UN authorization for military action against his country. To forestall this he attempted to find one permanent member of the Security Council prepared to veto such a resolution. It was with this objective in mind that he had the speaker of the Iraqi National Assembly propose a linkage between the release of all hostages and an undertaking by at least one permanent Security Council member against any military attack against Iraq. The ploy failed. Now, in his talks of 12 November with the foreign minister of

China – one of the two possible users of a veto against the US-sponsored move at the Security Council, the other being the Soviet Union – Saddam Hussein reportedly tried to get a promise of a veto from him by offering the most he could – Kuwait – as a 'sacrifice' for peace. The Iraqi News Agency report on the meeting hinted as much behind a veil of generalities. 'The concern of everybody should be how to establish peace, and not to impose conditions by war,' the Iraqi president told the Chinese foreign minister. 'When this becomes the focus of attention for those concerned, then dialogue should be their way to secure peace. Then Iraq would be . . . ready to make sacrifices for the sake of peace.'

Qian Qichen returned to Peking with the Iraqi proposal which was discussed at the highest level. During the next several days, it became clear to Baghdad that China would not veto a US-sponsored resolution at the Security Council and thus earn the ire of Washington.

On 18 November, therefore, Iraq made a unilateral, placatory move. It announced that it had authorized the 'foreign guests' to start leaving from 25 December onwards with the last departure on 25 March 'if nothing comes to disturb the climate of peace'. The offer applied to the remaining 3,500 Western and Japanese hostages. Saddam Hussein's assessment was that Western public opinion was likely to attach more significance to the freedom of Western hostages than to the immediate liberation of Kuwait. The timing, too, was well chosen. The window of opportunity for an assault by the allies extended from early January to mid-March. Apparently, by choosing the three-month period after Christmas the Iraqi leader was attempting to spike Washington's military option. Aware of this, the Western capitals responded coolly to the offer. Undeterred, the Iraqi parliament, acting on the president's recommendation on 20 November, decided to release all German hostages and 100 other Europeans as a goodwill gesture to the Conference on Security and Co-operation in Europe being held in Paris. Iraq's president cited long-standing good relations between Baghdad and Bonn, and repeated calls by Chancellor Kohl for a peaceful solution, as his reasons for the recommendation.

However, the change in his position could be traced to a process which Primakov had noticed earlier, and which he elaborated in an interview with the *New York Times* on 16 November. Primakov said that he had seen 'an evolution' of Saddam Hussein's position between their meetings of 5 and 28 October. During the first meeting the Iraqi leader spent 'much of their time together arguing his claim that Kuwait is an integral part of Iraq that was artificially separated from it by Britain in colonial days'. But when Primakov returned to Baghdad on 28 October for a second round of talks, he no longer appeared interested in defending the take-over. 'Instead, Saddam Hussein wondered how the Security Council could guarantee the [solution of the] Palestinian issue if he gave up Kuwait. He also worried about his personal safety, recalling several plots against him after he had agreed to a ceasefire with Iran two years ago. And he asked for guarantees that Iraq would not be attacked.' He also felt that certain Western powers were determined to destroy his regime regardless of his actions in Kuwait.[15]

These developments at home and abroad put Bush, and his recent policy of doubling US troops in the Gulf, on the defensive. The American public was losing faith in his crisis management. The *USA Today* poll statistics published on 13 November were typical. The approval rating on Bush's handling of the Gulf crisis was down to 51% from a peak of 82% on 20 August. The same percentage approved of his recent US deployments in the Gulf, with 38% disapproving. But only 10% were 'more comfortable' with US actions vis-à-vis 57% who were 'increasingly concerned'.

Disaffection among national legislators was even more pronounced. Bush's failure to consult leading members of Congress before ordering the latest build-up wiped out the bipartisan backing that he had received in Congress in early October for his management of the crisis until then. Now an increasing number of legislators became vehement about exercising their authority to declare war as enshrined in Article I, Section 8, paragraph 11 of the US constitution.[16] They also referred to the War Powers Resolution of 1973.

Bush argued that since the American forces did not face imminent hostilities in the Gulf the 1973 War Powers Resolution did not apply. As for the constitutional right, he opposed the Congressional demand on the grounds of principle and practicality. He was unwilling to give up any decision-making authority in the realm of national security. At a more mundane level, he was afraid that Congress might tie his hands by forbidding offensive actions in the Gulf. The fact that both houses of Congress had a Democrat majority certainly did not help the president.

Nor was he reassured by the assessments of the Security Council's permanent members and the American allies, which were conveyed to Baker during his whirlwind tour of seven important capitals. Among the US-led coalition, Turkey was equivocal, with Kuwait, Saudi Arabia, Egypt and Syria being supportive of the war option, but differing on the timing. Of the Security Council's permanent members, only Britain was solidly with the US in favour of a military attack. The remaining three – the Soviet Union, France and China – had reservations about the costs, human and material, of the war option, and stressed the benefits of 'alternative strategies'.[17]

The human cost of warfare was very much in the American mind. A study by the Centre for Defence Information, Washington DC, estimated that: (a) war would last four months and end with Iraq's surrender; (b) it would involve 300,000 US troops, and cost \$50 billion, including a year-long occupation of Kuwait; and (c) 10,000 American and 35,000 Iraqi troops would be killed, and another 35,000 US combatants injured. The worst scenario by the Pentagon visualized 30,000 military personnel dying in 20 days. An estimate made by the Washington-based Brookings Institute put the American military personnel dead at 15,000. According to a retired US army chief of staff, a 'head-on fight' between the Iraqis and the Americans would result in 10,000 to 30,000 US casualties. Paul Carren of KPMG Peat Marwick, a consulting firm, summarized various studies thus: 'Most estimates outside and inside the Pentagon range from six to ten weeks of intense fighting, with [American] casualties climbing past 15,000.'[18]

These figures were certainly an important factor in the determination of a policy on the issue by such mass organizations as churches. They took a critical stance. In mid-November, following an appeal for restraint in the Gulf addressed to President Bush by US Catholic bishops, the National Council of Churches, made up of 32 denominations representing 42 million Americans, unanimously adopted a resolution stating that military action may 'well violate the principles of proportionality and last resort'.[19] These principles are part of the Christian doctrine on war: punishment meted out to a wrongdoer must be proportional to the scale of his wrongdoing, and a war is just only when it is absolutely the last resort for resolving a problem.

The other major factor working against Bush was his muddled thinking and incompetent presentation of his case. Long before he ordered the doubling of US troops in the Gulf, he had confused politicians and commentators about the main purpose of their presence there. In his television address on 8 August he declared their mission to be 'wholly defensive'. On 23 October he stated, 'We're dealing with Hitler revisited, a totalitarianism and brutality that is naked and unprecedented in modern times. And it must not stand.'[20] He failed to explain how and why defending Saudi

Arabia could only be accomplished by reversing the Iraqi take-over of Kuwait.

There was further confusion in the administration on how to justify the massive build-up in the Gulf. Among the plethora of reasons Bush and his senior officials had offered singly or jointly were: defence of oilfields and safeguarding oil supplies; upholding international law; overthrowing aggression; overcoming the dangers of Iraq's possessing chemical and biological weapons, and prospective nuclear capability; maintaining the regional security system; creating a 'new world order' where the US would act under the UN umbrella to protect international peace; upholding American values; stamping on a new Hitler; safeguarding US embassy staff in Kuwait; securing the freedom of Western captives; and protecting American jobs.

Bush's basic problem was that he could not tap the built-in anti-Communist or anti-fundamental Islamic sentiment in the American public which had helped his predecessors to mobilize public opinion on a foreign issue. What compounded his predicament was the fact that until 1 August 1990 his administration, and the ones under his predecessor, Reagan, had presented Saddam Hussein as 'a moderate' and 'a pillar of stability' in a volatile region, who had served well Western interests by containing the carrion of Muslim fundamentalism in an area with two-thirds of the planet's petroleum reserves. On top of that, the general perception of Arabs, popularized by the mainstream media, was that they were either terrorists or greedy oil shaikhs. This created a further dilemma for the moulders of opinion and policy in the Bush administration. On the one hand was a super-terrorist, Saddam, and on the other an oil shaikh, the emir of Kuwait, in flowing robes. There was really not much to choose between the two.

Faced with such a daunting task, Bush and Baker (who had been his election campaign manager) fell back on the tactic they had employed during the presidential campaign: raise a different slogan each week to see which one strikes the right chord. This playing by ear made the administration's explanations look contradictory. On 16 October 1990, addressing an election rally, Bush declared that 'the fight' was not about oil but about 'naked aggression'. Four weeks later, on 13 November, Baker said that the reason for American military involvement in the Gulf was economic. 'If you want to sum it up in one word: it's jobs,' he said. 'Because an economic recession, worldwide, caused by the control of one nation, one dictator, of the West's economic lifeline [i.e. Gulf oil supplies] will result in the loss of jobs on the part of American citizens.'[21]

Bush elaborated the point two days later. 'With its speculative effect on the price of oil, the Iraq situation has complicated and worsened our economy and the economies of our neighbours and the economies of the rest of the world,' he said in an interview with Cable News Network. 'I'm worried about a continuation in the Gulf of this kind of a stand-off . . . adversely affecting our economy further and the economies of other countries further.' He added, 'The rise in oil prices that grew out of Iraq's invasion of Kuwait does mean jobs. Jobs, I'd say, comes under the heading of the economic security of the world, and it's a very important part of this.'[22] (The Iraqi officials, avid watchers of CNN, were quick to exploit Bush's statement to make the point they had made many times before. Citing Bush's words, Baghdad Radio said on 17 November that the US military presence in the Gulf had only one aim: 'to control oil wells and dictate oil policies'.)

However, the Bush–Baker tactic was not working. A *New York Times*–CBS poll published on 20 November showed that 51% felt that Bush had not given adequate reasons for the deployment of over 400,000 US troops in the Gulf. More specifically, 62% thought 'protecting oil supplies' an inadequate reason for fighting. While 56% considered 'restoring Kuwaiti government and protecting Saudi Arabia' as insufficient reasons to fight, only 35% considered them as sufficient. In contrast, 54% thought 'stopping Iraq develop nuclear weapons' was an adequate reason to fight. The approval of Bush's handling of the crisis had fallen to 50%, the lowest yet, and disapproval had risen to 41%.

Though no poll was conducted among US troops in the Gulf, there were press reports that the troops were upset at Baker's statement that oil was the primary reason for America's military involvement, having been told repeatedly that confronting 'naked aggression' by a 'new Hitler' was the foremost purpose.[23] This worried the administration since President Bush was all set to address the American forces in the Gulf on 22 November, Thanksgiving Day, and it was essential to make his visit a stunning success.

It was therefore important, in the interim, to present a macho image of America. This came in the form of six days of US–Saudi joint military exercises, codenamed Operation 'Imminent Thunder'. These began on 15 November, and involved Saudi forces and 1,000 American marines, 16 warships and more than 1,000 aircraft, about 100 miles south of the Kuwait–Saudi border.[24]

On 19 November, Iraq responded to Bush's decision of 8 November to despatch additional ground troops, calling it 'an acknowledgement of the importance of artillery and infantry if Iraq's force is to be challenged'. Now, in order to preserve the superiority of Iraq, the government was mobilizing an additional 250,000 troops: of these 100,000 (or 7 divisions) were being sent immediately to Kuwait with the remaining 150,000 to go there later. 'Given the normal ratio of attackers to defenders, the US will need 3 million troops to launch an offensive.' The need for extra troops arose when the Iraqi chief of staff decided to extend the defence line further west, 50 miles into Iraq, to thwart an allied flanking attack across the Saudi–Iraqi border.[25]

But this did not mean Baghdad had turned its face against negotiations. On the same day, 19 November, *Al Qadisiya*, the Iraqi military newspaper, said, 'Iraq wants an in-depth dialogue with the concerned parties, and each [party] should be ready to offer the appropriate sacrifices.' Earlier, in a long interview with ABC television, Saddam Hussein had proposed talks between Iraq and Saudi Arabia on regional problems, and between Iraq and America on wider issues.[26]

Washington was interested in talks, but of a different kind. Aware of the opposition in Congress and outside to his use of force in the Gulf, Bush decided to secure a UN mandate for the military option first, and then seek the approval of Congress: it was unlikely to reject a request by the US president *after* it had been granted by an international organization. This plan also had the advantage of meeting the Soviet demand that force should be used only under the UN umbrella. The ease with which Washington's will and initiative on the Kuwaiti issue had prevailed at the Security Council since early August made Bush fairly confident of acquiring the required majority for the most threatening and controversial of the numerous resolutions on Kuwait yet tabled at the Council. The onerous task fell, as before, on Baker who, on 16 November, left for Geneva on the first leg of his tour to lobby the nine Security Council members whose vote for the use of force against Iraq was in doubt.

Baker began his mission at a time when public opinion in America was running against military action – with 45 Democratic members of Congress having filed a lawsuit demanding that President Bush consult Congress before declaring war – and such foreign leaders as Presidents Mubarak and Gorbachev were counselling Bush to conduct further consultations. Mubarak specified a period of 'two to three months' to try and achieve a peaceful solution. In his meeting with Bush in Paris, the venue of the Conference on Security and Co-operation in Europe from 19 to 21 November, Gorbachev told Bush that the UN Security Council resolution on the use of force should be passed only after 'more international consultations'. His special envoy, Primakov, urged Washington to consider 'direct, high level contact' with Baghdad before committing itself to armed action.[27]

Meanwhile, the UN Security Council remained vigilant regarding developments in Kuwait. On 15 November the Kuwaiti ambassador to the UN passed on to the UN secretary-general the official population register – a set of computer disks – which had been smuggled out of Kuwait a fortnight earlier as a precaution against any alteration of the register by the Iraqi government.

By then about half of the Kuwaiti nationals had left Kuwait. (And more than two-thirds of the Palestinians had done the same, demonstrating that they were even more alienated from the occupying Iraqi forces than the Kuwaiti nationals.)[28] With this, a clearer picture of the Iraqis' pillage of Kuwait and their harsh treatment of the local people emerged. 'One must understand the systematic nature of destruction [of Kuwait City],' said one Kuwaiti doctor in exile in Tehran. 'This is the rape of a country by bureaucracy. Where rape of individuals has occurred, steps have been taken to eliminate its repeat. Often this has meant the death of the Iraqi soldier concerned. In the earliest days of the invasion, Iraqi troops were orderly and disciplined: regular troops who knew the rules of war. The crushing of the early resistance [by Kuwaitis] was brutal but targeted. The Iraqis were disciplined, the resistance ill-planned and woefully tactless.' According to this doctor, most of the resistance was backed by the Muslim League with a stronghold in the Mushrif area: they got their explosives from the Mina Abdullah industrial district. 'The Iraqis devastated the Mushrif area and concentrated on the strongholds of the Muslim League. Explosives stocks [held by the Kuwaiti resistance] are now rumoured to be low.' As for day-to-day life, all basic foodstuffs were scarce. 'The most disgraceful edict from Baghdad is the one which allows Iraqi soldiers to enter Kuwaiti property to search for hoarded goods, particularly food,' said the doctor. 'Iraqi units have blank papers which permit the right to search for stored produce. It is a warrant they use to remove all supplies.'[29]

However, some of the reports such as the killing of 312 premature babies by Iraqi soldiers and large-scale executions of Kuwaitis turned out to be either false or exaggerated. According to a report by Aziz Abu Hamad, a Saudi researcher, published by the Middle East Watch, a New York-based human rights organization, since the August invasion 5,000 Kuwaitis had been arrested arbitrarily, with 3,000 of them still in detention. Reports of 7,000 executions in Kuwait could not be substantiated: 250 executions had been traced. When Abu Hamad interviewed the Kuwaiti Red Crescent doctor who was reported to have alleged that 312 premature babies had died after the Iraqi soldiers had removed them from incubators at the Maternity Hospital in the al Sabah Medical Complex (in order to send the incubators to Iraq), and that he had personally buried 72 in al Rigga cemetery, he denied using the figure of 312, and mentioned only the burial of 72 – adding that he had no way of telling the causes of their deaths. The doctor, a Kuwaiti civil servant, was then living in the Sheraton Hotel, Taif, the headquarters of the Kuwaiti government-in-exile. Further inquiries showed that the highest estimate of incubators at the Maternity Hospital was 80 and, according to a Kuwaiti nurse in exile, in September about 20 babies at the Maternity Hospital were in incubators, and there were other empty incubators which had not been shipped to Iraq.[30]

No doubt the continuing human rights violations by Iraqi troops were discussed when President Bush met Shaikh Jaber al Sabah in Taif on 21 November on his way to address US troops stationed in the Saudi kingdom's Eastern Province.

On 22 November, Thanksgiving Day, Bush addressed four rallies, each 1,500 strong and consisting respectively of soldiers, seamen, air force personnel and marines. He reminded them that 46 years ago he had been a navy pilot on 'a similar mission to resist aggression'. His voice cracked with emotion as he spoke of the hostages and of the pillaging of Kuwait. He cited 'the need to free the West's hostages, liberate the people of Kuwait, establish a clear principle of global action against aggression', and stressed 'the economic threat to the West's oil'. He concluded the speech with a reference to the nuclear menace from Baghdad. 'Every day that passes brings Saddam Hussein one day closer to his goal of a nuclear weapons arsenal. And that is another reason, frankly, why more and more our mission is marked by a real sense of urgency.' It was significant that the last clause was not in the original text of Bush's speech which was broadcast live at breakfast time in America on Thanksgiving Day. Bush had hastily added it himself, apparently after he had seen the findings of the New York Times–CBS poll on the subject.[31] Here was an example of Bush being 'consumer responsive', tailoring his views to suit a prevalent popular mood: behaviour which led his critics to call him 'an unprincipled weathercock', and his admirers 'pragmatic'.

There was little doubt that Bush's trip had been stage-managed to an unprecedented extent. The gathering of some 1,500 troops at each of the sites consisted of military personnel who had been brought in from the camps all over the kingdom. Officials justified this on the ground that this spread the news of the president's trip among all of the US forces. The ranks were unconvinced: the selection of those allowed to attend the rallies was highly biased towards those who were known to their officers for their ardour and polite manners, or had won prizes as the unit's 'soldier of the year' and such-like. The selection of those handpicked to eat the Thanksgiving meal alongside the president was even more rigorous. The civil and military authorities, working under the direction of Sig Rogich, the president's assistant for special activities, were determined to see that there was no repeat of the carping which greeted James Baker and General Colin Powell during their encounters with the troops. And there was not.

'With the help of the Pentagon press office and the collusion of the American television networks, Rogich made sure the viewers back home saw only what they were meant to: loud cheering crowds and an American military that was lean, mean and menacing,' reported John Cassidy of the *Sunday Times*. 'From the moment Bush touched down in Dhahran until he took off for Cairo seven hours later, every camera shot had been carefully planned.' As a result, American viewers had watched live at breakfast time 'a jaunty, baseball-cap-wearing George Bush' eating Thanksgiving turkey with 'the American boys' half a world away. 'Never mind that, in reality, Bush was rambling, repetitive, embarrassingly unfunny in his attempted jokes, or that off-camera he looked increasingly old and frazzled,' wrote Andrew Stephen of the *Observer*. 'Rogich ... along with the four main US television networks spent millions ensuring that Bush would be seen in supposedly relaxed and spontaneous televisual moments. Not for the first time, the White House and media had conspired to fool the masses.'[32] There was no way that the widespread frustration among the troops at the lack of sex, beer and a return home date – which print journalists frequently reported – could find an outlet on American television networks.

Bush's warning about Saddam Hussein getting closer to his 'goal of a nuclear weapons arsenal' by the day did not stand up to serious scrutiny. On 13 November, Iraq, a signatory to the non-proliferation treaty, had called on the International Atomic Energy Agency (IAEA) in Vienna, which monitors compliance with the treaty, to make public the results of its latest inspection which showed no evidence of a military programme, and declared that its civil nuclear research facilities were open for inspection. Indeed, while Bush addressed his troops, two

IAEA inspectors were in Iraq inspecting the nuclear research facility near Baghdad. 'They found that all the highly enriched uranium stored by Iraq from the former Osirak reactor was where it should be, and none had been diverted,' the IAEA stated on 27 November.[33]

Iraq possessed 27.6 pounds of enriched uranium (U-235), about enough to produce one crude atomic bomb with the destructive power of the one the US dropped on Hiroshima, Japan, in August 1945 – hardly a foundation for the nuclear weapons arsenal Bush mentioned. In any case, according to the IAEA, the fissionable U-235 fuel was intact.

Moreover, Iraq did not refine the nuclear fuel – that is, separate fissionable U-235 from its inert isotope U-238 – but bought it in the enriched state from France. Carrying out this separation requires highly complex machines, called gas centrifuges. A gas centrifuge spins uranium gas at high speed and separates the unstable U-235 atoms from the stable U-238 atoms that form over 90% of natural uranium. It takes 1,000 such centrifuges a year to produce enough enriched uranium for one atomic warhead. By all accounts, Iraq possessed no more than a few of these centrifuges so far: something it had achieved by relying on imported technology. The basic point was that Iraq's military potential, including its nuclear potential, was derivative. 'There is no real short-term risk of an Iraqi nuclear weapon – at least based on what the Bush administration has told us so far,' stated Gary Milhollin, director of the Wisconsin Project on Nuclear Arms Control, to the Senate Armed Services Committee in late November. 'The administration should be ashamed of itself for misleading the public about the Iraqi bomb; there should be a reasonable limit to governmental disinformation when the stakes are so high.' A similar statement was made later by Frank Barnaby, author of *Weapons of Mass Destruction: A Growing Threat in the 1990s?* 'It would take Iraq at least five years, and possibly twice as long, to produce nuclear weapons suitable for military requirements,' he said. 'Stories recently released [by the US] are more propaganda than based on what is technically possible.'[34]

On the eve of Bush's visit to the American frontline in Saudi Arabia, Saddam Hussein undertook a two-day inspection of his troops in southern Iraq and Kuwait. 'Iraq and its faithful men do not seek war,' he told his soldiers. 'But, if fighting is imposed on them, they will fight in a way that will please friends and all believers, and anger the infidels and evil-doers.'[35]

With the call-up of the reserves, Iraq's mobilization reached a point where 9% of its 17.2 million nationals – nearly 1.5 million – were under arms, making Iraq the world's fifth largest military force. Of the 430,000 Iraqi troops in the field, nearly a third were élite forces whose motivation, training and combat readiness equalled those of the frontline American combat forces.

A recent study of the Iraqi military, co-authored by Lt-Colonel Douglas V. Johnson and published by the Strategic Studies Institute of the US Army War College, Carlisle Barracks, Pennsylvania, provided much useful information and analysis on the make-up of Iraq's armed forces as well as their strategy and tactics for countering US war plans, expected to combine air strikes against Iraq with offensives by ground forces and marines. It concluded *inter alia* that the Iran–Iraq War had taught Staff Field Marshal Saddam Hussein to delegate substantial decision-making powers to his field commanders, and that he planned to do so in the case of conflict with Washington. The recent promotion of General Hussein Rashid Wendawi – who had changed Iraqi fortunes in 1987–8 by combining flexible defences with innovative offensive assaults against Iran – to chief of staff (and later to defence minister) was a good indicator. Thus American and allied forces would be confronting experienced and resourceful commanders rather than sycophants blindly following the orders of the Iraqi president who lacked military training. Indications were that these field commanders were demonstrating the same innovation and industriousness they had shown in their successful operations against Iran, in both offensive and defensive planning, including extending the defensive belt further west, well into Iraq, to thwart an allied assault across the Saudi–Iraqi border, provision for the release of oil into the sea and setting it alight to frustrate amphibious attacks by US marines, and destroying Saudi oil wells as well as Israeli industrial targets with medium-range ground-to-ground missiles.[36]

The overall Iraqi strategy to counter both the American allies' air campaign and any ground offensive that emerged could be summarized thus. Instead of deploying its aircraft to confront the superior enemy combat planes, Iraq planned to protect its warplanes from destruction during the first phase of the war with a view to using them later in dogfights with the enemy aircraft and thus diverting them from their offensive tasks. To improve their chance of survival, the Iraqis had constructed three fortified shelters for each of their 700 warplanes. To counter America's B-52 bombers flying at altitudes of up to 30,000 feet, the Iraqi air force had conducted high-altitude interceptions with their MiG-25 fighters. They had improved their air defences against low-level attacks. Over the past two months they had moved hundreds of anti-aircraft batteries into the war zone. As for low-flying helicopters, the Iraqi forces would fire a barrage of ammunition with their rifles and anti-aircraft weapons into one quadrant of the sky to block an approaching aerial attack. This method, used by the Vietnamese against the American helicopters and called 'mining the sky', was virtually impossible to counter.

The essentially defensive nature of Iraq's war plans fitted well its ground forces. 'They [Iraqi troops] are doctrinally inclined to fighting set-piece battles, seeking to lure enemies into pre-arranged killing zones, capable of tenacious defence of their homeland, and well practised at intricate defence systems,' noted Lt-Colonel Johnson. The Iraqis were planning to depend on their defence barriers to safeguard their infantry and armoured divisions from aerial strikes. They had stored enough ammunition in their forward depots to sustain fighting for many weeks. They expected to match the annihilating power of the enemy's advanced cluster munitions delivered by air or artillery with inexpensive Fuel Air Explosives, which spread a cloud of explosive vapour that, when detonated, delivered the same lethal concussion as hundreds of conventional bombs. Finally, aware that the enemy would jam and disrupt their radio communication, the Iraqis had been trained by their officers to make minimum use of it.[37]

A composite study of radar surveillance and electronic data as well as satellite pictures had led Pentagon analysts to a conclusion which could be summarized thus: the overall strategy of Baghdad was to ensure that liberating Kuwait by force imposed a casualty figure high enough to drain away American public backing for war.

It was taken for granted that the Pentagon was engaged in devising a strategy to counter Iraq's military plans as well as its political implications regarding American casualties. Indeed, following the rejection of his Operation 'Night Camel', Schwarzkopf had, by his account, 'crystallized' a ground assault plan, tentatively codenamed Operation 'Hail Mary' (a term used in American football games), by early November: it visualized attacking Iraq from its western flank, the one it had left exposed.[38] All this was of course top secret. What was public, and presented in high profile, was Washington's diplomatic moves, whether by Bush or Baker.

After his meeting with President Mubarak in Cairo on 23 November, Bush flew to Geneva to meet President Assad on neutral ground. Following a three-hour meeting the two leaders issued a joint communiqué which stated that Iraq's occupation of Kuwait was unacceptable, and that it should not receive any reward for its aggression; Kuwait's territory and legitimate government must be restored 'fully'. The last US president who had met Assad (in May 1977, also in Geneva) was James Carter – to back the idea of reconvening the international peace conference on the Middle East.

This time a reluctant Bush yielded to pressures from Mubarak and Fahd to confer with Assad. After considerable delay, Assad had increased the size of the Syrian contingent in Saudi Arabia from the initial 3,000 to 7,500, with the arrival in Yanbu on 5 November of units from the 9th Armoured Division with T-52 and T-62 tanks and anti-aircraft guns. This was in line with the pledge he had given to King Fahd at the Cairo summit on 10 August, after he had received $500 million from the monarch with a promise of $500 million more over the next twelve months. At the same time, Damascus continued to snipe at Washington for using the crisis to strengthen further its strategic ally in the region, Israel. Just as Syrian troops were boarding ships bound for Saudi Arabia, the official Damascus newspaper *Al Thawra* accused the US of 'exploiting the Gulf Crisis to trap Arab power in a pincer hold that would lead to geographic and demographic changes' in favour of Israel.[39] There was another, more profound difference between Damascus and Washington. For Syria, Iraq represented strategic depth in its confrontation with Israel where, in case of war, retreating Syrian forces could withdraw and regroup. All it wanted to see in Iraq, therefore, was a change of leadership, with Iraq's armed forces and military industry left intact as potential partners in a future battle with their common foe: Israel. It was therefore opposed to seeing Iraq crushed and/or occupied by victorious American or multinational forces. So the state-guided Syrian press sent out contradictory signals, commending those Arab leaders who were seeking an Arab solution one day and decrying such an outcome as 'a snare and a delusion' the next.

Small wonder that Bush's talks with Assad were received with mixed feelings in the US and Israel. While prime minister Shamir reportedly sent a telegram to Bush saying he understood that he was meeting Assad in order to keep the anti-Iraq coalition firm, the pro-Israel lobbyists in America were not so understanding. 'For the second time in four months, the US is pandering to a Mideast dictator,' wrote A. M. Rosenthal, an American columnist, in the *New York Times*. He described Assad as 'a dictator, assassin of thousands of his own people, master of terrorists who specialize in bombing airplanes', and accused him of exploiting the Gulf crisis and 'American acquiescence to make Lebanon a colony' by turning a blind eye to Assad's successful assault (on 12 October) on Lebanon's rebellious Maronite general, Michel Aoun. There were others who distinguished between Hafiz Assad and Saddam Hussein. 'While no one can operate on the assumption that Mr Assad is a nice chap, he is a realist, as Israelis point out,' noted Anthony Lewis, an American columnist, in the *New York Times*. 'Ambitious though he is, he is not a megalomaniac like Saddam Hussein. He has an acute sense of limits.'[40]

No such differences of opinion about the Bush–Assad meeting were expressed in Syria. There the media unanimously acclaimed it as 'a major turning point on the regional and international levels'. Describing Assad as 'a model representative of the Arab nation' in Geneva, they pointed out that President Bush had concurred with him on the need for a 'comprehensive and just solution [of the Arab–Israeli conflict] based on the UN resolutions', and urged that 'This US endorsement of a well-known Syrian policy should be welcomed by the Arabs.'[41] However, the Arabs were far too engrossed in tackling the Gulf crisis to heed this advice.

There was an almost immediate diplomatic pay-off for Syria. On 28 November Britain decided to resume diplomatic ties forthwith. These had been severed in October 1986 after a British jury had found a London-based Jordanian, Nizar Hindawi, guilty of attempting to bomb an El Al aircraft, departing from London's Heathrow airport with 375 people aboard on 17 April 1986, by placing an incendiary device in the luggage of his would-be wife flying to Israel ahead of him. The British authorities believed that Hindawi had acted on orders from Syrian intelligence, travelled on a Syrian passport to London, and met the Syrian ambassador Loutfallah Haydar at the embassy after the bomb plot had been discovered. Damascus denied any involvement in terrorism on British soil. Its attempts to resume diplomatic links with London were repeatedly rebuffed by Prime Minister Thatcher, who held strong views on terrorism. The reason why Britain now reacted so positively and quickly to Assad's co-operation was that, responding to rising criticism of her domestic and European policies by the ruling Conservative MPs, Thatcher had resigned as leader of the Conservative Party in parliament on 22 November, and was replaced by John Major six days later. With the single outstanding hurdle to the resumption of Damascus–London ties gone, the British foreign secretary Douglas Hurd was free to act on his own initiative.[42]

Baghdad welcomed Thatcher's resignation since she had been

named, by Saddam Hussein in his ABC television interview of 15 November, as one of the four personalities who 'pushed' Bush to take a militantly anti-Iraqi line, the other three being Shamir, Mubarak, and Prince Bandar.[43] However, her departure made no difference to the strategy of Bush, who was set on winning a military mandate from the UN Security Council, whose ten non-permanent members were currently Canada, Colombia, Cuba, Ethiopia, Finland, Ivory Coast, Malaysia, Romania, Yemen and Zaire, and whose secretary of state was concentrating on those Council members from the Third World who were reluctant to go along with the military option: Colombia, Cuba, Malaysia, Yemen and Zaire.

'The UN Security Council was brought round by a mixture of intensive personal diplomacy, wheedling and bullying by the US,' reported Martin Walker of the *Guardian* on 3 December. 'Mr Bush even located, by telephone, the Malaysian prime minister, Mahathir Muhammad (1981–), in a Tokyo restaurant to swing his country's vote.' The vote of Colombia was secured with a White House pledge of an early concession to it in its dispute with the US on exports of cut flowers.[44]

However, impoverished Yemen refused to yield to Baker's threat, during his meeting with President Ali Abdullah Saleh in Sanaa on 22 November, to cancel $70 million US aid to it if it failed to support the US-sponsored resolution at the Security Council. Responding to the pressure from Baker, the Yemeni leader said that his country was opposed to the presence and possible use of force by foreign troops in the Gulf. He explained his position a few days later in an interview with the *Washington Post*. Confident that it was still 'possible' to find a peaceful solution for 'the complete withdrawal of all Iraqi troops from Kuwait and all foreign forces from the region', President Saleh said: 'I know Iraq is ready for dialogue. Why doesn't President Bush send a personal envoy to Baghdad or Geneva or any Arab capital to meet with a representative of the Iraqi leadership?' He was critical of US threats against Iraq. 'First the United States says it is coming to protect Saudi Arabia from aggression, and now the US says it wants to use force against Iraq and destroy its military capability. The entire world was against Iraq's invasion of Kuwait, but the foreign intervention and threats of force are leading some Arabs now to support Iraq.'[45]

Saleh was not swayed by the threat of Washington to withdraw its aid to Yemen – just as he was not intimidated by the vendetta of Riyadh against the nearly 1.6 million Yemenis resident in the Saudi kingdom, which meant a loss in the expatriates' remittances home of

$2 to $3 billion annually. During the initial stages of the Gulf crisis Sanaa balanced its condemnation of the Iraqi invasion with criticism of Saudi Arabia for inviting foreign forces. Angered by the criticism, Riyadh retaliated. On 19 September it announced that every Yemeni resident in the kingdom must find a Saudi sponsor (a requirement waived in the past for Yemenis) within two months, or leave. By the deadline, 651,000 Yemenis had left Saudi Arabia, with another estimated 150,000 crossing the border unofficially. That meant in effect expulsion from the Saudi kingdom of half of the Yemenis who, as manual workers, shopkeepers, drivers and petty contractors, served an economically beneficial purpose. Most of those leaving were obliged to sell their property at a fraction of its value. This engendered much bitterness against Saudi Arabia, and provided further backing for the principled stand that their government was taking on the crisis.[46]

In an unprecedented move, Baker had conducted talks on 28 November with the Cuban foreign minister, the first such formal meeting in 30 years, where he reportedly held out a promise of removing Cuba from the list of the nations that support international terrorism, thus making Cuba eligible for US humanitarian aid. This ploy failed.[47] But there were successes, too. His visit to the capital of Zaire, ruled by President Mobutu Sese Seko (1965–), a pro-Western leader, secured him the backing of that country at the Security Council after his failure to obtain it during his meeting with the Zairian foreign minister in Geneva on 17 November. The foreign ministers of Ethiopia and Ivory Coast, however, had proved amenable to Baker's request during their talks in Geneva on the same day.

Among the permanent members, China was unenthusiastic about the use of force against Iraq. Though a friend of Iraq, and a substantial supplier of weapons to it, China had supported all Security Council resolutions on the Gulf crisis so far. Citing recent 'confidential documents' on the crisis in Peking, an unnamed Chinese official was quoted as saying, 'Chinese leaders have seen the Gulf crisis as an opportunity to divert [world] attention from China's human rights problems.'[48] Also, by backing Security Council resolutions against Iraq, Peking hoped to win greater stature in the international community and to use this to normalize commercial and other links with America and other Western nations, thus reversing the economic sanctions that the West had imposed against it in the wake of the killings of pro-democracy demonstrators in Peking's Tiananmen Square in early June 1989. More specifically, China wanted its foreign minister to be invited to Washington for an official visit: Peking felt such a move would encourage Western companies to invest in China, something the country needed to overcome its economic recession. The Bush administration had suspended official exchanges in response to China's crackdown against peaceful protesters, and had banned military sales to China. Since early August 1990, however, aware that China was the one permanent Security Council member likely to use its veto against the US-sponsored resolutions concerning Iraq, Baker had tried his best to keep it in tow. As the time for voting on the resolution authorizing the use of force approached Baker struck a deal: the Chinese foreign minister would be invited to Washington for an official visit if Peking would promise not to veto the forthcoming resolution on Iraq.[49]

As for the Soviet Union, Bush and Baker had met Gorbachev in Paris at a time when (during the Conference on Security and Co-operation in Europe) he was preoccupied with securing multi-billion-dollar emergency food and other aid for the USSR, and therefore vulnerable to toeing the US line if the latter agreed to aid Moscow financially and diplomatically. Beset with the rising nationalist militancy of the three Baltic republics intent on breaking away from the USSR, and their declared intention of raising the issue at the CSCE in Paris, Gorbachev appealed to Bush for diplomatic assistance. It was offered in the form of blocking the attendance of the Baltic states at the CSCE conference in return for a Soviet promise to back the US-sponsored resolution on the use of force at the Security Council. Moscow agreed – but with one (unpublicized) proviso: before using the military option Washington would hold top-level talks with Baghdad. As subsequent events were to show, Bush conceded this.

Washington was not in a position to offer any financial aid to Moscow. So it called on affluent Riyadh to step in and help. After all, the Saudis were as anxious as the Americans to win a UN mandate for their use of force. Indeed a Saudi delegation, led by foreign minister Prince Saud al Faisal, was in Moscow to discuss Soviet support for the campaign to expel the Iraqis from Kuwait as the Security Council prepared to vote on what was to become Resolution 678. On 28 November when the Saudi foreign minister met President Gorbachev and his foreign minister, Shevardnadze, they also discussed a 'new financial co-operation agreement' under which the Soviet Union was to receive a loan of $4 billion from Riyadh, with an immediate payment of $1 billion. This was to be part of a financial aid package of $6 billion to be funded by Saudi Arabia, Kuwait, the UAE and Qatar. That day Abdul Muhsin al Duaji, the Kuwaiti ambassador to the USSR, told the

London-based *Al Sharq al Awsat* (owned by the Saudi royal family) that Kuwait would be contributing $1 bn to the package. According to Saudi banking sources, the UAE had already extended a loan of $500 million to the Soviet Union. And the finance minister of Qatar was then in Moscow apparently to finalize his country's contribution.[50]

Two days earlier, following several hours of talks between Shevardnadze and Tariq Aziz in Moscow, Tass released a statement by the Soviet foreign ministry. 'Tariq Aziz was told firmly that if Iraq really wants a settlement in the entire region, it must now openly declare and show in its actions that it is leaving Kuwait, freeing hostages, and in general is not preventing anyone from leaving Iraq,' it said. 'Otherwise a tough UN resolution [against it] would be adopted.' Later President Gorbachev, addressing the Soviet parliament, referred to the Iraqi behaviour on hostages thus: 'It is against the norms of ethics that people are being let out in groups of several dozen in some kind of trading.' Before 2 August 1990 there were about 8,000 Soviet citizens in Iraq, including several hundred military advisers. More than half, mostly women and children, had left since then. In November about 1,000 were expected to depart, but only 350 had done so – with Aziz blaming 'bureaucratic' problems for the hold-up. So there were still 3,315 Soviet citizens in Iraq.[51]

As for the hostages from other countries, their numbers were down too. There were practically no French, German or Greek captives left. On 26 November the Iraqi parliament decided to let the last 58 Swedes go – followed by a decision three days later to let all Belgians leave in response to the Belgian foreign minister's statement that Belgium would not participate in any military action in the Gulf. Apart from large contingents from Britain (1,400) and America (700), the other countries with more than 50 hostages were: Italy (270); Ireland (200); Japan (150); Netherlands (133); Switzerland (80); and Denmark (56). Their presence attracted visits by senior politicians from their countries, which in turn provided a certain legitimacy to Iraq's stance in the Gulf crisis and a highly publicized forum for the Iraqi president to explain his viewpoint. At the same time some kind of material trading had evolved. Following the arrival of 25 tons of donated medical supplies in Baghdad from Italy on 24 November, Baghdad Radio confirmed the next day that the release of a 'large number' of Italians was imminent. That day Iraqi papers reported that Tokyo was considering a similar move to gain the freedom of the remaining 150 Japanese captives.[52]

It was against this background that the Security Council adopted

Resolution 678 by 12 votes to two (Cuba and Yemen), with one abstention (China). It authorized 'member states co-operating with Kuwait' to use 'all necessary means to uphold and implement the Security Council Resolution 660 and all subsequent relevant resolutions' and restore 'international peace and security in the area' unless Iraq fully implemented all the relevant Security Council resolutions by 15 January 1991.[53]

Thirteen of the fifteen members were represented by their foreign ministers, with America's Baker in the chair. He compared, favourably, the Council's decision to use collective action against Iraq's aggression to the League of Nations' failure to challenge the Italian aggression against Ethiopia in 1936. Roland Dumas, the French foreign minister, noted that the world was on the edge of a 'new order' which, while 'respecting sovereignties and identities', was 'intended to promote solidarity and co-operation'.[54]

Just before the vote, the Iraqi ambassador to the UN, Abdul Amir al Anbari, called the Security Council 'a willing tool of the US' because President Bush had not yet been able to persuade his own Congress to support the use of force against Iraq. 'The resolution reflects a double standard by attacking Iraq while allowing Israel to occupy Palestine, and is a plot by Washington to dominate the Middle East,' he said. 'The Americans have succeeded in imposing their hegemony, and their only object is to defend their own and Israel's interests . . . Iraq wants peace not just for itself but for the whole Middle East, including Palestine.'[55]

A joint meeting of the Iraqi RCC and the Regional Command of the Baath Party held on 30 November described Security Council Resolution 678 as 'illegal, null and void', and added, 'The members of the Security Council voted for the resolution under pressure.' Accusing America of practising 'all forms of pressure, terrorism and bribes', it said, 'The Security Council has become the theatre for the American hegemony.' However, it warned that, 'in the heat of the battle', Iraq will 'wipe out the dwarfs who are supporting America, especially the treacherous Fahd regime'.[56]

Aware of Baghdad's extreme hostility towards it, and fearing a pre-emptive strike by Iraq on the eve of the Security Council vote, Saudi Arabia had put its forces on maximum alert. Later, the Saudi spokesman described Resolution 678 as 'one more step, one more chance for peace', and hoped that reason would prevail. 'The liberation of Kuwait is closer than at any time before,' said the Kuwaiti spokesman. 'Iraq must think carefully now to obey the decision of the UN to save Iraq and the area from being destroyed.'[57]

Far more importantly, having achieved its objective at the Security Council, the Bush administration decided to take a high profile on the subject at home, with the president ready to summon Congress leaders for consultations.

With this, the countdown towards an almost certain war started.

8   THE COUNTDOWN

'Bush is equipped to negotiate like a gentleman, and fight like a Texas roughneck.'

Martin Walker, British journalist[1]

'They are going to send our men and women into battle for those Kuwaitis who have taken over the Sheraton Hotel in Taif, and are sitting there in their white robes, drinking coffee, and urging us to go to war. What is the matter with George Bush?'

Senator Daniel Patrick Moynihan,
15 November 1990[2]

'While Iraq is prepared to compromise, it is not prepared to capitulate. The Iraqi calculation has been that a concession made too early will be interpreted as weakness.'

Patrick Cockburn, British journalist,
6 December 1990[3]

'Allah is on our side. That is why we will beat the aggressor.'

Saddam Hussein in an interview with ZDF
Television, Mainz, Germany, 21 December 1990[4]

While the international community was digesting the implications of Resolution 678, authorizing the states co-operating with the Kuwaiti government to 'use all necessary means to uphold and implement Security Council resolution 660 (1990) and all subsequent resolutions' and 'to restore international peace and security in the area', President Bush sprang a surprise on the world.

In an abrupt policy reversal, in a televised address to the nation, he invited Tariq Aziz to Washington during 'the latter part of the week of December 10' for talks, and suggested that President Saddam Hussein meet Baker in Baghdad some time between 15 December 1990 and 15 January 1991, the deadline mentioned in Resolution 678. However, he assured his audience that the US would refuse to negotiate anything less than 'Iraq's complete withdrawal from Kuwait and the release of all hostages'. He described his offer of direct talks as 'going the extra mile' in search of peace.[5]

Bush's gesture was warmly received by the financial markets. In New York the Dow-Jones Industrial Index rose 40.84 points to 2559.65. The oil price fell $4.06 to $28.85 a barrel, the second biggest drop since the beginning of the Gulf crisis, the largest decline being $5 on 21 October, when Prince Sultan was reported to have made a conciliatory statement.[6]

It emerged that Baker had raised the prospect of direct talks with Iraq during his whirlwind tour of the capitals of the Security Council members to win backing for the UN resolution authorizing force. More specifically, Moscow had insisted on high-level contact between Washington and Baghdad as a condition for its vote. At the private dinner with the foreign ministers of the USSR, Britain, France and China, after the Security Council vote on 29 November, Baker raised the matter. The Soviet and French ministers agreed with the idea of the US sending a high-level emissary to Baghdad. Baker telephoned Bush telling him of the agreement reached in principle on the subject.

Bush decided to announce Baker's mission the next morning. The speed with which he moved surprised many. Though his overall strategy, planned a month earlier, included an attempt at direct contact with Saddam Hussein to convince the American public that all avenues of peaceful resolution had been explored, the timing was forced on Bush by Congress – more specifically, by the Senate Armed Services Committee chaired by Sam Nunn, a Georgia Democrat, and the generally anti-administration drift of the testimonies.

Opening the four-day televised hearings on 27 November, Senator Nunn stated that the president's decision of 8 November to double US troops in the Gulf was a 'fundamental shift' away from the stated objectives: to deter further Iraqi aggression; defend Saudi Arabia; and enforce the UN embargo. It had raised new questions: (1) Has the liberation of Kuwait become a vital interest of the US? (2) Has the large-scale deployment of US forces created a situation in which a decision on an offensive action would be dictated by logistics rather than by deliberate policy? (3) Has the destruction of Iraq's military capability been added to the original list of objectives? Since America would be doing most of the fighting and taking most of the casualties, it was necessary to inform the American people of US objectives.[7]

By holding hearings Senator Nunn, a military expert, diverted

Congressional pressure for a special session to debate the Gulf crisis. The opposition to Bush's war-oriented policy was strong among politicians, and centred on two major points: why should a republican, democratic America shed blood for antiquated, autocratic Arab monarchies; and why should American troops die to ensure oil supplies for Japan and Europe. There was also strong resentment at the failure of Tokyo and Bonn to send troops to the Gulf and their willingness merely to provide cash, thus making US forces look like mercenaries. However, Nunn and his fellow-Democrats opted for the forum of public hearings. It allowed them to criticize, and perhaps influence, the White House without facing a vote on the Congressional floor, where the danger of sending mixed signals to Saddam Hussein would have weighed heavily on the minds of the lawmakers, putting them in a politically tricky situation.

Now, as the testimonies of highly respected military, intelligence and foreign affairs experts were recorded, the Democratic members of Congress found much material to beat President Bush with. James Schlesinger, former defence secretary and director of the CIA, stated that the sanctions were working more rapidly than anticipated, the period anticipated by the Bush administration being one year. 'To date, it [the sanctions option] has been a winning strategy, and I am puzzled by the administration's failure to take credit for its success on this slow route to its objectives,' stated General William Odom, former director of the National Security Agency. 'Every day Iraq pays a bigger price for its invasion. Saudi Arabia is secure. Oil production from the moderate Gulf states should increase. The international support for the blockade is holding.' Odom and Schlesinger based their statements on reports by US intelligence sources that the three-and-a-half-month UN embargo and blockade had cut Iraq's imports by 90%, including the flow of spare parts and military supplies, and its exports by 97%; reduced its industrial output by 40%; and caused shortages of such critical goods as lubricants and chemicals – and predicting that by next spring 'probably' only its energy-related industry and 'some' military factories would be functioning fully. 'If, in fact, the sanctions will work in 12 to 18 months instead of six months, a tradeoff of avoiding war, with its attendant sacrifices and uncertainties, would in my estimation be more than worth it,' said Admiral William J. Crowe, the chairman of the Joint Chiefs of Staff until September 1989.[8]

There were others who disagreed. Among them were Richard Cheney and General Colin Powell who, behaving as a typical military man, had fallen in line with his commander-in-chief, President Bush, and discarded his earlier preference for the economic option, described by him as the 'strangulation policy'. Cheney stated that the US could not wait 'indefinitely' for the sanctions to work while Saddam Hussein used this time to upgrade his military preparedness. Henry Kissinger, former secretary of state and national security adviser, offered a refined argument. 'I do not believe a clear-cut point will ever be reached in which we can tell the sanctions are working or not working,' he said. 'And it will certainly be Saddam's strategy, if he is at all skilful, to put us into that position,' he said. In any case, argued Powell, sanctions alone could not get Saddam Hussein out of Kuwait, and if the sanctions path was pursued the US could at a later stage find itself fighting 'a far more difficult war with an adversary who might by then be armed with nuclear weapons.' He added that if Iraq was given another 12–18 months' grace, 'they can put their army into somewhat of a state of hibernation and stretch their sustaining capability if they don't have to keep it finely tuned in anticipation of military action.'[9] In any event, if the US had to deploy a large number of troops in the Gulf for more than twelve months, they would have to be rotated; and there were not enough armed personnel available to do that.

Reasoned, expert voices were raised against the use of force. 'Certainly, many Arabs would deeply resent a campaign which would necessarily kill large numbers of their Muslim brothers and force them to choose sides between Arab nations and the West,' Admiral Crowe said. 'Even if we win, we lose ground in the Arab world and generally injure our ability to deal in the future with the labyrinth of the Middle East.' James Webb, navy secretary during the previous administration, was another expert witness cautioning against warfare. 'If we go to war, it is not inconceivable that the end result would be yet another cycle of ancillary confrontation including an Arab–Israeli war, Iran re-establishing itself as the dominant regional power, and the Soviets emerging as the intermediary of choice in the region,' he stated.[10]

Even those favouring military action, such as Richard Perle, assistant secretary of defence during the Reagan administration, called for an air offensive against Iraq, not a fully-fledged campaign to recapture Kuwait. Edward Luttwak of the Centre for Strategic and International Studies, Washington DC, doubted if the US army was 'capable of conducting a competent mobile ground war, something it had not tried in 46 years'.[11]

Senator Nunn had opened the hearings with strong pro-sanctions witnesses, who presented a carefully argued case against war, thus strengthening Congressional and public doubts about the causes, cost and consequences of fighting Iraq. The witnesses provided disturbing evidence about the lack of equipment and training to fight a sustained ground campaign in the Arabian desert. They questioned the White House's assertion that if America did not use force soon the anti-Iraq coalition would begin to fall apart, a position well articulated, *inter alia*, by Henry Kissinger. He feared that during the year it would take for the sanctions to bite, one or more of the critical countries – Iran, Syria and Jordan – provoked perhaps by Washington's backing for Israel, would break the embargo against Iraq – or that Riyadh, apprehensive of the survival of the Saddam Hussein regime, would sign a separate deal with Baghdad. By vindicating the Iraqi leader, such an outcome, he argued, would torpedo the prospects of regional and international security arrangements no less than a bloody land war. The sceptics were not convinced. If the alliance against Communism held during the 43 years of cold war, retorted Senator Albert Gore, a Democrat, why could not the present anti-Iraq coalition hold so long as Iraq was occupying Kuwait? Moreover, the hearings addressed for the first time the after-effects of the war, in the process making the public and politicians wonder whether the calamitous consequence of the military conflict might be too high a price for America and the rest of the world to pay.[12]

President Bush, who had been watching the televised testimonies with rising alarm, rushed to announce Baker's mission in the midst of the hearings. By so doing he regained the initiative and turned the limelight away from Senator Nunn. He demonstrated that he was not at the mercy of events, and that he was ready to act as a statesman and diplomat, not merely as the impetuous warmonger several senators and military and foreign affairs experts had portrayed at the Senate hearings. His decision to send Baker to Baghdad and invite Aziz to Washington proved immensely popular, with 90% of the public backing it.[13]

Having made a fast move, Bush tried to capitalize on it immediately. He wanted to rush the military action for several reasons. He was unsure that the coalition would hold for a year. There was a major problem looming about the presence of US forces in Saudi Arabia during the holy month of Ramadan (beginning on 17 March 1991) and then during the hajj pilgrimage three months later. Finally, the continued uncertainty in the Gulf was having an adverse impact on the world economy. At a two-hour meeting with Congress leaders on the night of 30 November he pressed them to provide him with a Congressional resolution authorizing force in the Gulf similar to the one passed at the UN Security Council. He failed. 'There is no justification for Congress to give approval to the president to conduct war at some indefinite future date under some unspecified future circumstance,' said Senator George Mitchell, leader of the Democratic majority.[14] He was in tune with majority public opinion. A *USA Today* poll published on 3 December showed that whereas 49% wanted the sanctions to continue after 15 January, only 42% wanted America to attack Iraq.[15]

On 1 December Iraq's Revolutionary Command Council met to consider Bush's proposal. 'Despite the arrogant language he used in his call,' said its communiqué, 'we accept the idea of the invitation and the meeting.' The RCC, it continued, would try to hold 'an in-depth, serious dialogue', not 'formal meetings as sought by President Bush to use as a pretext for American public opinion, US Congress, world opinion and the international community to achieve objectives that he [had] planned in the first place.'[16]

In a French television interview, broadcast on 2 December in France, Saddam Hussein put the chances of war and peace at 50:50. The outcome of the forthcoming meetings depended on 'Bush and those pushing him towards war'. If they wanted the meetings to be 'a simple formal show before the [US] Congress and international opinion in order to have a clear conscience and say: we have met the Iraqis but they have not changed their stand, so war is the only solution', then the world 'will be closer to the armed conflict'. Regarding the remaining Western and Japanese hostages, he said that they could be released now if 'we had an assurance that President Bush would not attack the Iraqi people between now and 25 March [the day by which all hostages were scheduled to be released]'.[17]

While formally accepting Bush's proposal, Saddam Hussein gave Joseph Wilson, the US chargé d'affaires in Baghdad, a series of questions that he wanted answered about the nature of the discussion to be held. Bush's public response was that he had not endorsed talks to initiate negotiations but rather merely to inform Iraq of the resolutions passed by the UN Security Council. On another major point, however, Bush backed down. Initially he had said that he would receive Iraq's foreign minister in Washington in the presence of the Kuwaiti, Saudi and Egyptian ambassadors. But when Iraq threatened that if he did so then President Saddam Hussein would invite a PLO delegation to his meeting with Baker in Baghdad, Bush quietly dropped the idea.[18]

As it was, in his haste to do something dramatic, Bush had failed even to inform King Fahd, Emir Jaber and President Mubarak, much less consult them. They were reportedly deeply upset about being ignored on such a vital matter, but refrained from expressing their displeasure publicly.[19]

By making his overture to Baghdad, Bush had contradicted his own assessment of Saddam Hussein as a political pariah. Also he stopped using the rhetoric of reparations, a war crimes tribunal, the curbing of Iraq's military might even if it withdrew voluntarily – demands normally associated with the unconditional surrender of an enemy defeated in war – to pressure Iraq. By making these demands earlier, he (and Thatcher) had gone beyond the UN Security Council resolutions, blurring UN objectives and, inadvertently, increasing the Iraqi leader's popularity in the Arab world by singling him out for unprecedented punishment.

On the other hand, despite repeated efforts, Saddam Hussein had failed to break the anti-Iraq coalition, which included 11 of the 21 members of the Arab League, the rest being sympathetic to Baghdad. After their meeting with the Iraqi president on 5 December, King Hussein, Yasser Arafat and Ali Salim al Baidh, the Yemeni vice-president, expressed satisfaction at the Bush initiative. Baidh added that his government proposed to hold meetings with all Arab leaders in order to restore unity in the Arab ranks.[20]

The next day, yielding to the pressures from these friendly Arab leaders, Saddam Hussein asked the National Assembly to let all hostages go immediately. There were then in Iraq and Kuwait more than 2,700 Western and Japanese captives, including about 500 at strategic sites, with two-thirds of the total being British and American nationals.[21]

'I recognize that despite what the foreigners had to endure, denying those people the freedom to travel has rendered a great service to the cause of peace,' Saddam Hussein wrote in his letter to the National Assembly. 'Because God has taught us that forbidden actions should never be undertaken except in very urgent cases and without excess, we should not maintain emergency measures, especially this one, any longer. The period through which our nation has passed has been such that our options ... were not open or without limits. Our valiant forces did not have the chance to complete their concentrations in order to confront the possibilities of military aggression against them in the Kuwaiti province. So any measure that was taken to delay the war ... has provided an opportunity for us to prepare for any eventuality. We have reached the stage when our blessed forces under the care of God are fully prepared . . . People of goodwill; men and women of different nationalities and political trends have come to Iraq; and dear brothers from Jordan, Yemen, Palestine, Sudan and the Arab Maghreb have also consulted us on this issue as on others . . . Time has come to give our decisive view on this subject. [Earlier] we had considered a timing different from the present one, namely, the occasion of Christmas . . . However, the appeal by certain brothers, the decision of the Democratic majority in the American Congress, the European Parliament's invitation to our foreign minister for dialogue: all these have encouraged us to respond to these positive changes which will have a major impact on world public opinion in general, and American public opinion in particular, in restraining the evil warmongers . . . We find that the exigencies . . . which prevented the travel of foreigners have been replaced by . . . positive change in public opinion everywhere, including America, which will restrain the intentions and decisions of evil-doers led by the enemy of God, Bush. Therefore I call on you to allow all foreigners on whom travel restrictions were imposed to enjoy freedom of travel, with our apologies for any harm done to anyone of them.'22

Yasser Arafat played a significant role behind the scenes. Having sent an urgent message to Saddam Hussein on 30 November urging acceptance of the Bush offer of an exchange of high-level visits, and the release of all hostages in order to prepare the ground for a wider dialogue with the Americans, Arafat flew to Amman for talks with King Hussein. Together they left for Baghdad, where they were joined by the Yemeni vice-president, Baidh. On 5 December they persuaded Saddam Hussein to release all the hostages.

Having achieved this objective, King Hussein and Arafat, working in conjunction with Sultan Qaboos of Oman and President Chadli Ben Jadid of Algeria, began laying the groundwork for an eventual meeting between Saddam Hussein and King Fahd in Algiers – to finalize an agreement whereby Kuwait would concede the disputed border strip to Iraq and lease two offshore islands to it for 99 years – followed by an Arab summit to replace the Iraqi troops in Kuwait with an Arab League peacekeeping force. The main reasons why King Fahd and Emir Jaber responded positively to these behind-the-scenes overtures were that they thought that President Bush had lost his will to fight, as shown by his readiness to talk directly with Saddam Hussein and his failure even to inform them of this dramatic policy change. Moreover, King Fahd felt that if Bush chose to hold direct talks with Saddam Hussein, he could too. Fearful of being abandoned by Washington, he and the Kuwaiti emir decided to negotiate with the Iraqi leader. Kuwait expressed its willingness to make territorial concessions to Oman, a fellow-member of the GCC, which had earlier tried to bring about a rapprochement between King Fahd and King Hussein and which maintained friendly relations with Baghdad. After some initial hesitation, King Fahd sent a special envoy, Shaikh Ali ibn Muslim, to Algiers twice in early December. However, no matter how much Fahd felt piqued by Bush's insensitive behaviour, he realized that he could meet Saddam Hussein only after advance clearance from the White House. Otherwise the meeting might be seen by the world as a Saudi rebuff to the US-led forces in the kingdom and undermine the legitimacy of the US military presence in the region, instantly sending the financial markets into the doldrums.[23] The White House seemed unlikely to give the green light to King Fahd.

Responding to the Iraqi leader's positive decision on the hostages, President Bush, then in Santiago, Chile, in the course of a Latin American tour, declared that US pressure was 'working'. Perhaps. Actually, Bush's shrewd strategy of making the inevitability of war compel Saddam Hussein to vacate Kuwait, and thus make warfare unnecessary, was being torpedoed by the tough new stance adopted by the Democrats in Congress, encouraged partly by the expert assessment made by former US military leaders. At the hearings on 4 December of the Senate Foreign Relations Committee, which included anti-war Senators Joseph Biden and Paul Sarbanes, Baker was given a rough ride by the Democrats. They argued that Baker had ignored expert opinion on economic sanctions and other matters, failed to explain the Bush administration's impatience, and failed to secure enough forces or funds from the allies for the common purpose. 'For the first time in recent history,' wrote R. W. Apple, an American columnist, 'public and political opinion in the US is split on the eve of a possible war – not halfway through it, as in Vietnam, or toward its end, as in Korea.'[24] The Democrats knew they could not lose. If war caused too many casualties they would say 'We told you so'; and if the American victory was total and casualties nominal, they would say that their Congressional leaders played their full part as laid down by the constitution.

With US commentators of all shades hailing the hostages' release as a turning point in the crisis, and the first 500 Western nationals flown out of Baghdad by 9 December, Saddam Hussein had a good chance of convincing the American public that being flexible

on the hostages indicated that he could be flexible on Kuwait as
well – thus using diplomacy to exploit Bush's weakness at home
and divide the multinational anti-Iraq alliance. Bush realized the
danger to his war-oriented strategy. Once all the captives had been
freed and there were no more American lives to be protected in
Kuwait or Iraq, popular backing for military action to liberate Kuwait
(running at around 40% before the hostages' release) was bound
to drop.

He therefore concentrated on dampening popular euphoria by
putting practical impediments in the way of finalizing the timetable
for high-level meetings, and letting General Powell and the Pentagon
give a high profile to the American war plans with a view to
intimidating Saddam Hussein. On 7 December the White House
announced that it would not fix a date for Bush's meeting with
Aziz (originally planned for the latter part of the week beginning
10 December) unless Saddam Hussein had first settled the date
for his meeting with Baker. Two days later the White House set
3 January as the cut-off date for the Baker–Hussein meeting,
having earlier proposed 'any time between 15 December and 15
January'.

In his testimony to the Senate Foreign Relations Committee,
General Powell rejected 'sole reliance' on surgical air strikes, carpet
bombing and other 'nice, tidy, low cost, incremental, may-work
options', and stated that a full-scale ground war would be 'the
centrepiece of US military strategy' if force became necessary to
expel Iraq from Kuwait. Only a 'violent, destructive overland
war' would 'destroy the Iraqi army or force it to retreat', he
asserted.[25]

The success of this strategy rested on two assumptions. One,
American aircraft would control the skies from the first day, and
continue to hit Iraqi and Kuwaiti military and economic targets day
after day, unhindered. Two, guided by up-to-the-minute intelligence
on enemy deployments, the highly mobile US troops would have the
advantage of surprise assault, whereas the dug-in Iraqi troops, being
comparatively immobile, would be unable to cover the holes that
their foes would punch in their defence lines. In any case, a war
fought on this strategy would last weeks, not days, with Admiral
Crowe putting the duration of the air campaign alone at four to seven
weeks.

There would be two distinct phases of the strategy. In the first
phase Tomahawk cruise missiles and F-117 Stealth warplanes would

annihilate the Iraqi air force's command and control network so as to deny Iraqi pilots radio guidance from ground controllers tracking American planes. Scores of F-111 fighters and A-6 attack bombers would fire missiles to destroy Iraqi radar. Then F-15 and F-16 fighters and the navy's F-14s and F-18s would attempt to sweep the sky of Iraqi airplanes while US bombers would raid almost every airfield in Kuwait and Iraq that could be used by the Iraqi planes. The objective would be to destroy aircraft on the ground as well as create such large craters in the runways that the undamaged aircraft would be unable to take off. Concurrently, US electronic warfare planes and other jamming devices would attempt to cut off Iraq's high command from the forward units.

For its success this scenario depended on tactical surprise, which immediately placed the initiative in American hands. There was always the possibility that Baghdad would launch a pre-emptive spoiling assault and deprive the US of initiative. (The evidence so far was to the contrary. Saddam Hussein had come to rely so heavily on a defensive posture and doctrine that, despite numerous violations of Kuwaiti airspace by US and allied aircraft, the Iraqi interceptors seldom took off. The idea was to ignore deliberate provocations by the allies and keep secret Iraq's defence tactics.) Secondly, since the Iraqis had mined oil wells in Kuwait, they would most probably respond to the American attack with widespread destruction of Kuwait's valuable resource.

The launching of the ground war would herald the second phase of the strategy. US army troops and marines would attempt to confuse the Iraqis with 'feints, deceptions and continued electronic jamming'. Squadrons of B-52 bombers would be brought nearer to the war zone from Diego Garcia (in the Indian Ocean) to the bases of an allied Arab country to drop 'hundreds of tons of bombs' on Iraqi artillery bases, command posts and supply roads. Having thus stunned and disoriented the Iraqis, the Pentagon would mount co-ordinated ground attacks to follow the bombing raids. The American land forces would be covered by low-flying A-10 tank-killing planes and Apache helicopters attacking Iraqi armour and infantry vehicles. By keeping sufficient warplanes in the air to destroy any Iraqi forces emerging from their reinforced bunkers the Pentagon expected to reduce enemy mobility. Since the Iraqi army units were known to lack the independence and initiative to operate effectively without precise direction from their regimental leaders, the US planned to separate the enemy units from them by *inter alia* jamming their communications systems and induce mass surrenders.[26]

There were weaknesses in this phase of the military operations. Firstly, low-flying aircraft would be highly vulnerable to anti-aircraft fire and surface-to-air missiles. Secondly, in land offensives, troops invariably fire, accidentally, at their own comrades, a hazard made worse in this case because of the lack of a centralized command.

As General Powell made clear, whatever the extent of aerial bombing, there was no substitute for a land war, with soldier pitted against soldier. Yet there was no way the US could field enough troops to meet the traditional 3:1 ratio for attacker versus defender, especially when, according to the Pentagon, Baghdad had increased its forces in the Kuwaiti theatre to 480,000 and equipped them with 3,700 tanks.[27] All it could do, and did, was to use the multiplier effect of monopoly over the skies, unparalleled air strength, superior firepower, and high mobility.

As Saddam Hussein hinted in his letter to the National Assembly, the Iraqi forces had by early December reached a high state of military preparedness in the Kuwaiti theatre. There was not much more he could do in that field. So his immediate interest shifted to the forthcoming high-level talks with Washington, something he had desired since the crisis erupted. Here he planned to reiterate his position: a solution to the Gulf crisis had to be tied to a solution to other regional problems, principally that of the Palestinians. 'The linkage draws Israel into the debate, always a convenient tool for an Arab leader,' wrote Joel Brinkley of the *New York Times*. 'By positioning himself as the strongest advocate of the Palestinian cause, Saddam Hussein automatically becomes Israel's *bête noire* and, as a result, a leader of great appeal to Arabs.'[28] If in the process of vacating Kuwait, the Iraqi leader could secure some concession for the Palestinians he would emerge from this crisis with enhanced standing in the popular Arab mind. That was precisely why Washington was determined to see that Saddam Hussein would never be able to claim that a gain for the Palestinians – such as an international conference on the Palestinian issue – was a result of the Kuwait crisis.

However, Saddam Hussein was not alone in wanting an international conference on the Palestinian–Israeli issue. Among those who took the same position were America's Arab allies as well as Britain, France, the USSR, China and most of the Third World countries.

The problem remained 'hot' as exemplified by the imposition of a curfew on one million Palestinians in the Occupied Territories on the eve of the third anniversary of the intifada on 9 December 1990. During those three years 1,025 Palestinians had been killed, all but 250 by the Israeli security forces. The Israeli toll was 56.[29] With 253 violent deaths registered in the eleven months of 1990 in a population of 1.75 million, the Occupied Territories were the most violent place in the world. At the rate of 144.6 deaths per million, the area was more violent than South Africa (population 32 million) at 109, the US (population 226 million) at 78, and Northern Ireland (population 1.5 million) at 49.3.[30]

At the Security Council too the subject remained under active scrutiny. On 6 December four non-aligned nations – Colombia, Cuba, Malaysia and Yemen – circulated a draft resolution which specified despatching a UN ombudsman to the Occupied Territories and calling a conference of the 164 signatories to the Fourth Geneva Convention to discuss protecting Palestinian civilians under Israeli military occupation. Given that about a month earlier President Bush had told American Jewish leaders that he would not veto such a resolution at the Security Council, the chances of success for the non-aligned nations were good.[31] Already Israel had modified its defiance of the Security Council resolution to receive a UN mission to investigate the killings on 8 October at Jerusalem's Temple Mount. On 12 November it told the UN secretary-general that it was prepared to receive a UN envoy to discuss the treatment of Palestinians provided he did *not* raise the issue of the Jerusalem killings. On 21 November the UN secretary-general accepted the Israeli offer.

In the course of their lobbying for the resolution on the Palestinians, the four non-aligned nations decided to add a clause to it incorporating Washington's statement of the previous spring that 'at an appropriate time' an international conference on the Middle East might be supported if it was 'properly structured with the participation of the parties concerned.' So the expanded resolution now declared that the Security Council 'considers that the convening at an appropriate time of an international conference, properly structured, with the participation of the parties concerned', would facilitate a peace settlement. Washington said that the change was acceptable. But before the new resolution could be put to the vote there was a leak. The media interpreted America's agreement to support the resolution as a basic change of policy (which it was not). The Israelis, backed by all the powerful Jewish groups in the US, cried betrayal. On the other side, Iraq's Arab and other friends, including the PLO, claimed that the Gulf crisis had compelled America to yield to Palestinian demands. Dismayed by these reactions, the Bush administration did a quick volte-face and returned to its traditional line.[32]

Nor did Israel's tactical compromise on receiving the UN mission mean any change in its hardline stance on the territorial issue. 'The past leaders of our movement left us a clear message to keep the land of Israel from the [Mediterranean] sea to the River Jordan for the generations to come, for the mass immigrations and for the Jewish people, most of whom will be gathered into this country,' Prime Minister Shamir said on 19 November.[33]

Iraq's National Assembly was quick to condemn Shamir's statement, just as the Israeli government, despite repeated exhortations from Washington to keep a low profile, let it be known that it had told the US that it was opposed to a solution to the Gulf crisis which left Iraq's war machine intact. Israel had been alarmed by Bush's decision to seek talks with the Iraqi president. Israeli officials considered Saddam Hussein's compliance with UN resolutions as an unsatisfactory resolution of the crisis. Avoiding a war now, they argued, would lead to a bloodier conflict later, almost certainly involving Israel. If Saddam Hussein's regime were not destroyed now, he would emerge as the hero of the Arabs, even if he were to evacuate Kuwait. He would then set the agenda on the Palestinian problem. He would also try to destabilize Saudi Arabia and Egypt, the former for having invited the Americans and the latter for having sided with the Saudi kingdom and having made unilateral peace with Israel in 1979. Now was the time to move against Iraq, militarily, before the unprecedented and fragile coalition against it collapsed, and/or the continued stalemate destabilized the pro-American Arab regimes.

During his meeting with Bush in Washington on 11 December, Shamir doubtlessly articulated Israel's official position. Their 'friendly exchange' of views lasted two hours. According to American columnists Rowland Evans and Robert Novak (as well as White House briefings after the Gulf War), President Bush reassured Shamir on Israel's security in the event of an Arab attack on it, and added that the US would like to launch a retaliatory counterattack on Israel's behalf. Shamir was not receptive to the idea, and insisted on maintaining Israel's freedom of action in military affairs. Bush said that the US was doing its utmost to avoid linkage between the Gulf crisis and the Palestinian issue, and that it was vital that Israel should do the same by refraining from retaliating against any Iraqi attack – an action which would, inadvertently, link the Gulf crisis with the wider Arab–Israeli conflict. Shamir promised not to mount a pre-emptive strike against Iraq, and to consult Bush before responding to any Iraqi attack. To facilitate this, Bush agreed to share US intelligence summaries with Israel – and, more importantly, to install a hot line, codenamed 'Hammer Rick', which was to be established between the Pentagon's Crisis Situation Room and the Israeli defence ministry in Tel Aviv so that the Pentagon could give instantaneous warning to Israel of any Iraqi missile launch monitored by US satellites. Of course, none of this came out at the press conference Shamir addressed after the meeting. 'President Bush said several times, and he said to me now again, that there will not be any deal at the expense of Israel,' Shamir stated. John Kelly, US assistant secretary for the Near East, told the press conference that President Bush had assured Shamir that Israel would continue to maintain its military dominance in the region, but that the US wanted 'to aid Arab nations as well'; and that the two leaders agreed that 'the wider regional peace process must be reinvigorated once the Gulf crisis is over.'[34]

It was against this background that the US agreed with the USSR at the UN Security Council to postpone voting on the Palestinian resolution for five days to allow more time for talks between the US and the Non-Aligned Group on the wording.[35]

However, Washington was not so accommodating on the dates for high-level meetings with the Iraqi government. On 13 December, while suggesting 17 December as a date for the Bush–Aziz meeting, Iraq's foreign ministry stated that it was ready to accept the American date for Aziz's meeting with Bush if the US would agree to its date for Baker's meeting with Saddam Hussein. Reneging on its earlier statement that any day between 15 December and 15 January would be suitable for Baker–Saddam Hussein talks, Washington now insisted on 3 January as the 'cut-off point', with the Iraqis sticking to their suggestion of 12 January, a date which the US considered too near the deadline mentioned in Resolution 678, a document which Baghdad had rejected. On 15 December Iraq's Revolutionary Command Council stated that Iraq alone had the right to set 'the appropriate dates' for its president to meet foreign officials, thus implying its rejection of Washington's proposal of 3 January as the date for the Baker–Saddam Hussein meeting.[36] That day the US cancelled the Aziz–Baker meeting scheduled for 17 December in Washington. Each of the two parties was seeking not peace but the best way of defeating the other at the least cost to itself. As such, a feeling quickly grew in each capital that talks would be on terms disadvantageous to it.

The situation at home for the Bush administration was mixed. On the positive side, by 13 December all American hostages who wanted to leave had done so, with the US ambassador to Kuwait, Nathaniel Howell, on his way back home.[37] Judge Harold Green of US District Court in Washington, DC, rejected a plea by 54 Democratic members of Congress to bar President Bush from waging war without Congressional approval, on the ground that the matter had been raised prematurely.[38]

On the negative side, for Bush, the *New York Times*–CBS poll of 1,044 people, conducted during 9–11 December, showed that while 45% of Americans wanted military action if Iraq did not withdraw by 15 January, 48% said that the US should 'wait and see' if the 15 January deadline was met. There was little 'generation gap' in the poll, but marked differences between sexes and races. Whereas 53% of men supported military action only 37% of women did so. While 48% of whites backed fighting only 23% of blacks did so. The *Los Angeles Times* poll of 2,205, conducted during 8–12 December, showed only 37% backing war if Iraq did not withdraw by 15 January. The overall picture presented by a series of opinion polls was that about 40% supported military action in most circumstances, with approximately the same percentage being equally broadly opposed. The remaining 'swing' segment of 20% changed its mind according to the exact phrasing of the question. When the UN was mentioned, backing for war rose; when the option of maintaining the economic embargo was mentioned, support for military action fell.[39]

Expert opinion, as expressed before the Senate Foreign Relations Committee on 13 and 14 December, was running heavily against war, with twelve out of fourteen witnesses arguing against swift US military action. Summarizing the first day of the hearings, Senator Joseph Biden said: 'There appears to be broad agreement that if force is used on 16 January, it will be perceived, rightly or wrongly, by most Arabs and the Arab world as primarily a US undertaking.' Therefore, argued four former US assistant secretaries for the Near East, an American-led offensive could stigmatize the US and complicate its pursuit of long-term stability in the region. The possible negative scenarios that were sketched were: destabilization of Saudi Arabia and/or Jordan, especially if the Islamic shrines in the Saudi kingdom were damaged, and/or if Israel, provoked by Iraq, joined the US-led offensive; the US finding itself in possession of Iraqi territory with no clear way of disengaging; and destruction of Iraq's military capability leading to its eventual dismemberment or control by fundamentalist Shias closely allied with Iran. Earlier, in another Congressional hearing, Zbigniew Brzezinski, former national security adviser and an active participant in the 1980 US military undertaking in the Gulf to rescue American hostages in Iran, had warned of the following 'undesirable and unanticipated side-effects' of the US-led war against Iraq: Iran's dominance in the Gulf; Syrian leadership of the Arab world; overthrow of moderate Arab regimes friendly with Washington; and temptation to Israel to use its military force more freely than before.[40]

Then there were the views of the editorial writers of America's influential dailies as well as those experts who published their articles in these newspapers. A highly original study of 657 such pieces in the *New York Times, Washington Post, Wall Street Journal* and *Christian Science Monitor* from 3 August to 30 November by Thomas P. Barnett, an American researcher, was illuminating. He gave each article one point, and classified the views expressed in it as (a) isolationist, (b) unilateralist, or (c) multilateralist.

Isolationists emphasized the negative aspects of Operation 'Desert Shield': unreasonable cost, unneeded entanglements abroad, and unpleasant moral dilemmas. In their militant variety, they were the 'new order isolationists': George McGovern–Patrick Buchanan type of liberal Democrats, and staunch conservatives. They wanted only limited US involvement, and disavowed any Washington-led military campaign if the UN embargo against Iraq failed. They argued that America must severely shed its foreign commitments in the post-Cold War world. They favoured a negotiated settlement, with several of them promoting an Arab solution encompassing the Palestinian question. Their ranks included columnists Rowland Evans and Robert Novak, and Tom Wicker of the *New York Times*. In their moderate variety, they were like 'refuseniks'. They disclaimed any American responsibility to get involved. They viewed the Gulf crisis as a regional issue and promoted energy independence as the best long-term strategy to avoid future Middle East conflicts. They stressed the human cost of the war with Iraq and questioned the morality of calling on young Americans to 'die for cheap oil'. They included Russell Baker of the *New York Times* and Mark Shields.

Unilateralists stressed the cost of Washington's indecisiveness in dealing with Saddam Hussein. They argued that military action was needed, given America's dependence on Gulf oil, commitment to allies, opposition to aggression, and the dangers stemming from Iraq's arsenal of weapons of mass destruction. In their militant variety (called the Hot Bloods by Barnett), they were wary of relying on international law, or the UN, to prevail. They were against any sell-out involving Kuwait or Israel. Their slogan was: 'Stop Saddam Now Before He Strikes Again'. Their ranks included A. M. Rosenthal of the *New York Times*, Charles Krauthammer of the *New Republic*, and the editorial writers of the *Wall Street Journal*. Their moderate variety (called the Cold Bloods by Barnett) favoured US military action but feared its cost. So they settled for surgical strikes by air to cripple Iraq without a bloody land offensive. This needed to be done soon as delay gave Iraq time to develop nuclear weapons. The Cold Bloods included William Safire of the *New York Times*, Henry Kissinger and Richard Perle.

Multilateralists highlighted the international payoff of collective security. They focused on Washington's inability to 'go it alone', the special legitimacy of multinational action, and the importance of co-ordinated action as a precedent for future international co-operation. The militant variety (called the New Order Warriors by Barnett) supported the UN embargo, arguing that it could work; but they were unwilling to wait for ever. They emphasized Washington's decisive diplomatic and military leadership of the anti-Iraq coalition. If push came to shove, the New Order Warriors supported the military option as sanctioned by the UN Security Council. The New Order Warriors were in tune with the predominant thinking at the Bush White House. The moderate variety of multilateralists (called the World Orderists by Barnett) were against a repetition of the League of Nations' failure to punish fascist Italy after it invaded Ethiopia in 1936. They stressed the significance of the allies' financial contribution to Operation 'Desert Shield'. Their ranks included Flora Lewis and Anthony Lewis of the *New York Times*, and the editorial writers of that newspaper.

The relative strengths of these three lobbies changed as the crisis continued. In the first month, August, the 233 published articles were classified as: multilateralist, 89; unilateralist, 76; and isolationist, 68. Multilateralists stressed the potential for global economic dislocation; unilateralists emphasized America's need for continued access to the leading strategic energy resource; and isolationists focused on rising petrol prices, fears of recession and soaring military costs while highlighting the advantages of a negotiated settlement. In the second month, September, the isolationists gained a definite lead over unilateralists. The 160 articles were categorized as: multilateralist,

78; isolationist, 48; and unilateralist, 34. The multilateralists concentrated on the UN embargo and the new international order; the
isolationists shied away from mentioning a negotiated settlement; and
unilateralists beat the drum of bombing Iraq into submission.

During the second half of the four-month crisis, the isolationists
gained a firm lead over their rivals, thanks partly to President Bush's
speech at the UN General Assembly where he opened up possibilities
for a peaceful solution. The 264 articles published in October and
November were classified as: isolationist, 114; multilateralist, 86; and
unilateralist, 64. 'The real story of the second half [of the crisis] was
the growing influence of the isolationists, whose scoreboard topped
50% in November,' noted Thomas P. Barnett. 'Their number soared
once the debate turned to the morality of force. The unilateralists
and multilateralists had trouble proving that Iraq represented an
imminent threat to America's national security. Neither Baker's
"jobs" nor Bush's "new world order" matched the potency of the
isolationists' warning "American blood for Arab oil".'

Small wonder that, having trailed way behind the multilateralists
(116 vs 167) during the first half of the crisis, the isolationists improved
their overall score to 230 – within earshot of the multilateralists' total
of 253 and well ahead of the unilateralists' 174.[41]

Barnett's study showed that the debate on the Gulf crisis was not
a repeat of the pre-Second World War debate between isolationists
and interventionists. This time there was an alternative to sitting
it out or going all out: multilateral action. Multilateralists started
strong, but only just managed to save their lead at the end. Their
voice was overtaken by the isolationists from the twelfth week of
the crisis onwards.

The most fruitful debate was conducted between the New Order
Isolationists (the militant isolationists) and the two varieties of
multilateralists – the militant New World Warriors and the moderate
World Orderists – and revolved around the efficacy of the UN embargo.
Unwilling to wait out the UN sanctions, the New Order Isolationists
preferred a negotiated resolution of the crisis. At the other end,
predicting the failure of the embargo in the long run, the New World
Warriors wanted to force the issue once the deadline was reached on
15 January 1991. (Unknown to them President Bush had adopted this
position on 31 October 1990.) In between were the World Orderists
who believed that the sanctions would achieve the objective of getting
Iraq out of Kuwait if allowed to continue.

All but the New World Warriors had reason to be concerned about the emotionalism displayed by President Bush when dealing with the words and deeds of Saddam Hussein. They remembered how he had handled General Manuel Noriega, the Panamanian leader. The official reasons for an all-out US invasion of Panama on 20 December 1989 were the safeguarding of American lives and overthrowing an oppressive dictatorship to restore democracy. But the single most important reason was Bush's personal hostility towards Noriega. On several occasions Noriega had affronted US authority and presidential pride, and thus earned the ire of Bush. The shooting of a US serviceman and the molesting of the wife of another proved to be the trigger for Bush's military campaign which lasted a mere three days. After Noriega had been forced out of his refuge inside the Papal nunciature, an elated Bush is said to have shouted to his wife Barbara, 'We got him! We got him!' like a greenhorn at a Texas turkey shoot.

'For all his efforts to portray the Gulf crisis as Saddam v. The Rest of the World, Bush appears hemmed in by his own bellicose, often emotive rhetoric, his own inflexible demands and his own political predicament,' noted Simon Tisdall of the *Guardian*. 'As matters grow more intractable and Saddam even more intransigent, Bush has regularly betrayed his own, apparently deeply-held feelings of animosity towards the Iraqi leader ... Even while announcing his willingness to go the "extra mile" for peace, by exchanging emissaries with Baghdad, Bush could not eschew the now routine references to Saddam's "immoral" and "unconscionable" brutality, to "rape, assassination, cold-blooded murder and rampant looting", to the violation of every "civilized principle".' Fresh impetus to Bush's crusade against Saddam Hussein came from the latest 79-page Amnesty International report on Iraqi human rights violations in Kuwait, published on 18 December. The document was based on interviews with more than 100 people in a dozen countries. 'We were told that the most common way [Iraqi] soldiers killed people was to take the victim to his family's doorstep, have his relatives identify him, and then shoot him in the back of his head,' the report said. The document incuded 38 methods of torture, including pulling out fingernails, beating the soles of feet, electric shocks to genitals, cutting off tongues, gouging eyes out, tying the accused to a ceiling fan and then running it, castration and rape, as well as rape or torture in the presence of relatives. It stated that the human rights violations in Kuwait were 'entirely consistent with abuses known to have been committed in Iraq over many years'. In other words, the Baghdad regime had extended its routine use of torture and other human rights violations to its 'nineteenth province'.

'It was standard language for an Amnesty International report, even for those on some of the key US allies,' noted Bob Woodward of the *Washington Post*. 'But Bush was horrified by the graphic accounts included.' Having read an advance copy of the document on 16 December, he retailed some of the details of the torture to his television interviewer, David Frost, adding that Barbara, his wife, had read two pages and said she could not read any more. It was against this background that an increasing number of observers noted that, as in the case of Noriega, Bush radiated personal revulsion and subjective hurt more than rational resolve in dealing with Saddam Hussein. 'In Congress, the sense among many Democrats, and not a few Republicans, is that the president, as if in pursuit of some family vendetta, is moving too fast, UN authorization notwithstanding,' reported Tisdall.[42]

Such a feeling was also abroad in the Arab world. Because of this, and because of the high stakes, Chadli Ben Jadid, the president of Algeria, a country with a high international reputation for mediation and which had been neutral in the crisis, began a peace mission after a series of talks with King Fahd's special envoy, Shaikh Ali ibn Muslim, in Algiers. He flew to Amman on 11 December for a meeting with King Hussein. From there he went to Baghdad where he had talks with Saddam Hussein. His next stop was Tehran. Then, on 15 December, he went to Cairo, and from there to Damascus. His last stop should have been Riyadh, where he had expected to set the scene for a Fahd–Saddam Hussein meeting; but King Fahd withdrew his invitation to the Algerian president under pressure from Bush, insisting that Saddam Hussein must first commit himself to withdrawal from Kuwait.[43] By then Bush had, through his intransigence on fixing the dates for high-level meetings with the Iraqi government, demonstrated (to the Saudi king among others) his lack of interest in serious dialogue with Baghdad.

If further evidence of the hardening of Washington's policy was needed it came on 17 December when Bush delivered a hardline speech to the first-ever meeting of the ambassadors of 28 countries which had contributed armed forces to the US-led effort to resolve the Gulf crisis. He reportedly told them that if he had to make the decision to go to war, he hoped he would have the support of Congress and the American people. If he did not have Congressional backing, he hoped he would have the support of the people. If he did not have the support of either, he continued, he would not be deterred from going to war if it was the 'right thing' to do.[44] On that day Prince Khalid, commander of the Arab and Muslim forces in Saudi Arabia, began a tour of the Gulf states, reportedly to prepare the ground for 'limited' air strikes against Iraq's military installations.

Equally significantly, on 17 December, while the foreign ministers of Nato (which included all the members of the twelve-strong European Community except Ireland), meeting in Brussels, endorsed Security Council Resolution 678, the foreign ministers of the European Community, gathering in the same city, showed their solidarity with the US by cancelling their invitation to Tariq Aziz for talks.

These signs bode ill for Baghdad. Not surprisingly, on 19 December the Iraqi press and radio advised citizens and traders to store paraffin, fuel and diesel oil to reduce the impact of possible US attacks on Iraq's twelve major petrochemical facilities, including three refineries, and instructed citizens on how to cope with chemical attacks and how to follow black-out procedures. Owners of apartment buildings were advised to clear out their cellars for use as air raid shelters. Furthermore, 250,000 Iraqi males, aged 30 to 33, were ordered to report to the military registration centres. On 20 December, as part of civil defence drills ahead of possible US-led attacks, an evacuation exercise was conducted in Basra, a settlement of one million people, followed by similar drills on the next two days by 3 million inhabitants of the eastern and western parts of Baghdad, a city with 370 civil defence centres. The purpose of the exercises, according to the Iraqi interior minister, was to test the government's ability to get people swiftly out of Baghdad if a nuclear strike or use of chemical weapons was expected.[45]

As tension rose, President Mitterrand carved out a position different from Bush's. At a press conference on 19 December he said that if US–Iraq dialogue did not materialize by 3 January, France would then seek direct talks with Saddam Hussein. Asserting that France had not despatched troops to the Gulf to destroy Iraq's military potential in a preventive war, he stated that if Iraq met UN demands for evacuating Kuwait and freeing hostages it would be entitled to assurances that it would not be attacked militarily. He thought it 'quite possible' that the Iraqi president would provide a definite timetable for withdrawal from Kuwait to forestall armed action by US allies. Finally, he added, territorial concessions by Kuwait to Iraq could only be made by a sovereign Kuwaiti government in 'full possession' of its territory.[46] French officials were not too hopeful of a voluntary pull-back by Saddam Hussein who, they feared, was overestimating his room for manoeuvre based on his assessment of the situation as conveyed to him by his sycophantic aides and the various self-designated emissaries from the West and Japan who had met him to obtain the release of hostages.

On the Palestinian issue, however, Mitterrand was forthright in his backing for an international peace conference, describing it as 'an indispensable means of reconciling peoples'. France was one of the six nations at the Security Council to oppose the postponement of the Non-Aligned Group's resolution on the Palestinians on 19 December. But with nine nations taking a contrary position, the vote on the resolution was postponed for the fourth time in ten days.[47] The Soviet Union voted with the US for the postponement in a bid to give more time to America and the Non-Aligned Group to hammer out a common position. Like the US, the USSR had refused to tie the Gulf crisis to the Palestinian problem. 'There is no strict linkage between the two issues,' stated Shevardnadze at the Security Council during the debate on Resolution 678. 'The enslavement of one nation in order to promote the freedom of another is absurd.'[48]

On the issue of letting go the mainly civilian Soviet experts in Iraq, Baghdad dragged its feet chiefly because it wanted Moscow to bear the material responsibility for the effects of a breach of their contracts. Within five months of the Gulf crisis the number of Soviet technicians and specialists had dwindled from about 7,000 to 3,232 – with 2,000 employed in the oil industry, 500 in power plant projects, 300 in irrigation projects, and 100 in the military. The USSR welcomed Iraq's decision on 6 December to let all its hostages go. On 16 December a delegation from Moscow arrived in Baghdad to negotiate suspension of the remaining 2,300 Soviet experts' contracts without involving penalties, to be resumed once the Gulf crisis was over and UN sanctions had been lifted.[49]

Baghdad had reason to feel satisfied with Moscow's policy on military involvement in the Gulf. Responding to calls by Soviet parliamentarians not to send forces to the region, Prime Minister Nikolai Ryzhkov told Interfax, a semi-official news agency: 'Our experience in Afghanistan and Czechoslovakia is too recent for the public to accept renewed military involvement abroad.' Earlier, members of Soyuz (i.e. Union), a 700-strong hardline parliamentary group (forming nearly a third of the total strength of the chamber), had vociferously accused the moderate Shevardnadze of being ready to despatch Soviet forces to the Gulf, and questioned his authority to back UN Security Council Resolution 678 without prior parliamentary approval. That the Kremlin had been reduced in status to the extent that it seriously considered despatching troops to participate in defeating Iraq, its ally of three decades, to secure American hegemony in the Gulf was, they argued, a deplorable contrast to the times when Soviet military might successfully checkmated the Pentagon at every strategic point on the globe. A defensive Shevardnadze stated that he had acted within his powers at the Security Council, arguing that prior parliamentary approval would have been needed only if the government had decided to get militarily involved in the Gulf – excepting in the case of an emergency arising in the form of, say, a Soviet citizen in Iraq being harmed, allowing President Gorbachev to exercise his emergency powers.[50]

The acrimonious debate in parliament left a deep mark on Shevardnadze. On 20 December he resigned as foreign minister. In his resignation speech he referred emotionally to the charge that he was prepared to commit Soviet forces for military confrontation in the Gulf, and repudiated it. His decision stunned many, including President Gorbachev. With six of the fifteen Soviet republics refusing to sign the new Union Treaty offered by Gorbachev, and the economy in the doldrums, the Soviet president was rapidly reaching a point where he had to choose between two stark options: to let the USSR disintegrate or to impose a crackdown. Under the circumstances he could scarcely afford the loss of such a valued colleague as Shevardnadze.

While Western capitals uniformly expressed regret at Shevardnadze's departure, the reaction in the Arab world was mixed. The pro-American Arab states were sorry to see him go while Iraq was pleased, as was the PLO. In Saddam Hussein's words, 'Shevardnadze was subservient to Baker: he did not show an understandable, distinct personality in his positions.' Abdullah Hourani, a member of the PLO executive committee, said, 'We hope Shevardnadze's replacement will adopt positions different in both form and content from those expressed by Shevardnadze . . . [and] his absence will be a chance for a review of [Soviet] policy, to make it more balanced and more distinct from US policy.'[51]

On 20 December the UN Security Council unanimously adopted Resolution 681. Deploring the decision of the Israeli government to resume deportations of Palestinian civilians living in the Occupied Territories, it urged 'the Government of Israel to accept *de jure* applicability of the Fourth Geneva Convention of 1949, to all the territories occupied by Israel since 1967, and to abide scrupulously by the provisions of the said convention'. It also called on 'the high contracting parties to the Fourth Geneva Convention' to 'ensure respect by Israel, the Occupying Power, for its obligations under the Convention', and requested the secretary-general to 'monitor and observe the situation regarding Palestinian civilians under Israeli occupation, making new efforts in this regard on an urgent basis' and to 'submit a first progress report to the Security Council by the first week of March 1991 and every four months thereafter'. Before the adoption of this resolution Yemen, the president of the Security Council, issued a non-binding statement: 'In this context they [Security Council members] agree that an international conference at an appropriate time, properly structured, should facilitate efforts to achieve a negotiated settlement and lasting peace in the Arab–Israeli conflict,' it said. 'However . . . there is not unanimity as to when would be the appropriate time for such a conference. In the view of the members of the Council, the Arab–Israeli conflict is important and unique and must be addressed independently, on its own merits.'[52]

The wording of the non-binding statement, and the fact of its dissociation from the main resolution, showed that weeks of bargaining between the US and the Non-Aligned Group had yielded nothing of substance from Washington. The US had succeeded in depriving Baghdad of anything that it might flaunt as diplomatic success stemming from the Gulf crisis it had created. This was confirmed when Saddam Hussein told Spanish television on 24 December: 'After all this period [of 84 days] the Security Council emerged with this absurd statement which cannot convince one honourable Arab citizen.' As for Israel, its prime minister described the resolution as 'another negative decision at the UN regarding Israel to join previous decisions in the UN archives'. However, while publicly deploring the Security Council resolution, senior Israeli officials noted with satisfaction that Washington had managed to remove from the resolution any suggestion of specific UN measures against Israel, a 'feat' that made the document 'tolerable'.[53]

Consequently, it was not difficult for Saddam Hussein to equate, once again, Israel with America. 'They [Zionist forces] are responsible for pushing the Bush administration towards the impasse in which it finds itself,' he said on Spanish television. 'Hence, if aggression [against Iraq] were to take place, we will assume that Israel has taken part in it. Therefore without [asking] any questions, we will strike at Israel. If the first strike is dealt to Baghdad or the front, the second strike will target Tel Aviv.'54

Shamir was quick to respond. 'Whoever dares to strike Israel will be struck hard and in the most severe way in return,' he said. The warning came on the heels of the Israeli defence minister's announcement that the army was in 'a higher state of readiness and alert than usual'. This was precisely what worried Senator George Mitchell, the Senate Democratic leader, after his trip to the Middle East. 'If Israel responds [to an Iraqi attack], Syria will probably change sides, abandon the coalition and fight against Israel; and this will place great stress on our other partners, Egypt and Saudi Arabia,' he said. 'If that occurs, American interests could be severely affected for decades to come.' He therefore urged the president to 'stay the course with the current economic sanctions, which are having a real effect in Iraq, and try to bring about the withdrawal that way. If we must use force ultimately ... I don't think January 15 is the time for that.'55

But President Bush thought otherwise. On 23 December US forces in Saudi Arabia went on a high state of alert for a week in case Iraq staged a sneak attack over the Christmas holiday. This was one way of diverting the minds of the troops from the resentment they were feeling at being barred by the Saudi authorities from celebrating Christmas in traditional fashion.

Of all the Muslim countries, Saudi Arabia is the only one which prohibits houses of worship for 'the people of the Book [i.e. the Quran]' – meaning Christians, Jews and Zoroastrians. 'This injunction is the result of an Islamic concept which holds the whole of the kingdom of Saudi Arabia to be considered within Islam as a mosque, where two religions cannot co-exist,' explained a Professor for Propagation of Islam at the Islamic University of Medina. On the same grounds the Saudi authorities forbid proselytizing for any religion other than Islam. Therefore, stated the Pentagon policy on religious practice in Saudi Arabia, 'Our personnel, whether Jewish, Christian or any other faith, are free to practise their religion as long as they do so in a discreet manner.' In practice, this meant that while there was a full range of religious services available on US military installations in Saudi Arabia, military personnel who wore a cross or star of David around their necks had to keep it hidden below their uniforms. Some commanders even limited the display of religious symbols at private gatherings. The red cross emblem for ambulances and hospital tents was replaced by the red crescent. US troops were constantly reminded not to discuss their religious beliefs with Saudis and not to take Bibles outside their compound. They were instructed to describe their religious services as fellowship meetings and identify their chaplains as 'morale officers'. As a special dispensation, the Saudi authorities allowed US troops to celebrate Christmas with church services and turkey dinner, with festively decorated trees and bands of carol singers obliged to restrict themselves to non-religious Christmas songs like 'Jingle Bells', but only on US military installations, far away from the Saudi public. These prohibitions on their religious freedom were resented by American military personnel, reported Philip Shenon of the *New York Times*, 'especially in a country that they are now being asked to defend with their lives'.[56]

The fact was that the Saudi kingdom which the Americans and other Westerners were safeguarding had been an Islamic fundamentalist state, ruled by the edicts of the Quran and the Hadiths (the sayings and doings of Prophet Muhammad), since its establishment in 1932. This was long before the Iranian revolution of 1979, an event which to most Westerners signified the rise of the first Islamic fundamentalist state in modern times run by fanatically anti-Western leaders. It had taken the arrival of more than 400,000 Western troops and hundreds of American and other Western journalists to dispel the popular misconception in the West about Iran having a near-monopoly on Islamic fundamentalism and fanaticism.

In the Islamic state of Saudi Arabia religious hierarchy is interwoven with secular authority at all levels. Locally, the religious establishment – the imam (prayer leader), the ulama (religious scholars) and the qadi (religious judge) – works in conjunction with the government administrators. The *muttawin*, religious police, execute the decisions of the local imam and qadi. They ensure that Islamic practices are observed, that businesses close during prayer times, that women are clad in modest, Islamic dresses and do not drive cars, that no alcohol is consumed in public or at home, and that during Ramadan there is no infringement of the ban on food and drink between sunrise and sunset.[57]

The arrival of hundreds of thousands of 'infidel' American and other Western forces, including female troops, in the Eastern Province and elsewhere made pious Saudis apprehensive that the traditional Saudi adherence to a strict form of Islam would be diluted by their presence.

To minimize the chance of clashes between the religious police and the American troops, the authorities in Riyadh transferred most of them from the Eastern Province to Jiddah, a thriving port city where many of the country's super-rich business families are based. The newly arrived *muttawin* did not like the relaxed, tolerant ways of Jiddah.

In late November the *muttawin*, armed with guns, raided a party at the house of a prominent Saudi businessman. They arrested many Saudis, including a member of King Fahd's staff, and foreigners, Arab and non-Arab, for drinking alcohol and mixing with members of the opposite sex to whom they were not related. The Westerners were rescued by their embassies. But all the fourteen non-Saudi Arab women were found guilty and jailed. Each of the two Saudi businessmen arrested was given a two-year jail sentence; and the member of King Fahd's staff ten months. Neither this raid nor an earlier one on the house of a French citizen in Riyadh was reported in the local media.[58] They had also ignored another dramatic incident on 6 November in Riyadh, which caught the imagination of the Western media. Inspired by the examples of American servicewomen driving cars and other vehicles in connection with their military duties, 49 women students, teachers and doctors from King Saud University, who had learned to drive abroad, dismissed their chauffeurs and drove their cars in a convoy, violating a traditional prohibition. Their move proved counterproductive. Shaikh Abdul Aziz ibn Baz, the highest religious authority, issued a fatwa, or religious decree, forbidding women to drive. 'Driving by women contradicts the Islamic traditions followed by Saudi citizens,' stated a decree issued by the ministry of interior. 'The ulama have determined that driving degrades and harms the sanctity of women.' Six of the women drivers, all of them professors, lost their jobs. Others faced harassment by their colleagues and zealot citizens. 'In a land where there is no tradition of freedom of speech,' noted James LeMoyne of the *New York Times*, 'the protest amounted to an act of political defiance at a time when there is talk in élite circles on the desirability of change following Iraq's invasion of Kuwait.' More specifically, the defiant gesture by women drivers was perceived by the ruling House of Saud as setting a dangerous precedent which could be emulated by other dissident groups.[59]

Saudi citizens lived in a country which did not have a constitution or parliament, elected or nominated, and which was ruled exclusively by royal decrees. When a draft constitution was presented to King Saud ibn Abdul Aziz (1953–64) in 1960 for approval, he rejected the document, saying: 'The Quran is the oldest and the most efficient of the world's constitutions.' But following the overthrow of the monarchy in the adjoining North Yemen in September 1962, the Crown Prince Faisal ibn Abdul Aziz promised the issuance of a 'Basic Law' (i.e. constitution), based on the Quran and the Hadiths, which would provide for the citizen's fundamental rights, 'including the right to freely express his opinion within the limits of Islamic belief and public policy'. Nothing came of it. Instead, in 1961 King Saud promulgated the State Security Act prescribing the death penalty, or 25 years' imprisonment, for anybody convicted of 'an aggressive act' against the state or the royal family. Following the seizure of the Grand Mosque in Mecca on 20 November (Islamic New Year) 1979 by some 300 well-armed militant Islamists in protest at the autocracy and corruption of the Saudi royal family, and the subsequent bloodshed, King Khalid ibn Abdul Aziz appointed a committee to produce a draft constitution, followed by an announcement by Crown Prince Fahd that a consultative council of 60 to 70 nominated members would be established 'in the near future'. But nothing happened.[60] Indeed, the government became more repressive. During the 1980s it widened the scope of the death penalty to include apostasy, conspiracy, robbery with violence, sabotage and corruption. Executions were carried out with a sword, often in a public square on a Friday. In the case of adultery, the culprits were stoned to death. In 1989 there were 65 executions, compared with 22 in the previous year. There were at least 100 political prisoners. 'No one is told why they have been arrested, and it is often weeks before families learn where their relatives are,' reported Caroline Moorehead, a British human rights specialist. 'Many remain [in jail] without being charged or tried for years. There is no appeal for wrongful arrest. Torture is routine.'[61]

It was becoming increasingly clear to the policy-makers in Washington that as unsavoury facts about the Saudi government and society became widely known among US troops, they would become restive. At the same time their continued presence on Saudi soil was acting as a destabilizing factor for a social system that was archaic, authoritarian and self-enclosed. The solution, therefore, lay in resolving the crisis sooner rather than later, and that meant there was no time to wait around for sanctions to succeed.

During his tour of the American military camps in the Saudi kingdom in mid-December, the US secretary of defence said as much when he told the troops that it was 'increasingly likely' that war would be needed to expel the Iraqi army from Kuwait. Regarding the actual timing, Washington deliberately tried to send confusing signals to Baghdad.

On 14 December General Powell told the House Armed Services Committee that it 'could be as late as mid-February before US forces have full capability for an offensive'. Five days later Lt-General Calvin Waller, deputy to General Schwarzkopf, said that the US army would not be ready by 15 January to attack the Iraqis, and that it could be mid-February before 430,000 soldiers, sailors, airmen and marines were ready for an offensive. 'I'd tell President Bush: No, I'm not ready to do the job,' he added. 'I would say to the president and the secretary [of defence] and the chairman of the joint chiefs of staff that until our full complement of forces are on the ground we should not initiate hostile activity.'[62] Unlike General Dugan, who was sacked instantly in September, Lt-General Waller stayed at his post. This was obviously a piece of disinformation directed at Saddam Hussein.

Matters were all the more confusing since, despite public announcements by both sides that high-level talks between them were off, efforts were afoot behind the scenes to find a compromise, which seemed to have been reached during the Christmas period. For on 26 December an Israeli newspaper, *Ha'Aretz*, reported confidently that 9 January had been agreed as the date for Baker's visit to Baghdad. Significantly, on the same day, Moscow announced that evacuation of the remaining 1,700 Soviet technicians and experts would be completed by 10 January 1991.[63]

On New Year's eve, Lt-General Saadi Tuma Abbas, the Iraqi defence minister, declared that Iraq had completed its war preparations, and warned of a fire burning 'the aggressors as soon as they start their aggression against our great Iraq'. Saddam Hussein accused Bush of betraying 'the teachings of Christ in the same way as Judas had betrayed Jesus'.[64]

As it was, Bush faced daunting problems both abroad and at home. In the Kuwaiti theatre of operations his forces would have to confront, according to Pentagon sources, 510,000 Iraqi troops equipped with 4,000 tanks, 2,500 armoured combat vehicles and 2,700 artillery pieces. At home the economic recession had deepened to the extent that the country was experiencing falling prices – something that had not happened for fifty years. The Christmas sales had been the worst for many years, and the unemployment rate had risen to 6.1%. The threat of big banks closing and large insurance companies going bankrupt loomed. More than half of the state and city governments faced serious budget deficits. Many were contemplating big cuts in

Left: The Iraqi Prime Minister, Abdul Karim Qasim (1958–63), whose demand on 25 June 1961 that Kuwait should be returned to Iraq set off a crisis a week after Kuwait's independence

Right: The UN Security Council unanimously adopts Resolution 664 on 18 August 1990, calling on Iraq to permit the immediate departure from Iraq and Kuwait of the nationals of other countries

Below: President Bush and Emir Jaber al Sabah of Kuwait outside the White House, Washington, DC, on 26 September 1990

Main picture: Palestinians carry an injured woman away from the holy Dome of the Rock on the Temple Mount, Jerusalem, following firing by the Israeli police on 8 October 1990
Inset: A Palestinian holds up a poster of the Dome of the Rock during a pro-Saddam Hussein demonstration in Amman

Right: General Norman Schwarzkopf, Dick Cheney and General Colin Powell (left) in Riyadh

Below: The US Secretary of State James Baker with King Fahd ibn Abdul Aziz in Riyadh on 5 November 1990

Right: President Bush with President Hafiz Assad of Syria in Geneva on 23 November 1990

Below: James Baker and the Iraqi foreign minister Tariq Aziz shake hands in Geneva on 9 January 1991

Above: Victims of an Iraqi
Scud attack on Tel Aviv
being removed, 20 January
1991
Left: Dead Iraqi soldiers and
their equipment scattered in
the desert

Below: Iraqi prisoners of war
in Kuwait

Foot: The aftermath of the
US-led coalition's attack on
the retreating Iraqis at the
Mitla ridge, Kuwait

Right: General Schwarzkopf and Prince Khalid ibn Sultan of Saudi Arabia at Kuwait City beach on 12 March 1991

Above: President Bush with the British foreign secretary Douglas Hurd in Washington, DC, on 27 February 1991

Below: A Kuwaiti welcomes the victorious troops of the US-led coalition forces on 27 February 1991

Above: Jalal Talabani (centre), a Kurdish leader, with Ayatollah Muhammad Taqi Moderasi, a Shia leader, and Aziz Muhammad, a Communist leader, at the conference of the Joint Action Committee of the Iraqi Opposition in Beirut on 11 March 1991

Right: Jalal Talabani with President Saddam Hussein at the presidential palace on 24 April 1991

A Kuwaiti soldier at a border post, with a
burning oil well in the background

social services and public works, and huge layoffs of their employees. 'I think you will have to go back to the Great Depression [of the 1930s] to find similar anguish,' said Henry Aaron of the Washington-based Brookings Institute.[65] The Gulf crisis, said Bush's critics, had come as a divine gift to the administration, enabling it to divert popular attention away from grave economic problems at home.

But there was a limit to the period over which Bush could keep the American public glued to the Gulf crisis, especially when he had proved himself incapable of formulating a coherent and convincing rationale for military intervention in the Gulf and communicating it to the US public. Secondly, he commanded a force which, though made up of volunteers, was scarcely composed of hardened professionals, and its poor morale, brought into sharper focus during the Christmas season by the media, had a dampening effect on the people back home. Thirdly, Bush, a team player, lacked the qualities of a leader who could inspire a nation and maintain its morale. Finally, the psychological warfare against Saddam Hussein was proving problematic so far as the American public and media were concerned. On the one hand the White House was hinting that it would be hard to maintain the anti-Iraq coalition for too long, and so the military option must be used sooner rather than later. On the other hand, General Schwarzkopf was saying that 'If the alternative to dying is sitting out in the sun for another summer, that's not a bad alternative.' The whole thrust of Washington's strategy to amass a vast force and awesome military hardware was to mount a massive attack and achieve quick victory. Yet there was General Schwarzkopf telling a news conference in mid-December, 'You can always get into a stalemate . . . I can't say it won't last more than six months.'[66] Virtually every signal sent to Baghdad bounced back to cause a different, and often adverse, effect in America, with the media tending to concentrate on the publicly expressed differences between President Bush and his commanders.

Saddam Hussein did not have to cope with fickle public opinion or privately-owned media. Yet he too had grave problems in sustaining an economy strangled by international sanctions, which were causing Iraq a monthly loss of $2.5 billion in oil revenue, and maintaining the morale of his people and troops. Besides the periodic speeches he delivered to shore up national morale, he made a point of visiting the soldiers at the frontlines. For instance, he spent a night with a Republican Guard unit in the Kuwaiti theatre of operations in late December, and was shown on television participating in communal cooking.[67] While maintaining strict secrecy about its military hardware and its

294 DESERT SHIELD TO DESERT STORM

capabilities, Iraq made a point of broadcasting any technical advances it made in developing its aircraft or missiles. On 3 January it showed on television its Adnan-2 surveillance aircraft modelled on Boeing's Awacs, claiming that its first test flight had been successful, and that it included improvements on Adnan-1, shown at the Baghdad trade fair in 1989, especially a new coating which made it harder to detect by radar.[68]

Upgrading Iraq's military preparedness, however, did not stop Saddam Hussein from keeping his diplomatic lines open. His secret consultations in Baghdad with two dozen Iraqi ambassadors to Western capitals and the UN in late December was indicative of this. Among those attending was his half-brother, Barzan Tikriti, Iraq's ambassador to Switzerland as well as to the United Nations in Geneva. A member of the Iraqi president's inner circle, he played a vital role in secret diplomacy. At the behest of Ahmad Ben Bella, the former Algerian president, he had met Edgard Pisani, an adviser to President Mitterrand, in Switzerland on 5 December. Pisani pressed Tikriti on the evacuation of Kuwait and the freeing of the remaining hostages. The release of the hostages announced shortly afterwards, though unconnected with the Pisani–Tikriti talks, improved the chances of a follow-up meeting. This occurred on 25 December in Switzerland. Pisani handed over to Tikriti a 'draft scenario' of a peace plan which had been endorsed by Mitterrand. It called for an evacuation of Kuwait – with the proviso that Saddam Hussein had the 'right' to declare that 'the fate of the Palestinian people was one of the main reasons which led Iraq to invade Kuwait', and that the withdrawal from Kuwait was being implemented to prepare the way for a resolution of the Palestinian question, the restoration of the sovereignty of Lebanon, and the devising of an agreement on a 'rational exploitation of petroleum resources'. The second proviso was that Saddam Hussein would have to approve Mitterrand's proposals on the Middle East international conference as outlined in his speech of 24 September to the UN General Assembly. Tikriti telefaxed the plan to Baghdad. The next day Saddam Hussein replied: 'Let Pisani come to Baghdad.' But Mitterrand refused to authorize the trip without a more explicit Iraqi response.[69]

Equally promising was the statement of 2 January by the Iraqi representative to the United Nations, Muhammad al Mashat, on his return from Baghdad, that if the US was prepared to accept the rules of protocol, whereby the host government sets a date for high-level meetings, then Iraq would consider a date other than 12 January.

More importantly, following his meetings with Saddam Hussein and Tariq Aziz in Baghdad on 29–30 December, the Non-Aligned Movement's envoy Budimir Loncar, the Yugoslav foreign minister, carried proposals from Iraq to the US, which showed its preparedness to withdraw from Kuwait on certain conditions. These were: (a) a US pledge not to attack Iraqi forces as they withdrew; (b) withdrawal of foreign troops from the region; (c) an agreement on solving the Palestinian problem; and (d) an agreement on banning all weapons of mass destruction in the region. While the White House dismissed the proposal as 'inadequate' because it contained preconditions for withdrawal, a state department Middle East expert called it 'a serious pre-negotiation position', noting that Iraq had dropped its previous claims to two Kuwaiti islands and the disputed border strip, and that it was ready for a negotiated settlement.[70] This was the second time that the White House spurned a serious attempt by Iraq to reach a peaceful settlement, the first being on 22 August. Significantly, in both instances, major American newspapers ignored the story, and it was left to *Newsday* alone to carry it.

Bush's hardline stance went down badly with Congressional leaders when they met him on 3 January. As the controllers of the federal purse-strings, they were unhappy at the doubling of the cost of the Gulf deployments during the fiscal year 1 October 1990–30 September 1991, from $15 billion to $31 billion. So far the allies (including Japan) had contributed only $7.5 billion to help pay for the military operations. (By providing $13.4 billion in aid to the states suffering the consequences of the UN embargo, the 24-member Gulf Crisis Financial Co-ordination Group had been more generous.) They refused to give the president unconditional authority to take military action against Iraq, with the Democratic leaders particularly urging him to explore all possible avenues of diplomatic solution. Even the Senate Republican leader, Bob Dole, could not refrain from expressing his 'gut feeling' that the American people were 'not yet committed to war'. It was in this context that Bush offered to despatch Baker to Geneva for talks with Aziz between 7 and 9 January.[71] Congress then decided to postpone debate on the issue until after the Geneva talks.

Baker had been partly instrumental in getting Bush to reverse his earlier decision on high-level talks. A skilled political tactician, he was not a profound believer in the president's moral crusade in the Gulf. From the start he advocated that the US should pursue all options for as long as possible, and that it should not lock itself too early into a stance which made war inevitable.

Bush was by now bent on starting hostilities, but had to curb his inclination for tactical reasons. Yet he needed to sound firm. 'This will not be secret diplomacy at work,' he assured his audience in a radio broadcast to the nation on 5 January after the Baker–Aziz meeting had been fixed for 9 January. 'Secretary Baker will restate in person a message for Saddam Hussein: withdraw from Kuwait unconditionally and immediately, or face the terrible consequences.' He added, however, that 15 January was 'a deadline for Saddam Hussein to comply with the United Nations resolution, not a deadline for our armed forces'. But time was running out. Each day that passed brought the Iraqi dictator further on the path to developing biological and nuclear weapons, and the missiles to deliver them. 'If Saddam corners the energy market, he can then finance further aggression, terror and blackmail,' Bush warned. 'Each day that passes increases Saddam Hussein's worldwide threat to democracy.' The struggling new-born democracies of Eastern Europe and Latin America already faced 'a staggering challenge' in making the transition to a free market, but the added weight of higher oil prices was 'a crushing burden' they could not bear, he stated. 'Our own economy is suffering, suffering the effects of higher oil prices and lower growth stemming from Saddam's aggression,' he continued. 'We risk paying a higher price in the most precious currency of all – human life – if we give Saddam more time to prepare for war.' Each day that passed was 'another day of fear, suffering, and terror' for Kuwaitis. 'At stake is not only some distant country called Kuwait,' he concluded, '[but] the kind of world we'll inhabit.'[72]

It happened to be Iraqi army day on 6 January, an appropriate date for Saddam Hussein to deliver a morale-boosting speech to his military in which he stressed the prime need to liberate the Arab territories occupied by Israel. 'Fortunately, this [Iraqi] army has become capable of confronting the enemies everywhere in the Arab homeland wherever there is danger,' he began. 'What a great honour that you are united this time under the banner of the Mother of Battles. You are now prepared for a single historic battle after the return of the branch [Kuwait] to the origin [Iraq] . . . The battle for the liberation of Palestine will not be a short one if we are serious about it, and we don't believe that the sacrifices will be small. It cannot be a battle which can be divided into several causes. This will divide ranks because if we fight divided battles, the forces working against could probably neutralize our efforts. But if we fight the battle as one battle, a battle which contains and embraces all the objectives of the Arabs at this particular juncture, then . . . this is the advantage of the great battle which we will fight. There are facilities of a strategic nature which could not be imagined elsewhere: flow and speed in communications, mobilization and military logistics. The Mother of Battles will also be [conducted] under an experienced, cohesive military leadership. It would be an honour for the believers to fight in this battle ... which aims at liberating Palestine and the Golan Heights under the banner: "God is great".'[73] Underlining the alliance of the PLO with Iraq, Yasser Arafat told a Palestinian rally in Baghdad: 'If the US and its allies want to fight Iraq over Kuwait, then I say, "Welcome, welcome, welcome to war". Iraq and Palestine represent a common will. We will be together side by side and after the great battle, God willing, we will pray together in Jerusalem.'[74]

However, like his adversary Bush, while breathing fire and brimstone the Iraqi president was simultaneously holding conciliatory talks. This time his interlocutor was Michel Vauzelle, a close associate of President Mitterrand and chairman of the French National Assembly's Foreign Affairs Committee. On 5 January Saddam Hussein and Vauzelle spent four-and-a-half hours together, with one hour in 'private' conversation, where apparently the Iraqi leader spelled out his bottom line. On his return to Paris the next day Vauzelle immediately briefed Mitterrand whose foreign minister, Roland Dumas, had presented to the EC foreign ministers conference on 4 January (when the EC's six-monthly presidency was transferred from Italy to Luxembourg) a three-point peace plan: Iraqi withdrawal from Kuwait, a pledge that Iraq would not be attacked by anti-Iraqi coalition forces, and an understanding that there would later be an international peace conference on 'all outstanding conflicts in the Middle East'. The French plan had emerged in the context of Mitterrand's response to the opposition to war in his ruling Socialist Party and among the general public, and epitomized in his cabinet by the defence minister, Chévènement.[75]

Washington watched with considerable unease the initiative of Mitterrand: a leader whom Bush had tried particularly to cultivate with frequent telephone conversations, taking care, for instance, to inform him in advance of his acceptance of the idea of a Baker–Aziz meeting in Geneva.[76]

As it was, the Bush administration had a delicate balancing act to perform at home: how to continue showing a desire for a peaceful solution without raising popular expectations at home or engendering pressure to make a deal with Baghdad. Since any slackening of support by its Western allies was likely to undermine its domestic position, the Bush administration was determined to keep them in line on the eve of the Geneva talks. As before Bush shared this task with his secretary of state, James Baker.

Baker's first stop was in London where, as before, he found a pliant ally in the person of Douglas Hurd, the British foreign secretary, serving under John Major who had succeeded Margaret Thatcher as prime minister in late November. Hurd had just expelled 75 Iraqis, eight of them diplomats, for making 'public threats' linked to possible war in the Gulf. Baker and Hurd spurned the idea of extending the 15 January deadline, which was favoured by the French. In Paris, Baker rejected the Mitterrand peace proposal because it tied Iraqi withdrawal from Kuwait to talks on solving the Arab–Israeli conflict. He did so before the proposal was formally embraced by Saddam Hussein or the EC, where it had gained wide support and whose foreign ministers had invited Tariq Aziz for talks in Luxembourg on 10 January.[77] Baker's stand was out of line with US public opinion. A *Washington Post*–ABC poll of 511 respondents showed that two-thirds felt that the Bush administration should be more flexible on the issue of the international peace conference on the Middle East and support such a gathering if Iraqi troops were to pull out of Kuwait.[78]

In Bonn, Baker heard Chancellor Helmut Kohl voice the widespread feeling in Germany against military involvement in the Gulf and for a peaceful settlement. In response Baker said that if his talks with Aziz failed, then the US would leave the door open for further diplomatic initiatives by others before the deadline.[79] Baker's concession was in line with the view of 53% in the most recent *Washington Post*–ABC poll who said that search for a diplomatic solution should continue after 15 January, the UN deadline.

On 9 January, six-and-a-half hours of talks between Baker and Aziz in Geneva failed. Baker stated that Aziz had told the American delegation that the Iraqi occupation of Kuwait was 'defensive', and that he had assured Aziz that if Iraq complied with the UN resolutions by withdrawing from Kuwait and allowing its monarchy to be restored, it would not be attacked. In response, said Baker, he had heard 'no signs of flexibility or new proposals' from Aziz that offered a peaceful alternative to a war to free Kuwait. 'There have been too many Iraqi miscalculations,' Baker continued. 'It miscalculated the international response to the invasion. It miscalculated the response to its barbaric policy of holding thousands of foreign hostages. Let us hope that Iraq does not miscalculate again . . . The 28 nations that have deployed forces to the Gulf in support of the United Nations Security Council resolutions have both the power and will to evict Iraq,' Baker concluded. 'Now the choice is with the Iraqi leadership.'[80]

'If we [had] had an earlier opportunity several months ago, I told the [US] Secretary, that we might have been able to remove a lot of misunderstandings between us,' Aziz told the press conference in Geneva. 'We know what the deployment of your forces in the region means. We know what the resolutions you [Americans] have imposed on the Security Council mean, and we know all the facts about the situation ... What is at stake is the fate of the whole region. If you are ready to bring about peace to the region we are ready to co-operate. He [Baker] says that he does not believe that what happened on 2 August and later was for the cause of the Palestinians or to help the Palestinians. I explained to him that the Palestinian question is a matter of national security to Iraq. If the Palestinian question is not resolved we do not feel secure.' He revealed that Iraq had been expecting an Israeli attack the previous March or April. 'What was happening [in the region] before 2 August has a strong relationship with what happened later.' Iraq was prepared 'for the worst', he concluded.[81]

How it would cope with such a contingency was outlined by Saddam Hussein in his speech to the Fourth Popular Islamic Conference – attended by about 1,000 delegates, a third from abroad – held in Baghdad on 9–11 January. Describing the impending armed conflict as a battle between believers and infidels, the Iraqi president said that there were thousands of Iraqi tanks and men dug into reinforced positions, and that Iraqi troops had trained for a year without using their radios, so that US plans to jam Iraqi military communications would have little effect. Moreover, he continued, the number of divisions massed by the US-led coalition in Saudi Arabia were only a quarter of the number deployed by Iraq in Kuwait. Enemy planes needed to get within three miles of their target in Iraq to inflict damage, but Iraq could shoot them down from eighteen miles away, he claimed.[82]

Run-up to Zero Hour

The remaining five days to zero hour were utilized differently by Bush and the duo of Mitterrand and Pérez de Cuellar. The American president used the time to secure authorization for the use of force in the Gulf from the US Congress while the French president and the UN secretary-general made last-minute attempts to hammer out a non-military solution.

The US Congress voted on the issue on 12 January after debating it for three days. The Senate as well as the House of Representatives voted on two motions. The first was presented by Senators George Mitchell and Sam Nunn (both Democrats) in the Senate, and Representatives Lee H. Hamilton and Richard Gephardt (both Democrats) in the House of Representatives. It read: 'The Congress believes that continued application of international sanctions and diplomatic efforts to pressure Iraq to leave Kuwait is the wisest course at this time and should be sustained, but does not rule out declaring war or authorizing the use of force at a later time should that be necessary to achieve the goal of forcing Iraqi troops from Kuwait.' It was defeated in the Senate by 46 votes to 53, and in the House by 250 votes to 183.

The second resolution, presented by Senators Bob Dole and John Warner (both Republicans) in the Senate and Representatives Stephen Solarz (a Democrat) and Robert Michel (a Republican) in the House of Representatives, read: 'The President is authorized ... to use United States Armed Forces pursuant to United Security Council Resolution 678 (1990) in order to achieve implementation of Security Council Resolutions 660, 661, 662, 664, 665, 666, 667, 669, 670, 674, and 677.' Before he could exercise the authority granted, the president was required to make available to the Speaker of the House of Representatives and the president pro tempore of the Senate his determination that the US 'has used all appropriate diplomatic and other peaceful means to obtain compliance by Iraq with the United Nations Security Council resolutions cited [above], and that those efforts have not been and would not be successful in obtaining such compliance.' It was passed in the Senate by 52 (42 Republicans and 10 Democrats) to 47 (45 Democrats and two Republicans), and in the House by 250 (164 Republicans and 86 Democrats) to 183 (179 Democrats, three Republicans and one Independent). The vote in the Senate kept Bush on tenterhooks. According to his National Security Adviser, President Bush worried 'most' that Congress would vote against authorizing the war. The Congressional vote was the 'most tension-filled moment' for the president.[83] In the end he got through with a slim majority in the Senate.

Bush did much better in the House of Representatives. Those voting for the military option included not only almost all of the 168 Republicans but also 86 of the 271 Democrats. At least 38 Democrats, including Stephen Solarz, stressed that their vote was a 'vote for peace'. Similar reasoning was offered by some of the Republicans. E. Clay Shaw Jr said, 'I believe very strongly that our last hope to avoid war is the immediate threat of war.' Another Republican, John Boehner, believed that 'the real threat of force' will make Saddam Hussein abandon his aggression. 'January 15 is not D-day,' said Don Sundquist. 'We are not going to abandon our efforts to resolve the crisis peacefully. But our diplomacy will carry more weight if Saddam understands that we are prepared to back up our words with deeds.'[84]

In practice, however, the Bush administration, assisted by the British government, did its best to dampen the last-minute diplomatic efforts by France which, in Mitterrand's words, had 'woven many threads' into the pattern of its Gulf diplomacy – that included not only the Security Council and UN secretary-general, but also the EC, Algeria and Iraq itself – to find a political solution before the deadline.

In early January, while pursuing his peace efforts through the EC, Mitterrand had also sent off a letter to the leading Arab mediator, President Chadli Ben Jadid of Algeria, in which he reportedly assured Iraq of an international conference on the Arab–Israeli question if Saddam Hussein first began to evacuate Kuwait. On his arrival in Paris on 9 January, Sid Ahmad Ghozali, the Algerian foreign minister, said that it was 'not too late to avoid war in the Gulf'. That day Mitterrand reiterated France's position. 'America and France do not have the same vision with regard to an eventual international conference to settle the Arab–Israeli conflict,' he stated. 'I well understand this position, but it does not entail a weakening of France's point of view on the same subject, especially as I have been calling for such a conference for six or seven years.' However, he added, the talks about an international conference would follow only *after* an Iraqi commitment to withdraw from Kuwait.[85]

Such a pledge was not forthcoming from Baghdad which had also, in retaliation for the EC's decision to cancel talks with Aziz in December, spurned the offer of a meeting between Jacques Poos, the foreign minister of the EC's current president, Luxembourg, with Aziz on 10 January. That was where the Algerian offer to host EC–Iraq talks in Algiers, an idea mooted by Mitterrand, came in. There was some hope that Aziz would fly to Algiers to meet Poos before returning to

Baghdad. But he returned directly to Baghdad. With this the mediatory efforts of France, Algeria and the EC reached a dead end.

Unlike Aziz, Baker did not return home directly. He visited the major capitals of Arab and Western allies, more or less to confirm the launching of the US-led attack soon after the deadline. In Riyadh Baker reportedly received permission for the US to begin military operations if necessary.

With this, efforts at last-minute peace-making were doomed. Yet, to keep its pledge given publicly to Germany, Washington did not openly discourage mediation, either from one of its leading Western allies, France, or the genuinely neutral UN secretary-general, Pérez de Cuellar, at 71 a statesman with half a century of experience in diplomacy, and in the last year of his second five-year term of office.

On 4 January, Pérez de Cuellar had backed the call by the Security Council's president, Bagbeni Adeito Nzengeya of Zaire, and President Mitterrand for a peaceful settlement, and their proposal for the summoning of a Council meeting before 15 January, only to have the idea dismissed by the Soviet ambassador to the UN. Throughout the crisis, at the instigation of Washington, the secretary-general, who should have acted as the central mechanism of the UN's involvement in the Gulf crisis, was sidelined. The basic flaw lay in Resolution 660, the first in the series, which, unlike Resolution 598 of 20 July 1987 on the ceasefire between Iran and Iraq, did not specifically request the secretary-general to carry out specific tasks concerning the operative clauses 2 and 3 of the resolution, dealing respectively with the withdrawal of Iraq from Kuwait, and 'intensive negotiations' between the two parties to resolve their differences. He therefore maintained a studied neutrality in the hope that he would be called upon by the Security Council at some point, during the long-drawn-out crisis, to mediate in the conflict. He never was. He saw a chance for his diplomacy once Security Council Resolution 678 was passed on 29 November. But it was spiked by Bush's sudden proposal of face-to-face talks with the Iraqi leaders. He was dismayed by five long weeks of 'ritualized sparring' between Washington and Baghdad, culminating in the predictable breakdown of talks in Geneva a week later. He was unhappy at the way the 15 January deadline engendered a psychosis of war, but remained silent. With the collapse of the Paris–Algiers–Luxembourg mediatory attempt, however, he became the last hope of peace.

After meeting Mitterrand in Paris and EC foreign ministers in Geneva on 11 January, Pérez de Cuellar flew to Baghdad. He met Tariq

Aziz on 12 January. The next day he had a two-and-a-half-hour meeting with Saddam Hussein in the evening. A transcript of the conversation between the two leaders was released by the Iraqi mission at the UN about a month later. The essence of their dialogue is well conveyed by the following excerpts.

Pérez de Cuellar: On the day I left for Baghdad I had discussion with President Bush . . . He said – in spite of the impression given by the information media – in considering me responsible for finding a peaceful international solution: 'I prefer the peaceful solution of the crisis' . . . You have taken certain initiatives. An important and constructive one was your decision to release the foreigners, by which you removed an obstacle in the way of relaxation of tension in the area. Your 12 August initiative has not been well understood, but it figured in one form or another in the first of the Security Council resolutions, which specifically referred to the Arab League and its participation in any solution. I believe that to be a positive thing. On that basis something can be done . . . I consider that you have done a great deal for the question of Palestine. You have put the fate of the Palestinian people on the agenda . . . Afterwards, I did not hesitate to call the attention of the United Nations to the Palestinian problem, working for the convening of an international conference in keeping with six or seven resolutions of the General Assembly of the United Nations . . . Mr President, you deserve all the credit for this achievement for the question of Palestine . . . I know your courage and generosity . . . and the unilateral initiatives you offered to put an end to the Iraqi–Iranian War. I hope you will in the same spirit offer something to put an end to this conflict. In order to do so we must see our way through to compliance with the United Nations resolutions, especially Resolutions 660 and 678. You will remember what was said by President Mitterrand of France. He said, 'If we are able to implement the Security Council resolutions, everything will be possible' . . . There is something else said by Mr Bush which I put down on a small piece of paper. It is this: 'The United States will not attack Iraq or its armed forces if withdrawal from Kuwait has been achieved and the situation has returned to what it was prior to 2 August. The United States does not want to keep ground forces in the region: it

will support negotiations between the parties concerned, and
I shall accept any decision taken by those parties' . . . Also, by
profiting from Your Excellency's initiative, we should work
for the elimination of all weapons of mass destruction in the
region . . . I am referring to the elimination of weapons of
mass destruction in Israel . . . I wish to be in a position to
go back with something we can build on to reduce tension
and deprive the warmongers of their opportunity . . .

Saddam Hussein: As to the issue of Kuwait, you, Secretary-
General, will know that up to 2 August 1990, you have
[had] no document signed by two parties that designates
boundaries between Iraq and Kuwait . . . While it is true
that we did not recognize the Security Council Resolution
660, we dealt with its contents . . . We actually withdrew a
whole brigade [from Kuwait] . . .

The Iraqi president complained that the Secretary-General had not
been able to 'ensure the arrival of the plane carrying the Iraqi foreign
minister to the US' for him to attend the UN and 'defend the point
of view of Iraq'.

Pérez de Cuellar: I tried. I said [to the US] that was not in
keeping with the UN's Headquarters Agreement with the
United States . . .

Saddam Hussein: The idea of protecting the Palestinians from the
occupiers has recently been put forward. You are aware that
it took 84 days for that idea to become a resolution. And you
know how the idea was squeezed and squeezed until it lost
its flavour and strength. Who has done this? It is America.
It declared openly that it 'opposed the idea of holding an
international conference to prevent Saddam Hussein from
scoring a political victory'. America has thus made justice
contingent upon political tactics. It does not seek peace with
justice . . . What are they saying now? Let Iraq withdraw from
Kuwait, then we shall convene an international conference to
discuss the issues involved. This is not a categorical promise.
It is only a possibility. On 12 August we offered an initiative.
We did not imagine that it would be accepted in its entirety.
But we did not imagine that it would be left without being
examined. The president of America rejected that initiative
while aboard his plane only two hours after it was announced,
and before learning anything about its contents . . .

Saddam Hussein then referred to the letter which Bush had addressed to him, and which Tariq Aziz had refused to accept from Baker in Geneva because of its threatening tone . . .

Saddam Hussein: Now look at the latest resolution which Bush has insisted on forcing out of the [US] Senate and House of Representatives. He had tried similar pressures to extract Resolution 678 [from the Security Council]. We know that he had told a number of Security Council members that what was intended by that resolution was to put pressure on Iraq, not to implement it. He has now played the same game with the Senate and House of Representatives by hinting that the resolution is not necessarily for implementation but to face the Iraqis with a threat which will make them withdraw. The Iraqis, however, will never withdraw in the face of threats . . . At present, we have good relations with Iran, and we praise God for this . . . All our people know that we have given half of the Shatt al Arab to Iran and have released all [their] prisoners of war without waiting for the release of ours. When Iraqis asked me: 'Why all this?' I answered: 'For the sake of peace. Now that Kuwait is part of Iraq, you have all that long coast of your own and there is no longer a need for us to fight one another for the Shatt al Arab' . . .

Pérez de Cuellar: As you have stated, those who want war and not peace will take advantage of the fact that I shall return with nothing. What I am asking for is . . . in the name of the international community, which wants you to give something which could relax tensions and become a way out not only for the region but also for the world.

Saddam Hussein: Every point we discussed involved giving you something.

Pérez de Cuellar: I am afraid I shall return with nothing along with the important matters you stated, that would not be enough to stop the slide towards confrontation not only in the region but in the world at large . . .

Saddam Hussein: Iraqis are willing to assume their responsibilities regarding peace if others are willing to do the same. But they are at the same time willing to fight if attacked, confidently relying on the depth of a fighting experience of eight years . . . Hence, even if we were granted all the privileges in the world, when the two armies – the Iraqi

and the American – are only a matter of hours away from
the likelihood of war, no one will ever utter the word
'withdrawal'. To utter the word 'withdrawal' when war is
likely is to prepare the psychological ground for the victory
of the enemy. Now isn't that what the Americans want? They
know what it means. This will never happen. Never . . .

Pérez de Cuellar: If I understood you well, your position in
Kuwait is irreversible, in which case the principle of the
package cannot be applied.

Saddam Hussein: I didn't say this. You said it. If you find the
Americans in a position wherein they are looking for a way
out of their impasse without losing – or gaining all that they
have in mind – then it is possible to set down certain principles, and charge the Arabs to look for a solution in keeping
with these principles. Or you as a capable, experienced diplomat might sound out other parties for their viewpoints.

Pérez de Cuellar: You are a party, too.

Saddam Hussein: Then you might submit proposals which you
will discuss with the principal parties, including us, in the
hope of an agreed solution.

Pérez de Cuellar: Do you authorize me to tell the Security Council that you want continuous discussions to be conducted
through the Secretary-General?

Saddam Hussein: I regard this as given on the basis of your offer.
That is why I have said there is a positive aspect to all the
points you discussed. There may emerge a package as a result
of continuity.

Pérez de Cuellar: Thank you for the trust you have shown in
me, as the Secretary-General. I must reflect on the points
and include them in my report to the Security Council . . . I
shall communicate that to all those concerned in this crisis,
especially in view of the fact that yours is a defensive, and
not an offensive, position.[86]

Saddam Hussein behaved in a predictable fashion. At first he laid
out a hard line, then offered a compromise. So the meeting ended on
a promising note. The talks were described by the Iraqi News Agency
as 'a deep dialogue on the situation in the region'. Pérez de Cuellar was
noncommittal, though. 'God only knows if there will be peace or war
in the Gulf,' he said after the meeting.[87]

That night Pérez de Cuellar flew to Paris. The next day, during his meeting with Mitterrand, he told the French leader that he had been 'badly treated' (referring probably to having been kept waiting by Saddam Hussein for most of the day on 13 January), and that the Iraqi president was unwilling to compromise. Consequently Mitterrand dropped the idea of despatching his foreign minister, Roland Dumas, and Edgard Pisani to Baghdad in response to the Iraqi government's invitation to them on 11 January.[88]

France launched a four-point peace plan at the Security Council, consisting of: (a) a call to Iraq to announce 'without further delay its intention to pull out of Kuwait according to a set timetable, and to begin now with a rapid and large-scale withdrawal'; (b) the Iraqi evacuation to be overseen by UN observers, with a UN peacekeeping force to replace the departing Iraqis; (c) 'a guarantee of non-aggression to be given to Iraq' by the anti-Iraqi coalition; and (d) a promise by the Security Council to 'call at an appropriate time an international conference (with the appropriate structure) according to the 20 December 1990 declaration of the Security Council president, with the goal of assuring the security, stability, and development in that part of the world'. Among the permanent members, the US, the USSR and Britain were opposed to the French draft resolution, but there was much support for it among the non-permanent members.[89]

When France formally unveiled its plan for peace on the morning of Tuesday 15 January, America and Britain opposed it strongly, despite widespread backing for it in the Security Council as a whole. They objected to its hint of reward for Iraq through linkage to a Middle East peace conference. France withdrew its motion, and then vetoed a resolution drafted by Britain, and seconded by America, which made 'a last urgent and solemn appeal' to Iraq 'to display wisdom and responsibility and . . . withdraw unconditionally from Kuwait'. The French ambassador said, 'We want substance, not lyrics.' At the end of this day of wrangling at the Security Council (which had on Monday received a secret report from Pérez de Cuellar on his mission to Baghdad), the secretary-general urged Saddam Hussein to 'turn the course of events away from catastrophe', adding that he was ready to deploy UN observers to monitor Iraq's withdrawal and ensure that the withdrawing Iraqi forces were not attacked by the anti-Iraq coalition forces, and that the Security Council would consider lifting sanctions. He pledged that 'with the resolution of the present crisis, every effort would be made to address, in a comprehensive manner, the Arab–Israeli conflict, including the Palestinian question.' He said that he was making these offers, 'on the basis of understandings that

I have received from governments at the highest level' and 'with the agreement of the Security Council'. A US spokesman said that though Pérez de Cuellar was acting 'on his own initiative', and 'not involving the US', Washington would not repudiate his promises to Iraq.[90]

Neither the French nor the British draft resolution meant much to Iraq. Its influential information minister declared that Kuwait was and would remain Iraq's nineteenth province. He was speaking on the day after the Iraqi National Assembly had voted unanimously to go to war, rather than pull Iraqi troops out of Kuwait. 'This is a historic confrontation,' stated the resolution adopted by the Assembly. 'Your steadfast Iraq led by President Saddam Hussein has resolved to fight.' It gave the president constitutional powers for 'whatever is needed'. In a televised speech before the vote, Saddam Hussein declared that Kuwait had become 'a symbol for the whole Arab nation', and urged his audience to 'hold it [i.e. Kuwait]'. Significantly, on that day, Saddam Hussein ordered that the Islamic credo, *Allahu Akbar* (God is Great), be inscribed on Iraq's red, white and black flag. The next day, the 15 January deadline, state-sponsored mass rallies, involving hundreds of thousands of people, were organized in Baghdad and other Iraqi cities to combine support for Saddam Hussein with defiance of the US, and to show the nation's determination to fight. Schools and factories were closed so that everybody could participate in the demonstrations; but the mood at these gatherings was festive rather than bellicose.[91]

There were demonstrations in Jordan on the eve of the UN deadline, with 20,000 people marching in Amman in support of Iraq, as Prime Minister Mudar Badran told the parliament that Baghdad had promised to send troops into Jordan if it came under attack by Israel, and if the Jordanian government requested it. Overall, some 100,000 Jordanians had volunteered to fight for Saddam Hussein. 'For the people there [in Jordan], the truly decisive moment in the shaping of this crisis was not Iraq's invasion of Kuwait, it was when the Americans, those incorrigible supporters of the latter-day usurper of Palestine, entered the fray,' noted David Hirst of the *Guardian*. 'What the present vast array of [Western] armed force so imminently portends is the Arabs' renewed subjugation to the foreigner.'[92]

With the Pentagon, on 15 January, putting the number of US troops in the Gulf at 415,000, and the British and French forces together amounting to another 45,000, there were more Western armed personnel in the Gulf than there were Allied troops landing on France's Normandy beaches on 6 June 1944 to challenge the military might of Germany. They were equipped with 2,200 tanks and 1,410 aircraft. And, according to the British–American Security Information Council, the US naval personnel among them were armed with 700-plus nuclear weapons on warships and submarines. All but four of the sixteen members of Nato were involved – the exceptions being Iceland, Luxembourg, Portugal and Turkey – deploying 107 warships in the Gulf, the northern Arabian Sea and Gulf of Oman, the Red Sea and the eastern Mediterranean, with most of them enforcing the UN embargo. Australia and Argentina deployed three and two warships respectively. Together with 220,000 Arab and Muslim troops, the anti-Iraq coalition had fielded 680,000 troops to confront, according to the Pentagon, 545,000 Iraqi troops in Kuwait and southern Iraq. Of the 425,000 US military personnel, 250,000 were army troops, 75,000 marines, 60,000 naval personnel and 45,000 air force personnel.[93]

In the Western camp, excepting Britain and France, which had ground troops in Saudi Arabia, none of the remaining twelve countries was prepared to place its military under US command and engage in fighting. This had mainly to do with public opinion at home. In Spain, a poll by *El Mundo* (The World) in early January showed that 85% were opposed to war, and over 50% wanted the three Spanish warships in the region to be withdrawn if hostilities erupted. Over the weekend of 12–13 January, over 100,000 people in Madrid and Barcelona protested against war. In Germany an estimated 250,000 people demonstrated in 120 cities and towns, with the demonstration in Berlin attracting 75,000. A similar event in Brussels brought 30,000 people on to the streets. On 15 January, 25,000 marched past the US consulate in Milan, Italy, to protest against armed conflict in the Gulf.[94]

Of the two European countries committed to fighting in the Gulf under US command, public sentiment in France was against warfare. An opinion poll conducted after the breakdown of the Baker–Aziz talks showed that 80% did not consider Kuwait worth dying for. The anti-war demonstrations during the 12–13 January weekend brought over 200,000 people out in 100 French cities and towns. A similar event in London attracted 50,000 people. A British opinion poll of 1,376 respondents conducted on 11–12 January showed 54% approving 'all action including force' (an increase of 4% over the August figure), 32% approving 'all action short of armed force' (a decrease of 9% over the August figure), and 13% saying that Britain should not get involved (a decline of 4% over the August figure). In other words, counting the isolationists in the same column as those favouring a non-military solution, British public opinion was divided between hawks and doves at 5:4.[95]

The division between hawks and doves was more level in America, the leader of the anti-Iraqi coalition. A Gallup poll, published on 15 January, showed 45% saying the Gulf was worth fighting over, and 44% disagreeing. Likewise, a *New York Times*–CBS telephone poll of 1,512 respondents, contacted between 11 and 13 January, showed 47% favouring immediate military action versus 44% who believed that Bush should have waited longer for sanctions to work. Half of those favouring immediate military action said they would not consider the war worth fighting if it dragged on with heavy casualties.[96] There were anti-war protests in all major American cities, the largest one being in Washington DC and the second largest in Chicago, where about 1,000 protesters were arrested after scuffles with police.

The leaders of this protest reminded the Bush administration that it had itself estimated that the sanctions would take about a year to bite, and that only five months had passed. 'Sanctions, given time, will produce a very much more favourable situation, either for a negotiated end to the conflict or, if we can't negotiate an end to the crisis, a much less damaging military action [later],' said Denis Healey, a former defence secretary in a British Labour government.[97] The anti-war protesters were critical of the switch-over from the sanctions to an arbitrarily set 45-day ultimatum.

Their other major argument concerned the economic and environmental damage that an armed conflict in the Gulf, containing two-thirds of global oil reserves, would cause. They cited the petroleum experts' estimate that war in the Gulf would raise oil prices from the current \$27–\$30 a barrel to about \$65 a barrel for up to a year. The consequent world recession would damage not only the economies of the Third World and Eastern Europe, but also play havoc with the fragile banking system in America, where the Bank of New England had recently collapsed.

Then there was the question of an environmental calamity if, as seemed most probable, the Iraqis ignited Kuwait's 850-plus oil wells. Petroleum experts estimated that fires in Kuwaiti wellheads could burn 3–6 mb/d, and could continue indefinitely, given the oil reserves of 95,000 million barrels, until and unless they were extinguished, a process likely to take up to a year. A threat to the environment would come from the major by-products of uncontrolled combustion: carbon monoxide, nitrogen oxides, sulphur dioxide (the cause of acid rain), and smoke. The smoke engendered by these fires, at an estimated rate of 500,000 to three million tonnes a month and released into the upper atmosphere, was reckoned by one expert to be enough to lower daylight temperature in summer by 10 to 20°C, and thus seriously interfere with the ecological balance in the region. The other fear was that smoke clouds – containing large parts of soot, almost pure carbon, exceptionally good at absorbing the sun's heat – could spread across the Indian sub-continent and South-east Asia, upset the energy balance and disrupt the Asian monsoon. There was a probability of the leakage of millions of barrels of oil from broken pipelines and oil wells into the Gulf, which would play havoc with marine life. All these facts were highlighted at a symposium of scientists in London in early January, which set up an emergency task force to produce a document on the subject for politicians before the deadline.[98]

The politicians that the participants in the London symposium had in mind encompassed both parts of the anti-Iraqi coalition: the Western component and the non-Western. Given the media coverage of the deliberations of these mainly Western scientists in London, it could be assumed that the event had some impact on public opinion in the West. But there was no way of gauging how these dire warnings by scientific experts had been received in the Middle East.

Quite simply, there was no reliable way of determining the state of public sentiment in those Arab and Muslim countries and regional organizations which had despatched their ground forces to Saudi Arabia and placed them under the command of Prince Khalid: Egypt (35,000 troops), Syria (19,000 troops), the GCC (10,000 troops of its Rapid Deployment Force), and Morocco (1,200 troops) from the Arab world; Pakistan (12,000 soldiers), Bangladesh (2,000 soldiers), Niger (480 soldiers) and Senegal (500 soldiers) from the non-Arab Muslim world. There was one exception: on 15 January Pakistanis took to the streets in 24 cities to mount an anti-American protest. Washington had ordered the dependants of its diplomats in Pakistan to leave. A poll commissioned by a Pakistani newspaper in early January showed that 77% were opposed to the US presence in the Gulf, up from 62% soon after the Iraqi invasion. The opposition to the government's despatch of troops to the Gulf had increased despite the official explanation that they were sent there to defend Saudi Arabia, not to attack Iraq or occupied Kuwait.[99]

As for Saudi Arabia, the linchpin of the coalition, its interior ministry announced that anyone responsible for 'unrest' or 'violations of national security' would receive 'the severest penalty' because of 'the current delicate situation'. It warned against 'rumour-mongering' which would face the 'full force of the Islamic law' – meaning death or mutilation.[100] Even though Riyadh and Dhahran remained within range of Iraqi missiles, the people there were blasé about the air-raid exercises, failing to take shelter when the sirens sounded.

There was no sense of panic in Egypt, where few thought that Saddam Hussein would target his missiles at Cairo or some other Egyptian city. The main fear was of terrorist actions against senior government officials and foreign diplomats. Despite repeated rebuffs, President Mubarak had kept up his periodic appeals to Saddam Hussein to leave Kuwait, but in vain. At the end of the GCC summit in Doha, Qatar, on 25 December, calling for an unconditional Iraqi withdrawal from Kuwait, King Fahd appealed to Iraq's president. 'We wish that he [Saddam Hussein], who was to us a brother, friend and ally, [should] know that the curtain is not yet drawn on the scorching war, and that he can spare himself and his people its horror,' King Fahd said. 'It is braver to opt for peace than for war.'[101] This appeal was apparently lost on the Iraqi leader.

Of the major Arab leaders lined up against Iraq, it was now President Assad's turn to address his Iraqi counterpart. In an 'open letter' to Saddam Hussein, read over Damascus Radio on 12 January, Assad declared that 'differences between brothers fade in such a dangerous situation', and added, 'I would like to make a brotherly pledge which cannot be doubted: that if an attack is launched against Iraq after it withdraws from Kuwait, Syria will stand alongside Iraq and fight until victory.' Assad told Saddam that history would judge a decision to 'end the crisis and spare Iraq and the Arab world a devastating war to be an appropriate, courageous action made at the right time.' He said that if Iraq withdrew from Kuwait immediately, then the Arab world could close ranks and confront Israel, which he described as the Arabs' true enemy. The final point was reiterated by Farouk al Shaara, the Syrian foreign minister, who said, 'We in Syria cannot accept Israeli intervention in this crisis.'[102]

Significantly, a few days earlier, President Mubarak had made the same point. 'We will not permit Israeli involvement, or [its] military involvement in the Gulf crisis,' Mubarak told a gathering of writers and intellectuals on 9 January. 'I don't think Israel would get involved, but if it did, Egypt would take a different position.'[103]

Conscious of how fraught the situation was, the next day President Bush urged Prime Minister Shamir, in a telephone conversation, to 'lie low', stay out of the potential Gulf conflict, and refrain from considering a pre-emptive strike against Iraq. He also despatched deputy secretary of state Lawrence S. Eagleburger to Israel to discuss the Gulf crisis. Eagleburger arrived to find the Israeli leaders relieved and satisfied that his boss, James Baker, had refused point-blank any linkage between the Kuwaiti and Palestinian crises at the Geneva talks, and Israel on the highest state of military readiness, with its combat and reconnaissance aircraft in the air around the clock and its 4.7 million population equipped with gas masks. While Shamir was grateful to have received two batteries of US-made Patriot anti-missile missiles he was in no mood to concede the American request that Israel refrain from military retaliation if it was attacked by Iraq. On his part, Eagleburger turned down Shamir's request for tactical co-ordination between the Israeli military and US forces in the Gulf.[104]

Such triangular tensions between Israel, America and its major Arab allies gave hope to Saddam Hussein that his military-political strategy of making Israel the first target of attack in case of war would succeed in fracturing the US-led anti-Iraq coalition.

The one country which, though not part of the Arab–Israeli equation, mattered a great deal because of its geopolitical importance, was Turkey, a member of Nato. It did not have to despatch troops to the Gulf to pressure Iraq. It could achieve the same result by massing troops along their extensive common border, thus compelling Baghdad to deploy more of its forces along that frontier. Washington saw that it did so. The result was that by Christmas 1990 there were 112,000 Turkish troops along the Iraqi border, equipped with gas masks, with Turkish radars facing southwards, not northwards, towards the Soviet Union. The Turkish president, Turgut Ozal, had opted for a high-profile policy in the Gulf, a stance which led to the resignation of the defence and foreign ministers in October. When Ozal successfully pressured parliament to empower the government to declare war, the chief of the armed forces, General Necip Torumtay, resigned in protest in early December. In his farewell message he called on military personnel to follow the path laid out by the founder of the Turkish Republic, Mustafa Kemal Ataturk: 'Peace at home, peace in the world'. Since opinion polls showed two-thirds of Turks being against involvement in the Gulf conflict, and since his government faced domestic problems of labour strikes and Kurdish insurgency, with its popularity rating down to 20%, Ozal would have been well advised to reverse his position on the Gulf crisis. But he did not do so. He persisted in pursuing a one-man gung-ho policy, believing that Saddam Hussein would back down at the last moment, thus enabling Turkey to emerge with a greater say in Middle Eastern affairs than before.[105]

Ozal was not the only one to conceive of a last-minute retreat by the Iraqi president. Other prominent leaders, including Muammar Qadhafi of Libya, thought he would do so.

But why did he not? Was he a 'madman' who saw himself as the saviour of the Arab people? No, according to Yevgeny Primakov, the special Soviet envoy to the Gulf. 'I've known Saddam Hussein for 21 years: enough time to figure out what someone is like, whether or not he has some eccentricities,' he said in a television interview in mid-January. 'I think that man, without a doubt, has a strong will – without a doubt he understands the game he is playing.'[106] .

The clues to his thinking could be found in the published transcript of his conversation with Pérez de Cuellar and the reported remarks he made to a senior member of the Algerian delegation in early January. These need to be viewed in the context of his conviction that there was an American–Israeli conspiracy afoot to destroy Iraq as a powerful military entity.

Saddam Hussein's key statements to the UN secretary-general were: (1) 'They [Iraqis] are at the same time willing to fight if attacked, confidently relying on the depth of a fighting experience of eight years ... Hence, even if we were granted all the privileges in the world, when the two armies – the Iraqi and the American – are only a matter of hours away from the likelihood of war, no one will ever utter the word "withdrawal". To utter the word "withdrawal", when war is likely, is to prepare the psychological ground for the victory of the enemy.' (2) 'If you [Pérez de Cuellar] find the Americans in a position wherein they are looking for a way out of their impasse without losing – or gaining all that they have in mind – then it is possible to set down certain principles, and charge the Arabs to look for a solution in keeping with these principles. Or you as a capable, experienced diplomat might sound out other parties for their viewpoints.' (3) 'When Iraqis asked me: "Why all these concessions to Iran?" I answered: "For the sake of peace. Now that Kuwait is part of Iraq, you have all that long coast of your own, and there is no longer a need for us to fight one another for the Shatt al Arab."' The last statement needed to be interpreted along with a remark he reportedly made to a senior Algerian official. 'I have two options: to be killed by US bombs or by Iraqi officers,' he said. 'In the first case I shall be a martyr, in the second a traitor. If I withdraw unconditionally from Kuwait, I shall certainly have to face the second scenario.' That is, by giving up Kuwait unconditionally, Saddam Hussein would have exposed himself to mortal risks from his senior military officers, who had seen him give away to Iran, unilaterally, whatever marginal gains Iraq had made in the Iran–Iraq War. Quite simply, by conceding the eastern half of the Shatt al Arab to Iran in mid-August, he had, in the domestic military context, negated the option of an unconditional evacuation of Kuwait. He needed at least to have secured Warba and half of Bubiyan on lease to survive the withdrawal from Kuwait. And this was not on *before* the pull-out. In short, his options were very limited. 'If Saddam Hussein is sure that the only choice is either to die or stand on his knees only to die afterwards, he would prefer war, where everybody loses,' said Yevgeny Primakov.[107]

If there was anything reassuring to the Iraqi leader in all this, it was his feeling, right or wrong, that it was President Bush who had got himself in an impasse due to his emotionalism and bellicosity. He believed that when the chips were down the Americans did not have the motivation or guts to fight a land war (which they regarded as inevitable) against an army which was battle-experienced and fighting on a familiar terrain, and a people who had withstood eight years of warfare.

Underlying all this was Saddam Hussein's mistrust of the American promise that the withdrawing Iraqis would not be attacked, and a conviction that there was a deep US–Israeli conspiracy to annihilate Iraq as a strong military power. 'Saddam Hussein believes that after his military success, as he calls it, against Iran, he became the object of conspiracy,' said Yevgeny Primakov. 'He feels there is a complex conspiracy to eliminate him, to surround Iraq, to strangle Iraq.'[108]

If so, it was better to stand and fight, rather than let the US or Israel destroy him and/or his military power by stealth. He knew the US had tried to assassinate Qadhafi in April 1986 by staging air raids on Tripoli. And he remembered only too well the manner in which Israel had knocked out Iraq's nuclear facility in June 1981. With world attention focused on him and Iraq, and with his popularity in the Arab world, outside the Gulf and Egypt, at an all-time high, now was the most suitable time to take a stand against the American–Israeli axis.

According to the Pentagon, Baghdad had deployed 590,000 troops

in Kuwait and southern Iraq (a figure which later Pentagon estimates
were to scale down to 350,000); and the total Iraqi hardware amounted
to 700 warplanes, 5,750 tanks, and 15 warships. They were facing a
total allied force of 700,000; and their military hardware amounted to
1,746 warplanes, 3,673 tanks and 149 warships.[109]

PART III

THE MILITARY SOLUTION

9 DESERT STORM: THE AIR CAMPAIGN

'If you are hoping that Iraq will yield to you after the air strikes . . . and if you believe that the [Iraqi] ground forces can be neutralized, then you are deluding yourself.'

President Saddam Hussein in an open letter to George Bush, 17 January 1991[1]

'Our strategy for dealing with this [Iraqi] army is very, very simple. First we're going to cut it off, then we're going to kill it.'

General Colin Powell, 23 January 1991[2]

'President George Bush was assured by his military advisers that Iraq would collapse within two days of the start of bombing two weeks ago. I have that from a member of the [US] Senate Foreign Relations Committee. Mr Bush was told by President Hosni Mubarak of Egypt that war would be over in two weeks. King Fahd of Saudi Arabia told him "two hours".'

William Pfaff, American columnist, 1 February 1991[3]

'Achieving our goals will require sacrifice and time, but we will prevail. Make no mistake about that.'

President George Bush, 1 February 1991[4]

'Bush said he had no dispute with the Iraqi people. It certainly looks different from Baghdad.'

A resident of Baghdad, 1 February 1991[5]

Operation 'Desert Storm' started on the night of 16–17 January with an air campaign. It was expected to achieve its objectives in a matter of days, but went on for more than six weeks. In contrast, the ground war, which most observers expected to last some weeks, ended in four days. The American success in the second phase of the war, codenamed 'Desert Sabre', was due to the length and effectiveness of the air offensive.

Week One: 16 January–23 January

Operation 'Desert Storm' began on 16 January at 23.30 GMT with F-117 radar-evading Stealth bombers aiming precise laser-guided Paveway bombs at key targets in Baghdad. Then came a series of co-ordinated allied air strikes into Iraq and Kuwait, and the firing of Tomahawk sea-launched cruise missiles by USS *Wisconsin* and USS *Missouri* stationed in the Gulf, seeking out such targets as command, control and communications centres, airports, missile launching sites and oil refineries. The first overall aim was to destroy Iraq's command, control and communications centres and to activate its air defence radars so that these could be knocked out by special anti-radar ALARM (Air Launched Anti-Radiation Missile) missiles carried by US Phantoms and Royal Air Force Tornados. The second major aim was to destroy Iraq's ability to launch Scud ground-to-ground missiles and utilize its air force. This was to be accomplished by US Stealth bombers equipped with accurate night bombing systems, F-15Es with the latest infra-red targeting equipment, and RAF Tornados with special JP-233 cluster bombs to wreck Iraqi runways.

American, British, French, Kuwaiti and Saudi air forces participated, using bases in Saudi Arabia and elsewhere – as well as the allied aircraft carriers stationed in the Gulf. In the first 24 hours they flew 2,000 sorties while USS *Wisconsin* and USS *Missouri* fired more than 100 Tomahawk cruise missiles. On the ground the allied forces began to move northwards inside Saudi Arabia towards the Kuwaiti and Iraqi borders. The allies claimed that for a loss of seven of their warplanes, they had destroyed five Iraqi aircraft and six Scud mobile missile launchers, and sunk three enemy patrol boats. Baghdad claimed to have shot down 44 allied aircraft.[6]

As required by the Congressional resolutions of 12 January, before implementing Operation 'Desert Storm', President Bush had addressed a letter to Congressional leaders, justifying military action on the grounds that 'Diplomatic and economic pressures have not diminished Iraq's intransigence, despite five-and-a-half months of unparalleled international effort.' He advanced the same argument in his television address to the nation on the night of 16 January. Not everybody was convinced. The next day anti-war protesters demonstrated in

Washington and other major cities. In San Francisco thousands of anti-war demonstrators laid siege to federal buildings, preventing government staff going to work.[7]

In Europe, President Mitterrand told the French National Assembly that since 'guns are going to speak' now, it was 'inconceivable' for France not to ally with other Western powers in a military action. He added that lines to the Arab world were being kept open, stressing that France's military activity was 'defensive': a term amplified by the defence minister Chévènement the next day when he told the deputies that Paris had agreed with Washington that its forces would strike only at targets inside Kuwait and not inside Iraq. Prime Minister Michel Rocard informed the Assembly that France would place its Gulf troops under US command 'for specific times and specific missions', thus reversing its previous policy of retaining sole command of its forces. The government's stance was supported by 523 deputies, and opposed by 42, with Chévènement abstaining.[8]

The Netherlands parliament too voted in favour of putting two Dutch frigates in the Gulf under US command. But the centre-left members of the coalition government blocked efforts by their conservative partners to send troops to the region. The other European country to place its warships (as well as warplanes) under the Pentagon's command was Italy. But, like France, taking Arab sensitivities into account, it pledged to attack only targets inside Kuwait.[9]

In contrast, the coalition government in Belgium stated that its minesweepers in the Gulf could not be used for any action against Iraq, and called for the appointment of a UN mediator to resolve the conflict. While promising 'humanitarian aid and logistical support' for the multinational troops in the Gulf, the Portuguese prime minister said, 'We will not send military forces to the war zone.' Reflecting popular feeling in his country, the Spanish prime minister, too, declared that Spain would not participate in any military attack.[10]

While expressing support for the anti-Iraq coalition, Chancellor Kohl reiterated that Germany would not despatch troops to join them (as such a step would contravene the constitution). Anti-war protesters, estimated at 300,000 nationally, marched in Berlin, Bonn and other cities on 17 January.[11]

The foreign ministers of the EC, meeting in an emergency session in Paris on 17 January, combined a 'pressing appeal' to the Iraqi government to withdraw completely from Kuwait to 'avoid new suffering for the people of Iraq' with an endorsement of French calls for an international peace conference on the Middle East.[12]

In Moscow, President Gorbachev said on Soviet television on 17 January that he had been informed only an hour in advance that military operations against Iraq were about to begin. He immediately contacted President Bush to insist that Saddam Hussein should be given a last chance to withdraw, and followed this up with a message to the Soviet ambassador in Baghdad to urge Saddam Hussein to declare his readiness to pull out. But Alexander Byelonogov, a Soviet deputy foreign minister, told him that communications to the Iraqi foreign ministry in Baghdad had broken down and attempts to contact Iraq's leadership had failed. Gorbachev said that the USSR would do everything 'in its power' to limit the conflict. 'We appealed to a number of influential countries, including France, Britain, Germany, Italy and India [then a non-permanent member of the Security Council] and most Arab states, to take steps to localize the conflict and prevent it spreading,' he said.[13] At its nearest point, the Soviet Union is only 200 miles from Iraq.

'Most Arab states' mentioned by Gorbachev certainly included the members of the Arab Maghreb Union where popular feeling was strongly pro-Iraq. Anti-US demonstrations swept through Algeria, Libya, Morocco, Mauritania and Tunisia. A million people took to the streets in Libya, a country of 4.5 million, to protest against the war, shouting 'Stop the bombardment of Iraq', and 'Kuwait has the right to self-determination'. Muammar Qadhafi, who participated in the march, called on the UN secretary-general to ensure that military operations did not go beyond the recovery of Kuwait. In the same vein, the Yemeni government called on the permanent members of the Security Council to 'put an end to the bloodshed and destruction'. The harshest judgement of the US-led alliance came from Amman. 'The Jordanian leadership, government and people denounce the brutal aggression against an Arab, Muslim country and people, who have always defended their Arab brethren without hesitation,' said an official spokesman.[14]

Much to the disappointment of the allies, Iraq did not respond to the aerial attacks by ordering its warplanes to engage the invading aircraft, choosing instead to conserve them by parking them in reinforced air shelters. It limited itself to the use of surface-to-air missiles and anti-aircraft fire. Claiming that the US-led air raids struck densely populated areas of Baghdad, an Iraqi military spokesman said on 17 January that 23 civilians had been killed and 66 wounded.[15]

Eye-witnesses reported thousands of buses, cars and taxis leaving Baghdad, either for the comparative safety of the countryside or the

Muslim holy cities of Najaf and Karbala, widely expected to be spared bombing by the allies. (But this was not to be. On 20 January the allies attacked Najaf twice, with bombs falling about two miles from the shrine of Imam Ali.) With shops and restaurants closed, streets empty, and schools silent, the Iraqi capital acquired an eerie atmosphere of calm.

In contrast, Baghdad Radio broadcast a defiant speech by Saddam Hussein on 17 January. 'With the escalation of the showdown and the steadfastness of the believers, relief will come and the whole nation will overthrow the thrones established on corruption,' he declared. 'It will also overthrow the renegade traitors who are followers of evil, and will cause the crumbling of the White House, the den of infidels and domination, and the den of the poisonous wasps and aggression in Tel Aviv.' He promised the liberation of 'Dear Palestine and its good and struggling people' as well as the Golan Heights and Lebanon. Baghdad Radio also reported that during his tour of the capital, Saddam Hussein visited the broadcasting studios and air force headquarters to acquaint himself with 'the high morale of his valiant hawks as they repulse the attacks of the invading forces of evil and atheism'.[16]

On that day, the allies added carpet-bombing of the Iraqi troops in Kuwait to their aerial activities. USS *Wisconsin* and USS *Missouri* fired almost 100 Tomahawk cruise missiles at enemy targets. The allies reported a loss of four warplanes.

Iraq carried out its long-promised attack on Israel by firing modified Scud missiles (called Al Hussein) at it. The Israeli authorities refused to give the exact number and locations of the hits. It emerged later that twelve Iraqi missiles had hit Tel Aviv and Haifa, and that at least two dozen people were injured.[17]

After months of talking, bragging and threats, the moment had arrived. Israel had been attacked, successfully, by Iraq with its ground-to-ground missiles. The actual damage done was small, both in human injury and in loss of property. Yet thousands of residents fled Tel Aviv for safer parts of the country, particularly Jerusalem which, being holy to Muslims, was expected to be spared the Iraqi Scuds. Industry, commerce and education came to a standstill. The news was warmly received by most Arabs. They were impressed by the fact that Saddam Hussein had hit Tel Aviv, the internationally recognized capital of Israel, thus demonstrating that the heart of the Jewish state was no longer impregnable. Iraqi officials rushed to agree with the interpretation offered by Iraq's ambassador to France, Abdul Razzak Hashimi, that 'The Scud attacks on Israel have turned the conflict into an Arab–Israeli one.' But had it? The answer lay with Israel. 'We have publicly said, and to the Americans, that if we were attacked we would retaliate,' said Moshe Arens, the Israeli defence minister. 'We were attacked.'[18]

Actually, according to the version released by Washington after the war, within minutes of the first Iraqi missile hitting Tel Aviv, senior officials of the US and Israel had a telephone conversation, in which the American side told the Israelis: 'We are going after western Iraq [the site of Iraqi missile launchers] full bore. There is nothing that your air force can do that we are not already doing. If there is, tell us, and we will do it. We appreciate your restraint, and please don't play into Saddam's hands.'[19]

Saddam Hussein would have welcomed Israeli retaliation, however severe, because that would have almost certainly caused a damaging split in the anti-Iraqi coalition, *and* drawn Iran into the fray on the Iraqi side to join the fight against Israel. Bush was only too aware of this. His administration had had ample time to rehearse its response. It acted both militarily and diplomatically. It intensified its efforts to locate and destroy mobile Iraqi missile launchers. According to NBC television, the Pentagon had assigned the task of seeking out and destroying 25 'remaining' Iraqi modified-Scud missile launchers in the western Iraqi desert to the 86 American warplanes stationed on aircraft carriers in the Red Sea and 96 US planes stationed at Incirlik in Turkey. (Also on 17 January the Turkish National Assembly passed by 250 votes to 148, with 52 abstentions, the War Powers Resolution which, *inter alia*, authorized the government to let members of the anti-Iraqi coalition use its military bases. While opposition leaders considered this decision as tantamount to Turkey's entering the war, President Ozal, aware of the unpopularity of participating in the conflict, disputed this interpretation, adding that Turkey would not join the fighting unless it was attacked by Iraq.) General Schwarzkopf, now designated commander-in-chief of the allied forces, claimed on 18 January that the allied forces had destroyed six launchers and targeted five more.[20] Whether true, false, or exaggerated, the main objective of highlighting the news about Iraq's missile launchers was to reassure Israel that Washington was doing its utmost to eliminate this danger to the Jewish state.

But more needed to be done to pacify Israel, or so the US was made to feel by Tel Aviv. Some days later, according to unconfirmed, news agency reports, broadcast by radio stations in Britain, Israeli warplanes were allowed to join the occasional sorties that the US aircraft were to carry out from Incirlik, Turkey. Thus Israel was able to retrieve its honour – surreptitiously. None of this was confirmed officially then or later. To pacify Israel publicly and immediately, Washington rushed its troops to operate the two Patriot anti-missile batteries it had decided to ship to Israel three months before, and to train Israelis.[21]

Moscow too reacted swiftly. It combined its 'definite' condemnation of Iraq with advice to Israel not to give in to provocation. 'For Israel to allow itself to be drawn in would only help the Iraqi leadership,' it stated.[22]

Popular reaction in the Arab world was ecstatic. Even in Damascus there was dancing in the streets. In Sanaa, the Yemeni capital, tens of thousands of people marched to acclaim the Iraqi achievement. The Palestinians and Lebanese in Lebanon celebrated the occasion with unrestrained joy. Summing up a general feeling, Amneh Menem, a Palestinian housewife in Sidon, said, 'Let them give Israelis a taste of what they have been inflicting on us for years.' This dovetailed with the statement of an Iraqi missile commander that the Scud attack on Israel had avenged 'the suffering of the Arab and Muslim people and of the Iraqis and Palestinians'. The press in Jordan splashed the story on the front page, with the Amman-based *Al Rai* (The Opinion) headline reading: 'The Iraqi missiles shake the Zionist and Saudi entities'.[23]

In contrast, the government-controlled or -guided media in Saudia Arabia either ignored or played down the Iraqi Scuds hitting Israel – with the Jiddah-based *Arab News* dismissing the event in less than five lines on an inside page. That day, 18 January, happened to be a Friday, the Islamic holy day when the preachers/prayer leaders, the imams, deliver sermons from the pulpit. In Saudi Arabia these sermons are required to be submitted to the government for clearance by 4 p.m. on Thursdays. On Thursday 17 January, the imams noticed that the authorities had re-interpreted certain verses in the Quran which attack the infidels. 'It is elective Islam now,' said an imam. 'The Quran [has been] expurgated to suit the present political purposes of the House of Saud and the war aims of General Schwarzkopf.' This was done to enable Shaikh Abdul Aziz ibn Abdullah ibn Baz, the head of the Supreme Religious Council, to issue a call for a jihad, holy struggle, by the Muslim and non-Muslim forces of the Custodian of the Holy Shrines (i.e. King Fahd) against the forces of Saddam Hussein, who was described as 'an enemy of God' and a blasphemer for claiming to be a descendant of Prophet Muhammad, something he had done years earlier in the course of the Iran–Iraq War. Small wonder then that on

18 January there was not a single mention in the sermons in Jiddah, Mecca or Medina, of the Iraqi missile attacks on Israel. Instead, the imams, taking their lead from Shaikh Abdul Aziz ibn Baz, condemned Saddam Hussein.[24]

In the neighbouring country of Jordan, where the ruler's claim to being a descendant of Prophet Muhammad was indisputable (since both belonged to the Hashemi clan), the government withheld comment on the Iraqi action against Israel. In contrast, the PLO, headed by a secular leadership, declared that Israel had effectively joined the Gulf War, and that Arabs could not justify taking part in a battle that included massive bombing of Iraq. In the Occupied Territories the popularity of Saddam Hussein seemed to have risen further, although the Palestinians could not demonstrate in support of Iraq. With the outbreak of war they were put under indefinite curfew, which was lifted only for three hours after ten days, on 27 January. Faisal Husseini, their East Jerusalem-based leader, however, was equivocal about the Iraqi action. 'We are not happy about those missiles on Baghdad and we are not happy about those missiles on Tel Aviv,' he said.[25]

There was no equivocation in the response of Syria, partly because by then it had received $2.2 bn in financial aid from Saudi Arabia, the Kuwaiti government-in-exile and the UAE. It said that Saddam Hussein would fail to enmesh other Arab countries into a conflict with Israel. 'If the Iraqi president is determined to fight on, betting on a reshuffling of the cards through firing a few missiles on Israel, then his bet is definitely a lost one,' stated the government newspaper *Al Thawra*.

Egypt agreed. Its ambassador to the US said that Egypt would stick with the anti-Iraqi coalition even if Israel retaliated against Iraq. 'Our position is very solid,' he said on 18 January. 'We are part of the coalition.' A day earlier Egypt's foreign minister, Esmat Abdel-Meguid, had appealed to Saddam Hussein to withdraw. 'There is still time to avoid more damage if Iraq begins an immediate and complete withdrawal from Kuwait,' he said.[26]

Such words fell on deaf ears. 'In the coming period,' declared Saddam Hussein on Baghdad Radio on 20 January, 'the response of Iraq will be on a larger scale, using all the means and potential that God has given us and which we have so far only used in part. Our ground forces have not entered the battle so far, and only a small part of our air force has been used. The army's air force has not been used, nor has the navy. The weight and effect of our ready missile force has not yet been applied in full.'[27] Politically, he tried to present the war as a struggle between the satanic Bush, aided by the traitors to Arabism and Islam (in the persons respectively of Mubarak and Fahd), and the glorious Iraqi people inspired by Islam and Arabism.

In this scheme of Baghdad there was hardly any role for countries like Turkey, a non-Arab state which was part of Nato, or Iran, a non-Arab state which was extremely wary of Washington. The Iranian president, Rafsanjani, was aware of the problem this created. He was bitter to see 'Muslims and their resources being destroyed by arrogant powers led by the hegemonist and aggressive America', but blamed Baghdad for the current situation. He told the US-led coalition forces that Iran would not allow them to use its airspace or territory to launch attacks against Iraq or Kuwait. At the same time his government decided to make an extensive diplomatic effort in the hope of bringing the war to a speedy end, and called for an emergency meeting of the 45-member Islamic Conference Organization for the purpose.[28] Jordan adopted a similar line. Its deputy prime minister, Salim Masadeh, said that Amman was in touch with many non-aligned, Islamic and pro-Iraqi Arab countries on the possibility of seeking a ceasefire call by the UN Security Council.

At the Council, on 20 January Pérez de Cuellar conveyed to the Iraqi ambassador to the UN, Abdul Amir al Anbari, three ceasefire proposals – from the USSR, India and Algeria. Each of these called for an immediate ceasefire and a UN peace-keeping force to oversee an Iraqi evacuation of Kuwait, with the Indian and Algerian proposals also mentioning the possibility of an early Middle East peace conference. However, because of the allied bombing of the Iraqi telecommunications systems, Anbari could not forward these proposals to Baghdad.

On 19 January, the third day of the war, the aggregate total of allied sorties flown so far reached 4,000, with half of these being bombing missions and the rest combat air patrol and other support missions. The allies put the day's aircraft losses at ten. As more Iraqi Scuds hit Tel Aviv and Haifa, President Bush urged restraint on Israel. The Pentagon claimed to have intercepted three Iraqi Scuds fired at Saudi targets.

No reliable casualty figures were available. However, an estimate of 4,000 Iraqi military personnel killed in the first three days of war given by a spokesman of the Kurdish Democratic Party – amounting to two persons killed for each allied bombing mission – seemed realistic.[29]

Iraq continued to follow its strategy of not responding to the allied aerial attacks with its air force, a situation which Group Captain David Henderson, commanding officer of the RAF Tornado bombers based in Bahrain, described as 'baffling'.[30] In the early hours of the battle the absence of Iraqi warplanes from the skies was presented by the allies as a result of their success in knocking out most of the Iraqi air force. Later allied communiqués began scaling down the damage the coalition's bombing missions had done to Iraq's warplanes. By the end of the second day of fighting the allies claimed to have destroyed eleven Iraqi aircraft. Apparently, Iraq's strategy of hunkering down and storing its aircraft in scattered heavily reinforced bunkers, and training its pilots to operate their machines without directions from ground controllers and radar, paid off.

Allied bombing of Iraq's water, fuel and electricity supplies and facilities had been more successful. This caused shortages in Baghdad and other cities. Many observers failed to see how the bombing of the economic infrastructure of Iraq could be presented as part of the 'surgical war' the allies claimed to be waging. This was one of the major points raised by the leaders of the anti-war protest.

The other point they made concerned the media coverage of the conflict. In this they were joined by the news executives of the major newspapers and television networks. The Pentagon adopted rules that limited coverage of warfare to reporters assembled in officially escorted groups, called 'pools'. Their reports were subject to 'security review' by military officers before being released for dissemination. The Pentagon described the censorship as 'necessary' to prevent 'any helpful information' from reaching the Iraqi military. The prime casualty of this policy was the truth. 'Journalists, particularly on television, have at times failed to distinguish fact from rumour, and the public has received false and misleading reports,' wrote David E. Rosenbaum of the *New York Times* on 21 January. 'The view prevails within the [US] military that the free rein the journalists had in Vietnam led to reporting that seriously damaged morale and turned the country against its own troops ... The second point growing out of Vietnam is that if the public knew how gruesome the fighting was, more people would turn against the war. There is even suspicion among journalists here [in Washington] that the government wants to keep news of the damage and casualties in Iraq to a minimum to keep Arab allies from turning against the United States out of horror.' The outright hostility of the US armed forces field commanders towards the press was aptly summed up by the remarks made by a senior US air force officer briefing the reporters in Dhahran on 21 January 1991. 'Let me say up front that I don't like the press,' he said. 'Your presence here can't possibly do me any good, and it can hurt me and my people.'[31]

These subjects were raised by those who addressed the anti-war demonstrations in major American cities, the largest one – organized by the National Coalition to Stop the War in the Middle East and attended by some 70,000 people – taking place in Washington, DC, on 19 January. It turned out to be the largest anti-war demonstration in the American capital since the Vietnam War ended in 1975.

In Europe tens of thousands of people joined anti-war protests on 20 January in Belgium, Switzerland, Yugoslavia and Spain. A poll taken in the previous week for El Cinco, a commercial television channel, showed that 52% of Spaniards living in provincial capitals thought the war was unjust. In Germany more than 80% backed the use of force, but 75% did not want Germany to fight. In France and Italy, the two countries on the European mainland officially engaged in hostilities, 80% of the French were against the war, and a similar proportion of Italians. In Italy, the anti-war stand of Pope John Paul, backed up by his statement on 22 January that the Gulf conflict did not meet the doctrinal definition of a just war, was an important factor, causing a rift between the Catholic church and the ruling Christian Democratic Party, the principal source of support in Italy for the Gulf War. The anti-war demonstrations, organized by both the Catholic church and the Communists, drew an estimated one million people during the first week of the hostilities.[32]

In contrast, in Britain, support for the Gulf War jumped abruptly from 54% in a poll (commissioned by the *Guardian*) taken on 12–13 January, to 80% in a poll conducted on 17–18 January (for the *Sunday Times*). This showed that so long as there was choice between war and peace, public opinion was almost evenly divided; but once the allied military campaign began, and it became a matter of life and death for hundreds of thousands of Western armed personnel, opinion turned decisively pro-war. This was particularly true of America which, having already deployed 431,000 service personnel, was adding another 25,000 troops each week. National surveys in the US showed that nearly half of those polled had a relative or friend in the Gulf. Secondly, in times of grave danger to a nation, as in an armed conflict, the public tends to rally round its government, whether it be morally wrong or right. This was as true of the people in the countries forming the anti-Iraq coalition as it was in Iraq.

On the fourth day of fighting, 20 January, Iraq showed seven allied airmen on its television: they said that the war must be stopped, and that they would be used as human shields at Iraq's economic and strategic sites so long as it continued. The allies strongly condemned the exposure of prisoners of war as contrary to Article 23 of the Third Geneva Convention on war. But that did not deter the Iraqis from putting two more captured allied airmen on television the next day and announcing that they were holding 20 allied air personnel as prisoners. Later an Iraqi military communiqué, broadcast on Baghdad Radio, sought to link the mistreatment of the allied prisoners of war to the Palestinian–Israeli issue, stating that Iraq would abide by the Geneva Conventions provided 'the same is applied to the people of Palestine'. Meanwhile, Saddam Hussein's mistreatment of the allied airmen increased support for Bush in America where his conduct of the Gulf War won the approval of 85%, the highest figure yet.[33]

Iraq fired eight Scuds at Riyadh and Dhahran on 20 January. All but one were reportedly intercepted by Patriot missiles, the lone Scud landing near the defence ministry in Riyadh. Iraq had now activated its air force, and this showed in the allies' claims of gains and losses: 17 Iraqi planes destroyed in air combats, with the loss of 16 allied aircraft.[34]

On the fifth day of hostilities, 21 January, aircraft losses on both sides were again even: 15 each. The total allied air missions (bolstered slightly by the joining of the Canadian aircraft based in Qatar) had by now reached 8,100. And, according to military sources in London, total Iraqi losses of aircraft amounted to 38 in five days of the air campaign. Iraq launched more Scuds at Dhahran, but these reportedly missed the mark and fell into the sea. The allies attacked Basra. Fierce artillery exchanges between the two sides along the Saudi–Kuwaiti border led to the blowing up of oil installations, including the storage tanks at Mina Abdullah refinery and Al Wafra oilfield, creating the danger of an oil slick. Two days later Baghdad announced that petrol sales were being suspended 'temporarily'.[35]

There was a virtual black-out of information as to the extent of human and material damage caused by the unprecedentedly heavy bombing by the allies. The official Iraqi total of 60 people dead, including 31 soldiers, was patently false. Both sides had an interest in withholding or falsifying these figures. Iraq did not wish to broadcast its true losses, in human casualties as well as economic and strategic targets, for fear of demoralizing its citizens and military forces. Since the Iraqi media were under the direct control of Saddam Hussein, this was easy to achieve. It did not occur to him, in the early days of the war, that by broadcasting the vast damage the allied bombing had done,

especially to civilian life and property, he would sway public opinion
in the West to his side. He would have perceived this sort of admission
as a sign of weakness on his part, and thus counterproductive: in the
Arab world opinion is swayed, whether in the clan, tribe or political
party, by demonstrating strength rather than weakness. Displaying the
allied pilots on television was a manifestation of strength; so too was
the success Iraq had in hitting Israel with Scuds.

For their part, the allies wanted to conceal the facts about casualties
so as not to horrify public opinion at home and abroad, particularly
in the Arab world, giving Syria or Egypt cause to leave the coalition.
Already the Islamic fundamentalists in Egypt, an important opposition
force, had begun urging the government to pull out.

While the estimate of 100,000 casualties, including 30,000 civilians,
given by Ayatollah Muhammad Taqi Moderasi, the leader of Iraq's Shia
Action Group, was grossly exaggerated, a figure of 15,000 casualties,
based on an average of two for every air sortie, seemed realistic.
Iran protested officially, arguing that the allied attacks on Iraq far
exceeded the UN mandate. 'Under no conditions can operations for
the liberation of Kuwait justify killing innocent people and destroying
economic resources,' said Iran's foreign minister, Velayati. 'Iraq is
being savagely attacked.'[36]

Despite this, according to Interfax, the semi-official Soviet news
agency, a Soviet military commander claimed that only about half of
Iraq's anti-aircraft defences had been destroyed. In a report in *Izvestia*
on 18 January 1991, Major-General G. Zhivits, deputy chief of the
research centre of the Soviet general staff, said: 'The combat potential
of the Iraqi army is still high enough. The basic groupings of its armed
forces and specifically land troops, reserves, rocket and artillery units
have remained undestroyed.'[37]

That assessment was confirmed by military sources in London.
According to them, much of Iraq's defence system remained intact,
with many of its 35 main airfields still functioning and most of
its mobile missile launchers operating. Admitting that the allied
bombers might have been annihilating decoy Scud missile sites made
of cardboard, the Pentagon conceded it was 'nowhere near wiping out
all the Scud facilities'.[38] It had started the war with a scenario by which
it would cut off the Iraqi military from its high command and destroy
the command, control and communications centres as well as other
strategic targets within a few days, so bringing the conflict swiftly to
a successful conclusion. This was not to be.

Setting aside the expensive 'smart' bombs, which only accounted for only 7% of the total explosive power and whose accuracy was put at 60%, the accuracy of the dumb bombs (according to a Pentagon briefing after the war) was less than 25%. This meant that many of the allied bombs had failed to destroy their targets. Iraqi aircraft and airfields proved more difficult to destroy than anticipated, with low-flying allied warplanes, dropping cluster bombs to damage runways, proving vulnerable to Iraqi ground fire. This enabled the Iraqi leaders to claim that while the US-led coalition had deluded itself into believing that the war would be 'quick and easy' they had known all along that it would be 'long and costly'. This assertion caused unease at both popular and expert levels in America. 'The Pentagon has nurtured disbelief by its relentless boasting about the historic dimensions of the air war without yet documenting its effectiveness,' wrote the *New York Times*.[39]

On the sixth day of the conflict, 22 January, Iraq (believed to possess 200 to 1,000 ground-to-ground missiles) hit the populated areas of Tel Aviv with three Scuds, killing three and injuring 70 people. The Israeli leaders vowed retaliation, but in measured tones. In reality, according to a version released by Washington after the war, after every Scud attack Israel's defence minister, Arens, would ask his American counterpart, Cheney, for the electronic identity codes (to distinguish between Iraqi and allied aircraft), and later for an air corridor through Saudi Arabia so that the Israeli warplanes could retaliate without going through Jordan – whose monarch had told the American ambassador, Richard Armitage, that the Jordanian air force would attack any Israeli planes flying over his country – but to no avail. President Bush would say he well appreciated Israeli restraint, and Prime Minister Shamir would 'weigh it all up and sit tight', and sound statesmanlike. 'To defend ourselves doesn't mean we have to do it without wisdom, intelligence, consideration, without evaluating the conditions we are acting in,' Shamir told Israeli Television. 'It isn't a question of ping-pong: you hit me, I'll hit you.'[40]

Innovative defence by Iraq made Washington and London decide to escalate the war and its aims publicly. On 22 January Douglas Hurd, the British foreign secretary, acknowledged that the multinational force would certainly have to enter Iraq, even if the Iraqi withdrawal from Kuwait had been achieved, to ensure that there would be no 'further threat to Kuwait', meaning thereby that the allies intended to annihilate Iraq's offensive potential. In a sense he was merely backing the position laid out earlier by the US defence secretary in a television interview: 'Our objective is to get Saddam Hussein out of Kuwait, and to destroy that military capability he has used to invade Kuwait and to threaten other nations in the Middle East.'[41]

While the leading Western members of the coalition were escalating their war aims, the regional powers were busily proclaiming that the territorial integrity of Iraq must be maintained after the war, with Iran publicly warning Turkey against seizing the Kurdish north of Iraq. With 200,000 Turkish troops massed along the Iraqi border, and several squadrons of warplanes of the US-led coalition operating from Incirlik, Turkey had emerged as an important element in the war equation.[42] This became apparent when on 22–23 January, the seventh day of warfare, the US launched two raids on Iraq from Incirlik. Iraq protested publicly, accusing Turkey of 'unjustified aggression'.[43]

The missions from Incirlik were part of the 2,000 allied air sorties mounted on that day, bringing the overall total during the first week of the war to 12,100. The allies' defensive systems were equally active, with the Patriot anti-missile missile batteries being the most alert. The Pentagon claimed that these missiles had intercepted Iraqi Scuds directed at Dhahran and Riyadh. More importantly, though, for the first time the US-manned Patriot batteries intercepted the Iraqi missiles directed at Israel.

The success and persistence with which the Iraqis continued to fire Scuds at Israel and Saudi Arabia showed that Saddam Hussein considered these missiles as an effective means of raising the anger and frustration of his two chief regional enemies to the point where they would urge publicly and emotionally the total annihilation of Iraq. He hoped, too, that Israel would join the war, thus causing Syria and/or Egypt to leave the anti-Iraq coalition.

But there was no sign of Saddam Hussein's gamble paying off. As the Saudi-funded, London-based *Al Sharq al Awsat* put it on 22 January: 'Israel thanks Saddam, for he has regained for it all it has lost as a result of its crimes against the patient Palestinian people.' The Syrian viewpoint was articulated by the Beirut-based *Al Safir* (The Ambassador), which argued that in giving America the pretext to supply Israel with Patriot missiles, Saddam Hussein had thrown away what had become the Arabs' most precious advantage – medium range missiles – and restored Israeli supremacy in the region.[44]

Apart from all this, the unprovoked Scud attacks on Israel had enhanced sympathy for Israel in Western capitals. In Europe, Bonn was in the forefront, with Chancellor Kohl combining his condemnation of the attacks with emergency humanitarian aid of $170 million on the ground that 'we Germans have a special responsibility' to protect

Israel's right to exist. This was followed by an aid package worth $670 million, including a battery of Patriot missiles and financial assistance in building two submarines.[45]

Overall, the first week of the Second Gulf War was a mixed bag, militarily and politically, for both sides. Most of the 216 US Tomahawk cruise missiles (out of the 500 deployed in the region) hit their targets: telecommunications centres and large, single buildings housing ministries, civilian or military. The fire following the bombing of the Dohra refinery near Baghdad on 18 January lit up the capital at night, facilitating allied bombing. The Iraqis responded by firing hundreds of anti-aircraft guns. Tens of thousands of people fled Baghdad, and normal life ceased. Despite the lack of electricity in the capital, however, the authorities managed to keep television and radio running, anxious to broadcast their version of the events. And the three newspapers, *Al Thawra, Al Jumhuria,* and *Al Qadasiya,* appeared regularly.

Despite the most intensive aerial bombing in history, amounting to over 12,000 air sorties in a week and involving six US aircraft carriers (as many as America would have deployed in case of war with the Soviet Union), the US-led allies had destroyed no more than 41 of Iraq's 700 warplanes (for their own loss of 31), and damaged the élite Iraqi Republican Guard only to the extent of 5–10% of what they wanted to do.[46] The allies quickly improved their air superiority over the enemy, by increasing their daily sorties from 1,200 to 2,000, with Iraq barely able to return to its pre-war daily average of 200 air sorties.

On the other hand, the Iraqis were successfully using (inflatable) dummy tanks and aircraft, and even fake runway craters to confuse the allies who therefore had to bomb Iraqi runways repeatedly. They had also realized that some important airfields were connected to roads serving as auxiliary runways. Iraq's military infrastructure, consisting of reinforced command and control bunkers, dispersal airfields, heavily protected aircraft bunkers and shelters, was much tougher than the Pentagon had reckoned. Its defensive strategy consisted of such tactics as deploying fake warplanes and missile launchers, dispersing munitions, transferring chemical weapons factories to underground sites. Its offensive strategy depended heavily on the use of mobile missile launchers which the allies found extremely hard to locate and destroy. The Iraqis had resorted to using civilian trucks as missile launchers, storing them underground during the daytime, driving them to sites many miles from the bunker at night, and then activating them.

All this was enough, according to Paul Rogers of Bradford University (in England), to frustrate 'US Air Force expectations that six days of intensive bombing would destroy the [Iraqi] air force, ballistic missiles and command system, bringing Iraq to its knees, or at least making an early ground battle for Kuwait an easy option with minimal casualties.' He attributed Iraq's well-preparedness to the premise that it had been readying itself for this type of warfare with Israel for some years. The trigger was the June 1981 Israeli strike against the Iraqi nuclear reactor, with military planning in Baghdad being speeded up after the lull in the Iran–Iraq War from the spring of 1987 onwards. Foreseeing a sudden Israeli air offensive against Iraq's nuclear, chemical and missile manufacturing and research sites in the early 1990s, the Iraqi high command planned on absorbing the initial strike, and then retaliating. This meant a strongly safeguarded command and control system, heavily protected air force, and an arsenal of missiles to be fired from mobile launchers.[47]

Politically, time seemed to be running in Iraq's favour. In Egypt, the only Arab ally of the US where opposition was allowed some freedom of expression, the public mood began to turn pro-Iraqi, especially after Washington's immediate and active assistance to Israel in the wake of the Scud attacks. The Muslim Brotherhood was foremost in fuelling pan-Islamic feelings against the West, while the leftist Progressive Unionist Party, enjoying strong support among workers, called for Egyptians to rally round Iraq. Addressing the Egyptian government, *Al Shaab* (The People), a leading opposition weekly, asked sarcastically whether 'all this destruction being sowed across Iraq' was 'in the name of liberating Kuwait or out of love for the ruling al Sabah family of Kuwait'. Eight opposition parties combined to circulate a mass petition calling for an end to the war. Afraid of the rising sympathy for Iraq (although not for Saddam Hussein) erupting into demonstrations, the government extended school and university holidays and cancelled plans for an anti-Iraq march. It also closed down all tourist sites and museums.[48]

In Syria, despite the repressive, efficient police state run by Assad, ordinary people openly aired their backing for Saddam Hussein. Distrusting Syrian or Western news reports, they turned to the Jordanian radio broadcasts, or even Israel's Arabic news bulletins. To ensure that 'subversive' images did not enter Syrian homes, the government jammed Jordanian television. It held back the information that 19,000 Syrian troops were assembled in Saudi Arabia along with US forces, or that these units had been withdrawn from the area adjacent to the Golan Heights and had not been replaced.[49]

Arguing that the multinational coalition had transgressed the UN mandate, and used the liberation of Kuwait 'as a pretext to destroy Iraq', the Algerian president, Chadli Ben Jadid, said: 'Algeria is at the side of brother Iraq.' In this he had the full backing of the Islamic and other opposition parties. In Morocco the opposition called on the government to withdraw its troops from Saudi Arabia, and called for a national day of fasting on 28 January to show backing for Iraq in the Gulf War. In response, King Hassan of Morocco joined his colleagues in the Arab Maghreb Union to request an urgent meeting of the UN Security Council to discuss the Gulf conflict. In response, the Council met in private, only to reject the North African states' proposal for a debate on the war.[50]

Week Two: 24 January–30 January

During the second week the allies stepped up the daily sorties to an unprecedented 3,000 while the Iraqi air force emerged from its bunkers to attack targets in Saudi Arabia and the Gulf. The early impression engendered by the Pentagon that the allies were carrying out 'surgical strikes' with negligible damage to human life was destroyed when the Pentagon conceded that precision bombs were not being used all the time, that their infra-red sensors were interrupted by rain and fog and smoke, and that not all aircraft were equipped to fire such weapons.

As the allies tried to focus fire on the Iraqi ground forces in and around Kuwait, there was a comparative thinning of bombing raids on Baghdad. Increasingly, the allies were targeting the Republican Guard units in Kuwait and southern Iraq. This élite force, which had evolved out of the Presidential Guard meant to safeguard the president and his palace, was recruited almost entirely from the inhabitants of the Tikrit region and paid twice the salary of ordinary soldiers and given extra perks. During the First Gulf War the force was expanded to a division, and deployed as a reserve to form a last line of defence in case the Iranians managed a breakthrough into the Mesopotamian plain. In October 1983 it was despatched to the Kurdish region to expel the Iranians from Iraqi territory, a task it failed to accomplish. It was sent to the frontlines again in September 1985 and March 1986, when it did better than before. By September 1986 the Presidential Guard consisted of 17 mechanized brigades, 25,000 strong, which were trained to use chemical weapons. It played an important role in frustrating a major Iranian offensive near Basra in early 1987. And in the series of lightning and successful offensives that Iraq undertook in the spring and summer of 1988 to recover its land from the Iranians, it played a crucial role. With a fourfold increase in its size in two years, entry to the force was opened up to almost all Iraqis who had had a college education, with the officer corps still from the Tikrit region and ideologically committed to the Saddam Hussein regime in the form of Baath Party membership. By then the Guard had emerged as a self-sufficient force with its own logistical units and air power.

The end of the First Gulf War saw an expansion of the force, now renamed the Republican Guard. By early 1990 the Guard was estimated to be 120,000 to 180,000 strong. As tension with Israel increased during the spring, Saddam Hussein was believed to have empowered Guard commanders to use chemical weapons and missiles without prior authorization. Given this, and the self-contained structure and equipment of the Republican Guard, the field commanders could devise their own strategy and continue fighting even if they were cut off from the central headquarters. As tension rose in the aftermath of the Iraqi occupation of Kuwait, Saddam Hussein deployed most of the Guard units in Kuwait and southern Iraq, their estimated strength being 120,000 to 160,000. They were believed to be Iraq's mobile force to be used as the strategic reserve – to fill in any holes that the allies might punch in the Iraqi defence line along the Kuwait–Saudi border. Since they had stopped using radio communication, their exact locations remained unknown to the allies. Therefore the Pentagon could not evaluate the effect of its continuous bombing of Iraqi positions in Kuwait with any accuracy.[51]

The other consequence of the allies' concentrating fire in and around the Kuwaiti theatre of operations was the inadvertent creation of an oil slick. From 22 to 24 January the allies bombed two Iraqi tankers, an oil platform (used by an Iraqi hovercraft as a hiding place), and a refinery in Kuwait. Iraq immediately complained to the Security Council about the resulting spillage of oil into the waters of the Gulf.

However, Baghdad seems to have decided to add its share of leaked oil by opening the taps of Kuwait's Sea Island terminal and/or its three loaded tankers still intact. There were military advantages to Iraq: the oil slick could clog the inductors that draw water into ships and – if ignited on beaches or on open water – pose a deadly threat to the attacking allied forces. It could also foul Saudi desalination plants that produced drinking water for the populace, and water for industry. The Bush administration blamed Iraq for deliberately creating the oil slick, describing it as an act of 'environmental terrorism'. In reality, Iraq probably added to the slick as part of its series of tactical probes to test allied forces with a view to disrupting and diverting their military activity, the other parts being the mounting of air raids on Saudi Arabia and attacks on allied targets in the Gulf with Exocet air-to-ship missiles. By 27 January, when the allies claimed to have hit oil facilities in Kuwait with 'smart' bombs to stem the flow, the oil slick was reported to be 35 miles long and 10 miles wide and moving southwards.[52]

Meanwhile, Iraqi Scuds continued to fall on Tel Aviv and Haifa as well as Riyadh and Dhahran, killing and injuring Israelis and Saudis, albeit on a modest scale, with the allies claiming some success in destroying the missiles in mid-air.

By 26 January, 51 Iraqi Scuds had been launched, with 25 directed at Israel and the rest at Saudi Arabia, killing four Israelis and one Saudi, and injuring 212 Israelis and 12 Saudis.[53]

While both Iraq and the allies were getting used to the Scud–Patriot war game, another surprise emerged. On 26 January, according to the National Security Council of Iran, following requests from seven Iraqi military pilots to make an emergency landing in Iran, they had been allowed to land and their planes had been confiscated. 'This policy would be applied to all parties which violate Iran's land, air and sea spaces,' it said. The next day the speaker of Iran's parliament, Mehdi Karubi, added that five passenger aircraft had also sought refuge. General Schwarzkopf disputed the figure, saying that 39 Iraqi aircraft had flown to Iran, and adding that Iran had given assurances that the planes would not be allowed to take off until the war was over.[54]

There were two theories about the event: one suggesting a clandestine agreement between Tehran and Baghdad, and the other claiming a spontaneous positive response by local Iranian commanders, known to be anti-American, to the Iraqi requests. During the next two days, as the number of Iraqi planes taking refuge soared to 100-plus, the explanation of spontaneity could not hold. It was apparent that this was part of Saddam Hussein's plan to save his air force from destruction by allied bombing. But what were the motives of Iran in being part of this plan? It could use them to bargain with Iraq over its compensation claims relating to the Iran–Iraq war. Or it could use them as a negotiating tool with the allies, threatening to release the aircraft if it felt that the allies' conduct of the war threatened to tilt the balance of power in the Gulf against it.[55] Much to the chagrin of the Pentagon, the fleeing Iraqi warplanes could not be intercepted and destroyed by the allied air force because most of them made only short trips across the border from small airfields in northern Iraq. (The White House spokesman said that the Iraqi jets in Iran would be watched continually, and would be destroyed if they left the Iranian sanctuaries.) To maintain a proper neutral stance, Tehran officially protested to Baghdad about its planes arriving in Iran without prior authorization.

On the political front, Mehdi Karubi launched a five-point plan to end the conflict. The plan consisted of: a halt to all military operations; withdrawal of Iraq from Kuwait, and all foreign forces from the region; lifting of the UN embargo against Iraq; stopping of Jewish immigration into Israel; and the establishment of an Islamic committee to oversee the plan.[56] To gain backing for his proposals he despatched a parliamentary delegation to important Muslim countries. As speaker of the Iranian parliament, Karubi did not have executive authority; and as such, his plan lacked an official stamp.

Another major country where differences at the top came to light was France. Defence minister Chévènement resigned on 29 January 1991 on the ground that 'the logic of war is driving us ever further from the objectives established by the UN'. His aides said that he was particularly alarmed that a military offensive authorized by the UN to expel Iraq from Kuwait now appeared aimed at overthrowing Saddam Hussein's regime and decimating much of Iraq. Chévènement represented a pro-Arab, anti-war trend within the government, which President Mitterrand tolerated until the outbreak of the war so as to avoid stirring up latent pacifism in France.[57]

Gianni de Michelis, the foreign minister of Italy, another European country engaged in hostilities in the Gulf, distanced himself from the Anglo-American position of destroying Iraq's military strength. He did so by opting for taking all necessary measures to dislodge Saddam Hussein.

In America, the leader of the anti-Iraq coalition, though, there was no overt sign of differences at the top. The debate was between those in power and their detractors, whose only effective means of expression was through street protest. They mounted demonstrations – primarily under the aegis of the National Campaign for Peace in the Middle East, a coalition of student, religious, labour and human rights groups. Its demonstration on 26 January in Washington drew 75,000 (police estimate) to 150,000 (the organizers' estimate) supporters.

There were similar marches and demonstrations in other major cities. Those participating in the anti-war protest far outnumbered the pro-war demonstrators on the same day. The protesters' main argument was that Americans could best back their armed forces by stopping hostilities which were not in the nation's interest.[58]

As in America, Germany experienced pro- and anti-war demonstrations on 26 January. In Bonn up to 200,000 young Germans marched peacefully, with the organizers making plain that their protest was as much against Iraq's invasion of Kuwait and its missile attacks on Israel as it was against the allied bombing of Iraq. The pro-allies demonstration was comparatively small. There were anti-war marches in Paris and Amsterdam, too.

There were also widespread pro-Iraq demonstrations in Algeria (whose foreign minister, Ghozali, offered proposals for a ceasefire and disengagement of forces in the Gulf), Tunisia and Mauritania as well as in Morocco. On 28 January there was a pro-Iraq general strike in Morocco that was backed by the government, which urged Moroccans to 'observe this day of solidarity with the brotherly Iraqi people'.[59] This extraordinary step by a government which had sent troops to Saudi Arabia showed the depth of pro-Iraqi feelings in the country.

A similar phenomenon manifested itself in Pakistan, a Muslim state which had committed 12,000 troops to the defence of Saudi Arabia. Its military chief of staff, General Mirza Aslam Beg, accused the Western powers of a conspiracy to undermine the Muslim world by encouraging Iraq to invade Kuwait in order to provide them with a justification to start a war, not giving peace attempts enough time to succeed, and now proceeding to destroy Iraq.[60]

'We do not seek the destruction of Iraq, its culture or its people,' President Bush told the National Religious Broadcasters Association on 28 January. 'We don't want to see the country so destabilized that Iraq itself will become a target.'[61]

By then the US and its allies had mounted 24,884 air sorties against Iraq. There was a shift in the choice of targets, with the allies no longer concentrating on airfields so intensively as before, and squadrons of US B-52s, British Tornados, and French Jaguars carpet-bombing the positions of Iraqi troops, particularly the Republican Guard, in Kuwait and southern Iraq round the clock with a view to reducing their effectiveness by 30 to 50% before attacking them on the ground – most probably by mid-February. By the end of the second week of fighting, the allies claimed that their attacks had damaged 11 out of 12 major Iraqi petrochemical facilities, including three refineries, destroyed Iraq's capacity to develop and produce nuclear arms, and reduced its capacity to manufacture chemical and biological weapons by half, and forced the Iraqi high command to abandon centralized control of its air defences within Iraq.[62]

On the other hand, according to 'well placed' US officials' briefing to the *Washington Post*, despite the Pentagon's claims the previous week that all the Iraqi airfields had been 'neutralized', two-thirds were still operational; about a fifth of Iraq's air defence radar, almost wholly taken out in the first week, was back in operation; all of Iraq's military and civilian aircraft, except about 50 destroyed by the allies and another 100-plus transferred to Iran, were safe in concrete and steel bunkers which could only be knocked out by a direct hit from a laser-guided 2,000-pound penetration bomb; most of Iraq's 8,000–9,000 high grade anti-aircraft artillery pieces were intact, and so too were 4,700 of its 5,500 tanks; 22 of the 30 Iraqi fixed Scud missile batteries were still functioning; and Saddam Hussein continued to communicate with his forces through a sophisticated network of command posts, some of them mobile, which used remotely placed antennas far removed from him to evade being located exactly by the allies.[63]

Little wonder that, in an interview with CNN's Peter Arnett on 28 January, Saddam Hussein summed up the military situation thus: 'We have maintained our balance using only conventional weapons', adding that any chance of 'negotiations to end the conflict' was up to Bush. That is, there was no possibility of Iraq surrendering and seeking a ceasefire. In the words of Crown Prince Hassan of Jordan, 'It would be totally dishonourable of Saddam Hussein as the leader of the Iraqi people in the middle of all this to say, "Look, I have been subjected to the most massive military attack in history and now I'm going to raise a white flag".'[64]

As the leader of a single nation involved in a conflict with a coalition of 28 states, Saddam Hussein had the advantage of being, and presenting himself as, clear-minded and firm. This was not the case with America or its president, who not only had to hold together an unwieldy coalition but also to keep the other superpower, the USSR, in line through constant consultations: an unenviable task, as exemplified by the visit to Washington of the newly appointed Soviet foreign minister, Alexander Bessmertnykh, in late January, and his statement before leaving Moscow.

'I have never put in doubt the commitment by the USSR, or the

US . . . to the Security Council resolutions [on Iraq],' Bessmertnykh said on 26 January in Moscow. 'I am concerned [however] there may be a danger of the conflict going more in the direction of the destruction of Iraq, which was not in the spirit of the UN resolutions.' In Washington, following his meeting with President Bush on 28 January, Baker and Bessmertnykh announced at a press conference that the planned superpower summit on 11–13 February was being postponed. The next day, in Moscow, Gorbachev's spokesman, Vitali Ignatenko, repeated Soviet fears that the conflict might escalate from its original objective of expelling Iraq from Kuwait into a broader and more devastating war, and said that the time might be right for a new peace initiative, something the North African and non-aligned nations had been demanding at the UN. Later that day, at the end of three days of talks in Washington, Baker and Bessmertnykh issued a joint communiqué on the Middle East. It stated that 'cessation of hostilities' in the Gulf would be possible only if Iraq made an 'unequivocal commitment' to withdrawing from Kuwait 'backed by immediate, concrete steps' leading to a full withdrawal and compliance with the UN Security Council resolutions. 'Both ministers agreed that in the aftermath of the crisis in the Persian Gulf, mutual US–Soviet efforts to promote Arab–Israeli peace and regional stability, in consultation with other parties in the region, will be greatly facilitated and enhanced.'[65] The overall effect of the communiqué was not only to link the two major crises in the Middle East but also to combine, confusingly, President Bush's pledge to defeat the 'evil tyrant', Saddam Hussein, with his secretary of state's offer of a deal that would keep the Iraqi president in power.

Next day, 30 January, as Israel denounced the statement as recognizing linkage between the Gulf crisis and the Palestinian–Israeli problem, the White House stepped in to reiterate that its policy on Iraq remained unchanged, and that there were no differences between it and the state department. The White House press secretary acknowledged, however, that the timing of the communiqué stemmed 'in large part' from Moscow's fears that Iraq might be destroyed, while the state department explained that Baker's move was designed to head off the prospect of an independent Soviet ceasefire proposal at the Security Council, or its backing for such a resolution by a non-aligned member. A state department briefing to the *New York Times* tried to put the joint communiqué in the context of the hardening of attitudes of the Soviet government in the face of rising nationalism in the three Baltic states: over the previous fortnight, the Soviet troops had shot dead 19 civilians in Latvia and Lithuania; the Soviet authorities had ordered armed soldiers to join police in patrolling all major cities; and President Gorbachev had granted sweeping powers to the police and intelligence services. The meaning of Bessmertnykh's statement in Moscow cautioning the US against destroying Iraq was that if America pressed the USSR on the Baltic issue, the Soviet Union would then back the Gulf War ceasefire proposals being offered by the non-aligned nations at the Security Council. In the event, the US did not publicly press the USSR on the Baltic question, and it succeeded in getting the Soviet foreign minister to commit himself to backing a ceasefire proposal only if it was tied to a total and immediate Iraqi evacuation of Kuwait.[66] Despite this explanation by the state department, there was a revival of informed speculation that Baker, an advocate of a peaceful resolution of the crisis, had been unhappy at the rhetoric of Bush and Hurd, the British foreign secretary, which called for the bringing of Saddam Hussein to 'justice' and stressed the need to cripple Iraq's military machine.

This divergence of views between the two superpowers and the different centres of power in Washington kept Saddam Hussein hopeful of success if only he could manage to withstand the punishment the allies were meting out to Iraq.

On his part he continued to implement the different phases of his overall strategy as planned, the latest phase being to unleash terrorist actions against allied targets. 'Any Iraqi, Arab or Muslim taking part in a commando attack against the nations participating in the barbaric aggression against Iraq, their interests or their allies, will be considered a martyr in the "Mother of All Battles",' said a statement issued by Iraq's Revolutionary Command Council, and broadcast by Baghdad Radio on 27 January. The next day Baghdad Radio threatened President Hosni Mubarak with assassination. 'The Egyptian people, who have a rich legacy of Arabism, struggle and history, have said their word and issued their verdict,' it said. 'They carried out their verdict on his predecessor, [Anwar] Sadat. Hence Hosni's date with death will not be far away.' It added, 'National and Islamic groups are moving to the phase of guerrilla activity to start delivering crushing hits on the interests of America and its allies and make Bush a hostage in his Black House.' Such groups had been active in Turkey and Greece, and had so far attacked 33 American, British and French targets, none of them spectacular, since the outbreak of hostilities. However, the threat of terrorist action was taken seriously both in the Gulf and in America, with the White House using decoy helicopters, and equipping its staff with gas masks, as security around Bush tightened. 'The immediacy of the television war and the threat of terrorism have left people [in the White House] tired and jittery,' reported Maureen Dowd in the *New York Times.* '"During the Vietnam War," a top Bush adviser said about the menace of terrorism, "people never thought there was the remotest chance that the North Vietnamese could actually reach out and touch someone [here]."'67

Following his visit to Basra on 27 January, Saddam Hussein ordered an assault on the port-town of Khafji, 12 miles inside Saudi Arabia, on 29 January. Baghdad claimed that the operation was successful and that its troops, estimated at 1,500 and possessing more than 40 tanks, had seized the town the same day, killing 12 US marines for their own loss of 13 taken as prisoners. The coalition forces tried to regain the town immediately. Fighting went on for three days. Ultimately, the allies recaptured the town, but only after issuing a series of inaccurate statements some of which amounted to lies, as documented by Robert Fisk of the *Independent.*

Fisk pointed out that while Prime Minister Major was declaring on 31 January that Khafji had been retaken, military reports said that the Iraqi troops were still fighting in the streets and had strengthened their position in one part of the town, with Staff Sergeant John Post of the US Marines stating on the morning of 1 February: 'The Iraqis are still in there – maybe two hundred of them.' A news bulletin of the allied troops in Saudi Arabia on 1 February reported 300 Iraqis dead in Khafji, only to amend the figure later to 30. General Schwarzkopf kept referring to Khafji as a village, whereas it is one of the largest towns of Saudi Arabia. The allied reports that 11 marines were killed trying to recapture Khafji were inaccurate. 'They died . . . more than 50 miles away, on the elbow of the frontier where Kuwait juts into Saudi Arabia far to the west of Khafji,' noted Fisk. 'Finally, the two marines taken prisoner in Khafji were not fighting but driving down a narrow street at the moment of the Iraqi attack.'68

The Iraqis were equally guilty of falsification and distortion. On 1 February Baghdad Radio highlighted the reluctance of Arab troops to fight alongside the Americans against Iraq by stating that US troops in Saudi Arabia had killed 'several' Moroccan troops who refused to fight the Iraqis. But Rabat Radio denied the story immediately. More particularly, Baghdad announced the withdrawal of its forces from Khafji on the afternoon of 1 February, but made no mention of its casualties, or of the fact that Saudi and Qatari troops had played a role in bringing about Iraq's withdrawal. Its radio described the outcome of the fighting at Khafji, which resulted in some 400 Iraqis being taken prisoner by the allies, thus: 'The battle with the enemy in the Khafji area, and the successful obstruction of the enemy's counter-offensive, will always be remembered as the gate to victory, the gate to thwarting the will of the devil in the face of the will of the faithful who rely on the will of God Almighty, the all-powerful.'[69]

Week Three: 31 January–6 February

Once Saddam Hussein had decided around 25 January to concede, and publicize, the damage done to the civilian sector of Iraq by the allied bombing, it was only a matter of days before his government would let in Western journalists (whose number had been reduced to two on the outbreak of war) to see the situation for themselves. Their reports provided an account of the impact on the Iraqis of the most intensive bombardment in history.

One of the major conclusions drawn by the Western journalists allowed back into Iraq in late January was that, while the expensive laser-guided bombs were fairly accurate, this could not be said of the 'dumb' bombs. In Diwaniya, for instance, the allied bombers had been trying to demolish a 150-foot-high telecommunications pylon since 17 January. In four raids they had blown the top storey off two hotels and wrecked about 60 small shops in the market, but had left the target untouched. In Hilleh the correspondents visited a children's clinic and a secondary school in a residential area which, said the Iraqi officials, had been hit by allied bombs on 18 and 26 January respectively, the last bombing killing five and injuring 25. In the village of Al Haswa there were three large craters in an area of one-storey houses caused by bombs dropped on 23 January, presumably meant to hit the nearby motorway.[70]

Nor were the Tomahawk cruise missiles as accurate as they had been claimed to be. Of the five Tomahawk missiles, 'looking like black aerial torpedoes', that struck Baghdad on 1 February, one hit houses and shops in Karada, a residential district of Baghdad, and another the nearby Masbah district, causing a deep crater in the road close to the city's largest open-air swimming pool. 'At these two sites I visited there was no sign of military facilities nearby, indicating that the Tomahawks are considerably less accurate than claimed by the allies,' reported Patrick Cockburn of the *Independent*.[71]

However, the Western correpondents' report of what they found at a devastated plant at Abu Ghreib on the outskirts of Baghdad proved controversial. According to the Iraqi officials, it had been 'an infant formula factory' producing milk powder before it was hit by an allied missile. The journalists saw inside the tangle of twisted steel girders and flattened walls milk powder, containers, stationery, and such signs as 'pasteurizing line' to give credence to the Iraqi claim. The Pentagon insisted that the site had been a disguised factory for biological weapons.[72]

Those missiles and bombs which had worked as intended had knocked out the city's communications, water, electricity, and fuel supply systems, with the smoke rising from the damaged Dohra refinery on the outskirts of the capital visible more than 60 miles away. Consequently, there was no electricity and little water available in Baghdad. Water supplies in Basra, the second largest Iraqi city, were cut off on 25 January. Petrol was rationed to 30 litres for 15 days per car, with people often queuing all night at filling stations.

However, it seems that Iraqis had learnt to take much of this in their stride. 'Thirteen days of bombing have bred a certain insouciance among ordinary Iraqis,' reported Patrick Cockburn. 'At Abu Ghreib, on the outskirts of Baghdad, a large street market was operating, and there appeared to be as many people in the streets as before the start of the war . . . There was little of the edginess of the opening days of the war, when the first rounds of anti-aircraft fire would send people running to [air raid] shelters. In the towns of Ramadi, Falluja and Abu Ghreib, about one in five shops were open . . . At Falluja some 350 cars were waiting patiently for petrol. There were also large numbers of people on foot waiting to buy paraffin, which Iraqis use for heating in the cold, wet winter weather . . . [A] sort of normality has appeared. Even two missiles passing over Al Rashid hotel soon after we arrived in Baghdad did not excite the alarm they would have caused two weeks ago.' Food was 'plentiful', with fruit and vegetables on sale in shops. Only about a quarter of Baghdad's four million residents had fled.[73]

The events on the ground had little, if any, impact on the coalition's military planners. They continued their air missions as before, pushing the total to 41,000 by 3 February 1991. The 2,500 air sorties staged on that day included 40 'packages' of 20 or more warplanes at a time aiming their payloads at Iraq's Republican Guard units. The Pentagon claimed that the latest round of allied bombing, using laser-guided penetration bombs, had destroyed the enemy's 68 reinforced aircraft shelters and 31 planes on the ground, the highest number of such 'kills' in a day yet. With this it could claim that it was on its way to upgrading its 'air superiority', which it had enjoyed all along, to 'air supremacy' over Iraq. It had reason to be satisfied with the outcome so far.

So too had those Western politicians who backed the military operations. Support for war was running high in America. After reaching 83% in a poll by the *Washington Post* and ABC News within the first few days of the hostilities, it had stabilized around 75%. In France the corresponding figures in a poll commissioned by *Le Figaro* were 75% and 70%. In Germany 66% backed the allied campaign compared to 50% in a survey conducted during the week when the war erupted. Accordingly, the government decided to increase its financial contribution to the war effort, and despatched missiles and 600 troops to Turkey, a fellow-member of Nato, to help protect it from possible Iraqi attack, an action allowed by its constitution. In Italy, according to the poll published in the Communist daily *L'Unità*, the opposition to war fell from 62% in the first week of January to 46%. But that did not inhibit the Pope from issuing his most forthright spiritual condemnation of those waging the Second Gulf War on Sunday 3 February 1991. He said that the combatants were in breach of the divine law and of the commandment 'that thou shalt not kill', which applied to every person. Spaniards seemed to agree with the Pope. There, anti-war opinion showed no sign of declining: 65% said that the allied troops had no justification for the use of force against Iraq. But the strong anti-war sentiment in Spain had no effect on the government, which acknowledged on 1 February that it had been allowing America's B-52 bombers to use its Moron airbase for raids on Iraq.[74] Indeed, US airbases in Spain continued to play an important role in transporting troops and supplies to the Gulf.

In contrast, just across the Straits of Gibraltar in Morocco, the government, despite its formal membership of the US-led alliance, proved sufficiently sensitive to public opinion to break with its authoritarian tradition and allow an anti-war demonstration in Rabat on 3 February. It drew half a million people. The Moroccan Red Crescent described its appeal for donations to buy tents, blankets and medicine for Iraq as a 'sacred duty'. In Tunisia the ruling party, the Constitutional Democratic Association, continued to organize anti-war demonstrations, making sure, however, that these did not turn into pro-Saddam Hussein marches. In Algeria the powerful opposition party, the Islamic Salvation Front, was in the forefront of organizing pro-Iraq demonstrations, the one on 31 January attracting 60,000 participants.[75] Even tightly run Syria produced its first confirmed report of backing for Saddam Hussein when a number of Islamic groups called on the faithful to confront the 'new Crusader invasion' being mounted by the forces led by 'the infidel America'.[76]

President Mubarak used a visit to Riyadh to reiterate that Egypt and Saudi Arabia had agreed that their forces would not engage in combat inside Iraq. He went on to predict that the war would be over in a month, having earlier put its duration at two weeks. Those who had counted on an early collapse of Iraq had been disappointed. But such a feeling was confined to top leaders, not to ordinary citizens even in cities such as Riyadh. Summing up a general sentiment prevalent there, Judith Miller of the *New York Times* wrote: 'Saudi and Arab diplomats said that in Riyadh, where support for the coalition is strong, many Saudis felt a begrudging respect for the Iraqi leader and enormous relief that he was not crushed in the initial days of the allied invasion.'[77]

Saddam Hussein's stock was of course much higher in cities such as Algiers where the government, aware of the popularity of the Iraqi leader, redoubled its diplomatic efforts to bring about a truce in the Gulf War. Its foreign minister, Ghozali, travelled to Tehran in late January to try to co-ordinate its peacemaking efforts with those of Iran, a country which became increasingly important as the Gulf War continued unabated.

Tehran stuck by its neutrality, with its ambassador to Pakistan declaring that Iran would not allow the tens of thousands of Pakistani volunteers to cross its territory to join Iraq's defence forces.[78] At the same time it pursued a policy of trying to alleviate the suffering of Iraq's predominantly Muslim population by encouraging interested countries to send relief aid, including food and medicine, to them in accordance with UN Security Council Resolution 666 under the supervision of the International Committee of the Red Cross. This was one of the major points conveyed by Iran's foreign minister, Ali Akbar Velayati, to Sadoun Hamadi, Iraq's deputy prime minister, during the latter's two-day visit to Tehran, beginning on 31 January. He also protested to Hamadi for failing to obtain Iran's agreement before sending Iraqi aircraft into Iran. The main purpose of Hamadi's trip was to discuss the implementation of certain clauses of UN Security Council Resolution 598, pertaining to the Iran–Iraq War ceasefire, particularly the one about reparations.[79]

In another important meeting – between Velayati's deputy, Mahmoud Vaezi, and François Scheer, secretary-general of the French foreign ministry, who was in Tehran for consultations on 'ways of finding a solution to the crisis, and on factors that can bring about an end to the conflict' – Iran expressed its views clearly on the allies' conduct of the war. 'We condemn the bombing of residential areas in Iraq and destruction of its economic installations,' Vaezi said. 'Iran is greatly concerned that the allies are overstepping the limits set by the UN Security Council for use of force to drive Iraq out of Kuwait.' Equally significantly, he repeated the Iranian position that it would fight alongside Iraq if Israel joined the fray.[80]

But, with the war already three weeks old, and the military options for Saddam Hussein narrowing – as exemplified by his decision to save his warplanes rather than see them destroyed in an unequal air confrontation, and the failure of his forces to fire Exocet missiles at allied naval targets – there was no need for Israel to join the allies.

The first sign that Baghdad sensed major trouble ahead came on 31 January when its foreign minister, Tariq Aziz, appealed for help from the leaders of the 103-member Non-Aligned Movement, arguing that Iraq was attempting to build a 'new world order' that would protect the Third World. In response, the NAM's secretariat in Belgrade announced that a 15-member committee of the NAM, including Algeria, India, Iran, Venezuela and Yugoslavia, would meet in Belgrade on 11–12 February to begin an initiative to end the Gulf War.

A few days later, on 4 February, a plenary session of the Soviet Communist Party's central committee urged President Gorbachev to 'take the necessary additional steps before the international community and the UN to end the bloodshed [in the Gulf]'. The party's concern stemmed partly from the failure of the allies to win a blitzkrieg against Iraq, leading to fears that if the conflict escalated into a land campaign, Saddam Hussein would be tempted to use chemical weapons. General Stanislav Petrov, commander of the Soviet troops specializing in chemical warfare, told *Izvestia* that Iraq had between 2,000 and 4,000 tons of chemical agents stored at ten or twelve sites, and that the attempts of the allied air forces to destroy Iraq's stocks of chemical and bacteriological weapons had not yet succeeded.[81]

While the Soviets and the Iranians were active diplomatically, there was a surprising silence from the UN secretary-general, which persisted for the first two-and-a-half weeks of the hostilities. This puzzled and angered Iraq. On 1 February, in his second letter to Pérez de Cuellar since the outbreak of war, Tariq Aziz referred to the 'horrendous and deliberate crimes' against the Iraqi people by the 'US–Nato–Zionist alliance', and found it 'strange that nothing had been done about this by the UN secretary-general'. Aziz's letter was broadcast on Baghdad Radio on 4 February.

That day Pérez de Cuellar seized his opportunity when the US state department acknowledged that Jordan had lodged a complaint with it the previous week over the deaths of eight Jordanian truck and tanker drivers resulting from the allied bombing of the Baghdad–Amman highway. 'Jordan is an innocent victim of what is happening,' he said. 'This is something inadmissible, why Jordan has to suffer in a war in which it is not a party. I do deplore these acts.' The state department claimed that the Jordanian trucks had been passing through a 'war zone . . . that has been the source of Scud attacks against neighbouring states'. It alleged that war materiel 'including some related to Scud missiles has been transported in convoy with civilian oil trucks': an allegation that had not been placed before the UN Sanctions Committee chaired by Finland. Responding to US accusations of breaking the UN embargo, Jordan stated that it had informed the UN Sanctions Committee about its oil deal with Iraq, and that since the Committee had chosen to ignore the information, no sanctions-busting was involved. 'The problem for Jordan is that it is an oil-dependent country,' said Crown Prince Hassan in a newspaper interview published in Amman on 6 February 1991. 'Already the Iraqi imports represent less than two-thirds of our requirements.' (Before the crisis the figure was 83%.) Jordan possessed limited oil reserves to counter further economic decline due to the Gulf crisis, which had deprived it of tourism, remittances of expatriate Jordanians working in the Gulf states, and most of its export markets, particularly Iraq.[82] In short, the situation was dire, and not only economically – as a televised address by the Jordanian monarch on 6 February amply illustrated.

Accusing the US-led coalition of killing women and children in its onslaught on Iraq, King Hussein said that the allies intended to 'destroy all the achievements of Iraq and return it to primitive life by using the latest technology of destruction'. He described the Gulf conflict as 'a war against all Arabs and Muslims, and not only against Iraq . . . The real purpose behind this destructive war . . . is to destroy Iraq and rearrange the area, putting it under foreign hegemony.' This, he warned, would be more dangerous to the Arab world than the secret agreement of April 1916 between Mark Sykes and Georges Picot, which carved up the region between Britain and France. 'When Arab and Islamic lands are offered as bases for the allied armies . . . to launch attacks to destroy Muslim Iraq,' he continued, 'any Arab or Muslim can realize the magnitude of this crime committed against his religion and his nation.' Describing his address as 'a cry from a Hashemite Arab to rally all efforts to end this tragedy, to save the Iraqi people from what is planned against them,' he called for an end to the conflict. 'If the war continues, it would only benefit those who covet our land and resources, with Israel at the forefront.'[83] Though King Hussein had elaborated this theme before, there was a marked change in his tone. His earlier despair had been transformed into helpless outrage and foreboding at the wanton destruction of a neighbourly ally and the enhanced strength of the neighbouring enemy, Israel.

Washington responded by declaring that the Baghdad–Amman highway was a 'legitimate' military target, and that US aid to Jordan, amounting to $55 million, was being reviewed. President Bush said that Jordan had 'moved over, way over, into Saddam Hussein's camp'.[84] There was apparently no question of reconsidering the allies' targets.

The bombing of Iraq continued unabated, with the allies announcing a staggering total of 49,000 air sorties, including carpet-bombing swoops by the deadly B-52s, and the firing of 284 cruise missiles in 21 days of a non-stop air campaign. They claimed the destruction of 27 of Iraq's 35 key bridges, the latest target being the Jumuhirya bridge across the Tigris in Baghdad. While the US was one of the nine nations engaged in combat missions against Iraq, it accounted for 84% of the sorties.[85] It had by now not only exhausted all of the prime targets – military facilities and economic infrastructure – but also a majority of its secondary, 'dual-use' targets, consisting mainly of bridges and roads. The Pentagon and its allies had bombed Iraq and Kuwait so severely that they now had considerable difficulty finding suitable targets. 'Accounts of pilots in the field suggest that a law of diminishing returns is fast setting in where air supremacy is concerned,' reported David Beresford of the *Guardian* from Dhahran. 'Pilots of Intruder bombers with a US marine squadron, for instance, report that they are having to "troll" Kuwaiti roads in search of targets.'[86]

Attempts by the Iraqi military to mount any offensive operation, whether on land or sea (as in its attempt to capture Khafji through an amphibious landing) or in the air, were quickly and thoroughly countered, thus leaving Iraq no option but to maintain a totally defensive strategy. Even the firings of its Scuds declined to about one a day. By now the allies had established uncontested supremacy in the air and on the high seas.

Angered and frustrated, the Iraqi government decided on 6 February to sever diplomatic links with America, Britain, Canada, France and

Italy as well as Egypt and Saudi Arabia. The decision was announced on Baghdad Radio. (Iraq had cut its diplomatic ties with Syria in 1980 after the outbreak of the First Gulf War.)

At the same time it showed rising interest in a ceasefire proposal being prepared by Iran in consultation with high Soviet officials in Tehran.

Week Four: 7 February–13 February

By the fourth week the allies were concentrating on destroying Iraq's transport infrastructure of roads and bridges, in order to eliminate logistical facilities for its frontline troops, and softening up the Republican Guard units in Kuwait and southern Iraq.

US officials expressed satisfaction with the conduct of the war, despite conflicting assessments of the effectiveness of bombing – with some reports claiming that allied bombing had reduced the effectiveness of the Republican Guard units by 30%, and others stating that the bombardment had merely forced the Republican Guard units to move from positions along the Kuwait–Iraq border to residential areas in Basra and Kuwait City. The British defence secretary, Tom King, summarized the results of the bombing thus: nuclear research and production capability almost totally destroyed; chemical and biological weapons research and production capacity severely damaged and stocks substantially cut; half of the oil refining capacity and 70% of the lubricant production capacity knocked out (leading to suspension of the sale of petroleum products to civilians from 6 February); national electrical grid disrupted and Baghdad blacked out; transport routes to Kuwait successfully attacked at choke points, repairs hindered and capacity cut by half; international and internal telecommunications severely damaged; and water shortage in Baghdad due to bomb damage (though water supplies as such were not targeted). On the other hand, despite herculean efforts to knock out all of Iraq's 30 fixed Scud missile launching sites, allied photo reconnaissance showed that half of them were still intact. While 135 Iraqi warplanes were reportedly destroyed, an almost equal number, including all of its 24 Sukhoi Su-24 Fencer penetration bombers, had escaped to Iran. Of its 5,500 battle tanks only 600 had been destroyed, and of its 3,500 artillery pieces, only about 400.[87]

There was, therefore, debate in Washington about the next phase of the war, with one faction arguing that the air campaign should

continue for 'at least several more weeks' until, in the words of
William Cohen, a Republican member of the Senate Armed Services Committee, 'we feel the ground casualties will be an absolute
minimum.' The proponents of this strategy as well as others were
unaware that the US Central Command was fast reaching the end
of its plan of 30 days of bombing – and that the list of the targets
in the Mesopotamian heartland of Iraq had been enlarged from the
initial 400 to more than 700. The opposing faction was conscious of
the Saudi insistence that hostilities should end before 17 March, the
onset of Ramadan (the holy month of fasting during which Muslims
are forbidden to bear arms), and the change of mood in the Saudi
kingdom which made possible the wounding by sniper fire of two
US military personnel in Riyadh on 4 February.[88] Aware, also, of
the restlessness in the US army and marine corps, wanting to get
'a piece of the action', it argued that the air campaign had passed
its optimum point, and that ground action was needed to expel the
Iraqis from Kuwait, and crown the conflict with victory.

Unable to decide, Bush despatched Cheney and Powell to Riyadh to
confer with the allied commanders.

The propaganda warfare, too, continued unabated. The allies resorted to bombarding Iraqi troops with leaflets urging them to desert.
But the result was poor. The air drop of some 14 million leaflets up
to 6 February induced 87 desertions by 10 February, indicating that
morale among the 360,000 Iraqis reportedly stationed in Kuwait was
still high.[89]

The Pentagon continually repeated its assurances that it was
doing its utmost to avoid civilian casualties, and described any
such result as 'collateral damage'. 'We are not, not, not, not, not
deliberately targeting civilian casualties, and we never will,' said
General Schwarzkopf on 4 February. 'We are a moral and ethical
people.'[90]

An example of the contrary in the allies' behaviour towards civilian
life was their attack on a bridge across the Euphrates in Nasiriyeh at
3 p.m., when traffic was heavy, killing 47 people and injuring 163.
Iraq resorted to backing up its allegations of air raids on civilians
with pictures of the victims as well as damaged houses, shops,
schools, mosques and churches. Following his visit to Iraq from 2
to 8 February, Ramsey Clark, a former US attorney general, submitted
a report to the UN secretary-general on 12 February. 'In all areas we
visited and all other areas reported to us, municipal water processing
plants, pumping stations and even reservoirs have been bombed,' he

wrote. 'Electric generators have been destroyed. Refineries and oil and gasoline facilities and filling stations have been attacked. Telephone exchange buildings, TV and radio stations, and some radio telephone relay stations and towers, damaged or destroyed. Many highways, roads, bridges, bus stations, schools, mosques and churches, cultural sites and hospitals have been damaged.' Earlier he had told a press conference in New York: 'We are raining death and destruction with our technology on the life of Iraq.' This was borne out by Barton Gellman of the *Washington Post*. His post-war inquiry into the air campaign against Iraq, which had been presented at the time as directed 'solely at Iraq's armed forces and their lines of supply and command' revealed that: (a) some targets were attacked to destroy or damage 'valuable facilities' which Iraq could not replace or repair without foreign assistance; (b) many of the targets chosen in the Iraqi heartland of Mesopotamia were selected to 'amplify the economic and psychological impact of international sanctions on Iraqi society ... and to incite Iraqis to rise against their leader'; and (c) the air force and navy target selectors 'deliberately did great harm to Iraq's ability to support itself as an industrial society'. The damage to Iraq's electrical facilities was so severe that its total output was down to 4% of its pre-war figure. Nearly four months after the conflict, repairs had raised the national power generation to only 20–25% of its pre-war total of 9,000 megawatts – about the level it had in 1920.[91]

On 8 February an Iraqi military communiqué said that the allies had carried out 138 missions against non-military targets on the night of 7–8 February. Little wonder that even the Iraqi Islamic opposition paper *Sout al Iraq* (Voice of Iraq) headlined its editorial on that day: 'The savagery of the civilized nations'. More importantly, Tehran Radio said on 9 February: 'Iran cannot be indifferent to the massacre of innocent Iraqi Muslims and the destruction being inflicted upon Iraq.'

This sentiment was shared by Alexander Byelonogov, Soviet deputy foreign minister, then in Tehran to discuss Iran's peace plan. 'Deliberate destruction of Iraqi residential areas cannot fulfil the tasks set by the UN Security Council resolutions,' he said. (Byelonogov was reflecting the concern of President Gorbachev, about to be aired on Soviet television, that allied military actions were in danger of going beyond the limits of the UN mandate.) After his talks with Iran's foreign minister he announced that Moscow and Tehran had identical views on the need for a swift end to the war.[92] Vsevolod Ovchinnikov, a veteran Soviet commentator, said in the *Pravda* of 8 February 1991,

'I fear that the mission approved by the UN could be transformed into neo-colonial action ... to occupy key positions in the fight for energy resources, thereby ensuring for the American monopolies a dominant position in the world economy.' He added that leading Soviet public figures were urging re-examination of 'the hasty way in which the Americans urged the world community to recognize military interference as the only way, with no alternatives.'

On 7 February, the London-based Kuwaiti newspaper *Sout al Kuwait* published an account of what Western diplomatic sources believed to be the official Iranian peace plan. The peace process would start with an appeal by Ayatollah Ali Khamanei, Iran's Supreme Leader, for a ceasefire. Iraqi forces would then start withdrawing from Kuwait while Tehran sought to 'persuade' the US-led coalition troops to pull out of the region simultaneously. An Islamic peacekeeping force would be despatched to Kuwait to act as a buffer between Iraq and the coalition; and a committee of Islamic notables would study all the disputes, territorial and non-territorial, between Iraq and Kuwait. An Islamic fund would be established to help repair the war damage in the region; and a regional non-aggression pact, covering economic, political and security questions, would be concluded.[93]

Sadoun Hamadi arrived in Tehran on 9 February to convey Iraq's response to the Iranian peace plan. He reportedly told his hosts that while their peace initiatives were 'not at the level that was anticipated in Baghdad' they were being discussed. He expressed his government's objection to the idea of the Iraqi withdrawal from Kuwait while nothing more substantial than an attempt by President Rafsanjani to 'persuade' the Americans and others to leave the region was being offered. As it was, President Bush had sent a letter to Rafsanjani through the Swiss embassy in Tehran saying that the US had 'no plans to stay in the region for long and will quit the region as soon as the crisis is over'. But, as the semi-official *Tehran Times* put it on 7 February, 'Iran cannot rely on Bush's statement.'[94]

Iranian officials were irked by Baghdad's equivocal response to their peace plan as well as its continued rhetoric. 'Iraq and its leader will not make peace with the infidels,' declared Baghdad Radio on 8 February. 'We will affirm day after day that the Iraqis are capable of a showdown and that their struggle and capabilities of confronting the enemies are boundless.'[95]

Yet, undeterred, Iran co-operated with India to produce a six-point peace proposal to be placed before the meeting of 15 foreign ministers of the Non-Aligned Movement in Belgrade on 11–12 February 1991.

The proposal consisted of: a declaration by Iraq of its intention to withdraw from Kuwait; simultaneous cessation of hostilities in the Gulf; establishment of a UN mechanism to monitor the Iraqi evacuation of Kuwait as well as the ceasefire; the UN to lift sanctions against Iraq; the UN to make security arrangements for the Gulf region; and the UN to hold an international conference to resolve the Middle East problems, including the Palestinian issue.[96]

The continued news of Iraqi death and destruction aroused widespread sympathy for Iraq in the Arab world – and even in Turkey where, according to the Tass news agency, Turkish officials agreed with the Soviet deputy foreign minister, Byelonogov, during his visit to Ankara on 9 February, that an end should be put to 'the destruction of Iraq'. The continued refusal of Iraq to bow to the unparalleled might of Western air forces elicited popular admiration for it and its leader, particularly in Morocco, Tunisia, Algeria, Mauritania and Libya, with speakers at public rallies calling for the despatch of troops and materiel to Iraq. Thus pressed, the authorities in Morocco, the only member of the Arab Maghreb Union with its soldiers in Saudi Arabia, revealed that the Moroccan force of 1,200 troops in the Saudi kingdom was performing a purely defensive act of guarding the oil refinery at Safaniya.[97] On 7 February Cairo witnessed its first demonstration against the Gulf War. The government repeated that none of its 35,000 soldiers deployed in Saudi Arabia was involved in fighting.

Even in Saudi Arabia, the centre of allied military activity, public opinion was gradually, but definitely, changing. The main reason was the severity and persistence of the American bombing of Iraq conveyed to Saudis through Cable News Network, a service bought by their government in the course of the Gulf crisis. 'Saudis do not like Saddam Hussein . . . but the seeds of destruction in Iraq are far more powerful and disturbing for them than to a Western audience,' reported Robert Fisk of the *Independent*. 'The Iraqis picking through the wreckage of their homes look much like the Saudis. They speak the same language . . . The civilians wounded in the Baghdad hospital remind them of their own families. Why do the Americans go on bombing?' This troubling question was on the minds of many Saudis. An answer was given to Fisk by a government-appointed religious preacher, who insisted on anonymity. 'We all hate Saddam Hussein,' he said. 'We always thought he was a bad man. But this war is now worse than Saddam. Why has it gone on so long? The Americans are testing their weapons on the Arabs. We are all guinea pigs.'[98] Fearful of the iron hand of the state, most Saudis dared not give vent to such thoughts in public.

Equally, the substantial body of Iraqis who in their heart of hearts blamed their leader, Saddam Hussein, for the death and destruction that was being rained on them by the US-led coalition dared not express their thoughts. This was of course not the case with the exiled Iraqis who opposed the Baathist regime of Saddam Hussein. As the Gulf crisis deepened the disparate opposition came together, thanks mainly to the efforts of the Kurdish nationalists. They persuaded the mainly Shia Islamic groups to drop their traditional antipathy towards the secular segment of the clandestine opposition – Communists, Pan-Arabists and dissident Baathists – and endorse the Damascus Declaration of 17 December 1990. The 17 opposition groups which signed this declaration had agreed to overthrow Saddam Hussein's regime and hold free and fair elections in post-war Iraq. For the present, the Damascus Declaration coalition opposed the US-led war against Iraq, which put it at odds with Syria, the country which spawned it.

The opposition to Saddam Hussein was not the only grouping riven with contradictions. Even the Iraqi regime began to develop a dichotomous personality, with the Iraqi president sounding resolute and hawkish, and his deputy prime minister, Sadoun Hamadi, presenting a compromising stance. On 10 February, while Saddam Hussein (in a speech described as 'historic' by the Iraqi News Agency) was applauding Iraq's resistance to 'the warplanes of shame', and describing the patience of the Iraqi people as 'the force of faith on the front line', Hamadi was telling a press conference in Amman that Baghdad was ready to negotiate an end to the Second Gulf War provided America was excluded from the talks.

Hamadi urged fellow-Arabs to pressure their governments to impose an economic and diplomatic boycott on the members of the US-led coalition and reject the UN Security Council resolutions on Kuwait which, he said, were 'dictated to the Council by the US' and were 'a cover for blatant aggression on Iraq and the Arab nation'.[99]

Although not an Arab state, India, a non-permanent member of the UN Security Council, played an active diplomatic role. On 9 February it strongly opposed the allied military operations against Iraq, and urged the Security Council to ensure that these did not go beyond what was provided in Resolution 678. Two days later it sought the backing of the foreign ministers of the 15 non-aligned nations, meeting in Belgrade, for a six-point peace plan it had formulated along with Iran. It failed to gain the backing of the Non-Aligned Movement because of disagreement among the conferees on the issue of linking peace in the Gulf with the holding of an international conference on the

Middle East, one of the points in its plan. Instead, the meeting agreed to send two missions – one to Baghdad and the other to Washington and the Western capitals allied to it – to spearhead a Non-Aligned 'action programme' for peace in the Gulf.[100]

At the UN Security Council, the efforts of the non-aligned members succeeded when at their behest the Council agreed to meet on 14 February to discuss the war. By then Pérez de Cuellar had publicly countered the charge of being party to the attainment of the objectives of the US-led coalition which went beyond the liberation of Kuwait by explaining that the Security Council had handed over control of the war to the three Western permanent members – America, Britain and France – and that he only learned of the military operations after their implementation. He added that he was most concerned about the loss of human life because 'as the secretary-general of the UN, I consider myself head of an organization which is first of all a peaceful organization, and secondly a humanitarian organization.'[101] However, the attempts of Yemen and Cuba to hold a debate on the war failed. Afraid that an open debate, carried live by television networks, would bolster rising criticism from the specialists as well as the public that the allies' war operations were going far beyond the terms of Resolution 678, and fracture the fragile alliance, Washington and London insisted on closed-door sessions, and won. It was the first time in fifteen years that the Security Council had decided to debate an issue behind closed doors, leading to speculation that the US and Britain had something to hide from public scrutiny.

In fact from 10 February the allies had been admitting to only one-fifth to a quarter of the daily total of 2,400 to 2,800 air sorties aimed at targets in the Kuwaiti theatre of operations. The extent and severity of allied bombing in southern Iraq was reported by the correspondents of the (Iranian) Islamic Republic News Agency based in Ahvaz and Bostan, and broadcast by Iranian radio. 'The US-led allied jet fighters bombed Basra's oil refinery and petrochemical complex for the third time since the war broke out,' they said. 'The US-led allied forces bombarded Kahla, Amara, Qala Salah, Uzayr, Aziziya, Qurna, Nashwa, Tanuma, Shuaiba, Fao, Abu Khasib, Nasiriyeh and Zubair in southern Iraq on Wednesday night and Thursday morning [13–14 February]. The sound of missile and bomb explosions are heard in most southern Iranian cities bordering Iraq including Susangard, Bostan, Hoveizeh, Shush, Khorramshahr and Abadan. The attacks are so severe that window panes are shaken in most of these [Iranian] cities.'[102]

What the allies did not disclose was that they had entered the final phase of their air campaign and begun the initial phase of the ground campaign by punching a few safe corridors through the four-tier Iraqi defence lines along the Kuwaiti–Saudi border. This was being achieved by a liberal use of Fuel Air Explosives (FAEs), which the US had used on a large scale in Vietnam, and 15,000-pound concussion bombs, which exploded just above ground creating overpressure of 1,000 lbs/square inch (or 33 times the normal atmospheric pressure) to clear minefield and barrier areas as well as destroy berms and bunkers.[103] On 11 February, between 4 a.m. and 7 a.m. local time, allied forces bombarded Iraq and Kuwait in the largest combined land-sea-air operation to date. During the night of 11–12 February allied air strikes hit the ministries of justice and local government near the densely populated Haifa Street, a business and residential route in the city centre of Baghdad, which was also damaged. According to the Baghdad correspondent of the (Iranian) Islamic Republic News Agency, the allied bombing levelled 15 houses and 100 shops near the justice ministry.

In short, the latter half of week four of the war marked the preparatory period for launching a fully-fledged ground offensive by the allies, planned for 14–15 February, a moonless night. As expected, nothing was being said officially, with President Bush declaring after his meeting with Cheney and Powell on 11 February, following their trip to Riyadh, merely that 'I am very satisfied, having heard their briefing, at the progress in the war.'

On 12 February Baghdad Radio broadcast a military communiqué which reported 30 allied air sorties on civilian targets, including a maternity hospital and a nursery, and – breaking with convention – reported 96 raids on Iraqi military targets in Kuwait and southern Iraq. It described the invaders as 'barbarians' who 'attack innocent, defenceless civilians and shell mosques, hospitals, residential areas, bridges and everything related to civilian life with unprecedented baseness'. A day earlier, Abdullah Fadel Abbas, Iraq's minister for religious affairs, had stated that 'thousands' of Iraqi civilians had been killed or wounded; a big jump from the official figures of 1,397 civilian casualties so far. He added that several mosques and churches had been damaged, as well as 80 homes in the Shia holy cities of Najaf, Karbala and Samarra.[104] However, the single most devastating attack by the US air force on Iraqi civilians was yet to come.

On 13 February at 4 a.m. local time, Iraq announced that more than 400 people had been killed in an allied air attack on a civilian air raid shelter in the Amiriya district of Baghdad. 'The bunker that was attacked last night was a military target, a command and control centre that fed instructions directly to the Iraqi war machine, painted and camouflaged to avoid detection, and well documented as a military target,' said Marlin Fitzwater, the White House press secretary. 'We don't know why civilians were at this location, but we do know that Saddam Hussein does not share our value for the sanctity of life ... Time and again he has shown willingness to sacrifice civilian lives and property that further his war aims.' He implied that Saddam Hussein had moved civilians to the bunker. [105] The incident caused a shudder of horror not only in the Arab world but also in Europe. The complacency with which most Europeans had accepted the Pentagon's statements about 'surgical strikes', which at worst caused minimum 'collateral damage', was severely jolted.

Summing up the feeling prevalent in pro-Iraq countries of the Arab world, the state-run radio in Tunisia said, 'The ugliness of the aggression of the US and its allies against Iraq today reached new heights.' In neighbouring Algeria the official news agency described 'this massacre committed today against our people in Iraq' as 'one of dozens of massacres that have been aimed at our Arab nation'. Jordanian television transmitted a film of burnt bodies and crying, hysterical relatives, and following its regular late news programme, broadcast a documentary focusing on civilian Iraqi casualties entitled, 'Does Might Make Right?'[106]

Week Five: 14 February–20 February

The fifth week of the war opened with reactions to the US bombing of Baghdad's civilian shelter, with Washington on the defensive and the Iraqi government using the incident as a cover to make its first offer of withdrawal, albeit conditional, from Kuwait.

Eye-witness accounts suggested that an American F-117 Stealth bomber had fired two 2,000-lb delayed-fuse, laser-guided bombs, one of which went down a ventilation shaft past a ten-foot-thick reinforced ceiling and detonated inside the bunker, which could accommodate up to 1,600 people, while the other bomb hit a spot two yards away from the ventilation shaft. The estimate of deaths which started with 400 finally climbed to 1,000-plus, the majority of them women and children. The next day, 14 February, thousands of Iraqis marched behind a truck piled high with the coffins of the victims of the bombing. Distraught women in black beat their breasts in distress while men in military uniforms wept and fired guns in the air. The mourners carried placards denouncing President Bush as a coward. 'After ... four weeks of fierce, large-scale aerial attacks, the leaders of the aggression have reached the brink of despair and frustration,' commented Baghdad Radio. Iraq's information minister criticized the UN secretary-general for being silent on 'the crimes of the Americans and their allies'.[107]

Declaring a three-day period of mourning in Jordan for the Iraqi victims, King Hussein urged an immediate ceasefire and the despatch of a fact-finding mission to Baghdad by the UN Security Council. Jordan's senate called on the monarch to abandon neutrality so that Jordanians could stand by 'our Iraqi brethren' with deeds, not just words. In Tunisia, the president announced a day of mourning, and his foreign minister condemned the bombing as 'this barbaric act'. The Algerian government called for special prayers for the victims. 'The Western–American aggression against the Iraqi people yesterday reached the paroxysm of terror and barbarism,' said the National Liberation Front, Algeria's ruling party. 'US aviation deliberately committed this crime to terrorize the civilian population.' The Sudanese foreign minister stated that the 'hideous, bloody massacre' proved the objective of the allies was to 'destroy the Iraqi people'.[108]

Iran's neutrality did not bar its foreign minister from condemning the attack on the Baghdad shelter and offering to treat Iraqi victims in Iranian hospitals in co-ordination with the International Committee of the Red Cross. He said that the situation in the Persian Gulf had surpassed the allies' UN Security Council mandate. 'The destruction of Iraq and Kuwait, as well as the economic resources of the region, is hardly compatible with the maintenance of regional peace and security,' he added.[109]

More worryingly for Washington, Spain combined its demand for an international inquiry into the Baghdad shelter bombing with a call that the allies should halt air attacks against Baghdad and other Iraqi cities, and concentrate their bombing on the Kuwaiti zone of operation. This made sense, particularly with regard to Baghdad. Allied pilots reported bombing the same targets in the capital five or six times, even after the structures had been almost destroyed. Yet the Pentagon continued to direct 150–200 sorties daily at the city.

The Bush administration was reportedly 'horrified and dismayed' by the television pictures of the bombed Amiriya shelter, fearing the adverse political impact on the rest of the world. It took to explaining how an error might have been made, in the process divulging what until then would have been considered 'classified information'. US intelligence analysts were quoted as saying that it was impossible for any target to be photographically monitored for more than a short time each day, because only a limited number of satellites were available and they had to orbit at close range to record the information needed. The time for watching targets in Baghdad was put at about two-and-a-half hours a day. (This ran counter to the impression which had been created hitherto, that all of Iraq and Kuwait was under continuous observation and nothing escaped the all-seeing US eyes in the sky.) What had been thought to be a military target might have changed its nature without being noticed by the time of being hit. This meant, simply, that until then the Pentagon had treated about 100 shelters used (according to it) for both civilian and military purposes as legitimate targets. After this blunder, it 'suggested' that it 'might' take these 'dual-purpose bunkers' off its target list.[110] However, the root of the problem did not lie in the shelters. It had to do with the American decision, taken at the very top, to assassinate Saddam Hussein. US intelligence officials had drawn up lists of potential targets connected with him, his family, and his close associates, particularly the members of the Tikriti clan. The most plausible reason for bombing the Amiriya bunker was a tip-off from an American agent to US intelligence that Saddam Hussein was sleeping there. (There was a parallel here to what had happened during the 1982 Israeli invasion of Lebanon. Intent on assassinating Yasser Arafat, the Israelis bombed an apartment block because of a tip-off from their agents that he would be there.) In a briefing to *Newsweek*, 'a senior allied Gulf War planner', citing intelligence sources, said that Saddam Hussein had been spotted at the Amiriya bunker at 'the beginning of February'; that the bunker was used by many senior military commanders and Baath Party officials and their families; and that 'leadership targets' were still high on the air campaign's objectives.[111]

As far as the American public was concerned, the Pentagon need not have bothered with explanations. A *Washington Post*–ABC News poll, published on 18 February, showed that eight out of ten Americans believed Bush's assertion that the shelter was a military target, and the same proportion blamed the Iraqi government for the deaths of the civilians. This happened in a context where a large majority backed Bush's handling of the Gulf crisis, more specifically the war – and not only in the US. In France, 64% expressed satisfaction with Bush's decisions, and the figure in Britain was 69%, up from 49% a month earlier.[112]

Actually, the explanatory exercise was directed primarily at Saudi Arabia, where there was rising anxiety that Washington wished to decimate Iraq as enthusiastically as it intended to liberate Kuwait. 'There is a great deal of feeling among the Saudis in the MODA [Ministry of Defence and Aviation] because of the Baghdad bombing,' said a US military source. 'They are distressed over the continued bombing . . . concerned that Iraq should not be destroyed – they are thinking of the post-war era – and the Saudis didn't want to go along with the Washington statement . . . [that the Baghdad shelter was a "legitimate military target"].'[113]

Saudi discomfiture contrasted with the almost callous response of President Mubarak. 'I am sorry to see civilians dying but, unfortunately, these things happen sometimes in war,' he said. He attacked Saddam Hussein for making 'propaganda hay from the corpses of his citizens'. Damascus Radio, similarly, blamed the Iraqi leader's 'arrogance and stubbornness' for the 'catastrophe'.[114]

The Amiriya shelter incident came at a time when Saudi Arabia, acutely aware of the approaching holy month of Ramadan, was growing impatient about the staging of the land offensive against Iraq. General Ahmad al Baheri, commander of the Royal Saudi Air Force, most probably privy to the fact that the US had planned a bombing campaign of 30 days' duration, was quoted as saying, 'We should get on with the ground war.' (The moonless night of 14–15 February and the next few nights were ideal for launching a land offensive.) Noting the Pentagon statements that the US forces in the region had reached 515,000 soldiers, sailors, marines and air force personnel, that the allies had destroyed 27 of the 31 main bridges on the supply route from Baghdad to Basra and Kuwait, and that they had knocked out 1,300 of Iraq's tanks and 1,100 of its artillery pieces, Riyadh could not understand the delay in mounting the land offensive.[115]

Saudi authorities and Pentagon officials were having considerable difficulty in defusing the rising frustration of many of the 1,200 Western correspondents, including 800 Americans, operating mostly from Riyadh and Dhahran. They had no choice but to rehash reports sent by officially selected pools of journalists from the front: an exercise they found increasingly demeaning. Time and again Pentagon press officers staged events for the benefit of television cameras. At other times they stopped on-camera interviews because they disapproved of what was being recorded. If and when they let reporters alone to talk freely to the troops, other problems arose. 'If the troops' frank comments angered senior Pentagon officials, reporters' access immediately suffered,' wrote James LeMoyne of the *New York Times*. 'The one article the Pentagon officials said they definitely did not like included quotes from army enlisted men who criticized President George Bush and who, after two months in the desert, questioned the purpose of their being sent to fight and perhaps die in Saudi Arabia. The day the article was published, the Pentagon press officer intimated it might well scuttle the interview with General Schwarzkopf. The interview was later cancelled with no explanation other than that the general's "schedule has changed".' An officer of the unit whose members had been quoted told LeMoyne that senior commanders had demanded 'explanations' of the soldiers' critical views. 'For the next six weeks almost all print news reporters were denied visits to army units,' reported LeMoyne.

On 10 February US military authorities picked up Chris Hedges of the *New York Times* just as he had finished talking to shopkeepers in a Saudi town fifty miles from the Kuwaiti border, detained him in Dhahran for a few hours, and confiscated his press credentials for attempting to report outside the official media 'pools' set up by the US defence department. This led to a row between W. R. Apple, head of the Dhahran bureau of the *New York Times*, and Colonel Bill Mulvey, the Pentagon official dealing with the press, with Apple accusing Mulvey of hindering his newspaper from covering the war. Leaving aside specific instances, the general complaint of the reporters, American and other, was that they had been denied access to prisoner-of-war camps, B-52 pilots, Awacs reconnaissance planes, battleships, military chaplains and hospitals.[116]

While the Pentagon had taken to exaggerating its success in destroying Iraq's infrastructure, it was coy about the success it was having in clearing minefields and blasting away berms, bunkers and clusters of trucks and armoured vehicles along the Kuwaiti–Saudi border with a liberal use of Fuel Air Explosives and BLU-82 'daisy cutter' concussion bombs. However, the Iraqi government seemed to have realized that the balance was shifting rapidly against it on land even before the US-led alliance had mounted its ground assault. It therefore decided to use the Amiriya shelter bombing as a cover to assume a placatory stance.

Following an overnight session Iraq's Revolutionary Command Council issued a statement on 15 February 1991 which departed from its hitherto uncompromising stand. 'In appreciation of the Soviet initiative conveyed by [Primakov], the envoy of the Soviet leadership', and in compliance with President Saddam Hussein's initiative of 12

August, the RCC declared 'Iraq's readiness to deal with Security Council Resolution 660' with the objective of 'reaching an honourable and acceptable political solution, including [Iraqi] withdrawal'. It then outlined its conditions. 'A pledge by Iraq regarding withdrawal' had to be linked to the following: a ceasefire; abrogation of Security Council Resolutions 661, 662, 664, 665, 667, 669, 670, 674, 677 and 678; the forces of the US-led coalition to withdraw from the region along with the weapons and equipment they brought (including weapons and equipment supplied to Israel 'under the pretext of the crisis in the Gulf') within a month; Israel to withdraw from Palestine and other Arab territories in accordance with the resolutions of the UN Security Council and General Assembly (with an Israeli failure to do so to be penalized by the Security Council in the same way as was Iraq's failure to withdraw from Kuwait); Iraq's 'historical rights' to be guaranteed on land and at sea in full in 'any peaceful settlement'; the nationalist and Islamic forces of Kuwait to participate in 'the political arrangement' for Kuwait to be agreed. Secondly, those countries that participated in or helped finance the 'aggression against Iraq' should undertake to rebuild what the aggression had destroyed ... without Iraq being burdened with any financial liability. Thirdly, all the debts of Iraq and other regional states harmed by the 'aggression' should be cancelled. Fourthly, Gulf countries, including Iran, should be left alone to undertake the necessary security arrangements 'without any foreign interference'. Finally, the Gulf region should be free of foreign military bases and 'any form of foreign military presence'.[117] Popular reaction to the RCC communiqué in Iraq was enthusiastic, with Iraqis firing rifles in the air and shaking hands to celebrate the statement, which they mistakenly saw as signalling the end of the war.

President Bush responded swiftly. Describing the Iraqi offer as 'a cruel hoax', he rejected it. 'Not only was the Iraqi statement full of unacceptable old conditions, but Saddam Hussein has added several new conditions,' he said. 'There is another way for the bloodshed to stop and that is for the Iraqi military and the Iraqi people to take matters into their own hands to force Saddam Hussein, the dictator, to step aside, and to comply with the UN resolutions, and then rejoin the family of peace-loving nations.' He stressed that 'Our differences are with Iraq's brutal dictator.' This blatant call for the overthrow of a head of a state stemmed from Bush's conviction that the current situation was the result of the 'evil work' of a single individual: Saddam Hussein. He had personalized a complex, international conflict, to an unprecedented extent, and taken to routinely calling the Iraqi president 'that guy', 'that brutal dictator', 'that lying s.o.b. [son of a bitch]' and so on.[118] Such an assessment ignored the historical fact that Saddam Hussein had been moulded by the Baathist regime in Iraq as much as he had moulded it, and that there was symbiosis between the leader and the system, the two interacting with each other.

Once again the American president had made important policy statements without consulting his partners in the coalition. Sir David Hannay, British ambassador to the UN, expressed his displeasure at Bush's hasty response to a senior US official. Another Western diplomat at the UN described Bush's statement as 'blatant interference in the affairs of a [foreign] country'.[119]

However Cairo, dependent on the US for its economic survival, was quick to follow the footsteps of Bush. It described Saddam Hussein's offer as 'a propaganda tool' to give him room to manoeuvre, to create 'confusion in the Arab [city] streets' so that he could escape a military defeat with 'a political victory'.[120] Equally swift was the response of Kuwait. Iraq's offer did not deserve to be taken seriously, it stated. 'The overriding fact is that Iraq has to unconditionally withdraw from Kuwait without bargaining,' said Abdullah Bishara, the Kuwaiti secretary-general of the Gulf Co-operation Council.[121]

Other Arab countries noticed, approvingly, the linkage between Iraq's evacuation of Kuwait with Israel's evacuation of Arab lands in Palestine, Syria and Lebanon. His original airing of this idea within a fortnight of his invasion of Kuwait had been seen as a cynical move. But now, after suffering terrible loss of life and property in Iraq from four weeks of non-stop US bombing, his claims of standing up for Palestinian rights seemed reasonable to most Arabs in the street. King Hassan of Morocco, a member of the US-led alliance, told a cabinet meeting that Iraq's statement was a 'positive step along the path to a just peace in the region,' and that for a peaceful settlement to be durable it must be based on 'the Iraqi people's dignity, and not their humiliation, and respect for their territorial integrity.' Positive reactions to the Iraqi offer also came from Tunisia, Algeria and Jordan.[122]

Iran welcomed Baghdad's move, with President Rafsanjani describing Iraq's 'readiness' to evacuate Kuwait as 'a beginning of the solution of the region's problems'. The semi-official *Tehran Times* criticized the West's 'outright rejection' of the Iraqi proposal as 'unbearably harsh'. Tehran had by now emerged as a key player in the diplomatic field, with Iraqi leaders using it as a staging place for their important trips to Moscow. It had come to co-ordinate its peace moves with the

Soviet Union – which, having failed to induce an Arab solution to the crisis, had now switched to striving for a regional settlement by including Iran as an active partner – and to stress the importance of its role. 'Iraq trusts Iran much more than Russia,' said a senior Iranian diplomat in Tehran. 'It needs the Kremlin because it has a right of veto at the UN Security Council. But at the same time it suspects the Russians of using the Gulf War as a bargaining card against the US in relation to the internal situation in the USSR, particularly the Baltic problem. This is not so with Iran, as our assistance for the Iraqi people is genuine, based on humanitarian, religious, historical and cultural considerations.'[123]

But, unlike Iran, the Soviet Union could claim unbroken friendship with Iraq over a period of three decades. Now its leaders lost no time in criticizing Washington for rejecting the Iraqi offer which, in the words of foreign minister Bessmertnykh, 'opened up a new stage in the development of the conflict'. Moscow had become the hub of diplomatic activity on the Gulf conflict, with Primakov engaged in shuttle diplomacy which took him to Baghdad on 11 February. During his meeting with Saddam Hussein, the Iraqi leader referred to the 'US and allied crimes' perpetrated 'under the cover of UN Security Council Resolution 678, endorsed by the USSR', and reminded him that the Soviet Union had 'a legal, political and moral responsibility, despite differing Iraqi–Soviet perspectives on the Gulf, to act to stop the crimes against Iraq and to stop the US manipulating the UN as a vehicle for imperialist objectives'.[124] Such an exhortation was also being directed at the Kremlin by orthodox Communists and military leaders. On 12 February the *Sovyetskaya Rossiya* stated that Moscow's decision to join the UN Security Council members against Iraq had ended 'the USSR's existence as a superpower and alienated the Kremlin's allies in the Middle East and Third World', and that this would underline American–Israeli hegemony in the Gulf 'for decades'. Next day the political directorate of the Soviet armed forces denounced the US-led military campaign against Iraq. It said that its 'real goal' was the killing of civilians and the destruction of Iraq. According to General Vladimir Lobov, the last commander of the Warsaw Pact troops, the US campaign posed a threat to the Soviet territory in Transcaucasia – Azerbaijan, Armenia and Georgia. Each day of the war increased the danger of its spilling over the southern Soviet borders. 'The fire of war is always dangerous, and wars themselves are not always predictable,' said General Vladimir Litvinov, first deputy commander of the anti-aircraft defences.[125]

Contrary pressures were applied on the Kremlin by the pragmatists within the Communist Party and outside, and by such affluent countries as Saudi Arabia and Kuwait, ready to buy Soviet diplomatic backing for a price. Not surprisingly, Kuwait's foreign minister, Shaikh Sabah al Sabah, met Gorbachev in Moscow on 14 February to urge him to stay firm in his demand for the full implementation of the Security Council resolutions by Iraq.

On the eve of his meeting with Tariq Aziz and Sadoun Hamadi on 18 February, Gorbachev summed up the Soviet position thus: 'It is important to avoid the tragedy of destroying Iraq as a state, of dismembering its territory, to say nothing of human deaths.'[126] Their talks went well. The Iraqi officials left for Baghdad, via Tehran, with a peace plan offered by the Soviet leader. The Iranian president, the third member of the Iraq–USSR–Iran triangle, expressed optimism.

Gorbachev forwarded his peace proposal to Bush, urging confidentiality. Bush was once again swift to respond. Without divulging the contents of the Gorbachev plan, he left little doubt as to his reply. 'Let me just reiterate, as far as I'm concerned, there are no negotiations,' he said. 'The goals have been set out. There will be no concessions . . . I've been frank with him [Gorbachev] on this – while expressing appreciation for his sending it [his peace plan] to us, it falls well short of what would be required.' In his telexed response to Gorbachev, sent on 19 February, Bush outlined minimum conditions for a truce: Iraq's withdrawal to happen *before* a ceasefire; the pull-back to be finished within four days (thus compelling Iraq to abandon most of its heavy military hardware in Kuwait); immediate release of all prisoners of war; restoration and recognition of the al Sabah regime in Kuwait by Baghdad; payment of reparations to Kuwait by Iraq; and continuation of the UN embargo even after the Iraqi withdrawal. Bush's virtual rejection of the Gorbachev plan was to receive endorsement by Britain and France, both of which insisted that the Iraqis must leave behind their heavy weaponry in Kuwait, and that toppling the present Iraqi regime was 'a matter of public safety and regional security' – but not by Italy, which backed the Soviet plan. Equally importantly, King Fahd said that there could be 'no settlement without an unconditional withdrawal, and making Saddam Hussein accountable for the losses inflicted upon Saudi Arabia.'[127]

If the requirement was Iraq's compliance with Security Council Resolution 660, it was now being offered by Saddam Hussein unconditionally – as was to be revealed by Iran's foreign minister. Following his meeting with Tariq Aziz in Tehran on 19 February, Velayati said: '[Aziz] told me, "We are determined to abide by that resolution [660]"

... The most important element in that resolution is the total and unconditional withdrawal from Kuwait.' He added that Aziz had conceded that what had formally been described as 'conditions' for Iraqi withdrawal, including the departure of allied forces from the region and evacuation by Israel of Arab territories, were not conditions but 'matters that could be addressed'.[128]

But apparently Bush had set his sights much higher than the Security Council resolution: his call on 15 February for the overthrow of Saddam Hussein said as much. The fact that Gorbachev was playing the peacemaker showed that he was willing to live with the Iraqi leader and his regime. An immediate ceasefire would leave Saddam Hussein in power with most of his military machine intact; he would emerge a political hero in the Arab and non-Arab segments of the Third World, for standing up to Washington, and become the rallying centre of anti-American and anti-Zionist forces in the region and outside. Bush reckoned that acceptance of a truce along the Soviet lines, guaranteeing Iraqi territorial integrity and sovereignty, would damage US relations with Saudi Arabia and Kuwait over regional security, and with Israel over the Palestinian issue. The American president needed not a Soviet-brokered, messy peace, but a clear-cut victory, if only as compensation for having compromised traditional US policy towards Syria, earned the anger of Pakistan and Yemen, and made promises of additional aid to Egypt and Turkey.

Such hawkish advisers to Bush as the increasingly influential deputy chief of the National Security Council, Robert Gates – a sceptic concerning Soviet perestroika who pointed to Gorbachev's use of force in suppressing nationalist movements in the various Soviet republics, and the rising prominence of the military and the state security police – now viewed the Gorbachev plan as a ploy to deny Washington a military victory in the Gulf. Outside the White House there were some dovish politicians who chose to speak out. Democratic Congressman Lee Hamilton advised the Bush administration not to press the war to the point of destroying the post-war 'New World Order' it was claiming to be fighting for. 'There is a lot at risk in US–Soviet relations, in US–Arab relations and in US–Europe relations if we pass up a real opportunity to end this war,' he said. The state department let it be known that an unconditional Iraqi withdrawal was at least worth exploring, explaining that the post-war guarantees to Iraq, given in the Gorbachev plan, were couched as Soviet promises and not as allied concessions. Then there were others, such as Senator Bob Dole, who argued that given the outstanding success of the air

campaign a ground assault was unnecessary.[129] In this debate the view
that prevailed was the one which perceived Gorbachev's peace move
as emanating from his decision to placate his hardline military leaders
combined with a calculation that even if it failed it would win back
some of Moscow's lost credibility in the region, particularly among
the radical Arab states.

The USSR was angered by Washington's accusation that it was
breaking ranks with the coalition against the Iraqi occupation of
Kuwait. It argued that there was nothing in the Security Council
resolutions to justify the dismemberment of Iraq or the overthrow
of Saddam Hussein, and that Gorbachev's peace plan had only put
the well-known elements of the UN resolutions in a more attractive
light. The Soviet foreign ministry referred to the two major elements
of the joint Baker–Bessmertnykh statement of 30 January: Iraq would
be offered a ceasefire if it made an 'unequivocal commitment' to
leave Kuwait; and once the crisis was over, the US and the USSR
would activate 'their joint efforts, in contact with other parties, to
promote peace between Arabs and Israel'. The unease in the Kremlin
with the hawkish stance of Washington was shared widely. 'One gets
the impression that someone has been blinded by the idea of revenge
against Saddam Hussein ... that the [US] military is not inclined
to stop [the war], whatever the success achieved by the politicians
and diplomats,' wrote *Pravda*, the Communist Party newspaper, on
19 February 1991.[130]

With no let-up in the ferocity of the US-led alliance's bombing
campaign, leading Soviet Communists, civilian and military, began
speaking out strongly against Washington's policy. 'The language of
guns, and death-dealing B-52 bombers, is something we have been
familiar with for a long time,' said Marshal Viktor Kulikov, a senior
adviser at the defence ministry, in an interview with the *Rabochaya
Tribuna* on 19 February. 'It has nothing to do with the "new thinking"
which the Americans applauded warmly but did little in a concrete
way to support.' The comments a few days later by Dan Quayle and
Dick Cheney that the nuclear option was still 'open' for the US in
the Gulf (against the background of reports that American warships
and submarines in the region carried nuclear weapons) – denounced
by Tass as 'reckless and ill-considered' and which could lead to 'very
dangerous military and political consequences throughout the world'
– further underlined the fears of the Soviet military. Small wonder that
Marshal Kulikov was backed by the *Krasnaya Zvezda*, which accused
the US-led coalition in the Gulf of exercising military force in the

Middle East to the extent that it threatened the East–West disarmament process. It was 'alarming', said the defence ministry daily on 19 February, that Nato was improving its military structure in southern Europe as a result of the preparations for the Gulf War, and had 'put in doubt all that had been achieved in the sphere of disarmament on the continent of Europe and in the world at large.'[131]

While the two superpowers were engaged in a diplomatic game, Iraq was under continued military pressure, with the allied air missions totalling 86,000 in the five weeks of fighting. After having lied about the number of war victims, Iraq released the true figures in a roundabout way. On 19 February, during Sadoun Hamadi's visit to Tehran, a local newspaper, *Jumhouri-ye Islami* (Islamic Republic), quoted him as saying that in the first 26 days of the Gulf War (i.e. until 12 February) the allied bombing had killed 20,000 Iraqis and injured 60,000, and caused estimated damage of $200 billion to Iraq's infrastructure. At 32,500 allied bombing sorties (amounting to half of the total 65,000 air missions until 12 February), this amounted to about 2.5 casualties per bombing mission, a credible figure.[132] These losses, combined with the success that the allies were having in establishing safe corridors through the Iraqi defence lines, led the RCC to decide (secretly) to start pulling out immediately the best Iraqi troops from Kuwait, and setting Kuwaiti oil wells on fire. As it transpired later, the process began on 17 February, the day Tariq Aziz and Sadoun Hamadi arrived in Moscow.[133]

But, true to his style, Saddam Hussein covered his retreat on the ground with mixed signals. On 17 February Iraq's government newspaper, *Al Jumhuriya*, described Bush's rejection of the RCC offer of conditional withdrawal as 'rabid and hasty', which unmasked 'the pact of aggression, its deviousness, double-dealing and criminal scheming to control and subjugate the Arab region.' Two days later, the military daily *Al Qadasiya* combined a warning to 'the Satanic alliance and the criminal Zionists' of 'horrible surprises' if they did not refrain from 'slaughtering Iraqi civilians', with a statement by the commander of the Republican Guard, General Ayad Khalifa, that the massive bombing raids against his men had 'hardly had any effect'. That day *Al Jumhuriya* summed up the government's policy of fighting and seeking peace simultaneously by referring to Yasser Arafat's statement in 1974 before the UN General Assembly: 'We will continue to hold the olive branch in one hand and the gun in the other.'

On Iraq's fighting front, what was new was its claim on 16 February that it had fired three of a longer-range variant of Scuds, named Al Hijaara al-Sijjil, at Israel's nuclear reactor at Dimona in the Negev desert. The Shamir government merely stated that two missiles landed in Israel.[134]

Week Six: 21 February–27 February

Week six started with the disclosure of the contents of Gorbachev's eight-point peace plan to which, Moscow announced, Iraq had responded 'positively'. The plan consisted of: (1) a formal Iraqi statement of intention to withdraw; (2) a ceasefire; (3) an immediate release of all prisoners of war; (4) beginning of the Iraqi evacuation within a day of the truce; (4) the withdrawal to occur over a fixed time frame (as yet unspecified); (5) once two-thirds of the Iraqi forces had left Kuwait, the UN sanctions would cease to apply; (6) when all Iraqi troops had departed, all other UN resolutions on the subject would become redundant; and (7) the ceasefire to be monitored by a UN force consisting of contingents from the countries uninvolved with the conflict. The details of the last, eighth, point were still being thrashed out by Gorbachev and Aziz during an all-day session in Moscow.[135]

The launching of a peace plan by the Soviet Union and Iraq – which conceded two major US demands of 'no linkage between Kuwait and the Palestine issue or Israel' and the release of prisoners of war immediately after the truce – created a dilemma for Bush. Were he to accept it, he would have to abandon the US war aims of destroying the Iraqi military machine and overthrowing Saddam Hussein. Were he to reject it, he risked splitting the coalition, and pitting himself against not only Iraq but also the USSR and much of the Arab world and Europe.

As for Saddam Hussein, he had to prepare his people for a compromise. This was to be done behind the usual torrent of rhetoric, presenting himself and his country as eager to sacrifice everything for the sake of peace and justice. 'There is no other course but the one we have chosen, except the course of humiliation and darkness,' he said in a 35-minute radio speech on 21 February 1991. 'We will proceed on this course irrespective of the nature of the political efforts which we are exerting and whose formulation and direction Tariq Aziz carried to Moscow – and which, if rejected, will expose all the cover-ups, and will only maintain the premeditated intentions of the aggression against us.' He referred to the 15 February initiative of Iraq, which was prepared to deal with UN Security Council Resolution 660 ('springing' from 'its sister initiative' of 12 August 1990), which was rejected by Bush and 'his servant Fahd'. 'Note how they now have ambitions for greater things,' Saddam Hussein continued. 'Remember how in the period before the [15 February] initiative they and others in the West used to say that as soon as the word withdrawal is said, everything will be possible . . . Now their media attacks are talking about stripping Iraq of strength and capability, stripping Iraq of all its characteristics, moral qualities and faith.' However, 'their designs will be frustrated', he vowed. 'Note how those who feared a ground battle have avoided the showdown for over a month, and instead concentrated on killing civilians, and destroying property with their long-range aircraft and missiles with rancour.' However, he went on, 'All this will make [Iraqis] more patient and steadfast, and better prepared for the battle which God blesses and good men support.'[136]

Among the countries which dismissed this speech of Saddam Hussein was Egypt. Cairo Radio described it as 'designed for local consumption', adding that 'such nonsense talk, only applauded by a minority of romantics high on the opium of nationalism, has no place in today's real world.' In contrast, the organ of the Labour Islamic Alliance, *Al Shaab*, said that the timing of Saddam Hussein's speech was designed to appeal straight to the masses. 'Where does Egypt stand in the choice between ground offensive and peace initiatives?' it asked. It claimed to have evidence that America was working secretly to get the allies to reject Iraq's peace offers regardless of any concessions that its leaders might make, and that General Schwarzkopf had received a confidential memorandum from Washington telling him to step up attacks to destroy Iraqi military hardware and ignore any talk of a peaceful settlement.[137]

Contrary to Cairo Radio's description of Saddam Hussein's speech, there was nothing romantic about it or its author. Actually, having realized that his forces had little chance of prevailing over the enemy in a bloody combat that was looming, he was busily pulling out his most able troops from Kuwait.

For all practical purposes, the ground battle was joined on 22 February 1991. Baghdad Radio on that day said as much. There followed a routine denial from allied headquarters in Riyadh. Likewise, that day, when the allies alleged that the Iraqi forces had set fire to about 100 oil wells and other facilities over the past 24 hours – action which the Iraqis had actually initiated four days before – Baghdad denied it. 'You could see the flames from three oil fires in the Wafra field,' reported Richard Dowden of the *Independent* on 22 February. 'The air smelt oily. In the past few days, the thud of bombs has been joined by the sharper sound of artillery fire from the American and British howitzers and the terrible, regular beat of the US multiple-rocket launchers firing several hundreds of rounds – 12 rockets [at a time] – each with 644 bomblets. When they land the roar goes on for over a minute sometimes.'[138]

At 06.00 hours GMT on 22 February, President Bush made public his rejection of the eight-point Soviet peace plan. 'The United States and its coalition allies are committed to enforcing the United Nations resolutions that call for Saddam Hussein to immediately and unconditionally leave Kuwait,' said President Bush. 'In view of the Soviet initiative, which very frankly we appreciate, we want to set forth this morning the specific criteria that will ensure Saddam Hussein complies with the United Nations mandate. Within the last 24 hours alone, we have heard a defiant, uncompromising address by Saddam Hussein, followed less than 10 hours later by a statement in Moscow that on the face of it appears more reasonable. I say "on the face of it" because the statement promised unconditional Iraqi withdrawal from Kuwait, only to set forth a number of conditions, and needless to say, any conditions would be unacceptable to the international coalition and would not be in compliance with the United Nations Security Council Resolution 660's demand for immediate and unconditional withdrawal. More importantly and more urgently, we learned this morning that Saddam had now launched a scorched earth policy against Kuwait, anticipating perhaps that he will be forced to leave. He is wantonly setting fire to and destroying the oil wells, the oil tanks, the export terminals and other installations of that small country. Indeed, they are destroying the entire oil production system of Kuwait. And at the same time that the Moscow press conference was going on and Iraq's foreign minister was talking peace, Saddam Hussein was launching Scud missiles. After examining the Moscow statement and discussing it with my senior advisers here late last evening and this morning, I have decided that the time has come to make public with specificity just exactly what is required of Iraq if ground war is to be avoided. Most important, the coalition will give Saddam Hussein until noon [EST] Saturday [23 February 1991] to do what he must do – begin his immediate and unconditional withdrawal from Kuwait. We must hear publicly and authoritatively his acceptance of these terms. The statement to be released [by Marlin

Fitzwater] . . . informs Saddam Hussein that he risks subjecting the Iraqi people to further hardship unless the Iraqi government complies fully with the terms of the statement.'[139]

That day US warplanes rained napalm and Fuel Air Explosives on the Iraqi positions in Kuwait. The role of napalm, according to a senior US marine officer, was to reach entrenched troops, 'just like in Vietnam'.[140]

At 15.45 hours GMT on 22 February, Marlin Fitzwater, the White House spokesman, regretted the peace moves by the Soviet Union, and issued the statement mentioned earlier by Bush, listing twelve demands. Iraq must begin 'large scale withdrawal' from Kuwait by noon New York time [17.00 GMT] 23 February, and complete the withdrawal in one week. Two, within the first 48 hours, Iraq must remove all its forces from Kuwait City and allow for the prompt return of the legitimate government of Kuwait. Three, it must withdraw from all prepared defences along the Saudi–Kuwaiti and Saudi–Iraqi borders, from Bubiyan and Warba Islands, and from Kuwait's Rumeila oil field. Four, within the one week specified, Iraq must return all its forces to their positions of 1 August. Five, in co-operation with the International Red Cross, Iraq must release all prisoners of war and third-country civilians being held against their will, and return the remains of killed and deceased servicemen. Six, this action must commence immediately with the initiation of the withdrawal, and must be completed within 48 hours. Seven, Iraq must remove all explosives or booby traps, including those on Kuwaiti oil installations, and designate Iraqi military liaison officers to work with coalition forces on the operational details related to Iraq's withdrawal. Eight, Iraq must provide all data on the location and nature of any land or sea mines. Nine, Iraq must cease combat air fire, aircraft flights over Iraq and Kuwait, except for transport aircraft carrying troops out of Kuwait, and allow coalition aircraft exclusive control over and use of all Kuwaiti airspace. Ten, Iraq must cease all destructive actions against Kuwait citizens and property, and release all Kuwaiti detainees. Eleven, the United States and its coalition partners reiterated that their forces would not attack retreating Iraqi forces, and would exercise restraint so long as withdrawal proceeded in accordance with the above guidelines and there were no attacks on other countries. Twelve, any breach of these terms would bring an instant and sharp response from coalition forces in accordance with United Nations Security Council Resolution 678.[141]

At 19.00 GMT, following several hours of talks between Gorbachev and Aziz, the Kremlin announced a refined six-point peace plan. One, Iraq agrees to implement UN Security Council Resolution 660 – that is, withdraw its forces immediately and unconditionally from Kuwait to the positions they occupied on 1 August 1990. Two, the troop withdrawal will start the day after a ceasefire encompassing all military operations on land, sea, and in the air. Three, the troop withdrawal will be completed within 21 days, including a pull-out from Kuwait City within the first four days. Four, once the withdrawal has been completed, all the pertinent UN Security Council resolutions will no longer be valid because the reasons for them will have been removed. Five, all prisoners of war will be freed and repatriated within three days after the ceasefire and the end of military operations. Six, control and monitoring of the ceasefire and withdrawal of troops will be carried out by observers or peacekeeping forces as determined by the UN Security Council.[142] In deference to strong US objections, the provision about the lifting of the UN embargo after two-thirds of the Iraqi troops had left Kuwait, which appeared in the earlier eight-point plan, was dropped.

At 20.45 GMT the Iraqi government accepted the six-point Soviet peace plan.

That day (22 February), Gorbachev had a telephone conversation with Bush; and, according to Tass, told him that 'No winds, no adversaries can influence our choice in favour of this course.' Apparently, 'this course' meant the path of peace. By actively pursuing the diplomacy of peace the Soviet president had kept the USSR within the orbit of the anti-Iraqi coalition without committing any Soviet troops or funds to the enterprise, and simultaneously pacified such powerful lobbies at home as the defence and foreign ministries as well as orthodox Communist and other members of parliament (who argued, convincingly, that by bombing Iraq's electric and water facilities and causing high civilian casualties, the US had clearly overstepped the UN mandate).[143] Gorbachev had been careful to involve the UN Security Council throughout the crisis.

On 23 February, Saturday, at a press conference in Moscow at noon GMT, Tariq Aziz announced that his government had decided to endorse the USSR's six-point peace plan, and to withdraw 'immediately and unconditionally' its troops from Kuwait to the positions they occupied on 1 August 1990. (Apprehensive that Baghdad's acceptance had come too late to satisfy Washington, which was in a hawkish mood, Gorbachev reportedly tried to get Aziz to combine his proposals with the points contained in Bush's ultimatum. He got somewhere: Aziz responded favourably to some of the demands contained in the American ultimatum. Two hours later he left Moscow for Baghdad.)

At 15.00 GMT, the White House dismissed the Soviet plan, and reiterated Bush's ultimatum that the Iraqi troops should start pulling out of Kuwait by 17.00 GMT. An hour later allied warplanes pounded Basra and other southern Iraqi cities and towns.

At 16.30 GMT (half an hour before the US deadline), at the Soviet initiative, the UN Security Council began a closed-door emergency session. The Soviet ambassador, Yuli Vorontsov, announced that Tariq Aziz had 'responded positively' to some of the American conditions for ending the war. But the Western ambassadors said that they were not interested in bridging the gap between the Soviet plan and the US conditions.[144] Vorontsov did not press the matter further as he knew that any Soviet motion would be vetoed by America, Britain and France. This derailed his plan, which was to get the Council to set a date for the Iraqi withdrawal and resolve the issue of confirming, verifying and monitoring the ceasefire and pull-out. As for China, the remaining permanent member of the Security Council, it had taken a passive role in resolving the crisis. When Sadoun Hamadi visited Peking on 20 February (after his stop-over in Tehran) to solicit backing for a resolution similar to the one now devised by Moscow, he was told by the Chinese leaders to take 'immediate and concrete actions to withdraw'.[145]

However, President Gorbachev did not give up. On 23 February he held telephone conversations with the leaders of Britain, France, Germany, Italy, Japan, Syria and Egypt, urging them to postpone the land offensive for 'a day or two' to give time for the Security Council to 'integrate' the Iraqi and American plans for ending the war. He realized that the decision rested solely with Bush. During his 28-minute telephone conversation, which ended at 16.30 GMT (just as the Security Council meeting began), Gorbachev told Bush that 'an acceptable compromise' was only one day away, if only he would postpone the ground invasion for the time being. But Bush did not budge. This time he behaved towards Gorbachev in the way he had done with Mitterrand on the eve of the air campaign on 15 January, but for a different reason. As a White House press briefing after the war made clear, Bush understood that 'for domestic reasons' Gorbachev needed 'to be seen to be playing a role', and that 'We had to reject that role, but not in a way that would embarrass him.'[146] In other words, Bush and his senior advisers were intent on exploiting the limitations of Gorbachev and the Soviet Union. They were prepared to jolly him along as the leader of the other superpower in the knowledge that he could not act as an equal and, if need be, stand up to the US. And that is precisely what happened at 17.10 GMT on 23 February: the Kremlin said it did not wish to strain relations with the White House because of the latter's rejection of the Soviet peace plan.

At 18.00 GMT (one hour after the US deadline), President Bush announced that since Saddam Hussein had made no move to withdraw from Kuwait the coalition's military action would proceed, 'according to plan'. He then issued an order to General Schwarzkopf to eject the Iraqis from Kuwait.

'The instinct for a military solution won through, despite the fact that Iraq's agreement to withdraw its forces from Kuwait in accordance with UN Security Council Resolution 660 created a qualitatively new situation, clearing the way for the conflict in the Gulf to be switched to the arena of political regulation,' said Vitaly Churkin, the Soviet foreign ministry spokesman, on 25 February. He referred to the Iraqi government's decision to leave Kuwait 'immediately and unconditionally' – induced largely by the Soviet Union – which provided an opportunity to prevent the conflict entering 'a sharper, bloodier phase'.[147]

The ground assault came after an air campaign that had lasted 38 days. During that period the US-led coalition staged 94,000 air sorties (divided evenly between bombing and support missions), and fired about 300 Tomahawk (offensive) and 130 Patriot (defensive) missiles. They claimed to have destroyed 135 Iraqi aircraft, 1,685 tanks, 925 amoured personnel carriers, 1,485 artillery pieces, and 73 ships. They put their aircraft losses at 47 while Iraq claimed to have downed 200-plus allied planes and missiles. Going by the Iraqi casualty rate given by its deputy prime minister, Sadoun Hamadi, for the first 26 days – 2.5 for each bombing sortie – the total by now should have been 117,400, with 29,275 dead and 88,125 injured. In contrast, the 36 Iraqi Scuds aimed at Saudi Arabia had killed one and wounded 30, and the 37 fired at Israel had killed four and injured 305. These figures confirmed the assessment made by many analysts, including Edward Luttwak of the Washington-based Centre for Strategic and International Studies, that the threat posed by the Iraqi Scuds – capable of carrying a payload of 400 lbs in contrast to 8,800 lbs by a modern fighter-bomber – had been grossly exaggerated.[148]

An opinion poll taken in America on 15 February, and published ten days later in *Newsweek*, showed that while 90% favoured continuing military operations until Saddam Hussein agreed to withdraw unconditionally, and 87% believed that President Bush should continue the air war, only 8% wanted him to start the ground offensive 'soon'.[149]

10 DESERT SABRE: THE GROUND WAR

'The Mother of Battles will be our battle of victory and martyrdom.'

President Saddam Hussein, 21 February 1991[1]

'The Iraqi forces are conducting the Mother of all Retreats.'

US defence secretary Dick Cheney,
27 February 1991[2]

'Iraqis will never forget that on 8 August 1990 Kuwait became part of Iraq legally, constitutionally and actually. It continued to do so until last night, when withdrawal began.'

President Saddam Hussein, 26 February 1991[3]

'As far as Saddam Hussein being a great military strategist, he is neither a strategist, nor is he schooled in the operational arts, nor is he a tactician, nor is he a general, nor is he a soldier. Other than that, he's a great military man.'

General Norman Schwarzkopf, 27 February 1991[4]

Operation 'Desert Sabre', the US-led coalition's ground offensive, began at 01.00 GMT on 24 February with the 16-inch guns of USS *Wisconsin* and USS *Missouri*, anchored off the Kuwaiti coast, firing a massive naval barrage as part of a pretence that the allies' amphibious forces were about to land on the beaches in order to link up with the ground troops ready to fight their main battle across the Kuwaiti–Saudi border. Simultaneously, to the west, well past the Kuwaiti–Saudi border, the artillery of US 18th Airborne Corps began shelling positions in southern Iraq. Since the allies had gained air supremacy, depriving Iraq totally of its use of airspace, the Iraqis found themselves unable to keep abreast of enemy positions.

At 04.00 GMT the allied ground troops started advancing on two axes: one (on the right) across the Kuwaiti–Saudi frontier, and the other (on the left) across the Iraqi–Saudi border. The right flank consisted of (a) five mechanized brigades of Saudi, Kuwaiti, Omani and UAE troops under the Joint Force Command East based along the coastal road, and (b) two US marine divisions and a brigade of an American armoured division based about 50 miles further inland. The immediate task of the US marines was to clear several lanes through the forward Iraqi minefields which had already been the targets of US 'Daisy Cutter' 15,000-lb bombs.

At 04.30 GMT the allies' left flank, consisting of the French 6th armoured division and a brigade of US 82nd airborne division, based 200 miles west of the US marines near the Saudi–Iraqi border, crossed into Iraq. It overpowered an Iraqi infantry division 36 miles to the north on its way to Salman airfield 35 miles further on. The aim was to capture the airfield and transform it into an advance operational base, codenamed 'Cobra', for the US 82nd airborne division. This was accomplished later in the day when 460 helicopters brought in troops from across the border. The major task of the 'Cobra' units was to cut off the roads along the Euphrates and Tigris valley – and seal off the Kuwaiti theatre of operations, thus severing the sole escape route of the Iraqis.

Having activated the forces on the two extremes of the frontline, General Schwarzkopf turned his attention to the ones in the middle: the Joint Force Command North, consisting of Saudi, Egyptian, Syrian, Kuwaiti and Pakistani units, poised along the Saudi–Kuwaiti frontier; and the US 7th Corps, backed by a British armoured division, stationed along the Saudi–Iraqi border. The latter was expected to provide the allies' major thrust into southern Iraq. Schwarzkopf directed the Joint Force Command North to cross over into Kuwait while backing it with fake US military radio communications to dress up its advance as the main operation of the ground offensive.[5]

Around noon on 24 February while the allied headquarters was claiming that its first 24-hour objectives had been achieved in half the time, the Iraqi high command claimed to have stopped the US-led offensive. 'At the time when the UN Security Council decided to discuss the Soviet peace initiative, which we endorsed, the treacherous committed treachery,' Saddam Hussein said in a radio broadcast. 'Fight them, oh brave, splendid men, oh men of the Mother of Battles . . . Fight them because, with their defeat, you will be at the last entrance of the victory of victories . . . If the opposite takes place, God forbid, there will only be the ignominious abyss to which the enemies are aspiring to push you.'[6]

Behind this bravado, Saddam Hussein was accelerating the pull-out of his best troops from Kuwait, a process he had begun several days before, and getting ready to raise a white banner. This was pointed out by *Baghdad*, an Iraqi opposition newspaper, on 24 February 1991. It said that the massive Iraqi propaganda machine was preparing the public for a withdrawal from Kuwait after a few limited battles, and presenting the outcome as a victory because of the preservation of the bulk of the Iraqi military.[7]

The Soviet Union expressed its disapproval of the allies' actions. Regretting that 'a real chance . . . to achieve the goals set out by the UN Security Council resolutions without further human casualties and material destruction' had been missed, its foreign ministry spokesman pointed out that 'The difference between the formulations agreed to by Iraq and the proposals of a series of other countries were not great' and that it was still 'not too late' to bridge the differences.[8]

Iran, the other country which had co-ordinated its peace moves with the USSR, was disappointed too. Regretting the start of the land offensive, President Rafsanjani said, 'The US and its allies proved that they are after something beyond a mere Iraqi pull-out from Kuwait.' Interestingly, a commentary on Tehran Radio criticized the Soviet plan for failing to address the question of the allied forces' withdrawal from the region following the Iraqi evacuation of Kuwait.[9]

The PLO called on the Soviet Union and China, as well as Arab, Islamic and non-aligned countries, to help Iraq confront 'the US-led allied aggression'. In a message to Saddam Hussein, Yasser Arafat said that his peace initiative and the Soviet plan 'unmasked for the entire world that the American–Zionist–Atlantic coalition wants neither peace nor the implementation of the UN resolution [660]' but rather 'the destruction of Iraq, its people, its army and its leadership'. Describing Iraq as 'the defender of the Arab nation of Muslims', he concluded: 'I pray for your victory and assure you the support of our people, who are in the same trench to defend the honour, dignity, security and existence of this [Arab] nation.'[10]

To stifle any pro-Iraqi protests in the Occupied Territories, Israel imposed a total and indefinite curfew, and declared the West Bank and Gaza military zones, thus barring them to journalists.[11]

Jordan expressed 'great sorrow and anger' over the allied offensive, and condemned it. Jordanian Radio regularly broadcast the details of Baghdad's military communiqués: these claimed that the Iraqis had 'repulsed' US-led attacks and were 'well in control'.[12] According to the Pentagon, however, there had been little resistance by the Iraqi troops, who had been surrendering in their thousands. By the end of

24 February, one US infantry division and one armoured division had advanced north into Iraq and linked up with the American forces at the 'Cobra' base.

This happened against the background of a heated closed-door session of the UN Security Council in New York. The Cuban ambassador to the UN described the Gulf conflict as 'an American war', and argued that it was 'not connected in any way with the UN'. The Indian ambassador said that the Security Council had 'abrogated its responsibility' by failing to press for a peaceful solution. Calling the allies' ground offensive 'unjustifiable' and 'unnecessary', Yemen's ambassador deplored the fact that the Security Council had been 'eclipsed', and walked out in protest.[13]

Monday 25 February began with Baghdad claiming that it had repulsed the allies' assaults, and Washington stating that it had captured more than 14,000 Iraqi troops. The US infantry and armoured units, operating from the 'Cobra' base, moved east to attack the northernmost Republican Guard positions. Half of the 3,000 air sorties flown that day provided cover for the ground forces as the US 7th Corps and British 1st armoured division provided the main allied thrust into southern Iraq, with an American infantry division breaching Iraqi defences west of Wadi al Batin. A Sea Dart missile fired by HMS *Gloucester* downed a Silkworm surface-to-ship missile launched by the Iraqis at USS *Missouri*. However, an Iraqi Scud hit a US base near Dhahran at 17.40 GMT, killing 28 American troops. By now the Iraqis had set on fire 590 oil wells in Kuwait.

At its closed-door session on 25 February, the UN Security Council ruled out a ceasefire until Iraq accepted in writing all the twelve resolutions the Council had adopted on the subject on and after 2 August 1990. While confirming Baghdad's intention to evacuate Kuwait in compliance with Resolution 660, the Iraqi ambassador to the UN refused to discuss 'questions that have nothing to do with that resolution'. The Soviet Union shifted its position on the subject. In its six-point peace plan it had stated that the resolutions subsequent to 660 would lapse once Iraq had accepted the central principle of withdrawal from Kuwait. Now its UN ambassador talked of Saddam Hussein abiding by all Security Council resolutions simultaneously with a ceasefire, but not before, as America, Britain and France insisted. However, he did not press the point.[14]

The Soviets presented a new peace plan at 21.30 GMT at the Security Council.

An hour later Baghdad Radio announced that the Revolutionary

Command Council had accepted the Soviet initiative, and ordered an Iraqi withdrawal from Kuwait. 'They have been engaged in an epic, valiant battle which will be recorded by history in letters of light,' said the official statement. 'On this basis, and because the leadership affirmed its agreement to withdraw in accordance with UN Security Council Resolution 660 through its approval of the Soviet initiative, orders have been issued to our armed forces to withdraw in an organized manner to the positions held prior to 1 August 1990.'

At 22.35 GMT (01.35 local time), the radio announcer read out a statement by Saddam Hussein. 'O valiant Iraqi men, O glorious Iraqi women,' it began. 'Kuwait is part of your country and was carved from it in the past. It is due to the current circumstances that Kuwait will return to the situation that will prevail after our withdrawal. It hurts you that this should happen . . . that, on this day, our armed forces will complete their withdrawal from Kuwait, God willing.' Announcing that the Iraqi withdrawal from Kuwait had already begun (around 21.00 local time), he tried to rationalize it. 'All that happened to us or which we have decided in certain circumstances [to happen], bowing to God's will, is an honourable record for the people and nation and Islamic and human values,' he said. 'Special conditions made the Iraqi army withdraw, including the aggression by 30 [i.e. 28 coalition members, America and Turkey] countries and their abominable blockade. Their repugnant siege has been led in evil and aggression by the machine and criminal entity of America . . . Everybody will remember that the gates of Constantinople were not opened to Muslims from the first attempt, and that the cause of dear Palestine, which has been neglected by the international community, is again knocking at the closed doors to force them to solve it, no matter how hard the aggressors tried to obstruct this, and thanks to the struggle of the Palestinians and the Iraqis. The confidence of the nationalists and the faithful Mujahedin [i.e. those who conduct jihad] and Muslims has grown bigger than before, and hope grew more and more . . . Therefore, victory is now and in the future, God willing. Shout for victory, O brothers. You have fought 30 countries, and all the evil and the largest machine of war and destruction in the world.'[15] Saddam Hussein's statement made little difference to the White House. Half an hour later, at 23.05 GMT, it said that, in the absence of 'an official contact' from Baghdad, 'the war continues'.

The Iraqi News Agency reported that foreign minister Tariq Aziz had informed the Soviet ambassador in Baghdad of Iraq's decision – which constituted compliance with UN Security Council Resolution

660 – and asked that a message be conveyed from President Saddam Hussein to President Gorbachev, requesting him to exert efforts at the Security Council to achieve a ceasefire and put an end to 'the criminal behaviour of the US and its allies and collaborators'. The Kremlin confirmed that, having received a letter from Saddam Hussein (in the early hours of 26 February), President Gorbachev passed it on to the Soviet envoy at the UN. 'We shall be working in accord with the United States at the Security Council' in seeking an end to the war, said Gorbachev's spokesman.[16] It was a forlorn hope.

On 26 February, at 04.25 GMT, the US rejected the Soviet peace proposal at the Security Council, thus continuing to cold-shoulder Gorbachev's mediation efforts.

Five minutes later, in Washington, President Bush disputed Saddam Hussein's statement that his troops were withdrawing. 'His defeated forces are retreating,' Bush said. 'He is trying to claim a victory in the midst of a rout. And he is not voluntarily giving up Kuwait. He is trying to save the remnants of power and control in the Middle East by every means possible.' Bush stated that Saddam Hussein was 'not interested in peace, but only to regroup and fight another day. And he does not renounce Iraq's claim to Kuwait. To the contrary, he makes clear that Iraq continues to claim Kuwait.' There was no evidence of 'remorse for Iraq's aggression', or any indication that 'Saddam is prepared to accept the responsibility for the awful consequences of that aggression', Bush continued. 'He still does not accept UN Security Council resolutions, or the coalition terms of February 22, including the release of all prisoners of war, third-country detainees, and an end to the pathological destruction of Kuwait. The coalition will, therefore, continue to prosecute the war with undiminished intensity.' Referring to Baghdad's announcement of the previous night about withdrawal, Bush said that 'we will not attack unarmed soldiers in retreat'. Then came the crucial qualification. 'We have no choice but to consider retreating combat units as a threat, and respond accordingly,' he said. 'Anything else would risk additional coalition casualties.' (This was soon translated into a warning to the Iraqis to leave all arms and tanks behind, and proceed on foot, if they wanted to avoid being attacked.) In Bush's view, 'the best way to avoid further casualties on both sides' was for the Iraqi soldiers to lay down their arms as nearly 30,000 of them had already done. 'It is time for all Iraqi forces in the theatre of operation – those occupying Kuwait, those supporting the occupation of Kuwait – to lay down their arms,' he said. 'That will stop the bloodshed.' More specifically, he insisted on Saddam Hussein's agreeing 'personally and publicly' to abide by all twelve UN Security Council resolutions, and Iraq's withdrawal from Kuwait, as preconditions for ending the hostilities.[17]

Having prevailed militarily and diplomatically, Bush was resolved to press his advantage to the fullest, and achieve everything he had promised. Admirers applauded his determined leadership and refusal to compromise. Critics saw him as hell-bent on crushing an unequal enemy, and humiliating a leader of a Third World country.

Nearly four hours later, at 08.20 GMT, Saddam Hussein announced on Baghdad Radio that Iraq was withdrawing from Kuwait in compliance with UN Security Council Resolution 660. But, refusing to yield completely to Bush's demands, he did not announce the unconditional acceptance of all Security Council resolutions.

At 09.15 GMT the Soviet Union suggested a ceasefire.

The Pentagon claimed that a huge helicopter-borne assault by its airborne troops had resulted in the capture of the crucial road junction near Nasiriyeh leading to Baghdad, that further south US armour had encircled the Republican Guard positions at the northern Iraqi–Kuwaiti border, and that the British 1st armoured division had swung right to attack and defeat in a night battle Iraq's 12th armoured division held in tactical reserve along the western Iraqi–Kuwaiti frontier. Iranian sources reported the 'heaviest bombing yet' of the Iraqi border areas around Basra. And the allies claimed that bridges vital to the Iraqi war effort had been destroyed.

As for the fighting in Kuwait, the Joint Force Command North, spearheaded by the Egyptians, engaged the Iraqis controlling the Salim military airbase west of Kuwait City while the combined column of the Joint Force Command East and US marines began approaching Kuwait City from the south.

At 11.50 GMT (on 26 February) Kuwaiti resistance sources said that Iraqi forces had evacuated Kuwait City and suburbs. The operation had begun 18 hours earlier: in an assorted convoy of Iraqi tanks, armoured personnel carriers, trucks, buses, and hijacked vans and cars, the occupation force left Kuwait City along the ring road and on to Highway 80, the main route to Basra. As it approached Mitla ridge, a sandy hill north of Jahra, 20 miles west of Kuwait City, its head and tail were hit by US ground-attack aircraft operating from USS *Ranger*. The convoy was immobilized and turned into a sitting duck. Bombing continued throughout the night and well past the normal 10 a.m. stopping time until early afternoon, when the weather became unsuitable for aerial attacks. The US navy's Intruder jets dropped

Rockeye cluster bombs, each weighing 500 pounds, releasing 247 bomblets and producing 500,000 high velocity shrapnel fragments, over an area of an acre. The US air force pressed into action its F-16s and B-52s, each B-52 dropping eighty 1,000-lb bombs. Apache helicopters fired their lethal anti-tank missiles. By the morning of 26 February the 2nd Marine division and the Tiger brigade of the US army's 2nd armoured division had reached their final objective: Jahra. There they received orders from General Schwarzkopf 'not to let anybody or anything out of Kuwait City'.

By 12.00 GMT, having completed a massive enveloping operation, which enabled US armour to outflank the Iraqi positions along the Kuwaiti–Saudi border and strike the Republican Guard units, the Pentagon claimed that all exits for the Iraqi troops in the Kuwaiti theatre of operations were blocked.

At about the same time Baghdad Radio reported that allied para-troopers had landed in southern Iraq, blocking the 'dignified with-drawal' of the Iraqis sought by Saddam Hussein.

The slaughtering of the Iraqis as they tried to retreat along the six-lane Highway 80 continued for the next 40 hours, until the truce at 05.00 GMT on 28 February, turning the road into a 'Highway to Hell'. The assault was so severe that it became, in the words of Colin Smith, the chief roving correspondent of the *Observer*, 'one of the most terrible harassments of a retreating army from the air in the history of warfare'. It was carried out to implement General Schwarzkopf's order 'to block enemy forces from withdrawing into Iraq', and involved all four service wings of the US military. In practice, this meant attacking the retreating Iraqis not only along Highway 80 and the Jahra–Umm Qasr coastal road in Kuwait, but also Highway 8 (connecting Umm Qasr with Nasiriyeh) and the Basra–Baghdad highway in Iraq.

According to a US military officer, the US air force was given 'the word to work over the entire area, to find anything that was moving and take it out', and every American pilot within 100 miles of the battle-zone heard the order. The density of air traffic became so thick, with the planes of the air force, navy and marines participating in the kill, that air traffic controllers had to divert aircraft to avoid mid-air collisions.[18] With the weather turning 'sour' in the afternoon of 26 February, the task of 'taking out' the retreating Iraqis fell largely on the US army and marines.

The 'Hounds of Hell' battalion of the Tiger brigade was assigned the job. 'We got there [to Highway 80] just before dusk [on 26 February], and essentially shot up the front of this column,' said Tony Clifton of

Newsweek. 'The group of vehicles we hit included petrol tankers and tanks, so the tanks exploded in these great fountains of white flame from the ammunition . . . You could see the little figures of soldiers coming out with their hands up. It really looked like a medieval hell – the hell you see in [the paintings of Hieronymus] Bosch, because of the great red flames and then these weird little contorted figures . . . It was all conducted at a distance of, say, half a mile, and in darkness . . . Next morning we went up to see what we'd done . . . there were bodies all over the place. And I remember at one point looking down at the car track and I was up to my ankles in blood. The tracks had filled with blood, and there were very white-faced men going round saying, "Jesus. Did we really do this?"'[19]

As for the US marines, Major Bob Williams summed up the situation in an interview on Sky Television. 'On the night of 26 February, it was apocalyptic,' he said. 'We had artillery, T-55s [tanks] exploding, a lot of small-arms fire, some tank rounds, and there was a pall of smoke from the burning fuel, and it was like night-time.'[20]

At 19.00 GMT the Soviet Union again called for a truce, but to no avail.

The next day, 27 February, at 01.30 GMT the Pentagon announced that American, Kuwaiti and Saudi troops controlled Kuwait City. By then the Kuwaiti emir had declared three months of martial rule in Kuwait and called on Shaikh Saad al Sabah, the crown prince, to administer it. In practice this job fell into the hands of the 352nd Civil Affairs Command, the US political-military authority in Kuwait, which had signed a contract with the Kuwaiti government-in-exile to put the Americans in positions of bureaucratic power.[21]

At 05.30 GMT Baghdad announced that it had completed its withdrawal from Kuwait.

Three-and-a-half hours later, the Pentagon claimed a helicopter-borne assault by allied airborne forces on Ali ibn Abi Talib airbase near Nasiriyeh with a view to gaining control of the main road from Basra – the headquarters of the Iraqi troops for the Kuwaiti theatre of operations – along the western bank of the Euphrates. By now, according to the allies, all the bridges across the Euphrates except one had been destroyed.[22]

Later that day, American sources said that US troops had used cluster bombs to attack Iraqi soldiers retreating 'bumper to bumper' from Kuwait and elsewhere. Among the victims of the cluster bombs and anti-tank missiles and rockets were the Medina armoured division and the Hammurabi division of the Republican Guard. Admitting that the allies were continuing to attack the Republican Guard 'to make sure [they] are rendered incapable of conducting the heinous crimes they have done in the past', General Schwarzkopf said: 'There is a lot more purpose to this war than getting the Iraqis out of Kuwait.'[23]

His statement gave no clue of the means being employed by US forces to render 'harmless' retreating Iraqi soldiers. This came from veteran American and British military officers. 'They [Iraqis] are defenceless troops,' said Gene La Roque, a former American admiral, and director of the Washington-based Centre for Defence Information. 'They're trying to escape with their lives . . . They are routed and the senseless killing of fleeing troops does not contribute in any way to the successful conclusion of this war.' Alistair Mackie, a former British air commodore, accused the allied forces of effectively shooting Iraqi troops in the back. 'Pilots' inability to distinguish surrendered soldiers from others is no excuse,' he said. Indeed, according to a US navy pilot quoted by Rowan Scarborough of the *Washington Post*, the Iraqis had fixed white flags to their tanks and were riding with turrets open, scanning the skies with binoculars, but were bombed because the allied rules of engagement required the pilots to bomb the tanks unless the soldiers had abandoned the vehicles and left them.[24]

With Highway 80 jammed, many of the retreating Iraqis had taken to the road from Jahra to the Iraqi border city of Umm Qasr. They met the same fate as their colleagues along the Jahra–Basra road at Mitla ridge which by the morning of 28 February had been turned into a gigantic scrap-yard, with some 2,000 military and civilian vehicles destroyed, some charred, some exploded, some reduced to heaps of tangled metal, with dead bodies and their severed limbs scattered all over, some corpses petrified in their vehicles, and others incinerated, with their faces reduced to grinning teeth. There was one difference, though. The Mitla ridge carnage was soon cleared up, but not the one along the Jahra–Umm Qasr road. 'For 60 miles, hundreds of Iraqi tanks and armoured cars, howitzers and anti-aircraft guns, ammunition trucks and ambulances are strafed, smashed and burned beyond belief,' reported Bob Dogrin of the *Los Angeles Times*. 'Scores of soldiers lie in and around the vehicles, mangled and bloated in the drifting desert sands. Most were retreating on this two-lane road before midnight on 25 February, one of two huge caravans to flee ravaged Kuwait City as their army collapsed under the fast-approaching blitzkrieg.' Dogrin had accompanied Major Bob Nugent, a US army intelligence officer, who searched the wreckage for Iraqi documents. 'Even in Vietnam, I didn't see anything like this,' Nugent said.[25]

The two-lane Highway 8, connecting Umm Qasr with Baghdad via Nasiriyeh and running parallel to the Euphrates, proved equally fatal for the retreating Iraqis. Here they ran straight into the US 24th mechanized infantry as the Americans drove south-east towards the Zubair–Basra area to attack the Republican Guard, while US military helicopters fired their anti-tank missiles at the Iraqi tanks or machine guns at the fleeing Iraqi soldiers heading for the marshes. Thousands of retreating Iraqis, who managed to reach the Basra beachhead on their way to the Iranian border, found themselves under aerial attack. As they tried to cross the marshes or the Shatt al Arab by jumping into fishing boats, or by devising makeshift pontoon bridges out of barges, they were tracked down by allied helicopters up to 100 miles inside Iraq and gunned down. The pilots of the Iranian patrol aircraft described the scene as 'a rat shoot'.

On 27 February, the last full day of the Gulf War, the US navy alone staged 660 air missions as, in the words of the *Navy Times*, 'they chased the retreating [Iraqi] army out of Kuwait and into the trap sprung by [allied] ground forces'.26

At 18.00 GMT on that day, a letter from Tariq Aziz reached the UN secretary-general in New York. In it he reportedly agreed to the release of the prisoners of war, and the acceptance of Resolutions 660, 662 (making the Iraqi annexation of Kuwait null and void) and 674 (regarding war reparations), while rejecting Resolutions 661, 665 and 670 (all of them concerning the UN embargo against Iraq) – the rest of the resolutions, except 678, which authorized military action against Iraq, being essentially unimportant because of their application to diplomatic missions and the population register in Kuwait. He asked for a commitment in advance that UN and EC sanctions against Iraq would be lifted following the ceasefire.27

While the Security Council's permanent members were debating Iraq's offer, President Bush received secret briefings from General Colin Powell and Dick Cheney at 19.30 GMT that 'all military objectives' had been achieved.28

At the Security Council its five permanent members found Aziz's letter unsatisfactory because it offered conditional acceptance of Security Council resolutions. 'They agreed we need an authoritative, unconditional acceptance of all twelve resolutions,' said a UN official at 20.45 GMT.29

By then, 23.45 Gulf time, General Schwarzkopf had unleashed the heaviest bombing yet on Baghdad, bringing the total allied air sorties to a staggering 106,000 in 42 days of war.

Neither Schwarzkopf nor Bush had any qualms about raining death and destruction on a defeated enemy. 'When enemy armies are defeated, they withdraw,' said US air force chief of staff General Merrill A. McPeak. 'It's during this time that the true fruits of victory are achieved from combat, when the enemy is disorganized . . . If we do not exploit victory, the president should get himself some new generals.' Schwarzkopf summed up his state of mind, later, by quoting the American Civil War general William Tecumseh Sherman, 'War is the remedy that our enemy has chosen: therefore, let them have as much of it as they want', and adding: 'You do that by inflicting the maximum casualties on the enemy.'[30] President Bush was exploiting victory; and his conduct of the war had proved so popular that it had dramatically transformed the overall view of him and the nation. A *Washington Post*–ABC poll conducted during 22–26 February, and published on 1 March, showed that the percentage of Americans who thought that the nation 'is going in the right direction' trebled, from 19 (in early January) to 58; and the percentage who thought things are 'going pretty seriously off, on the wrong track' halved, from 78 to 39.

The contrary was the case in the Soviet Union, both at the popular and specialist levels. In his report in the *Sovyetskaya Rossiya* of 27 February, Viktor Filatov denounced the allied bombers of Iraq as 'twentieth century barbarians', who wanted to 'drive the Iraqis, as they did the Vietnamese, back to the Stone Age'. Posing a rhetorical question, 'How much more blood do they want?', he answered: 'I don't know if there is anything left in Baghdad to bomb. They have cut out the liver and the kidneys, gouged out the eyes and pierced the ear-drums of Baghdad, once a healthy, flourishing being.' Writing in the same newspaper Yuri Gvozdyev, a Soviet commentator, blamed Britain for 'redrawing the map of Arab territory in the Persian Gulf according to its imperial will, sowing the seeds of future conflicts and divisions.' Now he blamed the Americans for pursuing both 'their imperialist interests, which have nothing in common with human values, and super-profits for their military-industrial complex'.

In Washington, having satisfied himself that all military aims of the US administration had been gained, President Bush decided to stop the fighting. 'Seven months ago, America and the world drew a line in the sand,' Bush said in his victory speech to the nation at 21.00 EST on 27 February 1991 (02.00 GMT on 28 February). 'We declared that the aggression against Kuwait would not stand, and tonight

America and the world have kept their word.' He told his audience that he had held consultations with the US secretary of defence, the chairman of the joint chiefs of staff, and the coalition partners. The US and coalition forces were ready to 'suspend offensive combat operations at midnight tonight, Eastern Standard Time [05.00 GMT on 28 February], exactly 100 hours since ground operations commenced, and six weeks since the start of Operation "Desert Storm",' if Iraq laid down its arms and ended its launchings of Scud missiles. Regarding a permanent ceasefire, Bush set the following conditions: (a) release of all coalition prisoners of war, third country nationals, and the remains of all those who had fallen; (b) release of all Kuwaiti detainees; (c) informing the Kuwaiti authorities of the location of all land and sea mines; (d) full compliance with all relevant UN Security Council resolutions, including abrogating Baghdad's decision to annex Kuwait and accepting the principle of responsibility for paying compensation for damage and injury; and (e) designating military commanders to meet within 48 hours with their coalition counterparts, at a place in the theatre of operations to be specified, to arrange military aspects of the ceasefire.[31]

Significantly, Bush made no mention of his earlier demand that Saddam Hussein should agree 'personally and publicly' to all twelve UN Security Council resolutions. While his press secretary, Fitzwater, attributed this concession to the fact that 'We won the war', another official said, 'Bush brought the conflict from the "bring-him-to-his-knees" rhetoric back to the military business of arranging [ceasefire] terms.'[32]

About an hour and a half later, at 03.40 GMT, Baghdad Radio responded. 'Iraq had fought, stood fast and triumphed,' said a commentator. 'It is a victory for our people and for our President Saddam Hussein. O Iraq, maker of victory, you teach the world struggle, patience, sacrifices and rare heroic fight.' According to a military spokesman, continued Baghdad Radio, the Republican Guard inflicted 'heavy losses on the forces of the infidels' in the fighting on 27 February. 'Iraq is the one that is in control and victorious,' said another commentator. 'Iraq is the master of the whole land, and the leader of the Muslims in the whole world.'[33]

At 04.40 GMT Iraq accepted the ceasefire conditions imposed by Bush, including all Security Council resolutions, and formally declared the annexation of Kuwait null and void, thus reversing the statement of Saddam Hussein made only two days earlier. In a sense, this was a trade-off for Bush's concession of dropping his insistence on a personal statement by Saddam Hussein accepting all Security Council resolutions.

At 05.00 GMT on 28 February, Thursday, a temporary ceasefire came into effect after 209 days of the crisis and warfare.

Iraq put a different gloss on the event from most other countries. 'The aggressors imagined that through the Iraqi high command decision to withdraw from Kuwait they were able to put our armed forces in a position that is contrary to the military and manly values for which the men of the Mother of Battles are reputed in this great showdown,' said an Iraqi military spokesman on Baghdad Radio soon after the truce. 'Many battles occurred in Basra district and other places in our great Iraq's territories after the withdrawal [from Kuwait]. Due to faith in our capability that is able to teach the enemy forces lessons that would make them worried militarily and politically if the war [had] continued, Bush announced his decision [to cease fire] early this morning. We are happy for the halt in fighting, which will save the blood of our sons and the safety of our people after God made them victorious by faith against their evil enemies, and save the blood of the sons of humanity who suffered due to Bush and his traitorous agents. Therefore, orders were issued to all our units at the battlefront not to open fire. God is great.' Contrary to Western and other reports, the newspapers in Baghdad asserted that Iraq had inflicted heavy losses on the allies, one headline saying: 'By God's will and the might of our leader Saddam Hussein we foiled the aggressor's plot.' They called on their readers to rejoice because their army had been able to keep its power intact.[34]

There was no rejoicing, however; only relief that an ordeal had ended. Many residents of the capital reacted with disbelief as the consequences of their government's decision sank in: they had been subjected to exhortations for a long and bloody battle. There was a consensus that Iraq had suffered grievously due to Saddam Hussein's invasion of Kuwait. Baghdad had been without electricity for six weeks. Water was scarce, and so was fuel. Only a few of the country's 1.25 million cars and trucks were on the road, and there were not enough buses to meet demand. Non-stop bombing for 42 days had severely disrupted Iraq's infrastructure, destroying power stations, bridges, factories, refineries, public buildings and telecommunications systems. Most Iraqis seemed to believe that the chief aim of the allied attacks was to humiliate Iraq, not liberate Kuwait. 'We're proud of our history, our heritage and we'll never let Bush impose his will,' said Suhad Salien, an Iraqi housewife. 'In the new world order, which

Mr Bush is so concerned with, he's not prepared to respect Iraq's strength and independence,' said Fawzi Hussein, a lawyer. However, despite all the intensity of the almost non-stop bombing, the Iraqi economy proved to be more resilient than most had expected. Allied aerial attacks impaired commercial activity, but failed to kill it. Retail trade continued, albeit on a smaller scale than in the pre-war days. While the prices of candles and eggs had risen fourfold since the war, those of other consumer items such as clothing, shoes, paper products, kitchen utensils, sweets, nuts and spices were virtually unaffected, and they were plentiful. Yet there were fears for the future. 'How can we rebuild our country, how can we do business if the economic embargo is to continue?' asked Ahmad Razak, a businessman. 'Iraq is an oil rich country, but war reparations are a very heavy burden,' said a civil servant in Baghdad. 'We need money to rebuild our country.'[35]

It was little comfort for Iraqi citizens to hear over their state-run radio on 1 March 1991 that, according to 'various sources', President Bush's decision to call a ceasefire stemmed from the losses suffered by his side in heavy tank battles with the Iraqis, which were described as 'the fiercest since the Second World War'.[36] It was apparent to most foreign observers that Saddam Hussein was trying to claim 'victory' by playing up the fact that he and his regime had survived the most intense air campaign in history, capped with a ground offensive, mounted by the most powerful alliance on earth.

Among Iraq's neighbours, the country which came nearest to sharing the Iraqi leader's sentiments and perceptions was Jordan. Popular opinion regarded Saddam Hussein as 'an innocent victim' whom 30 states headed by 'oil-thirsty superpowers' had set out to destroy. It also accepted Baghdad's claim to have scored 'a moral victory', not least because it had offered to withdraw from Kuwait *before* the allies launched their ground assault. In any case, to have survived continuous bombardment by the world's most powerful nations for six weeks was victory enough. Finally, straw polls showed that nearly two-thirds of Jordanians believed that Iraq's moves attracted global attention to the much neglected Palestinian cause.[37]

In the Arab segment of the US-led coalition, public opinion finally manifested itself in street violence in Egypt. The staging of the ground offensive by the allies unleashed simmering anti-regime and anti-American feelings in Egypt after a long period of low-key dissent in Cairo. Demonstrating university students called Mubarak 'a coward' and an 'American agent', and jeered and 'roughed up' Westerners in the streets. On the fourth day of the daily demonstrations the skirmishes between the protesters and riot police turned violent enough to cause the death of one student.[38]

In the five countries of North Africa, except Libya, crowds celebrated the ceasefire in each case by demonstrating in favour of Saddam Hussein, whereas the official media welcomed the liberation of Kuwait.

In the European sector of the coalition, Britain was quick to follow Bush's lead, sometimes making even stronger demands on Iraq than the American president. On 28 February 1991, for instance, Prime Minister John Major told the British parliament that Iraq would be required to destroy all its remaining ballistic missiles and chemical weapons, and promise not to acquire replacements before the allies would lift the embargo and evacuate southern Iraq. (Interestingly, on the same day, the Shamir government demanded that Iraq should be barred from possessing missiles or non-conventional weapons – and be compelled to declare its intention to make peace with Israel – before the trade embargo against it was lifted.)[39]

The Soviet Union welcomed the ceasefire. 'Every country which participated in the settlement of this crisis can claim part of the success,' said its foreign minister, Bessmertnykh. 'No party can claim the success single-handed.' He called for a meeting of the five permanent members of the Security Council as a first step towards a new security system in the Middle East, in which Iraq had to play a role; and added that the Palestinian issue was still 'the basic issue' in Middle East security and should be solved 'as soon as possible'. Regarding nuclear arms, he implied that Israel should give up its nuclear weapons if it expected Iraq to stop attempting to build a nuclear arsenal. 'We believe the problem [of nuclear arms proliferation in the region] lies in the lack of will, or unpreparedness, of some states [i.e. Israel] to extend their efforts.' Finally, he continued, it was up to the Iraqi people to decide whether to keep Saddam Hussein as their leader or not.[40]

On the last point Moscow was at variance with Washington. Bush said he had not yet felt the euphoria of victory because, for him, the end had not yet come: Saddam Hussein was still in power, and allied prisoners of war were still being held. This was in contrast to World War II, in which he had fought, and of which there had been a 'definite end'.[41]

In contrast, Iran's foreign minister, Velayati, was in agreement with Bessmertnykh on this subject. 'Iraqis should decide the future of Iraq,' he said. 'Iran is opposed to the partition of Iraq.' He urged the allies to withdraw their troops from the region 'as soon as possible', a call no other country had made so far. '[Security Council] Resolution 674, which requires Iraq to pay war damages to all parties affected by the Iraqi aggression against Kuwait, must not overshadow Resolution 598, which calls for the payment of war damages by Iraq to Iran,' stated the Tehran Times on 27 February 1991.[42] (This was not strictly true. Before the question of reparation can be considered, it needs to be established as to who started the First Gulf War in September 1980, Iran or Iraq.)

It is worth noting that during its eight-year war with Iran, Iraq saw some 70,000 of its soldiers taken prisoner. This time a six-week conflict resulted in 80,000 Iraqi prisoners of war. As for Iraqi casualties, no official statistics were released either by Iraq or by the allies, and no formal study to produce these was ordered by the Pentagon. 'Indeed, the allies intend to keep the statistics as vague as possible, in part because the true picture is so horrifying,' reported James Adams of the Sunday Times from Washington. He then quoted allied intelligence sources 'speculating' that as many as 200,000 Iraqis may have died in the Second Gulf War. A few weeks later General Schwarzkopf offered an estimate of 'as many as 150,000'. On 22 May the Defence Intelligence Agency issued its estimate of 100,000, with an 'error factor' of 50%, meaning that 50,000 to 150,000 might have been killed. The purpose of offering high casualty figures initially was to help create discontent against Saddam Hussein and his regime, and foment a popular uprising against them. A reasonable estimate could be arrived at by dividing the war into the 38-day air campaign until 23 February, and the ground offensive. Multiplying the 20,000 deaths in the first 26 days of the air war (as revealed by Sadoun Hamadi in Tehran) by 1.5 gives a figure of 30,000, with three-quarters being military personnel. The estimate of 25,000 Iraqi soldiers, forming about one-seventh of the 12 divisions attacked by the allies while retreating along the Jahra–Basra and Jahra–Umm Qasr routes, seems realistic. Then there were those Iraqi soldiers who were killed and maimed in the fighting that preceded the collapse of their army, and those who were attacked inside Iraq as they fled. Between them, the last two categories probably contributed another 35,000 dead, including more than 8,000 Iraqi troops, who were buried alive in their trenches by the earthmovers and ploughs mounted on the tanks of the attacking US 1st mechanized infantry division. This gives a grand total of 82,500 dead (a figure about midway between 50,000 and 100,000) in a war that lasted only six weeks. It amounts to one-third to one-half of the Iraqi dead during the Iran–Iraq War, which went on for 464 weeks.[43]

The human losses on the allied side were minor, with the US suffering 376 dead in combat and accidents during the seven-month crisis and war.

British military sources claimed that the allies had destroyed or captured 3,500 Iraqi tanks and 2,000 armoured personnel carriers, and knocked out 2,000 Iraqi artillery guns.[44]

Once the war had ended, and the military-approved media 'pools' had been allowed into the Kuwaiti theatre of operations, it became obvious that the allied intelligence and press officers had fed the world media a steady diet of disinformation. They had steadily built up a picture of a huge, monstrous army that had entrenched itself inside massive complexes of underground trenches behind huge sand berms and endless minefields, and equipped itself with stocks of chemical weapons near the frontline. The fact that every captured Iraqi soldier was shown carrying chemical protection equipment was presented as evidence that this was a precaution by the Iraqi army to safeguard its troops against 'blowbacks' when their comrades fired chemical weapons at the allies. 'Not so, we were to discover later,' reported David Beresford of the *Guardian*, who was not attached to the official media pools, after the war. 'The Iraqis were convinced that the allies were going to use chemical weapons and lived in mortal fear of it.'[45]

The size of the Iraqi forces in the Kuwaiti theatre of operations too had been inflated (by about 50%) to 540,000 – primarily to get more and more American and allied forces into Saudi Arabia. (Indeed by the time hostilities ended, the US had 541,000 troops in the region.) Taking into account the 80,000 Iraqis who surrendered and another 180,000 who were hammered by the allies, there was a shortfall of 280,000. Allowing for the 180,000 soldiers who had been added on (for effect) by the Pentagon, the missing 100,000 were the troops that the Iraqi high command had started withdrawing from the Kuwaiti theatre of operations from 18 February onwards.[46]

The one area where there was no need for padding was the actual cost of the war. Despite the brevity of the ground fighting it totalled $61 billion (the estimate made for the war ending in late March 1991), with the allies providing $43.1 billion, and America $17.9 billion, amounting to 0.34% of its annual gross domestic product.[47]

In contrast, Riyadh put the costs of the war, direct and indirect, including its subsidies to the states stationing troops on Saudi soil and suffering the effects of the UN embargo against Iraq, at $45 billion, amounting to 57.3% of its annual gross domestic product. The swift rise in oil price approaching $40 a barrel after the Iraqi invasion, and the large jump in the Saudi output to more than 8 mb/d, provided Saudi Arabia with an increased oil revenue of $8 billion a month. However, the high petroleum prices did not last. After a spurt at the beginning of the air war in mid-January, due to fears of damage to Saudi oil installations by Iraqi weapons or agents, the price of oil per barrel settled down to less than $20, reducing Saudi Arabia's extra cash intake by almost half. The situation deteriorated to the extent that in mid-February 1991 Riyadh sought a loan of $3 billion from international banks, an unprecedented step.[48]

The comparative financial burden borne by Kuwait was even higher. Its government-in-exile paid $22 billion towards financing the allies' military operations, more than three times the annual gross product of Kuwait. And its restored administration faced the daunting task of repairing the damage done to 732 oil wells, 640 of which had been set ablaze by the retreating Iraqi troops. It talked of reparations from Iraq of the magnitude of $100 billion: an unrealistic prospect, since Iraq's oil revenue in 1989 amounted to $14 billion, and it was indebted to foreign governments and banks to the tune of some $75 billion. Taking into account the $10 billion that the UAE and Qatar contributed towards the allies' military operations, the total cost of the six-week Second Gulf War to the oil-rich Gulf monarchies at $77 billion was nearly twice the financial aid they had given to Iraq during the eight-year First Gulf War.[49]

Baghdad, however, had a more pressing problem on hand: how to consolidate the temporary ceasefire into a permanent one. On 2 March the UN Security Council passed Resolution 686 by 11 votes to one (Cuba), with three abstentions (China, India and Yemen), setting out precise steps that Iraq should take to do so. Meanwhile, the UN secretary-general prepared plans to send 8,000 peace-keeping troops to the Iraqi–Kuwaiti border.

Next day, Lt-General Sultan Hashem Ahmad, Iraq's chief of operations, and Lt-General Saleh Abbud Mahmoud, commander of Iraq's 3rd Army Corps, met General Schwarzkopf and General Khalid ibn Sultan at the Safwan airstrip, six miles from the Kuwaiti–Iraqi border. They agreed to meet the conditions for a permanent ceasefire in the Second Gulf War.

While the Iraqi government pressed on with ceasefire arrangements with a view to returning the domestic situation to normality, the anti-Saddam Hussein forces became active, seeing in the acute crisis facing the Iraqi leader an unprecedented opportunity to overthrow him.

11 THE AFTERMATH

'Nothing we had seen or read [about Iraq] had quite prepared us for the particular form of devastation which had now befallen the country ... The recent conflict has wrought near-apocalpyptic results on the economic infrastructure of what was until recently a highly urban and mechanized society.'

Martti Ahtissari, UN undersecretary-general, in
his report on the state of post-war Iraq[1]

'From now on, Iraq and Saddam incarnate the spirit of resistance and the rejection of a [Western] desire to bring Arabs to their knees.'

Sid Ahmad Ghozali, Algerian foreign minister,
2 March 1991[2]

'We tried to overthrow the government and we failed. They tried to crush us and they failed. Now we must find a political and peaceful solution.'

Jalal Talabani, Kurdish rebel leader, 24 April 1991[3]

'To this day, no Israeli government has decided or committed itself to stop building in Judea, Samaria and Gaza – and this will not happen. We will continue to build there. This is an issue that has no relation with the negotiations between us and the Arab states. This has no connection. It is an internal affair.'

Prime Minister Yitzhak Shamir on
Israeli television, 10 April 1991[4]

'What did we win? We've got Saddam. We've to adopt the Kurds. We have strengthened Iran. Down in Kuwait, torture and rape continue under the emir.'

Senator Ernst Hollings to James Baker,
13 June 1991[5]

At the meeting of their military leaders at Safwan airstrip on 3 March, Iraq and the allies formalized the terms of a truce, including the demarcation of the ceasefire line. It placed about one-sixth of Iraq's territory under the control of allied forces, consisting among others of 100,000 US troops. Each side was required to keep its ground forces one kilometre and its aircraft six kilometres from the line. Allied aircraft were allowed to continue their reconnaissance flights over all of Iraq.

The ink had hardly dried on this document when Saddam Hussein's regime found itself facing a rebellion by Shia insurgents in the south. A revolt began in Nasiriyeh on 2 March, when reportedly a group of armed men, freshly arrived from Suq al Shuyukh, a town under American control, organized hundreds of Iraqi army deserters. Together, they battled the government forces and won. A similar phenomenon occurred in Basra, the headquarters of Iraq's 3rd Army Corps.

Aware of the danger that thousands of army deserters might join the Shia rebels in the south, the Iraqi government announced on 4 March that it was pardoning all deserters, and appealed to them to rejoin their units. But this had little effect on the uprising. It spread rapidly to other Shia-majority towns and cities: Amara, Kut, Hilleh, Karbala, Najaf and Samawa. By 7 March all these places had fallen into the hands of the Shia insurgents.

Saddam Hussein was alarmed by these events. He decided to use his well-tried strategy of stick and carrot for both the military and civilian segments of Iraqi society. His government ordered the demobilization of all soldiers aged 35 to 38 and all the retired army officers who had been called up during the Gulf crisis. It gave monthly bonuses of 20 Iraqi dinars each to conscripts and ID 100 to Republican Guardsmen. It increased food rations by a quarter.[6] At the same time, Saddam Hussein appointed the much feared Ali Hassan Majid, who had been co-ordinating the five intelligence services since mid-1988, as interior minister.

Initially, those who participated in the insurgency in southern Iraq, or sympathized with it, considered it to be a purely Iraqi concern. But this changed when, on 7 March, President Rafsanjani of Iran intervened. 'You know well that you are undesirable in your country as well as in the region,' Rafsanjani said, addressing Saddam Hussein. 'So, don't further stain your bloodied hands by killing more innocent Iraqis. Yield to the people's will, and step down.' He warned the Iraqi leader that 'crushing the popular uprising will be your deadliest mistake and a much greater folly than the one which got you into this miserable situation.' He appealed to the Iraqi opposition to close ranks.[7]

Rafsanjani's public call to Saddam Hussein to resign came at a time when there were persistent reports that 'tens of thousands' of armed men had crossed into Iraq from Iran. They reportedly included not only members of Iran's Revolutionary Guards Corps but also the forces of the Tehran-based Supreme Assembly of Islamic Revolution in Iraq. Formed in November 1982 with the primary assistance of the al Daawa al Islamiya and the Islamic Action Organization, SAIRI was led by Baqir Hakim, a Shia cleric with a long history of resistance to the Iraqi regime. During the Iran–Iraq War it built up an armed force of over 20,000 men, consisting of volunteers from among the Iraqi exiles and prisoners of war.[8] Along with this went statements by SAIRI leaders which stressed the Islamic nature of the uprising. This was contrary to the undertaking that SAIRI and other Shia leaders had given to the Damascus-based Joint Action Committee of Iraqi Opposition: their struggle was aimed at overthrowing Saddam Hussein and establishing a democratic state. Many Shias in southern Iraq, who had participated in a popular uprising to gain democratic freedoms, were angered and alienated when they realized that the aim of the leaders of the insurgency was to create an Islamic state on the Iranian model. After all, most of them had fought Iran for eight years to prevent such an outcome. Iran's open intervention, and SAIRI's dominance of the Shia uprising, also alarmed Saudi Arabia, Kuwait and America. The prospect of a fragmented Iraq, with the Shia south lining up with Iran, worried the rulers of Saudi Arabia and Kuwait, not to mention the US administration. Inimical though they were to Saddam Hussein, they did not wish to see his regime replaced by an Iranian-style one, with Tehran extending its influence to the Kuwaiti and Saudi borders, and emerging as the uncontested leader of the Gulf.

It was against this backdrop that the Baghdad government reassembled its forces in the south, particularly the Republican Guard, which was almost wholly Sunni, and its military hardware, including the 700 tanks and 1,400 armoured personnel carriers it had managed to withdraw from the Kuwaiti theatre of operations before the ceasefire.[9] It launched a counterattack against the Shia rebels on 9 March. The ensuing fight was particularly bloody in Basra, Najaf and Karbala.

On 13 March, Iran's Supreme Leader, Ayatollah Ali Khamanei, told the Iraqi army not to fire at believers as this was forbidden in

Islam. He urged Iraqis to resist the Republican Guard, and called for the establishment of an Islamic state in Iraq.[10] Khamanei issued this statement because he knew that Saddam Hussein's forces were gaining the upper hand in their drive against the Shia rebels.

Indeed, by then, they had regained all the towns and villages except Najaf and Karbala, where they encountered the stiffest resistance. Karbala, a city of 250,000 people and the site of two holy shrines of the Shias – the tombs of Imam Hussein and Imam Abbas – had fallen into the rebels' hands on 5 March after an uprising in which tens of thousands of residents had participated. The insurgents had attacked the army headquarters and seized weapons. Once in control, they destroyed the security police headquarters as well as municipal offices, and emptied the warehouses of food and medicine. They decapitated or hanged 75 military officers and Baathist officials, some of them Shia, and tortured many more, often using rooms and halls inside the precincts of the holy shrines. This lasted until 14 March, when the Iraqi soldiers and Republican Guardsmen attacked using mortars and occasionally ground-to-ground missiles. They faced stiff resistance, with the insurgents fighting the regular troops in the streets and houses. In the end, the hardcore of 2,000 to 3,000 rebels retreated to the shrine of Imam Abbas. Some 1,500 Iraqi soldiers and Guardsmen laid siege to the rebel stronghold, and fought for two days before overrunning it. The toll of human life and property was heavy. 'All along Al Abbas Street, which leads to the Shia shrine of Imam Abbas, buildings were burnt out or smashed by gunfire,' reported Patrick Cockburn of the *Independent* a month later. 'At the end of the street a tank stands in front of the porch of the shrine, whose top has been hit.' This shrine as well as Imam Hussein's suffered damage, including bullet marks and gaping artillery holes.[11]

On 16 March Saddam Hussein delivered an hour-long speech on radio and television, his first since the end of the war. 'Herds of rancorous traitors, falsely bearing Iraqi identity, infiltrated from inside and outside the country to spread devastation, terror, sabotage and looting in a number of Iraq's southern cities and villages, helped by mobs who strayed from the right path in Basra, Amara, Nasiriyeh, Karbala, Najaf and Hilleh,' he said. 'Those renegade traitors began to attack some army units and barracks which were remote and withdrawing ... to capture weapons and equipment, burn the people's property, loot government offices, schools, hospitals and houses, and dishonour women ... [and] kill some of the state and party officials, [military] officers and citizens in those cities.' Lamenting the behaviour of Iraq's neighbours, he said, 'We did not expect neighbours with whom we had sincerely determined to establish peace ... to turn their territories into a springboard for such harm and treachery against Iraq.' He contested the view that these events were part of 'a popular uprising' against the regime. 'Any attempt of whatever nature to change the system of government in any country during war with foreign forces cannot be, in substance and consequence, a nationalist attempt.' He alluded to the sectarian nature of the events. 'Iraq has never been and never will be a farm belonging to a certain sect or faction, thus making possible sectarian rivalry or the raising of divisive slogans among the sons of the same country,' he said. 'The transformation of Iraq's diversity into divisions and a political situation that leads to the fragmentation of Iraq ... would be like entering a dark maze that Lebanon has been in for 15 years.' He then turned to the Kurdish north which, he claimed, was also infiltrated by 'armed elements' from 'the same place', that is, Iran. 'Just as the rancorous elements raised slogans of sectarian division in southern cities, the elements that entered northern cities raised slogans of national division, and committed similar acts of terror, revenge, killing, pillage and arson to promote the same failed purpose,' he said. '[In the past 30 years] every Kurdish movement that was linked to the foreigner or relied on him politically, militarily or materially brought only loss and destruction to our Kurdish people. All these movements ended in failure when the political stances in the region changed.' He laid out 'the basic facts of the situation' for 'our genuine' Kurdish people. 'What the renegade and adventurous traitors are calling for, and the slogans they raise, will never be achieved for several reasons including the fact that the Kurds exist in larger numbers in Turkey and Iran, and also in Syria and the Soviet Union,' he stated. 'Eventually, these states will not be able to allow the achievement of the calls that are being raised. The objective of these calls [therefore] is to harm and destroy Iraq.' He reminded his audience that 'the time has come to begin building the pillars of the new phase' despite the current difficulties. 'Our decision as a leadership to build a democratic society based on the constitution, the rule of the law, and pluralism now, just as we were determined to do in 1990, is an irrevocable and final decision.' The first step in this direction would be to appoint a new government which, besides undertaking reconstruction, would supervise a debate on the draft constitution and a referendum on it.[12]

While the Iranian leaders intervened directly, the American president was in two minds. He did not wish to see Iran's power enhanced, nor did he want Saddam Hussein's hand strengthened. He therefore ended up doing nothing more than issuing a verbal warning on 15 March to Iraq's president to stop combat operations against the insurgents.

Having retaken Karbala, Saddam Hussein concentrated on Najaf. Emulating the example of the insurgents in Karbala, the Shia rebels in Najaf had set up their headquarters in the shrine of Imam Ali, father of Imam Hussein. And that was where the final battle was waged when they were attacked by Baghdad's forces. By the time Najaf reverted to government control some 1,400 civilians had lost their lives, according to Iraqi Shia sources. There was a mass exodus from Najaf as well as Karbala. Those who fled reported bloody retribution by the relatives of the victims of the Shia insurgents against the families of the rebels, with the Republican Guardsmen being merciless towards the defeated Shias.[13]

Iran announced a day of mourning on 18 March for those Iraqis who fell in their government's military onslaught in the south, and the desecration of the holy shrines in Najaf and Karbala. Tehran Radio stepped up news of the Shia rebellion, claiming that Saddam Hussein's forces had killed 12,000 to 16,000 civilians in recapturing Najaf and Karbala. Addressing visiting Palestinian and Lebanese groups, Khamanei said, 'Saddam cannot remain in power for long and the continuation of his rule is impossible because of the arms that have fallen into the hands of the people', and he expressed hope that 'an Islamic and truly popular government based on the wishes of the innocent people of Iraq will come to power in that country'.[14]

That seemed to be a forlorn hope. By then Baghdad's forces had virtually regained the south, ending the Shia rebels' 10–14-day rule of Najaf, Karbala and Basra. Indeed, on 21 March Saddam Hussein was able to show the 94-year-old Shia cleric Grand Ayatollah Abol Qasim Khoei on television congratulating him on crushing the rebellion in Najaf. 'Thanks be to God that you succeeded in stamping out this sedition,' Khoei said.[15]

While Saddam Hussein's attention was focused on the south, the Kurdish nationalists struck, building on the success that Masud Barzani's Kurdish Democratic Party had had in freeing the town of Ranya on 4 March. Kurdish leaders were simultaneously participating in the conference of the Joint Action Committee of Iraqi Opposition in Beirut from 11 to 13 March. Its main purpose was to forge a common programme of action to overthrow Saddam Hussein's regime and outline the kind of state the participants wished to create.

A Kurdish nationalist coup took place on 14 March, when most of the troops of the Fursan, the 100,000-strong local Iraqi army auxiliary force made up of Kurds, changed sides. On the morning of that day the regular Iraqi forces found themselves facing ultimatums from their Kurdish auxiliary units. Some fought, others surrendered. By the evening, thanks to the action of tens of thousands of Kurdish auxiliaries, in twelve major towns in a 100-mile-long arc, administrative and other authority passed to the Kurdish insurgents, called *peshmargas* (lit., those who stand in the face of death). Ever since the invasion of Kuwait by Saddam Hussein, the Kurdish nationalist parties had been cultivating the auxiliaries, most of them young recruits who had joined the force either at the behest of their tribal chiefs, who received money and favours from the government, or because they had been dispossessed of land and jobs in the forced settlement of Kurds into protected villages. Omar Sindi, leader of the Fursan in the region of Zakho, and feudal lord of 120 villages, was typical. He changed sides because he sensed that America was backing the Kurdish rebels, and that they were on their way to victory.[16]

Within a week, the insurgents controlled not only the three provinces of Suleimaniya, Arbil and Doahak, which formed the official Autonomous Region of Kurdistan, but also large parts of the governate of Tamim, with the oil city of Kirkuk as its capital.[17] However, this did not last long.

The loyalties of the Kurdish tribal leaders, who had underpinned the success of the *peshmarga* guerrillas, were fickle. But the more serious problem was the absence of geographical proximity and organizational linkage between the insurgencies in the north and the south. By the time the Shia and Kurdish leaders confabulating in Beirut left the city on 22 March to take charge of their respective movements inside Iraq and co-ordinate the two uprisings, it was too late. On that day Saddam Hussein despatched Ali Hassan Majid to Mosul to reorganize the government troops in the Kurdish region, an ominous sign for the Kurdish guerrillas.

The next day the Iraqi president carried out the promised reshuffle of the government, making seven major changes. He promoted Sadoun Hamadi, a US-educated Shia, to prime minister, a position he had held himself so far. Tariq Aziz remained deputy prime minister, but handed over the foreign ministry to Ahmad Hussein Khodayir, the erstwhile head of the president's secretariat. He promoted the army chief of staff, Lt-General Saadi Tuma Abbas, to defence minister.[18]

George Bush dismissed the cabinet changes as cosmetic. But his remark was peripheral to the dilemma he faced. Should the US intervene militarily in what seemed to be an incipient civil war in Iraq by severing Baghdad's supply lines to the Republican Guard, compelling Saddam Hussein to keep his air force grounded, and arming the insurgents with anti-tank and anti-aircraft missiles? There was intense debate on the subject in Washington, with input from Riyadh, Ankara and Cairo.

All the regional capitals advised America against intervention. The prospect of southern Iraq under Shia control alarmed Saudi Arabia – as the prospect of an independent Kurdistan worried Turkey, with a large Kurdish population concentrated in its south-eastern region. Indeed, during his meeting with President Bush at Camp David on 24 March, President Turgut Ozal of Turkey reportedly explained how an independent Iraqi Kurdistan would become the nucleus for a Greater Kurdistan for the Kurdish populations of Turkey, Iran and Syria, thus destabilizing the whole region. 'We're playing no part in that [Iraqi uprising], but it shows great unrest with the rule of Saddam Hussein,' said Bush after this meeting. President Ozal was more direct. He urged outside powers 'not to intervene in Iraq', adding that 'Iraqis will find the best way for themselves.'[19] Letting the Iraqis sort it out for themselves meant, in policy terms, that the US should settle for something less than achieving its stated objective of overthrowing the Saddam Hussein regime. If Ozal did not press this point, then apparently King Fahd did, during his meeting with Brent Scowcroft and his deputy for Near Eastern affairs, Richard Haas, during their secret visit to Saudi Arabia on 26 March at Fahd's invitation.

Following the National Security Council meeting on 27 March, the White House spokesman announced that Bush had no intention of putting his administration in the middle of a civil war in Iraq, adding that it had made 'no promises to the [Iraqi] Shias or Kurds'. Reflecting the public mood, he said, 'The American people have no stomach for a military operation to dictate the outcome of a political struggle in Iraq.' This was a setback for the pro-Israeli lobby, which advocated a new US drive to Baghdad to overthrow Saddam Hussein, an objective to which Washington remained committed but not with much enthusiasm. 'If Iraq is just a country that treats its people decently and [does] not attack its neighbours, it'd be great progress,' said Paul Wolfowitz, policy undersecretary at the Pentagon, after attending the NSC meeting.[20]

By now, the Iraqi military high command felt confident that the Shia revolt in the south no longer threatened the future of the regime, and turned its full attention to the Kurdish insurgency. On 28 March, using heavy artillery, multiple rocket launchers and helicopter gunships, the Iraqi armoured and infantry divisions mounted an all-out assault on Kirkuk. By the evening they had driven out the rebels, who were lightly armed.

The success of Baghdad's forces in overpowering the popular Kurdish insurgents and the renegade Kurdish auxiliaries led to a massive exodus of the Kurds to the mountainous Iranian and Turkish borders. By Easter Saturday, 30 March, Charles Glass, an American journalist touring the area, found '[Kurdish] villagers and townspeople on the march, living in captured Iraqi army tents in the mountains, driving north to the borders, the poorest among them walking mile after mile in search of safety'.[21] As the Iraqi army recaptured town after town, the size of the Kurdish exodus increased, finally involving over 1.5 million people, or about half the total population of the region. The Kurds feared brutal and extensive reprisals by Baghdad, a repeat of its behaviour in the mid-1970s and late 1980s.

On 1 April Masud Barzani made a desperate appeal to America, Britain and France to act through the UN to save his people from 'genocide and torture'. But the Western allies failed to respond, primarily because the events did not fit the scenario they had hastily conceived for post-war Iraq: a military coup against Saddam Hussein which would leave the army in control of a united Iraq.

During the first week of April Baghdad's forces retook Arbil, Dohak and Zakho. On 6 April the Revolutionary Command Council declared: 'Iraq has totally crushed all acts of sedition and sabotage in all cities of Iraq.'[22] Despite repeated pleas by Barzani and other Kurdish leaders to fellow-Kurds not to leave their settlements, they fled in droves. So intense was their terror of Saddam Hussein and his army that they risked death by exposure, exhaustion and disease on the mountain passes rather than stay behind and become victims of the brutality of the Iraqi troops.

These developments occurred against the background of a bleak economic situation in Iraq, encapsulated in a report by the UN undersecretary-general, Martti Ahtissari, published on 22 March. It said *inter alia* that the UN sanctions 'seriously affected' Iraq's ability to feed its people. This was noted by the drafters of the Security Council's Resolution 687, a long and comprehensive document of thirty-four paragraphs. It was adopted on 3 April by 12 votes to one (Cuba), with two abstentions (Yemen and Ecuador).[23] It removed the embargo on foodstuffs, eased restrictions on essential civilian needs, and unfroze Iraq's foreign assets. However, the lifting of the remaining restrictions was tied to the elimination of Iraq's non-conventional weapons, and the establishment of a mechanism for Iraq to compensate those who had suffered from its actions. The other provisions of the resolution concerned a formal ceasefire, borders between Iraq and Kuwait, peacekeeping, and international terrorism.

The document could be summarized as follows. One, a formal ceasefire would come into effect when Iraq officially accepted the resolution. Two, Iraq and Kuwait must respect the disputed 1963 border until the UN demarcated it. Three, UN military observers would monitor a demilitarized zone extending six miles into Iraq and three miles into Kuwait, and their deployment would allow the allies to remove their troops from Iraq. Four, Iraq must agree unconditionally to destroy or remove under international supervision all chemical and biological weapons, and all ballistic missiles with ranges greater than 95 miles, and related production facilities. A similar procedure would be instituted to remove all nuclear weapons-usable material. Iraq must provide lists of locations, amounts and types of these arms and materials as well as chemical and biological weapons by 17 April. The UN secretary-general would set up a commission charged with making on-site inspections by 17 May. These actions represented steps towards the goal of establishing in the Middle East a zone free from weapons of mass destruction. Five, Iraq was liable for damages, without prejudice to its foreign debts, arising from its invasion of Kuwait. A fund would be created to meet the claims, and a commission established by 2 May to administer it. The amount to be paid into the fund would be based on a percentage of Iraq's oil revenues. Payment levels would take into account the needs of Iraq's people, its economy and foreign debts. Six, Iraq must pledge not to support international terrorism.

After protesting that Resolution 687 aimed at establishing US hegemony over the region, and that its terms impinged on Iraq's sovereignty, Baghdad accepted it on 6 April.

By then, setting aside Iraq's protest about interference in its internal affairs, the Security Council had passed another resolution, Number 688, by ten votes to three (Cuba, Yemen and Zimbabwe), with two abstentions (China and India). It dealt primarily with the Kurdish problem. It condemned the repression of the Iraqi civilian population in many parts of Iraq, including most recently in Kurdish-populated areas, and demanded that Iraq should immediately end this repression, and open dialogue with the concerned parties to ensure that the human and political rights of all Iraqi citizens were respected. It called on Baghdad to allow immediate access by international humanitarian organizations to those in need of assistance in all parts of Iraq and make available all necessary facilities for their operations. It requested the secretary-general to pursue his humanitarian efforts in Iraq and report forthwith, if appropriate, on the basis of a further mission to the region, on the plight of the Iraqi civilian population, and in particular the Kurds.

Resolution 688 was adopted on 5 April, a day before the RCC claimed that the central government had crushed 'all acts of sedition and sabotage' in all Iraqi cities, and offered amnesty to rebellious Kurds. At the same time Saddam Hussein appointed Hussein Kamil Hassan Majid – his son-in-law and cousin, who was a member of the RCC and ran the ministry of industry and military industrialization – as defence minister.[24]

Hussein Kamil Hassan Majid took over from Ali Hassan Majid in Kurdistan. He carried out mopping-up operations there which, according to opposition sources, involved the use of heavy artillery and helicopter gunships, and caused the massacre of a few thousand civilians.[25] This action accelerated the mass exodus, which in its final stage left a million Kurds taking refuge either inside Iran or along the Iraqi–Iranian border, and another half a million inside Turkey or along the Iraqi–Turkish frontier.

The high death toll that exhaustion and exposure to the elements inflicted on the children and old men and women among the Kurdish refugees, coupled with the appalling conditions prevalent at the makeshift refugee camps, conveyed to the Western public through television pictures, aroused much sympathy for the Kurds in the West. Media commentators and politicians were unanimous in demanding action.

Responding to this outcry, on 9 April, the British prime minister John Major unveiled a four-point plan at the EC summit in Luxembourg. As well as a proposal to set up a 'transparent' register under which the UN would be notified of all weapons sales throughout the Middle East, in order to prevent a revival of an arms race in the region, his plan included additional humanitarian aid for Kurdish refugees in Turkey and Iran; the creation of a safe haven for the Kurds in two stages; and tying the lifting of the economic blockade against Iraq to the cessation of Saddam Hussein's atrocities against civilians. The two stages of safeguarding the Kurds were: to bring them down from the mountains to a relatively small enclave inside Iraq (probably above the 36th parallel) under UN protection; and then to help them to return to their settlements.[26]

Iraq rejected the safe haven idea. 'The proposal to set up a zone under UN supervision inside Iraq to deal with the so-called refugee problem is a suspicious proposal that Iraq categorically rejects and will resist with all means,' said Sadoun Hamadi, now the prime minister of Iraq. 'Creating and inflating this problem is deliberate, and is part of the chain of plots against Iraq's sovereignty.'[27]

On 11 April the Security Council president, Paul Noterdaeme of Belgium, handed over a letter to the Iraqi ambassador, notifying him that a ceasefire in the Gulf was now in effect, and that a 1,440-strong United Nations Iraq–Kuwait Observation Mission had been deployed to monitor the ceasefire and prevent border violations in the nine-miles-wide demilitarized zone as well as the 25-mile-long Khor Abdullah waterway.

However, the situation in the north remained tense, with the Iraqi government rejecting Washington's efforts to circumscribe the actions of its army, and insisting that it would not agree to a ceasefire in the region. On 16 April the three Western permanent members of the Security Council announced their interpretation of Resolution 688. Under it, they said, they were entitled to send troops to northern Iraq and establish secure encampments to provide supplies for Kurdish refugees. 'They have no right to send troops to our territory,' said Tariq Aziz on 17 April. 'This is interference in our internal affairs.'[28]

Significantly, at 08.30 GMT on that day, an undeclared ceasefire between the Kurdish rebels and the Iraqi army came into effect as a prelude to negotiations between the Baghdad government and the delegates of the Iraqi Kurdistan Front (IKF), a coalition of seven Kurdish parties. The news of the Kurdish leaders' assent to talks with Saddam Hussein came as a surprise to most outsiders. Jalal Talabani, the leader of the Patriotic Union of Kurdistan who headed the Kurdish delegation, explained the reasons for the volte-face. 'We have no friends to help us,' he said. 'Iran, Turkey, Saudi Arabia, Syria – none of them stood by us. The Shias had the help of Iran, a big neighbour. Our people are begging, and Iran is not helping us at all. If we were supported by others, we could fight for a long time, but without the Kurdish people at home, we can't do anything.'[29] In other words, the first priority was to get the Kurdish refugees to return home. Also, the Kurdish leaders saw Saddam Hussein's current weakness as providing a good opportunity to strike a deal. The talks began in Baghdad on 18 April.

On that day Iraq's foreign minister, Ahmad Hussein Khodayir, signed a memorandum of understanding on the role of UN Humanitarian centres (UNHUCs). Baghdad welcomed UN efforts to promote the voluntary return home of Iraqi displaced persons and to take humanitarian measures to avert new waves of refugees, and allowed the UN to set up UNHUCs, staffed by UN civilians, all over the country in agreement with Baghdad, to provide food aid, medical care, agricultural rehabilitation and shelter. It promised to make cash contributions in local currency to help cover the UN's in-country operational costs. The arrangement was 'without prejudice to the sovereignty, and territorial integrity, political independence, security and non-interference in the internal affairs of Iraq'.[30]

Yielding to Western pressures, Saddam Hussein deputed two Iraqi generals to meet the US commander in charge of Operation 'Provide Comfort' to set up safe havens for the Kurdish refugees inside Iraq on 19 April. They agreed to withdraw Iraqi security forces, including police, from the Zakho area.

Following several days of talks between the Kurdish leaders and the Iraqi delegation, headed by Izzat Ibrahim, vice-chairman of the Revolutionary Command Council, Jalal Talabani told a press conference (attended by the Iraqi information minister Hamid Yusuf Hamadi) that his delegation had concluded an agreement in principle with Saddam Hussein providing for Kurdish autonomy in Iraq. 'The agreement affirmed the principle of democracy in Iraq, press freedoms, and allowing all Kurds to return to their towns and villages,' said Talabani. He added that the pact was based on the 1970 agreement, and that it granted 3.5 million Iraqi Kurds autonomy in northern Iraq. It permitted them to return to, and revive, about 3,800 villages and towns which had been razed by the Baathist regime over the past 17 years. It included the government's promises to end the policy of trying to Arabize Kurdistan, and to release all Kurdish political prisoners. Talabani stated that the agreement would be dependent upon the advent of 'free elections to a national assembly in [all of] Iraq'. That evening, Iraqi television showed Saddam Hussein kissing each of the four Kurdish leaders on both cheeks.[31]

This agreement had little impact on the thinking of the Western powers at the Security Council as they considered the idea of a 'UN police force' in northern Iraq as a reassurance for Kurdish refugees who were being encouraged to return home. However, under the UN charter such a force could not be despatched to Iraq without its consent. On 9 May Baghdad rejected the proposal. It also protested against John Major's statement of 10 May that Britain would veto any easing of UN sanctions against Iraq while Saddam Hussein remained in power. Its letter on the subject to the UN secretary-general described Major's statement as going beyond the UN resolutions against Iraq and constituting meddling in Iraq's internal affairs.[32]

On the whole, Iraq was on the defensive, a position it had found itself in following its acceptance of Resolution 687. Just before the deadline of 17 April it provided information about its chemical, nuclear and missile programmes to the UN secretary-general and the International Atomic Energy Agency in Vienna. When the IAEA asked Iraq to provide further details it did so in a letter. It claimed that 'all its fissionable material' was buried in the ruins of its two small nuclear reactors at Tuwaitha, 20 miles south-east of Baghdad, which were destroyed in the allied bombings, and that this material was not emitting radiation. It stated that Iraq had relocated some of its nuclear materials during the war to escape allied bombing, and that the government would disclose the new whereabouts only if IAEA officials guaranteed their safety from further allied aerial attacks.[33] Having read the Iraqi letter, US sources leaked their version. According to them, Iraq's letter to the IAEA contained 13 items under the listing of nuclear materials. Of these, six had been moved within the Tuwaitha nuclear research complex 'for reasons of safety'; and four had been moved to a site near Tuwaitha. The remaining three items, including uranium powder and pellets as well as natural uranium fuel bundles and rods, were described as 'completely destroyed' in the allied air campaign. US officials claimed that the ten items unaffected by the bombing included the bulk of Iraq's enriched uranium.[34]

A visit by the IAEA's 34-member team to Iraq was in progress when the contents of the Iraqi letter were leaked by US sources. It lasted five weeks. IAEA inspectors found the country's entire stockpile of 98 pounds of enriched uranium (including 47.5 lbs supplied by France and the Soviet Union) at Tuwaitha. About a third of this was under the ruins of the destroyed Iraqi nuclear reactors, and was not emitting radiation. The rest had been stored in special bunkers to safeguard it from the allied bombing, and had survived intact.[35]

Regarding the payment of reparations by Iraq, on 20 May the Security Council passed Resolution 692, establishing a war damage fund to be financed by Iraq's oil revenue, by 14 votes to none, with Cuba abstaining. The resolution set Geneva as the site of the governing board, consisting of representatives from the 15 Security Council members. It requested the UN secretary-general to set the ceiling on the percentage of Iraq's oil income to be used to pay claims from individuals, corporations and governments. While Baghdad asked for a five-year moratorium on compensation payments, arguing that its foreign debts and reconstruction costs were exorbitant, the non-aligned nations on the Security Council suggested that 5% of Iraqi petroleum revenue should be used to pay claims while the US proposed that the figure should be 50% of Iraq's oil income. A UN report on the procedures, published on 3 May, had stated that Iraq's foreign assets, frozen under the UN sanctions, would not be part of the fund to be administered by the UN Compensation Commission. The task of settling damages would include such items as the costs to Saudi Arabia of cleaning up the oil pollution in the Gulf, the claims of tens of thousands of foreign workers who fled Kuwait after the Iraqi invasion, and Kuwaiti losses due to the Iraqis' setting alight nearly 640 oil wells, consuming an estimated 6 mb/d.[36]

Extinguishing the oil well fires was a top priority for the government in Kuwait, which began its rule by imposing martial law for three months, with Crown Prince Saad al Sabah acting as the military governor-general. The 210,000 Kuwaiti nationals (about a third of the total) who endured the Iraqi occupation felt that they had the right to a greater say in the running of their country. They were critical of the al Sabahs as well as the Kuwaitis returning from a comfortable exile and telling them what they should do. The possession of some 500,000 small arms by the Kuwaitis, and the lack of water, electricity and telephones heightened political tension. Abdullah Nibbari, a politician and economist, announced the formation of the Kuwait Democratic Forum, and demanded the restoration of the National Assembly dissolved in 1986 and the formation of a government of national unity. It was not until 14 March that the emir returned to Kuwait after his temporary palace had been refurbished with golden taps. On 20 March came the resignation of the government, in which the al Sabahs had held all the seven important ministries.

When the crown prince consulted various groups on the formation of the new cabinet he found the opposition reluctant to join. He argued that reconstruction and security should take precedence over democratization, whereas the opposition – consisting mainly of the Kuwait Democratic Forum, the Second August Movement, dominated by local Shias who stayed behind and resisted the Iraqi occupation, and the Islamic Constitutional Movement – wanted specific promises about reviving the National Assembly and holding fresh elections. Two meetings between Crown Prince Saad and a KDF delegation ended in a deadlock. 'The ruling al Sabahs are very stubborn,' said a KDF leader on 28 March. 'They are repeating the same things they used to say before the Iraqi invasion.' Two days later a joint delegation of all opposition groups told the crown prince that they would join the new government only if they were given a timetable for parliamentary elections. It got the backing of 96 eminent citizens who urged the ruler to promise an elected parliament, an independent press and judiciary, freedom of association and speech, and the appointment of a panel of Kuwaitis of 'honesty and integrity' to review all the contracts that the government had awarded recently.[37]

On 7 April, in a television address to the nation, Shaikh Jaber III al Sabah said that after 'things settle down and life resumes its [normal] course', elections would be held 'next year' in accordance with the constitution. He said that the issue of granting the franchise to women and second-class citizens (i.e. those who could trace their origins in the emirate to 1945) should be 'studied'. The emir praised the Kuwaiti people for their steadfastness in facing the brutality of the Iraqi occupation as well as the Gulf states and other members of the anti-Iraqi coalition. 'The tyrant of Baghdad is fast on signing agreements but at the same time very quick in suspending them,' he said. 'So I ask our brothers and friends to keep their forces here.'[38]

The 'brothers' concerned were Egypt and Syria. Following the hostilities they had not pulled out their troops from Kuwait. Their foreign ministers met their counterparts from the Gulf Co-operation Council in Damascus on 5 and 6 March. Together they issued a communiqué, known as the Damascus Declaration, agreeing to form a joint peacekeeping force to maintain post-war security in the Gulf, with an understanding that it would consist chiefly of Egyptian and Syrian troops. The declaration also made a statement of intent about pursuing joint economic policies aimed at achieving 'balanced social and economic development' in the region, and eventually establishing some form of Arab economic community.[39]

At a meeting in Kuwait City in late March, GCC ministers decided to provide Egypt and Syria with financial aid of $5 billion to integrate them into the recently proclaimed 'new Arab order'. This was in addition to the GCC grants to these two countries for the deployment of the 35,000 Egyptian and 20,000 Syrian troops as part of the backbone of an expanded Gulf defence force.[40]

By then Egypt and Syria were at the centre of Baker's shuttle diplomacy to reactivate the moribund Middle East peace process involving Israel and the Arabs. Among the parties Baker consulted were the Palestinian leaders in the Occupied Territories, including Faisal Husseini, an eminent pro-PLO figure. They insisted on being able to choose their own delegates to the peace conference.[41]

Israel's prime minister Shamir agreed to an international conference chaired by the US and the USSR on two conditions: the opening session should lead immediately to bilateral negotiations between Israel and individual Arab states; and the conference should not have the power to decide solutions or impose them on Israel. Furthermore, the Palestinian delegation should not include members of the PLO or persons resident in East Jerusalem, since all of Jerusalem was part and parcel of Israel. On the other side was President Assad of Syria. He wanted all concerned parties to seek a comprehensive and just peace based on Security Council Resolutions 242 and 338 through an international conference where the UN would play an important role. Secondly, the basic mandate of the conference should be to implement these resolutions. Thirdly, the conference should have an ongoing structure and responsibilities so that the parties to the dispute could turn to the two co-chairmen of the conference – the US and the USSR – if they got into a deadlock at some point.[42]

Later, each side made peripheral concessions, with Shamir saying that he was prepared to concede the establishment of Palestinian 'ministries' in the Occupied Territories to take charge of Palestinian (and not Jewish settlers') health, education, justice and trade, but not security or foreign affairs; and Syria offering Israel internationally-backed guarantees of peace in return for withdrawal from the Arab lands it occupied in June 1967.[43] But there was no movement in the Israeli and Syrian positions on the procedures and scope of the international peace conference.

As Baker prepared to meet Assad in Damascus, Israel added more mobile homes to its Talmon-B settlement near Ramallah in the West Bank, a move widely seen as a rebuff to Baker's peace efforts. He criticized Israel for its action, and appealed to it to stop creating new Jewish settlements in the Occupied Territories.[44]

Ten hours of talks between Baker and Assad on 24 April failed to resolve the differences between Syria and Israel. The situation was back to square one on the Arab–Israeli conflict. The hopes aroused by President Bush and his senior aides that once the Iraqi invasion of Kuwait had been reversed they would apply themselves wholeheartedly to resolving the Arab–Israeli problem were virtually dashed. This provided a field day to the sceptics who said, 'I told you so'. Among them was Tariq Aziz. 'I really doubt that the situation is

[now] better than before last January 15 for the United States and its
Arab allies,' he told the *Washington Post* on 6 May 1991. 'Israel is
more ambitious and expansionist than ever before, and you will see
in a few years how the Arab members of the so-called coalition will
suffer seriously because of it.'45

Tariq Aziz and other Iraqi leaders were now feeling more confident
than they had since their defeat two months before, especially as the
American forces prepared to withdraw from southern Iraq. They did so
on the night of 6 May. And, within a couple of days, Saddam Hussein
was back in the recently evacuated border town of Safwan, with his
smiling portrait adorning the streets and calendars portraying him in
various costumes on sale in the market. Freshly scribbled street graffiti
read: 'Yes, yes Saddam', 'No East, no West, Saddam Hussein is Best',
and 'Death to traitors of Iraq'.46

On 7 May the Baghdad government began its second round of
negotiations with a four-man delegation of the Iraqi Kurdistan Front
led by Masud Barzani, the head of the Kurdish Democratic Party. The
official delegation was headed by Izzat Ibrahim. These talks continued
for several weeks, with the Iraqi side not being as accommodating as
it had been in the first round.

Meanwhile, the UN began establishing its presence in the 3,600
square mile security zone that the allies had created in the Iraqi–
Turkish border region and where they had by late May deployed
16,000 troops from a dozen nations. UN personnel took over the
administration of Zakho refugee camp from the US military. By
mid-May at least half of the 500,000 Kurdish refugees who had fled
to this region after the Iraqi military crackdown in late March (about
half as numerous as those who had sought refuge inside Iran or along
its border with Iraq) had returned home. On 23 May Iraq signed a
memorandum with the UN to allow 100 to 500 security guards into
Kurdistan to protect UN civilian workers and equipment. But this
did not stop the allied task force of engineers, doctors and munitions
clearance experts from rehabilitating the municipal services of Dohak,
located outside the security zone, to reassure the remaining Kurdish
refugees that it was safe to return home. Saddam Hussein saw it
differently. In an interview with the Turkish daily *Milliyet* (People),
published on 28 May, he denounced the US-led operation to protect
Kurds. 'Separatism is being fuelled by the foreign powers,' he said.
'They are aiming to set up a small oil state.'47

However, the allied troops began leaving gradually, officially handing over all humanitarian tasks to the UN High Commissioner for

Refugees (UNHCR) on 7 June. When the Kurdish tribal leaders invited Lt-General John Shalikashvili, the US army officer who had been put in charge of the 12-nation Operation 'Provide Comfort' since its launch on 19 April, to stay on, he refused the offer. This was the background against which the talks between the Kurdish leaders and the government delegation in Baghdad proceeded.

With each passing week, the economic situation in Iraq eased somewhat, petrol rationing ending nationally on 28 April, Saddam Hussein's birthday, and electricity and water services being restored almost fully to Baghdad. Life in Basra, the second largest city, had improved sufficiently by late May to allow the local governor, General Latif Hammoud, to claim: 'We have been able to restore normal life to the city.' Other urban centres had their electricity and water restored partially. The official decisions, taken in the latter half of May, to abolish the revolutionary courts (established after the Baathist seizure of power in mid-1968) and demobilize the Popular Army, were warmly received by the public. So too were the long prison sentences meted out to profiteers in order to control runaway inflation.[48]

By all accounts, Saddam Hussein had by now consolidated his power, with the inner circle of his senior advisers, called the Special Bureau, virtually intact. It included Izzat Ibrahim, his loyal deputy; Tariq Aziz; Ali Hassan Majid (interior minister); Sibawi Hussein Tikriti, the president's half-brother, who controlled military intelligence; Hussein Kamil Hassan Majid, the president's son-in-law and the newly appointed defence minister.

It was significant that three of the four Iraqi leaders negotiating an agreement with the Kurdish delegation belonged to Saddam Hussein's Special Bureau, the exception being Saadi Mehdi Saleh, the speaker of the National Assembly. They bargained hard. And it was not until 16 June that Barzani and his team were able to return to Kurdistan with a draft agreement.

On the eve of Eid al Adha, an important Muslim festival falling on 22 June, Masud Barzani unveiled the agreement he had struck with Baghdad to other leaders of the Iraqi Kurdistan Front. Overall, Barzani claimed that he had secured 70 per cent of the original demands he had made. Where he had failed was in getting the Iraqi government to include certain cities and areas in the Kurdistan Autonomous Region, hold free and fair elections to a national constituent assembly charged with drafting a new constitution, and underwrite the agreement with international guarantees. The draft agreement gave Kurds predominant military and political authority over the provinces of

Dohak, Arbil and Suleimaniya, with the control of the army and police shared jointly by the Kurdish authorities and the central Iraqi government. Kurdistan was to have a separate budget funded by Iraqi oil revenues, with an urgent plan to rebuild Kurdish villages. Kirkuk was to be jointly administered by the Iraqi government and the Kurds, as a temporary measure, with discussions on its future to continue after Kurdish autonomy had been implemented. Elections in Kurdistan were to be held within three months of the signing of the agreement, with elections in the rest of Iraq to be conducted within six months to a year. The new national constitution was to guarantee a multi-party system, freedom of the press, and separation of judicial, executive and legislative powers.[49] Opinion among the Kurdish leaders was divided, with Barzani recommending acceptance and Talabani advocating further negotiations.

On its part, Baghdad demanded that, besides closing down their two radio stations, the Kurds should lay down their heavy weapons, throw their weight behind the regime by fighting domestic and foreign enemies, and sever all links with the outside powers. Its fears were increased when the US announced on 25 June that it and its Gulf War allies had decided, subject to Turkish approval, to deploy a brigade-size force in southern Turkey ready to intervene in Iraq to protect the Kurds.[50] While Baghdad described the move as 'an anti-Iraqi plot', the Kurdish leadership felt encouraged to stiffen its stance. It decided on 29 June that the draft agreement needed 'further discussion' with the central government.

Feeling betrayed by the Kurds' negotiations with Baghdad, the other constituents of the Joint Action Committee of Iraqi Opposition met in Damascus on 29–30 June to develop new strategies to bring about the downfall of Saddam Hussein.

The Bush administration, too, was committed to overthrowing Saddam Hussein by any means: a coup, or slow strangulation of the economy. Indeed, it was so confident of a military coup against Saddam Hussein that it reportedly let Majid Khoei, a son of the Grand Ayatollah Khoei with a plan to topple Saddam Hussein, cool his heels in a border town of Saudi Arabia in mid-March. It was not until late April that Majid Khoei was received by Richard Haas of the National Security Council in Washington. Haas advised Khoei to avoid escalating the Shia insurgency so as not to threaten a pending coup that the US was planning with Iraqi officers. If Washington was the prime instigator behind the attempt reportedly made by Lt-General Bareq Abdullah (a Sunni officer who, following his brilliant performance in repulsing the Iranian attempts to cross the Shatt al Arab in early 1987, had been promoted to command the Republican Guard) to overthrow Saddam Hussein in early May, then it was certainly disappointed. For the coup attempt failed, and Bareq Abdullah lost his life.[51]

Then there was the strategy of squeezing the Iraqi economy so hard that it would fuel public discontent to the point of repeated mass demonstrations against the regime in Baghdad, leading to the downfall of Saddam Hussein. President Bush repeatedly stated that the US opposed lifting the UN embargo against Iraq until the Iraqi dictator was forced out. 'All possible sanctions will be maintained until Saddam Hussein is gone,' said Robert Gates, director-designate of the CIA, on 21 May. 'Any easing of the sanctions will be considered only when there is a new government.'[52] Since Iraq needed to import 70% of its foodgrains, the government was unable to provide enough to its citizens through its rationing system. This, and the lack of electricity for water purification and sewerage treatment, had resulted in typhoid, hepatitis, meningitis and gastroenteritis reaching epidemic levels. While the UN lifted its sanctions against food imports to Iraq on 22 March, its continued embargo on Iraq's foreign financial transactions, combined with its ban on Iraqi exports of crude oil, made it extremely hard for Baghdad to import food and medicine.

As if this were not enough, America, actively backed by Britain, sponsored a resolution at the Security Council which required Iraq to pay the cost of eliminating its arsenal of non-conventional arms under international supervision. It was passed unanimously as Resolution 699 on 17 June 1991. Earlier Iraq had informed the UN that it possessed 1,005 tons of liquid nerve gas stored in vats, and 11,381 chemical warheads. Of these 30 were fitted for Scud missiles, and the rest for bombs or artillery shells. It added that at least 2,700 chemical warheads were buried under debris from allied attacks. The UN commission appointed to undertake the task of destroying Iraq's non-conventional weapons sent a team of 28 experts to Iraq to investigate its stockpiles of chemical weapons. The cost of eliminating Iraq's arsenal of weapons of mass destruction, which could reach $800 million, would be deducted from the Iraqi assets frozen in Western banks since August 1990.[53]

America's regional allies were almost equally hostile towards Saddam Hussein. Tariq Aziz's appeal to Turkey during his visit to Ankara on 12–13 June to send its diplomats back to Baghdad and reopen Iraq's pipelines to the Mediterranean fell on deaf ears. By then Iraq knew that the limit for its oil revenue to be channelled into the

UN compensation fund was not to exceed 30%, as recommended by the UN secretary-general.

On 12 June the Security Council's sanctions committee decided that 31 countries could release more than $3.75 billion in Iraqi assets frozen in their banks to enable Baghdad to buy food and other essential consumer goods. A month earlier the committee had authorized the unfreezing of about $1 billion in Iraqi assets in American, Swiss, British and Japanese banks at the discretion of their governments. Iraq badly needed this money. According to a study by a team of Harvard University doctors, the official Iraqi ration was half the size required to maintain normal health; and child mortality had doubled since the UN sanctions were imposed. Though the electricity supply was running at 22% of the pre-war level it was not sufficient to ensure water purification and sewerage treatment.[54]

Iraq needed $8 billion annually just to service its foreign loans of $75 to $80 billion. It faced a repair bill of up to $30 billion, about half of that to be paid in hard currency earned from resumed shipments of oil.[55] But at least its oil extraction facilities were almost intact. This was not the case with Kuwait. With only about 50 of its burning oil wells being extinguished each month, some 500 were still alight in mid-June. As for oil production, the plan was to extract 50,000 b/d by summer, and double the figure by late 1991, reaching about 7% of Kuwait's pre-war OPEC quota. Full recovery was not expected until the mid-1990s. The cost of rebuilding the country and its infrastructure was estimated at $80 billion, over the next five years, with government plans to borrow up to $34 billion at home and abroad.[56]

Many of the contracts for post-war reconstruction had been awarded to American companies. American personnel were also in the forefront of performing civil and administrative functions of the Kuwaiti state. Indeed, James Baker reportedly hinted to the emir during their meeting in Kuwait City on 22 April that his government was becoming too dependent on US forces for non-military functions, and not getting its own machinery working again properly.[57] Baker also pointed to the violations of human rights in the emirate. These were summarized by Amnesty International in its report on 18 April: it charged that since 26 February scores of people, mostly Palestinians and Iraqis, had been murdered, and hundreds arrested and tortured by Kuwait's military and the members of the Kuwaiti resistance during the Iraqi occupation. 'Although revenge for alleged collaboration appears to have been the motive in some cases, many people seem to have been targeted simply because of their nationality,' the report said. Referring to some 600 detainees held at a military prison outside Kuwait City, the report stated: 'Torture is said to have been rife, including beatings, electrical shocks and prolonged deprivation of food and water, and medical care virtually non-existent.'[58] Under pressure from Baker, the emir agreed to allow human rights organizations to visit Kuwait and interview the Palestinians and other minorities. However, by all accounts, human rights were low on the emir's agenda, his primary concerns being ensuring the external security of his emirate and pacifying an increasingly vocal opposition at home.

By getting America and Britain to agree to keep their troops in Kuwait for the time being, the emir felt that he had made his emirate secure. But long-term security for Kuwait as well as other Gulf states depended on how the Damascus Declaration of 6 March was to be implemented.

If the US and its Western allies had their way, they would have liked to see GCC states provide bases for 100,000 troops from Egypt and Syria, and pay for their upkeep, with the whole arrangement to be formally named the Mutual Defence Organization. In addition, Washington would have liked to place an advance headquarters of its Central Command in Bahrain and, more importantly, pre-position enough tanks, trucks, artillery and ammunition, preferably in Saudi Arabia, to arm an armoured division of 15,000–20,000 US troops. However, on 29 April Riyadh turned down Washington's proposals. Prince Khalid ibn Sultan said that Saudi history, traditions and culture weighed against a substantial American presence in his country, and that the Pentagon should not expect Saudi Arabia to agree that the most efficient way of deterring a future threat to it would be to leave behind a stockpile of weapons in case US forces had to return.[59]

When foreign ministers of the GCC met in Kuwait City on 5 May to discuss security arrangements in the region, they announced that they were holding 'intensive contacts' with Iran over regional security. This went down badly with Egypt, which wanted to keep Gulf security as an exclusively Arab affair. Moreover, Cairo had been disappointed by the lack of Kuwaiti contracts for Egyptian companies and the emir's decision to limit severely the number of Egyptians to be allowed back into his emirate to work. On 8 May President Mubarak announced that the pull-out of the Egyptian troops from Saudi Arabia, which had begun in April, would be completed by August.

Following this, General Schwarzkopf said that the US intended to station 5,000 US troops in Kuwait 'indefinitely'. However, Dick Cheney announced on 21 May that American troops would remain in

the emirate for 'several more months'. He said this after having completed trips to GCC capitals as well as Cairo to discuss a framework
for a US–Arab military relationship in the region. He found Bahrain
and the UAE wanting closer military co-operation with America than
before, and Kuwait pleading for more US forces and weapons, and
offering a permanent base on its soil to the Pentagon.[60]

As for pacifying opposition inside Kuwait, the emir announced
that parliamentary elections would be held in October 1992, and
that meanwhile the pre-invasion National Council, an advisory body,
would be reconvened from 9 July onwards.

A joint statement by all seven political parties criticized the ruler's
decision, and demanded parliamentary elections by the new year
and a broad-based government to organize them. Calling on the
National Council members to resign, the Islamic Constitutional
Movement revealed that the ruling family's continued resistance to
political reform had disillusioned military officers as much as it had
politicians. 'The stakes in the current domestic contest are higher than
ever before,' noted Nadim Jaber, an Arab commentator, in mid-June
1991. 'The government and its critics both keep warning that the
tensions over the [National] Council that were simmering this time
last year may not have been irrelevant to Saddam Hussein's decision
to invade [Kuwait]. But they draw diametrically opposite lessons from
the experience.'[61]

Part of the reason for the emir's prevarication and resistance to
political reform lay in the fact that the Saudi royal family was averse
to the idea of a fully-fledged democratic system in Kuwait, or anywhere
else in the Arabian Peninsula.

However, Saudi society itself was undergoing change. 'The war
brought into focus so many things: it raised our consciousness and
gave us an opportunity for soul-searching,' said Khalid Maeena, editor
of the Jiddah-based *Arab News*. 'All sections of society are having
this experience. Right now, the pot is bubbling, not boiling.'[62] As
a member of the Saudi establishment, and someone prepared to be
named, Maeena was underplaying the change that had occurred. In
a closed society such as Saudi Arabia, the truth often appears in
statements made by the speaker who insists on anonymity. Such
was the case with a Saudi source knowledgeable about the goings-
on in the army. 'There are more and more bearded soldiers,' he
said. 'More and more leaflets and clandestine letters criticizing the
behaviour of the royal princes, the perverse way the [Saudi] embassies
are run, the widespread corruption among high-ranking officials

and members of the royal family are distributed in the army's garrisons.'63

Then there were public manifestations of the stirrings in the Saudi kingdom. The best known of these were in Buraidah. On 17 May the governor of the province, Prince Abdul Ilah ibn Abdul Aziz, half-brother of King Fahd, banned two eminent preachers, Shaikh Abdullah Jallali and Shaikh Fahd Salman Oudah, from delivering their Friday sermons because earlier they had been stridently critical of the autocracy of the House of Saud and the continued presence of the American forces on Saudi soil. Two days later thousands of their supporters, led by the local ulama and religious police, mounted a noisy demonstration in Buraidah, an event that would have been unthinkable in the pre-war period. The security forces broke up the protest march and made many arrests. To the consternation of the ruling family, Shaikh Abdul Aziz ibn Baz, the supreme religious authority, addressed a letter to the preachers backing them against the royal governor. An influential group of ulama petitioned the monarch to dismiss Prince Abdul Ilah while nearly 100 telegrams of protest arrived daily at the royal palace.64

On 24 May it was revealed that during his meeting with King Fahd a week earlier, Shaikh Abdul Aziz ibn Baz had passed on to him a petition signed by more than a hundred leading religious scholars, judges and academics, demanding a consultative assembly, fully Islamic laws and a loosening of Saudi Arabia's close ties with the West.

This unprecedentedly comprehensive petition demanded: (1) the establishment of a consultative assembly to 'debate and decide on all domestic and foreign affairs, with its members chosen from the most competent candidates without any kind of exception or distinction'; (2) the Islamization of all social, economic, administrative and educational systems and the closing down of all non-Islamic structures; (3) reform of the military and arms suppliers to carry out the Islamization of the military with a view to creating 'modern, strong and independent Islamic armed forces', backed by a sophisticated armament industry and military academies to form military cadres, personnel and soldiers 'on the pattern of the Prophet Muhammad's armies' as well as the 'diversification of modern arms procurement sources'; (4) reform of the judicial system, including the establishment of a Supreme Judiciary Council with the responsibility of implementing Islamic laws; (5) introduction of comprehensive social justice based on 'equality for all citizens without any exception or exclusion' within the framework of

Islamic laws; (6) punishment of all those who enriched themselves by illegal means 'whoever they are, wherever they are, without any exception of rank'; (7) reform of the press and media, including the closure of the 'corrupt press' to ensure a 'strong, independent Islamic press and propaganda tool in the service of Islam', and creation of Islamic cultural centres throughout the Muslim world with the task of challenging the Western, non-Islamic press and propaganda; (8) assuring freedom of expression within the Islamic law, with the government striving to 'abolish all institutions that limit the people's freedom' within Islam; (9) preservation of the interests, purity and unity of the *umma* (Islamic community) by 'keeping it out of non-Islamic pacts and treaties'; and (10) a thorough reform of the Saudi embassies abroad to bring them in line with the laws and interests of Islam.[65]

The demands to diversify sources of arms procurement and stay out of treaties and alliances with non-Muslim states implied damning criticism of Saudi Arabia's alliance with leading Western powers to fight Iraq. The religious luminaries, whose support is crucial to provide legitimacy to the rule of the House of Saud, were thus strongly advising King Fahd ibn Abdul Aziz to end close military ties with the West, particularly the US. They had the support of Crown Prince Abdullah ibn Abdul Aziz and Prince Salman ibn Abdul Aziz, the influential governor of Riyadh. Princes Abdullah and Salman were opposed by Prince Sultan ibn Abdul Aziz, the defence minister, and his two sons, Prince Khalid and Prince Bandar, all of them favouring close ties with the US. They also advised King Fahd to take firm action against the rebellious preachers in Buraidah.

In the middle stood King Fahd, unwilling as often to face the issue and reach a decision. But the direction of his thinking could be inferred from the way he treated the foreign minister of Iran, Ali Akbar Velayati, during and after the hajj pilgrimage to Mecca, lasting from 17 to 22 June. The fact that Saudi Arabia had acted swiftly to restore its diplomatic links with Iran in March, shortly after the Second Gulf War, and concede the Iranian demands on the number of hajj pilgrims to be allowed and their right to demonstrate peacefully in Mecca,[66] was remarkable enough. What was equally noteworthy was the fact that twice in three days King Fahd fêted Velayati, who left the kingdom expressing 'great optimism' regarding the future of ties between the two countries. In early August Saudi Arabia and Iran decided to exchange ambassadors.

As it happened, the Saudi clerical leaders' demands in their petition were in line with the practices and policies of the Islamic Republic of

Iran in domestic and foreign affairs. Since its 1979 Islamic revolution Iran had advocated that the security of the region should be the sole concern of the regional countries. After more than a decade an important section of Saudi society had accepted this doctrine and was pressuring the ruler to adopt it. Fahd's courting of Tehran indicated that there was a more than even chance that he would do so. The experience of having half a million 'infidel' troops on their soil had created a delayed backlash among most Saudis who seemed intent on wiping clean this stain on their history by making their society more truly Islamic, and more tightly linked with the Muslim world.

In short, while the military outcome of the Second Gulf War was clear-cut and unsurprising, its political and social consequences were turning out to be complex and unpredictable.

To some extent, this has been true of all the major conflicts in the Middle East since the Second World War: the 1948–9 Arab–Israeli War, the 1956 Suez War, the 1967 Arab–Israeli War, the 1973 Arab–Israeli War, the 1980 Iran–Iraq War, and the 1982 Israeli invasion of Lebanon.

12 CONCLUSIONS

'It [the Gulf War] has been a very good lesson, and a hard
and tough lesson, to those who break the rule of law and
order, to those who come to a point of over-confidence so
that they occupy the land of their neighbours.'

President Hosni Mubarak, 22 July 1991[1]

'We look at [our] victory in perspective as a historical duel,
not as a fight between one army and several others. You
are victorious because you have refused humiliation and
suppression . . . and clung to a state that will strengthen
the people and the [Arab] nation forever.'

President Saddam Hussein, addressing the nation,
29 July 1991[2]

'The most important factor of stability and peace in the
Middle East is the resolution of the Palestinian question.'

General Norman Schwarzkopf, 24 February 1991[3]

'If anyone tells you America's best days are behind her,
they're looking the wrong way.'

President George Bush, 28 January 1991[4]

The history of the Middle East since the Second World War has been
shaped largely by the founding in May 1948 of Israel in the midst of
Arab–Jewish hostilities, and the subsequent conflicts. Each military
confrontation after the 1948–9 war proved to be a seismic event, which
radically rearranged the political landscape.

By failing to defeat the newly born Jewish state in the First
Arab–Israeli war, the Arab regimes lost prestige at home. The ease
with which Colonel Hosni Zaim was able to overthrow Syria's
parliamentary system in 1949 showed the extent to which the recent
Arab–Israeli conflict had eroded the Syrian government's popularity.
But the event which properly heralded the first of several revolutions
in the region was the Egyptian Free Officers' coup on 23 July 1952; it

brought about a dramatic transfer of power from the corrupt, decadent Egyptian monarchy of King Farouk to republican military officers of modest social background. Their leader, Colonel Gamal Abdul Nasser, emerged as a charismatic figure epitomizing Arab nationalism, and became the focus of hostility not only of Israel but also of Britain and France, unwilling to surrender the last vestiges of imperial power in the Middle East.

Israel, in secret alliance with Britain and France, attempted to bring about the downfall of Nasser by invading the Sinai Peninsula and the Suez Canal. Their aggression, which lasted from 29 October to 6 November 1956, proved counter-productive, thanks to the energetic intervention of the Soviet Union and America, backed by the UN Security Council.

Arab nationalism thrived at the expense of pro-Western monarchies in the region. On 14 July 1958 the Iraqi king, Faisal II ibn Ghazi, lost his throne and his head to the Free Officers group of Iraq. Four years later, in September 1962, the monarch of North Yemen fell under similar circumstances, giving the Nasserite forces a strategic entry into the oil-rich Arabian Peninsula ruled by pro-Western feudal autocracies.

The subsequent increase in the popularity of President Nasser and radical Arab nationalism, not only in Egypt but also in Syria, raised the temperature in the region. It created a tense environment conducive to a military clash between Egypt and Israel, which had watched the rise of Nasser and the Palestine Liberation Organization (established in 1964) with growing apprehension, worried that it would lose the military superiority it had acquired over its Arab adversaries.

Israel's pre-emptive strikes on 5 June 1967 against Egypt and Syria, which destroyed their air forces on the ground, determined the outcome of the next Arab–Israeli War, which lasted a mere six days, and ended with Israel occupying Egypt's Sinai Peninsula, Syria's Golan Heights as well as the Palestinian territories of the West Bank and Gaza. Israel's occupation of the West Bank (which had been part of Jordan since 1949) and Gaza (which had been part of Egypt since 1949) created a specific Palestinian problem within the overall context of Arab–Israeli hostility.

The defeat in the Six Day War chastened Nasser and blunted the force of radical Arab nationalism. At the same time, by exposing the pusillanimity of the Iraqi president, Abdul Rahman Arif, who failed to intervene in the hostilities early and effectively, it prepared the ground for his overthrow by Baathist officers, in league with the non-Baathist officers in his personal entourage, on 17 July 1968.

Overall, therefore, during the first generation of its existence, Israel's two successes and one failure in military combats with its Arab neighbours resulted in radicalizing three major Arab countries – Egypt, Syria and Iraq – and completely deprived Palestinians of their land by placing all of the Palestine of the British mandate under Israeli control. Since 1967, therefore, the attainment of a sovereign state for the Palestinians has become the cutting edge of Arab nationalism: an objective which all Arab countries, whether republican or monarchical, conservative or radical, secular or theocratic, are committed to achieving.

Because the overthrow of the pro-Western Iraqi monarchy in 1958, and the Baathist seizure of power a decade later, are both by-products of the Arab–Israeli conflict, centred on the Palestinians and their land, the rise to supreme power by Saddam Hussein is related to the same phenomenon. Thus the linkage between the Palestinian problem and the Gulf crisis of 1990 (resulting from Saddam Hussein's aggression) is organic and indisputable.

It was to recover the Egyptian and Syrian territories lost in the Six Day War that Egypt, led by President Anwar Sadat, and Syria, headed by President Hafiz Assad, attacked Israel on 6 October 1973, thus starting the next Arab–Israeli War. It lasted until 22 October. Though the military result was 'no victory, no defeat' for either side, politically and militarily Israel lost more than it gained.

An important and lasting by-product of the 1973 conflict was the quadrupling of the oil price within a matter of months. This changed the balance of forces within the Arab world, with oil-rich Saudi Arabia emerging as a leading player in Arab politics, and Kuwait trailing behind.

Later, in 1980, when Saddam Hussein initiated a military conflict with Iran, he was able to secure the financial backing of these affluent monarchies in the name of Arab nationalism, with the specific objective of protecting them from collapse under the weight of a victorious Iran. In the process he built up a powerful military-industrial complex, thanks to the active co-operation of the governments and arms merchants of the Soviet Union, France, China, West Germany, America, Egypt and Brazil.

In the final analysis, therefore, the unprecedented armed might of Iraq in the late 1980s, at the end of the second generation of Israel's existence, was a by-product of the October 1973 Arab–Israeli War.

Given the ambition and vengefulness of Saddam Hussein, it was only a matter of time before he made use of his newly acquired strength against his adversaries, Arab and non-Arab. He was dissuaded by President Mubarak from attacking Syria for having sided with Iran during the First Gulf War, and thus *inter alia* undermining his claim of battling on behalf of all Arabs. He then settled for getting even with President Assad by arming his foe in Lebanon, General Michel Aoun. But this was small-league stuff.

If hefty subsidies from the oil states had helped the Iraqi leader become militarily powerful, might not economic pressure be used to reduce his power? The idea was certainly discussed in the aftermath of the Iran–Iraq War ceasefire in August 1988 at the headquarters of the Gulf Co-operation Council in Riyadh. In early 1990 it was actively pursued by Kuwait, the small neighbour of Iraq, and the UAE, too far down the Gulf to feel the heat of Saddam Hussein's wrath. They chose the instrument which Kuwait and Saudi Arabia had used, successfully, against Iran in late 1985–early 1986: flooding the market with oil to depress its price. It worked. The result was the fluctuation of oil price in the $11–14 range in June 1990 – versus OPEC's reference price of $18 a barrel. Since Kuwait derived more than half of its foreign income from its investments abroad, a low oil price made only a minimal difference to its revenue in hard currencies. Conscious of the beneficial effects of cheap oil on the Western economies, and of the enormous petroleum reserves under their soil and sea, the Kuwaiti and UAE governments could well afford the strategy.

At the same time Kuwait pressured Iraq to return the funds it had borrowed during the First Gulf War. (Significantly, Saudi Arabia, which had provided more money to Iraq during that conflict than Kuwait, never raised the subject of the repayment of its loans, implicitly accepting Baghdad's argument that Iraq had fought the Iranians on behalf of all the Arab states on the western side of the Gulf.) Kuwait's persistent demand was a recipe for confrontation, whether its emir realized it or not. He most likely saw it as a lever to compel Baghdad to demarcate the Kuwaiti–Iraqi frontier he and his predecessors had sought since 1932.

As for Saddam Hussein, the domestic disaffection in Kuwait, which surfaced before and during the June elections for the National Council, an advisory body, augured well for pressuring the emir in the severest possible way. But when he sent troops to the border to get the Iraqi debts written off and Kuwait's oil output brought down to the OPEC quota level, the Kuwaiti emir turned to Washington, London and Cairo for advice. Evidence suggests that they all encouraged him to stand up to Baghdad, and not allow history to repeat itself: a financially strapped Iraq threatening Kuwait by moving its troops to the border, getting a subsidy from the rich neighbour, and then withdrawing.

The last time this scenario had been enacted was in March 1973. Since then Kuwait had seen America and Britain stand by it when it needed their aid. In the spring of 1987, after Iran had resorted to attacking Kuwaiti oil tankers for aiding Iraq in its war effort, Washington agreed to let Kuwait place half of its fleet of 22 oil tankers under the American flag in order to secure US naval protection, with Britain following the American lead. This prepared the way for the assembling of warships from various European naval forces, and the intervention of the American navy against Iran: a fact that was recalled by President Rafsanjani with much bitterness at the height of the 1990 Gulf crisis.[5]

In the 1980s Kuwait figured as prominently in Washington's Middle East policy as it did in London's during the 1950s, when it was a British protectorate. British prime minister Macmillan's note in his private papers in 1961 that Britain's 'irreducible interest in the Gulf' was the safeguarding of Kuwait's oil summed up Britain's policy aptly. Petroleum was, and remains, central to the energy needs of the advanced economies of Europe, America and Japan.

Given these historical facts, Saddam Hussein clearly underestimated the force and determination that Washington and London were bound to apply to reverse his take-over of Kuwait.

He seemed to have missed the point, too, that the prime reason for America's intervention in the Iran–Iraq War was oil. As leader of the West, the US is highly conscious of the importance of the Gulf as the leading *and* the most concentrated source of petroleum essential for the healthy growth of the Western and Japanese economies. Possessing proven oil reserves of 655.5 billion barrels out of the global total of 1,012 billion barrels, the eight states bordering the Gulf are in a unique position to control the oil market directly and through OPEC.[6] It was this potential of the Muslim countries of the Gulf that Ayatollah Khomeini's Iran wished to see realized: something that would have stemmed from its victory in the First Gulf War, many observers believed. At the very least a victorious Iran would have pressured the Gulf monarchs to fall in line with its professed policy of cutting oil output to raise the price as a means of transforming the region into a hub of industry and high technology, and setting up a Gulf Common Market as a stepping stone to a larger Islamic Common Market. This prospect was much dreaded by the West, particularly the US which, through Saudi Arabia, exercises crucial influence on the rate of extraction and price of petroleum. While the price levels and output have been satisfactory recently (except during the 1990–91 Gulf crisis and war), the prospects for the near future are not. At the 1989 rate of production of nearly 4 billion barrels a year in North America, the total oil reserves of America (34.1 billion barrels) and Canada (8.3 billion barrels) will be exhausted in 10 years.[7] On present trends, by 1995 the West would be dependent on the Gulf oilfields for 40–45 per cent of its petroleum needs. For the welfare of the Western economic system, therefore, the US simply could not afford to let Iran prevail in the First Gulf War. It could not allow the ultimate power to fix the rate of the extraction and price of oil to slip from the hands of its close ally, Saudi Arabia, to revolutionary Iran under Ayatollah Khomeini.

So when, by annexing Kuwait in August 1990, Saddam Hussein increased the total petroleum reserves under his control to 194.5 billion, nearly rivalling Saudi Arabia's 255 billion barrels and thus placing himself in a position to challenge Riyadh's dominance in OPEC, he should have known that Washington would not let the altered state of affairs stand.

On top of the availability of or control over oil was the question of the recycling of petrodollars. With over $100 billion of Kuwait's state funds invested in Western and Japanese financial institutions, the economic importance of the emirate could not be overstated. For Washington to acquiesce to Baghdad's take-over of Kuwait would have meant approving the transfer of this vast sum to Iraq, ruled by a megalomaniac and independent-minded president: a recipe for disaster for the West in more ways than one.

It is hard to visualize Saddam Hussein not comprehending the enormity of his action when he occupied and annexed Kuwait. As early as 1975 he had realized that oil had become 'a decisive element in American global policies', but had concluded that 'America's involvement in an area of conflict as a party hostile to the will of the [local] peoples' would turn them against the US regardless of the 'strong grip of America's local allies, the reactionary regimes' of the Gulf region.[8] At that time Iran under the Shah was one of the two leading reactionary regimes in the Gulf, the other being Saudi Arabia. Iran's people did turn against America, but did not adopt a secular, radical ideology akin to Baathism. Contrary to Saddam Hussein's calculation, the change against the US in Iran did not prove beneficial to his regime. Indeed, it turned into a mortal threat to Baathist Baghdad. In short, Saddam Hussein was not a leader given to complex, subtle thinking, a weakness which cost him and his country dear in 1990–91. He was a blunt man, prone to short-term thinking and making fast moves, with a view to solving his immediate problem with a clean swoop: a gambler at heart.

Having realized the overwhelming strength of the forces arrayed against him in the wake of the invasion of Kuwait, he tried to make amends by offering a peace initiative on 12 August. This sought to link together all the Middle East crises – including the Palestinian issue, the Lebanese civil war and the unfinished Iran–Iraq peace talks – and proposed tackling them in the order in which each had emerged. It was a clever move, and won him much popular backing in the Arab world, but did not appeal either to the Kuwaiti or Saudi rulers or their American and British backers. Undeterred, a few days later he made a unilateral concession to Iran by agreeing to share the Shatt al Arab, and return to the March 1975 Algiers Accord that he had ceremonially torn up on television on 17 September 1980. This was typical Saddam Hussein at work: dramatic, unpredictable.

While he thereby secured Iraq's eastern front he had lost any area of manoeuvre on Kuwait. Having conceded half of the Shatt al Arab to Iran, to the surprise and disappointment of his people and officer corps, Saddam Hussein simply could not afford to pull back from Kuwait, the acquisition of which had provided his country with a long shore-line along the Gulf: a much cherished aim of the rulers of Iraq since its independence in 1932.

An anecdote attributed to Saddam Hussein by an Arab diplomat, who dined with the Iraqi president in mid-September 1990 at a military camp 40 miles from Baghdad, summed up his dilemma. 'One day a dog from a bedouin camp stole a chicken from a neighbouring camp. The people asked their chief for revenge, but he told them to forget it. A week later, the dog stole the chief's baby son. No one said a word. Furious, the chief asked, "You wanted revenge for à chicken, why are you silent when my son is stolen?" The people replied, "You did not care for our concerns, why should we stand with you when you have trouble?"' Saddam Hussein concluded, 'This is what I'd have faced [from the Iraqi people] if I had not punished Kuwait for conspiring against its mother, Iraq – and what I would face now if I leave Kuwait having gained nothing, and given back to Iran the Shatt al Arab.'[9]

There were those, such as King Hussein of Jordan, who argued that the Iraqi president occupied Kuwait with a view to using it as a bargaining counter to secure the disputed border strip and one or both of the offshore islands of Warba and Bubiyan. The fact that

Iraq withdrew one brigade from Kuwait soon after the invasion was cited as evidence of his intention, which changed when the Arab League condemned his aggression on the night of 3 August. However, Saddam Hussein would have insisted on a place for the pro-Iraq Kuwaitis in any negotiations that followed under the aegis of the Arab League or any other mediator. As late as mid-February 1991 the Iraqi Revolutionary Command Council included the demand for the involvement of 'nationalist and Islamic' elements of Kuwait in deciding the political future of Kuwait. Given the uncompromising stance that Washington and London had taken on restoring the al Sabah regime in Kuwait, there was no chance of Saddam Hussein being allowed to inject a pro-Iraqi element into the domestic Kuwaiti equation.

Saddam Hussein's best bet would have been to limit his aggression to the two uninhabited offshore islands and the disputed border strip. In that case he would have faced nothing more severe than half-hearted and poorly enforced economic sanctions by the UN Security Council.

In practice, having marched into Kuwait supposedly in response to calls by 'revolutionaries' and installed the Provisional Free Government of Kuwait, he dissolved it and annexed the emirate on 8 August. He thus fell into the trap that Washington had set for him. If he had persisted with the charade of the 'Free Government' of Kuwait, he would have ultimately secured its recognition by some radical Arab states and thus a semblance of legitimacy.

Saddam Hussein underestimated not merely the determination of the Bush administration to fight if need be, but also its power greatly to influence the world media, and thus international public opinion, as well as key Arab rulers, like King Fahd, by such subterfuges as the doctoring of satellite pictures. This was all the more surprising since, as the recipients of US satellite pictures during the Iran–Iraq War, the Iraqis were aware of the way the Americans manipulated the photographic intelligence they supplied, and had complained about it.

The Iraqi leader's other major miscalculation was that he reckoned that when push came to shove Moscow, an ally of Baghdad for nearly 30 years and signatory to an existing Friendship and Co-operation Treaty with it, would veto all anti-Iraq resolutions at the Security Council. He failed to predict that with the end of the Cold War in favour of Washington, the Soviet Union would not be prepared to confront the US at the Security Council. His appeal in September 1990 to President Gorbachev, on the eve of his meeting with President Bush in Helsinki, to act like a superpower, when the objective conditions militated against any such stand, was a further example of his failure to grasp reality and accept it.

In a way this had to do with his life experiences. Saddam Hussein had grown up in deprived circumstances, both material and emotional. He had to struggle hard to get what he wanted; and he had achieved the highest position in Iraq by the time he was 42. He was a strong-willed man, who had come to believe that he could overcome a problem through sheer willpower. An obstinate man, he seemed to thrive on crisis, whether in opposition or power. He used the Shia unrest of 1977–8 to usurp ultimate authority from President Bakr.

During the eight years of warfare with Iran he had faced several acute crises including periodic assassination attempts, two of which nearly succeeded, and weathered them, emerging ever stronger and more indestructible than before. The First Gulf War steeled him, and he thought that it had steeled his nation as well. But he failed to make a distinction between armed confrontation with a Third World neighbour – in which *both* superpowers ended up siding with him – and with the combined military might of the three leading Western nations funded by the riches of Saudi Arabia, Kuwait, Japan and Germany.

Finding himself in a corner, Saddam Hussein resorted to the methods he had used before. Taking hostages was one such, a tactic he had practised on political opponents at home. His security forces would take hostage family members of a man who proved too elusive to be caught. Its application to thousands of Western and Japanese hostages proved a double-edged sword. It won him the time he needed to consolidate his military grip over Kuwait, but it also provided the cement to hold together what at first seemed an unwieldy coalition.

Saddam Hussein also underestimated the personal animosity and hatred he had aroused in President George Bush by invading Kuwait. Until 2 August 1990 Bush had expressed his wish to have friendly relations with Iraq. This policy was based on a long-term US aim of integrating Iraq, economically and otherwise, into the American global system, with the pro-Western regimes of Egypt and Jordan assisting Washington through their membership of the Arab Co-operation Council formed in early 1989. The overall objective was to diminish Saddam Hussein's independent-mindedness and tame him by softening his stance on the Middle East peace process, nuclear non-proliferation and international terrorism. Washington's encouragement to Kuwait and the UAE to put an economic squeeze on Baghdad was part of the same strategy.

When the Iraqi leader invaded Kuwait, President Bush felt he had been cheated and lied to. Despite Saddam Hussein's explanations that his promise not to attack Kuwait pertained to the period before the final Iraqi–Kuwaiti meeting in Jiddah, Bush concluded that the Iraqi leader was unreliable. In this he was not wrong. Yevgeny Primakov, who had known Saddam Hussein for more than a generation, referred to his 'dangerous unpredictability' as one of his leading characteristics.[10] After his aggression against Kuwait, the Iraqi president could do nothing right in Bush's eyes. Every tale of Iraqi brutality that emerged from Kuwait horrified Bush, strengthening his instantly acquired view that Saddam Hussein was evil incarnate, a brutal dictator, conveniently forgetting that the doings of the Iraqi troops in Kuwait were a replica of what the Iraqi security and intelligence forces had been doing in Iraq itself for decades, something which Bush and his predecessors had chosen not to notice and comment on before.

On the whole, however, as someone who by upbringing and experience had become interested and adept in handling foreign affairs, Bush conducted himself adroitly. He immediately understood that Saddam's absorption of Kuwait was more than a strong Third World country gobbling up a weak neighbour: it was a matter of grave importance to the economic fabric of the West. He got his priorities right. To ensure that Iraq did not invade Saudi Arabia was a top priority. He set out to achieve this by using all the means at his disposal including, and most importantly, the manipulation of the media with doctored and concocted 'information'. He apparently did not shy away from resorting to a similar tactic (including, most probably, the furnishing of doctored satellite pictures) in trying to convince King Fahd that Iraq was about to invade his kingdom when no such evidence existed on the ground. Once Bush had succeeded in scaring King Fahd into inviting American forces to Saudi Arabia he could afford to relax a little: he had planted a seed and ensured it enough water and sunshine to sprout.

Very properly, the American president used the UN Security Council as the prime vehicle for isolating and punishing Iraq for its aggression. He constantly consulted the Soviet president, Gorbachev, thus ensuring his co-operation. At the Helsinki summit in September he went so far as to invite Gorbachev to take further interest in Middle Eastern affairs, aware that the Kremlin no longer had the power or the inclination to challenge the near-hegemony of the US in the region.

Whether by accident or design, the crucial Security Council Resolution 660 made no mention of the UN secretary-general (who happened to be on a tour of Latin America at the time). By thus keeping the secretary-general on the sidelines, Bush maintained full control over the direction and content of the subsequent resolutions. Given the total lack of resistance from the USSR or China, the US had an unhindered run at the Security Council.

Bush managed to assemble and hold together a formidable coalition of Western and Arab allies. Here again he used carrots and sticks. He kept up pressure on such affluent allies as Germany and Japan (whose constitutions forbade the despatch of their troops to a region as distant as the Gulf) to contribute substantial funds towards the military operation and economic aid to the regional states suffering the consequences of a UN embargo against Iraq. He managed to squeeze $9 billion from Japan alone. His pressure on Saudi Arabia and Kuwait to contribute to the allied enterprise cost them a total of $67 billion. Together with another $10 billion paid by the UAE and Qatar, the total contributions by the Gulf states during the seven-month crisis and war were twice as much as those they had made to Iraq in its eight-*year* military conflict with Iran.

The American president also pressured Saudi Arabia and Kuwait to win the active backing of such countries as Turkey and the USSR by offering them material inducements. By the time the Security Council was ready to debate a motion authorizing the member states co-operating with Kuwait to use 'all necessary means' to reverse the Iraqi aggression, Saudi Arabia and Kuwait, along with the UAE and Qatar, had put together a $6 billion aid package for Moscow. So dire was the need for hard currencies in the Kremlin that it was grateful to have these funds partly in return for backing Resolution 678 at the Security Council.

George Bush was so intent on achieving his objective of reversing the Iraqi aggression – something he put on the agenda later in the crisis in order to take US public opinion with him – that he did not shrink from courting President Assad, despite the fact that Syria was on the US state department's list of nations which support international terrorism. Indeed, this was one of the reasons for taking Syria into the anti-Iraq coalition, and keeping it there. Its knowledge of the terrorists' networks was to be used to counter the threats of terrorism emanating from Baghdad. The other main reason was the insistence of Egypt and Saudi Arabia on including Syria. Among other things, they saw this as one way of blunting Assad's already jaded radicalism. It was to pay dividends after the war when Assad agreed (in mid-July 1991) to have talks with Israel without any preconditions.

Nor did Bush ignore Iran. He made it a point to reassure Tehran through the Swiss embassy (which has been looking after US interests there since 1979) that America had no intention of staying on in the Gulf, militarily, once Kuwait had been restored to the al Sabahs. His administration reacted to Ayatollah Khamanei's mid-September attack on the US more in sorrow than in anger, saying that Tehran had 'misunderstood' the American position. On their part, the Iranian leaders did not translate into action Khamanei's fatwa (religious decree) against the US presence in the Gulf. In fact, despite repeated calls by radical Islamic politicians to side with Iraq to confront the infidel, imperialist America, President Rafsanjani refused to do so. He argued that his government had no intention of taking steps which would ultimately help Iraq to expand its influence in the Gulf. As the president of a country which had been a victim of Saddam Hussein's aggression, Rafsanjani was in tune with popular feeling on the subject. Iran was pleased to see Saddam Hussein concede half of the Shatt al Arab, and saw it as the vindication of its principled stand on the matter. It announced that it would abide by UN sanctions while making clear that the Muslim people of Iraq must not be deprived of food and medicine. Throughout the crisis Iran maintained its opposition to the overwhelming military presence of the US in the Gulf while condemning the Iraqi action and insisting on the return of Kuwait to the al Sabahs. This policy seemed to have the widespread backing of Iranian people and politicians.

In America, while there was consistent approval of Bush's handling of the crisis at the UN Security Council and in the capitals of the coalition partners, voices of dissent rose sharply as he tried to implement his 8 November 1990 decision to double US forces in the Gulf to 430,000. It became clear to many that Bush was switching over to the military option without letting the sanctions do the job they were expected to do within about twelve months. This ended the bipartisan support in the US Congress that the chief executive had so far enjoyed for his handling of the crisis. The resulting Congressional hearings conducted in late November revealed a high proportion of experts, many of them former senior administration officials, favouring the continuation of

the UN embargo which had proved far more effective than anticipated.

These televised testimonies alarmed President Bush, who had
mapped out a strategy of first getting UN Security Council sanc-
tion for military force and then approaching the US Congress
for authorization to make war against Iraq. The start of highly
critical Congressional hearings a few days before the 29 November
adoption of Resolution 678, which set the deadline of 15 January
1991 for the Iraqi withdrawal, upset Bush's plans. For the first time
since the outbreak of the Gulf crisis he lost the initiative to his
critics.

To snatch it back from them he rushed to announce on the morning
after the passing of Resolution 678 that he was offering high-level
talks to Baghdad, with secretary of state Baker meeting Saddam
Hussein in Baghdad during the next fortnight, and the Iraqi foreign
minister Tariq Aziz meeting Bush in Washington any time between
15 December and 15 January. The dramatic move helped him to
project himself as a statesman-diplomat, and not a warmongering ogre
as his critics had done, especially during the Congressional hearings.
It also proved extremely popular with the American public as well as
Congress.

The effect of the statement on the Arab allies of the US, however,
was wholly negative, due to both its content and the manner in
which it was made public. Bush had not even bothered to inform the
Egyptian, Saudi and Syrian leaders of his impending announcement,
much less consult them. As a result, the effort of Algeria to bring about
a meeting between Saddam Hussein and King Fahd made progress. The
Saudi ruler saw no reason to spurn offers of talks with the Iraqi leader
while President Bush was despatching his secretary of state to Baghdad
to meet him.

These developments kept Saddam Hussein hopeful that his strategy
of dividing the anti-Iraqi coalition would succeed, and that time was
on his side. The talks with him by various prominent (although
out of power) West European and Japanese politicians to secure
the release of their nationals held hostage, and their assessment
of public opinion in their countries as being against war, provided
the Iraqi president with another hopeful sign. To dissuade Bush and
Thatcher from choosing the military option he raised the spectre
of a long, bloody war – accompanied by terrorist actions against
American and British targets worldwide – in the event of an attack
on Iraq.

Until his decision on 6 December to let all Western and Japanese captives leave, Saddam Hussein had succeeded to a substantial extent in diverting media attention from the Iraqi occupation of Kuwait and focusing it on the staggered release of the hostages. This ploy had upset the White House: it detested the unprincipled exploitation of the media by the Iraqi leader.

The White House's frustration was all the more since President Bush had proved inept in communicating his thoughts to large audiences. His television manner was appalling, a stark contrast to that of his predecessor, Ronald Reagan, who was a consummate communicator. Bush's weakness in this field was compounded by his lack of clarity on what the main issue was, and why America must fight, if need be. His reasons for confronting Saddam Hussein militarily varied from his being a 'new Hitler' to protecting American jobs to securing the release of American hostages. He lacked the vision and charisma of President Franklin Roosevelt (1932–45), or even President John Kennedy (1961–3), to inspire his fellow-citizens to fight for a moral cause. His political career had been built on the expedient of being all things to all people, and leading by consensus rather than through sheer force of personality or conviction. He had thus become adept at exploiting opportunities for short-term aims.

Having won the plaudits of the American public and politicians for offering to make high-level contacts with Baghdad, Bush quietly sabotaged the enterprise by getting into a fatuous argument with Baghdad about the fixing of the dates for the talks. This was in part to discourage King Fahd from meeting Saddam Hussein. All along Bush and his close advisers were apprehensive that while they drummed up support for military intervention in the US, the Saudi and Kuwaiti rulers, following the pattern of the past, would strike a deal with Saddam Hussein behind their backs, and make redundant the American military presence in the Gulf, particularly in the Saudi kingdom. They were hell-bent on seeing that such a scenario never materialized, and even the faintest hint that it might do so made them nervous.

The other possible prospect which made them nervous was of Saddam Hussein withdrawing from Kuwait – either completely or up to the disputed border strip – just before the 15 January 1991 deadline. Significantly, such a move, which would have saved much death and destruction in Iraq and Kuwait, was described by the White House as 'a nightmare scenario'.

There was enough of a hint in this description that the end-purpose of the military operation being prepared by Washington was more than a reversal of the Iraqi occupation of Kuwait: it was to destroy Iraq's military and economic infrastructure, and overthrow Saddam Hussein. This was borne out amply by the conduct of the 38-day air campaign by the allies, with the US deploying six aircraft carriers (as many as it would have done in case of a full-scale war with the Soviet Union) and providing nearly seven-eighths of the air sorties in the bombing of Iraq and Kuwait.

Those who criticized the war argued that its conduct was disproportionate and excessive in relation to the declared aim of liberating Kuwait. Secondly, they said that since the economic sanctions had not been given enough time to prove or disprove their efficacy, the war was not the last resort it should always be. Thirdly, in the final analysis, the armed action had less to do with the recovery of Kuwaiti sovereignty than with ensuring supplies of cheap oil and the continued influence of the West in the Gulf. Finally, the detrimental effect of the armed conflict on the ecology of the region was unjustifiable.

Those who backed the military option at the time it was taken did so on practical and moral grounds. They could not see how the morale of US troops could be maintained for twelve long months in the desolation of the Saudi desert and its puritanical society. Nor could they visualize the forthcoming hajj pilgrimage in June, to be undertaken by nearly two million Muslims, passing off peacefully with some half a million American, British and French troops stationed on Saudi soil. Above all that was the awareness in the White House of the volatility of Middle Eastern politics. Who could say when the next large-scale eruption of violence would occur in the Occupied Territories, or that some sensational event would not break out in Jordan, Egypt, Lebanon or Iran, causing the withdrawal of Syria or Egypt from the US-led coalition or bringing Iran and Iraq together?

Then there was the moral-legal aspect of the crisis. Proponents of the war were to argue that it was the first time since the Second World War that one member of the United Nations had occupied and annexed another member. Such behaviour called for a determined response. By punishing Iraq for its naked aggression a clear warning had been issued to all potential aggressors, and the world made safer. If Saddam Hussein had not been punished as severely as he was he would have threatened Saudi Arabia, further destabilizing regional security and establishing himself as the unchallenged leader of the oil-rich Gulf. In the final analysis, therefore, the leader responsible for the raining of death and destruction on Iraq and Kuwait was Saddam Hussein.

But the irony was that while his military and his country got a severe beating, Saddam Hussein was still in power several months after the ceasefire on 28 February 1991. His supporters argued that by standing up to the deadliest war machine ever assembled for 42 days – more than the total duration of the three major Arab–Israeli conflicts of 1956, 1967 and 1973 – the Iraqi president had proved that his regime was more solid and immune to military pressures than had been assumed by most outsiders. They argued too that, contrary to the popular view abroad, Saddam Hussein had begun to withdraw his troops before the start of the ground war, as most of his well-wishers, Arab and non-Arab, wanted him to do. If so, the Iraqi leader's calculation ignored the fact that wars create their own dynamic, and that had he begun pulling out before the air campaign started, he would have saved fully his troops and hardware, something he was unlikely to achieve once the air war had been initiated.

On the allied side, many of the negative consequences of the war predicted by experts failed to materialize. In contrast to the estimates of 12,000 to 30,000 American dead, the actual toll was 376, with only 79 dying in combat. Consequently, warnings of the Vietnam syndrome repeating itself proved superfluous. This happened partly because the air campaign went on for many weeks, partly because Saddam Hussein decided to withdraw his best troops several days before the start of the ground war, and partly because the Iraqi defences were not as formidable or extensive as the Pentagon had portrayed them to be.

The expected oil price rise to $60 to $80 a barrel, as foreseen among others by Chris Flavi, vice-president of the World Watch Institute, did not take place. The price fluctuated around $19 a barrel, primarily due to the failure of Iraq or its Iraqi agents to damage Saudi oil installations. When no such incidents occurred during the first few days of the allied air campaign, the markets discounted the possibility and the oil price settled down at around $20 a barrel.

Baghdad's failure to play its terrorist card stemmed from several factors. US intelligence claimed to have discovered that, following the Gulf crisis, Iraq had transformed its worldwide intelligence service into a terrorist support enterprise with a view to linking up with established local terrorist groups. The American operators therefore concentrated on disrupting any lines of support these terrorist groups might have established with Iraqi intelligence, a tactic which apparently worked. America joined Saudi Arabia and Kuwait in successfully pressuring Hafiz Assad to co-operate in preventing terrorist actions. Washington warned Colonel Qadhafi of military reprisals if any terrorist activities were traced to Libya. On its own initiative, Tehran seems to have instructed the pro-Iranian terrorist groups not to co-operate with Iraq. Because of the long-drawn-out crisis before the war the CIA had a long lead time to render harmless Iraq's terrorist plans.[11]

The widespread calculation that successful Iraqi Scud attacks on Israel would lead to Israeli reprisals, which in turn would result in Syria, and probably even Egypt, quitting the coalition, and Iran lining up with Iraq, did not materialize. The news agency reports broadcast on 22 January by radio stations in Britain that Israel was allowed to participate in intermittent allied bombing missions from Turkey largely explained why it desisted from overt retaliation against Iraq.

Equally, the fear that the deaths of Arabs caused by the American bombs would create sufficient pressures on the regimes in Jordan and Egypt to destabilize them, proved unfounded.

The expectation that week after week of relentless American bombing would compel Gorbachev to break ranks with Bush also proved empty. Those making such a prediction had underestimated the weakness of the Soviet position, stemming primarily from its acute domestic problems.

The overall success of the American military operation was due to President Bush's policies and the use of high-technology weapons by US armed forces. Bush accepted the military doctrine offered by General Powell: avoid the damaging incrementalism of the Vietnam War, assemble troops and hardware to the fullest, and use them decisively, massively and swiftly. By rejecting the argument that avoiding the use of force and seeking a political solution should be the overall objective of the US administration, Bush shielded himself from getting bogged down in endless negotiations.

Regarding the use of sophisticated weaponry, mainly by US forces, it emerged that precision-guided arms, particularly when launched from the air, not only functioned well but also proved to be a decisive factor in land battles. Enemy armour proved vulnerable to anti-tank missiles fired from helicopters. Secondly, the ability to fight at night by using special equipment nearly doubled the force of the allied troops. Finally, the allies' electronic jamming of the Iraqi surface-to-air missiles proved highly successful. No doubt these results will play an important role in the manufacture and deployment of the high-technology weapons of the future.

However, the end-purpose of winning military battles is to rearrange the distribution of political power. How the political configuration of the region works out will depend on: (a) whether and for how long Saddam Hussein survives as the ruler of an enfeebled, chastened Iraq; (b) whether Iran is integrated into the refurbished Gulf security arrangement; and (c) whether political settlements can be forged between Israel and Syria, and between Israel, the Palestinians, and Jordan, with Saudi Arabia playing an important role publicly.

At the time of the first anniversary of the Iraqi invasion of Kuwait, on 2 August 1991, Saddam Hussein was still in power. His statement to friendly Arab leaders before the conflict – 'If I survive, I win' – acquired fresh significance, and buoyed the spirits of his supporters at home and abroad.

Repeated attempts by the US to overthrow him through a military coup had failed. He was aware of these efforts, and acted to thwart them. Within a week of the ceasefire he established a bipolar equilibrium in the defence forces, placing the defence ministry and the Republican Guard in the hands of officers who were from outside the Tikriti area, his home base: General Saadi Tuma Abbas and General Mukhlif Iyad al Rawi. They were balanced by leading officers who were Tikritis: General Hussein Rashid Wendawi as the military chief of staff; General Mezahim Saib as the air force commander; and Hussein Kamil Hassan Majid as the minister of military industrialization. The military intelligence, political intelligence and public security services remained as before under Saddam Hussein's half-brothers: Sibawi Hussein Tikriti, Wathban Tikriti and Barzan Tikriti. The appointment of a cousin, Ali Hussein Majid, as interior minister in early March completed the grip of Saddam Hussein over the formidable intelligence and security apparatus of Iraq. Such a division of power in the military, intelligence and security services made a successful attempt to overthrow Saddam Hussein dependent on a highly unlikely alliance between the two poles of Tikritis and non-Tikritis, or the neutralization of one by the other.

Washington's other strategy of making living conditions for ordinary Iraqis so wretched as to provoke an internal revolt against the regime has also failed so far.

Falling living standards coming on the heels of the most intense bombing in history succeeded in causing depression among most of the Iraqi urban dwellers, who have little energy left after they have waged a daily battle for survival. 'If 30 countries could not kick Saddam out, how can we poor, oppressed, scared Iraqi people do it?' said a Baghdad merchant to a British journalist in mid-July.[12] Like most ordinary Iraqis, he was aware that adversity had brought the ranks and officials of the ruling Baath Party together, determined to keep the Saddam Hussein regime going. They and the Iraqi media were able to convince the public at large that the continuation of economic sanctions – blocking imports of food and medicine by maintaining a ban on the sale of Iraqi oil – long after Kuwait had been restored to the al Sabahs, was directed at the Iraqi people. This gave rise to growing anti-Western feeling in Iraq.

Even if a majority of Iraqis felt that the root cause of their present plight was the aggressive adventure of their leader, Saddam Hussein, they had no means of expressing their view publicly, or transforming it into a popular vote to oust his government peacefully.

In this respect Iraq is more the rule than the exception in the Arab world. The basic problem is that power sharing and public accountability, the essentials of democracy, do not exist in the Arab Middle East. In the leading republics of Egypt, Syria and Iraq, the power of the state escalated after the Second World War, with the president emerging as an all-powerful ruler. In these countries the size of the civil service increased almost ninefold within a generation, making the government the single largest employer. Taking into account the military, security and intelligence services as well, the government in these republics now employs more than a quarter of the national workforce.[13] The power of patronage of the president is therefore enormous and so is his power of manipulation, both of the upper echelons of the civil, military and intelligence services and of popular perceptions through the control of the mass media. Saddam Hussein has by now proved himself to be a past master in this. In the tightening economic circumstances in the wake of the Gulf crisis, he ensured the well-being of the upper and middle echelons of the military, intelligence and security services as well as the Baath Party in order to insulate them from the practical consequences of his Kuwaiti adventure.

But that does not negate or mitigate the fact that Iraq has lost heavily: militarily, diplomatically and economically. From being the most powerful Arab military force with an advanced industrial-military complex, Iraq has been reduced to second-rate status in the region. It can no longer claim to have achieved strategic military parity with Israel as it did before 17 January 1991. At the cost of receiving several hits by Iraqi Scuds, and the loss of a dozen lives, Israel gained enormously both in public sympathy in the West and material aid from the US and Germany.

The other gainers at the expense of Iraq were not only the al Sabahs, who regained their emirate, but also Saudi Arabia, Egypt, Syria and Iran. With Iraqi military power reduced considerably, Saudi Arabia had only one rival in the Gulf to contend with: Iran. This bipolarity simplified the power equation in the region. Little wonder that Riyadh re-established diplomatic ties with Tehran shortly after the war, and offered a warm welcome to the Iranian foreign minister during the hajj pilgrimage. Outside the region, Saudi Arabia improved its relations with Moscow, which had for long been the superpower backer of Baghdad.

Egypt was another major gainer among the Arab countries. Rivalry between Egypt and Iraq for the leadership of the Arab world has a long history. In more recent times it was the suspension of Egypt from the Arab League in the wake of its unilateral peace with Israel in March 1979 which provided an opportunity for Iraq to fill the leadership vacuum. It was in this context that Iraq went to war with Iran, and during the long years of that conflict built itself up as a formidable military power and a virtual leader of the Arab camp. Egypt cultivated Iraq during the 1980s as a means to readmittance to the Arab League, a long, tortuous process. This was one of the major reasons for Egypt's agreeing to join the Arab Co-operation Council proposed by King Hussein of Jordan in early 1989, a step which won it the readmittance to the Arab League it craved. But the rivalry between Iraq and Egypt, even though subdued, had not ended. They now competed for the soul of the PLO and the Palestinians, the Egyptians advising moderation, the Iraqis militancy. Washington's suspension of low-level talks with the PLO in early June 1990 showed the Palestinian leadership the limits of moderation, and settled the competition between Baghdad and Cairo. Baghdad won. Cairo was unhappy to see the PLO drift away from its orbit towards Iraq as tension rose in the region in the wake of a sudden jump in Soviet Jewish immigration into Israel. (It was in the context of widespread despair among Palestinians, who were rejected by Washington despite the PLO's disavowal of violence, that Saddam Hussein struck at the Kuwaiti emir and then produced his 12 August initiative linking the Gulf crisis with the Palestinian issue.) Now, with Iraq cut down to size, Egypt saw the moment as opportune to assume leadership of the Arab world. The shifting of the Arab League headquarters from Tunis to Cairo in December 1990 endorsed the leading role of Egypt. The appointment of Esmat Abdel-Meguid, the erstwhile foreign minister of Egypt, as secretary-general of the Arab League in May 1991 underlined the Egyptian role.

There were also financial rewards for Egypt for its active participation in the anti-Iraq coalition. Along with the cancellation of $7.1
billion US military loans went the abrogation of Saudi credits of $4
billion. In addition the Paris Club of Western donor nations agreed to
write off $10 billion of Egypt's outstanding debts and to reschedule
the remaining $10 billion over 25 years.[14]

Syria too made financial gains out of its military stance in the
Gulf Crisis. It received subsidies not only from Saudi Arabia but also
from Kuwait, the UAE and Qatar. More importantly, it received the
go-ahead from Washington to bolster the power and prestige of the
Syrian-backed President Elias Hrawi of Lebanon by attacking the
forces of the rebel Maronite General Michel Aoun in October 1990.
This complaisance continued after the Gulf War ceasefire, when the
Lebanese government, at the instigation of Damascus, seized control
of the important Palestinian refugee camps in southern Lebanon from
the PLO.

Iran benefited merely by seeing its regional rival reduced in military
strength. With Iraq now branded as the anti-Western outlaw in
the Gulf, Western pressure on Tehran eased, helping the pragmatic
Rafsanjani to liberalize the economy and mend his fences further
with Europe, and set the scene for the visit to Iran by President
Mitterrand later in the year. In the Gulf, it gained much diplomatic
ground, with all GCC states now positively friendly towards it and
interested in considering a way of getting Iran involved in Gulf security
arrangements.

Any rational security system for the Gulf must include all the eight
Gulf countries, including Iraq. But so long as Saddam Hussein is the
president of Iraq, it will be excluded from any such scheme.

Beyond the security arrangements for these states, all of them
possessing petroleum, there is the problem of equitable relations
between oil and non-oil Arab countries which needs to be addressed
seriously. Given the enormous petroleum reserves available in the
thinly populated countries of the Gulf, their rulers should show concern for the non-oil Arab states with comparatively large populations,
and share their wealth with them. The best way to do so would be
through a common aid agency funded by the affluent states on the
basis of an equitable formula. Instead, the oil shaikhs, particularly
from Saudi Arabia, have used their riches and their power to control
the oil price as a means of coercion and bribery, intent on controlling
the politics of the non-oil Arab states and nipping in the bud any signs
of democracy, particularly in the Arabian Peninsula.

In the absence of any power-sharing between the rulers and the ruled in these monarchies, the wealth accruing from the extraction of petroleum, accomplished by tens of thousands of local and expatriate workers, ends up as the private property of the ruling oligarchies. Since the total oil reserves in Kuwait, Oman, Qatar, Saudi Arabia and the UAE (more specifically three of its seven constituent principalities) amount to 462.6 billion barrels,[15] and since all these countries are run as feudal autocracies, seven ruling families now possess oil which, priced at $20 a barrel, is worth $9,252 billion. Such outrageously skewed ownership of property in the world's most heavily armed region, with its long history of volatility and violence, can only be a continuing recipe for destabilization and violent upheavals.

Small wonder that in the early and mid-1960s the oil shaikhs became the focus of subversion and destabilization by the leader of radical Arab nationalism: Nasser. After he was cut down to size by Israel in June 1967, there was a respite for these potentates. But after the petroleum price rise of 1973–4 had inflated their riches to unimagined heights, they became the target of another radical figure, Ayatollah Khomeini, the leader of the 1979 Islamic revolution in Iran. He condemned them for their corrupt, autocratic ways; for refusing to share power with their subjects as enjoined by the Quran; for selling oil cheaply to the West, particularly to America, the Great Satan; and, finally, for having failed to liberate Palestine, including Jerusalem which contains Islam's third holiest shrine. Khomeini's attacks, based on his interpretation of the Quran and Hadiths, were a source of great worry to the oil shaikhs, who claimed to derive their political legitimacy from Islam and Islamic precepts. So acute was their fear of the propaganda by revolutionary Iran that the Saudi rulers, the single most important group in the Arabian Peninsula, encouraged Saddam Hussein to attack Iran in September 1980. The Iraqi leader accomplished what he set out to do even though it took him eight years: he contained the tide of revolutionary Islam, and made the future of the Gulf monarchs safe. But less than two years after the end of the Iran–Iraq War, Saddam Hussein adopted, consciously or subconsciously, the two-point programme for the Gulf that Khomeini had conceived but failed to implement: raising the oil price and overthrowing the Gulf monarchs.

Why did this happen? Was there something subjective, such as the megalomaniac tendencies of Khomeini and Saddam Hussein (and before them Nasser), which led them to behave as they did? Or, was (and is) there something objective – the vast wealth owned and

misused by a handful of autocratic ruling families – that moved a
radical leader to attempt to put right an enormous wrong? If it is the
latter, which seems to be the case, then the recurrence of attacks,
ideological and/or physical, on one or more Gulf monarchies is only
a matter of time. The solution therefore lies in these Gulf states
acquiring *internal* security by the ruling families sharing power and
wealth with their fellow-citizens through representative government,
public accountability, and the granting of civil rights to all.

It is worth noting that Washington, the leading upholder of civil
and human rights and democracy, has all along refrained from cajoling,
or even persuading, the Saudi royals towards political pluralism.
Among the millions of words that were unleashed by Washington and
other Western capitals during the seven-month Gulf crisis, the word
'democracy' was conspicuously absent. Two major reasons explain
this stance. First, it is much simpler to deal with seven ruling families
than with the varied personalities and policies bound to be thrown up
by a democratic system. Second, elected governments in the Arabian
Peninsula would reflect the ideologies of Arab nationalism and Islamic
militancy prevalent among large sections of the population, and veer
away from the West, stressing self-reliance and Islamic fellowship.[16]

The example of Jordan is illustrative. There, free and fair elections
held in November 1988 produced 32 Islamic fundamentalists in
a house of 80, and about half as many Arab nationalists. King
Hussein had little choice but to act, for all practical purposes, as
a constitutional monarch, and reflect the popular will in the Gulf
crisis and war. For this he was pilloried by the Western capitals.

Yet, once the fighting stopped, the Jordanian monarch, with a
long record of pro-Western alignment, lost no time in saying 'Let
bygones be bygones', as a prelude to mending fences with the West.
The US responded positively, with Baker consulting King Hussein
during each of his several tours of the Middle East in search of
Arab–Israeli peace.

The PLO, the only other ally of Iraq during the crisis, was not so
agile, partly because it lacks a history of pro-Western inclination, and
partly because it is a composite of different political tendencies among
the Palestinians, most of them antipathetic to the West because of its
insensitivity towards the continued plight of the Palestinians and its
indulgent attitude towards Israel. Its leader, Arafat, based his pro-Iraqi
position on the fundamental premise that the PLO is bound to side
with an Arab country prepared to confront Israel on the issue of
the Palestinian right to self-determination. By all accounts Arafat's

stand had widespread support among the residents of the Occupied Territories. Whatever may have been the means, aggressive and opportunistic, employed by Saddam Hussein, the end result of his actions was to force the Palestinian issue to centre stage, American protestations notwithstanding. Even such a neutral personality as the UN secretary-general admitted this in his conversation with the Iraqi president on 13 January 1991.[17] Indeed, after the ceasefire, Arafat claimed that the Second Gulf War had 'strengthened' the PLO because it had shown that 'the prime cause in the Middle East is the Palestinian one'.[18]

It is noteworthy that even the US president and secretary of state, while refusing to link the convening of an international peace conference on the Middle East with the resolution of the Gulf crisis, always added that once the Gulf crisis had been resolved satisfactorily America would apply itself to securing a lasting and just peace in the Middle East. Bush repeated this on 27 February 1991.

The US tried, but nothing came of Baker's four tours of the Middle East between March and June 1991 to assemble the parties to the Arab–Israeli conflict for negotiations. Israel showed no inclination for talks except on its own terms of keeping the United Nations out of the proceedings (refusing to cede its national interests to an international body), insisting on strictly bilateral talks with its Arab neighbours, and imposing such restrictions on the Palestinians' delegates as their residential status (with those based in East Jerusalem to be barred) and their membership of the PLO.

Israel's reasons for taking a tough line were varied. It was ruled by Prime Minister Shamir, a hardliner of long standing, who believed passionately in the concept of Eretz Israel, and the legitimacy of the Israeli government's policy of building Jewish settlements in the Occupied Territories of 'Judea, Samaria and Gaza'. Moreover, he also believed that, with millions of Soviet Jews settling in Israel over the next several years, time was on the Israeli side; and that the prospect of the Palestinians emerging as a majority in Eretz Israel by the turn of the century, due to their higher birth rate, as had been widely predicted, would be averted. He also knew that with Iraq, the only Arab military power in a position to challenge Israel, reduced to a fraction of its previous strength and robbed of its nuclear facilities, chemical weapons and intermediate-range Scud missiles, there was no prospect of the Arabs being able even to conceive an armed confrontation with Israel on the Palestinian issue.

Then there was the objective fact that public opinion in the Jewish state favoured Shamir's party, Likud, over Labour, committed to the exchange of 'land for peace'. A survey of 1,200 Israeli voters in early June 1991 showed that while support for Labour had dropped from 31.5% after the 1988 parliamentary elections to 23%, that for Likud had decreased only marginally, from 34% to 32%. The support for small right-wing and religious parties in coalition with Likud remained firm.[19]

On the other hand, the three-year intifada, followed by the Gulf crisis and war, which brought Iraqi Scuds landing in Israeli cities, engendered a growing feeling that the price of holding on to the West Bank and Gaza was escalating. A study in April 1991 by the Jaffee Centre for Strategic Studies at Tel Aviv University showed that 58% of Israelis favoured ending direct rule of the West Bank and Gaza compared to 50% a year before and 46% five years before.[20] Of course 'ending direct rule' needed to be defined. If it meant giving autonomy to the Palestinians to run basically municipal services for the community, then the Palestinians were unlikely to take the offer seriously. They remained aware that even if recognition of their inalienable right to self-determination were to lead to an independent Palestinian state, they would have regained only 22% of the land they possessed under British mandate, and about half of what was offered to them by the United Nations' partition plan of September 1947.

Conscious of the dangers that lay ahead for them, the Palestinians and their leaders seemed to have resolved to stand by the PLO in its hour of depression and defeat. Plans were afoot in the pro-Western Arab camp to remove Yasser Arafat as the leader of the PLO. The GCC states decided to suspend their subsidies to the PLO so long as Arafat was its chairman. Throughout its history, dating back to 1964, various Arab governments singly and jointly had tried to control the PLO, but had failed. The spirit of independent-mindedness seemed to be alive among the Palestinians and their leaders. 'If anyone wants to talk to the representatives of the Palestinians, he will have to talk to those who have been chosen and accepted by the Palestinian people,' said Muhammad Milhem, a member of the PLO Executive Committee. 'It is the Palestinian people who must decide who represents them, not the UN, the USA, Europe, other states or Israel.'[21]

The matter of Palestinian representation became significant when the chance of an international peace conference on the Middle East improved in mid-July. Reversing his earlier position, President Assad responded positively on 14 July to an earlier letter by President Bush in which he proposed the international conference to be co-chaired by the US and the USSR, with the UN present as a silent observer (with the proviso that the conference would reconvene every six months if *all* parties agreed), and with the conference giving way to direct talks between Israel and each of its Arab neighbours without any preconditions.

This dramatic shift in Syria's position was the cumulative result of the collapse of its superpower backer, the Soviet Union, as a competing force in the international arena, and the defeat of Iraq, which until then had been seen as providing Syria with strategic depth in its confrontation with Israel. Assad made his move knowing that, following the decimation of Iraq, there was no credible radical Arab state left to challenge or derogate his decision. In a sense his action in mid-July 1991 was foreshadowed by the policy he pursued during the Gulf crisis, when he lined up firmly with Egypt, Saudi Arabia and America. Significantly, between writing his letter to Bush and meeting Baker in Damascus on 18 July, Assad had six hours of talks with President Mubarak in the Syrian capital in order to forge a common Syrian–Egyptian stand on the international peace conference on the Arab–Israeli conflict.

While the role of the United Nations in the forthcoming negotiations for Arab–Israeli concords was being downgraded, overall the UN had emerged stronger from the Gulf crisis and Iraq's defeat in the subsequent war. There are some who argued that the Bush administration resorted to this forum only because it knew in advance that it would get what it wanted, and that the United Nations had become a fig-leaf for the United States. This was certainly true at the time of the Korean crisis in 1950 – mainly because of the absence of the Soviet Union from the proceedings at a crucial moment. In the recent crisis, however, the Soviet Union was an active participant in the deliberations of the Security Council and often concurred with the US and other Western permanent members. As for China, the only Third World country to have a permanent seat on the Council, it maintained a low profile, and in the main went along with what the other four permanent members decided. On the crucial Resolution 678 it abstained.

China also abstained on Resolution 688 which pertained to the behaviour of the Iraqi government towards its citizens, particularly the Kurds, and demanded entry of 'international humanitarian organizations' into Iraq. So did India, another important Third World state. Three non-permanent members, all of them from the Third World, opposed the motion, on the ground that it amounted to interference in the domestic affairs of a member state. Of all the resolutions on the Gulf crisis and its aftermath, Resolution 688 emerged as the one which met with most opposition, with five of the 15 members either voting against it or abstaining.

Many Third World countries saw Resolution 688 as the beginning of a process by which the Western powers, using the forum of the UN Security Council, meant to diminish their political independence and sovereignty. To them, this signalled the direction the 'New World Order' – a term launched by the US during the course of the Gulf crisis – was to take under the hegemony of America. The events during the Gulf crisis and war established clearly that Washington was willing and able to use the big stick, and that its memory of defeat by Vietnam was receding fast. In a sense Bush resorted to the military option, confident that moral right was on his side, to exorcize America of the Vietnam syndrome.

It is ironic that Saddam Hussein, the one Arab leader who was intent on seeing that the American writ did not run in the Gulf or anywhere else in the Arab world, became the cause of further enhancement of American power and prestige in the Arab world and elsewhere. As it was, he objected vehemently to the naval presence of the US in early 1990, forgetting that Washington had maintained such a presence since 1949 in Bahrain, which was then a British protectorate. On the eve of British military withdrawal in December 1971, the US had signed a secret agreement with the Bahrain ruler, Shaikh Issa al Khalifa. It included leasing naval facilities, previously used by the British, to America for an annual rent of £300,000. With this, Bahrain became the headquarters of the US Middle East Force. During the Arab–Israeli War of October 1973, angered at Washington's backing for Israel, the Bahraini ruler stated that he had abrogated the agreement. But what he had actually done was to cancel the provision about providing fuelling facilities to the US navy, and raised the annual rental for the use of remaining naval facilities to £2 million. Later, the Bahraini–American military agreement, specifying naval and air facilities, was clandestinely renewed beyond its expiry date of June 1977.[22]

There was a marked difference in how Saddam Hussein and Hafiz Assad, both considered radical leaders, handled reality. Assad, a supple operator, comprehended the fact that his superpower backer, the Soviet Union, had been beaten in its competition with the US, and adjusted his policies accordingly, extracting as much gain as he could from the US to improve Syria's standing in Lebanon, its 'younger sister'. Saddam Hussein, on the other hand, conceived a scenario where Iraq would lead an independent bloc of oil-rich Arab states, emerging as the strategic power broker in the post-Cold War era. In his drive to impose his will on Kuwait, he overlooked the fact that the threat of force can often be more effective than its actual use. In dealing with Israel he had used this strategy well, claiming that his threats to use chemical weapons against it had aborted any Israeli plans to launch pre-emptive strikes against Iraq, Jordan or Libya.

The brutal haste with which he implemented the first phase of his overall plan for the Gulf – the invasion of Kuwait – created a situation which reduced the international position of Iraq itself to halfway between independence and the status it had under British mandate after the First World War.

This will remain the supreme irony of the Second Gulf War and the crisis that preceded it.

EPILOGUE

In July two areas of tension emerged: Baghdad's relations with its Kurdish minority, and its dealings with the UN. Bush pursued his demand on 1 July that Iraq give free access to UN inspectors seeking to check its nuclear facilities, while a joint statement with Mitterrand a fortnight later threatened new air attacks against Iraq if Saddam Hussein continued trying to make nuclear weapons or persecuted Iraqi Kurds or Shias.

Following a demand by the UN Security Council in mid-July that Baghdad should disclose full information about its nuclear, chemical and biological weapons facilities by 25 July, and a letter to Saddam Hussein from Mubarak warning him of grave consequences if Iraq continued to breach the terms of the ceasefire, the Iraqi leader invited a team from the Arab League to show that nothing was being concealed from the UN. On 16 July Iraq gave a second new list of nuclear sites, followed by an admission a few days later that it had been building two superguns.

This was not enough to dissuade the White House from declaring that the US had made a list of 120 Iraqi targets to be hit if Iraq failed to meet the UN demand. Iraq took the warning seriously with its prime minister saying that the danger of being bombed by the US was real. In the event, no military action was taken, primarily because Bush failed to get the backing of his regional allies to bomb Iraq again,[1] and secondarily because the attention of his administration turned to convening a Middle East peace conference in the wake of Assad's dramatic climb-down in mid-July on his terms for attending it.

Following Baker's four-day visit to the Middle East, beginning with a meeting with Assad on 18 July, he succeeded in getting Israel's consent on 1 August to attend a Middle East peace conference.

Concerned about the reports of growing malnutrition in Iraq, the UN Security Council agreed on 15 August to let Iraq sell up to $1.6 billion-worth of oil in a six-month period under UN auspices. Iraq described the resolution as interference in its internal affairs.[2]

On 4 September Saddam Hussein signed a law which, while allowing a multi-party system, outlawed parties based on 'atheism, religion, race and ethnicity'. Following his speech to the Baath Party congress advocating liberalization of all aspects of life, and strict adherence to UN resolutions to enable Iraq to end its isolation, Sadoun Hamadi was replaced as prime minister by one of his deputies, Muhammad Hamza Zubaidi.[3]

In mid-September as Baghdad refused to give unlimited freedom of movement to UN helicopters based in Iraq, and a 44-strong team of UN inspectors prepared to arrive in Iraq to investigate further Iraq's nuclear programme, Bush announced that he was planning to send warplanes to Saudi Arabia to press Saddam Hussein to comply with the ceasefire terms.

When on 24 September the UN inspectors began copying documents at the Atomic Energy Commission building in Baghdad, the Iraqi authorities protested that they were not following 'Iraqi procedures' and were violating Iraqi sovereignty and security. Following their refusal to hand over the documents to the Iraqis, and their return to their vehicles in the car park, they were surrounded by Iraqi security men. The impasse ended on 27 September when the two sides agreed to make a joint inventory of all the documents, film and videotapes before the UN inspectors could remove them from Iraq.

A preliminary perusal of the 25,000 pages of documents, 700 rolls of film and 19 hours of videotape reportedly gave the UN Special Disarmament Commission and the IAEA a complete picture of the Iraqi Atomic Energy Commission's personnel and procurement of materials. However, this did not alter the earlier conclusion reached by the IAEA. 'There is no physical evidence that the Iraqis had produced a detonator and there is no evidence yet that they had accumulated enough uranium on their own,' said David Kydd of the IAEA. 'It would have taken Iraq until at least 1995 or 1996 to acquire the ability to manufacture [nuclear] weapons at a rate of two or three a year.'[4]

NOTES

Introduction

1 *Sunday Times*, 27 January 1991.
2 The 1950 UN military action against North Korea's invasion of South Korea happened because the Soviet Union had walked out of the Security Council in protest against the continued presence of Nationalist China as a permanent member of the Security Council after its defeat by the Chinese Communists in October 1949.
3 Micah L. Sifri and Christopher Cerf (eds), *The Gulf War Reader*, Times Books, New York, 1991, pp. 369, 371; *New Statesman and Society*, 21 June 1991, p. 24. Britain and France too introduced their 'pool' systems. See also pp. 363–4.
4 The League of Arab States was established in 1945. Its members in 1978 (in chronological order) were: Egypt (1945), Iraq (1945), Jordan (1945), Lebanon (1945), North Yemen (1945), Saudi Arabia (1945), Syria (1945), Libya (1953), Sudan (1956), Morocco (1958), Tunisia (1958), Kuwait (1961), Algeria (1962), South Yemen (1967), Bahrain (1971), Mauritania (1971), Oman (1971), Qatar (1971), United Arab Emirates (1971), Somalia (1974), Palestine Liberation Organization (1974), and Djibouti (1977).

1 Iraq and Kuwait

1 Cited in Alan Rush, *Al-Sabah: History and Genealogy of Kuwait's Ruling Family. 1752–1987*, Ithaca Press, London and Atlantic Heights, N.J., 1987, p. 44.
2 Cited in Peter Mansfield, *Kuwait: Vanguard of the Gulf*, Hutchinson, London, 1990, p. 128.
3 Fred Halliday, *Arabia Without Sultans*, Penguin Books, Harmondsworth, 1974, p. 429.
4 Richard Schofield, *Kuwait and Iraq: Historical Claims and Territorial Disputes*, The Royal Institute of International Affairs, London, 1991, pp. 45, 47.
5 *Ibid.*, p. 61; H. R. P. Dickson, *Kuwait and Her Neighbours*, Allen & Unwin, London, 1956, pp. 278–80.
6 The Iraqi letter was forwarded to the Kuwaiti shaikh on 21 July 1932, and he accepted the Iraqi statement in his letter of 10 August 1932. Fifty-eight years later, in August 1990, the Iraqi government argued that the 1932 agreement was invalid because it was signed when Iraq was still under British mandate.
7 *The Times*, 7 August 1990.
8 Adel Darwish and Gregory Alexander, *Unholy Alliance: The Secret History of Saddam's War*, Victor Gollancz, London, 1991, p. 12.
9 The Free Officers' Group commanded the loyalties of

some 200 activists and 100 sympathizers. Majid Khadduri, *Republican Iraq: A Study of Iraqi Politics since the Revolution of 1958*, Oxford University Press, London and New York, 1969, p. 17.

10 Alan Rush (ed.), *Records of Kuwait 1899–1961, Vol. 7; Foreign Affairs II*, Archive Editions, Farnham Common, 1989, pp. 649–50. After the political union of Iraq and Jordan, both ruled by Hashemite kings, in early 1958, the Iraqi prime minister, Nuri al Said, proposed that Kuwait should join the union. Britain rejected the proposal.

11 The 10,000 US marines exceeded the number of soldiers and officers in the Lebanese military. Robert W. Stookey, *America and the Arab States: An Uneasy Encounter*, John Wiley, New York and London, 1975, p. 155.

12 Cited by Noam Chomsky, 'A Stand on Low Moral Ground', *Guardian*, 10 January 1991. In 1963 when Egypt's President Nasser threatened to attack Saudi Arabia from North Yemen, then in the throes of a civil war, America moved many of its warplanes from Frankfurt to Dhahran.

13 Chomsky, loc. cit.

14 *Guardian*, 1 January 1991.

15 Cited in *Independent Magazine*, 26 January 1991, p. 55.

16 *Ibid.*

17 Mansfield, op. cit., p. 52.

18 *Guardian*, 3 August 1990.

19 Cited in *The Middle East*, March 1977, p. 42.

20 Marion Farouk-Sluglett and Peter Sluglett, *Iraq Since 1958: From Revolution to Dictatorship*, I. B. Tauris, London and New York, 1990, p. 136.

21 *Pravda*, 12 February 1972.

22 Majid Khadduri, *Socialist Iraq: A Study in Iraqi Politics since 1968*, The Middle East Institute, Washington, DC, 1978, p. 145.

23 Darwish and Alexander, op. cit., pp. 34–5.

24 *New Times*, no. 1, 1966, p. 11.

25 *Middle East Economic Digest*, August 1977, 'Special Report on Kuwait', p. 43.

26 Committee Against Repression and For Democratic Rights in Iraq, *Saddam's Iraq: Revolution or Reaction?*, Zed Press, London, 1986, p. 66.

27 Cited in *Independent*, 26 September 1990.

28 Ralph Shaw, *Kuwait*, Macmillan, London, 1976, p. 26.

29 Of the 440,000 Kuwaiti nationals in 1975, fewer than 40,000 were eligible to vote. Five years later the total electorate amounted to 41,700. *The Middle East*, July 1980, p. 32; *8 Days*, 28 February 1981, p. 15; and Shaw, op. cit., p. 48.

30 *Guardian*, 30 August 1976.

31 The disputed Article Three of the draft constitution read: 'Internal concessions and lease monopolies as well as external agreements and treaties cannot be considered legal and binding unless approved by the elected legislative assembly.' Hassan A. al Ebraheem, *Kuwait: A Political Study*, Al Qabas Printing Press, Kuwait, 1971, p. 134.

32 *The Times*, 12 July 1977.

Taking into account their investments in Kuwait, the total may well have exceeded $10,000 million.

33 *The Middle East*, July 1980, p. 30.

34 *Vanity Fair*, November 1990, p. 159.

35 Ruh Allah Khumayni, *Islam and Revolution*, trans. Hamid Algar, Mizan Press, Berkeley, CA, 1981, p. 202.

36 *The Middle East*, July 1980, p. 30.

37 *Al Rai al Aam*, 10 December 1980; *Al Siyasa*, 10 December 1980. Between 1979 and 1982 the cargo bound for Iraq from Kuwait increased almost threefold to 3.5 million tons a year. Christine Moss Helms, *Iraq: Eastern Flank of the Arab World*, The Brookings Institution, Washington, DC, p. 49.

38 *International Herald Tribune*, 4 October 1982; *Economist*, 9 October 1982.

39 *Foreign Broadcast Information Service*, 23 March 1983.

40 Dilip Hiro, *The Longest War: The Iran–Iraq Military Conflict*, Grafton Books, London, 1989, and Routledge, New York, 1991, p. 115.

41 *Ibid*.

42 The Gulf Co-operation Council was established in May 1981. See further Dilip Hiro, *Inside the Middle East*, Routledge & Kegan Paul, London, 1982, and McGraw-Hill, New York, 1982, pp. 347, 348, 352–4.

43 *Guardian*, 28 August 1987. The unnamed Saudi official was identified by a British journalist present at the briefing as Prince Bandar ibn Sultan, the Saudi ambassador to the US.

44 Tehran Radio, 31 May 1984.

45 *Ibid*., 10 March 1986; *Al Watan al Arabi*, 18 April 1986.

46 The Beirut-based Islamic Jihad Organization claimed responsibility for the attack and demanded the release of the 17 people arrested in connection with the December 1983 bombings in Kuwait, six of whom had been sentenced to death in March 1984.

47 *Middle East Economic Digest*, 19 April 1986, p. 20.

48 Cited in *Vanity Fair*, November 1990, p. 160.

49 *Middle East Economic Survey*, 3 March 1986.

50 Laura Guazzone, 'Gulf Co-operation Council: The Security Policies', *Survival*, March–April 1988, p. 143.

51 *The Times*, 15 October 1990.

52 A few weeks later Iraq's First Deputy Premier, Taha Yassin Ramadan, visited Kuwait with a message of support for Shaikh Jaber III from Saddam Hussein. Iraqi News Agency, 23 July 1986.

53 Kuwait News Agency, 5 April 1986.

54 Caspar W. Weinberger, 'A Report to the Congress on Security Arrangements in the Persian Gulf', Department of Defense, Washington, DC, 15 June 1987.

55 *Keesing's Record of World Events*, Vol. XXXIII, p. 35546.

56 In December 1990, 'Captain Karim', who had until recently been one of the 'close and intimate' bodyguards of Saddam Hussein for five years, claimed on French television that the 17 May 1987 attack on USS *Stark* was ordered by the Iraqi president himself,

and that he had decorated the pilot who lodged two Exocet missiles in the ship's flanks with the highest military order. *Independent*, 22 December 1990.

57 Cited in *MERIP Middle East Report*, September–October 1987, p. 4.

58 *Independent*, 6 August 1987.

59 *Keesing's Record of World Events*, Vol. XXXIII, p. 35598.

60 See Hiro, *The Longest War*, p. 250, p. 285, note 13.

61 *Mednews: Middle East Defence News*, 22 February 1988, p. 1; The International Institute of Strategic Studies, *The Military Balance 1987–1988*, pp. 98, 100, 101. The armed forces figures included both the active and reserve personnel. Only Iran's (active) Basij militia of 350,000 was far stronger than the Iraqi volunteer force of 120,000.

62 BBC World Service, 30 November 1987; *Arab News*, 9 February 1988.

63 Hiro, *The Longest War*, p. 119.

64 *Sunday Times*, 16 March 1985.

65 *Washington Post*, 7 February 1991. This arrangement seems to have followed the October 1982 meeting between George Shultz, the US secretary of state, and Tariq Aziz in Paris, the first high-level encounter between America and Iraq since June 1967. See Hiro, *The Longest War*, pp. 119, 159–60.

66 *Ibid.*, pp. 36–7.

2 Prelude to the Crisis

1 Jordanian Television, Amman, 24 February 1990.

2 *Middle East International*, 2 March 1990, p. 10.

3 *BBC Summary of World Broadcasts*, 19 July 1990.

4 *Independent*, 3 August 1990.

5 Martin Short and Anthony McDermott, *The Kurds*, Minority Rights Group, London, 1977, p. 19; *Guardian*, 25 April 1991.

6 *Washington Post*, 24 August 1990; *Foreign Broadcast Information Service*, 29 and 30 August.

7 *The Proliferation of Chemical Warfare: The Holocaust at Halabia*, People for a Just Peace, Washington, DC, 1988, p. 8, citing UN Document No. S/19816, 21 April 1988.

8 *Guardian*, 6 January 1989.

9 *Sunday Times*, 11 September 1988; *Foreign Broadcast Information Service*, 14 September 1988.

10 Dilip Hiro, *The Longest War*, p. 201.

11 *Washington Post*, 10 and 12 September 1988.

12 *Guardian*, 16 September and 21 October 1988; *Middle East International*, 21 October 1988.

13 Cited in *The Middle East*, October 1988, p. 16.

14 *Guardian*, 16 October 1988. As late as 14 October, an Iraqi chemical attack in Suleimaniya province was reported. *Ibid.*, 19 October 1988.

15 In mid-June 1989 at the second ACC summit in Alexandria, Mubarak found himself pressured again to add a military clause to the ACC Charter. He refused. Later Egyptian officials construed the Iraqi–Jordanian move as a 'conspiracy' to entangle Egypt with Iraq militarily so as to curtail Egypt's area of manoeuvre and effectively

destroy it after the Iraqi
invasion of Kuwait. *New York
Times,* 12 November 1990.

16 *Foreign Broadcast Information
Service,* 28 March 1989.

17 Adel Darwish and Gregory
Alexander, *Unholy Babylon:
The Secret History of Saddam's
War,* p. 236. In late 1988, after
Kuwait had restored diplomatic
links with Iran, the Iraqis
had made at least one illegal
incursion over the border into
Kuwait. Another incursion
occurred soon after the Iranian
ambassador had presented his
credentials in Kuwait on 29
September 1989. *Ibid.*

18 *Foreign Broadcast Information
Service,* 4 November 1988;
Guardian, 24 March 1989.

19 Marion Farouk-Sluglett and
Peter Sluglett, *Iraq Since
1958,* p. 275. According to
'Captain Karim', Generals
Salah Ghazi, Taher Abdul
Majid, Aziz Hadithi, Hamad
Abdullah Kamil Ali were
executed. *Independent,* 22
December 1990.

20 *Washington Post,* 7 May 1989;
Independent, 22 December
1990 and 28 January 1991.

21 These figures were
mentioned by King Fahd
in his conversation with
Shaikh Khalifa ibn Hamad
al Thani, the ruler of Qatar,
on 9 July 1990. See p. 86. In
his disclosures published in
October 1986, Mordechai
Vanunu, who had worked at
the Israeli nuclear plant at
Dimona from 1976 to 1985,
stated that Israel was producing
annually 40 kilograms of
weapons-grade plutonium,
enough for 10 nuclear bombs
of 20 kiloton capacity (the type

dropped on Nagasaki, Japan),
and that it had also developed
means to produce more
lethal neutron and hydrogen
warheads. *Sunday Times,* 5
October 1986.

22 *Washington Post,* 1 April 1989;
*Foreign Broadcast Information
Service,* 31 March 1989. The
missile project, known as
Condor-2, was being pursued by
Iraq in conjunction with Egypt
and Argentina.

23 *The Middle East,* December
1989, p. 30. In his message to
President Bush of 25 July 1990,
Saddam Hussein put Iraq's
war burden at 'a $40 billion
debt, excluding the aid given
by Arab states'. Micah L. Sifri
and Christopher Cerf (eds), *The
Gulf War Reader,* Times Books,
New York, 1991, p. 123.

24 *Independent,* 8 June 1989.

25 *Ibid.,* 12 September 1990; *New
York Times,* 23 December 1990.
See also Dilip Hiro, *Inside the
Middle East,* p. 329; Victor
Ostrovsky and Claire Hoy, *By
Way of Deception: The Making
and Unmaking of a Mossad
Officer,* St Martins Press, New
York, 1990, pp. 22–3, 26–7.

26 *Guardian,* 16 March 1990; *The
Middle East,* June 1990, p. 25.

27 *Ibid.,* November 1989, p. 19.

28 *The Times,* 7 December
1989; *Sunday Times,* 10
December 1989; *Guardian,*
18 December 1989; *The
Middle East,* February 1990,
p. 18. The flaw was reportedly
traced to a faulty wind tunnel
at the missile research and
development centre at the
Saad-16 complex near Mosul.
Darwish and Alexander, op. cit.,
p. 242.

29 *Guardian,* 15 December 1989;

The Middle East, May 1990, pp. 11–12.

30 *Ibid.*, December 1989, p. 30.

31 *New York Times*, 15 November 1989; *Foreign Broadcast Information Service*, 20 November 1989.

32 *New York Times*, 11 February 1990; *Foreign Broadcast Information Service*, 6 March 1990.

33 *New York Times*, 23 February 1990.

34 In the 1948–9 Arab–Israeli War, the Palestinians lost 77 per cent of Palestine to Israel, established on 15 May 1948, with the (remaining) West Bank going under Jordan's jurisdiction and Gaza under Egypt's.

35 *New York Times*, 1 and 8 February 1990.

36 Baghdad Radio, 2 February 1990.

37 *Indian Express*, 8 February 1990.

38 Iraqi News Agency, 16 February 1990.

39 *The Middle East*, April 1990, p. 7.

40 Jordanian Television, Amman, 24 February 1990. Four months later, in an interview with an American paper, Saddam Hussein summed up the situation thus: 'It is now clear the US can exert influence over the Soviets and make them abandon any position contrary to the US. So, America thinks it can cast things anyway it wants in the region and in alliance with Israel can suppress any voice in support of Arab rights.' *Wall Street Journal*, 28 June 1990.

41 *New York Times*, 25 and 31 January 1990.

42 Simon Henderson concludes that Bazoft had spied for Britain during his five earlier visits to Iraq, and that Iraqi intelligence had monitored his handing over of the soil samples to his contact at the British embassy. Yet he notes that 'At no time did the British admit that Bazoft had been spying, nor did Iraq flesh out its allegations.' This, he explains, was done in order to avoid diplomatic rupture, which would have been commercially damaging to both countries. *Instant Empire: Saddam Hussein's Ambition for Iraq*, Mercury House, San Francisco, CA, 1991, pp. 204–10.

43 Cited in *Independent*, 16 March 1990. The main source of information on Bazoft for the Iraqis was probably a Briton, Rocky Ryan. In July 1988, after he had threatened Bazoft and the editor of the *Observer*, Donald Trelford, he was bound over for a year. In August 1989, he claimed to have phoned the Iraqi embassy in London three times alleging that Bazoft was an agent for Israel and Iran. Again on 26 October Ryan claimed to have transmitted further information on Bazoft to the Iraqi mission, saying that his source was 'a contact in MI5 [Military Intelligence–5, which deals with subversive elements in Britain]'. Bazoft's televised confession in Baghdad came five days later.

44 Iraqi News Agency, 12 March 1990.

45 *Guardian*, 16 March 1990; Darwish and Alexander, op. cit., p. 249.

46 However, the British

ambassador returned to
Baghdad after two months.

47 Voice of the Masses Radio,
Baghdad, 16 March 1990.

48 *Sunday Times*, 16 March
1990. In the summer of
1986, in the course of doing
a story on Cyrus Hashemi,
an Iranian arms dealer, who
died in London in mysterious
circumstances, Bazoft had
reportedly interviewed Yaacov
Nimrodi, an Israeli arms dealer,
who headed the Israeli mission
in Tehran during the last years
of the Shah.

49 *Ibid.*

50 *Ibid.*

51 *The Middle East*, April
1990, p. 6.

52 The Saudi statement
implicitly drew parallels with
the controversial execution
of 16 Kuwaiti Shias found
guilty of planting bombs in
Mecca in July 1989. *Middle
East International*, 30 March
1990, p. 9.

53 Three months later Saddam
Hussein expressed himself
thus on the subject: 'The US
and Britain began to talk about
ruthless Saddam with no heart
when a spy was executed to
avoid a return to the time when
foreigners ran rampant in this
country. We will not allow any
foreigner to steal intelligence.'
Wall Street Journal, 28
June 1990.

54 *Guardian*, 16 March 1990.

55 Cited in *Middle East
International*, 30 March
1990, p. 10.

56 BBC-TV's *Panorama*, 18
February 1991.

57 *Washington Post*, 30 and 31
March 1990. In mid-April
the Iraqi government said

that the devices confiscated
by the British and American
officials on 28 March were
destined for use in a carbonic
laser system at Baghdad's
Technological University.
*Foreign Broadcast Information
Service*, 18 April 1990. On 9
May Saddam Hussein displayed
the devices on television,
with a spokesman later stating
that these had been obtained
legally from the US in 1988
by Baghdad's Technological
University. *Foreign Broadcast
Information Service*, 9 and
10 May 1990. Of the three
defendants put on trial in
Britain, one was found 'not
guilty' and the remaining
two given a five-year prison
sentence each. *Independent*, 13
June 1991.

58 Dilip Hiro, *Inside the Middle
East*, p. 223; *Middle East
International*, 13 April 1990,
p. 15. Israel also possessed a
much smaller nuclear reactor at
Nahal Sorek inside an airbase
south of Tel Aviv. Ostrovsky
and Hoy, op. cit., p. 150.

59 Some commentators
interpreted this move as a
deliberate ploy by Iraq to deter
Israel from launching a strike
against one or more Iraqi
targets.

60 Darwish and Alexander, op. cit.,
p. 251.

61 Cited in *Middle East
International*, 13 April
1990, p. 4. Saddam Hussein
raised the issue of negative
media coverage of Iraq in the
American media. 'I wonder,
as you may wonder, if the
US government was not
behind such reports,' he said.
'How else could all this have

occurred in such a short period of time?' To this Senator Alan Simpson replied: 'It's very easy ... They all live off one another. Everyone takes from the other. When there is a major news item on the front page of the *New York Times*, another journalist takes and publishes it.' Cited in Sifri and Cerf (eds), *The Gulf War Reader*, p. 120.

62 *The Middle East*, March 1990, p. 17.

63 In mid-May 1990, the Italian authorities said they had confiscated 90 tons of steel parts thought to be part of a supergun for Iraq. *Financial Times*, 16 May 1990. Christopher Cowley and Peter Mitchell, managing director of Walter Somers, were arrested in April 1990; but, significantly, charges against them were dropped in November.

64 BBC-TV's *Panorama*, 18 February 1991.

65 Baghdad Radio, 18 April 1990.

66 *New York Times*, 23 May 1990.

67 *Independent*, 13 September and 16 December 1989; *The Middle East*, October 1989, p. 23.

68 *Washington Post*, 5 June 1990.

69 *Ibid.*, 21, 23 and 27 May 1990.

70 Baghdad Radio, 28 May 1990. The summit was boycotted by Syria and Lebanon. At a closed session, attended only by the Arab rulers, Saddam Hussein urged his audience to pressure the US by boycotting American financial institutions.

71 *Washington Post*, 30 May 1990; *Independent*, 31 May 1990.

72 Baghdad Radio, 30 May 1990.

73 *Foreign Broadcast Information Service*, 4 June 1990.

74 *Ibid.* At the subsequent PLO executive committee meeting in Baghdad, Abu al Abbas confirmed that the PLF operation had not targeted civilians. *Ibid.*, 8 June 1990.

75 *New York Times*, 31 May 1990.

76 *Washington Post*, 27 June 1990; *Wall Street Journal*, 28 June 1990.

77 *Financial Times*, 19 June 1990; *Washington Post*, 21 June 1990.

78 *Wall Street Journal*, 28 June 1990.

79 *Foreign Broadcast Information Service*, 8 and 15 May 1990; *Echo of Iran*, July 1990, p. 9. The texts of Saddam Hussein's 21 April and 19 May letters and 21 June telegram of condolences to Rafsanjani on the earthquake victims in Iran were broadcast on Baghdad Radio on 15, 18 and 21 August 1990.

80 *The Middle East*, April 1990, p. 5.

81 Cited in Mansfield, *Kuwait*, p. 116.

82 *Middle East International*, 11 May 1990, p. 12.

83 *Ibid.*, 22 June 1990, p. 12.

84 Baghdad Radio, 18 July 1990.

85 Hiro, *The Longest War*, p. 175; Daniel Yergin, *Prize: The Epic Quest for Oil, Money and Power*, Simon and Schuster, New York and London, 1991, pp. 749–50.

86 *Foreign Broadcast Information Service*, 28 June 1990; *New York Times*, 28 June 1990; Pierre Salinger with Eric Laurent, *Secret Dossier: The*

Hidden Agenda behind the Gulf War, Penguin Books, Harmondsworth, 1991, p. 32.

87 Cited in John Bulloch and Harvey Morris, *Saddam's War: The Origins of the Kuwait Crisis and the International Response*, Faber, London and Boston, 1991, pp. 143–6. The reference to the meeting in September pertained to the annual GCC summit.

88 The English translation of this memorandum, discovered at the headquarters of Kuwait's State Security Department by the Iraqis, was placed before the UN secretary-general by Iraq's ambassador to the UN on 24 October 1990. The CIA said that the document was a forgery.

89 *Wall Street Journal*, 12 July 1990.

90 *Al Thawra*, 21 July 1990.

91 Baghdad Radio, 18 July 1990.

92 *Wall Street Journal*, 18 July 1990; *Guardian*, 26 February 1991.

93 Baghdad Radio, 17 July 1990; *Guardian*, 19 July 1990.

94 *Independent on Sunday*, 29 July and 5 August 1990; *Guardian*, 4 and 6 August 1990.

95 Kuwait Radio, 18 July 1990.

96 *Ibid.*, 19 July 1990. In its response to the Iraqi memorandum, the UAE described Iraq's attack on its oil policy as 'void of truth', and repeated the Kuwaiti argument about 'the collective responsibility of the oil-producing countries inside and outside OPEC' regarding the fall in oil prices. *BBC Summary of World Broadcasts*, 23 July 1990.

97 *Guardian*, 24 July 1990. The other, unstated, objective of the joint exercise was to provide the US with a ruse to supply two aerial-refuelling tankers to the UAE so that it could keep its patrol planes in the air around the clock. Bob Woodward, *The Commanders*, Simon and Schuster, New York and London, 1991, p. 210.

98 See p. 85. This is a reference to the GCC summit to be held in September.

99 The complete transcript of the meeting was released by the Iraqi government on 12 September 1990. The US state department neither confirmed nor denied its accuracy. The full text is reprinted in Sifri and Cerf (eds), *The Gulf War Reader*, pp. 122–33. In her testimony to the US Senate Foreign Relations Committee, chaired by Senator Claiborne Pell, on 20 March 1991, Ambassador Glaspie said that she repeatedly warned President Saddam Hussein against using violence to settle his border dispute with Kuwait and that he was too 'stupid' to understand how the US would react if he did. Later, this was disputed by three members of the Senate Committee – Claiborne Pell, Jesse Helms and Alan Cranston – after they had read the secret cables that Glaspie had sent to the state department and the message that President Bush had sent to Saddam Hussein. 'Ms Glaspie had deliberately misled Congress,' said Senator Cranston. 'Her testimony is at great variance with [the] reporting cables on her meetings with Saddam

Hussein.' Referring to the joint US–UAE naval exercise, Glaspie said in her cable that 'We have caught Saddam Hussein's attention', and added: 'I believe we would now be well-advised to ease off on public criticism of Iraq until we see how the [Iraq–Kuwait] negotiations develop.' *New York Times*, 21 March 1991; *Washington Post*, 13 July 1991.

100 *Washington Post*, 21 October 1990.

101 *Independent*, 28 July 1990; *Wall Street Journal*, 19 December 1990.

102 Salinger with Laurent, op. cit., pp. 70–75.

103 *Guardian*, 15 February 1991, citing the Amman-based *Al Rai*, 14 February 1991.

104 Cited in *The Times*, 3 August 1990. On 31 July, appearing before the Middle East sub-committee of the House of Representatives Foreign Affairs Committee, John Kelly said, 'We don't have any defence treaty with the Gulf states.' To the question, 'If Iraq crossed the Kuwaiti border, is it correct to say that we have no treaty, no commitment, which would oblige us to use American forces?', he replied: 'That's exactly right.' See Salinger with Laurent, op. cit., pp. 68–9.

105 According to PLO sources, Saddam Hussein's decision to invade Kuwait was taken around midnight on 31 July–1 August 1990. *Independent*, 2 October 1990. See also Salinger with Laurent, op. cit., p. 76.

106 *Financial Times*, 2 August 1990; *Guardian*, 2 August 1990; *The Times*, 3 August 1990.

3 Saddam's Blitzkrieg, Bush's Line in the Sand

1 *Vanity Fair*, November 1990, p. 160.

2 *Guardian*, 9 August 1990.

3 *Independent*, 10 August 1990.

4 *Guardian*, 13 August 1990.

5 *Los Angeles Times*, 19 August 1990.

6 *Guardian*, 3 August 1990; *The Times*, 3 August 1990; *Vanity Fair*, November 1990, p. 156; *New York Times*, 4 March 1991; Pierre Salinger with Eric Lauret, *Secret Dossier*, pp. 83–4.

7 According to hospital sources in Kuwait, some 700 Kuwaitis were killed in the invasion and its aftermath. *Sunday Times*, 5 August 1990; *Independent*, 8 August 1990.

8 *Independent*, 7 August 1990; *New York Times*, 25 May 1991. After the liberation of Kuwait, Colonel Matar Said al Matar, a diplomat at Kuwait's consulate in Basra, claimed that he had told foreign and defence ministries on 25 July 1990 that Iraq would invade, and had conveyed to his superiors his prediction of immediate invasion after the failure of the Kuwaiti–Iraqi talks on 31 July, but to no avail. *Washington Post*, 8 March 1991.

9 *The Times*, 3 August 1990; *Independent*, 3 August 1990.

10 *New York Times*, 3 August 1990.

11 *Guardian*, 20 August 1990.

12 Baghdad Radio, 3 August 1990.

13 *Guardian*, 5 August 1990. Except Iraq, no other country recognized the Provisional Free Government of Kuwait.

14 *Washington Post*, 4 August

1990. On the same day Gulf
Co-operation Council foreign
ministers meeting in Cairo also
condemned Iraqi aggression
against Kuwait.

15 *New York Times*, 16 October
1990; Salinger with Laurent,
Secret Dossier, pp. 102, 113.

16 See Dilip Hiro, *Inside the
Middle East*, pp. 346–50.

17 Bob Woodward, *The
Commanders*, pp. 226–7.

18 *Washington Post*, 9 March
1991; *Independent*, 9
March 1991.

19 In early October 1990 Prince
Bandar related this story to
Stephen Solarz, a member of
the House of Representatives
Foreign Affairs Committee,
who leaked it to the *New York
Times*. Significantly, the Saudi
official refused to say how
many Iraqis were involved.
(Most probably, not many.)
Guardian, 5 October 1990.
A slightly modified version,
omitting certain important
details, appeared in Woodward,
op. cit., pp. 240–44.

20 *Ibid.*, pp. 247–53; *New York
Times*, 4 March 1991.

21 Woodward, op. cit., pp. 258–9.

22 *In These Times*, 26
September–2 October
1990, p. 14.

23 Cited in *Guardian*, 15 October
1990.

24 *Washington Post*, 6 August
1990.

25 *Financial Times*, 10 August
1990. It was the State Reserve
Fund of Kuwait which gave
interest-free loans to Iraq
during the First Gulf War. It
was also meant to cover budget
deficits.

26 *The Times*, 3 August 1990. A
row over how much control

the al Sabahs should have
over the Kuwait Investment
Authority's overseas funds led
to the resignation of twelve
KIO executives in January 1991.
New Statesman and Society, 1
March 1990.

27 *BP Statistical Review of
World Energy*, June 1990, The
British Petroleum Company,
London, p. 2.

28 Actually, this order was issued
on 3 August. See Woodward,
op. cit., p. 237.

29 *Financial Times*, 6 August
1990.

30 *New York Times*, 6 August
1990; *Guardian*, 6 August
1990; *New York Times*, 7
March 1991.

31 Cited in *Independent*, 11
September 1990; *Guardian*, 12
September 1990; Salinger with
Laurent, op. cit., pp. 139–47. In
his message to President Bush,
Saddam Hussein said that Iraq
had offered a non-aggression
pact to Kuwait which had
been rejected, 'probably on
the advice of a foreign power,
possibly Britain', and added that
if there had been such a pact,
Iraq could not have supported
'the revolutionary group in
Kuwait'.

32 *New York Times*, 4 March
1991; Woodward, op. cit.,
p. 273.

33 *New York Times*, 8 August
1990.

34 *Independent on Sunday*, 12
August 1990.

35 Baghdad Radio, 7 August 1990.

36 *Guardian*, 13 August 1990.
Saddam Hussein mentioned
no figure in his letter to Bush,
but there was speculation that
he was seeking $50 billion for
post-war reconstruction of Iraq.

37 *Guardian*, 9 August 1990.
38 *Independent*, 14 August 1990.
39 Woodward, op. cit., pp. 213, 243.
40 *New York Times*, 17 August 1990.
41 John Tower, Edmund Muskie and Brent Scowcroft, *The Tower Commission Report: The Full Text of the President's Special Review Board*, Bantam Books and Times Books, New York, 1987, p. 417.
42 Cited in *In These Times*, 27 February–19 March 1991, p. 7.
43 *In These Times*, 19–25 September 1990, pp. 4–5.
44 This tied in with what Saddam Hussein told the American chargé d'affaires, Joseph Wilson, on 6 August. See pp. 114–15. According to King Hussein, the Iraqi president seized all of Kuwait as a bargaining counter to get the disputed areas of the emirate.
45 *Guardian*, 20 August 1990.
46 Baghdad Radio, 8 August 1990.
47 *Independent*, 11 August 1990.
48 Baghdad Radio, 8 August 1990.
49 *Washington Post*, 9 August 1990.
50 *Independent*, 9 August 1990.
51 *Ibid.*, 10 August 1990.
52 Saudi Arabia Television, Riyadh, 9 August 1990.
53 Baghdad Radio, 10 August 1990. Pro-Saddam Islamic rallies were held in Amman, Sanaa and the West Bank. *Washington Post*, 11 August 1990.
54 Saudi Press Agency, 11 August 1990; *Independent on Sunday*, 12 August 1990.
55 *Guardian*, 14 August 1990; *New York Times*, 4 March 1991; Woodward, op. cit., p. 266.
56 Cairo Radio, 10 August 1990; *Washington Post*, 11 August 1990.
57 Cited in *The Times*, 10 August 1990.
58 Baghdad Radio, 13 August 1990.
59 *New York Times*, 11 August 1990.
60 *The Times*, 8 August 1990.
61 *Washington Post*, 14 August 1990.
62 *Guardian*, 13 and 15 August 1990.
63 Baghdad Radio, 12 August 1990.
64 In contrast, 4,000 Egyptians volunteered to fight for Saudi Arabia and Kuwait. *Guardian*, 14 August 1990; *Independent*, 15 August 1990.
65 *Washington Post*, 15 August 1990. These members referred to UN sanctions against Rhodesia (now Zimbabwe) in 1965 when Britain approached the UN for permission to stop a ship sailing with goods for Rhodesia.
66 Baghdad Radio, 12 August 1990.
67 *Independent*, 14 August 1990. Of the 1.4 million foreign workers, about 850,000 were Egyptian, some 200,000 Sudanese, with the rest being other Arabs, South Asians and Filipinos.
68 *New York Times*, 14 August 1990.
69 *Washington Post*, 15 August 1990. Earlier, Washington had pressured the Kuwaiti emir to promise financial aid to Ankara to persuade it to close the Iraqi oil pipeline. *New York Times*, 7 August 1990.
70 *Ibid.*, 14 and 16 August 1990.
71 The severing of links stemmed from the riot by Iranian pilgrims in Mecca during the hajj on 31 July 1987, which resulted in the death of 402

mainly Iranian pilgrims at the hands of the Saudi security forces, and angry demonstrations in Tehran outside Saudi and Kuwaiti embassies. See Hiro, *The Longest War*, p. 225.

72 *Washington Post*, 8 and 10 August 1990.

73 Islamic Republic News Agency, 16 August 1990.

74 Baghdad Radio, 15 August 1990.

75 *New York Times*, 21 March 1991. The source of this information was Hassan Rabani, the spokesman of Iran's National Security Council. He leaked it to 'several Arab officials' at a time when Iran had openly resorted to arming Iraqi Shia rebels to overthrow the Saddam Hussein regime. *Ibid.*

76 *Los Angeles Times*, 15 August 1990. Evening newscasts of the three major US television networks drew a combined 60% of the audience while prime time television attracted only 53%. *Guardian*, 16 August 1990.

77 *Ibid.*; *Independent*, 16 August 1990.

78 Baghdad Radio, 16 August 1990; and see pp. 114–15.

79 Hiro, *Inside the Middle East*, p. 146; Samir al Khalil, *Republic of Fear*, University of California Press, Berkeley, 1989, and Hutchinson Radius, London, 1989, pp. 70–72; Farouk-Sluglett and Sluglett, *Iraq Since 1958*, p. 209.

80 *Economist*, 4 December 1982 and 29 January 1983; author's interview with an Iraqi opposition leader in London, April 1988. For further assassination attempts on

Saddam Hussein, see Hiro, *The Longest War*, pp. 51, 98, 197.

81 *New York Times*, 17 August 1990; *Guardian*, 18 August 1990. The figures for Western and Japanese nationals in Iraq (and Kuwait) were: Britain, 4,000 (+640); America, 2,500 (+600); Canada, 522 (+200); West Germany, 290 (+450); France, 290 (+270); Japan, 270 (+230); Italy, 152 (+330); Greece, 150; Spain, 106; Sweden, 100. Below 100: Australia, Austria, New Zealand, Denmark etc. Iraq allowed the 570 nationals of Austria, Finland, Portugal, Sweden and Switzerland to leave because their governments had not joined the military build-up against Iraq. *Independent*, 20 August 1990; *New York Times*, 21 August 1990.

82 *Ibid.*, 18 August 1990; *Washington Post*, 19 August 1990.

83 *Independent on Sunday*, 19 August 1990. According to Mizhir Affat, a former bodyguard of Saddam Hussein, the order to take foreign hostages had come from the Iraqi president. In domestic affairs, in order to secure the arrest of an elusive opponent, Saddam Hussein often ordered the taking of family members as hostages.

84 *New York Times*, 19 August 1990; *Washington Post*, 19 and 20 August 1990. Following the failure of the US warships to impose their will on the Iraqi tankers, an agitated Bush telephoned Thatcher for consultation. It was in the course of this conversation

that, according to Bush, she said to him, 'George, this is not the time to go wobbly'; words which, Bush claims, stayed with him throughout the crisis. *Ibid.*, 9 March 1991.

85 Cited in *Independent on Sunday*, 2 September 1990.

86 Baghdad Radio, 19 August 1990.

87 *Newsday*, 29 August 1990.

88 *Ibid.*, 30 August 1990.

89 *New York Times*, 22 August 1990; *USA Today*, 22 August 1990.

90 Cited in *Guardian*, 20 August 1990.

91 *Ibid.*

92 *Sunday Telegraph*, 12 August 1990.

93 *Washington Post*, 22 August 1990; *Independent*, 23 August 1990; *Sunday Times*, 26 August 1990.

94 *Guardian*, 22 August 1990; *Independent*, 4 September 1990.

95 *Guardian*, 20 and 21 August 1990. Later, of OPEC members, the UAE and Venezuela announced increased output of 500,000 b/d each. Allowing for another 500,000 b/d to be squeezed out of non-OPEC producers, the global shortfall was expected to be 800,000 b/d, or 1.25% of the total world production of 64 mb/d. *Daily Telegraph*, 23 August 1990.

96 *Ibid.* What Gorbachev found particularly galling was that Saddam Hussein had used Soviet weapons, provided for defensive purposes, to carry out an aggression in 'flagrant contempt for international law and the United Nations'. *Guardian*, 23 August 1990.

97 Hiro, *Inside the Middle East*, pp. 290–92.

98 *New York Times*, 21 and 23 August 1990; *Financial Times*, 22 August 1990.

99 *Guardian*, 23 August 1990.

100 *New York Times*, 22 August 1990; *Daily Telegraph*, 23 August 1990; *Guardian*, 23 August 1990; Woodward, op. cit., p. 249.

101 *Independent on Sunday*, 2 September 1990.

102 *Independent*, 24 August 1990; *Guardian*, 24 August 1990.

103 *Ibid.*, 25 August 1990.

4 Diplomacy, Hostages and Military Build-ups

1 *Financial Times*, 29 August 1990.

2 *Ibid.*

3 *Sunday Times*, 23 September 1990.

4 *Financial Times*, 17 September 1990.

5 *Sunday Times*, 23 September 1990.

6 Cited in *Independent on Sunday*, 9 September 1990.

7 *New York Times*, 18 August 1990.

8 Cited in *Guardian*, 25 August 1990.

9 *New York Times*, 21 August 1990.

10 *Guardian*, 29 August 1990; *Daily Telegraph*, 30 August 1990.

11 Cited in *Guardian*, 29 August 1990; *Sunday Times*, 2 September 1990.

12 Baghdad Radio, 25 August 1990.

13 *Independent on Sunday*, 26 August 1990.

14 *Sunday Times*, 26 August 1990; *Washington Post*, 27 August 1990.

15 Hiro, *Inside the Middle East*, pp. 349–50.
16 Tehran Radio, 24 August 1990; *Independent*, 25 August 1990.
17 *Guardian*, 27 August 1990.
18 *Washington Post*, 20 August 1990; *Foreign Broadcast Information Service*, 20 August 1990.
19 *Independent*, 30 August 1990.
20 *New York Times*, 30 August 1990; *The Times*, 30 August 1990; *Foreign Broadcast Information Service*, 30 August 1990. Syrian troops reportedly moved to the south-east after pro-Iraqi demonstrations occurred in Abu Kamal and Deir al Zor.
21 *Guardian*, 24 August 1990; and see p. 62 earlier.
22 *Independent*, 29 August 1990; *Guardian*, 29 August 1990.
23 *Ibid.*, 6 September 1990.
24 By late August Washington had reached 'Threshold A' – that is, it had enough troops to deter, or counter, further aggression by Iraq. It needed another six to eight weeks to reach 'Threshold B' – to be able to mount an offensive to expel the Iraqis from Kuwait.
25 *Sunday Times*, 2 September 1990.
26 *Daily Telegraph*, 31 August 1990. In contrast, the Iraqi government had no qualms about periodically jamming the BBC's Arabic broadcasts.
27 Tehran Radio, 24 August 1990.
28 Earlier, instead of insisting on keeping its embassy open after the deadline of 24 August, as the US did, the USSR vacated its diplomatic mission without closing it down. It also promptly evacuated its 880 citizens from Kuwait.
29 *Guardian*, 26 September 1990.
30 *Daily Telegraph*, 31 August 1990.
31 Cited in *Sunday Times*, 2 September 1990.
32 *Guardian*, 1 September 1990.
33 *Washington Post*, 3 September 1990.
34 Cairo Radio, 1 September 1990; *Washington Post*, 2 September 1990.
35 *Independent*, 6 September 1990.
36 *New York Times*, 3 September 1990; *Guardian*, 7 September 1990.
37 Hiro, *The Longest War*, pp. 309–10.
38 *New York Times*, 31 August 1990; *Washington Post*, 5 September 1990. After it was released by the US navy, *Zanubia* proceeded to Aden. *Financial Times*, 6 September 1990. The two Iraqi tankers, whose movements earlier had upset President Bush, were now anchored off the Yemeni coast, and were being watched by the French navy.
39 *Financial Times*, 28 August and 15 September 1990; *Washington Post*, 5 September 1990.
40 *Ibid.*, 30 August 1990; *New York Times*, 8 September 1990.
41 *Independent*, 6 September 1990.
42 Baghdad Radio, 5 September 1990.
43 *Guardian*, 6 September 1990.
44 *Ibid.* To counter these doubts, the state-controlled media played up the release of about half of the 70,000 Iraqi prisoners of war, which occurred during 18–27 August and which brought joy to as many families. *Foreign*

Broadcast Information Service, 28 August 1990.

45 *New York Times*, 20 September 1990 and 21 March 1991.

46 *Washington Post*, 30 August 1990.

47 *Guardian*, 7 September 1990; Hiro, *Inside the Middle East*, pp. 143, 280–1, 282, 373.

48 Cited in *Independent*, 8 September 1990.

49 Baghdad Radio, 8 September 1990.

50 *Washington Post*, 10 September 1990. 'The UN Sanctions Committee will decide under what conditions humanitarian aid should go to Iraq, and will then supervise its allocation and distribution,' said Brent Scowcroft. 'International control over Iraq's food imports is acceptable to our administration.' *Guardian*, 10 September 1990.

51 *Washington Post*, 10 September 1990; *Independent*, 10 September 1990; *Guardian*, 10 September 1990.

52 *New York Times*, 29 August 1990; *Independent*, 29 August 1990.

53 *Washington Post*, 2 and 4 September 1990; *The Times*, 5 September 1990; *Independent on Sunday*, 9 September 1990. This was in line with the Saudi conditions on which the US troops were invited. See p. 116.

54 *New York Times*, 5 September 1990.

55 *Ibid.*, 10 and 11 September 1990; *Guardian*, 13 September 1990.

56 *New York Times*, 13 and 14 September 1990.

57 Iraqi Television, Baghdad, 10 September 1990.

58 Tehran Radio, 12 September 1990.

59 *Independent*, 13 September 1990.

60 *Washington Post*, 11 and 14 September 1990.

61 *Independent*, 15 September 1990.

62 Saudi Press Agency, 13 September 1990.

63 Riyadh Radio, 13 August 1990.

64 *Independent*, 14 September 1990.

65 *Independent on Sunday*, 16 September 1990.

66 The other reason for the delay was the Pentagon estimate of 30,000 casualties to free Kuwait, a figure which had shocked the White House. *Washington Post*, 13 September 1990.

67 *Independent*, 14 September 1990.

68 *Ibid.*

69 Damascus Radio, 16 August 1990; *Independent*, 14 September 1990.

70 Cited in Hiro, *Inside the Middle East*, p. 311.

71 *Washington Post*, 15 September 1990.

72 *Independent*, 19 September 1990. Later it was revealed that Saudi Arabia had also promised to resume the annual subsidy to Syria that it had suspended following its differences with Damascus on resolving the Lebanese crisis.

73 Hiro, *Inside the Middle East*, p. 107; Patrick Seale, *Asad: The Struggle for the Middle East*, I. B. Tauris, London, and California University Press, Berkeley, 1988, pp. 332–4.

74 *Guardian*, 14 September 1990.

75 *Ibid.*, 18 September 1990.

76 *Washington Post*, 16 September

1990; *Guardian*, 19 September 1990. The fact that of the 150,000 US troops then in the Gulf, 30,000 were air force personnel with 420 warplanes and 250 support aircraft showed the importance the Pentagon attached to air superiority.

77 The last time a serving chief of staff was dismissed was in 1949 when President Truman sacked Admiral Louis Denfeld, Chief of Naval Operations.

78 *Independent*, 17 and 18 September 1990; *Guardian*, 18 September 1990.

5 Bush and the Domestic Front

1 *Guardian*, 28 August 1990.
2 *Independent on Sunday*, 7 October 1990.
3 *Time*, 7 January 1991.
4 *Washington Post*, 20 September 1990.
5 In the event, following the massacre of 241 marines as a result of a truck-bomb explosion in October 1983, the marines were withdrawn from Lebanon in January 1984.
6 Gabriel Kolko, *Anatomy of a War*, Pantheon Books, New York, 1985, pp. 124–5, 609.
7 *Guardian*, 20 August 1990.
8 Gary Hufbauer and Kimberley Ann Elliot, *Iraq Sanctions*, Washington Institute for International Economics, Washington, DC, 1990, cited in *Financial Times*, 17 September 1990.
9 *Guardian*, 18 September 1990; *Sunday Times*, 23 September 1990.
10 *Guardian*, 20 and 21 September

1990; *Independent*, 22 September 1990.
11 *Washington Post*, 16 September 1990; *Independent*, 21 September 1990. Baghdad's later explanation that its troops had mistaken the French diplomat's residence for an al Sabah property, and its apology for the incident, failed to pacify Paris.
12 Hiro, *The Longest War*, pp. 172, 197. According to Iraqi officials, harbouring a foreigner meant that the local host was a spy, and spying was a capital offence; hence hiding a foreigner was a capital crime.
13 *Washington Post*, 18 September 1990. The voluntary outflow of Kuwaitis slowed down when they realized they would lose their possessions at the border and might have to sign away their property rights in Kuwait.
14 *Washington Post*, 30 August 1990; *Independent on Sunday*, 16 September 1990; *Independent*, 21 September and 9 October 1990.
15 *Independent on Sunday*, 16 September 1990.
16 *Guardian*, 3 October 1990.
17 *Financial Times*, 6 September 1990; *Independent*, 9 October 1990.
18 *Washington Post*, 7 September 1990.
19 *New York Times*, 20 September 1990; *Independent*, 22 and 28 September 1990.
20 *Ibid.*, 24 September 1990. By signing the Treaty of Muslim Friendship and Arab Fraternity with Saudi Arabia in 1934, North Yemen ceded its provinces of Asir, Jizan and Najran to the Saudi kingdom for 40 years. But in 1974 Saudi Arabia did not return these

provinces to North Yemen as it should have. See Hiro, *Inside the Middle East*, p. 34.

21 *Independent*, 24 September 1990.

22 *Guardian*, 27 September 1990. This compared well with the British deployment of 54 warplanes, three surveillance aircraft, three warships and two minesweepers, and 6,000 soldiers with 136 tanks. *Independent on Sunday*, 16 September 1990.

23 *New York Times*, 25 September 1990. Mitterrand's anti-war position was in line with popular feeling in France: a poll by *Le Monde* published on 2 October showed 83% agreeing with the statement: 'No cause can justify war in the Gulf'.

24 Baghdad Radio, 27 September 1990.

25 *Guardian*, 24 and 25 September 1990.

26 *Independent*, 29 September 1990.

27 Judith Miller and Laurie Mylroie, *Saddam Hussein and the Crisis in the Gulf*, Times Books, New York, 1990, pp. 146, 150; *Washington Post*, 12 March 1991. The US–Iraq Business Forum had a membership of 70 American companies, including some big names in US technology.

28 Woodward, *The Commanders*, p. 287; *Guardian*, 25 September 1990.

29 Hiro, *Inside the Middle East*, pp. 83–5.

30 *Guardian*, 28 September 1990.

31 *International Herald Tribune*, 29–30 September 1990.

32 *Independent*, 26 September 1990; Baghdad Radio, 26 September 1990.

33 *Financial Times*, 19 September 1990; *Washington Post*, 26 September 1990; Iraqi News Agency, 26 September 1990.

34 *Washington Post*, 29 September 1990. Tens of thousands of Iranians participated in a demonstration called by the Islamic Propagation Organization in Tehran on Friday, 28 September. Calling for an Islamic jihad against 'alien forces' in the region, they shouted: 'The Persian Gulf is the base of Islam/There is no place in it for America.' *International Herald Tribune*, 29–30 September 1990.

35 *Washington Post*, 29 September 1990.

36 *Independent*, 28 September 1990. These figures were supplied by the 21-member International Energy Agency, which includes all the 24 members of the Organization of Economic Co-operation and Development, except Finland, France and Iceland.

37 *New York Times*, 22 and 29 September 1990; *Financial Times*, 27 September 1990; *Independent*, 28 September 1990.

38 *Washington Post*, 22 September 1990. It is worth noting that this arms deal as well as others, including a $26 billion-worth package signed with Britain in 1986, was made through Prince Bandar and his father Prince Sultan, the Saudi defence minister.

39 *Guardian*, 8 October 1990.

40 *Ibid.*, 1 October 1990; *Independent*, 1 October 1990; *Sunday Times*, 7 October 1990.

41 *Ibid.*, 7 October 1990 and 24 March 1991.

42 *Guardian*, 1 October 1990.
43 *Sunday Times*, 7 October 1990.

6 Blood on the Mount

1 *Independent*, 5 October 1990.
2 *Guardian*, 10 October 1990.
3 *Independent*, 11 October 1990.
4 Cited in *Middle East International*, 26 October 1990, p. 5.
5 *New York Times*, 9 October 1990.
6 *Middle East International*, 12 October 1990, p. 3.
7 Amman Radio, 9 October 1990; *Washington Post*, 10 October 1990.
8 *Guardian*, 10 October 1990.
9 *International Herald Tribune*, 11 and 13–14 October 1990.
10 *Middle East International*, 12 October 1990, p. 3.
11 According to Zeev Schiff, 'new evidence' showed that the Palestinians had intended merely to defend themselves against the Temple Mount Faithful, and that stones supposedly gathered in advance were in fact easily available because of construction work on the site, suggesting behaviour more spontaneous than had been previously believed. *Ha'Aratez*, 10 October 1990. B'Tselem, an independent Israeli human rights group, stated, 'The firing continued even while the crowd was dispersing, as well as at the stage in which medical teams arrived at the scene.' Cited in *Guardian*, 15 October 1990.
12 *Independent on Sunday*, 14 October 1990.
13 *Guardian*, 18 October 1990.
14 *The Times*, 15 October 1990.
15 *Washington Post*, 15 October 1990.
16 *Guardian*, 15, 16 and 17 October 1990.
17 *Independent*, 20 October 1990; *Middle East International*, 26 October 1990, p. 5.
18 *Washington Post*, 19 October 1990. Those rejecting the PLO resolution were: six GCC states, Djibouti, Egypt, Lebanon, Somalia and Syria. Interestingly Morocco, which had deployed troops in Saudi Arabia, did not vote with this faction.
19 *Financial Times*, 20–21 October 1990.
20 *Guardian*, 19 October 1990. However, Levy confirmed that he stood by his letter of 2 October to Baker that the $400 million US housing construction loan would not be used beyond the Green Line.
21 *The Times*, 18 and 19 October 1990. Earlier Hurd had criticized Israel for refusing to co-operate with the Security Council.
22 *New York Times*, 21 October 1990; *Financial Times*, 23 October 1990. On 24 October the UN Security Council unanimously passed Resolution 673 calling on Israel to reverse its refusal to receive the UN mission, and asking the secretary-general to report back before 31 October. *New York Times*, 25 October 1990.
23 *L'Express*, 19 October 1990; *New York Times*, 4 March 1991; Woodward, *The Commanders*, pp. 304–7.
24 Cited in *Washington Post*, 9 October 1990.

25 Cited in *Guardian*, 18 October 1990.

26 *Washington Post*, 15 October 1990.

27 A study by the *Economist* Intelligence Unit, published in early October 1990, predicted that the sanctions would not be damaging to Iraq 'before late 1991 summer' on the assumption that the gold it had looted from Kuwait's Central Bank was worth $2 billion and could be smuggled out and converted into hard currency. After the war, it emerged that the gold reserves of Kuwait were worth only $700 million. *International Herald Tribune*, 19 August 1991.

28 *Sunday Times*, 23 September 1990.

29 The remainder consisted of 141 Japanese, 80 French and 77 Germans. *Independent*, 9 October 1990.

30 *Sunday Times*, 21 October 1990; *Guardian*, 22 October 1990. Following her meeting with the emir of Kuwait in London, Thatcher repeated that Saddam Hussein must withdraw totally, and added: 'Then we shall have to deal with the problem of [Iraqi] chemical weapons and nuclear weapons to see that the problem does not arise again.' *Independent*, 24 October 1990.

31 *Ibid.*, 23 October 1990; *Guardian*, 25 and 26 October 1990.

32 Saudi Press Agency, 22 October 1990. The next day Saudi television broadcast a clarifying statement by Prince Sultan in which he said that in the past 'through good intentions' Saudi Arabia had managed to solve its border problems with Iraq, Jordan and the UAE.

33 *The Times*, 24 October 1990.

34 *Guardian*, 22 October 1990; *Independent*, 27 October 1990.

35 *Ibid.*, 14 October 1990; *Middle East International*, 26 October 1990, pp. 8–10.

36 The US made sure that there was no misunderstanding between Syria and Israel: through its embassy in Nicosia, Cyprus, it cleared the flight plan of the Syrian warplanes that bombed Aoun's palace. *Middle East International*, 26 October 1990, p. 8.

37 Damascus Radio, 28 October 1990; *Independent*, 7 November 1990.

38 *Washington Post*, 6 October 1990; Woodward, op. cit., p. 42.

39 *Guardian*, 12 October 1990. Prince Sultan's statement of 21 October on territorial concessions to Iraq after its evacuation of Kuwait needs to be viewed in the above context.

40 *New York Times*, 17 October 1990; *Guardian*, 17 October 1990; *Independent*, 19 October 1990. Later testimonies to the US Senate Foreign Relations Committee established that sanctions were causing shortages of spare parts and other supplies in Iraq. *Washington Post*, 21 October 1990. Since the embargo was imposed on 6 August, the allied naval forces had issued more than 2,500 challenges to the ships sailing to or from Iraq, and interdicted about 10 per cent. *Financial Times*, 23 October 1990.

41 *Guardian*, 17 and 18 October 1990; *Independent*, 26 and 27 October 1990. Since the CIA

relied heavily on the Israeli secret service, Mossad, for its intelligence on the Middle East, Webster's assessment tallied with Israel's.

42 Woodward, op. cit., p. 312. At 210,000, the American troops were then 60% of the total strength of the anti-Iraqi coalition at 350,000. *Independent*, 26 October 1990.

43 In Oman 15,000 US marines were undertaking their third amphibious landing involving 18 US landing vessels with 90 fixed-wing jets. *Independent*, 29 October 1990.

44 *Los Angeles Times*, 30 October 1990. Baker's statement was taken seriously by Baghdad, which put its forces on 'extreme alert'. *Washington Post*, 31 October 1990.

45 *Washington Post*, 2 December 1990; *New York Times*, 4 March 1991; Woodward, op. cit., pp. 306, 319–20.

46 *Independent*, 30 October 1990; *Guardian*, 30 October and 8 November 1990.

47 *Guardian*, 31 October 1990.

48 *International Herald Tribune*, 1 November 1990.

49 *Washington Post*, 1 November 1990; *Guardian*, 1 and 2 November 1990. The Iraqi ambassador to the US denied Bush's charges, and said, 'All foreigners are being well looked after.'

50 Baghdad Radio, 31 October 1990. Among those who were publicly critical of Bush on this count were Edward Heath and Claude Chausson, former French foreign minister.

51 Iraqi News Agency, 31 October 1990. 'We expect war to erupt at any moment, and we are ready for that,' said Iraq's information minister. *Guardian*, 2 November 1990. This served Washington's purpose, aware that frequent deployments of Iraq's ground forces and scrambling of its aircraft depleted its finite supply of spare parts. Also, by forcing the Iraqi military to go on a near-permanent alert, the US hoped to degrade its effectiveness if and when a real attack materialized.

52 *Guardian*, 23 October and 6 November 1990.

53 *Independent on Sunday*, 4 November 1990. This was a modification of the earlier proposal by Baghdad to free all 'foreign guests' if the US gave an assurance not to use force against Iraq.

54 *Sunday Times*, 28 October 1990.

55 *New York Times*, 6 November 1990; *Independent*, 7 November 1990.

56 *Sunday Times*, 28 October 1990. An earlier telephone poll conducted by Gallup (for the London-based Free Kuwait Association) in five European countries showed the highest support for Bush's decision to send troops to the Gulf in Britain, the figures for individual countries being: Spain, 53%; Italy, 59%; France, 73%; Germany, 75%; and Britain, 80%. *Guardian*, 19 October 1990.

57 In contrast, 90% thought that the presence of the French task force in the Gulf was 'a sign of French determination to uphold respect for international law'. Cited in *Independent on Sunday*, 28 October 1990.

58 *Washington Post*, 27 October 1990.

59 *Independent*, 31 October 1990. Concluding a nine-month investigation, Judge Ezra Kama ruled that the police initially provoked the violence at the Temple Mount and called the police explanation that they had opened fire out of fear for their lives as 'exaggerated and strange'. *New York Times*, 19 July 1991.

60 During the debate on the UN secretary-general's report, the four non-aligned members of the Security Council – Colombia, Cuba, Malaysia and Yemen – proposed sending a UN peacekeeping force to the Occupied Territories to replace Israel as the occupying power.

61 *New York Times*, 6 November 1990.

7 Desert Shield into Desert Sword

1 *New York Times*, 23 November 1990.

2 *Independent*, 13 November 1990.

3 *International Herald Tribune*, 23 November 1990.

4 *Washington Post*, 9 November 1990. The highest US deployment during the Vietnam War was 570,000.

5 International Institute of Strategic Studies, *The Military Balance 1990–1991*, London, Autumn 1990, p. 17.

6 *Guardian*, 5 November 1990. Even the British, with a much smaller commitment, faced the same problem. 'We just don't have enough troops to rotate the ones who have actually got there,' said Archie Hamilton, minister for the armed forces. 'For that reason it will not be possible to go on for that long [12 months, as wished by the US Congress]. The Americans have the same problem.' *Ibid.*, 18 December 1990.

7 *Independent*, 6 November 1990; *USA Today*, 12 November 1990.

8 *Sunday Times*, 4 November 1990; *Los Angeles Times*, 6 November 1990.

9 Cited in *Independent*, 7 November 1990. Similar conclusions were drawn by Lt-Colonel Douglas V. Johnson, Stephen C. Pelletiere and Leif R. Rosenberger, *Iraqi Power and US Security in the Middle East*, US Army War College, Carlisle Barracks, Pa., 1990, pp. 37–40.

10 *Sunday Times*, 4 November 1990; *Guardian*, 6 November 1990.

11 After Lt-General Khazraji's retirement in August came the resignation of another old hand: Sadoun Shakir, an associate of Saddam Hussein since 1963, and a member of the Revolutionary Command Council since 1977. *Wall Street Journal*, 13 November 1990; *International Herald Tribune*, 13 December 1990.

12 *New York Times*, 10 November 1990. Just as Brandt left, Anker Jørgenson and David Lange, former prime ministers of Denmark and New Zealand respectively, arrived in Baghdad.

13 Middle East News Agency, 12 November 1990.

14 Iraqi News Agency, 13 November 1990; *Washington*

Post, 13 November 1990;
New York Times, 15 and 16
November 1990.

15 *Washington Post,* 9 November
1990; *New York Times,* 16
November 1990. Since the
Iran–Iraq ceasefire in August
1988 there had been an average
of three coup attempts a year to
overthrow Saddam Hussein.

16 In 202 years of the republican
constitution, US presidents
have despatched forces abroad
between 130 and 200 times,
with Congress declaring
formal war only five times: in
1812 against the British, the
Mexican War (1846–8) and the
Spanish–American War (1898);
and during the First World
War (1916–18) and the Second
World War (1939–45). In some
instances Congress passed
laws authorizing presidents to
take action, but fell short of
declaring war. In August 1964
the Gulf of Tonkin resolution
empowered President Johnson
to defend US forces against
North Vietnamese aggression.
Later, courts ruled that even
after US Congress had repealed
the 1964 resolution the war
could not be challenged as long
as the Congress was funding
the military.

17 *Independent,* 12 November
1990.

18 *USA Today,* 12 November
1990; *Wall Street Journal,* 15
November 1990. According
to Michael Dewar, deputy
director of the London-based
International Institute of
Strategic Studies, casualties
would be 8% to 15% of the
combat forces, depending on
the length of the war.

19 *New York Times,* 13

and 16 November
1990.

20 Cited in *Ibid.,* 16 November
1990.

21 *Ibid.*

22 Cited in *Wall Street Journal,* 16
November 1990.

23 *Guardian,* 21 November 1990.
The American troops' lack
of patriotism in joining the
military was apparent from a
study published in the *New
York Times* of 13 November
1990. Only 10% of the recruits
said they were looking to 'serve
the USA', with 26% saying they
wanted increased training or
money, and 39% stating that
they needed money for college
education. Nor was patriotism
high among Kuwaitis. Of the
350,000 Kuwaitis in exile
in November, no more than
3,000 had volunteered to fight
Iraq. In pre-invasion Kuwait,
with resident nationals twice
as numerous as those in
exile by mid-November, the
defence forces were 20,000
strong. *Sunday Telegraph,* 18
November 1990.

24 *New York Times,* 16 November
1990. Unsurprisingly, Iraq
called the military exercises
'provocative', showing that the
US was preparing feverishly
for war.

25 Iraqi News Agency, 19
November 1990; *The Times,* 24
November 1990. The Pentagon
put the current total of the Iraqi
troops in Kuwait and the Basra
area – the Kuwaiti theatre of
operations – at 430,000.

26 Iraqi News Agency, 17
November 1990.

27 *New York Times,* 17
November; *Independent,* 17
November 1990; *Guardian,*

20 November 1990. Calling for a peaceful solution to the Gulf crisis, Chancellor Helmut Kohl of Germany said on 22 November: 'Time is ripe to solve the Arab–Israeli tension and the Lebanese conflict as well.'

28 By early October, 250,000 of the original 350,000 Palestinians had quit Kuwait. *New York Times*, 17 November 1990.

29 *Independent*, 16 November 1990.

30 *Guardian*, 19 November 1990; *Nation*, 4 February 1991, p. 114. A Palestinian doctor at a major hospital in Kuwait, exiled in Amman, told Judith Miller of the *New York Times* that while, contrary to the assertions of the Kuwaiti officials in Washington, Iraqi soldiers did not throw babies out of incubators, they did ship empty incubators, hospital beds and hospital equipment to Baghdad, 17 November 1990.

31 *Guardian*, 23 November 1990; *Sunday Times*, 25 November 1990.

32 *New York Times*, 23 November 1990; *Sunday Times*, 25 November 1990; *Observer*, 25 November 1990.

33 *International Herald Tribune*, 14 November 1990; *New York Times*, 28 November 1990.

34 See Micah L. Sifri and Christopher Cerf (eds), *The Gulf War Reader*, pp. 249–50; *Guardian*, 12 December 1990.

35 Baghdad Radio, 22 November 1990. On the day of Bush's tour of the US frontline in the Saudi kingdom, there were mass demonstrations in Iraq against his trip.

36 *The Times*, 24 November 1990;

Sunday Times, 25 November 1990; *New York Times*, 26 November 1990; Johnson, Pelletiere and Rosenberger, op. cit., pp. 38–40.

37 *New York Times*, 26 and 27 November 1990.

38 *Ibid.*, 28 March 1991. In mid-November, however, realizing this weakness, the Iraqi high command decided to extend their defence line to cover this flank.

39 *Guardian*, 6 and 13 November 1990.

40 *International Herald Tribune*, 26 November 1990; *New York Times*, 26 and 27 November 1990.

41 *Guardian*, 29 November 1990.

42 It has not been established whether Assad himself or one of his top henchmen, Muhammad al Khouli, head of air force intelligence, had intended to blow up the Israeli airliner with the assistance of Nizar Hindawi. But it is beyond doubt that Assad has made systematic use of terrorism as an instrument of state policy. See Patrick Seale, *Asad*, pp. 475–82. Syria continued to be included in the US state department's list of countries that support international terrorism. The EC eased passage of a $190 million loan to Syria, but did not lift other sanctions. Its member countries kept all Syrian diplomats under surveillance. *Independent*, 7 November 1990; *International Herald Tribune*, 29 November 1990.

43 Iraq News Agency, 17 November 1990.

44 *Independent on Sunday*, 2 December 1990.

45 *International Herald Tribune*, 23
November 1990; *Washington
Post*, 26 November 1990;
Guardian, 3 December 1990.
46 *Independent*, 24 November
1990. Relations between Yemen
and Saudi Arabia had begun
to sour before the crisis when
Sanaa refused to sign a treaty
resolving a border dispute in a
region where over one billion
barrels of oil reserves had been
discovered.
47 *Independent*, 30 November
1990.
48 *New York Times*, 27 November
1990.
49 *Independent*, 30 November
1990.
50 Tass, 28 November 1990;
International Herald Tribune, 28
and 29 November 1990; *New
York Times*, 2 December 1990.
The Soviet Union's borrowings
from the Gulf states had to be
seen in the context of its loans
from Italy totalling $6.3 billion,
and food aid worth $2.5 billion
from Spain and France, all of
these meant to shore up its
faltering economy.
51 *Washington Post*, 27 November
1990.
52 *International Herald Tribune*,
27 November 1990; *New York
Times*, 28 November 1990;
Baghdad Radio, 29 November
1990; *Independent*, 30
November 1990.
53 *Ibid.*, 30 November 1990. 29
November happened to be
the United Nations' Day of
Solidarity with the Palestinian
People. Ironically, on the eve
of that day, while the Security
Council unanimously passed
Resolution 677 asking the UN
secretary-general to safeguard
a smuggled copy of Kuwait's
population register to foil
attempts by Iraq to repopulate
Kuwait with Iraqis, the PLO
and its non-aligned backers in
the Council failed to persuade
the Council to vote on their
draft resolution pertaining to
the treatment of Palestinians
under Israeli occupation before
the US-sponsored resolution on
the use of force to expel Iraq
from Kuwait.
54 The French government's
decision to back the use of
force ran contrary to public
opinion. A poll by *Le Figaro*
published on the day of the
Security Council vote showed
that 57% opposed French
participation in a Gulf war
(up from 45% in the previous
month), and only 36%
supported it.
55 *Guardian*, 30 November
1990.
56 *Independent*, 1 December
1990.
57 *Guardian*, 30 November 1990;
International Herald Tribune, 30
November 1990.

8 The Countdown

1 *Guardian*, 28 August 1990.
2 *Wall Street Journal*, 16
November 1990.
3 *Independent*, 6 December
1990.
4 Baghdad Radio, 22 December
1990.
5 To show that there was
some softening in Baghdad's
stance, Bush revealed that
the Iraqis had delivered fruit,
vegetables and cigarettes to
the US embassy in Kuwait.
Independent, 1 December 1990.

6 *Financial Times*, 1–2 December 1990.

7 *Guardian*, 28 November 1990.

8 *Washington Post*, 29 November 1990; *Guardian*, 5 December 1990; *New York Times*, 6 December 1990; Micah L. Sifri and Christopher Cerf (eds), *The Gulf War Reader*, p. 236.

9 *Washington Post*, 29 November 1990; *New York Times*, 4 December 1990; *Guardian*, 4 and 5 December 1990.

10 *Ibid.*, 30 November 1990.

11 *Independent*, 30 November 1990.

12 *In These Times*, 21 November–4 December 1990, p. 14; *Independent*, 1 December 1990.

13 At the same time the respondents in a *Washington Post*–NBC poll doubted, by 2:1, that Resolution 678 would persuade Saddam Hussein to leave Kuwait. *Washington Post*, 4 December 1990.

14 *Sunday Times*, 2 December 1990. On the other hand lawmakers were insistent on exercising their war powers, with a private meeting of Democrats in the House of Representatives voting by 177 to 37 to require President Bush to 'seek a declaration of war from Congress before attacking Iraqi troops in the Gulf'. Among those who hailed this decision was President Hussein. *Guardian*, 5 December 1990; Baghdad Radio, 5 December 1990.

15 However, 80% believed that the US would 'eventually' go to war. *USA Today*, 4 December 1990.

16 Baghdad Radio, 1 December 1990. Thousands of Iraqis turned the celebration of their Martyrs' Day, to commemorate those killed in the First Gulf War, into anti-US demonstrations, chanting anti-American slogans and transforming the occasion into pro-government demonstrations. *Independent on Sunday*, 2 December 1990.

17 *BBC Summary of World Broadcasts*, 4 December 1990.

18 *Guardian*, 1 and 3 December 1990; *International Herald Tribune*, 3 December; Baghdad Radio, 5 December 1990.

19 *Sunday Times*, 2 and 9 December 1990.

20 Iraqi News Agency, 5 December 1990.

21 The major groups held in Kuwait and Iraq respectively were: Britain (443+725=1,168); America (0+700); Japan (6+233=239); Italy (0+195); Netherlands (0+133); Canada (19+69=88); Switzerland (0+80); Denmark (29+27=56); Norway (1+21=22); Australia (0+21); and Finland (0+9). *International Herald Tribune*, 7 December 1990.

22 Baghdad Radio, 6 December 1990. The next day Iraq's 250-member National Assembly decided by a show of hands, with 15 deputies dissenting, to lift travel restrictions on all hostages and let them go. The Iraqi foreign minister called on those foreigners hiding in Kuwait not to be afraid and declare themselves.

23 *Guardian*, 7 and 10 December 1990; *Independent on Sunday*, 9 December 1990. The idea of leasing one or both of the two offshore islands was first mooted in 1965, and revived

in 1973, with the leasing to
be applied to half of Bubiyan
Island. See p. 25.

24 *New York Times*, 7 December
1990.

25 *Washington Post*, 10 December
1990. In his testimony to
the House Armed Services
Committee on 14 December,
Powell said that the strategy
of air strikes alone would
allow Saddam Hussein to
concentrate on a single
threat. He could have his
army dig in or disperse. 'The
Iraqi army can ride out such
a devastating attack . . . but
when the attack is over, the
decision still remains with
Saddam Hussein' whether or
not to withdraw from Kuwait.
International Herald Tribune,
15–16 December 1990.

26 *Washington Post*, 10 December
1990.

27 *Independent*, 8 December
1990.

28 *New York Times*, 8 December
1990.

29 BBC World Service, 9 December
1990. Those Palestinians
not killed by the Israelis
met their death at the hands
of fellow-Palestinians for
alleged collaboration with the
occupying power.

30 *Sunday Times*, 16 December
1990.

31 *Independent*, 14 November
1990. On 27 November,
however, when Cuba, Malaysia
and Yemen offered a resolution
to the Security Council to
protect Palestinian civilians
under Israeli occupation
and provide for a series of
international conferences on
the Arab–Israeli problem,
the vote was postponed at

American insistence. *Guardian*,
28 November 1990.

32 *International Herald Tribune*, 11
December 1990; *Guardian*, 11
December 1990.

33 *Ibid.*, 20 November 1990.

34 *International Herald Tribune*, 12
December 1990; *Washington
Post*, 26 December 1990; *New
York Times*, 2 January and
5 March 1991. Shamir was
upset at not being told by the
US of the three Iraqi missile
test-firings that had occurred on
2 December 1990. To reassert
Israel's freedom of action in
military affairs, he and his
defence minister did not warn
the Pentagon of the test-firing
of Israel's Arrow missile on
21 December. Consequently,
following the monitoring of
an unannounced test-firing of
a missile, US air and ground
troops in the region went
on 'condition red' footing.
Guardian, 24 December
1990; *Washington Post*, 26
December 1990.

35 *Guardian*, 13 December 1990.
Roland Dumas, the French
foreign minister, said that
France would not vote for the
Security Council resolution
on the Palestinians unless it
contained an explicit reference
to an international peace
conference on the Middle East.

36 Iraqi News Agency, 15
December 1990. Earlier the
US had mentioned 20/21/22
December as its first choice
for the Baghdad meeting, and 3
January as its second choice.

37 Whereas, of the 1,168 British
hostages in Iraq and Kuwait,
only 206 chose to stay behind
of their free will, 509 of the
700 American hostages did so.

International Herald Tribune, 13
December 1990; Guardian, 14
December 1990.
38 International Herald Tribune, 14
December 1990.
39 Independent, 15 December
1990; International Herald
Tribune, 15–16 December
1990. The Los Angeles Times
poll showed 61% approving
Bush's overall handling of the
crisis with 33% disapproving.
40 Washington Post, 15 December
1990; International Herald
Tribune, 7 December 1990.
41 Washington Post, 20 December
1990.
42 Guardian, 19 and 24 December
1990; International Herald
Tribune, 19 December
1990; Bob Woodward, The
Commanders, p. 343.
43 New York Times, 21 December
1990.
44 Washington Post, 30 December
1990. The 28 countries were:
Argentina (naval); Australia
(naval); Bahrain (ground, air);
Bangladesh (ground); Belgium
(air – in Turkey, naval); Canada
(air, naval); Czechoslovakia
(ground); Denmark (naval);
Egypt (ground); France (ground,
air, naval); Germany (air – in
Turkey); Greece (naval); Italy
(air, naval); Kuwait (ground,
air, naval); Morocco (ground);
Netherlands (naval); New
Zealand (air); Niger (ground);
Norway (naval); Oman (ground,
air); Pakistan (ground, naval);
Qatar (ground, air); Saudi
Arabia (ground, air, naval);
Senegal (ground); Spain (naval);
Syria (ground); United Arab
Emirates (ground, air); and
United Kingdom (ground, air,
naval).
45 Baghdad Radio, 19 and 20

December 1990; Iraqi News
Agency, 21 December 1990;
Independent, 21 and 22
December 1990.
46 International Herald Tribune, 20
December 1990.
47 Ibid.
48 Independent, 1 December 1990.
49 International Herald Tribune,
5 December 1990; New York
Times, 17 December 1990. The
presence of Soviet military
experts was particularly
valuable to the Iraqis, who
knew that their advice would
be important in enabling them
to devise means to work around
the anticipated shortages of key
military spares.
50 The Times, 7 December 1990.
On 11 December the Russian
Federation's parliament,
presided over by Boris Yeltsin,
urged President Gorbachev
'not to allow the USSR to be
drawn into a military conflict
which could have the most
serious consequences for peace
and stability on the planet.'
Guardian, 12 December 1990.
51 International Herald Tribune, 21
December 1990; Baghdad Radio,
26 December 1990.
52 Guardian, 21 December 1990.
53 Independent, 22 December
1990; Washington Post, 22
December 1990; Baghdad Radio,
26 December 1990.
54 Iraqi News Agency, 24
December 1990; Baghdad
Radio, 26 December 1990.
Reflecting the deep fear and
hatred between Iraq and Israel,
Tariq Aziz told La Reppublica,
an Italian newspaper, a few
days later: 'If America does
not attack us now, sooner or
later, Israel will.' Cited in
International Herald Tribune,

31 December 1990. In early December, Israel had said that it wanted Saddam Hussein removed from power, otherwise it would not maintain a 'low profile'. *The Times*, 6 December 1990.

55 *International Herald Tribune*, 24–25 December 1990; *The Times*, 26 December 1990.

56 Restrictions were imposed on journalists, who were forbidden to observe religious services at US military facilities and were routinely denied access to military chaplains. *New York Times*, 23 December 1990. Matters were much worse for the British and the French, who had to put up with a ban on chaplains and midnight mass on Christmas eve. 'Describing life as austere, spartan or monastic is an understatement,' said a French military doctor. 'This is a prison atmosphere.' *Guardian*, 24 December 1990.

57 See Dilip Hiro, *Islamic Fundamentalism*, Paladin Books, London, 1988/*Holy Wars: The Rise of Islamic Fundamentalism*, Routledge, New York, 1990, pp. 108–41.

58 *Washington Post*, 14 December 1990.

59 *Wall Street Journal*, 15 November 1990; *New York Times*, 15 November 1990.

60 See Hiro, *Inside the Middle East*, p. 13; *Islamic Fundamentalism/Holy Wars*, pp. 130–34.

61 *Independent*, 29 October 1990.

62 *International Herald Tribune*, 19 and 20 December 1990. According to Bob Woodward, Waller's remarks made General Powell 'furious'. Cheney

felt that since Waller lacked experience of dealing with the media, it was wrong to have arranged his interview with the press. 'Nonetheless, the remarks and the ensuing uproar served Cheney's purposes, conveying the impression that it was not likely the United States would go to war until February.' Woodward, *The Commanders*, p. 346.

63 *International Herald Tribune*, 27 December 1990.

64 Iraqi News Agency, 30 and 31 December 1990.

65 *Independent*, 31 December 1990; *Guardian*, 5 January 1991.

66 *Washington Post*, 17 December 1990 and 3 January 1991.

67 Iraqi News Agency, 1 January 1991; *Financial Times*, 4 January 1991.

68 *Daily Telegraph*, 4 January 1991.

69 *Le Canard Enchaîné*, 6 March 1991, cited in *Guardian*, 7 March 1991, and *Independent*, 7 March 1991.

70 *Newsday*, 3 January 1991.

71 *New York Times*, 11 December 1990. The members of the Gulf Crisis Financial Co-ordination Group were: Austria, Belgium, Canada, Denmark, European Commission, Finland, France, Germany, Iceland, Ireland, Italy, Japan, Republic of Korea, Kuwait, Luxembourg, Netherlands, Norway, Saudi Arabia, Spain, Switzerland, United Arab Emirates, United Kingdom and United States of America. Of the $13.4 billion allocated, $10.9 billion went to Egypt, Turkey and Jordan, with the rest going to Syria, Lebanon and Morocco. *Financial Times*,

12 December 1990 and 4 January 1991.

72 *New York Times*, 6 January 1991; *Guardian*, 7 January 1991.

73 *Guardian*, 7 January 1991. The next day, addressing military commanders, Saddam Hussein said: 'The main weight of the military battle may be Iraq, but the war will reach every struggler and fighter whose hand can reach out to harm the aggressor in the whole world.' Baghdad Radio, 7 January 1991.

74 *International Herald Tribune*, 8 January 1991.

75 *New York Times*, 8 January 1991; *Guardian*, 8 January 1991.

76 *Financial Times*, 4 January 1991.

77 The Mitterrand peace plan had a real chance of success since it satisfied Saddam Hussein's precondition, from the beginning, that any compromise proposal had to emanate from the other side or a third party before he could adopt it.

78 *Washington Post*, 12 January 1991.

79 Earlier, under US pressure, Germany had agreed to send 18 Alpha warplanes to Erhac military base in eastern Turkey, 270 miles from the Iraqi border, as part of a Nato force of 42 aircraft, the rest being Belgian and Italian, to defend Turkey in case of an Iraqi attack. *Independent*, 4 January 1991. Germany had also been pressured to deploy its warships in the eastern Mediterranean to replace some of the US warships despatched to the Gulf region from the Mediterranean.

80 *International Herald Tribune*, 10 January 1991; *Guardian*, 10 January 1991.

81 *Ibid.*, 10 January 1991; *Independent*, 10 January 1991; *The Times*, 10 January 1991.

82 *Independent*, 10 and 12 January 1991. Among those attending the conference were delegates of the Muslim Brotherhood from various Arab countries, an organization which, financed largely by Riyadh, had hitherto been pro-Saudi. See Hiro, *Islamic Fundamentalism/Holy Wars*, pp. 61–107.

83 *Sunday Times*, 13 January 1991; *International Herald Tribune*, 14 January and 14 June 1991; Sifri and Cerf (eds), op. cit., pp. 287–9.

84 Cited in *Nation*, 18 February 1991, p. 189.

85 *New York Times*, 10 January 1991; *Independent*, 10 January 1991.

86 The Permanent Mission of Iraq to the United Nations, *Transcript of Meeting held on Sunday evening, 13 January 1991, between H.E. President Saddam Hussein and H.E. Pérez de Cuellar, Secretary-General of the United Nations*, New York, 15 February 1991.

87 *Guardian*, 14 January 1991.

88 *Le Canard Enchaîné*, 6 March 1991.

89 French sources said that Riyadh approved of France's peace moves after a visit there by President Mitterrand's chief assistant, Jean-Louis Bianco. *Guardian*, 15 January 1991; *Independent*, 15 January 1991.

90 *Guardian*, 16 January 1991; *Independent*, 16 January 1991. Though Pérez de Cuellar's plan included most of the

elements in the Mitterrand
proposal, both America and
Britain let it pass since, unlike
the French president, the UN
secretary-general had not tried
to get his initiative stamped
with the authority of the
Security Council. On the other
hand, this may have been the
reason why Iraq did not respond
positively to Pérez de Cuellar's
initiative.

91 Iraqi News Agency, 14
January 1991; *International
Herald Tribune*, 15 and 16
January 1991; *Guardian*, 16
January 1991.

92 *Ibid.*, 15 and 16 January 1991.

93 *International Herald Tribune*, 15
January 1991; *Independent*, 16
and 17 January 1991.

94 *Guardian*, 7 and 14 January
1991; *International Herald
Tribune*, 16 January 1991.

95 *Guardian*, 14 and 16 January
1991. Public opinion was not
reflected in parliament. A vote
on the subject in the House
of Commons on 15 January,
in the form of an adjournment
motion placed by those opposed
to military action, had 57
MPs supporting it and 534
opposing it. *Independent*, 16
January 1991.

96 *New York Times*, 16 January
1991; *Guardian*, 16 January
1991; *Independent*, 16
January 1991.

97 *Ibid.*, 15 January 1991.

98 *Ibid.*, 3 January 1991; *New
Scientist*, 12 January 1991,
pp. 30–31; *In These Times*, 27
March–2 April 1991, pp. 12–13.

99 *International Herald Tribune*, 10
January 1991.

100 *Guardian*, 15 January 1991.

101 *The Times*, 26 December
1990.

102 *New York Times*, 14 January
1991.

103 *Ibid.*, 10 January 1991.

104 *Washington Post*, 11 and 14
January 1991.

105 *Guardian*, 4 December 1990;
Independent on Sunday, 30
December 1990.

106 Cited in *International Herald
Tribune*, 14 January 1991.

107 The Permanent Mission of Iraq
to the United Nations, op. cit.;
Observer, 6 January 1991;
International Herald Tribune, 11
and 14 January 1991.

108 *Guardian*, 14 January 1991.

109 *Independent*, 17 January 1991;
Woodward, op. cit., p. 249.

9 Desert Storm: the Air Campaign

1 Baghdad Radio, 17 January
1991.

2 *International Herald Tribune*, 24
January 1991.

3 *Los Angeles Times*, 1 February
1991.

4 *International Herald Tribune*,
2–3 February 1991.

5 *Ibid.*

6 *Ibid.*, 18 January 1991;
Independent, 19 January 1991.
In the first 24 hours of fighting
Iraq was hit by a greater
explosive force than that which
flattened Hiroshima in 1945.
Guardian, 22 January 1991.

7 *New York Times*, 18 January
1991. There were larger
anti-war demonstrations on
Saturday 19 January, with
100,000 people participating in
the protest in San Francisco.
Independent on Sunday, 20
January 1991.

8 Seven members of the ruling

Socialist Party voted against the government. *International Herald Tribune*, 17 January 1991; *Financial Times*, 17 January 1991.

9 *International Herald Tribune*, 17 and 18–19 January 1991.

10 *Ibid.*, 17 January 1991.

11 *Independent*, 19 January 1991.

12 *Guardian*, 18 January 1991.

13 *Washington Post*, 18 January 1991.

14 *Guardian*, 18 January 1991; *Independent on Sunday*, 20 January 1991.

15 *International Herald Tribune*, 18 January 1991.

16 Baghdad Radio, 17 January 1991.

17 *Independent*, 19 January 1991; *Independent on Sunday*, 20 January 1991.

18 *International Herald Tribune*, 19–20 January 1991; *Independent on Sunday*, 20 January 1991.

19 *New York Times*, 5 March 1991.

20 *International Herald Tribune*, 18 January 1991; *New York Times*, 19 January 1991; *Independent*, 19 January 1991.

21 The infra-red telescopes of two US satellites picked up the intense heat of the Scuds as they took off. This was monitored by a ground station in central Australia, and transmitted to a communications network which included the Patriot batteries in Israel and Saudi Arabia. A Patriot missile, 17 feet long and weighing 2,000 pounds, was not designed to obliterate a Scud, 41 feet long and weighing 16,000 pounds, but to damage it in flight.

22 *International Herald Tribune*, 19–20 January 1991.

23 Baghdad Radio, 18 January 1991; *Independent*, 19 January 1991; *International Herald Tribune*, 19–20 January 1991.

24 *New York Times*, 18 January 1991; *Independent*, 19 January 1991. In contrast, the supreme religious leader of the Palestinians, Saad Eddin Alami, the Mufti of Jerusalem, called for a jihad against the US and its allies. *International Herald Tribune*, 24 January 1991.

25 *Ibid.*, 19–20 January 1991. Despite a Supreme Court order to distribute gas masks to the Palestinians in the Occupied Territories, the Israeli army issued them only to hospital workers and employees of emergency services. *Independent*, 29 January 1991.

26 *Guardian*, 18 January 1991; *Independent*, 19 January 1991.

27 Baghdad Radio, 20 January 1991.

28 *Guardian*, 18 January 1991; *International Herald Tribune*, 18 and 21 January 1991. Only 10 members responded positively.

29 *Independent*, 22 January 1991.

30 *Guardian*, 21 January 1991.

31 *New York Times*, 19, 21 and 22 January 1991.

32 *Guardian*, 21 and 24 January 1991.

33 *Guardian*, 23 January 1991; *International Herald Tribune*, 24 January 1991.

34 *New York Times*, 21 January 1991.

35 *International Herald Tribune*, 24 January 1991; *Independent on Sunday*, 27 January 1991.

36 *International Herald Tribune*, 22 January 1991.

37 Cited in *Independent*, 19

January 1991. Washington stated later that the USSR was closely monitoring the war activities of the allies.

38 *Independent*, 22 January 1991.

39 *Washington Post*, 18 March 1991; *Guardian*, 23 January 1991; *New York Times*, 23 January 1991.

40 *Guardian*, 21 January 1991; *Washington Post*, 29 January 1991; *New York Times*, 5 March 1991. What this version omitted was the arrangement by which Israeli warplanes were reportedly allowed to join air strikes against Iraq from Turkey, with an Israeli spokesman saying that information on the subject would be made available at 'the right moment'. BBC Radio 4, 22 January 1991.

41 *Guardian*, 23 January 1991. On 21 January, Sir Patrick Mayhew, the British attorney-general, told the war cabinet that Saddam Hussein, being the head of Iraq's military, was 'a legitimate target' (for assassination). *Independent*, 22 January 1991. When questioned on the extension of war aims, British defence secretary Tom King replied that the Security Council resolutions placed 'a duty' on the allies to ensure that the Iraqis would not strike after the war ended, and referred to the phrase 'to restore international peace and security in the area' in Clause 2 of Resolution 678. *Guardian*, 28 January 1991.

42 With 89% of Turks opposed to direct involvement in the war, however, there was little chance of Ankara formally joining the US-led coalition. *Guardian*, 23 January 1991.

43 *International Herald Tribune*, 24 January 1991.

44 Cited in *Guardian*, 24 January 1991.

45 *International Herald Tribune*, 24 and 31 January 1991.

46 *Washington Post*, 24 January 1991; *Jane's Defence Weekly*, 2 February 1991, p. 135.

47 *Guardian*, 24 January 1991.

48 *New York Times*, 24 and 25 January 1991; *Washington Post*, 28 January 1991. The debt-ridden government was keen to capitalize on its military commitment, with the Egyptian foreign minister personally appealing to President Bush for further debt concessions.

49 Assad had despatched these troops only after he had sought, and received, assurances from Israel, through President Bush, that it would not take advantage of the consequent military vacuum.

50 *International Herald Tribune*, 24 January 1991; *Independent*, 25 January 1991.

51 *Independent*, 26 January 1991. See also Dilip Hiro, *The Longest War*, pp. 102, 137, 138–9, 146, 168, 178, 182, 206, 210, 241.

52 *Washington Post*, 26 January 1991; *Independent on Sunday*, 27 January 1991; *International Herald Tribune*, 28 January 1991. The oil slick was also fed by the leakage from the storage tanks hit earlier by Iraqi artillery. *Guardian*, 28 January 1991.

53 *Independent on Sunday*, 27 January 1991; *Jane's Defence*

Weekly, 2 February 1991, p. 134.

54 *Independent*, 28 January 1991.

55 According to Mizhir Affat, a former bodyguard of Saddam Hussein, agreements between Iraq and Iran that the latter would provide Iraq with 'substantial food, medical and military assistance' and safe sanctuaries for the Iraqi forces were worked out earlier in the month during Izzat Ibrahim's visit to Tehran. Statements by captured Iraqi sailors that they had been issued with high-level orders to head for Iran if caught in the Gulf, and berth their vessels in Iranian waters until the war ended, confirmed that what was happening was not spontaneous. *Independent*, 28 January 1991; *Jane's Defence Weekly*, 9 February 1991, p. 168. Washington acknowledged that Iran had allowed some food shipments to cross into Iraq, but chose to ignore this transgression of the UN blockade. *Washington Post*, 30 January 1991.

56 *International Herald Tribune*, 28 January 1991.

57 After Chévènement had declared on 17 January that France would not engage in hostilities inside Iraq, Mitterrand reversed his decision three days later in a television address. *International Herald Tribune*, 30 January 1991.

58 A survey of the marchers by the *Washington Post* showed that one out of two had participated in at least one other demonstration against the Gulf War, four out of five had previously attended a protest for some political or social issue; and one out of four had a friend or relative serving in the Gulf. *Washington Post*, 27 January 1991. Nationally, however, about half of the Americans polled had a friend or relative in the Gulf. *Guardian*, 28 January 1991.

59 *International Herald Tribune*, 29 January 1991.

60 General Beg's unprecedentedly open condemnation of America, a long-term patron of Pakistan, widened the rift between the civilian government and the armed forces. *Independent*, 29 January 1991.

61 *International Herald Tribune*, 29 January 1991.

62 *Washington Post*, 29 January 1991; *Financial Times*, 30 January 1991; *International Herald Tribune*, 31 January 1991.

63 *Washington Post*, 29 January 1991.

64 *Los Angeles Times*, 29 January 1991; *Guardian*, 29 January 1991.

65 *New York Times*, 28 January 1991; *International Herald Tribune*, 29, 30 and 31 January 1991. Expressing a genuine apprehension in Soviet military circles, Major-General Sergi Bogdanov told *Krasnaya Zvezda* that he feared the war in the Gulf could spill over into Soviet territory. 'Even if we discount the idea of an international nuclear strike, we cannot exclude a simple accident, a computer error or sabotage,' he said. *International Herald Tribune*, 1 February 1991.

66 *Guardian*, 31 January 1991; *Independent*, 31 January 1991; *International Herald Tribune*, 31

January 1991; *New York Times,* 1 February 1991.

67 *Ibid.,* 30 January 1991.

68 *Independent,* 2 February 1991.

69 *Ibid.; Guardian,* 2 February 1991.

70 *Independent on Sunday,* 3 February 1991; *International Herald Tribune,* 4 February 1991. According to Iraq, the latest victims of allied bombing had been an animal vaccination plant and a potato crisp factory. *Sunday Times,* 3 February 1991.

71 *Independent,* 2 February 1991.

72 *International Herald Tribune,* 2–3 February 1991. Michel Wery, director of Pierre Guérin, the French company which constructed the disputed plant as an infant formula factory, told the *Washington Post* on 9 February that it could not be used to make chemical products. Two New Zealand technicians, who had visited the factory, said that they saw it 'actually canning milk powder' as recently as May 1990. However, after the ceasefire, Alfonso Rojo of the Spanish daily *El Mondo,* the only Western print journalist to cover the whole crisis and war from Iraq, reported from Madrid that he had been told by a reliable Western diplomatic source in Baghdad that the site was a nuclear research facility.

73 *Independent,* 1 February 1991; *International Herald Tribune,* 4 February 1991.

74 *Sunday Times,* 3 February 1991; *Guardian,* 4 February 1991; *Jane's Defence Weekly,* 9 February 1991, p. 169.

75 *International Herald Tribune,*

1 February 1991; *Guardian,* 4 February 1991.

76 *Independent,* 5 February 1991.

77 *New York Times,* 2 February 1991; *International Herald Tribune,* 3 February 1991.

78 The Jamait-ul-Ulama, an Islamic party of Pakistan, claimed that 110,000 Pakistanis had volunteered to fight for Iraq. *New York Times,* 4 February 1991.

79 *Independent,* 2 February 1991. Due to the proximity of such Iraqi cities as Basra to the Iranian border, there were inevitably numerous violations of Iranian airspace by allied aircraft, a fact embarrassingly and repeatedly pointed out by Baghdad Radio. *Guardian,* 5 February 1991.

80 *International Herald Tribune,* 2–3 February 1991; *Jane's Defence Weekly,* 9 February 1991, p. 169.

81 *Guardian,* 1 and 5 February 1991. According to General Petrov, Iraq was believed to possess strains of anthrax, cholera and 'some obscure lethal African viruses' as well as botulin toxin – so lethal that 100 grammes of it could kill 'hundreds of millions of people'.

82 *Independent,* 5 and 6 February 1991; *New York Times,* 7 February 1991.

83 *Independent,* 7 February 1991; *Guardian,* 7 February 1991. For Sykes–Picot agreement, see Hiro, *Inside the Middle East,* pp. 50, 247.

84 *International Herald Tribune,* 9–10 February 1991; *Jane's Defence Weekly,* 16 February 1991, p. 206.

85 The other eight countries were:

Canada, France, Italy, Kuwait, New Zealand, Saudi Arabia, United Arab Emirates and United Kingdom.

86 *Guardian*, 7 February 1991.

87 *Ibid.*, 29 January and 8 February 1991; *Independent*, 8 February 1991; *International Herald Tribune*, 9–10 February 1991; *Jane's Defence Weekly*, 16 February 1991, p. 168.

88 *Independent*, 6 February 1991; *Washington Post*, 24 June 1991.

89 *Jane's Defence Weekly*, 16 February 1991, p. 207.

90 *Independent*, 5 February 1991.

91 *Guardian*, 8 and 12 February 1991; *Mainstream*, 2 March 1991, p. 14; *Washington Post*, 24 June 1991. Another example of the allies' callousness in bombing was their air raid on an Iraqi helicopter base inside a Kurdish settlement at Harir, east of Arbil, which, according to Kurdish opposition sources, led to 3,000 casualties. *Washington Post*, 12 February 1991.

92 Islamic Republic News Agency, 8 February 1991; *Independent on Sunday*, 10 February 1991.

93 *Washington Post*, 8 February 1991.

94 *International Herald Tribune*, 8 February 1991; *Independent*, 11 and 16 February 1991.

95 *International Herald Tribune*, 9–10 February 1991.

96 *Guardian*, 11 February 1991.

97 *Independent*, 4 February 1991. In contrast a Syrian contingent had engaged in combat on 3 February, when a unit of 30 Iraqi soldiers penetrated the Saudi kingdom where the Syrians were deployed.

98 *Independent*, 4 February 1991.

99 *International Herald Tribune*, 11 February 1991.

100 The 15 non-aligned foreign ministers had the benefit of hearing the Iraqi and Kuwaiti envoys in a closed-door session, as well as the Chinese deputy foreign minister, Yang Fuchang, on his way to Syria, Turkey and Iran in his search for peace. *Independent*, 12 and 13 February 1991.

101 *Independent*, 11 February 1991.

102 *BBC Summary of World Broadcasts*, 15 and 16 February 1991.

103 *Jane's Defence Weekly*, 23 February 1991, p. 247. One of the consequences of increased allied military activity in Kuwait was that 50 oil wells had been set alight. *Guardian*, 13 February 1991.

104 *Guardian*, 12 February 1991; *International Herald Tribune*, 12 February 1991. On the night of 13–14 February the allied air sorties against civilian targets rose to 135 while those against military targets in Kuwait and southern Iraq increased to 251. Baghdad Radio, 14 February 1991.

105 *International Herald Tribune*, 14 February 1991. On the same day allied bombs hit a refugee bus carrying Jordanian refugees out of Kuwait, killing 30 and injuring 24.

106 *Guardian*, 14 February 1991.

107 Baghdad Radio, 14 February 1991; *Independent*, 15 February 1991; *Newsweek*, 25 February 1991.

108 *Guardian*, 15 February 1991; *International Herald Tribune*, 15 February 1991; *Jane's Defence Weekly*, 23 February 1991, p. 246. A day earlier, in

the first face-to-face meeting between representatives of Iraq and a member of the anti-Iraqi coalition, Sadoun Hamadi had urged King Hassan to withdraw his troops from Saudi Arabia. *New York Times*, 14 February 1991.

109 *International Herald Tribune*, 15 February 1991. Another neutral country, India, also accused the allies of going beyond the UN mandate. *Independent*, 15 February 1991.

110 *Independent*, 15 February 1991. As an example of the dual-purpose bunker, the Pentagon mentioned the basement of the Rashid Hotel, where most Western journalists stayed, as 'a major military communication system'. The Associated Press reporter, who along with other journalists was allowed to make an unrestricted tour of the hotel, visited the communications room in the basement but found 'nothing highly sophisticated' to indicate 'a military communications centre'. *New York Times*, 15 February 1991.

111 *Newsweek*, 25 February 1991, p. 12. Israel disclosed later that it had an assassination squad near Saddam during the war, but failed to find an opportunity to kill him. *Sunday Times*, 4 August 1991.

112 *International Herald Tribune*, 12 February 1991; *Independent*, 16 February 1991.

113 *Ibid.*, 15 February 1991.

114 *Guardian*, 15 February 1991.

115 *International Herald Tribune*, 14 February 1991; *New York Times*, 15 February 1991; *Jane's Defence Weekly*, 23 February 1991, p. 246; *Washington*

Post, 24 June 1991. However, destroying main bridges did not mean cutting off supply routes. A few days earlier Western journalists in Iraq were shown that the main supply road between Baghdad and Basra was still open. The Iraqis were apparently rebuilding temporary bridges as fast as the allies destroyed them, something they had become adept at during their war with Iran. *Independent*, 12 February 1991.

116 *New York Times*, 18 February 1991; *Washington Post*, 11 and 12 February 1991. The frustration among Western journalists who were neither American nor British reached a point where 300 of them threatened to go to the front on their own. *International Herald Tribune*, 19 February 1991.

117 Baghdad Radio, 15 February 1991.

118 *International Herald Tribune*, 16–17 February 1991; *Los Angeles Times*, 18 February 1991.

119 *Independent*, 16 February 1991.

120 *International Herald Tribune*, 16–17 February 1991. Privately, though, Egyptian diplomats at the UN were upset about Bush's call for Saddam Hussein's overthrow since it meant that the US was going to dictate the kind of government that would take over in Iraq after the war, as it did in Panama after ousting General Manuel Noriega in December 1988. *Independent*, 16 February 1991.

121 *International Herald Tribune*, 16–17 February 1991.

122 *Guardian*, 18 February 1991.

123 *Independent*, 18 February 1991.
124 *International Herald Tribune*, 16–17 February 1991; Baghdad Radio, 13 February 1991.
125 *International Herald Tribune*, 22 February 1991. USSR military monitored the Gulf War by repositioning Soviet satellites over the region for maximum view, and collecting valuable data on US intelligence-gathering, use of such 'smart' weapons as laser-guided bombs, communication links and general military doctrine. *Los Angeles Times*, 21 February 1991.
126 *Guardian*, 18 February 1991.
127 *International Herald Tribune*, 20 February 1991; *Independent*, 21 and 22 February 1991.
128 *New York Times*, 20 February 1991.
129 *Independent*, 21 February 1991; *Washington Post*, 22 February 1991.
130 *Independent*, 21 February 1991.
131 Cited in *Ibid.*, 20 and 23 February 1991.
132 *New York Times*, 20 February 1991. These figures were 20 times higher than previous official statistics for that period. Interestingly, on 12 February Iraqi deserters were reported to have said that 20,000 Iraqi troops had been killed. *Jane's Defence Weekly*, 23 February 1991, p. 246.
133 'The Iraqis started to blow them [oil wells] the day the Iraqi foreign minister went to Moscow, the week before the final offensive,' said [Kuwaiti] drilling engineer Ayad al Kanderi in late March. *In These Times*, 27 March–2 April 1991, p. 12. This date was also confirmed by military sources in Iran, whose spotter planes along the Iraqi border in the south had noticed preparation for a retreat in the form of pontoon bridges.
134 *Independent*, 18 February 1991; *Jane's Defence Weekly*, 23 February 1991, p. 247.
135 *Guardian*, 22 February 1991; *Independent*, 22 February 1991.
136 Baghdad Radio, 21 February 1991.
137 Cited in *Independent*, 21 and 23 February 1991. Among the important regional states to respond positively to Baghdad's acceptance of the Soviet peace plan were Iran and Jordan.
138 *International Herald Tribune*, 22 February 1991; *Independent*, 23 February 1991.
139 *International Herald Tribune*, 23 February 1991.
140 Napalm is a gel, consisting of aluminium napthenate and aluminium palmitate (i.e. nap+palm), mixed with petroleum, and dropped in bombs. Highly effective in raising temperatures, depleting oxygen supplies, and burning up everything in its path, it is not covered by any controls or arms treaties, and is specifically excluded from the negotiations to ban chemical weapons.
141 Micah L. Sifry and Christopher Cerf (eds), *The Gulf War Reader*, pp. 351–2.
142 *International Herald Tribune*, 23 February 1991.
143 'There is growing pressure in the Soviet Union to stop supporting the multi-national coalition,' said Sergi Stankevich, deputy mayor of Moscow and a leading radical. 'This internal pressure is becoming unbearable for

our president.' *Guardian*, 26 February 1991.

144 Bush's ultimatum to Saddam Hussein at 15.45 GMT on 22 February had been endorsed by the nine-member Western European Union, a regional defence body, including Britain, France, Germany, Italy and Spain, arguing that Baghdad's attempt to attach conditions to its offer to pull out of Kuwait was unacceptable. *New York Times*, 23 February 1991. The impotence of the Security Council to bring about a truce created discontent among United Nations staff. In an unprecedented move, more than 500 of them addressed a petition to the secretary-general, urging him to call for 'an immediate ceasefire'. The UN staff bulletin, *Secretariat News*, quoted staff members complaining that the Security Council had been misused 'especially by the permanent members', and that it lacked 'a will of its own'. *Guardian*, 22 February 1991.

145 *Independent*, 23 February 1991.

146 *Independent on Sunday*, 24 February 1991; *Guardian*, 25 February 1991; *Washington Post*, 25 February 1991; *New York Times*, 5 March 1991.

147 *Guardian*, 25 February 1991. Interestingly, a *Newsweek* poll, taken on 15 February, showed that 49% thought that the Soviet Union was playing a 'positive role' in seeking an end to the war. 25 February 1991, p. 8.

148 *Independent*, 23 February 1991; *Jane's Defence Weekly*, 2 March 1991, p. 287; *New York Times*, 14 January 1991. See also p. 360. Later, the number of the Israelis killed by Scuds rose to 12.

149 *Newsweek*, 25 February 1991, p. 14.

10 Desert Sabre: the Ground War

1 Baghdad Radio, 21 February 1991.

2 *International Herald Tribune*, 28 February 1991.

3 Baghdad Radio, 26 February 1991.

4 *Guardian*, 28 February 1991.

5 *Jane's Defence Weekly*, 9 March 1991, p. 327.

6 Baghdad Radio, 24 February 1991.

7 Cited in *Independent*, 25 February 1991.

8 *Guardian*, 25 February 1991.

9 Tehran Radio, 24 February 1991.

10 *International Herald Tribune*, 25 and 26 February 1991.

11 *Independent*, 25 February 1991.

12 *International Herald Tribune*, 25 February 1991.

13 *New York Times*, 25 February 1991.

14 *Guardian*, 27 February 1991.

15 Baghdad Radio, 26 February 1991.

16 *Ibid.*; *Guardian*, 26 February 1991; *Independent*, 27 February 1991.

17 *International Herald Tribune*, 27 February 1991; *Washington Post*, 27 February 1991.

18 Cited in *New Statesman and Society*, 21 June 1991, p. 23.

19 BBC-2 television's 'Late Show', 8 June 1991.

20 Cited in *New Statesman and Society*, 21 June 1991, p. 23.

21 *International Herald Tribune*, 27 February 1991; *Guardian*, 1 March 1991. Unsurprisingly, American companies received over 70% of the value of 72 contracts worth $1,259 million that were signed immediately by the Kuwaiti government to rebuild the emirate. *Independent*, 26 February 1991.

22 *Ibid.*, 28 February 1991.

23 *Guardian*, 28 February 1991.

24 *Washington Post*, 27 February 1991; *Guardian*, 28 February 1991.

25 *Los Angeles Times*, 10 March 1991.

26 Cited in *New Statesman and Society*, 21 June 1991, p. 25.

27 *International Herald Tribune*, 28 February 1991; *Jane's Defence Weekly*, 9 March 1991, p. 327.

28 Four weeks later when General Schwarzkopf said, in a television interview with David Frost, that if the war had gone on for 24 hours more, 'we could have inflicted terrible damage on them [the retreating Iraqis] with air attacks and that sort of thing on the far side of the [Euphrates] river', Cheney replied that Schwarzkopf and Powell were consulted, and that 'they made the recommendation to me and to the president that we had achieved our military objectives, and agreed that it was time to end the campaign'. *New York Times*, 28 March 1991.

29 *Independent*, 28 February 1991; *Jane's Defence Weekly*, 9 March 1991, p. 327.

30 Cited in *New York Times*, 28 March 1991; *New Statesman and Society*, 21 June 1991, p. 27.

31 *New York Times*, 28 February 1991; *Guardian*, 28 February 1991.

32 *Washington Post*, 1 March 1991.

33 *International Herald Tribune*, 1 March 1991; *New York Times*, 1 March 1991.

34 Baghdad Radio, 28 February 1991; *International Herald Tribune*, 1 and 2 March 1991.

35 *Guardian*, 28 February 1991; *International Herald Tribune*, 1 March 1991.

36 *Ibid.*, 2 March 1991.

37 *Independent*, 27 February 1991.

38 *Ibid.*, 28 February 1991.

39 *Washington Post*, 1 March 1991; *New York Times*, 1 March 1991.

40 *Independent*, 1 March 1991.

41 *Ibid.*, 2 March 1991.

42 *International Herald Tribune*, 28 February 1991 and 1 March 1991.

43 *Ibid.*, 2 March 1991; *Sunday Times*, 3 March 1991; *New York Times*, 28 March 1991; *New Statesman and Society*, 21 June 1991, p. 26; *Washington Post*, 24 June 1991; *Newsday*, 12 September 1991.

44 *Guardian*, 1 March 1991.

45 Cited in *New Statesman and Society*, 21 June 1991, p. 24.

46 See p. 371.

47 *Independent*, 27 July 1991; International Institute of Strategic Studies, *The Military Balance, 1990–1991*, p. 17.

48 *Washington Post*, 13 February 1991; *Independent*, 14 February 1991; *Jane's Defence Weekly*, 16 February 1991, p. 207; International Institute of Strategic Studies, op. cit., p. 115.

49 *International Herald Tribune*, 16 July, 30 July and 12 August

1991; International Institute of Strategic Studies, op. cit., p. 108.

11 The Aftermath

1 *Independent on Sunday*, 22 March 1991.
2 *Le Figaro*, 3 March 1991.
3 *Guardian*, 25 April 1991.
4 Cited in *Middle East International*, 19 April 1991, p. 22.
5 Cited in *Sunday Times*, 16 June 1991.
6 *Ibid.*, 10 March 1991; *Guardian*, 11 March 1991.
7 *New York Times*, 8 March 1991; *Independent*, 8 March 1991.
8 See Dilip Hiro, *The Longest War*, pp. 97, 150, 179, 197. In late March US intelligence reports mentioned 'more than 20,000' former Iraqi soldiers, who had refused to go home after the First Gulf War, being assembled in eight border camps in Iran, armed, and sent into Iraq. *Washington Post*, 30 March 1991. According to the Baghdad-based Mujahedin Khalq, an exiled Iranian opposition party, Iran's revolutionary guards entered Iraq twice at Jalloula in March and April, and its troops repulsed their attack. *Guardian*, 1 May 1991.
9 *Sunday Times*, 31 March 1991.
10 Islamic Republic News Agency, 13 March 1991.
11 *Independent*, 17 March and 16 April 1991; *Middle East International*, 19 April 1991, p. 10. 'At the Imam Abbas mosque . . . a small reception hall has a smashed glass frame that once held Saddam Hussein's picture,' reported Caryle Murphy. 'Next to the empty frame is a wall engraving titled, "Saddam Hussein's Family Tree", meant to show his purported descent from Prophet Muhammad. Of the hundreds of names on the leaves of the family tree, the rebels scratched out only three: Saddam Hussein and his two sons, Uday and Qusay.' *Washington Post*, 1 July 1991.
12 Baghdad Radio, 16 March 1991.
13 *Middle East International*, 19 April 1991, p. 10; *Guardian*, 1 May 1991.
14 Islamic Republic News Agency, 18 March 1991.
15 The Iraqi opposition claimed that the government had kidnapped Khoei and other ulama in Kufa and Najaf, and taken them to Baghdad on 19 March. *Independent*, 22 March 1991. Addressing visiting Western journalists in mid-April at his home in Kufa, near Najaf, Khoei said, 'What has happened in Najaf and other cities is not allowed and is against God'; but added, 'Nobody visits me, so I don't know what is happening.' *Ibid.*, 16 April 1991.
16 *Guardian*, 25 March 1991; *Independent Magazine*, 13 April 1991, p. 34. When asked 'If the Iraqi army comes back, would the auxiliaries rejoin it?', a *peshmarga* guerrilla replied without hesitation, 'Yes'. *Ibid.*
17 *Independent on Sunday*, 24 March 1991.
18 *Washington Post*, 24 March 1991.
19 *Daily Telegraph*, 25 March

1991; *International Herald Tribune,* 25 March 1991.

20 *Guardian,* 28 March 1991. Earlier, the White House had said that the US would shoot down Iraqi helicopters used against the rebels *only* if they posed a threat to the allied troops. *New York Times,* 27 March 1991.

21 *Independent Magazine,* 13 April 1991, p. 32.

22 *Independent,* 7 April 1991.

23 See Appendix III for a full text of the resolution.

24 *New York Times,* 6 April 1991; *Sunday Times,* 7 April 1991. His earlier appointment of another cousin, Ali Hassan Majid, as interior minister had served to abort any plotting by the higher ranks of the intelligence services.

25 According to Kurdish sources, the government had been systematically rounding up Kurds living in Baghdad in reprisal for the Kurdish uprising.

26 *Guardian,* 10 April 1991.

27 *New York Times,* 10 April 1991.

28 *Ibid.,* 18 April 1991.

29 Cited in *Middle East International,* 3 May 1991, p. 3.

30 The UN programme was to last until 31 December 1991. *Guardian,* 19 April 1991.

31 *International Herald Tribune,* 25 April 1991; *Middle East International,* 3 May 1991, p. 3. But since Kurdistan lacked electricity, and therefore television, the people there did not see these pictures.

32 *Middle East International,* 17 May, p. 11.

33 *Independent,* 26 April 1991; *Guardian,* 1 May 1991.

34 *Washington Post,* 2 May 1991.

35 *Ibid.,* 24 May 1991.

36 *International Herald Tribune,* 2 and 4–5 May 1991.

37 *Ibid.,* 29 March 1991; *Middle East International,* 5 April 1991, p. 7.

38 *Guardian,* 8 April 1991.

39 *Independent,* 7 March 1991; *International Herald Tribune,* 7 April 1991.

40 *New York Times,* 1 April 1991; *Washington Post,* 6 April 1991. GCC states also decided to stop paying subsidies to Jordan and the PLO because of their stand during the Gulf crisis and war.

41 On 20 April Baker met three representatives of the Fatah, the leading constituent of the PLO, which like its umbrella organization is headed by Yasser Arafat. *Guardian,* 22 April 1991.

42 *Guardian,* 10 April 1991; *Washington Post,* 10 April 1991; *New York Times,* 13 April 1991; *International Herald Tribune,* 16 April 1991.

43 *Independent,* 15 April 1991; *New York Times,* 19 April 1991.

44 *Guardian,* 23 and 24 April 1991. By then Israel had settled more than 88,000 Jews on the West Bank. *New York Times,* 7 March 1991.

45 *Washington Post,* 17 May 1991.

46 *Independent,* 10 May 1991.

47 Cited in *International Herald Tribune,* 29 May 1991. Of Iraq's pre-war oil output of 3.4 mb/d, 800,000 came from the area around Kirkuk. *Ibid.,* 31 May 1991.

48 Censorship of foreign journalists was abolished on 5 May 1991.

49 *Independent*, 22 and 25 June 1991; *International Herald Tribune*, 24 June 1991.

50 About 6,300 allied troops, including 1,975 Americans, remained in northern Iraq, but they were all expected to leave by mid-July. *New York Times*, 23 June 1991.

51 *Observer*, 19 May 1991; *Independent*, 21 May 1991. 'If a man like General Abdullah with his following could not pull off a takeover, we don't honestly believe anyone could,' said a senior Kurdish leader. *Ibid*.

52 *New York Times*, 22 May 1991.

53 *Middle East International*, 14 June 1991, p. 9; *Washington Post*, 19 June 1991. On 31 May the UN secretary-general fixed 30% of Iraq's oil exports earnings as the upper limit of Iraq's liability for war reparations.

54 *Independent*, 7 and 13 June 1991.

55 *New York Times*, 4 June 1991.

56 *Independent*, 4 May 1991; *International Herald Tribune*, 16 July 1991.

57 *Middle East International*, 3 May 1991, p. 9.

58 *Guardian*, 19 April 1991. Amnesty International withdrew the charge made in its report of 18 December 1990 that 312 premature Kuwaiti babies had been killed by the Iraqi military, stating that during their visits to Kuwait its investigators found no evidence of this. *Ibid*.

59 *New York Times*, 30 April 1991; *International Herald Tribune*, 6 May 1991. After his meeting with King Fahd in Saudi Arabia in mid-May, Dick Cheney said that 'the shape of future military relationships' in the region would not emerge 'for months'. *Ibid.*, 13 May 1991.

60 *Guardian*, 13 May 1991; *Independent*, 22 May 1991; *Washington Post*, 3 June 1991. London announced that 1,300 British soldiers would stay on in Kuwait 'temporarily'.

61 *Middle East International*, 14 June 1991, p. 10.

62 Cited in *The Middle East*, July 1991, p. 8.

63 Cited in *Middle East International*, 14 June 1991, p. 11.

64 A few days later, the religious police, *muttawin*, increasingly intent on performing their job zealously, raided a mansion in Riyadh and arrested all those found drinking alcohol, including King Fahd's official interpreter, Muhammad Annai. *Independent*, 29 May 1991.

65 *Independent*, 25 May 1991; *New York Times*, 27 May and 6 July 1991. In late February a group of 43 liberal Saudis had issued a petition for democratic reform, proposing a change-over to constitutional monarchy with a multi-party political system, votes for women, and the freedom of expression and the press. *Middle East International*, 14 June 1991, p. 11. Both the petitions were later published in full in the Egyptian press.

66 Whereas every other country was allowed 1,000 pilgrims per million Muslims, Iran, with a population of nearly 54 million, was given twice the normal quota: 110,000. See Hiro, *The Longest War*, pp. 224–5.

12 Conclusions

1 *Independent*, 23 July 1991.
2 Baghdad Radio, 29 July 1991.
3 *Los Angeles Times*, 25 February 1991.
4 *New York Times*, 29 January 1991.
5 See p. 165.
6 The proven oil reserves of the Gulf countries in billion barrels at the end of 1989 were: Iran, 92.9; Iraq, 100; Kuwait, 94.5; Saudi Arabia, 255; Saudi–Kuwaiti Neutral Zone, 5.2; Qatar, 4.5; UAE, 99.1; and Oman, 4.3. *BP Statistical Review of World Energy*, June 1990, p. 2.
7 *Ibid.*, pp. 2, 5.
8 See p. 27.
9 *Sunday Times*, 23 September 1990.
10 *New York Times*, 16 November 1990.
11 *Washington Post*, 4 March 1991. The only sensational terrorist action, the mortar-bombing of the British prime minister's residential office at 10 Downing Street in London on 7 February 1991 was the work of the Irish Republican Army, and had nothing to do with the Gulf crisis.
12 *Sunday Times*, 21 July 1991.
13 See Muhammed Muslih and Augustus Richard Norton, 'The Need for Arab Democracy',

Foreign Policy, vol. 83, Summer 1991, pp. 3–19.
14 BBC World Service, 25 May 1991. In contrast, Egypt claimed to have lost $16.5 billion in foreign exchange due to the fall in tourism and the remittances of its workers in Kuwait and Iraq, and the rise in oil price. *Independent*, 27 July 1991.
15 *BP Statistical Review of World Energy*, June 1990, p. 2.
16 See Dilip Hiro, 'A Few of Our Favourite Kings' in Micah L. Sifri and Christopher Cerf (eds), *The Gulf Reader*, pp. 408–11.
17 See p. 303.
18 *Guardian*, 4 March 1991.
19 *Independent*, 8 June 1991.
20 *Washington Post*, 30 April 1990.
21 *Independent*, 22 February 1991.
22 Dilip Hiro, *Inside the Middle East*, p. 350.

Epilogue

1 *New York Times*, 29 July 1991.
2 Iraq claimed a loss of $17 billion in the first six months of the UN embargo. *International Herald Tribune*, 19 August 1991.
3 *Ibid.*, 16 September 1991; and *Middle East International*, 27 September 1991, p. 10.
4 *Independent*, 5 October 1991.

APPENDIX I:
Chronology

BEFORE THE SECOND GULF WAR

1987

July

20 The UN Security Council passes Resolution 598 calling for a ceasefire in the Iran–Iraq War, and withdrawal of warring forces. The ten-article text is comprehensive, and includes a clause for an impartial commission to determine war responsibility. Iraq accepts the resolution on the condition that Iran does the same.

October

2   The Americans destroy three Iranian patrol boats near Farsi Island after claims that the Iranians fired on a US patrol boat.
19 US warships destroy two Iranian offshore platforms in retaliation for mining damage to an American-flagged oil tanker.
22 Iran hits Kuwait's Sea Island oil terminal.

1988

March

15 Assisted by its Kurdish allies, Iran captures Halabja in Iraqi Kurdistan.
16 The Iraqi air force drops chemical bombs on Halabja, killing at least 4,000 people.

April

14 An American frigate strikes a mine in international waters off Bahrain.
16–18 The Iraqis recapture the Fao peninsula, using chemical weapons.
18 US warships blow up two Iranian oil rigs, destroy an Iranian frigate and immobilize another, and sink an Iranian missile boat.

May

23–25 Iraq mounts offensives in the northern and central sectors, and then in the Shalamche region in the south. It retakes Shalamche, using chemical weapons.

June

25 The Iraqis recapture the Majnoon Islands, using chemical weapons.

July

3   An American cruiser shoots down an Iran Air airbus with 290 people on board, mistaking it for an F-14 warplane.

17 On the twentieth anniversary of the Baathist coup Saddam Hussein repeats his five-point peace plan, including a ceasefire and return to the international frontier, the signing of a peace treaty and a non-aggression pact, and a mutual agreement not to meddle in each other's domestic affairs.

18 Iran accepts UN Security Council Resolution 598 unconditionally.

20 Iraq insists on direct negotiations with Iran, which the latter refuses.

22–29 The Iraqis mount offensives in the northern, central and southern sectors. These are partly successful.

August

1 A United Nations investigation concludes that Iraq made intensified use of chemical weapons in its military operations in the spring and summer.

6 Iraq withdraws its demand for direct talks with Iran.

20 A ceasefire comes into effect.

September–October

Negotiations between Iraq and Iran in Geneva under the chairmanship of the UN secretary-general stall.

November

8 George Bush is elected president of America, and Dan Quayle vice-president.

1989

February

16 The Arab Co-operation Council, consisting of Iraq, Egypt, Jordan and North Yemen, is formed.

18 Iran's foreign minister, Velayati, reveals that Iraq is occupying 920 square miles of Iranian territory.

April

1 General elections to the Third National Assembly of Iraq are held.

June

3 Ayatollah Khomeini dies.

4 President Ali Khamanei is elected the Supreme Leader of Iran by the Assembly of Experts.

17 The Arab Co-operation Council backs Iraq's claims to both banks of the Shatt al Arab and calls on the United Nations to clear the waterway of debris.

July

28 Rafsanjani is elected president of Iran.

September

15 Farzad Bazoft, a correspondent of the London-based *Observer*, is arrested in Baghdad on charges of spying.

November

20 A memorandum by the director-general of Kuwait's State Security Department to the interior minister refers to his meetings at the US CIA headquarters, and states: 'We agreed with the American side that it was important to take advantage of the deteriorating economic situation in Iraq in order to put pressure on that country's government to delineate our common border.' The CIA describes the document as a forgery.

December

5 Iraq claims to have launched its first space rocket.

1990

January

22 Kuwaiti police break up protest meeting in the capital calling for the restoration of parliament.

February

24 At the ACC summit in Amman, Saddam Hussein warns that Israel might embark on 'new stupidities' in the wake of the recent US supremacy in international affairs.

March

15 Israel's National Unity government falls because of the defection of Labour due to its differences with Prime Minister Shamir on how to proceed with the peace process.
Farzad Bazoft is hanged in Baghdad.

22 Gerald Bull, a Canadian expert on long-range artillery, involved in Iraq's military projects, is murdered near his flat in Brussels.
Britain arrests five persons in London for trying to smuggle into Iraq 40 high-speed electronic capacitors, powerful enough to be used as nuclear triggers, from the US.

April

2 Denying that Iraq intends to produce nuclear arms, Saddam Hussein says, 'Don't they know that we have the binary chemical weapons to cause fire to devour half of the Zionist entity if the Zionist entity, which has atomic bombs, dared attack Iraq?'

11 Britain confiscates a consignment of long steel tubes, believed to be part of a supergun, destined for Iraq.

21 Saddam Hussein writes a letter to Ayatollah Khamanei and President Rafsanjani of Iran proposing a meeting in Mecca to reach a peace accord.

May

20 A young Israeli shoots and kills seven Palestinian workers, setting off rioting in the Occupied Territories where seven more Palestinians are killed by Israeli security forces.

21 Washington suspends Iraq's request for a $500 million loan guarantee from the US Commodity Credit Corporation.

26 US vetoes a Security Council resolution, backed by 14 out of 15 members, to send a UN team to the Occupied Territories to investigate the condition of the Palestinians.

30 The extraordinary Arab League summit in Baghdad describes the settlement of Soviet and other Jews in Palestine and other Occupied Arab Territories as 'a new aggression against the rights of the Palestinian people' and 'a dangerous threat to pan-Arab security'.

At a closed session of the summit Saddam Hussein refers to 'the failure by some of our brothers to abide by the OPEC decision' and thus depressing the oil price through oversupply, and warns that 'this is in fact a kind of war against Iraq'.

An attempt by the Palestine Liberation Front, a pro-Iraqi group, to land its guerrillas at Tel Aviv's beaches fails, resulting in four deaths.

June

10 Elections to the Kuwaiti National Council, an advisory body, are boycotted by the opposition.

11 The Likud-led coalition government of Shamir receives 62 out of 120 votes in the Israeli parliament.

20 President Bush suspends talks with the PLO due to its failure to condemn the 30 May aborted attack on Israel, or discipline those responsible for it.

July

9 King Fahd of Saudi Arabia and Shaikh Khalifa al Thani of Qatar decide to instruct their oil ministers 'not to pay attention to what the Iraqi [oil] minister said' at the 11 July meeting of the Arab Gulf oil ministers.

14 President Assad of Syria visits Cairo after an interval of 13 years, and meets President Mubarak.

15 Iraqi foreign minister Tariq Aziz complains to the Arab League that the oil glut caused by Kuwait and the UAE has caused the oil price to fall to $11 to $13 a barrel, far below the OPEC's reference price of $18, and that a drop of $1 a barrel reduces Iraq's annual revenue by $1 billion.

17 On the 23rd anniversary of the Baathist seizure of power, Saddam Hussein warns Arab countries against conspiring to hurt Iraq.

19 Kuwait's foreign minister calls on the Arab League to settle the Kuwait–Iraq border dispute.

US expresses 'strong commitment' to 'supporting the individual and collective self-defence of our friends in the Gulf'.

23 US confirms that its six warships in the Gulf have been put on alert, and that they have joined an exercise with the UAE navy.

25 US ambassador April Glaspie has a meeting in Baghdad with Saddam Hussein, who says that he hopes for a peaceful settlement of the dispute with Kuwait. Glaspie tells Saddam Hussein, 'We have no opinion on the Arab–Arab conflicts, like your border disagreement with Kuwait . . . [T]he issue is not associated with America.'

The OPEC meeting in Geneva raises the oil reference price from $18 to $21 a barrel.

27 US Senate decides by 80 votes to 16 to impose an arms and technology embargo against Iraq. The White House opposes the move.

28 President Bush sends a message to Saddam Hussein expressing a wish to improve relations with Iraq, but advising him against pursuing threats involving military force or conflict.

31 Iraqi and Kuwaiti representatives hold talks in Jiddah, Saudi Arabia, against the background of some 100,000 Iraqi troops positioned along the Kuwaiti border.

August

1 The talks in Jiddah collapse either because (according to the Kuwaitis) Kuwait refused to concede the Iraqi demands to write off its debts and relinquish some of its territories, or because (according to the Iraqis) Iraq saw no serious sign by Kuwait of willingness to repair the damage it had inflicted on Iraq.

2 At 2 a.m. local time Iraqi forces invade Kuwait and occupy it. Baghdad claims that it intervened on behalf of local revolutionaries, who form the Provisional Free Government of Kuwait. The emir, Shaikh Jaber III al Sabah, and most other members of the royal family flee to Saudi Arabia with the assistance of the US embassy.
   UN Security Council passes Resolution 660 by 14 votes to none, condemning Iraq, urging a ceasefire and withdrawal of the Iraqi troops from Kuwait.
   US condemns the Iraqi aggression, freezes Iraqi and Kuwaiti assets, and bans trade with Iraq. Britain and France freeze Kuwaiti assets. The Soviet Union halts arms deliveries to Iraq.

3 Iraq says that its troops will start withdrawing from Kuwait from 5 August 'unless something happens which would threaten the security of Kuwait and Iraq'.
   Egypt condemns Iraqi invasion of Kuwait.
   The Arab League foreign ministers' meeting in Cairo condemns the Iraqi action by 14 votes to one, with five abstentions and one walk-out.
   The names of the nine members of the Provisional Free Government of Kuwait are announced.
   2,000 Egyptian troops are airlifted to Saudi Arabia.

5 Bush urges the Arab states to condemn the Iraqi aggression against Kuwait which, he says, 'will not stand'.

6 Saddam Hussein tells US chargé d'affaires, Joseph Wilson, that the withdrawal of the Iraqi army from Kuwait has to be based on an 'international agreement'; that it is not 'in anyone's interest' that Iraq should withdraw 'in a hurry, leaving Kuwait to the warring parties'; and that he does not intend to attack Saudi Arabia.
   UN Security Council passes Resolution 661 by 13 votes to none, imposing mandatory sanctions and embargo on Iraq and occupied Kuwait.
   US secretary of defence Cheney is in Jiddah to meet King Fahd, who invites American forces to his kingdom to bolster its defences. President Bush orders fighter aircraft and troops to leave for Saudi Arabia.

7 Cheney pledges to see Egypt's military debts of $6.75 billion to the US written off.

Israel warns Jordan that it would regard the entry of Iraqi troops into Jordan as a 'threatening move', and would respond 'appropriately'.

8 The Provisional Free Government of Kuwait calls for the merger of Kuwait into Iraq. Baghdad annexes Kuwait and calls it the 'nineteenth province' of Iraq.

Addressing the nation on television, President Bush describes the role of some 40,000 US troops in Saudi Arabia as 'wholly defensive'.

9 UN Security Council passes Resolution 662, unanimously, declaring Iraq's annexation of Kuwait null and void.

In a television address King Fahd condemns the Iraqi invasion of Kuwait as 'the most vile aggression known to the Arab nations in its modern history', and says that the foreign forces participating in 'joint training between them and the Saudi military' will be present 'temporarily'.

10 In a radio broadcast Saddam Hussein attacks the Saudi rulers for placing Mecca and Medina under 'foreign protection', and calls on 'Arabs, Muslims, believers in God' to revolt against 'the spears of the foreigners'.

The Arab League summit in Cairo (boycotted by Tunisia) decides by 12 votes to three, with five members expressing reservations or abstaining, to condemn Iraq for its invasion and annexation of Kuwait, and to accept the request of Saudi Arabia and other Gulf states to despatch Arab forces to assist their armed forces.

12 Saddam Hussein offers a peace initiative, including 'preparation' of withdrawal of 'Israel from the occupied Arab territories in Palestine, Syria and Lebanon; Syria's withdrawal from Lebanon; a withdrawal between Iraq and Iran; and the formulation of arrangements for the situation in Kuwait' in line with the UN resolutions.

Bush rejects the Saddam Hussein initiative.

13 Pakistan agrees 'in principle' to join the 'Islamic contingent' to defend Saudi Arabia.

14 In a letter to Rafsanjani, Saddam Hussein agrees to abide by the 1975 Algiers Accord, to withdraw Iraqi forces from the occupied Iranian territory, and undertake exchange of prisoners of war immediately. The Iranian president accepts the offer.

15 In an interview with an American television network, Tariq Aziz offers US open-ended talks on the Gulf crisis.

17 Iraq's National Assembly decides to detain the nationals of those governments which have decided to participate in the embargo against Iraq and are planning to attack it. Most of the 8,000 Western and Japanese nationals in Kuwait and another 3,400 in Iraq are affected.

18 UN Security Council passes Resolution 664, unanimously, demanding that Iraq 'permit and facilitate the immediate departure from Kuwait and Iraq' of all foreigners.

41 Britons in Kuwait are moved to unknown destinations, adding to the 35 Americans who had been sent to undisclosed destinations earlier.

19 Saddam Hussein offers to free foreigners if the US pledges to withdraw

from Saudi Arabia, not to attack Iraq, and lift the blockade against Iraq 'by all sides'. Bush rejects the proposal.

21 Syria confirms that it is sending 1,200 troops to Saudi Arabia.
     Iraq evacuates all occupied Iranian territory.

22 Oil price reaches $30 a barrel.

23 Using an intermediary Saddam Hussein offers a deal to the White House through its national security adviser, Brent Scowcroft: Iraqi withdrawal from Kuwait and release of all foreigners in exchange for the lifting of UN embargo against Baghdad, and securing of Iraq's access to the Gulf through Warba and Bubiyan Islands. Bush does not pursue the proposal.

24 Defying the Iraqi deadline, the three Western permanent members of the UN Security Council – America, Britain and France – refuse to close down their embassies in Kuwait City.

25 UN Security Council passes Resolution 665 by 13 votes to none, authorizing 'such measures commensurate to the specific circumstances as may be necessary' to halt all ships trading with Iraq in order to implement Resolution 661.

28 Saddam Hussein decides to let go all Western and Japanese women and children.

28 King Hussein of Jordan unveils a peace plan: simultaneous withdrawal of Iraqi troops from Kuwait and US forces from Saudi Arabia, followed by an election in Kuwait to choose a new government which will sign an agreement with Iraq giving it 'certain rights over Kuwait'. Iraq accepts it, but Saudi Arabia and Kuwait reject it.

30 America puts together a $25 billion 'Economic Action Plan' to defray the costs of deployment of US forces in the Gulf and aid the states hurt by the UN embargo against Iraq.

31 In Amman the UN secretary-general Pérez de Cuellar and Tariq Aziz conclude two days of talks, described as 'inconclusive'.
     Arab League foreign ministers meeting (boycotted by 8 members) in Cairo endorses UN Security Council resolutions on the Kuwaiti crisis by 12 votes to one (Libya).

September

1   Libya, having consulted Iraq, Jordan and Sudan, unveils a seven-point peace plan, including the withdrawal of Iraqi troops from Kuwait and US and other non-Muslim troops from Saudi Arabia, the lifting of embargo against Iraq, the ceding of Warba and Bubiyan Islands to Iraq, and the people of Kuwait deciding their own political system through a plebiscite. Kuwait and Saudi Arabia reject it.

5   Saddam Hussein renews his call to 'the Iraqi people, faithful Arabs and Muslims everywhere' to wage a holy struggle against the Saudi rulers and their backers.
     Tariq Aziz meets President Gorbachev in Moscow.

6   Jordan says that an estimated 605,000 people have entered the kingdom from Kuwait and Iraq since 2 August, and that 105,000 are being held in 17 refugee camps.

8   Saddam Hussein urges 'the concerned politicians' worldwide to 'choose this critical issue and time to restore to the Soviet Union its superpower

status' by adopting 'a just and fair position' on the Gulf crisis, and rejecting 'America's shunning' of his 12 August peace initiative.

9 At the end of a summit meeting in Helsinki, Bush and Gorbachev call on Iraq to withdraw unconditionally from Kuwait, allow the restoration of the legitimate government of Kuwait, and free all hostages held in Iraq and Kuwait.

10 Iraq and Iran decide to renew diplomatic relations.
Saddam Hussein offers Third World countries free oil so long as they can arrange the transportation at their own expense.

12 Ayatollah Khamanei condemns the US military presence in the Gulf, and declares that those who confront 'America's aggression and greed' in the Persian Gulf will have participated in a holy war in the path of Allah.
The Saudi-funded World Muslim League declares at the end of a three-day conference in Mecca that the foreign help sought by Saudi Arabia to bolster its self-defence was necessitated by 'a legitimate need'.

16 UN Security Council adopts Resolution 667 by unanimous vote, condemning Iraq's acts of violence against diplomatic missions and their personnel in Kuwait.
In a *Washington Post* interview, General Michael Dugan, US air force chief of staff, says that US air power is the only effective way of expelling Iraq from Kuwait, that Baghdad will be on 'the cutting edge' of the bombing, and that, according to Israeli advice, Saddam Hussein should be at 'the focus of our efforts'.

17 US defence secretary Cheney sacks General Dugan.
Iraq's deputy prime minister, Taha Yassin Ramadan, says Iraq is prepared to withdraw from Kuwait if it leads to an international conference to solve the Palestinian problem.

19 King Hassan of Morocco, after consulting Jordanian and Algerian rulers, offers a peace plan, including Iraqi evacuation of Kuwait, withdrawal of non-Arab troops from Saudi Arabia, a 'special relationship' between Iraq and Kuwait, and an international conference on the Middle East to consider the Palestinian and Lebanese problems.
Washington and Riyadh reject the proposal.

21 The Popular Forces Conference for Solidarity with Iraq, attended by 20 radical Arab parties in Amman, condemns Saudi alliance with the US.

23 In Tehran, Syrian President Assad reiterates his call for the withdrawal of Iraqi troops from Kuwait. While endorsing this demand President Rafsanjani says that the presence of foreign force in the Persian Gulf is hindering the regional Arab countries from finding a solution to the crisis.

24 At the UN General Assembly, President Mitterrand proposes a four-phase peace plan, including an Iraqi declaration of 'intent' to withdraw from Kuwait; tackling the problems of Lebanon, the Palestinians and security for Israel; and reduction of arms in the region. Iraq responds positively; and also China.

25 UN Security Council adopts Resolution 670 by 14 votes to none, extending the applicability of sanctions against Iraq to all means of transport, including aircraft, and threatens Iraq with 'potentially severe consequences' if it fails to withdraw from Kuwait.

At the UN General Assembly Soviet foreign minister Eduard Shevard-nadze says that the USSR may support the use of force if Iraq continues to occupy Kuwait.

27 Following the statement by Shaikh Yamani, former Saudi oil minister, that in case of war the Kuwaiti oil wells will be set on fire, and that Iraq can inflict damage on Saudi oil installations, the price of oil rises to $40 a barrel, the highest in 12 years.

29 A senior White House official says, 'Our message number one, two and three to Israel is to keep out of this [crisis] at all costs.'

October

1 At the UN General Assembly, President Bush says that the US seeks 'a peaceful outcome' to the Gulf crisis, and that once Iraq has evacuated Kuwait, there may be opportunities to settle the differences between Iraq and Kuwait as well as the conflict that divides the Arabs from Israel.

2 Amnesty International publishes a report portraying widespread arrests, torture under interrogation, summary executions and mass extra-judicial killings in Kuwait by the occupying Iraqi forces.

4 During the French president's visit to Riyadh, King Fahd backs the Mitterrand peace plan, provided the restoration of the al Sabah family to power is assured.

5 Yevgeny Primakov, a Soviet Presidential Council member, has a meeting with Saddam Hussein in Baghdad, and says he is 'not pessimistic' about a political solution to the Gulf crisis.
Following its rejection of the federal budget for 1 October 1990–30 September 1991 presented by Bush, US Congress adopts a temporary spending bill to cover the expenses for the next fortnight.

7 The commander of the Syrian forces in Saudi Arabia says that his forces will not participate in any offensive.

8 The commander of the Egyptian troops in Saudi Arabia says that his forces will not participate in any offensive.
Israeli police shoot dead 18 to 20 Palestinians and injure another 150 during rioting at the Temple Mount on Jerusalem triggered by the plans of the Temple Mount Faithful to lay a foundation stone for the Third Jewish Temple. Iraq orders three days of mourning.

9 Rioting in the Occupied Territories results in the death of three more Palestinians and the imposition of curfew on large areas of the Occupied Territories.

10 French foreign minister Dumas calls on the world community to support 'the Palestinian aspirations'.

12 UN Security Council adopts Resolution 672 by unanimous vote, expres-sing alarm at the 8 October violence at the Temple Mount, Jerusalem, and calling on Israel to abide by the Fourth Geneva Convention, and requesting the secretary-general to submit, by 30 October, the findings of a UN mission to be sent to the region.

13 Crown Prince Saad al Sabah tells the Popular Conference of the Kuwaitis in Jiddah that in a liberated Kuwait the al Sabah regime will 'consolidate' the freedoms granted by the 1962 constitution.

13 In Lebanon Syrian troops attack and defeat the troops of General Michel

Aoun, who takes refuge at the French embassy. The forces of Elias Hrawi, the Lebanese president, occupy the captured presidential palace near Beirut.

16   At a Congressional hearing US secretary of state Baker says that the sanctions against Iraq are 'tightening with increasing severity', and that blockades and sanctions have a chance of bringing about the desired outcome 'short of war'.

18   The Arab League foreign ministers combine their condemnation of Israel for its violence against the Palestinians with a call to the US to change its policy to favour 'the national rights of the Palestinians and Arabs'.

19   Paris-based *L'Express* publishes details of America's Operation 'Night Camel' to launch air and ground offensives against Iraq, resulting in the estimated deaths of 20,000 troops. Bush rejects the plan.

The deadline for adopting the annual federal budget passes without any agreement between Bush and Congress, and is extended to 24 October.

21   Former British prime minister Heath meets Saddam Hussein in Baghdad, and secures the release of 38 sick and elderly British hostages.

Saudi defence minister Prince Sultan says that 'There is no harm in an Arab country giving its sisterly Arab country anything – be it land, money or a sea inlet.' Oil price drops by an unprecedented $5 a barrel in a day.

24   UN Security Council adopts Resolution 673 by unanimous vote, calling on Israel to reconsider its refusal to accept the mission of the UN secretary-general to Israel.

Iraq's National Assembly decides to release all French hostages.

Bush reaches a compromise with US Congress on the federal budget.

25   US chairman of joint chiefs of staff General Powell returns to Washington from a tour of Saudi Arabia with a request by the commander of the US Central Command, General Schwarzkopf, to double the US troop strength of 210,000.

26   General Zvi Zamir commission's report on the 8 October Jerusalem killings absolves the Israeli police of using excessive live ammunition to control rioting by the Palestinians.

28   Following Primakov's talks with Saddam Hussein in Baghdad, President Gorbachev says that Iraq has modified its previous intransigent position on Kuwait.

29   UN Security Council adopts Resolution 674 by 13 votes to none, reminding Iraq that it is liable for any loss, damage or injury to Kuwait and third states, and their nationals and corporations resulting from its occupation of Kuwait.

Condemning the use of 103 American hostages by Iraq as human shields, Baker says, 'We will not rule out a possible use of force if Iraq continues to occupy Kuwait.'

31   Bush decides secretly to double the US troops in the Gulf to 430,000 with a plan to mount an air campaign against Iraq in mid-January. He also decides to secure a UN Security Council mandate for war against Iraq.

Bush compares the behaviour of the Iraqi troops in Kuwait to Nazi Germany's in occupied Poland.

November

2   UN secretary-general recommends that the Security Council should convene a conference of all 164 signatories to the Fourth Geneva Convention to discuss its compliance by Israel. The support for the recommendation in the Occupied Territories leads to widespread rioting, resulting in injuries to 300.

4   Baker undertakes a seven-nation tour to discuss possible military action against Iraq.

6   Mid-term elections in America lead to the loss of 9 Republican seats in the House of Representatives and one seat in the Senate to Democrats, who continue to control both houses of Congress.

8   Bush makes public his decision to double the US troops in the Gulf to 430,000.

9   Former German chancellor Brandt leaves Baghdad with 206 Western hostages, including 140 Germans, after talks with Saddam Hussein.

12   China's foreign minister, Qian Qichen, meets Saddam in Baghdad.
Israel tells the UN secretary-general that it is ready to receive a UN envoy to discuss the treatment of the Palestinians if he does not raise the question of the Jerusalem killings.

13   An initiative by King Hassan of Morocco to hold an extraordinary Arab summit to resolve the Gulf crisis fails.

15   In an interview with ABC-TV, Saddam Hussein proposes talks between Iraq and Saudi Arabia on regional problems, and between Iraq and the US on wider issues.
In an interview with CNN, Bush says that the Gulf crisis is damaging US economy and threatening jobs and economic security.
A six-day US–Saudi joint military exercise begins 100 miles south of Kuwaiti–Saudi border.

16   Baker undertakes a tour to lobby nine members of the UN Security Council to authorize use of force against Iraq.

18   Saddam Hussein decides to let all 'foreign guests' leave between 25 December and 25 March 'if nothing comes to disturb the climate of peace'.

19   Iraq mobilizes additional 250,000 troops, with 100,000 to be sent to Kuwait immediately.
Gorbachev tells Bush in Paris that the UN Security Council resolution on use of force against Iraq should be adopted only after 'more international consultations'.
Israel's prime minister Shamir vows 'to keep the land of Israel from the [Mediterranean] sea to the River Jordan for the generations to come'. Iraq's parliament condemns the statement.

21   The UN secretary-general accepts the Israeli condition for the despatch of his envoy to Israel.

21   Bush meets Shaikh Jaber al Sabah and King Fahd in Saudi Arabia.

22   On Thanksgiving Day, Bush addresses US troops in Saudi Arabia and aboard a warship in the Gulf.

Saddam Hussein visits Iraqi troops in southern Iraq and Kuwait. There are anti-US demonstrations in Iraq.

23 Bush meets President Mubarak in Cairo, and President Assad in Geneva.

27 Four-day-long televised testimonies of expert witnesses before the US Senate Armed Services Committee show a large majority favouring the economic option over the military option.

28 Saudi foreign minister Prince Saud al Faisal meets President Gorbachev and his foreign minister in Moscow, and they discuss a 'new financial co-operation agreement' between their countries. An aid package of $6 billion by Saudi Arabia, Kuwait, Qatar and the UAE for the USSR is being put together.

UN Security Council adopts Resolution 677 by unanimous vote, mandating the secretary-general to take custody of an authenticated copy of the population register of Kuwait.

John Major takes over from Thatcher as British prime minister.

29 Britain decides to resume diplomatic relations with Syria broken off in April 1986.

UN Security Council adopts Resolution 678 by 12 votes to two (Cuba and Yemen), with one abstention (China), calling on Iraq to implement all the earlier 11 resolutions, and authorizing 'all necessary means' to uphold and implement these resolutions, and 'to restore international peace and security in the area' to the states co-operating with Kuwait, unless Iraq fully implements these resolutions before 15 January 1991.

30 Bush invites Tariq Aziz to Washington for talks before 15 December, and offers to send Baker to Baghdad for talks with Saddam Hussein between 15 December and 15 January. Oil price falls $4 to $29 a barrel.

December

1 Iraq's Revolutionary Command Council accepts Bush's offer of talks.

3 Shaikh Ali ibn Muslim, a special envoy of King Fahd, goes to Algiers to see the Algerian president, who is trying to arrange a meeting between King Fahd and Saddam Hussein.

4 Baker faces critical questioning by the members of the US Senate Foreign Relations Committee for ignoring expert opinion on the economic sanctions against Iraq.

5 Barzan Tikriti, a half-brother of Saddam Hussein, accredited as the Iraqi ambassador to Switzerland, secretly meets Edgard Pisani, an adviser to President Mitterrand, in Switzerland.

Israel says it wants Saddam Hussein removed from power, otherwise it will not maintain a 'low profile'.

6 Saddam Hussein recommends to the National Assembly that all foreigners be released.

8 On the eve of the third anniversary of the Palestinian intifada, Israel imposes curfew on one million Palestinians in the Occupied Territories.

9 The US rejects Iraq's date for Baker–Saddam Hussein talks in Baghdad as too late, and names 3 January as the cut-off date.

11 During Bush–Shamir talks in Washington, Bush agrees to share US intelligence with Israel, and install a hotline between the Pentagon and the Israeli defence ministry.

13 The last of the American hostages who want to leave Iraq do so.
14 Twelve of the 14 witnesses before the US Foreign Relations Committee's two-day hearings argue against war with Iraq.
   General Powell tells the House Armed Services Committee that it 'could be as late as mid-February' before US forces have full capability for an offensive.
15 The US cancels the Aziz–Baker meeting scheduled for 17 January in Washington.
16 A Soviet delegation arrives in Baghdad to arrange for the departure of the remaining 3,232 Soviet experts, down from the original 7,000.
17 President Bush addresses the ambassadors of the 28 nations which have contributed armed forces to the US-led effort to resolve the crisis.
   Foreign ministers of Nato, meeting in Brussels, endorse UN Security Council Resolution 678.
   Foreign ministers of EC, meeting in Brussels, cancel their invitation to Tariq Aziz for talks.
18 A report by Amnesty International details brutalities by the Iraqi troops in Kuwait.
19 President Mitterrand says that if US–Iraq talks do not materialize by 3 January, France will seek direct talks with Iraq.
20 Shevardnadze resigns as Soviet foreign minister, following attacks by the hardline parliamentary group, Soyuz, on his Gulf policies.
   UN Security Council adopts Resolution 681 by unanimous vote, urging Israel to abide by the Fourth Geneva Convention, and requesting the UN secretary-general to submit a progress report on Israeli behaviour towards the Palestinians under its occupation.
23 US forces in Saudi Arabia go on a high state of alert for a week.
24 Expressing his disappointment with Resolution 681, Saddam Hussein blames Israel for pushing America towards the 'impasse' it finds itself in, and adds that if there is an attack on Iraq, we will 'assume that Israel has taken part in it', and 'we will strike at Israel'.
25 Shamir says that 'Whoever dares to strike against Israel will be struck hard and in the most severe way in return.'
   King Fahd appeals to Saddam to withdraw unconditionally from Kuwait.
   Pisani hands over to Tikriti a peace plan approved by Mitterrand, which provides for Saddam Hussein to say that he is withdrawing from Kuwait in order to prepare the way for a resolution of the Palestinian question and the restoration of the sovereignty of Lebanon, and that he is endorsing Mitterrand's 24 September peace proposals. Saddam Hussein asks Pisani to come to Baghdad, but Mitterrand wants a more explicit Iraqi response.
26 *Ha'Aretz*, an Israeli newspaper, says that 9 January has been agreed as the date for Baker's visit to Baghdad.
30 Following his meetings with Saddam Hussein in Baghdad, the Yugoslav foreign minister Budimir Loncar, acting as the Non-Aligned Movement's envoy, carries Iraqi proposals for an evacuation of Kuwait to the US. The White House describes them as 'inadequate' because of the pre-conditions. But a US state department spokesman calls them a

'serious pre-negotiation position', saying that Iraq has dropped its previous claims to Kuwaiti offshore islands and the disputed border strip.

1991

January

3   Bush offers to send Baker to Geneva for talks with Aziz between 7 and 9 January.

4   Iraq agrees to Aziz–Baker talks in Geneva on 9 January.

5   In Baghdad Saddam Hussein has a meeting with Michel Vauzelle, chairman of the French parliament's foreign affairs committee.

6   In his address on the Iraqi army day, Saddam Hussein says that the 'Mother of Battles' will be conducted under an experienced, cohesive military leadership.

7   Baker meets British foreign minister Hurd in London, and they reject the idea of extending the 15 January deadline.

PLO chairman Arafat says that if America and its allies attack Iraq, they will find Iraq and the Palestinians together 'side by side'.

9   Six-and-a-half hours of Baker–Aziz talks in Geneva fail. Baker says there is no flexibility from Iraq. Aziz says that Iraq is prepared 'for the worst'.

Algerian foreign minister Sid Ahmad Ghozali arrives in Paris saying it is 'not too late to avoid war in the Gulf'.

10   The last batch of Soviet experts in Iraq leaves.

Baker undertakes a tour of the capitals of the Arab and Western allies confirming the launching of a US-led attack on Iraq soon after the 15 January deadline.

11   US deputy secretary of state Lawrence Eagleburger arrives in Israel to urge Prime Minister Shamir not to retaliate if Israel is attacked by Iraq. Shamir refuses the advice. In turn Eagleburger rejects his request for tactical co-ordination between the Israeli military and US forces in the Gulf.

After meeting Mitterrand in Paris and EC foreign ministers in Geneva, the UN secretary-general, Pérez de Cuellar, flies to Baghdad. Saddam Hussein invites French foreign minister Dumas, and Pisani, to Baghdad.

The Third Popular Islamic Conference in Baghdad calls for a holy war if Iraq is attacked by the US-led coalition.

12   US Congress authorizes President Bush to use US military pursuant to UN Security Council Resolution 678. The vote in the Senate is 53 to 47, and in the House of Representatives 250 to 183.

Pérez de Cuellar meets Tariq Aziz in Baghdad.

In a radio broadcast President Assad appeals to Saddam Hussein to withdraw from Kuwait, and promises that if an attack is launched against Iraq after its withdrawal, then Syria will stand by Iraq and fight 'until victory'.

12–13 Anti-war demonstrations are held in all major European cities.

13   The meeting between Pérez de Cuellar and Saddam Hussein ends, with Pérez de Cuellar asking, 'Do you authorize me to tell the Security

Council that you want continuous discussions to be conducted through the secretary-general?', and Saddam Hussein replying, 'I regard this as given on the basis of your offer ... There may emerge a package as a result of continuity.'

14   Pérez de Cuellar tells Mitterrand in Paris that he was 'badly treated' by Saddam Hussein.

Mitterrand decides not to send Dumas and Pisani to Baghdad.

Iraqi parliament unanimously decides to go to war rather than withdraw from Kuwait, and gives President Saddam Hussein constitutional powers to conduct it.

Saddam Hussein orders that the Islamic credo, *Allahu Akbar* (God is Great), be inscribed on Iraq's national flag.

15   At the Security Council, facing strong American and British opposition, France withdraws its four-point peace plan, including a UN guarantee of non-aggression by the UN-led coalition forces and a promise by the Security Council to call an international conference on the Middle East at an appropriate time.

France vetoes a British resolution making a last-minute appeal to Iraq to withdraw unconditionally from Kuwait.

The US-led coalition has fielded 680,000 troops to confront, according to the Pentagon, 545,000 Iraqi troops in Kuwait and southern Iraq.

THE SECOND GULF WAR

January

16   The air campaign of the US-led coalition, codenamed Operation 'Desert Storm', begins at 23.30 GMT. It involves aerial bombing as well as the firing of Tomahawk cruise missiles from US warships.

17   EC foreign ministers, meeting in Paris, combine an appeal to Iraq to withdraw from Kuwait with an endorsement of French calls for an international peace conference on the Middle East.

Baghdad Radio broadcasts a defiant speech by Saddam Hussein.

President Gorbachev says that he was informed only an hour before the military operations began.

Large anti-US demonstrations are staged in the five member-states of the Arab Maghreb Union: Algeria, Libya, Morocco, Mauritania and Tunisia.

Turkish parliament passes the War Powers Resolution by 250 votes to 148, with 52 abstentions, allowing the government to let the US-led coalition use its military bases.

Egypt repeats its appeals to Iraq to withdraw unconditionally.

18   Twelve Iraqi Scud ground-to-ground missiles land in Tel Aviv and Haifa.

In their Friday prayers, the preachers in Saudi mosques issue a call for a holy war by Muslim and non-Muslim forces against the forces of Saddam Hussein, 'the enemy of God'.

19   Allied air sorties reach 4,000. Allied bombing of Iraq's water, fuel and electrical supplies has caused shortages in Baghdad and other cities.

Anti-war demonstrations are staged in American cities, including the largest such protest in Washington since the Vietnam War.

20 Iran calls for an emergency meeting of the 45-member Islamic Conference Organization. Only 10 members support its initiative.

Pérez de Cuellar conveys to the Iraqi ambassador at the UN ceasefire proposals by the USSR, Algeria and India, but the ambassador is unable to communicate these to Baghdad due to the allied bombing of Iraq's telecommunications systems.

Iraq shows seven captured allied airmen on television, who say that the war must be stopped.

Iraq fires eight Scuds at Riyadh and Dhahran.

Cheney says that US objective is to get Saddam Hussein out of Kuwait *and* destroy the military capability he has used to invade Kuwait and threaten other Middle Eastern nations.

21 Iran protests that the allied attacks on Iraq far exceed the UN mandate to liberate Kuwait.

Each side loses 15 aircraft in fighting.

22 Three Iraqi Scuds hit populated areas in Tel Aviv, killing three and injuring 70.

23 Germany offers Israel $170 million in humanitarian aid. Later additions raise the total to $670 million.

US confirms launching air raids against Iraq from Incirlik, Turkey.

Iraq suspends petrol sales 'temporarily', then rations it.

Total allied air sorties in the first week amount to over 12,000, and Tomahawk cruise missile firings to 216.

26 The first seven of the 135 Iraqi aircraft seek refuge in Iran.

Large anti-war demonstrations are held in American and European cities.

27 War damage creates an oil slick 35 miles long and 10 miles wide.

Iraq's RCC says that any Iraqi, Arab or Muslim taking part in 'a commando attack' against the interests of the US-led coalition members will be considered a martyr in the 'Mother of All Battles'.

28 A pro-Iraqi general strike in Morocco is backed by the government.

General Mirza Aslam Beg, military chief of staff of Pakistan, with its troops in Saudi Arabia, accuses the West of a conspiracy to undermine the Muslim world by encouraging Iraq to invade Kuwait to provide it with a justification to start a war against Iraq to destroy it.

In an interview with CNN, Saddam Hussein says that any chance of 'negotiations to end the conflict' is up to Bush.

29 Iraqi forces capture the Saudi border town of Khafji. The allies counterattack to regain it.

French defence minister Chévènement resigns, saying that the allies now aim to overthrow Saddam Hussein's regime and decimate much of Iraq.

In Moscow, President Gorbachev's spokesman repeats Soviet fears that the conflict may escalate into a broader war, and says that time may be right for a new peace initiative.

After three days of talks in Washington Baker and Alexander Bessmertnykh, the Soviet foreign minister, state that a ceasefire in the Gulf War will be possible only if Iraq follows its commitment to withdraw with

concrete steps, and add that US–USSR efforts to promote Arab–Israeli
peace will be enhanced in the aftermath of the ceasefire.

30   Israel denounces the Baker–Bessmertnykh statement. The White House
     says that there are no differences between it and the state department.
31   Tariq Aziz appeals to the Non-Aligned Movement for help to resolve the
     conflict.

February

1   The allies regain Khafji.
     Iraq's deputy prime minister, Hamadi, ends his two-day visit to Tehran
     to discuss the implementation of certain clauses of UN Security Council
     Resolution 598 pertaining to the Iran–Iraq War.
     Iran's deputy foreign minister, Vaezi, repeats that Iran will fight alongside
     Iraq if Israel joins the war.
     In his second letter to the UN secretary-general, Aziz complains that he
     has done nothing about 'the horrendous and deliberate crimes' against
     Iraq by the US-led alliance.
2   President Mubarak meets King Fahd in Riyadh. They both declare that
     their forces will not engage in combat inside Iraq.
3   Allied air missions reach a total of 41,000.
     Pope John Paul issues his most forthright condemnation of war yet.
     Half a million people march in an anti-war demonstration in Rabat,
     Morocco.
     Iran's ambassador in Pakistan states that Iran will not allow tens of
     thousands of Pakistani volunteers to cross its territory to join Iraq's
     defence forces.
4   The central committee of the Soviet Communist Party urges Gorbachev
     to take 'necessary additional steps' at the UN to end the bloodshed in
     the Gulf.
5   Bush sends a letter to President Rafsanjani saying that America has no
     plans to stay in the region for long and will leave 'as soon as the crisis
     is over'.
     UN secretary-general protests against the death of eight Jordanian truck
     drivers caused by the allied bombing of the Baghdad–Amman highway.
6   Iraq severs diplomatic relations with US, Britain, Canada, France, Italy,
     Egypt and Saudi Arabia.
     King Hussein says that the 'real purpose' of this war against 'all Arabs
     and Muslims' is to 'destroy Iraq and rearrange the area, putting it under
     foreign hegemony'.
7   US says that the Baghdad–Amman highway is a legitimate military target,
     and it is reviewing $55 million aid to Jordan.
     Allied air missions reach 49,000 in three weeks, with America responsible
     for 84% of the total. Allies claim they have destroyed 27 of Iraq's 35
     bridges. The air drop of some 14 million leaflets has induced 87 desertions
     from the Iraqi ranks.
     A London-based Kuwaiti paper publishes an Iranian peace plan. Following
     an appeal by Ayatollah Khamanei Iraq will start withdrawing from Kuwait
     while Iran tries to 'persuade' the US-led coalition forces to pull out of
     the region simultaneously. An Islamic peacekeeping force will act as a

buffer between Iraq and its enemy, and an Islamic committee will study all disputes between Iraq and Kuwait.

8 Bush says that Jordan has moved 'way over, to Saddam Hussein's camp'. Iraq says that during the previous night the allies carried out 138 air missions against non-military targets.

9 During his visit to Ankara, Turkish officials agree with Byelonogov, a Soviet deputy foreign minister, that an end must be put to 'the destruction of Iraq'.
India, a non-permanent member of the UN Security Council, urges the Council to ensure that the allies' military operations do not exceed the mandate of Resolution 678.
Hamadi arrives in Tehran saying that the Iranian peace plan is being studied seriously in Baghdad even though Iran can promise nothing more definite than trying to 'persuade' the US and its allies to leave.

10 Allied breakdown of the air missions says that 20% to 25% of the daily air sorties, totalling 2,400 to 2,800, are aimed at targets in Kuwait and southern Iraq.
In Amman, Hamadi says that Iraq is prepared to negotiate an end to the Gulf War if America is excluded from the talks.

11 Allies bomb Iraq and Kuwait in the largest land–sea–air operation to date.
UN secretary-general says he is concerned about the loss of life in the Gulf conflict.

12 In Belgrade 15 foreign ministers of the Non-Aligned Movement consider a peace plan offered jointly by Iran and India, starting with declaration of the Iraqi intention to withdraw from Kuwait and ending with an international peace conference on the Middle East. They fail to adopt it because of its linkage between the Gulf conflict and the Palestinian issue.

13 Allied bombing of an air raid shelter in the Amiriya district of Baghdad kills 1,000-plus civilians, majority of them women and children.
The White House insists that the Amiriya bunker was a military target, 'a command and control centre that fed instructions directly into the Iraqi war machine, painted and camouflaged to avoid detection'.

14 Iraq's information minister criticizes the UN secretary-general for being silent on 'the crimes of the Americans and their allies'.
North African countries, Sudan, Jordan and Iran protest at the US bombing of a civilian shelter. Jordanian Senate calls on the king to abandon neutrality so that Jordanians can join their Iraqi brethren with deeds.
Spain urges a halt to air attacks on Baghdad and an international inquiry into the Baghdad shelter bombing.
President Mubarak says that 'unfortunately, these things happen sometimes in war'. Damascus Radio blames Saddam Hussein's 'arrogance and stubbornness' for the 'catastrophe'.
UN Security Council meets behind closed doors, at the insistence of America and Britain, to review the Gulf conflict.
Kuwaiti foreign minister Shaikh Sabah al Sabah meets Gorbachev in Moscow to urge him to stay firm in his demand for the full implementation of Security Council resolutions by Iraq.

15   Iraq's RCC expresses readiness to 'deal with Security Council Resolution
     660' provided the subsequent resolutions are abrogated, the US-led
     coalition forces leave the region, Israel withdraws from the Occupied
     Arab Territories, the nationalist and Islamic forces of Kuwait are allowed
     to participate in settling the emirate's future, and those countries which
     have attacked Iraq undertake to rebuild what they have destroyed.
     Bush calls the Iraqi offer 'a cruel hoax', and calls on the Iraqi military and
     people to force Saddam Hussein to 'step aside', and then comply with the
     UN resolutions.
     Kuwait, Egypt and Saudi Arabia reject the Iraqi proposals.
     Soviet foreign minister says that Iraq's offer opens up 'a new stage in the
     development of the conflict'.
     Iraq claims it fired three of a longer-range variant of Scud, called Al Hijaara
     al Sijjil, at Israel's nuclear reactor at Dimona in the Negev desert.
17   Morocco, Tunisia, Algeria, Jordan and Iran welcome the Iraqi statement
     as a positive step along the path to a just peace in the region.
     Iraq starts pulling out its best troops from Kuwait surreptitiously, with
     the withdrawing forces setting Kuwaiti oil wells on fire.
18   In Moscow Tariq Aziz meets Gorbachev, who forwards his peace plan to
     Bush, urging confidentiality.
     In a telexed message to Gorbachev, Bush outlines minimum conditions for
     a truce: Iraq's withdrawal to happen before the ceasefire; the evacuation to
     be finished in four days; restoration and recognition of the al Sabah regime
     by Baghdad; payment of reparations to Kuwait by Iraq; and continuation
     of the UN embargo even after the Iraqi withdrawal. Britain and France
     back Bush's peace plan.
19   Italy endorses Gorbachev's peace plan.
     In an interview with an Iranian newspaper in Tehran, Hamadi says that
     in the first 26 days of the war the allied bombing killed 20,000 Iraqis and
     injured 60,000, and caused an estimated damage of $200 billion to Iraq's
     infrastructure.
     Following his meeting with Tariq Aziz in Tehran, Iran's foreign minister
     says that Aziz told him that what Iraq had described as 'conditions' for
     withdrawal were 'matters that could be addressed'.
20   King Fahd says there should be no settlement without an unconditional
     Iraqi withdrawal and Baghdad's agreement to pay reparations for the losses
     inflicted upon Saudi Arabia.
     Allied air missions reach 86,000 in five weeks.
     In Peking Hamadi is told to take 'immediate and concrete' actions to
     withdraw from Kuwait.
21   Iraq responds positively to Gorbachev's eight-point peace plan, including
     the Iraqi statement of intention to withdraw; a ceasefire; the actual
     withdrawal; the abrogation of the UN sanctions once two-thirds of the
     Iraqi forces have left, and the rest of UN resolutions once all Iraqi troops
     had departed; and the monitoring of the ceasefire by a UN force.
22   At 06.00 GMT Bush rejects the Gorbachev peace plan. He gives Saddam
     Hussein until 17.00 GMT on 23 February to accept publicly the con-
     ditions to be listed by the White House spokesman before a ceasefire
     is ordered.

At 15.45 GMT the White House press secretary, Fitzwater, lists twelve conditions, including complete withdrawal within a week; departure of all Iraqi forces from Kuwait City, facilitating the arrival of the legitimate Kuwaiti government in Kuwait City, and the release of all prisoners of war within the first two days; removal of all explosives from Kuwaiti oil installations, and providing the allies with data on all land and sea mines; and surrendering control over Kuwaiti airspace to the allies. In return the coalition forces will not attack retreating Iraqi soldiers.

At 19.00 GMT the Kremlin announces a refined six-point plan agreed by Gorbachev and Aziz, including immediate and unconditional Iraqi withdrawal; the evacuation to occur within a day of a ceasefire; the withdrawal to be completed within three weeks, with a pull-out from Kuwait City within the first four days; and abrogation of all Security Council resolutions once the withdrawal is complete.

At 20.45 GMT Iraqi government accepts the Soviet plan.

23   At 12.00 GMT Aziz says that following the acceptance of the Soviet peace plan, the Iraqi government has decided to withdraw from Kuwait immediately and unconditionally.

At 15.00 GMT, the White House dismisses the latest Soviet plan, and repeats Bush's ultimatum that Iraqi troops must start pulling out of Kuwait by 17.00 GMT.

At 15.30 GMT in a 28-minute telephone conversation Gorbachev tries to convince Bush that since 'an acceptable compromise' between the Soviet plan and his conditions was only one day away, he should postpone the ground attack on the Iraqi forces. Gorbachev fails. His telephone conversations with the leaders of Britain, France, Germany, Italy, Japan, Syria and Egypt to get them to postpone the ground fighting are equally futile.

At 16.30 GMT the UN Security Council begins a closed door session. Western ambassadors declare that they are not interested in bridging the gaps between the Soviet plan and US conditions as suggested by their Soviet counterpart.

At 18.00 GMT Bush orders Schwarzkopf to eject the Iraqis from Kuwait.

24   At 01.00 GMT the US-led coalition launches its ground offensive, codenamed Operation 'Desert Sabre', with shelling from US warships.

At 04.00 GMT allied ground troops start advancing on two axes.

Soviet Union publicly regrets the allied action.

Jordan and Iran criticize the allied ground offensive.

At the UN Security Council, Cuba, India and Yemen deplore the allied action and the failure of the Council to press for a peaceful solution.

Israel imposes total and indefinite curfew on the West Bank and Gaza, and declares the areas as 'military zones' closed to journalists.

25   Half of the 3,000 air sorties by the allies are staged to give cover to the ground forces.

At 21.30 GMT the Soviet Union presents a new peace plan.

At 22.30 GMT, accepting the Soviet plan, Iraq's RCC orders an Iraqi withdrawal from Kuwait as part of its acceptance of Resolution 660. Five minutes later a radio announcer reads a statement by Saddam

Hussein saying that the Iraqi withdrawal from Kuwait has already begun.

26 At 04.25 GMT the US rejects the latest Soviet peace initiative.

At 04.30 GMT, disputing Saddam Hussein's statement that the Iraqi forces were withdrawing, Bush says, 'His defeated forces are retreating.' He adds that nearly 30,000 Iraqi soldiers have surrendered, and advises the rest to do so.

At 08.20 Saddam Hussein announces on Baghdad Radio that Iraq is withdrawing from Kuwait in compliance with the UN Security Council Resolution 660.

At 09.15 the Soviet Union proposes a ceasefire.

At 11.50 GMT Iraqi forces are out of Kuwait City and suburbs.

At 12.00 GMT the Pentagon says that all exits for the Iraqi troops in the Kuwaiti theatre of operations are blocked. Slaughtering of the retreating Iraqis along Jahra–Basra highway, Jahra–Umm Qasr road and Umm Qasr–Nasiriyeh–Baghdad road continues until the ceasefire 40 hours later.

At 19.00 GMT the Soviet Union proposes a truce, but to no avail.

27 At 01.30 GMT the Pentagon says that Kuwaiti and Saudi troops control Kuwait City. The Kuwaiti emir declares martial law and appoints Crown Prince Saad al Sabah as martial law administrator.

At 05.30 GMT Baghdad announces that it has completed its withdrawal from Kuwait.

At 18.00 GMT the UN Security Council receives a letter from Aziz in which he accepts Resolutions 660, 662 (declaring the Iraqi annexation of Kuwait as null and void) and 674 (making Iraq responsible for war reparations), and rejecting 661, 665 and 670 (all of them concerning the UN embargo against Iraq), the rest being redundant. The five permanent members demand unconditional acceptance of all 12 resolutions.

Total allied air sorties reach 106,000 in 42 days of war.

28 At 02.00 GMT Bush delivers a victory speech to the nation, and orders a ceasefire at 05.00 GMT if Iraq puts down its arms and ends its launching of Scud missiles. He outlines four conditions before the temporary ceasefire is turned into a permanent one.

At 04.40 GMT Iraq accepts Bush's conditions for a ceasefire.

At 05.00 GMT a temporary ceasefire comes into effect after 209 days of the Gulf crisis and warfare.

Moscow welcomes the ceasefire.

AFTER THE TRUCE

March

2 The UN Security Council adopts Resolution 686 by 11 votes to one (Cuba), with three abstentions (China, India and Yemen), setting out the steps Iraq should take to consolidate the temporary ceasefire.

A revolt by Shia dissidents begins at Nasiriyeh.

3 Iraqi commanders Ahmad and Mahmoud meet Schwarzkopf and Khalid at Safwan airstrip six miles from the Kuwait–Iraq border.

4 The town of Ranya is taken over by Kurdish nationalists.

4–7 Shia rebellion spreads to other urban centres, including Basra, Najaf and Karbala.

6 In Damascus the foreign ministers of Egypt, Syria and the Gulf Co-operation Council agree to form a joint peacekeeping force to maintain post-war security in the Gulf.

7 Rafsanjani calls on Saddam Hussein to resign.

9 Reassembled government forces launch a counterattack against Shia insurgents.

13 Ayatollah Khamanei urges the Iraqi army not to fire on the people.
A three-day conference of the Joint Action Committee of Iraqi Opposition in Beirut ends with a programme to overthrow Saddam Hussein's regime.

14 Iraqi troops retake Karbala.
Kuwaiti emir Shaikh Jaber III al Sabah returns to Kuwait.
The defection of the 100,000-strong Iraqi army auxiliary force of Kurds enables the Kurdish nationalists to take over 12 major towns in a 100-mile-long arc.

15 Bush warns Saddam Hussein to desist from combat operations against Iraqi insurgents.

16 In a radio and television speech, Saddam Hussein accuses 'rancorous traitors' of spreading terror and devastation in southern towns and cities. He attributes the Kurdish uprising to infiltration of armed elements from 'the same place' (meaning Iran) as in the south.

17 Iraqi troops regain Najaf.

20 The Kuwaiti government, with seven al Sabahs running the most important ministries, resigns.

21 Kurdish nationalists control the Suleimaniya, Arbil and Dohak provinces of the Autonomous Region of Kurdistan and parts of Tamim province, including its capital, Kirkuk, altogether forming 10% of the Iraqi territory.

22 Saddam Hussein despatches Ali Hassan Majid to Mosul to reorganize the government troops in the Kurdish region.

23 Saddam Hussein makes seven major changes in the government, promoting Hamadi, a Shia, as the prime minister, and the army chief of staff, Lt-General Abbas, as the defence minister.

24 Bush says that 'We're playing no part in that [Iraqi uprising], but it shows great unrest with the rule of Saddam Hussein.'

26 King Fahd has secret talks with US national security adviser Scowcroft in Saudi Arabia.

28 Iraqi troops retake Kirkuk.

30 Kurdish exodus begins.

April

1 Kurdish leader Masud Barzani appeals to the US, Britain and France to act through the UN to save the Kurds from 'genocide and torture'.

3 UN Security Council adopts Resolution 687 by 12 votes to one (Cuba), with two abstentions (Ecuador and Yemen). A 34-paragraph document, it deals with the details of the ceasefire and war reparations, and sets

out the main condition for the complete lifting of economic sanctions against Iraq: destruction of its non-conventional weapons.

5   UN Security Council adopts Resolution 688 by 10 votes to three (Cuba, Yemen and Zimbabwe), with two abstentions (China and India), demanding that the Iraqi government end the repression of its citizens.

6   Iraq accepts Resolution 687.
    Iraq's RCC claims that the government has 'crushed all acts of sedition and sabotage in all cities of Iraq'. It offers amnesty to Kurdish rebels.

7   Kuwait's emir says that parliamentary election will be held 'next year' according to the constitution.
    The mopping-up operations by the Iraqi military under the newly appointed defence minister, Hussein Kamil Hassan Majid, accelerates the exodus of Kurds. In their hundreds of thousands they seek safety in the border areas with Turkey and Iran – away from the vengeful Iraqi troops.

9   In his meeting with Baker, Shamir sets out his conditions for participation in an international conference on Arab–Israeli conflict.

11 UN Security Council president informs the Iraqi ambassador that a ceasefire in the Gulf conflict is now in effect, with 1,400-strong UN peacekeeping force deployed to monitor it.

16 At 08.30 GMT an undeclared ceasefire between the Iraqi military and Kurdish guerrillas comes into force.
    Announcing that Resolution 688 allows them to send troops to northern Iraq and secure encampments to provide supplies to Kurdish refugees, US and Britain prepare to do so.

17 Complying with Resolution 687, Iraq provides information to the UN Security Council and the International Atomic Energy Agency about its chemical, nuclear and missile programmes.

18 An Amnesty International report details instances of scores of murders and widescale torture mainly of the Palestinians and Iraqis since the recapture of Kuwait by the allied forces on 26 February.
    A delegation of the Iraqi Kurdistan Front, led by Talabani, begins talks with the government in Baghdad.

19 Saddam Hussein deputes two Iraqi generals to meet the US commander in charge of the Operation 'Provide Comfort' to set up safe havens for the Kurdish refugees inside Iraq.

20 In the course of his shuttle diplomacy to convene an international conference on the Arab–Israeli conflict, Baker meets three representatives of the Fatah, the leading constituent of the PLO.

21 Robert Gates, the director-designate of the CIA, says, 'All possible sanctions [against Iraq] will be maintained until Saddam Hussein is gone.'

22 In his meeting with the Kuwaiti emir, Baker points out the violations of human rights in Kuwait.
    Israel decides to add more mobile homes to its Talmon-8 settlement near Ramallah as Baker prepares to meet Assad in Damascus. Baker criticizes the move.

24 Ten hours of talks between Baker and Assad fail to resolve the differences between Syria and Israel regarding an international conference.
    Talabani announces tentative agreement with the Saddam Hussein

government on Kurdish autonomy, designed to encourage the return of 1.5 million Kurdish refugees to revive some 3,800 villages that had been razed to ground by the Iraqi government over the past 17 years.

28 Petrol rationing ends in Iraq.

29 In Riyadh Prince Khalid says that Saudi history, traditions and culture weigh against substantial American presence in the Saudi kingdom.

May

4 An anti-Saddam coup attempt by Lt-General Bareq Abdullah is foiled.

5 GCC foreign ministers meet in Kuwait to discuss security arrangements in the region.

6 American forces withdraw from southern Iraq, thus ending their occupation of 16% of total Iraqi territory.

7 A delegation of the Iraqi Kurdistan Front led by Barzani begins a second round of talks in Baghdad.

8 President Mubarak says that the withdrawal of the Egyptian troops from Saudi Arabia, which had begun in April, would be completed by August.

15 About half of the 500,000 Kurdish refugees in the border area with Turkey have returned home.

17 Demonstrations in the Saudi city of Buraidah against the ban preventing two prominent religious preachers from delivering sermons which in the past have been critical of the autocratic ways of the Saudi royal family and the presence of US troops in Saudi Arabia.
Shaikh Abdul Aziz ibn Baz, the highest religious authority in Saudi Arabia, hands over a petition signed by over 100 leading religious scholars, judges and academics, demanding a consultative assembly, fully Islamic laws and a loosening of the kingdom's close ties with the West.

20 UN Security Council sets up a war damage fund to be financed by Iraq's oil revenue.

21 Cheney says that American troops will remain in Kuwait for 'several more months'.

22 King Fahd has a meeting with the Iranian foreign minister, Velayati, in Saudi Arabia.

28 Some 16,000 allied troops have created a 3,600-square-mile security zone for the Kurds.

June

12 The Security Council's sanctions committee decides that 31 countries can release more than $3.75 billion in Iraqi assets frozen in their banks following Iraq's invasion of Kuwait.

13 In Ankara Tariq Aziz's invitation to the Turkish government to send its diplomats to Baghdad is turned down.

16 Barzani returns to Kurdistan with a draft agreement for consultations with local Kurdish leaders.

17 UN Security Council adopts Resolution 699 by unanimous vote, requiring Iraq to pay the cost of eliminating its arsenal of non-conventional arms under international supervision.

July

3 Iraqi forces start shelling marshes in the south where 30,000 to 40,000 Shia rebels and their families are hiding.

14 Bush and Mitterrand threaten to order new air attacks against Iraq if Saddam Hussein persecutes Iraqi Kurds or Shias.

15 1,400 US troops leave northern Iraq to become part of a 3,000-strong multinational force to be based in southern Turkey.
UN Security Council gives Iraq until 25 July to reveal information about its nuclear, chemical and biological weapons facilities.

16 Saddam Hussein invites a team from the Arab League to prove that nothing is being concealed from the UN.

18 Following Assad's dramatic concession on the terms for attending a Middle East peace conference, Baker meets him in Damascus.

18 In a fight between the Iraqi soldiers and Kurdish guerrillas in Suleimaniya, 200 Iraqis are killed and 2,500 taken prisoner.

August

1 Israel agrees to participate in a Middle East peace conference.

15 Security Council adopts Resolution 706 by 13 to one (Cuba) and one abstention (Yemen), authorizing Iraq to sell up to $1.6 billion worth of oil in a six-month period under UN auspices. Iraq describes it as interference in its internal affairs.

20 Barzani presents a deal he has agreed with Saddam Hussein on Kurdish autonomy to his colleagues in the Iraqi Kurdistan Front.

September

13 Sadoun Hamadi is replaced as prime minister by one of his deputies, Muhammad Hamza Zubaidi.

18 As the latest UN inspection team arrives in Iraq, Bush says he is preparing to send warplanes to Saudi Arabia to press Saddam Hussein to comply with the Gulf ceasefire terms.

20 Kuwait signs a 10-year defence cooperation agreement with the US, allowing it to stockpile military supplies and conduct training exercises, as well as have access to Kuwait's ports and airfield.

24 When UN inspectors at the Iraqi Atomic Commission building in Baghdad refuse to surrender all the documents they have acquired, their vehicles are surrounded by Iraqi security men.

27 Iraq releases UN inspectors after agreement is reached to make a joint inventory of all the documents, film and videotapes before the UN inspectors can remove them from Iraq.

28 The PLO's National Council agrees to attend a Middle East peace conference.

October

4 The IAEA spokesman says that the latest inspection has revealed that it would have taken Iraq until 1995 or 1996 to acquire the ability to produce nuclear weapons at a rate of two to three a year.

APPENDIX II

Armed Forces of Iraq, Kuwait, Saudi Arabia and United States: 1990*

COUNTRY	IRAQ	KUWAIT	SAUDI ARABIA	UNITED STATES†
Total Regular Armed Forces				
(A) Active	1,000,000	20,300	67,800	2,117,900
(B) Reserves	–	–	–	1,819,300
GROUND FORCES				
(A) Regular Army				
Active	955,000	16,000	40,000	761,100
Reserves	–	–	–	1,043,000
(B) Para-military				
Active	250,000	10,500	7,000	–
Reserves	600,000	–	–	–
In Service Equipment				
Battle Tanks	5,500	245	550	15,440
Armoured Combat Vehicles	7,500	445	1,600	31,435
Major Artillery	3,500	72	475	5,725
Combat Helicopters	159‡	–	–	1,612
Aircraft	–	–	–	696
AIR FORCES				
Regular Air Force	40,000	2,200	22,000	571,000
In Service Equipment				
Combat Aircraft	689	35	189	3,921
Combat Helicopters	–	18	–	–
NAVAL FORCES				
Regular Navy	5,000	2,100	9,500	590,500
In Service Equipment				
Surface Combatants (Aircraft Carriers, Cruisers, Destroyers, and Frigates)	5 (frigates)	– –	8 (frigates)	220
Patrol and Coastal Combatants	38	23	12	30
Mine Warfare Vessels	8	–	5	29
MARINE FORCES				
Regular Marine Corps	–	–	1,500	195,300
In Service Equipment				
Battle Tanks	–	–	–	716
Armoured Combat Vehicles	–	–	140	2,025
Major Artillery	–	–	–	1,054

* Adapted from *The Military Balance 1990–1991*, International Institute of Strategic Studies, London, Autumn 1990.
† Coast Guard, a branch of the US military, is not included here.
‡ In 1985 the helicopter fleet was transferred from the Iraqi air force to the army.

APPENDIX III:

United Nations Security Council resolutions on the Gulf crisis and the Gulf War: 660, 661, 662, 664, 665, 666, 667, 669, 670, 674, 677, 678, 686, 687, 688, 689, 692, 699 and 700.

United Nations Security Council Resolution 660
2 August 1990

The Security Council,

Alarmed by the invasion of Kuwait on 2 August 1990 by the military forces of Iraq,

Determining that there exists a breach of international peace and security as regards the Iraqi invasion of Kuwait,

Acting under Articles 39 and 40 of the Charter of the United Nations,

1. Condemns the Iraqi invasion of Kuwait;
2. Demands that Iraq withdraw immediately and unconditionally all its forces to the positions in which they were located on 1 August 1990;
3. Calls upon Iraq and Kuwait to begin immediately intensive negotiations for the resolution of their differences and supports all efforts in this regard, and especially those of the League of Arab States;
4. Decides to meet again as necessary to consider further steps to ensure compliance with the present resolution.

Adopted by 14 votes to none, with one abstention (Yemen)*

United Nations Security Council Resolution 661
6 August 1990

The Security Council,

Reaffirming its resolution 660 (1990) of 2 August 1990,

Deeply concerned that the resolution has not been implemented and that the invasion by Iraq of Kuwait continues with further loss of human life and material destruction,

Determined to bring the invasion and occupation of Kuwait by Iraq to an end and to restore the sovereignty, independence and territorial integrity of Kuwait,

Noting that the legitimate Government of Kuwait has expressed its readiness to comply with resolution 660 (1990),

Mindful of its responsibilities under the Charter of the United Nations for the maintenance of international peace and security,

* Of the 15 Security Council members, five are permanent: China, France, Soviet Union, United Kingdom and United States. In 1990, the remaining members, elected by the General Assembly to serve two-year terms, were: Canada, Colombia, Cuba, Ethiopia, Finland, Ivory Coast, Malaysia, Romania, Yemen and Zaire.

Affirming the inherent right of individual or collective self-defence, in response to the armed attack by Iraq against Kuwait, in accordance with Article 51 of the Charter,

Acting under Chapter VII of the Charter of the United Nations,

1. Determines that Iraq so far has failed to comply with paragraph 2 of resolution 660 (1990) and has usurped the authority of the legitimate Government of Kuwait;

2. Decides, as a consequence, to take the following measures to secure compliance of Iraq with paragraph 2 of resolution 660 (1990) and to restore the authority of the legitimate Government of Kuwait;

3. Decides that all States shall prevent:

   (a) The import into their territories of all commodities and products originating in Iraq or Kuwait exported therefrom after the date of the present resolution;

   (b) Any activities by their nationals or in their territories which would promote or are calculated to promote the export or transshipment of any commodities or products from Iraq or Kuwait; and any dealings by their nationals or their flag vessels or in their territories in any commodities or products originating in Iraq or Kuwait and exported therefrom after the date of the present resolution, including in particular any transfer of funds to Iraq or Kuwait for the purposes of such activities or dealings;

   (c) The sale or supply by their nationals or from their territories or using their flag vessels of any commodities or products, including weapons or any other military equipment, whether or not originating in their territories but not including supplies intended strictly for medical purposes, and, in humanitarian circumstances, foodstuffs, to any person or body in Iraq or Kuwait or to any person or body for the purposes of any business carried on in or operated from Iraq or Kuwait, and any activities by their nationals or in their territories which promote or are calculated to promote such sale or supply of such commodities or products;

4. Decides that all States shall not make available to the Government of Iraq or to any commercial, industrial or public utility undertaking in Iraq or Kuwait, any funds or any other financial or economic resources and shall prevent their nationals and any persons within their territories from removing from their territories or otherwise making available to that Government or to any such undertaking any such funds or resources and from remitting any other funds to persons or bodies within Iraq or Kuwait, except payments exclusively for strictly medical or humanitarian purposes and, in humanitarian circumstances, foodstuffs;

5. Calls upon all States, including States non-members of the United Nations, to act strictly in accordance with the provisions of the present resolution notwithstanding any contract entered into or licence granted before the date of the present resolution;

6. Decides to establish, in accordance with rule 28 of the provisional rules of procedure of the Security Council, a Committee of the Security Council consisting of all the members of the Council, to undertake the following tasks and to report on its work to the Council with its observations and recommendations:

(a) To examine the reports on the progress of the implementation of the present resolution which will be submitted to the Secretary-General;

(b) To seek from all States further information regarding the action taken by them concerning the effective implementation of the provisions laid down in the present resolution;

7. Calls upon all States to co-operate fully with the Committee in the fulfilment of its task, including supplying such information as may be sought by the Committee in pursuance of the present resolution;

8. Requests the Secretary-General to provide all necessary assistance to the Committee and to make the necessary arrangements in the Secretariat for the purpose;

9. Decides that, notwithstanding paragraphs 4 through 8 above, nothing in the present resolution shall prohibit assistance to the legitimate Government of Kuwait, and calls upon all States:

(a) To take appropriate measures to protect assets of the legitimate Government of Kuwait and its agencies;

(b) Not to recognize any regime set up by the occupying Power;

10. Requests the Secretary-General to report to the Council on the progress of the implementation of the present resolution, the first report to be submitted within thirty days;

11. Decides to keep this item on its agenda and to continue its efforts to put an early end to the invasion by Iraq.

Adopted by 13 votes to none,
with two abstentions (Cuba and Yemen)

United Nations Security Council Resolution 662
9 August 1990

The Security Council,

Recalling its resolutions 660 (1990) and 661 (1990),

Gravely alarmed by the declaration by Iraq of a 'comprehensive and eternal merger' with Kuwait,

Demanding, once again, that Iraq withdraw immediately and unconditionally all its forces to positions in which they were located on 1 August 1990,

Determined to bring the occupation of Kuwait by Iraq to an end and to restore the sovereignty, independence and territorial integrity of Kuwait,

Determined also to restore the authority of the legitimate Government of Kuwait,

1. Decides that annexation of Kuwait by Iraq under any form and whatever pretext has no legal validity, and is considered null and void;

2. Calls upon all States, international organizations and specialized agencies not to recognize that annexation, and to refrain from any action or dealing that might be interpreted as an indirect recognition of the annexation;

3. Further demands that Iraq rescind its actions purporting to annex Kuwait;

4. Decides to keep this item on its agenda and to continue its efforts to put an early end to the occupation.

Adopted by unanimous vote

United Nations Security Council Resolution 664
18 August 1990

The Security Council,

Recalling the Iraqi invasion and purported annexation of Kuwait and resolutions 660, 661 and 662,

Deeply concerned for the safety and well being of third state nationals in Iraq and Kuwait,

Recalling the obligations of Iraq in this regard under international law,

Welcoming the efforts of the Secretary-General to pursue urgent consultations with the Government of Iraq following the concern and anxiety expressed by the members of the Council on 17 August 1990,

Acting under Chapter VII of the United Nations Charter,

1. Demands that Iraq permit and facilitate the immediate departure from Kuwait and Iraq of the nationals of third countries and grant immediate and continuing access of consular officials to such nationals;

2. Further demands that Iraq take no action to jeopardize the safety, security or health of such nationals;

3. Reaffirms its decision in resolution 662 (1990) that annexation of Kuwait by Iraq is null and void, and therefore demands that the Government of Iraq rescind its orders for the closure of diplomatic and consular missions in Kuwait and the withdrawal of the immunity of their personnel, and refrain from any such actions in the future;

4. Requests the Secretary-General to report to the Council on compliance with this resolution at the earliest possible time.

Adopted by unanimous vote

United Nations Security Council Resolution 665
25 August 1990

The Security Council,

Recalling its resolutions 660 (1990), 661 (1990), 662 (1990) and 664 (1990) and demanding their full and immediate implementation,

Having decided in resolution 661 (1990) to impose economic sanctions under Chapter VII of the Charter of the United Nations,

Determined to bring an end to the occupation of Kuwait by Iraq which imperils the existence of a Member State and to restore the legitimate authority, and the sovereignty, independence and territorial integrity of Kuwait which requires the speedy implementation of the above resolutions,

Deploring the loss of innocent life stemming from the Iraqi invasion of Kuwait and determined to prevent further such losses,

Gravely alarmed that Iraq continues to refuse to comply with resolutions 660 (1990), 661 (1990), 662 (1990) and 664 (1990) and in particular at the conduct of the Government of Iraq in using Iraqi flag vessels to export oil,

1. Calls upon those Member States co-operating with the Government of Kuwait which are deploying maritime forces to the area to use such measures commensurate to the specific circumstances as may be necessary under the authority of the Security Council to halt all

inward and outward maritime shipping in order to inspect and verify their cargoes and destinations and to ensure strict implementation of the provisions related to such shipping laid down in resolution 661 (1990);

2. Invites Member States accordingly to co-operate as may be necessary to ensure compliance with the provisions of resolution 661 (1990) with maximum use of political and diplomatic measures, in accordance with paragraph 1 above;

3. Requests all States to provide in accordance with the Charter such assistance as may be required by the States referred to in paragraph 1 of this resolution;

4. Further requests the States concerned to co-ordinate their actions in pursuit of the above paragraphs of this resolution using as appropriate mechanisms of the Military Staff Committee and after consultation with the Secretary-General to submit reports to the Security Council and its Committee established under resolution 661 (1990) to facilitate the monitoring of the implementation of this resolution;

5. Decides to remain actively seized of the matter.

Adopted by 13 votes to none, with two abstentions (Cuba and Yemen)

United Nations Security Council Resolution 666
13 September 1990

The Security Council,

Recalling its resolution 661 (1990), paragraphs 3 (c) and 4 of which apply, except in humanitarian circumstances, to foodstuffs,

Recognizing that circumstances may arise in which it will be necessary for foodstuffs to be supplied to the civilian population of Iraq or Kuwait in order to relieve human suffering,

Noting that in this respect the Committee established under paragraph 6 of that resolution has received communications from several Member States,

Emphasizing that it is for the Security Council, alone or acting through the Committee, to determine whether humanitarian circumstances have arisen,

Deeply concerned that Iraq has failed to comply with its obligations under Security Council resolution 664 (1990) in respect of the safety and well-being of third State nationals, and reaffirming that Iraq retains full responsibility in this regard under international humanitarian law including, where applicable, the Fourth Geneva Convention,

Acting under Chapter VII of the Charter of the United Nations,

1. Decides that in order to make the necessary determination whether or not for the purposes of paragraph 3 (c) and paragraph 4 of resolution 661 (1990) humanitarian circumstances have arisen, the Committee shall keep the situation regarding foodstuffs in Iraq and Kuwait under constant review;

2. Expects Iraq to comply with its obligations under Security Council resolution 664 (1990) in respect of third State nationals and reaffirms that Iraq remains fully responsible for their safety and well-being in accordance with international humanitarian law including, where applicable, the Fourth Geneva Convention;

3. Requests, for the purposes of paragraphs 1 and 2 of this resolution, that the Secretary-General seek urgently, and on a continuing basis, information from relevant United Nations and other appropriate humanitarian agencies and all other sources on the availability of food in Iraq and Kuwait, such information to be communicated by the Secretary-General to the Committee regularly;

4. Requests further that in seeking and supplying such information particular attention will be paid to such categories of persons who might suffer specially, such as children under 15 years of age, expectant mothers, maternity cases, the sick and the elderly;

5. Decides that if the Committee, after receiving the reports from the Secretary-General, determines that circumstances have arisen in which there is an urgent humanitarian need to supply foodstuffs to Iraq or Kuwait in order to relieve human suffering, it will report promptly to the Council its decision as to how such need should be met;

6. Directs the Committee that in formulating its decisions it should bear in mind that foodstuffs should be provided through the United Nations in co-operation with the International Committee of the Red Cross or other appropriate humanitarian agencies and distributed by them or under their supervision in order to ensure that they reach the intended beneficiaries;

7. Requests the Secretary-General to use his good offices to facilitate the delivery and distribution of foodstuffs to Kuwait and Iraq in accordance with the provisions of this and other relevant resolutions;

8. Recalls that resolution 661 (1990) does not apply to supplies intended strictly for medical purposes, but in this connection recommends that medical supplies should be exported under the strict supervision of the government of the exporting State or by appropriate humanitarian agencies.

Adopted by 13 votes to two (Cuba and Yemen)

United Nations Security Council Resolution 667
16 September 1990

The Security Council,

Reaffirming its resolutions 660 (1990), 661 (1990), 662 (1990), 664 (1990), 665 (1990) and 666 (1990),

Recalling the Vienna Conventions of 18 April 1961 on diplomatic relations and of 24 April 1963 on consular relations, to both of which Iraq is party,

Considering that the decision of Iraq to order the closure of diplomatic and consular missions in Kuwait and to withdraw the immunity and privileges of these missions and their personnel is contrary to the decisions of the Security Council, the international Conventions mentioned above and international law,

Deeply concerned that Iraq, notwithstanding the decisions of the Security Council and the provisions of the Conventions mentioned above, has committed acts of violence against diplomatic missions and their personnel in Kuwait,

Outraged at recent violations by Iraq of diplomatic premises in Kuwait and at the abduction of personnel enjoying diplomatic immunity and foreign nationals who were present in these premises,

Considering that the above actions by Iraq constitute aggressive acts and a flagrant violation of its international obligations which strike at the root of the conduct of international relations in accordance with the Charter of the United Nations,

Recalling that Iraq is fully responsible for any use of violence against foreign nationals or against any diplomatic or consular mission in Kuwait or its personnel,

Determined to ensure respect for its decisions and for Article 25 of the Charter of the United Nations,

Further considering that the grave nature of Iraq's actions, which constitute a new escalation of its violations of international law, obliges the Council not only to express its immediate reaction but also to consult urgently to take further concrete measures to ensure Iraq's compliance with the Council's resolutions,

Acting under Chapter VII of the Charter of the United Nations,

1. Strongly condemns aggressive acts perpetrated by Iraq against diplomatic premises and personnel in Kuwait, including the abduction of foreign nationals who were present in those premises;

2. Demands the immediate release of those foreign nationals as well as all nationals mentioned in resolution 664 (1990);

3. Further demands that Iraq immediately and fully comply with its international obligations under resolutions 660 (1990), 662 (1990) and 664 (1990) of the Security Council, the Vienna Conventions on diplomatic and consular relations and international law;

4. Further demands that Iraq immediately protect the safety and well-being of diplomatic and consular personnel and premises in Kuwait and in Iraq and take no action to hinder the diplomatic and consular missions in the performance of their functions, including access to their nationals and the protection of their person and interests;

5. Reminds all states that they are obliged to observe strictly resolutions 661 (1990), 662 (1990), 664 (1990), 665 (1990) and 666 (1990);

6. Decides to consult urgently to take further concrete measures as soon as possible, under Chapter VII of the Charter, in response to Iraq's continued violation of the Charter, of resolutions of the Council and of international law.

Adopted by unanimous vote

United Nations Security Council Resolution 669
24 September 1990

The Security Council,

Recalling its resolution 661 (1990) of 6 August 1990,

Recalling also Article 50 of the Charter of the United Nations,

Conscious of the fact that an increasing number of requests for assistance have been received under the provisions of Article 50 of the United Nations,

Entrusts the Committee established under resolution 661 (1990) concerning the situation between Iraq and Kuwait with the task of examining requests for assistance under the provisions of Article 50 of the Charter of the United Nations and making recommendations to the President of the Security Council for appropriate action.

Adopted by unanimous vote

United Nations Security Council Resolution 670
25 September 1990

The Security Council,

Reaffirming its resolutions 660 (1990), 661 (1990), 662 (1990), 664 (1990), 665 (1990), 666 (1990) and 667 (1990),

Condemning Iraq's continued occupation of Kuwait, its failure to rescind its actions and end its purported annexation and its holding of third State nationals against their will, in flagrant violation of resolutions 660 (1990), 662 (1990), 664 (1990) and 667 (1990) and of international humanitarian law,

Condemning further the treatment by Iraqi forces of Kuwaiti nationals, including measures to force them to leave their own country and mistreatment of persons and property in Kuwait in violation of international law,

Noting with grave concern the persistent attempts to evade the measures laid down in resolution 661 (1990),

Further noting that a number of States have limited the number of Iraqi diplomatic and consular officials in their countries and that others are planning to do so,

Determined to ensure by all necessary means the strict and complete application of the measures laid down in resolution 661 (1990),

Determined to ensure respect for its decisions and the provisions of Articles 25 and 48 of the Charter of the United Nations,

Affirming that any acts of the Government of Iraq which are contrary to the above-mentioned resolutions or to Articles 25 or 48 of the Charter of the United Nations, such as Decree No. 377 of the Revolution Command Council of Iraq of 16 September 1990, are null and void,

Reaffirming its determination to ensure compliance with Security Council resolutions by maximum use of political and diplomatic means,

Welcoming the Secretary-General's use of his good offices to advance a peaceful solution based on the relevant Security Council resolutions and noting with appreciation his continuing efforts to this end,

Underlining to the Government of Iraq that its continued failure to comply with the terms of resolutions 660 (1990), 661 (1990), 662 (1990), 664 (1990), 666 (1990) and 667 (1990) could lead to further serious action by the Council under the Charter of the United Nations, including under Chapter VII,

Recalling the provisions of Article 103 of the Charter of the United Nations,

Acting under Chapter VII of the Charter of the United Nations,

1. Calls upon all States to carry out their obligations to ensure strict and complete compliance with resolution 661 (1990) and in particular paragraphs 3, 4 and 5 thereof;

2. Confirms that resolution 661 (1990) applies to all means of transport, including aircraft;

3. Decides that all States, notwithstanding the existence of any rights or obligations conferred or imposed by any international agreement or any contract entered into or any licence or permit granted before the date of the present resolution, shall deny permission to any aircraft to take off from their territory if the aircraft would carry any cargo to or from Iraq or Kuwait other than food in humanitarian circumstances, subject to the authorization by the Council or the Committee established by resolution 661 (1990) and in accordance with resolution 666 (1990), or supplies intended strictly for medical purposes or solely for UNIIMOG [United Nations Iran–Iraq Military Observer Group];

4. Decides further that all States shall deny permission to any aircraft destined to land in Iraq or Kuwait, whatever its State of registration, to overfly its territory unless:

(a) The aircraft lands at an airfield designated by that State outside Iraq or Kuwait in order to permit its inspection to ensure that there is no cargo on board in violation of resolution 661 (1990) or the present resolution, and for this purpose the aircraft may be detained for as long as necessary; or

(b) The particular flight has been approved by the Committee established by resolution 661 (1990); or

(c) The flight is certified by the United Nations as solely for the purposes of UNIIMOG;

5. Decides that each State shall take all necessary measures to ensure that any aircraft registered in its territory or operated by an operator who has his principal place of business or permanent residence in its territory complies with the provisions of resolution 661 (1990) and the present resolution;

6. Decides further that all States shall notify in a timely fashion the Committee established by resolution 661 (1990) of any flight between its territory and Iraq or Kuwait to which the requirement to land in paragraph 4 above does not apply, and the purpose for such a flight;

7. Calls upon all States to co-operate in taking such measures as may be necessary, consistent with international law, including the Chicago Convention, to ensure the effective implementation of the provisions of resolution 661 (1990) or the present resolution;

8. Calls upon all States to detain any ships of Iraqi registry which enter their ports and which are being or have been used in violation of resolution 661 (1990), or to deny such ships entrance to their ports except in circumstances recognized under international law as necessary to safeguard human life;

9. Reminds all States of their obligations under resolution 661 (1990) with regard to the freezing of Iraqi assets, and the protection of the assets of the legitimate Government of Kuwait and its agencies, located within their territory and to report to the Committee established under resolution 661 (1990) regarding those assets;

10. Calls upon States to provide to the Committee established by resolution 661 (1990) information regarding the action taken by them to implement the provisions laid down in the present resolution;

11. Affirms that the United Nations Organization, the specialized agencies and other international organizations in the United Nations system are required to take such measures as may be necessary to give effect to the terms of resolution 661 (1990) and this resolution;

12. Decides to consider, in the event of evasion of the provisions of resolution 661 (1990) or of the present resolution by a State or its nationals or through its territory, measures directed at the State in question to prevent such evasion;

13. Reaffirms that the Fourth Geneva Convention applies to Kuwait and that as a High Contracting Party to the Convention Iraq is bound to comply fully with all its terms and in particular is liable under the Convention in respect of the grave breaches committed by it, as are individuals who commit or order the commission of grave breaches.

Adopted by 14 votes to one (Cuba)

United Nations Security Council Resolution 674
29 October 1990

The Security Council,

Recalling its resolutions 660 (1990), 661 (1990), 662 (1990), 664 (1990), 665 (1990), 666 (1990), 667 (1990) and 670 (1990),

Stressing the urgent need for the immediate and unconditional withdrawal of all Iraqi forces from Kuwait, for the restoration of Kuwait's sovereignty, independence and territorial integrity and of the authority of its legitimate government,

Condemning the actions by the Iraqi authorities and occupying forces to take third-State nationals hostage and to mistreat and oppress Kuwaiti and third-State nationals, and the other actions reported to the Security Council, such as the destruction of Kuwaiti demographic records, the forced departure of Kuwaitis, the relocation of population in Kuwait and the unlawful destruction and seizure of public and private property in Kuwait, including hospital supplies and equipment, in violation of the decisions of the Council, the Charter of the United Nations, the Fourth Geneva Convention, the Vienna Conventions on Diplomatic and Consular Relations and international law,

Expressing grave alarm over the situation of nationals of third States in Kuwait and Iraq, including the personnel of the diplomatic and consular missions of such States,

Reaffirming that the Fourth Geneva Convention applies to Kuwait and that as a High Contracting Party to the Convention Iraq is bound to comply fully with all its terms and in particular is liable under the Convention in respect of the grave breaches committed by it, as are individuals who commit or order the commission of grave breaches,

Recalling the efforts of the Secretary-General concerning the safety and well-being of third-State nationals in Iraq and Kuwait,

Deeply concerned at the economic cost and at the loss and suffering caused to individuals in Kuwait and Iraq as a result of the invasion and occupation of Kuwait by Iraq,

Acting under Chapter VII of the Charter of the United Nations,

Reaffirming the goal of the international community of maintaining international peace and security by seeking to resolve international disputes and conflicts through peaceful means,

Recalling the important role that the United Nations and its Secretary-General have played in the peaceful solution of disputes and conflicts in conformity with the provisions of the Charter,

Alarmed by the dangers of the present crisis caused by the Iraqi invasion and occupation of Kuwait, which directly threaten international peace and security, and seeking to avoid any further worsening of the situation,

Calling upon Iraq to comply with the relevant resolutions of the Security Council, in particular resolutions 660 (1990), 662 (1990) and 664 (1990),

Reaffirming its determination to ensure compliance by Iraq with Security Council resolutions by maximum use of political and diplomatic means,

A

1. Demands that the Iraqi authorities and occupying forces immediately cease and desist from taking third-State nationals hostage, mistreating and oppressing Kuwaiti and third-State nationals and any other actions, such as those reported to the Security Council and described above, that violate the decisions of the Council, the Charter of the United Nations, the Fourth Geneva Convention, the Vienna Conventions on Diplomatic and Consular Relations and international law;

2. Invites States to collate substantiated information in their possession or submitted to them on the grave breaches by Iraq as per paragraph 1 above and to make this information available to the Security Council;

3. Reaffirming its demand that Iraq immediately fulfil its obligations to third-State nationals in Kuwait and Iraq, including the personnel of diplomatic and consular missions, under the Charter, the Fourth Geneva Convention, the Vienna Conventions on Diplomatic and Consular Relations, general principles of international law and the relevant resolutions of the Council;

4. Also reaffirms its demand that Iraq permit and facilitate the immediate departure from Kuwait and Iraq of those third-State nationals, including diplomatic and consular personnel, who wish to leave;

5. Demands that Iraq ensure the immediate access to food, water and basic services necessary to the protection and well-being of Kuwaiti nationals and of nationals of third States in Kuwait and Iraq, including the personnel of diplomatic and consular missions in Kuwait;

6. Reaffirms its demand that Iraq immediately protect the safety and well-being of diplomatic and consular personnel and premises in Kuwait and in Iraq, take no action to hinder these diplomatic and consular missions in the performance of their functions, including access to their nationals and the protection of their position and interests and rescind its orders for the closure of diplomatic and consular missions in Kuwait and the withdrawal of the immunity of their personnel;

7. Requests the Secretary-General, in the context of the continued exercise of his good offices concerning the safety and well-being of third-State

nationals in Iraq and Kuwait, to seek to achieve the objective of paragraphs 4, 5 and 6 above and in particular the provision of food, water and basic services to Kuwaiti nationals and to the diplomatic and consular missions in Kuwait and the evacuation of third-State nationals;

8. Reminds Iraq that under international law it is liable for any loss, damage or injury arising in regard to Kuwait and third States, and their nationals and corporations, as a result of the invasion and illegal occupation of Kuwait by Iraq;

9. Invites States to collect relevant information regarding their claims, and those of their nationals and corporations, for restitution or financial compensation by Iraq with a view to such arrangements as may be established in accordance with international law;

10. Requires that Iraq comply with the provisions of the present resolution and its previous resolutions, failing which the Security Council will need to take further measures under the Charter;

11. Decides to remain actively and permanently seized of the matter until Kuwait has regained its independence and peace has been restored in conformity with the relevant resolutions of the Security Council.

B

12. Reposes its trust in the Secretary-General to make available his good offices and, as he considers appropriate, to pursue them and to undertake diplomatic efforts in order to reach a peaceful solution to the crisis caused by the Iraqi invasion and occupation of Kuwait on the basis of Security Council resolutions 660 (1990), 662 (1990) and 664 (1990), and calls upon all States, both those in the region and others, to pursue on this basis their efforts to this end, in conformity with the Charter, in order to improve the situation and restore peace, security and stability;

13. Requests the Secretary-General to report to the Security Council on the results of his good offices and diplomatic efforts.

Adopted by 13 votes to none, with two abstentions (Cuba and Yemen)

United Nations Security Council Resolution 677
28 November 1990

The Security Council,

Recalling its resolutions 660 (1990) of 2 August 1990, 662 (1990) of 9 August 1990 and 674 (1990) of 29 October 1990,

Reiterating its concern for the suffering caused to individuals in Kuwait as a result of the invasion and occupation of Kuwait by Iraq,

Gravely concerned at the ongoing attempt by Iraq to alter the demographic composition of the population of Kuwait and to destroy the civil records maintained by the legitimate Government of Kuwait,

Acting under Chapter VII of the Charter of the United Nations,

1. Condemns the attempts by Iraq to alter the demographic composition of

the population of Kuwait and to destroy the civil records maintained by the legitimate Government of Kuwait;

2. Mandates the Secretary-General to take custody of a copy of the population register of Kuwait, the authenticity of which has been certified by the legitimate Government of Kuwait and which covers the registration of the population up to 1 August 1990;

3. Requests the Secretary-General to establish, in co-operation with the legitimate Government of Kuwait, an Order of Rules and Regulations governing access to and use of the said copy of the population register.

Adopted by unanimous vote

United Nations Security Council Resolution 678 29 November 1990

The Security Council,

Recalling and reaffirming its resolutions 660 (1990) of 2 August 1990, 661 (1990) of 6 August 1990, 662 (1990) of 9 August 1990, 664 (1990) of 18 August 1990, 665 (1990) of 25 August 1990, 666 (1990) of 13 September 1990, 667 (1990) of 16 September 1990, 669 (1990) of 24 September 1990, 670 (1990) of 25 September 1990, 674 (1990) of 29 October 1990 and 677 (1990) of 28 November 1990,

Noting that, despite all efforts by the United Nations, Iraq refuses to comply with its obligation to implement resolution 660 (1990) and the above-mentioned subsequent resolutions, in flagrant contempt of the Security Council,

Mindful of its duties and responsibilities under the Charter of the United Nations for the maintenance and preservation of international peace and security,

Determined to secure full compliance with its decisions,

Acting under Chapter VII of the Charter,

1. Demands that Iraq comply fully with resolution 660 (1990) and all subsequent relevant resolutions, and decides, while maintaining all its decisions, to allow Iraq one final opportunity, as a pause of goodwill, to do so;

2. Authorizes Member States co-operating with the Government of Kuwait, unless Iraq on or before 15 January 1991 fully implements, as set forth in paragraph 1 above, the foregoing resolutions, to use all necessary means to uphold and implement resolution 660 (1990) and all subsequent relevant resolutions and to restore international peace and security in the area;

3. Requests all States to provide appropriate support for the actions undertaken in pursuance of paragraph 2 of the present resolution;

4. Requests the States concerned to keep the Security Council regularly informed on the progress of actions undertaken pursuant to paragraphs 2 and 3 of the present resolution;

5. Decides to remain seized of the matter.

Adopted by 12 votes to two (Cuba and Yemen), with one abstention (China)

United Nations Security Council Resolution 686
2 March 1991

The Security Council,

Recalling and reaffirming its resolutions 660 (1990), 661 (1990), 662 (1990), 664 (1990), 665 (1990), 666 (1990), 667 (1990), 669 (1990), 670 (1990), 674 (1990), 677 (1990) and 678 (1990),

Recalling the obligations of Member States under Article 25 of the Charter,

Recalling paragraph 9 of resolution 661 (1990) regarding assistance to the Government of Kuwait and paragraph 3 (c) of that resolution regarding supplies strictly for medical purposes and, in humanitarian circumstances, foodstuffs,

Taking note of the letters of the Foreign Minister of Iraq confirming Iraq's agreement to comply fully with all of the resolutions noted above (S/22275), and stating its intention to release prisoners of war immediately (S/22273),

Taking note of the suspension of offensive combat operations by the forces of Kuwait and the Member States co-operating with Kuwait pursuant to resolution 678 (1990),

Bearing in mind the need to be assured of Iraq's peaceful intentions, and the objective in resolution 678 (1990) of restoring international peace and security in the region,

Underlining the importance of Iraq taking the necessary measures which would permit a definitive end to the hostilities,

Affirming the commitment of all Member States to the independence, sovereignty and territorial integrity of Iraq and Kuwait, and noting the intention expressed by the Member States co-operating under paragraph 2 of Security Council resolution 678 (1990) to bring their military presence in Iraq to an end as soon as possible consistent with achieving the objectives of the resolution,

Acting under Chapter VII of the Charter,

1. Affirms that all twelve resolutions noted above continue to have full force and effect;

2. Demands that Iraq implement its acceptance of all twelve resolutions noted above and in particular that Iraq:

(a) Rescind immediately its actions purporting to annex Kuwait;

(b) Accept in principle its liability under international law for loss, damage, or injury arising in regard to Kuwait and third States, and their nationals and corporations, as a result of the invasion and illegal occupation of Kuwait by Iraq;

(c) Immediately release under the auspices of the International Committee of the Red Cross, Red Cross Societies, or Red Crescent Societies, all Kuwaiti and third country nationals detained by Iraq and return the remains of any deceased Kuwaiti and third country nationals so detained; and

(d) Immediately begin to return all Kuwaiti property seized by Iraq, to be completed in the shortest possible period;

3. Further demands that Iraq:

(a) Cease hostile or provocative actions by its forces against all Member States, including missile attacks and flights of combat aircraft;

(b) Designate military commanders to meet with counterparts from the forces of Kuwait and the Member States co-operating with Kuwait pursuant to resolution 678 (1990) to arrange for the military aspects of a cessation of hostilities at the earliest possible time;

(c) Arrange for immediate access to and release of all prisoners of war under the auspices of the International Committee of the Red Cross and return the remains of any deceased personnel of the forces of Kuwait and the Member States co-operating with Kuwait pursuant to resolution 678 (1990); and

(d) Provide all information and assistance in identifying Iraqi mines, booby traps and other explosives as well as any chemical and biological weapons and material in Kuwait, in areas of Iraq where forces of Member States co-operating with Kuwait pursuant to resolution 678 (1990) are present temporarily, and in the adjacent waters;

4. Recognizes that during the period required for Iraq to comply with paragraphs 2 and 3 above, the provisions of paragraph 2 of resolution 678 (1990) remain valid;

5. Welcomes the decision of Kuwait and the Member States co-operating with Kuwait pursuant to resolution 678 (1990) to provide access and to commence immediately the release of Iraqi prisoners of war as required by the terms of the Third Geneva Convention of 1949, under the auspices of the International Committee of the Red Cross;

6. Requests all Member States, as well as the United Nations, the specialized agencies and other international organizations in the United Nations system, to take all appropriate action with the Government and people of Kuwait in the reconstruction of their country;

7. Decides that Iraq shall notify the Secretary-General and the Security Council when it has taken the actions set out above;

8. Decides that in order to secure the rapid establishment of a definitive end to the hostilities, the Security Council remains actively seized of the matter.

Adopted by 11 votes to one (Cuba),
with three abstentions (China,
India and Yemen)*

United Nations Security Council Resolution 687
3 April 1991

The Security Council,

Recalling its resolutions 660 (1990), 661 (1990), 662 (1990), 664 (1990), 665 (1990), 666 (1990), 667 (1990), 669 (1990), 670 (1990), 674 (1990), 677 (1990), 678 (1990) and 686 (1990),

Welcoming the restoration to Kuwait of its sovereignty, independence and territorial integrity and the return of its legitimate government,

Affirming the commitment of all Member States to the sovereignty, territorial integrity and political independence of Kuwait and Iraq, and

---

* Beginning 1 January 1991 the non-permanent members of the Security Council were: Austria, Belgium, Cuba, Ecuador, Ivory Coast, India, Romania, Yemen, Zaire and Zimbabwe.

noting the intention expressed by the Member States co-operating with Kuwait under paragraph 2 of resolution 678 (1990) to bring their military presence in Iraq to an end as soon as possible consistent with paragraph 8 of resolution 686 (1991),

Reaffirming the need to be assured of Iraq's peaceful intentions in light of its unlawful invasion and occupation of Kuwait,

Taking note of the letter sent by the Foreign Minister of Iraq on 27 February 1991 (S/22275) and those sent pursuant to resolution 686 (1990) (S/22273, S/22276, S/22320, S/22321, and S/22330),

Noting that Iraq and Kuwait, as independent sovereign States, signed at Baghdad on 4 October 1963 'Agreed Minutes Regarding the Restoration of Friendly Relations, Recognition and Related Matters', thereby recognizing formally the boundary between Iraq and Kuwait and the allocation of islands, which were registered with the United Nations in accordance with Article 102 of the Charter and in which Iraq recognized the independence and complete sovereignty of the State of Kuwait within its borders as specified and accepted in the letter of the Prime Minister of Iraq dated 21 July 1932, and as accepted by the Ruler of Kuwait in his letter dated 10 August 1932,

Conscious of the need for demarcation of the said boundary,

Conscious also of the statements by Iraq threatening to use weapons in violation of its obligations under the Geneva Protocol for the prohibition of the Use in War of Asphyxiating, Poisonous or Other Gases, and of Bacteriological Methods of Warfare, signed at Geneva on 17 June 1925, and of its prior use of chemical weapons and affirming that grave consequences would follow any further use by Iraq of such weapons,

Recalling that Iraq has subscribed to the Declaration adopted by all States participating in the Conference of States Parties to the 1925 Geneva Protocol and Other Interested States, held at Paris from 7 to 11 January 1989, establishing the objective of universal elimination of chemical and biological weapons,

Recalling further that Iraq has signed the Convention on the Prohibition of the Development, Production and Stockpiling of Bacteriological (Biological) and Toxin Weapons and on Their Destruction, of 10 April 1972,

Noting the importance of Iraq ratifying this Convention,

Noting moreover the importance of all States adhering to this Convention and encouraging its forthcoming Review Conference to reinforce the authority, efficiency and universal scope of the convention,

Stressing the importance of an early conclusion by the Conference on Disarmament of its work on a Convention on the Universal Prohibition of Chemical Weapons and of universal adherence thereto,

Aware of the use by Iraq of ballistic missiles in unprovoked attacks and therefore of the need to take specific measures in regard to such missiles located in Iraq,

Concerned by the reports in the hands of Member States that Iraq has attempted to acquire materials for a nuclear-weapons programme contrary to its obligations under the treaty on the Non-Proliferation of Nuclear Weapons of 1 July 1968,

Recalling the objective of the establishment of a nuclear-weapons-free zone in the region of the Middle East,

Conscious of the threat which all weapons of mass destruction pose to peace and security in the area and of the need to work towards the establishment in the Middle East of a zone free of such weapons,

Conscious also of the objective of achieving balanced and comprehensive control of armaments in the region,

Conscious further of the importance of achieving the objectives noted above using all available means, including a dialogue among the states of the region,

Noting that resolution 686 (1991) marked the lifting of the measures imposed by resolution 661 (1990) in so far as they applied to Kuwait,

Noting that despite the progress being made in fulfilling the obligations of resolution 686 (1991), many Kuwaiti and third country nationals are still not accounted for and property remains unreturned,

Recalling the International Convention against the taking of hostages, opened for signature at New York on 18 December 1979, which categorizes all acts of taking hostages as manifestations of international terrorism,

Deploring threats made by Iraq during the recent conflict to make use of terrorism against targets outside Iraq and the taking of hostages by Iraq,

Taking note with grave concern of the reports of the Secretary-General of 20 March 1991 (S/22366) and 28 March 1991 (S/22409), and conscious of the necessity to meet urgently the humanitarian needs in Kuwait and Iraq,

Bearing in mind its objective of restoring international peace and security in the area as set out in recent Council resolutions,

Conscious of the need to take the following measures acting under Chapter VII of the Charter,

1. Affirms all thirteen resolutions noted above, except as expressly changed below to achieve the goals of this resolution, including a formal cease-fire;

A

2. Demands that Iraq and Kuwait respect the inviolability of the international boundary and the allocation of islands set out in the 'Agreed Minutes Between the State of Kuwait and the Republic of Iraq Regarding the Restoration of Friendly Relations, Recognition and Related Matters', signed by them in the exercise of their sovereignty at Baghdad on 4 October 1963 and registered with the United Nations and published by the United Nations in document 7063, United Nations Treaty Series, 1964;

3. Calls on the Secretary-General to lend his assistance to make arrangements with Iraq and Kuwait to demarcate the boundary between Iraq and Kuwait, drawing on appropriate material including the map transmitted by Security Council document S/22412 and to report back to the Security Council within one month;

4. Decides to guarantee the inviolability of the above-mentioned international boundary and to take as appropriate all necessary measures to that end in accordance with the Charter;

B

5. Requests the Secretary-General, after consulting with Iraq and Kuwait,

to submit within three days to the Security Council for its approval a plan for the immediate deployment of a United Nations observer unit to monitor the Khor Abdullah and a demilitarized zone, 10 kilometres into Iraq and 5 kilometres into Kuwait from the boundary referred to in the 'Agreed Minutes Between the State of Kuwait and the Republic of Iraq Regarding the Restoration of Friendly Relations, Recognition and Related Matters' of 4 October 1963; to deter violations of the boundary through its presence in and surveillance of the demilitarized zone; to observe any hostile or potentially hostile action mounted from the territory of one State to the other; and for the Secretary-General to report regularly to the Council on the operations of the unit, and immediately if there are any serious violations of the zone or potential threats to peace;

6. Notes that as soon as the Secretary-General notifies the Council of the completion of the deployment of the United Nations observer unit, the conditions will be established for the Member States co-operating with Kuwait in accordance with resolution 678 (1990) to bring their military presence in Iraq to an end consistent with resolution 686 (1991);

C

7. Invites Iraq to reaffirm unconditionally its obligations under the Geneva Protocol for the Prohibition of the Use in War of Asphyxiating, Poisonous or Other Gases, and of Bacteriological Methods of Warfare, signed at Geneva on 17 June 1925, and to ratify the Convention on the Prohibition of the Development, Production, and Stockpiling of Bacteriological (Biological) and Toxin Weapons and on Their Destruction, of 10 April 1972;

8. Decides that Iraq shall unconditionally accept the destruction, removal, or rendering harmless, under international supervision, of:
   (a) all chemical and biological weapons and all stocks of agents and all related subsystems and components and all research, development, support and manufacturing facilities;
   (b) all ballistic missiles with a range greater than 150 kilometres and related major parts, and repair and production facilities;

9. Decides for the implementation of paragraph 8 above, the following:
   (a) Iraq shall submit to the Secretary-General, within fifteen days of the adoption of this resolution, a declaration of the locations, amounts and types of all items specified in paragraph 8 and agree to urgent, on-site inspection as specified below;
   (b) the Secretary-General, in consultation with the appropriate Governments and, where appropriate, with the Director-General of the World Health Organization (WHO), within 45 days of the passage of this resolution, shall develop, and submit to the Council for approval, a plan calling for the completion of the following acts within 45 days of such approval:
   (i) the forming of a Special Commission, which shall carry out immediate on-site inspection of Iraq's biological, chemical and missile capabilities, based on Iraq's declarations and the designation of any additional locations by the Special Commission itself;
   (ii) the yielding by Iraq of possession to the Special Commission for

destruction, removal or rendering harmless, taking into account the requirements of public safety, of all items specified under paragraph 8 (a) above including items at the additional locations designated by the Special Commission under paragraph 9 (b) (i) above and the destruction by Iraq, under supervision of the Special Commission, of all its missile capabilities including launchers as specified under paragraph 8 (b) above;

(iii) the provision by the Special Commission of the assistance and co-operation to the Director-General of the International Atomic Energy Agency (IAEA) required in paragraphs 12 and 13 below;

10. Decides that Iraq shall unconditionally undertake not to use, develop, construct or acquire any of the items specified in paragraphs 8 and 9 above and requests the Secretary-General, in consultation with the Special Commission, to develop a plan for the future ongoing monitoring and verification of Iraq's compliance with this paragraph, to be submitted to the Council for approval within 120 days of the passage of this resolution;

11. Invites Iraq to reaffirm unconditionally its obligations under the treaty on the Non-Proliferation of Nuclear Weapons, of 1 July 1968;

12. Decides that Iraq shall unconditionally agree not to acquire or develop nuclear weapons or nuclear-weapons-usable material or any subsystems or components or any research, development, support or manufacturing facilities related to the above; to submit to the Secretary-General and the Director-General of the International Atomic Energy Agency (IAEA) within 15 days of the adoption of this resolution a declaration of the locations, amounts and types of all items specified above; to place all of its nuclear-weapons-usable material under the exclusive control, for custody and removal, of the IAEA, with the assistance and co-operation of the Special Commission as provided for in the plan of the Secretary-General discussed in paragraph 9 (b) above; to accept in accordance with the arrangements provided for in paragraph 13 below, urgent on-site inspection and the destruction, removal and rendering harmless as appropriate of all items specified above; and to accept the plan as discussed in paragraph 13 below for the future ongoing monitoring and verification of its compliance with these undertakings;

13. Requests the Director-General of the International Atomic Energy Agency (IAEA) through the Secretary-General, with the assistance and co-operation of the Special Commission as provided for in the plan of the Secretary-General in paragraph 9 (b) above, to carry out immediate on-site inspection of Iraq's nuclear capabilities based on Iraq's declarations and the designation of any additional locations by the Special Commission; to develop a plan for submission to the Security Council within 45 days calling for the destruction, removal, or rendering harmless as appropriate of all items listed in paragraph 12 above; to carry out the plan within 45 days following approval by the Security Council; and to develop a plan, taking into account the rights and obligations of Iraq under the Treaty on the Non-Proliferation of Nuclear Weapons, of 1 July 1968, for the future ongoing monitoring and verification of Iraq's compliance with paragraph 12 above, including an inventory of all nuclear material in Iraq subject to the Agency's verification and inspections to confirm

that IAEA safeguards cover all relevant nuclear activities in Iraq, to be submitted to the Council for approval within 120 days of the passage of this resolution;

14. Takes note that the actions to be taken by Iraq in paragraphs 8, 9, 10, 11, 12 and 13 of this resolution represent steps towards the goal of establishing in the Middle East a zone free from weapons of mass destruction and all missiles for their delivery and the objective of a global ban on chemical weapons;

D

15. Requests the Secretary-General to report to the Security Council on the steps taken to facilitate the return of all Kuwaiti property seized by Iraq, including a list of any property which Kuwait claims has not been returned or which has not been returned intact;

E

16. Reaffirms that Iraq, without prejudice to the debts and obligation of Iraq arising prior to 2 August 1990, which will be addressed through the normal mechanisms, is liable under international law for any direct loss, damage, including environmental damage and the depletion of natural resources, or injury to foreign Governments, nationals and corporations, as a result of Iraq's unlawful invasion and occupation of Kuwait;

17. Decides that all Iraqi statements made since 2 August 1990, repudiating its foreign debt are null and void, and demands that Iraq scrupulously adhere to all of its obligations concerning servicing and repayment of its foreign debt;

18. Decides to create a Fund to pay compensation for claims that fall within paragraph 16 above and to establish a Commission that will administer the Fund;

19. Directs the Secretary-General to develop and present to the Council for decision, no later than 30 days following the adoption of this resolution, recommendations for the Fund to meet the requirement for the payment of claims established in accordance with paragraph 18 above and for a programme to implement the decisions in paragraphs 16, 17, and 18 above, including: administration of the Fund; mechanisms for determining the appropriate level for Iraq's contribution to the Fund based on a percentage of the value of the exports of petroleum and petroleum products from Iraq not to exceed a figure to be suggested to the Council by the Secretary-General, taking into account the requirement of the people of Iraq, Iraq's payment capacity as assessed in conjunction with the international financial institutions taking into consideration external debt service, and the needs of the Iraqi economy; arrangements for ensuring that payments are made to the Fund; the process by which funds will be allocated and claims paid; appropriate procedures for evaluating losses, listing claims and verifying their validity and resolving disputed claims in respect of Iraq's liability as specified in paragraph 16 above; and the composition of the Commission designated above;

F

20. Decides, effective immediately, that the prohibitions against the sale or supply to Iraq of commodities or products, other than medicine and health supplies, and prohibitions against financial transactions related thereto, contained in resolution 661 (1990) shall not apply to foodstuffs notified to the Committee established by resolution 661 (1990) or, with the approval of that Committee, under the simplified and accelerated 'no-objection' procedure, to materials and supplies for essential civilian needs as identified in the report of the Secretary-General dated 20 March 1991 (S/22366), and in any further findings of humanitarian need by the Committee;

21. Decides that the Council shall review the provisions of paragraph 20 above every sixty days in light of the policies and practices of the Government of Iraq, including the implementation of all relevant resolutions of the Security Council, for the purposes of determining whether to reduce or lift the prohibitions referred to therein;

22. Decides that upon the approval by the Council of the programme called for in paragraph 19 above and upon Council agreement that Iraq has completed all actions contemplated in paragraphs 8, 9, 10, 11, 12, and 13 above, the prohibitions against the import of commodities and products originating in Iraq and the prohibitions against financial transactions related thereto contained in resolution 661 (1990) shall have no further force or effect;

23. Decides that, pending action by the Council under paragraph 22 above, the Committee established by resolution 661 (1990) shall be empowered to approve, when required to assure adequate financial resources on the part of Iraq to carry out the activities under paragraph 20 above, exceptions to the prohibition against the import of commodities and products originating in Iraq;

24. Decides that, in accordance with resolution 661 (1990) and subsequent related resolutions and until a further decision is taken by the Council, all States shall continue to prevent the sale or supply, or promotion or facilitation of such sale or supply, to Iraq by their nationals, or from their territories or using their flag vessels or aircraft, of:

(a) arms and related material of all types, specifically including conventional military equipment, including for paramilitary forces, and spare parts and components and their means of production, for such equipment;

(b) items specified and defined in paragraph 8 and paragraph 12 above not otherwise covered above;

(c) technology under licensing or other transfer arrangements used in production, utilization or stockpiling of items specified in subparagraphs (a) and (b) above;

(d) personnel or materials for training or technical support services relating to the design, development, manufacture, use, maintenance or support of items specified in subparagraphs (a) and (b) above;

25. Calls upon all States and international organizations to act strictly in

accordance with paragraph 24 above, notwithstanding the existence of any contracts, agreements, licences, or any other arrangements;

26. Requests the Secretary-General, in consultation with appropriate Governments, to develop within sixty days, for approval of the Council, guidelines to facilitate full international implementation of paragraphs 24 and 25 above and paragraph 27 below, and to make them available to all States and to establish a procedure for updating these guidelines periodically;

27. Calls upon all States to maintain such national controls and procedures and to take such other actions consistent with the guidelines to be established by the Security Council under paragraph 26 above as may be necessary to ensure compliance with the terms of paragraph 24 above, and calls upon international organizations to take all appropriate steps to assist in ensuring such full compliance;

28. Agrees to review its decisions in paragraphs 22, 23, 24, and 25 above, except for the items specified and defined in paragraphs 8 and 12 above, on a regular basis and in any case 120 days following passage of this resolution, taking into account Iraq's compliance with this resolution and general progress towards the control of armaments in the region;

29. Decides that all States, including Iraq, shall take the necessary measures to ensure that no claim shall lie at the instance of the Government of Iraq, or of any person or body in Iraq, or of any person claiming through or for the benefit of any such person or body, in connection with any contract or other transaction where its performance was affected by reason of the measures taken by the Security Council in resolution 661 (1990) and related resolutions;

G

30. Decides that, in furtherance of its commitment to facilitate the repatriation of all Kuwaiti and third country nationals, Iraq shall extend all necessary co-operation to the International Committee of the Red Cross, providing lists of such persons, facilitating the access of the International Committee of the Red Cross to all such persons wherever located or detained and facilitating the search by the International Committee of the Red Cross for those Kuwaiti and third country nationals still unaccounted for;

31. Invites the International Committee of the Red Cross to keep the Secretary-General apprised as appropriate of all activities undertaken in connection with facilitating the repatriation or return of all Kuwaiti and third country nationals or their remains present in Iraq on or after 2 August 1990;

H

32. Requires Iraq to inform the Council that it will not commit or support any act of international terrorism or allow any organization directed towards commission of such acts to operate within its territory and to condemn unequivocally and renounce all acts, methods, and practices of terrorism;

I

33. Declares that, upon official notification by Iraq to the Secretary-General and to the Security Council of its acceptance of the provisions above, a formal cease-fire is effective between Iraq and Kuwait and the Member States co-operating with Kuwait in accordance with resolution 678 (1990);

34. Decides to remain seized of the matter and to take such further steps as may be required for the implementation of this resolution and to secure peace and security in the area.

Adopted by 12 votes to one (Cuba),
with two abstentions (Ecuador and Yemen)

United Nations Security Council Resolution 688
5 April 1991

The Security Council,

Mindful of its duties and responsibilities under the Charter of the United Nations for the maintenance of international peace and security,

Recalling Article 2, paragraph 7, of the Charter of the United Nations,

Gravely concerned by the repression of the Iraqi civilian population in many parts of Iraq, including most recently in Kurdish populated areas which led to a massive flow of refugees towards and across international frontiers and to cross border incursions, which threaten international peace and security in the region,

Deeply disturbed by the magnitude of the human suffering involved,

Taking note of the letters sent by the representatives of Turkey and France to the United Nations dated 2 April 1991 and 4 April 1991, respectively (S/22435 and S/22442),

Taking note also of the letters sent by the Permanent Representative of the Islamic Republic of Iran to the United Nations dated 3 and 4 April 1991, respectively (S/22436 and S/22447),

Reaffirming the commitment of all Member States to the sovereignty, territorial integrity and political independence of Iraq and of all States in the area,

Bearing in mind the Secretary-General's report of 20 March 1991 (S/22366),

1. Condemns the repression of the Iraqi civilian population in many parts of Iraq, including most recently in Kurdish populated areas, the consequences of which threaten international peace and security in the region;

2. Demands that Iraq, as a contribution to removing the threat to international peace and security in the region, immediately end this repression and expresses the hope in the same context that an open dialogue will take place to ensure that the human and political rights of all Iraqi citizens are respected;

3. Insists that Iraq allow immediate access by international humanitarian organizations to all those in need of assistance in all parts of Iraq and to make available all necessary facilities for their operations;

4. Requests the Secretary-General to pursue his humanitarian efforts in Iraq and to report forthwith, if appropriate on the basis of a further mission to the region, on the plight of the Iraqi civilian population, and in particular the Kurdish population, suffering from the repression in all its forms inflicted by the Iraqi authorities;
5. Requests further the Secretary-General to use all the resources at his disposal, including those of the relevant United Nations agencies, to address urgently the critical needs of the refugees and displaced Iraqi population;
6. Appeals to all Member States and to all humanitarian organizations to contribute to these humanitarian relief efforts;
7. Demands that Iraq co-operate with the Secretary-General to these ends;
8. Decides to remain seized of the matter.

> *Adopted by 10 votes to three (Cuba,*
> *Yemen and Zimbabwe), with two*
> *abstentions (China and India)*

United Nations Security Council Resolution 689
9 April 1991

The Security Council,
   Recalling its resolution 687 (1991),
   Acting under Chapter VII of the Charter of the United Nations,
1. Approves the report of the Secretary-General on the implementation of paragraph 5 of Security Council resolution 687 (1991) contained in document S/22454 and Add. 1–3 of 5 and 9 April 1991, respectively;
2. Notes that the decision to set up the observer unit was taken in paragraph 5 of resolution 687 (1991) and can only be terminated by a decision of the Council; the Council shall therefore review the question of termination or continuation every six months;
3. Decides that the modalities for the initial six-month period of the United Nations Iraq–Kuwait Observation Mission shall be in accordance with the above-mentioned report and shall also be reviewed every six months.

> *Adopted by unanimous vote*

United Nations Security Council Resolution 692
20 May 1991

The Security Council,
   Recalling its resolutions 674 (1990), 686 (1990) and 687 (1991), concerning the liability of Iraq, without prejudice to its debts and obligations arising prior to 2 August 1990, for any direct loss, damage, including environmental damage and the depletion of natural resources, or injury to foreign Governments, nationals and corporations, as a result of Iraq's unlawful invasion and occupation of Kuwait,

Noting the Secretary-General's report of 2 May 1991 (S/22559), submitted in accordance with paragraph 19 of resolution 687 (1991),

Acting under Chapter VII of the Charter,

1. Expresses its appreciation to the Secretary-General for his report of 2 May 1991 (S/22559);

2. Welcomes the fact that the Secretary-General will now undertake the appropriate consultations requested by paragraph 19 of 687 so that he will be in a position to recommend to the Security Council for decision as soon as possible the figure which the level of Iraq's contribution to the Fund will not exceed;

3. Decides to establish the Fund and Commission referred to in paragraph 18 of resolution 687 (1991) in accordance with Part I of the Secretary-General's report and that the Governing Council shall be located at the Offices of the United Nations in Geneva and that the Governing Council may decide whether some of the activities of the Commission shall be carried out elsewhere;

4. Requests the Secretary-General to take the action necessary to implement paragraphs 2 and 3 above in consultation with the members of the Governing Council;

5. Directs the Governing Council to proceed in an expeditious manner to implement the provisions of Section E of resolution 687 (1991), taking into account the recommendations in Part II of the Secretary-General's report;

6. Decides that the requirement for Iraqi contributions shall apply in the manner to be prescribed by the Governing Council with respect to all Iraqi petroleum and petroleum products exported from Iraq after 3 April 1991 as well as petroleum and petroleum products exported earlier but not delivered or not paid as a specific result of the prohibitions contained in resolution 661 (1990);

7. Requests the Governing Council to report as soon as possible on the actions it has taken with regard to the mechanisms for determining the appropriate level of Iraq's contribution to the Fund and the arrangements for ensuring that payments are made to the Fund, so that the Security Council can give its approval in accordance with paragraph 22 of resolution 687 (1991);

8. Requests that all States and international organizations co-operate with the decisions of the Governing Council taken pursuant to paragraph 5 of this resolution and further requests that the Governing Council keep the Security Council informed on this matter;

9. Decides that if the Governing Council notifies the Security Council that Iraq has failed to carry out decisions of the Governing Council taken pursuant to paragraph 5 of this resolution, the Security Council intends to retain or to take action to reimpose the prohibition against the import of petroleum and petroleum products originating in Iraq and financial transactions related thereto;

10. Decides to remain seized of this matter and that the Governing Council will submit periodic reports to the Secretary-General and the Security Council.

Adopted by 14 votes to none, with
one abstention (Cuba)

United Nations Security Council Resolution 699
17 June 1991

The Security Council,

Recalling its resolution 687 (1991),

Taking note of the report of the Secretary-General of 17 May 1991 (S/22614), submitted to it in pursuance of paragraph 9 (b) of resolution 687 (1991),

Also taking note of the Secretary-General's note of 17 May 1991 (S/22615), transmitting to the Council the letter to him under paragraph 13 of the resolution by the Director-General of the International Atomic Energy Agency (IAEA),

Acting under Chapter VII of the Charter,

1. Approves the plan contained in the report of the Secretary-General;
2. Confirms that the Special Commission and the IAEA have the authority to conduct activities under section C of resolution 687 (1991), for the purpose of the destruction, removal or rendering harmless of the items specified in paragraphs 8 and 12 of that resolution, after the 45-day period following the approval of this plan until such activities have been completed;
3. Requests the Secretary-General to submit to the Security Council progress reports on the implementation of the plan referred to in paragraph 1 every six months after the adoption of this resolution;
4. Decides to encourage the maximum assistance, in cash and in kind, from all Member States to ensure that activities under section C of resolution 687 (1991) are undertaken effectively and expeditiously; further decides, however, that the Government of Iraq shall be liable for the full costs of carrying out the tasks authorized by section C; and requests the Secretary-General to submit to the Council within 30 days for approval recommendations as to the most effective means by which Iraq's obligations in this respect may be fulfilled.

Adopted by unanimous vote

United Nations Security Council Resolution 700
17 June 1991

The Security Council,

Recalling its resolutions 661 (1990) of 6 August 1990, 665 (1990) of 25 August 1990, 670 (1990) of 25 September 1990 and 687 (1991) of 3 April 1991,

Taking note of the Secretary-General's report of 2 June 1991 (S/22660) submitted pursuant to paragraph 26 of resolution 687 (1991),

Acting under Chapter VII of the Charter of the United Nations,

1. Expresses its appreciation to the Secretary-General for his report of 2 June 1991 (S/22660);
2. Approves the Guidelines to Facilitate Full International Implementation of paragraphs 24, 25 and 27 of Security Council resolution 687 (1991), annexed to the report of the Secretary-General (S/22660);
3. Reiterates its call upon all States and international organizations to act in a manner consistent with the Guidelines;

4. Requests all States, in accordance with paragraph 8 of the Guidelines, to report to the Secretary-General within 45 days on the measures they have instituted for meeting the obligations set out in paragraph 24 of resolution 687 (1991);

5. Entrusts the Committee established under resolution 661 (1990) concerning the situation between Iraq and Kuwait with the responsibility, under the Guidelines, for monitoring the prohibitions against the sale or supply of arms to Iraq and related sanctions established in paragraph 24 of resolution 687 (1991);

6. Decides to remain seized of the matter and to review the Guidelines at the same time as it reviews paragraphs 22, 23, 24 and 25 of resolution 687 (1991) as set out in paragraph 28 thereof.

Adopted by unanimous vote

APPENDIX IV

Important United Nations Security Council Resolutions on the Palestinian issue: 242, 338, 465, 476, 478, 672, 673 and 681

United Nations Security Council Resolution 242
22 November 1967

The Security Council,

Expressing its continuing concern with the grave situation in the Middle East,

Emphasizing the inadmissibility of the acquisition of territory by war and the need to work for a just and lasting peace in which every State in the area can live in security,

Emphasizing further that all Member States in their acceptance of the Charter of the United Nations have undertaken a commitment to act in accordance with Article 2 of the Charter,

1. Affirms that the fulfilment of Charter principles requires the establishment of a just and lasting peace in the Middle East which should include the application of both the following principles:

   (i) Withdrawal of Israel armed forces from territories occupied in the recent conflict;

   (ii) Termination of all claims or states of belligerency and respect for and acknowledgement of the sovereignty, territorial integrity and political independence of every State in the area and their right to live in peace within secure and recognized borders free from threats or acts of force;

2. Affirms further the necessity

   (a) For guaranteeing freedom of navigation through international waterways in the area;

   (b) For achieving a just settlement of the refugee problem;

   (c) For guaranteeing the territorial inviolability and political independence of every State in the area, through measures including the establishment of demilitarized zones;

3. Requests the Secretary-General to designate a Special Representative to proceed to the Middle East to establish and maintain contacts with the States concerned in order to promote agreement and assist efforts to achieve a peaceful and accepted settlement in accordance with the provisions and principles in this resolution;

4. Requests the Secretary-General to report to the Security Council on the progress of the efforts of the Special Representative as soon as possible.

Adopted by unanimous vote

United Nations Security Council Resolution 338
22 October 1973

The Security Council,

1. Calls upon all parties to the present fighting to cease all firing and terminate all military activity immediately, no later than 12 hours after the moment of adoption of this decision, in the positions they now occupy;
2. Calls upon the parties concerned to start immediately after the ceasefire the implementation of Security Council resolution 242 (1967) in all of its parts;
3. Decides that, immediately and concurrently with the cease-fire, negotiation shall start between the parties concerned under appropriate auspices aimed at establishing a just and durable peace in the Middle East.

Adopted by 14 votes to none, with
one abstention (China)

United Nations Security Council Resolution 465
1 March 1980

The Security Council,

Taking note of the reports of the Security Council Commission established under resolution 446 (1979) to examine the situation relating to settlements in the Arab territories occupied since 1967, including Jerusalem, contained in documents S/13450 and Corr. 1 and Add. 1 and S/13679,

Taking note also of letters from the Permanent Representative of Jordan and the Permanent Representative of Morocco, Chairman of the Islamic Group,

Strongly deploring the refusal by Israel to co-operate with the Commission and regretting its formal rejection of resolutions 446 (1979) and 452 (1979),

Affirming once more that the Geneva Convention relative to the Protection of Civilian Persons in Time of War, of 12 August 1949, is applicable to the Arab territories occupied by Israel since 1967, including Jerusalem,

Deploring the decision of the Government of Israel officially to support Israeli settlements in the Palestinian and other Arab territories occupied since 1967,

Deeply concerned by the practices of the Israeli authorities in implementing that settlements policy in the occupied Arab territories, including Jerusalem, and its consequences for the local Arab and Palestinian population,

Taking into account the need to consider measures for the impartial protection of public and private land and property, and water resources,

Bearing in mind the specific status of Jerusalem and, in particular, the need to protect and preserve the unique spiritual and religious dimension of the Holy Places in the city,

Drawing attention to the grave consequence which the settlements policy is bound to have on any attempt to reach a comprehensive, just and lasting peace in the Middle East,

Recalling pertinent Security Council resolutions, specifically resolutions 237 (1967), 252 (1968), 267 (1969), 271 (1969) and 298 (1971), as well as the consensus statement made by the President of the Council on 11 November 1976,

Having invited Mr Fahd Qawasma, Mayor of Al Khalil (Hebron), in the occupied territory, to supply it with information pursuant to rule 39 of the provisional rules of procedure,

1. Commends the work done by the Security Council Commission established under resolution 446 (1979) in preparing the report contained in document S/13679;

2. Accepts the conclusions and recommendations contained in the report of the Commission;

3. Calls upon all parties, particularly the Government of Israel, to co-operate with the Commission;

4. Strongly deplores the decision of Israel to prohibit free travel of Mayor Fahd Qawasma in order to appear before the Security Council and requests Israel to permit his free travel to United Nations Headquarters for that purpose;

5. Determines that all measures taken by Israel to change the physical character, demographic composition, institutional structure or status of the Palestinian and other Arab territories occupied since 1967, including Jerusalem, or any part thereof have no legal validity and that Israel's policy and practices of settling parts of its population and new immigrants in those territories constitute a flagrant violation of the Geneva Convention relative to the Protection of Civilian Persons in Time of War and also constitute a serious obstruction to achieving a comprehensive, just and lasting peace in the Middle East;

6. Strongly deplores the continuation and persistence of Israel in pursuing those policies and practices and calls upon the Government and people of Israel to rescind those measures, to dismantle the existing settlements and in particular to cease, on an urgent basis, the establishment, construction and planning of settlements in the Arab territories occupied since 1967, including Jerusalem;

7. Calls upon all States not to provide Israel with any assistance to be used specifically in connexion with settlements in the occupied territories;

8. Requests the Commission to continue to examine the situation relating to settlements in the Arab territories occupied since 1967, including Jerusalem, to investigate the reported serious depletion of natural resources, particularly the water resources, with a view to ensuring the protection of those important natural resources of the territories under occupation, and to keep under close scrutiny the implementation of the present resolution;

9. Requests the Commission to report to the Security Council before 1 September 1980 and decides to convene at the earliest possible date thereafter in order to consider the report and the full implementation of the present resolution.

Adopted by unanimous vote

United Nations Security Council Resolution 476
30 June 1980

The Security Council,

Having considered the letter of 28 May 1980 from the representative of Pakistan, the current Chairman of the Organization of the Islamic Conference, contained in document S/13966,

Reaffirming that the acquisition of territory by force is inadmissible,

Bearing in mind the specific status of Jerusalem and, in particular, the need to protect and preserve the unique spiritual and religious dimension of the Holy Places in the city,

Reaffirming its resolutions relevant to the character and status of the Holy City of Jerusalem, in particular resolutions 252 (1968), 267 (1969), 271 (1969), 298 (1971) and 465 (1980),

Recalling the Geneva Convention relative to the Protection of Civilian Persons in Time of War, of 12 August 1949,

Deploring the persistence of Israel in changing the physical character, demographic composition, institutional structure and the status of the Holy City of Jerusalem,

Gravely concerned about the legislative steps initiated in the Israeli Knesset with the aim of changing the character and status of the Holy City of Jerusalem,

1. Reaffirms the overriding necessity of ending the prolonged occupation of Arab territories occupied by Israel since 1967, including Jerusalem;
2. Strongly deplores the continued refusal of Israel, the occupying Power, to comply with the relevant resolutions of the Security Council and the General Assembly;
3. Reconfirms that all legislative and administrative measures and actions taken by Israel, the occupying Power, which purport to alter the character and status of the Holy City of Jerusalem have no legal validity and constitute a flagrant violation of the Geneva Convention relative to the Protection of Civilian Persons in Time of War and also constitute a serious obstruction to achieving a comprehensive, just and lasting peace in the Middle East;
4. Reiterates that all such measures which have altered the geographic, demographic and historical character and status of the Holy City of Jerusalem are null and void and must be rescinded in compliance with the relevant resolutions of the Security Council;
5. Urgently calls on Israel, the occupying Power, to abide by the present and previous Security Council resolutions and to desist forthwith from persisting in the policy and measures affecting the character and status of the Holy City of Jerusalem;
6. Reaffirms its determination, in the event of non-compliance by Israel with the present resolution, to examine practical ways and means in accordance with relevant provisions of the Charter of the United Nations to secure the full implementation of the present resolution.

Adopted by 14 votes to none, with one abstention (United States of America)

United Nations Security Council Resolution 478
20 August 1980

The Security Council,

Recalling its resolution 476 (1980),

Reaffirming again that the acquisition of territory by force is inadmissible,

Deeply concerned over the enactment of a 'basic law' in the Israeli Knesset proclaiming a change in the character and status of the Holy City of Jerusalem, with its implications for peace and security,

Noting that Israel has not complied with resolution 476 (1980),

Reaffirming its determination to examine practical ways and means, in accordance with the relevant provisions of the Charter of the United Nations, to secure the full implementation of its resolution 476 (1980), in the event of non-compliance by Israel,

1. Censures in the strongest terms the enactment by Israel of the 'basic law' on Jerusalem and the refusal to comply with relevant Security Council resolutions;

2. Affirms that the enactment of the 'basic law' by Israel constitutes a violation of international law and does not affect the continued application of the Geneva Convention to the Protection of Civilian Persons in Time of War, of 12 August 1949, in the Palestinian and other Arab territories occupied since June 1967, including Jerusalem;

3. Determines that all legislative and administrative measures and actions taken by Israel, the occupying Power, which have altered or purport to alter the character and status of the Holy City of Jerusalem, and in particular the recent 'basic law' on Jerusalem, are null and void and must be rescinded forthwith.

4. Affirms also that this action constitutes a serious obstruction to achieving a comprehensive, just and lasting peace in the Middle East;

5. Decides not to recognize the 'basic law' and such other actions by Israel that, as a result of this law, seek to alter the character and status of Jerusalem and calls upon:

   (a) All Member States to accept this decision;

   (b) Those States that have established diplomatic missions at Jerusalem to withdraw such missions from the Holy City;

6. Requests the Secretary-General to report to the Security Council on the implementation of the present resolution before 15 November 1980;

7. Decides to remain seized of this serious situation.

Adopted by 14 votes to none, with one abstention (United States of America)

United Nations Security Council Resolution 672
13 October 1990

The Security Council,

Recalling its resolutions 476 (1980) and 478 (1980),

Reaffirming that a just and lasting solution to the Arab–Israeli conflict must be based on its resolutions 242 (1967) and 338 (1973) through an active negotiating process which takes into account the right to security for all States in the region, including Israel, as well as the legitimate political rights of the Palestinian people,

Taking into consideration the statement of the Secretary-General relative to the purpose of the mission he is sending to the region and conveyed to the Council by the President on 12 October 1990,

1. Expresses alarm at the violence which took place on 8 October at the Al Haram al Shareef and other Holy Places of Jerusalem resulting in over 20 Palestinian deaths and to the injury of more than 150 people, including Palestinian civilians and innocent worshippers;

2. Condemns especially the acts of violence committed by the Israeli security forces resulting in injuries and loss of human life;

3. Calls upon Israel, the occupying Power, to abide scrupulously by its legal obligations and responsibilities under the Fourth Geneva Convention, which is applicable to all the territories occupied by Israel since 1967;

4. Requests, in connection with the decision of the Secretary-General to send a mission to the region, which the Council welcomes, that he submit a report to it before the end of October 1990 containing his findings and conclusions and that he use as appropriate all the resources of the United Nations in the region in carrying out the mission.

Adopted by unanimous vote

United Nations Security Council Resolution 673
24 October 1990

The Security Council,

Reaffirming the obligations of Member States under the United Nations Charter,

Reaffirming also its resolution 672 (1990),

Having been briefed by the Secretary-General on 19 October 1990,

Expressing alarm at the rejection of Security Council resolution 672 (1990) by the Israeli Government, and its refusal to accept the mission of the Secretary-General,

Taking into consideration the statement of the Secretary-General relative to the purpose of the mission he is sending to the region and conveyed to the Council by the President on 12 October 1990,

Gravely concerned at the continued deterioration of the situation in the occupied territories,

1. Deplores the refusal of the Israeli Government to receive the mission of the Secretary-General to the region;

2. Urges the Israeli Government to reconsider its decision and insists that it comply fully with resolution 672 (1990) and to permit the mission of the Secretary-General to proceed in keeping with its purpose;

3. Requests the Secretary-General to submit to the Council the report requested in resolution 672 (1990);

4. Affirms the determination to give full and expeditious consideration to the report.

Adopted by unanimous vote

United Nations Security Council Resolution 681
20 December 1990

The Security Council,

Reaffirming the obligations of Member States under the Charter of the United Nations,

Reaffirming also the principle of the inadmissibility of the acquisition of territory by war set forth in Security Council resolution 242 (1967) of 22 November 1967,

Having received the report of the Secretary-General submitted in accordance with Security Council resolution 672 (1990) of 12 October 1990 on ways and means of ensuring the safety and protection of the Palestinian civilians under Israeli occupation, and taking note in particular of paragraphs 20 to 26 thereof,

Taking note of the interest of the Secretary-General to visit and send his envoy to pursue his initiative with the Israeli authorities, as indicated in paragraph 22 of his report, and of their recent invitation to him,

Gravely concerned at the dangerous deterioration of the situation in all the Palestinian territories occupied by Israel since 1967, including Jerusalem, and at the violence and rising tension in Israel,

Taking into consideration the statement made by the President of the Security Council on 20 December concerning the method and approach for a comprehensive, just and lasting peace in the Arab–Israeli conflict,

Recalling its resolutions 607 (1988) of 5 January 1988, 608 (1988) of 14 January 1988, 636 (1989) of 6 July 1989 and 641 (1989) of 30 August 1989, and alarmed by the decision of the Government of Israel to deport four Palestinians from the occupied territories in contravention of its obligations under the Fourth Geneva Convention of 1949,

1. Expresses its appreciation to the Secretary-General for his report;

2. Expresses its grave concern over the rejection by Israel of Security Council resolutions 672 (1990) of 12 October 1990 and 673 (1990) of 24 October 1990;

3. Deplores the decision by the Government of Israel, the occupying Power, to resume the deportation of Palestinian civilians in the occupied territories;

4. Urges the Government of Israel to accept the *de jure* applicability of the Fourth Geneva Convention of 1949, to all the territories occupied by Israel since 1967 and to abide scrupulously by the provisions of the said Convention;

5. Calls upon the high contracting parties to the Fourth Geneva Convention of 1949 to ensure respect by Israel, the occupying Power, for its obligations under the Convention in accordance with article 1 thereof;

6. Requests the Secretary-General, in co-operation with the International Committee of the Red Cross, to develop the idea expressed in his report of convening a meeting of the high contracting parties to the Fourth Geneva Convention and to discuss possible measures that might be taken by them under the Convention and for this purpose to invite the parties to submit their views on how the idea could contribute to the goals of the Convention, as well as on other relevant matters, and to report thereon to the Council;

7. Also requests the Secretary-General to monitor and observe the situation regarding Palestinian civilians under Israeli occupation, making new efforts in this regard on an urgent basis, and to utilize and designate or draw upon the United Nations and other personnel and resources present there, in the area and elsewhere, needed to accomplish this task and to keep the Security Council regularly informed;

8. Further requests the Secretary-General to submit a first progress report to the Security Council by the first week of March 1991 and every four months thereafter, and decides to remain seized of the matter as necessary.

Adopted by unanimous vote

SELECT BIBLIOGRAPHY

For a name starting with Al, El, Le or The, see its second part.

Abir, Mordechai, *Saudi Arabia in the Oil Era: Regime and Elites: Conflict and Collaboration*, Croom Helm, London, 1988.

Ansari, Hamied, *Egypt: The Stalled Society*, State University of New York Press, Albany, NY, 1986.

Axelgard, Frederick W., *A New Iraq? The Gulf War and Implications for US Policy*, Praeger, New York and London, 1988.

Batatu, Hanna, *The Old Social Classes and the Revolutionary Movements of Iraq*, Princeton University Press, Princeton, NJ, 1978.

Bromley, Simon, *American Hegemony and World Oil: The Industry, the State System and the World Economy*, Polity Press, Cambridge, 1991.

Bulloch, John, and Morris, Harvey, *The Gulf War*, Methuen, London, 1989.

Bulloch, John, and Morris, Harvey, *Saddam's War: The Origins of the Kuwait Crisis and the International Response*, Faber, London and Boston, 1991.

Chubin, Shahram, and Tripp, Charles, *Iran and Iraq at War*, I. B. Tauris, London, 1988.

Committee Against Repression and For Democratic Rights in Iraq, *Saddam's Iraq: Revolution or Reaction?*, Zed Press, London, 1986.

Crystal, Jill, *Oil and Politics in the Gulf: Rulers and Merchants in Kuwait and Qatar*, Cambridge University Press, Cambridge and New York, 1990.

Darwish, Adel, and Alexander, Gregory, *Unholy Alliance: The Secret History of Saddam's War*, Victor Gollancz, London, 1991.

Dickson, H. R. P., *Kuwait and Her Neighbours*, Allen & Unwin, London, 1956.

Al Ebraheem, Hassan A., *Kuwait: A Political Study*, Al Qabas Printing Press, Kuwait, 1971.

Farouk-Sluglett, Marion, and Sluglett, Peter, *Iraq Since 1958: From Revolution to Dictatorship*, I. B. Tauris, London and New York, 1990.

Ghareeb, Edmund, *The Kurdish Question in Iraq*, Syracuse University Press, Syracuse, NY, 1981.

Graz, Leisl, *The Turbulent Gulf*, I. B. Tauris, London, 1990.

Helms, Christine Moss, *Iraq: Eastern Flank of the Arab World*, The Brookings Institution, Washington, DC, 1984.

Henderson, Simon, *Instant Empire: Saddam Hussein's Ambition for Iraq*, Mercury House, San Francisco, CA, 1991.

Hiro, Dilip, *Inside the Middle East*, Routledge and Kegan Paul, London, 1982; and McGraw-Hill, New York, 1982.

Hiro, Dilip, *Islamic Fundamentalism*, Paladin Books, London, 1988/ *Holy Wars: The Rise of Islamic*

Fundamentalism, Routledge, New York, 1989.

Hiro, Dilip, *The Longest War: The Iran–Iraq Military Conflict*, Paladin Books, London, 1990; and Routledge, New York, 1991.

Holden, David, and Johns, Richard, *The House of Saud*, Sidgwick & Jackson, London, 1981.

Hussein, Saddam, *Iraqi Policies in Perspective*, Translation and Foreign Languages Publishing House, Baghdad, 1981.

Johnson, Lt-Colonel Douglas V., Pelletiere, Stephen C., and Rosenberger, Leif R., *Iraqi Power and US Security in the Middle East*, US Army War College, Carlisle Barracks, Pa., 1990.

Khadduri, Majid, *Republican Iraq: A Study of Iraqi Politics since the Revolution of 1958*, Oxford University Press, London and New York, 1969.

Khadduri, Majid, *Socialist Iraq: A Study in Iraqi Politics since 1968*, The Middle East Institute, Washington, DC, 1978.

Al Khalil, Samir, *Republic of Fear: Saddam's Iraq*, University of California Press, Berkeley, 1989; and Hutchinson Radius, London, 1989.

Khumayni, Ruh Allah, *Islam and Revolution*, translated by Hamid Algar, Mizan Press, Berkeley, CA, 1981.

Kolko, Gabriel, *Anatomy of a War: Vietnam, the United States and the Modern Historical Experience*, Pantheon Books, New York, 1985.

McDermott, Anthony, *Egypt from Nasser to Mubarak: A Flawed Revolution*, Croom Helm, London and New York, 1988.

McDowell, David, *Palestine and Israel: The Uprising and Beyond*, I. B. Tauris, London, 1989.

McDowell, David, *The Kurds,*

Minority Rights Group, London, 1985.

Peter Mansfield, *Kuwait: Vanguard of the Gulf*, Hutchinson, London, 1990.

Miller, Judith, and Mylroie, Laurie, *Saddam Hussein and the Crisis in the Gulf*, Times Books, New York, 1990.

Nonneman, Gerd, *Iraq, the Gulf States and the War: A Changing Relationship 1980–1986 and Beyond*, Ithaca Press, London and Atlantic Highlands, NJ, 1986.

Ostrovsky, Victor, and Hoy, Claire, *By Way of Deception: The Making and Unmaking of a Mossad Officer*, St Martins Press, New York, 1990.

Rabinovich, Itamar, and Shaked, Haim (eds), *Middle East Contemporary Survey: Vol. XII, 1988*, Westview Press, Boulder, Colo., and London, 1990.

Rush, Alan, *Al-Sabah: History and Genealogy of Kuwait's Ruling Family, 1752–1987*, Ithaca Press, London and Atlantic Heights, NJ, 1987.

Rush, Alan (ed), *The Records of Kuwait 1899–1961, Vol. 7: Foreign Affairs II*, Archive Editions, Farnham Common, 1989.

Salinger, Pierre, with Laurent, Eric, *Secret Dossier: The Hidden Agenda behind the Gulf War*, Penguin Books, Harmondsworth, and Viking Penguin, New York, 1991.

Schofield, Richard, *Kuwait and Iraq: Historical Claims and Territorial Disputes*, Royal Institute of International Affairs, London, 1991.

Seale, Patrick, *Asad: The Struggle for the Middle East*, I. B. Tauris, London, 1988, and University of California Press, Berkeley, CA, 1989.

Short, Martin, and McDermott,

Anthony, *The Kurds*, Minority Rights Group, London, 1977.

Sifri, Micah L., and Cerf, Christopher (eds), *The Gulf War Reader: History, Documents, Opinions*, Times Books, New York, 1991.

Stookey, Robert W., *America and the Arab States: An Uneasy Encounter*, John Wiley, New York and London, 1975.

Tower, John, Muskie, Edmund, and Scowcroft, Brent, *The Tower Commission Report: The Full Text of the President's Special Review Board*, Bantam Books and Times Books, New York, 1987.

Woodward, Bob, *The Commanders*, Simon and Schuster, New York and London, 1991.

Yergin, Daniel, *Prize: The Epic Quest for Oil, Money and Power*, Simon and Schuster, New York and London, 1991.

News Agencies, Newspapers and Periodicals

Arab News (Jiddah)
BBC Summary of World Broadcasts (Reading)
Daily Telegraph (London)
Economist (London)
Le Figaro (Paris)
Financial Times (London and New York)
Foreign Broadcast Information Service (Washington)
Guardian (London)
In These Times (Chicago)
Independent (London)
Independent on Sunday (London)
International Herald Tribune (London)
Iraqi News Agency (Baghdad)
Islamic Republic News Agency (Tehran)
Jane's Defence Weekly (Coulsdon)
Al Jumhuriya (Baghdad)
Keesing's Record of World Events (Harlow)
Los Angeles Times (Los Angeles)
Mainstream (New Delhi)
MERIP Middle East Report (Washington)
Middle East Economic Digest (London)
Middle East International (London)
Middle East Journal (Washington)
Middle East Report (Washington)
Le Monde (Paris)
Nation (New York)
New Statesman and Society (London)
New Times (Moscow)
New York Times (New York)
Newsday (New York)
Newsweek (New York)
Observer (London)
Al Qadasiya (Baghdad)
Al Quds al Arabi (London)
Saudi Press Agency (Riyadh)
Al Sharq al Awsat (London)
Sunday Telegraph (London)
Sunday Times (London)
Tass (Moscow)
Al Thawra (Baghdad)
Time (New York)
The Times (London)
Vanity Fair (New York)
Wall Street Journal (New York and Brussels)
Washington Post (Washington)

INDEX

For a name starting with Al, El, L', Le, or The, see its second part. A person's religious or secular title has been omitted.